THE CHINESE ECONOMY

D0923970

THE CHINESE ECONOMY
SECOND EDITION
Adaptation and Growth

Barry Naughton

The MIT Press
Cambridge, Massachusetts
London, England

© 2018 Massachusetts Institute of Technology

All rights reserved. No part of this book may be reproduced in any form by any electronic or mechanical means (including photocopying, recording, or information storage and retrieval) without permission in writing from the publisher.

This book was set in Times Roman by Westchester Publishing Services. Printed and bound in the United States of America.

Library of Congress Cataloging-in-Publication Data is available.
Names: Naughton, Barry, author.
Title: The Chinese economy : adaptation and growth / Barry Naughton.
Description: Second edition. | Cambridge, MA : MIT Press, [2017] | Includes bibliographical
    references and index.
Identifiers: LCCN 2017021096 | ISBN 9780262534796 (pbk. : alk. paper)
Subjects: LCSH: China—Economic policy.
Classification: LCC HC427.95 .N38 2017 | DDC 338.951—dc23
LC record available at https://lccn.loc.gov/2017021096

10 9 8 7 6 5 4 3 2 1

Contents

Acknowledgments

In preparing this revised edition of *The Chinese Economy*, I had invaluable assistance from Henrique Barbosa, Li Xin, and Kieran Naughton. It was challenging, to say the least, to try to update and expand a general work to encompass the enormous changes that have occurred in China over the past decade. I benefited greatly from the close reading and generous comments I received from Ralph Huenemann, Peter Lorentzen, and Louis Putterman. Three anonymous readers from MIT Press helpfully showed me where more work was needed and shaped the final product. At the Press, Emily Taber stepped ably into John Covell's shoes and shepherded the whole process to completion.

The students at the School of Global Policy and Strategy (GPS) at the University of California, San Diego served as the test bed, lead market, and inspiration for the work. In addition, as scholarly exchanges and interactions with China have multiplied, I have increasingly benefited from the comments and reactions of colleagues at Chinese universities. Presentations at Tsinghua University, Peking University, and Fudan University in particular helped me to refine and modify arguments in this text.

The first edition of this book included two full pages acknowledging practical and intellectual debts I had accrued over the years. Those still stand; although the debts have been acknowledged, they have not been repaid.

Introduction: The Chinese Economy in Context

For the past 35 years, China has been the best-performing economy in the world. China's gross domestic product (GDP) has grown faster for longer than that of any other economy in history. Furthermore, the Chinese economy is now huge, comparable in size and global impact only to that of the United States. China is now a driver of the world economy, in part because it has benefited enormously from the wave of globalization that has washed over the world in the past three decades.

How has China achieved this extraordinary economic success? China is not an obvious candidate for prosperity, in the way that the United States and other "lucky countries" are. China has faced development problems that today's rich countries never had to face. Bringing its massive population out of poverty required China to overcome daunting geographic and resource limitations. China entered its rapid growth period far behind technologically and without the institutional framework and rule of law that rich countries had developed over centuries to support their sophisticated market economies. Yet China dismantled the socialist "command" system, created a dynamic market economy, and vaulted into the ranks of upper-middle-income economies. China has forged its own development strategy in a way that no country has ever done before, independent of the simplistic prescriptions of some brands of orthodox economics. Today, after more than three decades of extraordinary success, China must adapt its strategy to dramatically changed conditions that point to significantly slower growth. A newly middle-class society demands new goods and services, a better environment, and more robust social policies. Can policymakers deliver? Do they have the will to overhaul their approach to development, given the success it has brought them thus far? How big is the danger that hidden vulnerabilities will bring China's miraculous growth to a screeching halt? The Chinese economy continues to display both unmatched dynamism and unrivaled complexity.

It is useful to think of economic development as made up of two fundamental processes: structural change and institutional transformation. Structural change refers to real changes in the distribution of resources and activity. At the macro-structural level, the most fundamental change is the movement of labor and capital out of agriculture into the cities, and indeed China has transformed into a primarily urban industry and service-oriented economy over the past 35 years. Institutional transformation refers to changes in the organizations, information, and incentives that guide economic decision-makers. Governments, businesses, and households respond to the "rules of the game" in pursuing their objectives. China has undergone a dramatic institutional transformation from a "command economy" to a predominantly market economy. Both structural change and institutional transformation are sources of productivity improvement and income growth, and thus of economic development.

The objective of this book is to trace these broad processes of structural change and institutional transformation through the most important areas of the economy. From 1978 through 2010, both structural change and institutional transformation had their maximum possible effect on economic growth: the result was the extraordinary period we label the "miracle growth" period. Today, China has advanced to upper-middle-income status, and there is less opportunity for structural and institutional changes to drive growth: the miracle growth period is over. However, China still has robust growth potential, and medium-rapid growth over the coming decades will drive substantial catch-up and improvement in Chinese standards of living.

Structural change displays some common patterns in all growing economies. Although China has some distinctive features, China's industrialization can be easily situated in common structural processes. But structural change, as we shall see, is not just a "macro" phenomenon, but also an intermediate, or "meso" phenomenon, affecting specific sub-sectors, and also incorporating changes in demographic and technological structure. Institutional change by contrast, evolves from a specific context, and Chinese institutions are utterly distinctive. As a result, institutional change plays out in China in even more complex ways, in an incentive environment quite different from that in most economies. The objective of this volume, then, is to make China's ascent comprehensible by integrating the specific realities of China today with the broad patterns of structural and institutional change. Throughout, we hope to convey both the sources of strength and the challenges and vulnerabilities that have confronted China, including those overcome in the past and those that still face China today.

1.1   Enabling Conditions

China could not have achieved such dramatic growth without important advantages. Underpinning China's success are at least four favorable factors that influence nearly every aspect of Chinese economic performance:

1. Extraordinary human resources: China's people have a strong entrepreneurial drive, a cultural repertoire of market-friendly behaviors, and a powerful desire for educational achievement and increased knowledge. Moreover, they were already relatively healthy and literate at the end of the 1970s, so they were well positioned to take advantage of the sudden, massive increase in opportunities brought about by economic reform.

2. Global division of labor: China's opening corresponded precisely with a stage in the evolution of the global economy that permitted the dis-aggregation (or de-localization) of global manufacturing. This allowed the smooth transfer of labor-intensive export manufacturing from the already successful East Asian miracle economies to a newcomer—China—with low-cost, high-quality human resources and skills. China's factor endowment in the 1980s was a perfect complement to the world economy at that stage.

3. Enormous "catch-up" potential: Economists recognize that there are advantages of backwardness: the bigger the distance from the technology frontier, the more rapid the potential growth during the catch-up period. However, this potential can be realized only if there are sufficient enabling conditions, such as those provided by the two previous factors. China's enormous economic potential and human resources attracted interest and investment, enabling China to catch a wave of technological advance, most obviously in the spread of telecommunications and Internet technology.

4. A government with the capacity to learn: The Chinese government carried out an incremental and adaptive program of economic reform. This creativity was especially evident in the 1980s and 1990s, when China broke away from the command economy and created the fundamental institutions necessary to develop a robust market economy.

In other words, China in 1978 was in many respects well positioned for economic development. But many apparently well-positioned countries have stumbled in the development process, and some have stumbled repeatedly. China has been able to maintain a rapid pace of transformation. To accomplish this, China had to undergo a process of structural transformation, a technological revolution, the conversion from one demographic regime to another, and system reform that became systemic transformation. These concrete processes make up the subject matter of this book.

1.2   Growth and Development Level

From the beginning of the reform era in 1978 through 2010, China sustained an average annual economic growth rate of 10% according to official statistics. Rapid growth and huge population have long implied that China would one day emerge as one of the world's largest economies. As table 1.1 shows, this promise has now become reality. China's GDP reached US$11 trillion in 2015, valued at the prevailing exchange rate. China is the world's second-largest GDP after the United States ($18 trillion). If the figures are adjusted for purchasing power differences, according to the World Bank's international comparison project, China is already the world's largest GDP. In constant 2011 dollars—adjusted for purchasing power parity (PPP) based on the 2011 bench-marking exercise—China's GDP reached $18.6 trillion in 2015, surpassing the United States figure of $16.9 trillion (in 2011 prices). In PPP terms, China and the United States each account for one-sixth of total global output (see box 7.2 on page 163).

The growth that has made China a great economic power has not yet made it a rich country. China is the most populous country in the world, despite a declining growth rate: its population reached 1.375 billion in 2015. When the vantage point shifts to per capita values, the landscape changes dramatically. From a global stand-point, China is remarkably average. In terms of income, China's PPP-adjusted GDP per capita is close to the world mean value. Although China is still below the global mean, its growth rate is well above the global rate, so China will likely reach the global average in 2018 at about $16,000 in PPP terms.[1] China is a typical "upper-middle-income" country according to the World Bank's classification, right in the middle of that range. Other indicators related to the structure of the economy tell a consistent story. Urbanization—the share of population in cities—exactly equaled the global average of 53% in 2013, after decades of catch-up growth, and reached 57% in 2016. China's human resource indicators are a little better than global aver-ages; for example, life expectancy at birth in China in 2015 was calculated at 76, significantly above the global average of 71.7 and above the upper-middle-income average of 74.7 (but below the high-income average of 80.7, or the United States at 78.7). Overall, China is fairly representative of world average development levels; it is no longer poor but is still a long distance from being a rich country. After adjust-ment for PPP, per capita GDP is exactly one-quarter of that in the United States.

This position in the global economy could be problematic. In simple terms, the upper-middle-income neighborhood that China now inhabits is rather crowded, while the range just above it is sparsely populated. Over 2.5 billion people live in countries

---

1. As table 1.1 shows, the gap is larger if it is calculated at current exchange rates, and the catch-up time is correspondingly longer. The comparisons in this paragraph and table 1.1 use the World Bank World Development Indicators.

Table 1.1
China's 2015 GDP in international context.

	2015 GDP (trillions of US$ at current exchange rates)	2015 GDP (trillions of US$ at constant PPP 2011 prices)	2015 per capita GDP (US$ at current exchange rates)	2015 per capita GDP (US$ at constant PPP 2011 prices)
China	11.1	18.6	8,069	13,572
United States	18.0	16.9	56,116	52,704
World	74.3	108.2	10,112	14,724

with PPP-adjusted per capita GDP between $10,000 and $18,000, including China, Brazil, Mexico, Iran, Egypt, and Indonesia. China's objective is to break out of the pack and make it into the group of high-income countries (above $30,000). Above $18,000, the terrain between upper-middle- and high-income status is rather thinly populated and may be especially hard to traverse. Only 400 million people live in countries with per capita GDPs between $18,000 and $30,000. Moreover, most of these are in the former Soviet republics and countries that have recently joined the European Union. Outside these categories, the only large countries (over 5 million population) in this range are Turkey, Malaysia, and Chile. The small number of countries in this range partially reflects the difficulty that a few countries (Mexico, Brazil, and Thailand, for example) have had in breaking out of the $10,000–$18,000 range. This has led to discussion of a "middle-income trap." The essential idea of the middle-income trap is that while it is reasonably straightforward for an economy to develop the skills to industrialize, urbanize, and move out of poverty, it is more difficult to find a path to high-income status. Reaching high-income status requires stronger technical capabilities, better institutions, and more innovation. These factors pose challenges to China as well.

Yet it is obviously possible for China to overcome the middle-income trap. There are already 1.07 billion people living in high-income countries, with per capita GDP over $30,000. All these wealthy countries, without exception, fall into one of three categories: Europe and the four countries of predominantly European settlement (the United States, Canada, Australia, and New Zealand); oil producers; and East Asian high-performance economies. The East Asian growth stars are clearly the relevant comparison group for China. Japan, Korea, Taiwan, Hong Kong, Singapore, and Macao have all made it to upper-income status. China is more like these economies than any other in all respects except size. The growth miracle China experienced from 1978 through 2010 was similar to that experienced by other East Asian economies, such as Japan and Korea, but bigger and longer. China started from similar economic conditions (but lower per capita income) and underwent similar demographic and structural changes. It adopted related programs of opening and market reform. We should expect that China also has the capability to follow these former growth miracles into high-income status. However, we should also expect China to run into some of the same obstacles and encounter the same pitfalls as these fore-runner economies. Moreover, each of these economies experienced unanticipated difficulties when its miracle growth phase ended. China is not fated to repeat the experience of any given forerunner economy. Still, the question that defines China's big economic challenges today is: Can China adapt its policies and institutions to the requirements of slower growth so that it can sidestep crisis and disruption and smoothly enter another decade of moderately rapid growth?

1.3   Growth: Looking Backward and Forward

The first edition of this book was published a decade ago, in 2007. At that time, the relationship between China's growth prospects and the twin processes of struc-tural change and institutional transformation was unusually straightforward. China was undergoing the structural transformation from a rural to a predominantly urban, industrial economy, but it was not yet complete and there was still substan-tial impetus to be derived from further structural change. China had undertaken the institutional transition from bureaucratic socialism to a market economy and achieved substantial success, but there were still obvious opportunities and pro-ductivity improvements to be reaped from further reform and institutional change. Based on data through 2005, then, the first edition pointed out that both fundamental processes were strongly underway, and argued that since "these two transitions [are] both far from complete" (4), the prospects were good for continued rapid growth: "We should expect China's rapid growth to continue for another decade [i.e., through 2015] and then begin to moderate as labor force growth slows and rural-to-urban shifts wind down" (140). This is indeed what happened. Overall growth from 2005 to 2015 was rapid, averaging 9.5% annually, but after 2010 growth rates began a steady, gradual decline to 6.7% in 2016.

Today, the two processes of structural and institutional change are just as funda-mental as ever, but neither process can be counted on to deliver growth to the extent that it did a decade ago. The period of the most rapid structural change is now over. The commitment of policy-makers to market-oriented reforms has weakened, and it is uncertain to what extent institutional changes will drive future productivity gains. Each process has become a less powerful driver of development, and the two no longer work together in such an obviously consistent and mutually reinforcing fashion. Combined, they will make a weaker contribution to economic growth in the years ahead. The changed relationship among structural change, systemic reform, and growth is an underlying theme that unifies the diverse chapters in this volume.

This "new normal" is bringing slower growth and heightened risk, but recognition of these essential facts should not lead to a pessimistic appraisal of the Chinese economy. Slower growth should be understood as a deceleration from the 10% annual rates of the past 30 years, which obviously could not have been sustained indefinitely in any case. China's population is already much better off and has escaped the most severe forms of poverty. Moreover, the labor force has stopped growing, so the slowdown in output per worker will be less marked than the slowdown in total output. Anything growing at 6% doubles in 12 years. If China's output per worker grows at 6% annually, successive generations of 24 years will continue to see dramatic change as children enjoy wage incomes around four times those of their parents. Risks can be managed if economic reform continues and challenges are faced proactively. Slower growth is completely compatible with a highly productive and successful economy and a steadily improving standard of living.

1.4   Structural Transformation and the End of the Miracle-Growth Era

Structural transformation in China can be benchmarked against developing economies, since there are general patterns of structural change (chapter 7). However, an even more revealing comparison is that to the select group of so-called "miracle economies" described in section 1.2. These economies compressed the key structural transformations into a roughly 30-year period of extraordinarily rapid growth. These "forerunner economies" are almost all in East Asia, and they provide an obvious framework of comparison for China.

1.4.1   Features of Growth Miracles

There is no precise definition of a growth miracle. The Commission on Growth and Development (2008) covered 13 countries that grew at 7% or more for 25 years. Another common definition is economies with GDP growth above 8% for 20 years, or GDP per capita growth above 6% for the same period. Along with China, these definitions all include Japan, Korea, Taiwan, Hong Kong, and Singapore in the first generation of growth miracles; and Malaysia, Thailand, and Indonesia among a second generation of incomplete growth miracles. These nine economies, all in Asia, are the primary inhabitants of the growth miracle category.[2] In the most basic sense, these economies share four common features. Besides sustained rapid growth, these characteristics are:

2. In addition, the Commission on Growth and Development includes Brazil (1950–1980), Botswana, Malta, and Oman as sustained high-growth economies. Some definitions include Chile as well. In this volume, the comparison is primarily with East Asian forerunner "growth miracles."

1. Rapid labor-force growth as population dynamics change and economies enjoy a "demographic dividend";

2. Rapid structural change as workers leave agriculture and move to higher-productivity urban industry and services;

3. High investment rates that provide the infrastructure and industrial facilities needed to carry out this structural change; and

4. An open economic policy that allows rapid growth of export-oriented manufacturing.

China obviously displays all these characteristics. These features interact in a way that creates a virtuous circle in the development process. However, there is no clear consensus on which features are the most important. A great deal of attention has been paid to the policy lessons of export-oriented development, since that is potentially transferable to other countries. There is no dispute that the growth of labor-intensive export-oriented manufacturing plays a crucial role, since it allows the economy to absorb rapid labor-force growth and generate broad-based growth of incomes. Orientation to the world market means that growth does not run into demand-side constraints imposed by the size of the domestic market. Manufacturing may also be uniquely effective as a vehicle for importing and learning modern technologies. Export-oriented industrialization is a key part of the miracle growth process.

Since the 1990s, scholars have paid increasing attention to the centrality of the "demographic dividend" as well (chapter 7). Demographic change provides an abundant supply of young workers while also giving households an increased ability to save. High economy-wide saving and investment are essential to facilitate migration and rapid structural change. It is clear that each of these elements enables the positive impact of the other elements. They are complementary, and when they come together can produce phases of explosive growth.

Growth miracles cannot go on forever. They end when the structural and demographic conditions conducive to miracle growth are exhausted, and when economies move close enough to the global frontier that they can no longer succeed through imitative catch-up growth. The demographic and labor-force changes are inevitable and unavoidable. Rapid labor-force growth and the demographic dividend (chapters 8, 9) end after birth rates decline and as the population ages; structural change from workers moving out of low-productivity agriculture is exhausted when all young workers have left the farm. Other elements may also make less effective contributions to growth as the miracle ages. Dependence on export-oriented manufacturing does not automatically end, but as the supply of low-skilled workers dwindles, costs of labor-intensive manufactures rise quickly, and exporters lose competitiveness in traditional industries. Global markets for some specific commodities may become saturated by a huge exporter like China. Whether manufacturers can maintain growth by shifting to new capital- and skill-intensive industries depends on a host of sector- and product-specific factors.

Countries also face challenges in continuing to use high investment rates to drive growth. High investment rates can support demand in the short run, but to contribute to long-run growth this investment must be used productively. It was relatively easy to find productive investment projects during the period of massive structural change and rapid growth, but it is harder to find productive investments after the miracle ends. Some domestic markets are saturated (home appliances); infrastructure networks like high-speed rail are completed; and the stock of developed country innovations that can be cheaply copied is depleted. None of these opportunities are completely exhausted, but investors are forced to be more selective, and must search harder for productive and profitable opportunities. More generally, the end of the miracle-growth era reshapes the economic landscape in such fundamental ways that new approaches and policies are necessary to sustain moderately rapid growth.

1.4.2   The Abrupt Endings of Growth Miracles

The complexity of the relationships among demographics, migration, investment, and trade policy may illuminate one aspect of the end of miracle-growth eras that is otherwise difficult to explain. In all miracle-growth economies, gradually slowing labor-force growth and structural change would have been consistent with a smooth slowdown. Indeed, economic theory leads us to expect a gradual deceleration of growth as the growth of factor inputs (labor and capital) decelerates while productivity growth remains stable. However, the historical experience of previous growth miracles shows that growth transitions often happen quite abruptly and usually with significant economic disruption. For example, Japan grew at 10.4% per year for 23 years, between 1950 and 1973, but after 1973 growth dropped sharply, and Japan never sustained growth above 6% again. Less than 20 years later, Japan entered a profound economic crisis that saw its growth rate drop close to zero for another two decades. In the case of Japan, the end of the miracle was marked by short-term economic disruptions that were surprisingly severe and followed by a long-term slowdown that seems unduly protracted.

Korea grew robustly into the 1990s and tried to keep growth high even as labor costs rose and structural transformation slowed. The eruption of the Asian financial crisis in 1997 brought Korean growth to a temporary halt and forced deep and painful restructuring. Korea's post-1998 growth was more vigorous than that of Japan, but there was no mistaking the abrupt end of the miracle-growth era. GDP growth never retained previous highs and decelerated to 3% annually from 2010 to 2016. Other East Asian economies had less dramatic growth slowdowns, but each in its own way has experienced substantial difficulties in making a smooth transition to slower growth.

Economists have not developed a general understanding of these abrupt slowdowns. In each case, a sharp external shock produced lasting changes in long-term growth trajectories. The first world oil crisis in 1973–1974 shook up the Japanese miracle-growth model, and the Asian financial crisis in 1997 derailed Korea's growth. However, nobody has convincingly shown why these transitory external shocks, however severe, should lead to a permanent fall in the growth rate. China is not fated to follow a similar trajectory, but these experiences should alert us to the complexity of the end of the growth-miracle phase. China's level of development today is similar to that of Japan and Korea when their growth miracles ended. Looking just at GDP per capita, China in 2017 is at the level of Japan in 1973 ($15,000 in 2011 PPP U.S. dollars). By 2023, if growth remains strong, China will reach the level of Korea in 1997 ($20,800), and in another decade reach the $30,000 of Japan in 1992. Many factors are at play, and policy must adapt effectively to a number of new challenges, but the broad context is given by the end of the miracle-growth era.

1.4.3   Multiple Turning Points

The preceding discussion has made clear that the end of the growth-miracle phase is not simply a single dimensional quantitative change; an economy does not simply downshift from 10% to 6% growth. Instead, a society undergoes a multi-dimensional shift. Reaching middle-income status, the economy begins to mature, and changes take place in economic, social, and institutional arenas. Indeed, it is striking how many fundamental, long-run trends in the economy changed and reversed course, especially in the 2007–2010 period. For example, some of the unambiguous turning points that have occurred in the last decade include the following:

• Labor force growth had been robust as late as the 1990s, but gradually ceased and went into reverse after 2011 (chapters 8 and 9).

• Rural-to-urban migration had accelerated until 11 million new migrants were annually moving across provincial boundaries in the 2005–2010 period, but from this peak migration has dropped to less than 5 million annually in 2010–2015, and continues to fall (chapter 6).

• Exports as a share of GDP increased for three decades to a peak in 2006, and have declined steadily since to about half their peak level (chapter 16).

• The share of manufacturing in GDP and the share of investment in GDP, both among the highest ever attained by an economy, increased further before beginning to decline. The manufacturing share finally peaked in 2007 at 33% of GDP and investment plateaued from 2010 through 2013 at 45% of GDP. Both have now begun to drift downward (chapter 7).

• The economic center of gravity shifted steadily toward the coastal regions for decades, but the coastal share peaked in 2006 and the center of gravity is now slowly shifting inland (chapter 2).

• From being one of the world's largest host countries for inward foreign direct investment (FDI), China has become a large source of outward FDI. FDI outflows surpassed inflows for the first time in 2016. More generally, China now resembles a developed country with balanced inward and outward FDI flows (chapter 17).

• Income inequality, which had increased relentlessly to a peak Gini coefficient of 0.49 in 2008, has finally stabilized and begun a moderate decline (chapter 9).

Accompanying these profound reversals of economic trends, long-established policies have begun to change as well. A selection of these policy changes includes:

• The One-Child Policy, in place since 1980, was finally abolished and replaced in 2016 by a general two-child policy (chapter 8).

• China stopped taxing farmers and began to subsidize and protect agriculture (chapters 6, 12).

• The long-term process of rebuilding a social safety net, including health insurance and universal education, was undertaken in earnest after 2005 (chapter 20).

These policy changes are important adaptations to the "new normal" that China faces after the growth miracle. Chinese policy-makers have recognized for a decade that they will need to rebalance the economy, and find new drivers of growth in service and knowledge-intensive sectors.

1.4.4   Shift in Development Strategy After the Growth Miracle

One important difference between China and its forerunners in the Asian miracle-growth club is already apparent. Japan and Korea responded to the end of the miracle-growth phase by reducing government steerage of the economy. China, by contrast, has responded by increasing the activist role of the government in promoting new growth sectors. "Industrial policy" was most important in Japan and Korea in the 1950s through the 1980s and much less important thereafter. By contrast, industrial policy is a hot discussion topic in China today, and China has been increasing the scope and intensity of its industrial policy since 2006. As discussed in chapter 15, China has rolled out a series of activist industrial policies designed to foster the emergence of so-called "strategic emerging industries," industrial automation, and internet-based services. At the same time, government investments in infrastructure and research and development have been increased. In other words, rather than stepping back, letting market-based actors select investments in the young shoots of new industries, China has aggressively sought to foster new infant industries.

It remains to be seen whether China's approach will prove effective, but it is certainly different. Most mature economies have already moved to a "light touch" industrial policy, investing in research and seeding new sectors with modest amounts of funding. Some eschew industrial policies altogether. China has instead elected to spend a significant amount of government money and deploy a wide range of intrusive instruments to shape the emerging economic structure.

At a minimum, China's policy approach reveals a great deal of confidence in the government's ability to pick winners, and a somewhat surprising lack of confidence in the market's ability to generate dynamically efficient outcomes. This is surprising, because marketization has been so profoundly involved in the most important successes of the Chinese economy over the past 40 years. To understand this point, we must consider the fate of market-oriented reform in China today.

1.5 System Reform: An Increasingly Contested Transformation

System reform has contributed powerfully to growth in China since 1978. Yet it is a curious fact that growth has not completely vindicated the market, nor has it necessarily improved the fortunes of further market-oriented reforms. After about 2005, the Chinese government's commitment to market-oriented reform was noticeably scaled back. To be sure, the government's rhetorical commitment to the idea of reform has never wavered. However, the formulation and implementation of concrete reform programs has slowed since 2005. Market-oriented reforms seem to face more opposition than before from conservatives, big-government advocates, and interest groups. Moreover, policy-makers are clearly concerned with balancing objectives of at least equal priority with market-oriented reform, including rebuilding social security nets and fostering high-technology industry.

This is very different from the commitment to market reforms during most of the miracle-growth era. For most of the period from 1978 through 2005, top policy-makers saw the problem of reform as being central to the quest for growth, and inseparable from it. Chapter 5 argues that the desire to foster growth was an integral part of reform strategy from 1978 on; it is equally true that market reform was an essential part of growth strategy as well. Most key economic policy-makers took it for granted that China could not achieve the wealth and power it wanted without profound market-oriented reforms. As of 1978, the command economy had failed; that system was rotten to the core. The economic reforms of the 1980s represented a thorough effort to reconstruct and revitalize the system from the ground up. In the 1990s, a crisis of state capacity stared Chinese policy-makers in the face, and the reforms of the 1990s rebuilt institutions and the capabilities of the government and the economy at large. Reform was always difficult, and policy-makers debated and fought over reform policy. In the end, though, China overcame each successive economic crisis through thorough market-oriented reform.

Moreover, these reforms were successful. Each wave of reform was followed by a wave of re-invigorated growth and development. Reforms revealed information about economic potential that allowed China's development strategy to be tailored to the economic development stage China had achieved at the time. No other economy ever went through the initial stages of development more rapidly, more effectively, or with as much single-minded determination as China did. With the highest sustained investment rate ever experienced, China built infrastructure and factories, urbanized rapidly, and developed into an export powerhouse. This approach was thoroughly intertwined with market reforms, which provided the incentives that changed behavior and put hundreds of millions of people in motion.

After 2005, the unity between market reform and economic growth began to come apart. Chinese policy-makers faced new trade-offs. They could allow market forces to drive the emergence of new sectors, or they could force the process through government action. While they understandably tried to do both, they gradually began to tilt more toward government steerage then market reform. As a result, systemic transition slowed down after 2005.

In fact, successful growth after about 2003–2004 greatly reduced the urgency of reform. The experience of rapid growth and profound economic success made policy-makers complacent: What was the need for further reform? In the 1990s, a profound sense of crisis pushed forward painful changes, but what pressing crisis demanded painful reforms in the twenty-first century? Without compelling answers to these questions, further reforms stalled out. The absence of crisis may have coincided with a stronger commitment to the existing system among various interest groups. State-owned enterprises returned to profitability, so they were worth holding on to. Moreover, the system was in many respects further strengthened by the creation of a set of complementary social institutions—neglected in the previous reform phase—that began to provide basic medical insurance, improved education, and basic social security. The balance of forces was altered: sources of dissatisfaction were reduced, and defenders of the status quo were strengthened. Inclinations toward stronger government steerage were strengthened when the global financial crisis hit in 2008–2009, and a robust stimulus program vindicated government intervention, at least in the short run.

Thus, the market transition framework is less convincing today than it was 10 years ago. Around 2005, it was reasonable to see China as moving toward a form of mixed-market economic system, the basic framework of which was familiar and understood in similar ways by most Chinese and foreign observers. Today, a Chinese economic system has emerged that indeed relies predominantly on the market, especially in the downstream and foreign-trade sectors, but also retains a robust, relatively centralized state sector in some industrial and service sectors, including finance. Moreover, a powerful government intervenes extensively in microeconomic processes throughout the economy in pursuit of increasingly ambitious goals. Ten years ago, the achievements of economic reform were already evident, and it was easy to extrapolate their (positive) impact on the economy. The direction of change was clear, even if the exact end state of reform was unknown. Today, it seems more appropriate to see the Chinese system as having taken on a relatively stable form, a distinctively Chinese economic system based on the market, but with extensive direct government intervention and substantial discretionary control in the hand of government and Communist Party bureaucrats. Of course, this system will still undergo substantial change as policy-makers and the Chinese population adapt to new capabilities, opportunities, and challenges, but it is not obviously in transition to something else.

Since the Third Plenum of the 18th Communist Party Central Committee in November 2013, Chinese leaders have announced a broad program calling for the revitalization of reform. The Plenum more or less officially adopted the view that economic reform stagnated during the 2002–2012 Hu Jintao–Wen Jiabao administration. The Plenum marks a welcome recommitment to the goal of market-oriented reform, but it is not easy to restore momentum to a process interrupted for many years. It will take time to see where the new round of reforms leads, especially since many promising reforms were suspended during the market turmoil of 2015. Because it makes less sense to think of China as a transitional economy, the subtitle of this second edition has been changed. While the first edition was called *The Chinese Economy: Transitions and Growth*, this second edition is entitled *The Chinese Economy: Adaptation and Growth*. While China will continue to go through multiple transitions, the key challenge will be to adapt to the complex realities of the new normal, after the period of high-speed growth.

1.6   Growth Acceleration and Slowdown

From a long-term perspective, we can look at the years from 2005 to 2016 as the end of miracle growth and the transition to the new normal. However, the short-run experience was more complex: after 2005 the economy first accelerated and only then slowed down. Looking backward from 2005, GDP had grown at 9.2% per year for a decade. Optimists believed rapid growth could be maintained, but scarcely anybody expected that it would accelerate. In fact, though, from 2005 through 2010, growth increased to a remarkable 11.2% annually, an acceleration of two full percentage points. Moreover, since population growth dropped from 0.8% to 0.5% annually, per capita GDP growth accelerated from 8.3% to 10.7%, a difference that was probably perceptible in the daily life of households. This really was a golden era in the experience of the average Chinese household. Moreover, the acceleration of this five-year period occurred despite the impact of the global financial crisis that raged from late 2008 into 2010. This is also the period in which China's economic success burst into international recognition, and China began to play a significantly altered and expanded role on the international stage. This is one of the most extraordinary economic outcomes of modern times.

Why did growth accelerate after 2005? System reform played a crucial role. In 2005, the Chinese economy was emerging from the milestone reforms of the Zhu Rongji years (1993–2002), a period of fundamental transformation from a command economy to a market economy (chapter 5). The relationship between the Zhu Rongji reforms and the growth acceleration exemplifies the general logic of economic reform. Reform is difficult and costly, and it produces productivity and growth benefits with a lag. In the case of the Zhu Rongji reforms, painful reforms in the late 1990s cut back the state sector, releasing factors of production for more productive uses and reducing the drag on the government from subsidizing inefficient firms. It also cleared the way for the emergence of qualitatively more efficient producers who understood the new rules of access that enabled their growth. The evidence is overwhelming that substantial productivity growth occurred during the first decade of the century, encompassing both private firms and newly reformed state firms (Brandt, Van Biesebroeck, and Zhang 2012). The liberation of the potential of Chinese producers led to a massive positive supply-side productivity shock. China's growth acceleration after 2005 is inconceivable without the prior achievement of the Zhu Rongji reforms.

A successful growth acceleration is realized through specific sectoral changes. Two were most important in this period. First, China's entry into the World Trade Organization (WTO) was the culmination of several years of market-liberalization measures. By dismantling the barriers that had prevented domestic firms, especially private firms, from accessing international markets, WTO membership was crucial in facilitating the phenomenal surge of exports that occurred after 2004 (chapter 16). China's trade growth then became a constituent part of a virtuous circle of global growth fueling development in commodity exporters such as Brazil and Chile as well. Second, the urban housing boom was the result of the privatization of existing housing owned by work units, combined with a practical resolution of the problem of landownership in the cities through the development of tradable long-term use rights. As urban households traded up to more modern apartments and invested in a second or third apartment, demand for housing exploded. Rising prices in turn fueled investment demand, sparking dramatic growth in construction and then in upstream heavy industries such as steel and cement. Investment rates rose again as households contributed to increased national saving and investment. Growth acceleration was the deferred gift of the Zhu Rongji economic reforms to the Chinese economy.

Since institutional reforms had cleared away most of the barriers to macro-structural change, high investment was enough to facilitate restructuring. Migration from the countryside to China's cities peaked during the 2005–2010 period: inter-provincial migration reached a staggering 11 million per year during this period (chapter 6). An extraordinary investment effort provided factories for these migrants to work in, as well as shelter and transportation. Frenetic growth also pushed China more rapidly toward the conclusion of its period of maximum structural change.

Chinese policy-makers eventually began to worry seriously about economic over-heating caused by excessively rapid expansion of exports and housing. Inflation surged above the 5% warning line in the third quarter of 2007. Economic imbalances were exacerbated by a fateful policy choice of maintaining an almost fixed exchange range between the renminbi (RMB) and the U.S. dollar even as large export surpluses began to develop in 2005. In the fourth quarter of 2007 China finally began to allow faster appreciation, but within a couple of months, the global financial crisis upset everyone's calculations. The collapse of Lehman Brothers in October 2008 brought global crisis to China's front doorstep. China's reaction was to unleash an enormous wave of domestic stimulus spending. This domestic stimulus succeeded in buffer-ing China against the worst of the global crisis and pushed investment rates to new highs. The surge of credit rebalanced China's foreign-trade account by dramatically expanding domestic demand (through increased investment demand), and China's GDP growth rate bounced back after spending only one quarter below 8%.

Only after the global financial crisis had been weathered did China directly face the challenge of the secular decline in the growth rate. GDP growth slid steadily from 10.6% in 2010 to 6.7% in 2016. In this circumstance, the stimulus program of 2009 marked the beginning of a period of rapid expansion of credit designed to keep the growth rate from declining too precipitously. The credit spigots that were opened during the 2009 crisis have never really been closed. As a result, the problem of man-aging the long-term structural changes has been compounded by the challenges of dealing with a debt overhang and the need to de-leverage the corporate economy. These issues are discussed in chapters 18 and 19. As the experience of earlier growth-miracle economies demonstrates, the transition to slower growth is never simple or easy.

1.7   Responding to the "New Normal"

China's economic future will continue to be shaped primarily by the impact of structural change and institutional transformation. However, it no longer makes sense to portray these as essentially well-known and ongoing transitions. China's postindustrial economy beckons, but at the same time technological changes loom that may fundamentally shift the relationship between industry and other types of economic activity. In some respects, China has become a typical upper-middle-income emerging market, but in other respects, Chinese institutions and policies have become even more distinctive and more settled into a "Chinese system."

On the developmental side, China has come further and faster than expected. However, the structural changes that have brought China to where it is today, while far from exhausted, will not drive the same kind of growth in the future. One stage of development transition, in other words, has been mostly completed, and the prospects for the next stage are inevitably less clear.

The ultimate result of these changing trends is that the Chinese system is under increasing pressure to adapt to a new stage of growth. The necessary transitions are now multiple: demographic, technological, macroeconomic, and institutional. Can China rebalance its economy? Can it avoid the middle-income trap? Can it make the leap to an innovative society and economy? These are all questions that confront economic policy-makers with new challenges and new risks.

1.8   Using This Book

The chapters of this book are organized in a bottom-up fashion. Chapters 2 through 6 cover endowments, legacies, and economic systems and their evolution through the present. Chapters 7 through 10 approach the developmental process through four complementary perspectives: structural change, population, labor, and living standards. This is followed by seven chapters that cover specific sectors, beginning with agriculture and progressing through industry and technology and foreign trade and investment. Three chapters consider macroeconomic, financial, and fiscal issues. A final chapter on the environment concludes. The book is designed to be a platform, covering much of the essential information about the Chinese economy and thereby serving as a starting point for further in-depth study of any specific topic. Each chapter is a descriptive essay. The chapters are extensively cross-referenced, but each is designed to stand on its own. Some chapters have been changed and renumbered since the first edition. Chapter 18 is a new chapter on macroeconomic policy, discussing the dramatic macro events of the past decade and introducing three chapters on macro and financial issues. Coverage of macroeconomic and financial issues is much stronger than in the first edition. The section on energy that was included in a chapter on sectoral change in the first edition has been moved into chapter 21 on the environment, and the sectoral chapter (the former chapter 14) has been eliminated.

Because the chapters in the book are intended to stand alone, courses should be able to assemble the chapters in different sequences to accord with different approaches to the material.

Program 1. If the chapters are covered in order, the result is a strong focus on China, with the opening chapters on China's geography and history first. The progression is straightforward and provides in-depth coverage appropriate for a course specifically on China's economy or political economy, or as part of a course on East Asian economies.

Program 2. An alternative approach is to start with the core chapters on China's economic transition and contemporary developmental experience. Chapters 5–8 cover this material. Chapter 15 on technology and industrial policy and chapter 20 on the fiscal system would be natural complements.

Program 3. A strong focus on economic systems and socialist transition would begin with chapters 4 and 5 (the socialist economy and the transition economy), and then skip to chapters 13 and 14 for treatment of township and village enterprises and ownership and corporate governance reforms in industry.

Subject clusters. There are three chapter clusters: Chapters 12–14 on the rural economy, chapters 16–17 on international trade and investment, and chapters 18–20 on macroeconomics and the financial and fiscal systems.

Chapter 21 covers energy, the environment, and environmental policy. This can also be used as a policy case study, combined with the coverage of the political economy of local governments in section 5.6 and chapter 20. Chapters 12 and 20 raise the policy implications of increased welfare spending for rural and urban local governments and the central government.

The choice has been made throughout to present as much China-specific content as possible. Inevitably, the space spent on economic principles is limited, and this creates opportunities to combine text readings with in-class discussion. For example, a discussion of the relation among the current account, capital account, and the balance of payments identity will enrich chapter 17 on foreign investment. Similarly, in-depth discussion of the aggregate production function would enrich chapter 7 on growth. Since this material is familiar to trained economists, it should be straightforward to introduce supplemental materials in class and integrate it with the China-specific material from the text.

The book presents many charts and graphs. The data for these graphics, regularly updated, are available at the book's website, **chinaeconomicoutlook.com**. Supplementary materials and occasional opinion pieces and blog posts also appear there from time to time.

Bibliography

Suggestions for Further Reading

Kroeber (2016) is a brisk and insightful introduction to many of the topics covered in this text. Johnson (2004) manages to capture much of the realistic feel of contemporary China in three detailed and moving accounts. Lin, Cai, and Li (1996) is especially good on the socialist era. Feng and Yao (2014) is a realistic but optimistic take on China's current challenges.

Sources for Data and Figures

The majority of the data in this text are drawn from official Chinese sources. By far the most accessible source is data in the *Statistical Yearbook of China* (*SYC*) and the *Statistical Abstract of China* (*SAC*), published annually by the National Bureau of Statistics. The *SYC* has the additional advantage of having English headings for all tables. Chinese GDP figures have been repeatedly revised; this text uses data from the 2017 revision exclusively, given in *SAC* (2017, 21–37). These adopt the international convention of reclassifying research and development expenditures as investment, rather than an intermediate input, so they increase GDP slightly.

In table 1.1, for consistency, all data are taken from World Bank, World Development Indicators, last revision, June 1, 2017.

References

Brandt, Loren, Johannes Van Biesebroeck, and Yifan Zhang (2012). "Creative Accounting or Creative Destruction? Firm-Level Productivity Growth in Chinese Manufacturing." *Journal of Development Economics* 97:339–351.

Commission on Growth and Development (2008). *The Growth Report: Strategies for Sustained Growth and Inclusive Development.* Washington, DC: The World Bank.

Feng, Yingjie, and Yang Yao (2014). "The Middle-Income Trap and China's Growth Prospects." In Ligang Song, Ross Garnaut, and Cai Fang, eds., *Deepening Reform for China's Long-Term Growth and Development*, 133–158. Canberra: Australian National University Press. http://press.anu.edu.au/titles/china -update-series/deepening-reform-for-chinas-long-term-growth-and-development/pdf-download/.

Johnson, Ian (2004). *Wild Grass: Three Stories of Change in Modern China.* New York: Pantheon Books.

Kroeber, Arthur (2016). *China's Economy: What Everyone Needs to Know.* New York: Oxford University Press.

Lin, Justin Yifu, Fang Cai, and Zhou Li (1996). *The China Miracle: Development Strategy and Economic Reform.* Hong Kong: Chinese University Press.

SAC (Annual). *Zhongguo Tongji Zhaiyao* [Statistical abstract of China]. Beijing: Zhongguo Tongji.

LEGACIES AND SETTING

Plowing with traditional tools in Dengfeng, Henan 1982.

The Geographic Setting

China is the most populous nation, and it is also one of the largest countries, with the third-biggest landmass, after Russia and Canada. Its land area is 2% greater than that of the United States, which it resembles geographically. The two countries cover similar latitudes and a similar range of climatic conditions, and these similarities lead to numerous parallels between regions in the eastern half of both countries. The climate of Guangzhou is like that of Miami, and the climate of the Northeast (Manchuria) is similar to that of Minnesota. The biggest difference between China and the United States is that China is far more rugged. Only one-quarter of China is low lying, below 500 meters (1,640 feet) above sea level, compared with 60% of North America and 80% of Europe. Most of China consists of hills, mountains, and high plateaus, broken by river valleys and a few plains and basins. In the west, China borders on the vast deserts of inner Asia. Mount Everest, the highest mountain in the world, is on the China-Nepal border, while the Turfan depression in Xinjiang, 155 meters below sea level, is the third-lowest place on earth. Although China historically was a nation of farmers, only a small proportion of the land is arable. The largest plains in China cover only a fraction of the area of the vast central plain of the American Midwest. China is big, rugged, and diverse. As a result, modernization in China has meant overcoming geographic isolation and high transport costs, and the creation of an integrated national market and economic space has been a key part of development.

China has only a single seacoast. Moreover, China's eastern seaboard is not particularly accessible. Most of the southern part of the coast is rugged and hilly, so the occasional good harbors tend to be cut off from the inland regions. In the north, especially between the Yangtze River and the Shandong Peninsula, the coast is low and swampy, with few good harbors. Reflecting these geographic conditions, China's traditional economy was inwardly oriented. There were outward-oriented, seafaring subcultures, but these tended to be fenced off in the southeastern coast, which was economically peripheral. China thus contrasts sharply with northern Europe and with

Japan, Taiwan, and Korea, with their strong seagoing and commercial traditions. The lack of a coastal orientation contributed to China's late start in economic modernization. China's links to the modern world economy began to multiply only when foreign-dominated Treaty Ports were forcibly implanted into China's key economic regions after 1842. Even today, the vast interior continues to place huge demands on China's economic capacity, demands that will have lasting ramifications on future development. Since 1999, China has committed to an array of regional development programs, beginning with the Western Development Program, targeting investment and giving policy preferences to the western and inland regions. These efforts reflect the fact that the West lagged economically, while the coasts, benefiting from early favorable policies, have surged ahead and have been firmly linked to the ocean transport web and the global economy.

2.1 Landforms

The entire Chinese landmass tilts from west to east. The Himalayas are a young mountain range, still rising by several feet per century because of the collision of the Indian subcontinent with the Asian landmass. This mountain-building process has recently caused devastating earthquakes in Sichuan (2008) and Nepal (2015); more generally, it shapes the whole topography of China. Mountain ranges are high and rugged in the west and taper off to low hills in the east, so the land of China forms three great "steps" in elevation. The top step is made up of the frigid Tibetan Plateau, which averages more than 4,000 meters (over 13,000 feet) above sea level and contains the world's highest mountains. The second step consists of a series of plateaus and basins with an elevation of between 1,000 and 2,000 meters (between 3,000 and 7,000 feet). These include the basins in arid northwestern China (such as the Tarim and Junggar Basins), the Inner Mongolian Plateau and the Loess Plateau in northern China, and the Yunnan-Guizhou Plateau in southwestern China. The third step consists of the plains and low hills of eastern China, where the elevation is generally below 500 meters. Even in the east, ranges of relatively low mountains create barriers to north-south transport and separate different climate and vegetation areas.

The three most important rivers in China, the Yangtze (Changjiang), Yellow (Huang), and Pearl (Zhujiang) Rivers, all flow from west to east in accord with the basic topography. Even the great rivers of South and Southeast Asia, including the Mekong and the Ganges, originate within China on the Tibetan highland and initially flow east before turning south and cutting through mountain ranges on the way to the southern seas (see figure 21.3). The western half of China is high and arid, and the population is sparse. A line drawn from the town of Aihui in the northeastern

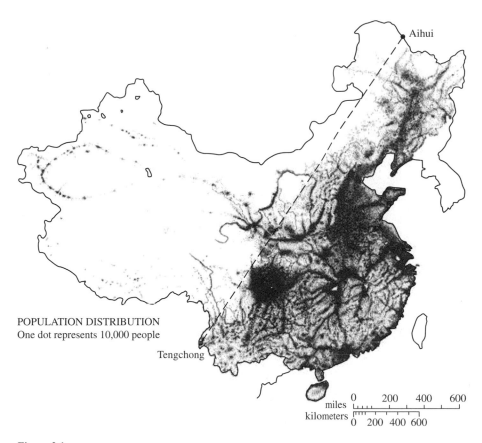

POPULATION DISTRIBUTION
One dot represents 10,000 people

Figure 2.1
Population distribution and the Aihui–Tengchong line.
Source: Based on Sun (1988).

province of Heilongjiang to Tengchong in the southwestern province of Yunnan (the Aihui–Tengchong line; see figure 2.1) divides the area of China in half, but only 6% of the population lives in the dry, mountainous west; 94% of the population lives in the eastern half of the country. The area west-northwest of the Aihui–Tengchong line has a population density of only 15 people per square kilometer, about the same as that of Utah or Argentina. Within this vast area, the Tibetan Plateau contains a quarter of the land area of China but less than 1% of the population. The northwestern region supports about 4.5% of the population, mostly in a few basins and scattered oases. A shortage of available water sharply limits the population potential of the western regions. East-southeast of the Aihui–Tengchong line, the country is lower in elevation and has ample water. This half is considered "monsoon China" because it receives seasonal summer rains that bring abundant water in most

Table 2.1
Land and population, 2012.

	Land area (millions of hectares)	Arable land (millions of hectares)	Arable land (percent)	Population (millions)	Arable land per capita (hectares)
China	939	135.4	14.4	1,351	0.10
India	297	156	52.5	1,237	0.13
United States	915	156	17.0	314	0.50
Russia	1,638	120	7.3	143	0.83
Indonesia	181	24	13.0	247	0.10

Sources: China arable land: Second National Land Survey (December 31, 2009). See chapter 12 for discussion. Other countries: World Bank, World Development Indicators, http://devdata.worldbank.org /dataonline. Arable land computed from WDI Arable Land Percent.
Note: A hectare is a square 100 meters on each side, equal to about 2.5 acres.

years. The population density in this eastern half of China is about 290 people per square kilometer, less than that of India (368) or Japan (337) but higher than that of the United Kingdom (255) or those U.S. states that are part of the Northeast Crescent from Boston to Washington, D.C. (186).

China's terrain is mainly mountainous or hilly (65%), which means that relatively little of the land is suitable for cultivation. Only 19% of China's surface is judged "suitable for human habitation" by Chinese surveyors. The good agricultural land lies in the fertile plains and valleys of the major river systems, separated from one another by hills and mountains. Less than 15% of China is arable (table 2.1), and there is very little land potentially suited for cultivation that is not already exploited. Because of its rugged topography, China has less arable land per capita than India, even though India is much more densely populated overall. The United States, with one-fourth of China's population, has more arable land than China and could easily bring much more land into cultivation if it were profitable to do so. Per capita arable land in China is only 0.10 hectare, or one-fifth of an acre. This is the average size of a new suburban home lot in the United States. Over the centuries, China has adapted to the scarcity of arable land by developing labor-intensive agricultural techniques that enable it to wrest more total food grain from the soil than any other country.

2.2   Climate and Water

The climate of China is dominated by the southeast monsoon, which sets the distinctive pattern of wet summers and dry winters. In winter, there is little rain or snow anywhere in China. A high-pressure zone is established over central Asia, creating

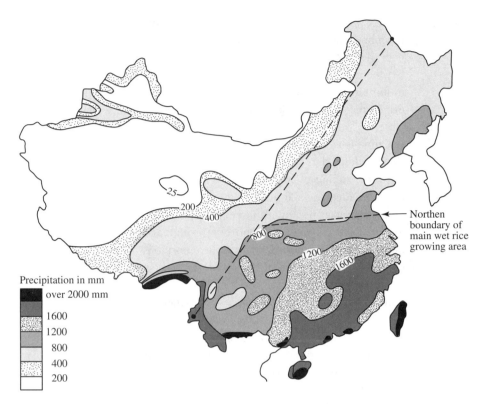

Figure 2.2
Annual precipitation.
Sources: Based on Leeming (1984) and Institute of Geography (2000).

a steady flow of cold, dry air over all of eastern China. But in the summer, heating of the entire Asian landmass creates a low-pressure area over central Asia that draws tropical maritime air, saturated with moisture, into southeastern China. As this air encounters mountain ridges and cooler air masses, rains fall abundantly on southern China. As a result, the coast stays relatively cool while the inland basins become very hot, particularly in the "four furnaces" of central China (Chongqing, Wuhan, Changsha, and Nanjing) and in the western deserts.

As the summer monsoon moves northwest, it loses strength and delivers less rain (figure 2.2). Overall, the north is dry, while the south is lush and drained by numerous waterways. The difference is reflected in an ancient saying about traditional means of transport: "South, boat; North, horse." This long-standing geographic difference increased at the end of the twentieth century, possibly because of the impact of global climate change (Climate Change Report 2015, 22–24). Usually, the monsoons push over the belt of mountains between the Yangtze and Yellow River basins, providing moderate summer rains in northern China. In bad years, however, the monsoons are too weak to cross over to the Yellow River valley and become stuck over the central mountain belt. In those years, northern China is struck by drought, while the rains hover over southern China, flooding the countryside. This central mountain range, then, creates another fundamental dividing line between southern China, with abundant water, and northern China, which is chronically short of water.

China is an arid country overall. In the Northwest, the margin of human habitation is defined by a continual tug-of-war with the desert, which threatens to advance, rolling over farmlands. The Aihui–Tengchong line marks this frontier between adequate and insufficient water. The precipitation gradient shapes the different character of China's three great west-to-east river systems. In the north, the Yellow River flows almost entirely through arid and semiarid country. The large population of northern China creates enormous demands on Yellow River water. One of the great rivers of the world, 4,800 kilometers long, but of only moderate total volume, the Yellow River literally runs dry in many years as withdrawals take all the available water. A record was reached in 1997, when there was no water in the downstream stretches of the Yellow River for 226 days (Liu 1998, 899). Furthermore, the Yellow River carries a heavy load of dissolved mud and sand, 2.6 billion tons every year, one-fourth of which is deposited on the riverbed. This raises the river bed about 10 centimeters each year, so that today the river—held between a line of dikes on either side—flows along an elevated path, always threatening to flood the surrounding, lower countryside when water does come. By contrast, the Yangtze River in lush southern China carries 20 times as much water. The Yangtze flows abundantly year-round and carries only one-third as much total sediment as the Yellow River. Even the Pearl River system carries six times as much water as the Yellow River. The distribution of water resources has led the Chinese government to create a massive south-to-north water-transfer system of aqueducts and canals (chapter 21). All the rivers rise and fall in rhythm with the monsoon. From their low point around February the rivers rise steadily until August or September, covering vast floodplains or barely held within dikes, until the flood begins to ebb again.

In relation to its enormous population, China is short of arable land, forests, and water, ensuring that its environmental problems will be severe and persistent. When account is taken of the highly uneven distribution of resources and population—especially the scarcity of water in the north and west—it is clear that enormous problems of environmental degradation challenge China. Climate change will affect this fragile balance in difficult-to-predict ways. Indeed, China will live on the margins of environmental crisis for the next 50 years or so, as economic growth pushes up against the limits of what the land can support (chapter 21).

2.3   Provinces and Regions

The most familiar way to divide China's vast space is into provinces. China currently has 31 diverse province-level administrative units, each of which is as big as a European country. The smallest population is in Tibet, with 3.2 million, according to 2015 data, and the largest is in Guangdong, with 108.5 million. China maintains an official distinction between provinces (22), municipalities under national supervision (4), and autonomous regions of ethnic minorities (5). These all have province-level "rank" in the national administrative system, and we will use the term "province" to refer to all of them. Some provinces have identities that trace back more than two millennia; two of them, however, are recent creations: Hainan Island was carved out of Guangdong Province in 1988, and Chongqing Municipality was separated from Sichuan Province in 1997. In addition, there are now two Special Administrative Regions (SARs) of China, Hong Kong (since 1997) and Macau (since 1999). These are never treated as provinces. Figure 2.3 shows the provinces and islands of China.

Provinces are not always the most natural way to divide up China's economic space. Another approach, following anthropologist William Skinner, is to divide Chinese territory into "macroregions" defined by the rugged topography. Each macroregion spreads over more than one province and consists of a densely settled core area and a less densely settled and often hilly periphery. Although it is possible to divide all of China into macroregions, not all macroregions are equal; we will look at several of the most important (see figure 2.4). The most important macroregion is North China, which can be thought of as the most central region of the Chinese economy. The North China Plain is by far the largest flatland area in China and contains a little over one-quarter of China's total farmland, as well as slightly over one-quarter of the total population (in figure 2.4, densely populated core areas show up as dark areas). The national capital, Beijing, serves as the urban center of North China and, along with its sister city, Tianjin, has a population well over 20 million. Size, location, and the national capital make North China the most important region of China. Despite the importance of the Beijing-Tianjin metropolis, the level of urbanization in the plain as a whole is slightly below the national average. Agriculture is still important, and large villages are spread thickly and fairly evenly over the entire expanse. Many areas in the plain are not irrigated; as a result, they depend on unreliable seasonal rains and are subject to periodic droughts and floods. The primary staple crop is wheat, although some areas produce economic crops such as cotton and peanuts. Although sheer size gives North China a predominant position among China's regions, it is rather average in terms of overall development levels, with 22% of China's population producing 23.4% of GDP in 2015.

Figure 2.3
China's provinces (includes provinces, autonomous regions, and municipalities with provincial rank).
Source: Based on Institute of Geography (2000).
SAR: special administrative region.

The most developed part of China is the Lower Yangtze macroregion. The Yangtze River delta, covering 50,000 square kilometers, is one of the great river deltas of the world. Wet rice cultivation is dominant, and typically two or more crops are harvested per year. The intensely cultivated countryside, comprising 7% of China's arable land, produces 9% of crop output. The country is lush and green, with water everywhere. For centuries, this has been the richest part of China. Canals provided efficient transportation throughout the delta, and many rich cities grew up over the years. Today, Shanghai is at the center of the region and is the largest and economically most important city in China, but the entire region is densely urbanized. Several important medium-sized cities serve the delta, ranging from Ningbo and Hangzhou in the south through Suzhou and Wuxi near Shanghai, to Nanjing in the west. With 12% of China's population, the three core Lower Yangtze provinces of Shanghai, Jiangsu, and Zhejiang produced 23% of China's industrial output and 19%

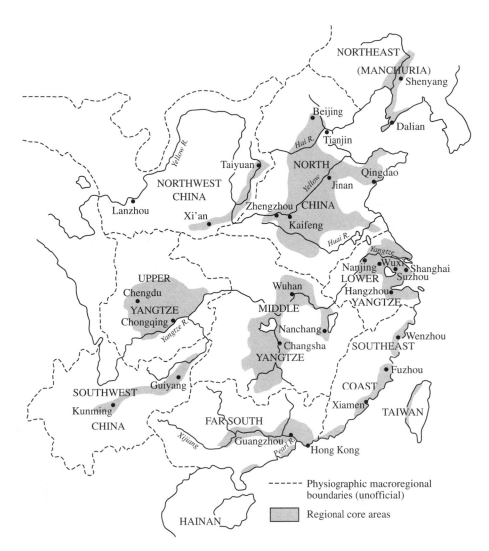

Figure 2.4
Macroregions and major cities of eastern China.
Source: Based on Fairbank and Goldman (1998).

of GDP in 2015. Since the 1970s, industrial production has spread so rapidly into the countryside that many areas classified as rural are more realistically thought of as urbanized countryside. The Lower Yangtze is also a foreign-trade powerhouse, with 2015 exports equal to 37% of GDP, nearly twice the national average.

Adjacent to the North China Plain and tied to it by numerous economic links is the region of the Northeast, or Manchuria. The Northeast is a region of abundant natural resources: farmers here have twice as much arable land per capita as the Chinese average, and rich reserves of iron ore, coal, and petroleum once made the Northeast the center of China's heavy industry. The relative abundance of land has encouraged migration from other parts of China since the beginning of the twentieth century, and the Northeast today has relatively high levels of agricultural mechanization and exports food grains to the rest of China. The industrial center is at Shenyang, in Liaoning, which is surrounded by a ring of eight medium-sized industrial cities, including Anshan, the site of China's oldest steel mill. But over the past three decades, the Northeast has struggled: the number of factory jobs in state-run industry has shrunk; the region has lost the important role it played in the national planned economy; and growth has lagged. From being a richer part of China, the Northeast has become precisely average, with 8% of China's population producing 8% of GDP in 2015.

The North, Northeast, and Lower Yangtze macroregions together accounted for 50.5% of national GDP in 2015. The economic relationship among the three regions has changed dramatically over many decades. Historically, the link between the North China Plain and the Lower Yangtze made China into a single economic entity: the Grand Canal was built to ship the food-grain surpluses of the Lower Yangtze to the national capital region in the northern plain. For a period in the mid-twentieth century, the mineral and land resources of the Northeast, along with the creation of its heavy industrial base, led it to be highly integrated into socialist, industrializing China. But over the past decades, the Northeast has become somewhat marginalized, losing its centrality to the Lower Yangtze, which has a better connection to the global economy and has grown rapidly. Today, the Beijing–Shanghai connection—now a high-speed rail link—once again defines the central axis of the economy.

The remaining Chinese macroregions were traditionally less tightly integrated into a single national economic system. The provinces in the middle reaches of the Yangtze—Hubei, Hunan, and Jiangxi—entered the reform era at Chinese average levels of development but lagged behind the rapidly growing coastal regions and have only partially caught up. These provinces hold 12.6% of China's population but produced only 10.4% of 2015 GDP. The land is well irrigated and intensely cultivated, but in contrast to the diversified agricultural economy of the Lower Yangtze, the Middle Yangtze primarily produces grain. This grain monoculture enables the region to export significant surpluses of grain to other regions of China. The major urban center is Wuhan, which has trade and industrial roles that extend beyond the region.

Following the Yangtze farther upstream, one arrives in Sichuan, a huge inland basin entirely surrounded by high mountains that is the core of the Upper Yangtze macroregion. Fertile and densely populated, there is no similar geographic feature anywhere in the world. The Sichuan basin is now divided into two provinces, Chongqing Municipality and Sichuan Province, which together had a 2015 population of 112 million. There is no natural route into or out of the Sichuan basin, and even the Yangtze River, as it flows out of Sichuan, cuts its way through a spectacular series of gorges, capped by the huge Three Gorges Dam. Chongqing and Chengdu (the capital of Sichuan Province) divide between them the functions of urban centers for the Upper Yangtze macroregion. In this region, out-migration has exceeded natural population growth since the turn of the century, and the population has declined by about 6% from its peak. Near the Sichuan basin and linked to it by extensive economic and transport ties is the Yunnan-Guizhou Plateau, labeled the "Southwest China" macroregion in figure 2.4. Although geographic conditions there are quite different from those in the Sichuan basin, the Chinese government usually includes Yunnan and Guizhou with Sichuan and Chongqing to form a greater Southwest China region. All four provinces are densely populated, have a common low income, and face serious development challenges. Here 14% of China's population produced 10% of GDP in 2015.

Two separate macroregions along the southeast coast can together be called "maritime China." John King Fairbank suggested long ago that "maritime China" was a distinct region and subculture within Chinese civilization, oriented outward toward ocean-borne trade, while most of China has been oriented inward. Maritime China is the homeland of most of the overseas Chinese who left China before 1949 (Fairbank and Goldman 2006). It is cut off from much of the rest of China by the mountain chains that define a narrow coastal strip. There is little hinterland, and communication was traditionally up and down the coast by boat. The one large core area along the coast is the fertile Pearl River Delta, the heart of Guangdong Province. The delta has long supported an extremely rich, diversified agriculture and a correspondingly dense population, with both Guangzhou and Hong Kong serving as urban centers.

The rapid growth of an externally oriented economy since 1978 has transformed Southeast China. Over the past 40 years, the politically divided segments of maritime China have grown together, constituting a single economic powerhouse. Investment from Hong Kong and Taiwan has built factories and new trading relationships. The close cultural, economic, and geographic ties among Taiwan, Hong Kong, and other regions of maritime China were temporarily broken under Maoist China after

1949. As a result, those parts of maritime China within the boundaries of the People's Republic of China were surprisingly poor and backward at the end of the 1970s, and one of the first priorities of reformers after 1978 was to reestablish traditional economic links among parts of maritime China. The early phases of China's economic opening after 1978 were largely steps in the reconstitution of these traditional links.

Four special economic zones (SEZs) were set up in 1979–1980 to attract investors to China. Each SEZ targeted a particular group of "maritime Chinese" as a source of investment and trade ties. The largest SEZ, Shenzhen, was set up adjacent to Hong Kong to attract spillover investment from what was then still a British colony. Shenzhen today has grown to become a large and independent city, the center of a metropolitan area of 10 million people. The gradual dismantling of the barriers that separated Hong Kong from the rest of the Pearl River delta has meant that multiple urban areas are progressively growing into a single integrated economic region. Housing, export factories, and diversified agricultural fields crowd the entire eastern delta. Meanwhile, the Zhuhai SEZ was set up across the Pearl River next door to the then Portuguese colony of Macau. Guangdong's exports were 55% of provincial GDP in 2015, down from earlier years but still by far the highest ratio among China's provinces. Up the coast, the Shantou SEZ was established in the Chaozhou (Teochiu) ethnic homeland to attract investment from this group, which is especially important economically in Southeast Asia. Finally, the Xiamen SEZ was designed to revive overseas links among the south Fujian (Minnan) people. People in Taiwan speak the same variety of Minnan that is spoken around Xiamen, from where their ancestors migrated after the 1600s. The Minnan have long been an oceangoing, trading people, and the distinctive Minnan dialect of Chinese is spoken also in extensive commercial networks throughout Southeast Asia, as well as in Taiwan and Fujian itself. As China opened up, investment from Taiwan increased dramatically, and Taiwan has begun to serve as one of the economic centers of the whole southeast region. Thus Taiwan and the Pearl River delta today serve as the dual cores of maritime China.

In western China, the macroregion concept is less applicable because the population is spread across vast, relatively arid regions. Skinner identified a Northwest macroregion with large concentrations of population in a few fertile river valleys—the Wei River in Shaanxi around Xi'an and the Fen River in Shanxi around Taiyuan. These rivers cut into the loess plateaus accumulated from centuries of sediment blowing in from central Asia. The loess can form a rich soil, but it is very susceptible to erosion and requires water. The Northwest region contains 10% of China's population, farming 18% of China's arable land, but the land is arid and overall of poor quality. During the coal boom of 2008–2012, parts of Shanxi and Inner Mongolia got rich quickly, but the region produced just 8% of China's GDP in 2015. To the west of this plateau country, people live primarily in oases or a few fertile valleys in the far northwest. Outside the valleys and oases, the land is arid and of poor quality, mainly used by nomadic herdspeople. As one ascends to the high plateau of Tibet and Qinghai, one finds vast stretches of virtually uninhabited land.

2.4   Natural Resources

Overall, China is a land-scarce and labor-abundant economy. With 18.7% of the world's population, China occupies only 7% of the world's land area. China's share of world mineral wealth is roughly proportional to its share of land area, so per capita mineral reserves are typically half of world averages or less. Even reserves of coal, which China mines and burns in abundance, amount to only 11% of total verified world reserves. China was the eighth-largest extractor of petroleum in 2016, but proven reserves of petroleum and natural gas amount to only 2.1% and 2.8% of the respective world totals. China may be able to develop its abundant shale gas deposits, but it is not yet clear whether complex geologic structures can be economically exploited. There are, however, rich deposits of nonferrous minerals, such as tin and copper and especially tungsten and rare earth.

The distribution of mineral and energy resources in China is extremely uneven. Fossil fuels are predominantly in the north, which has 90% of the oil and 80% of the coal reserves. Hydroelectric potential is substantial where there is water (the South) and relief (the West): 68% of the hydropower potential is in the Southwest macroregion. The rapidly growing southern coastal regions have virtually no energy resources. Geographic constraints, therefore, foreclose resource-based and land-intensive development strategies; China must develop along a labor-intensive and, ultimately, knowledge-intensive path. Moreover, unforgiving environmental constraints will make economic trade-offs more difficult and complex for the foreseeable future.

2.5   The Built Landscape

Geography provides a baseline, describing the spatial conditions and resources that give a structure to what is possible and a form to economic activity. However, geographic conditions are not fixed and immutable; human activity is constantly reshaping geographic possibility. Even in premodern China, a significant part of the geography was "man-made." The rich landscape of the Lower Yangtze is the product of many years spent draining swampland and fertilizing new fields, and the striking terraced hills and irrigation networks of upland southern China are also the outcome of centuries of hard work. A modern economy has a much larger capacity to reshape landscapes, and modern economic growth constantly creates new patterns of habitation and transportation. This is particularly true in China given the extraordinarily large investments that have accompanied rapid economic growth (see chapter 7), which has accelerated the pace at which landscapes are being reconstructed. The rapid build-out of modern infrastructure in China is changing the meaning of space and the impact of geographic conditions. China is becoming much "smaller": areas that were remote 20 years ago are now accessible to tourists, merchants, and government functionaries, and local people in those areas find it much easier to get out, migrate, or travel for business or experience.

Internationally, China was relatively isolated during the Mao years, but during the first years of reform and opening, a massive infrastructure effort was directed particularly toward reestablishing links with ocean-borne trade networks. Today, China is by many measures the most connected country in the world. It has 6 of the world's 10 busiest ports (Shanghai is the largest). The United Nations computes a Liner Shipping Connectivity Index based on shipping lines, capacities, and volumes; the 2015 edition assigned China by far the highest value, 167, compared with next-best Singapore at 117 and the United States, the United Kingdom, and the Netherlands in the 95–98 range. The reintegration of maritime China and the success of China's export drive would have been impossible without this massive investment effort.

Since 2000, the focus of infrastructure construction has shifted to domestic land transport. China has now built a national expressway network that is the world's largest, at 123,500 kilometers, compared with 76,000 kilometers in the United States. Since 2004, China has added 8,000 kilometers of expressway every year. Interregional car travel is now feasible, while traffic fatalities have dropped in half, notwithstanding the explosion in private vehicles. A new wave of transformation is occurring with the advent of high-speed rail. A nationwide grid of four north-south and four east-west main lines is planned for 2020, and about half of this grid was operational in 2015, shrinking the time required to get from Beijing to Shanghai, for example, to under six hours (figure 2.5). Like the rest of the world, China is getting wired: 1.27 billion mobile phone subscribers (more than one for every adult), and 577 million broadband Internet connections were in use at the end of 2015. It is clear that these changes in infrastructure will have significant ramifications for nearly every aspect of economic growth.

Moreover, the impact of these dramatic changes in communication and mobility is still just beginning to be felt. China has consistently followed a strategy of building out infrastructure ahead of demand. As a result, in some cases, infrastructure investments have been overly hasty and poorly planned, leading to low utilization rates and poor efficiency. Logistics within China are still relatively expensive, the result of rugged terrain, less efficient infrastructure, and administrative delays. However, thus far, the economy has steadily grown into the infrastructure created. As the cost

Figure 2.5
High speed rail network (operational July 2017).
Source: Xi'an Marco Polo International Travel Service. Accessed at https://www.travelchinaguide.com
/images/map/train/high-speed-railway.jpg.

of land transport declines, it will change urbanization patterns, create new linkages
that blur boundaries among macroregions, and facilitate the redistribution of economic activity across the expanse of China.

2.6   Changing Regional Dynamics

For almost 30 years after the beginning of China's market transition, economic
growth was more rapid in the coastal provinces than in inland provinces. At first,
this reflected catch-up growth on the part of the coastal regions: the development
strategy under the planned economy had neglected the coastal provinces, which
entered the reform era significantly underperforming their obvious potential.
However, the economic transformation went far beyond this. The Chinese government extended preferential policies to coastal regions and poured resources into

the infrastructure necessary to link maritime China to world markets. Moreover, as restrictions on population movement were gradually relaxed, a steady and growing stream of migrants came to the coastal provinces. The result was that China's economy tilted to the coast. The nine coastal provinces that participated fully in the explosive development of China's external economy—Beijing and Tianjin down through Guangdong—produced 43% of China's GDP in 1978 and increased their share to 55% by 2006. By that time, all the highest per capita GDP provinces were on the coast, and the coast-inland gap had become one of the most widely remarked features of the Chinese economy.

A few years into the twenty-first century, the tilt toward the coastal regions stopped and gradually went into reverse. Growth in the coastal provinces slowed, and by 2015, the nine core coastal provinces' share of national GDP had declined from its 2006 peak of 55% to 51%. There are many reasons for this fundamental turning point in China's regional development, but the most important is the change in relative costs caused by growth and development. Changing labor markets led to rapidly increasing wages (chapter 9), and world and domestic prices of energy and raw materials spiked. The value of land soared, and congestion and pollution costs increased. These changes in relative scarcities were quickly reflected in the costs faced by businesses selling in highly competitive markets, and two market shifts followed. First, the overall competitiveness of China's existing exports eroded. It is not coincidental that 2006, the year in which coastal GDP peaked as a share of national GDP, was also the year in which China's exports reached their peak value as a share of GDP. Subsequently, exports continued to grow in absolute terms but less rapidly than overall GDP, so exports as a share of GDP declined (chapter 16). Second, businesses began to move production inland in search of cheaper land and lower wages. Even some businesses that produced entirely for export (such as the huge electronics assembler Foxconn) set up inland factories to benefit from lower costs.

This shift, driven primarily by market forces, was also strongly encouraged by Chinese government policy. In 1999, the Chinese government officially launched the Western Development Program to give preference to western and inland provinces in investment projects and other economic development policies. The massive infrastructure build-out described in the previous section was part of this policy shift. Some inland provinces, including Chongqing, Hubei, and Guizhou, have been beneficiaries of massive national investment programs. Moreover, the government crafted many policies to redistribute investment and fiscal resources away from the coast and toward inland provinces (chapter 20). In addition, the government influenced the distribution of activity in more subtle ways. For example, it is much easier to convert agricultural land to industrial uses around inland cities than around coastal cities because the central government assigns stricter land-conversion quotas in coastal areas. Pollution standards are relatively lax inland, while the increasingly middle-class residents of coastal cities have begun to demand a healthier environment. Although production has begun to shift inland, households have continued to move toward the coast. So far, migration to coastal regions has continued, with the nine core coastal provinces increasing their share of national population from 33.4% in 1978 to 36% in 2006 and further to 37.7% in 2015. The coastal cities still boast higher wages and more amenities than most inland areas.

Broad generalizations about a coast-inland gap are too simple to capture the complexities of China's economic geography. In the first place, there is a north-south gap in growth rates that is just as significant as the east-west gap: the South is growing much faster. The Chinese government rolled out the Northeast Revitalization Plan in 2003 but still had to deal with a new round of problems in the Northeast after 2014. Moreover, different inland areas have very different resource endowments and face different developmental challenges. The best performers in recent years have been some northern resource-rich provinces, such as Inner Mongolia and Shaanxi. These provinces rode a boom in hydrocarbon production from 2006 to 2012 and exploited their proximity to Beijing but found growth fragile when prices for coal and oil dropped after 2013. In the far west, the half of the country west of the Aihui–Tengchong line that contains only 6% of the total population, the development challenge derives from limitations of water and fertile land, a sparse population, and a lack of economic agglomeration and accessible markets. A completely different challenge comes in what we might call the "near west," the areas where a dense population pushes up against rugged topography and limited carrying capacity of the land. China's most intractable problems of poverty are concentrated in a broad belt just east of the southern half of the Aihui–Tengchong line, running through Gansu, Sichuan, Guizhou, and Yunnan, where a huge population struggles to eke out a living from the ungenerous land. This is also a belt of environmental degradation, including deforestation and soil erosion, and of especially severe economic challenges: environmental, social, and economic problems all come together in this region. Geographic conditions and the associated environmental challenges will continue to shape China's developmental challenges and possibilities even as new opportunities emerge.

2.7   Conclusion

As economic conditions change, and particularly as labor costs rise in the coastal regions (chapters 6 and 9), some economic activity will move inland, and China's vastly improved infrastructure will facilitate the redistribution of activity and new patterns of urban development. Moreover, in the period around 2020, China's land connections to its neighbors will also begin to expand dramatically, creating communications and transport corridors in regions long thought of as frontiers and barriers. The Chinese government in 2014 launched an ambitious international program to bundle together various programs to improve infrastructure in Asia. Called the "Belt and Road Initiative" to evoke the ancient Silk Road while covering both land and maritime transport, the program has been given steadily increasing visibility through 2017. Containing many different initiatives, it will have important economic effects. A high-speed rail corridor will likely extend from Yunnan down through Southeast Asia to Singapore; and connections with Russia and inner Asia will multiply. Many of these regions have never had efficient transport networks, and we think of them as remote borderlands, but this is set to change. Given China's economic heft, these new transport networks will greatly increase China's centrality in the Asian region. The geographic endowment is continuously being rebuilt through ceaseless economic activity, and this process will continue in the foreseeable future.

Bibliography

Suggestions for Further Reading

Veeck et al. (2011) is a highly readable introduction to China's geography. Van Slyke (1988) is a lively introduction to Chinese geography through the perspective of the Yangtze River. Chi (1963 [1936]) is still an excellent account of different regions. Several excellent atlases of China are now available in English, but perhaps the most beautiful is Institute of Geography (2000).

Sources for Data and Figures

Data on Chinese landforms in this chapter come primarily from Zhao Ji (1990), with additional material from Zhao Songqiao (1994) and Li (1984). CIA (1971, 52–53) has interesting maps that explicitly show the analogies between the United States and China.

The macroregion approach was created by Skinner (1977), although the map reproduced in figure 2.4 is from Fairbank and Goldman (2006). Statistics on macroregions are drawn from Li (1984), updated from *SYC*.

Details on the links between specific groups of Chinese overseas and their source areas in China are given in Zhang et al. (1990). The UN Liner Shipping Connectivity Index is at http://unctadstat.unctad.org/wds/TableViewer/tableView.aspx?ReportId=92.

References

Chi, Ch'ao-ting (1963 [1936]). *Key Economic Areas in Chinese History: As Revealed in the Development of Public Works for Water Control*. New York: Paragon Book Reprint Corporation.

CIA (Central Intelligence Agency) (1971). *People's Republic of China: Atlas*. Washington, DC: U.S. Government Printing Office. Most of these maps can be accessed at http://www.lib.utexas.edu/maps/china.

Climate Change Report 2015. Ministry of Science and Technology. *Disanci Qihou Bianhu Guojia Pinggu Baogao* [Third national climate change assessment report]. Beijing: Kexue Chubanshe.

Fairbank, John King, and Merle Goldman (2006). *China: A New History*. 2nd, enl. ed. Cambridge, MA: Belknap Press of Harvard University Press.

Institute of Geography, Chinese Academy of Sciences, and China Population and Environment Society, eds. (2000). *The Atlas of Population, Environment and Sustainable Development in China*. New York: Science Press.

Leeming, F. (1984). *Selected China Maps*. Leeds: Department of Geography, University of Leeds.

Li Ruluan, ed. (1984). *Ziran Dili Tongji Ziliao* [Natural geography statistical materials]. New ed. Beijing: Shangwu Yinshuguan.

Liu Changming (1998). "Environmental Issues and the South–North Water Transfer Scheme." *China Quarterly*, no. 156 (December): 899–910.

Skinner, G. William (1977). "Regional Urbanization in Nineteenth-Century China." In G. William Skinner, ed., *The City in Late Imperial China*, 211–252. Stanford, CA: Stanford University Press.

Sun Jingzhi (1988). *The Economic Geography of China*. Hong Kong: Oxford University Press.

SYC (Annual). *Zhongguo Tongji Nianjian* [Statistical yearbook of China]. Beijing: Zhongguo Tongji.

Van Slyke, Lyman P. (1988). *Yangtze: Nature, History, and the River*. Reading, MA: Addison-Wesley.

Veeck, Gregory, Clifton W. Pannell, Christopher J. Smith, and Youqin Huang (2011). *China's Geography: Globalization and the Dynamics of Political, Economic, and Social Change*. 2nd ed. Lanham, MD: Rowman & Littlefield.

Zhang Xianghan et al. (1990). *Huaqiao Huaren Daguan* [Encyclopedia of the overseas Chinese], 11–18. Guangzhou: Jinan Daxue.

Zhao Ji, ed. (1990). *The Natural History of China*. New York: McGraw-Hill.

Zhao Songqiao (1994). *Geography of China: Environment, Resources, Population and Development*. New York: Wiley.

The Chinese Economy Before 1949

China's economic history over the last century has been marked by dramatic discontinuities, in particular the revolution of 1949 and the shift toward a market economy after 1978. This chapter and chapter 4 organize their discussion of economic development around those dramatic political and policy turning points. Before 1949, China never launched into rapid, modern economic growth; since 1949, growth has been consistently strong, rebounding quickly even after disastrous policy mistakes in the Maoist years. For more than a century—from the late eighteenth to the early twentieth century, China's economic performance was mediocre at best. Moreover, under pressure from the West, China disintegrated politically. The traditional interpretation has been that China's economy failed in the nineteenth and early twentieth centuries, and that 1949, therefore, was a fundamental turning point. The enormous differences in economic performance before and after 1949 certainly suggest changes in economic fundamentals.

A contrasting interpretation stresses that economic development is a long-term process that consists of the accumulation of human and physical capital, together with the evolution of institutions appropriate to a modern economy. The economic success of China after 1949, combined with the economic success of Chinese under different political systems in Taiwan and Hong Kong, indicates that there were features of the traditional economy that were supportive of economic development (Rawski 1989; Brandt, Ma and Rawski 2014). To those following this logic, China could have grown rapidly under any economic system and, lacking a socialist revolution, could have been expected to engage in development along capitalist lines. By contrast, those emphasizing the 1949 turning point argue that the revolution not only established domestic peace but also redistributed land and empowered poor people politically and economically in a way that was necessary for economic takeoff (Richardson 1999).

Interpretation of the 1949 turning point also requires an assessment of the performance of the traditional Chinese economy. Many scholars have engaged in interpreting the different historical experiences of China and the economically advanced countries of Western Europe. If we look at China after the collapse of the Qing in 1911 or after the conclusion of the civil war in 1945, the gap with the industrialized West looks enormous. Yet, as Pomeranz (2000) points out, most of this "great divergence" opened up relatively late, during the nineteenth century, rather than reflecting long-term differences in productivity or economic sophistication between China and the West. Did the Chinese economy "fail" before 1949, and if it did, why? Was the Chinese traditional economy well suited to economic development? If so, why was the actual response to the Western challenge so feeble? Was a basis laid in the pre-1949 era for the vigorous growth after 1949? Finally, the economic takeoff since 1978 has revived many traditional economic elements. To what extent has China's shift to a market economy involved the resurrection of traditional social and economic practices? To begin to address these questions, we first examine the traditional Chinese economy during three broad time periods and then evaluate the legacy of the traditional economy.

3.1   The Traditional Economy, 1127–1911

3.1.1   High-Productivity Traditional Agriculture

Chinese traditional society was overwhelmingly rural, with over 90% of the population living in the countryside. Farmers employed a sophisticated agricultural technology to wrest high crop yields per unit of land cultivated (King 1911). These yields depended on the massive application of human labor to small plots of farmland, so high productivity per unit of land coexisted with low productivity per worker. A complex and highly productive agricultural technology developed, based not on modern science but on the trial-and-error practice of generations of farmers. A "traditional triad" of farm technology consisted of three key elements: selected seed varieties, organic fertilizer, and irrigation. Early-ripening rice was adopted from Southeast Asia as early as the Southern Song dynasty (AD 1127–1279); the extraordinary early wealth and cultural development of the Southern Song, centered in the Lower Yangtze, clearly depended on this technological breakthrough. The short growing season of early-ripening rice allowed farmers to plant two or more crops of grain annually on a single plot of land. Organic fertilizers were applied to fields to maintain soil fertility. Every available nutrient was recycled into the soil; the most important was manure from humans ("night soil") and animals, but farmers also added pond mud, lime, and green algae to the soil. Even the clay bricks used to make chimneys were crushed and spread on fields after they had absorbed enough smoke to build up organic compounds. Finally, sophisticated irrigation systems allowed farmers to precisely control the water on their fields and take full advantage of better crop varieties and fertilizer. Rice shoots were sprouted in seedbeds and then transplanted to flooded fields. As the rice plants matured, fields were drained and the ripe plants were harvested. The productivity of each element of the traditional triad was enhanced by the presence of the others.

This highly productive traditional agricultural system could function only through the massive and intensive application of labor. Preparing fields and irrigation canals, hauling fertilizer, and transplanting seedlings were all backbreaking work. The average product per unit of land was high, but the average product per unit of labor input was low, and so incomes were low. Many farmers produced barely enough to feed their families. But farmers were always able to find some work for an additional hand: the marginal product of labor was below the average product, but it did not drop quickly to zero as more laborers were added. A growing population was supported, but population growth kept constant pressure on incomes and consumption, which remained low. One of the most striking characteristics of this agricultural system—in contrast to the one that evolved in Europe over the same period—was the limited role of animals in farm work and human diet. Meat was a luxury for most Chinese, protein consumption was inadequate, and almost all calories and protein came from grain.

The intensive application of human labor to small plots of land reminded early Western visitors to China of gardening rather than of farming as they knew it, but these observers were also uniformly impressed by the high yields and the intense utilization of resources they observed. The persistent recycling of wastes changed the composition of soils and served to maintain productivity. "Owing to many centuries of cultivation, there were no natural soils left [by the nineteenth century in China]. All soils were man-made in varying degrees" (Vermeer 1988, 224). The high-productivity system was created first in the Lower Yangtze and then gradually spread to lowland and riverside areas where irrigation was feasible. Population growth pushed farmers into the hills, where they built terraces up the slopes. The introduction of New World crops, especially corn (maize) and potatoes, allowed farmers to spread onto new lands less suited to the traditional growing technologies.

3.1.2 The Commercialized Countryside

The densely populated countryside supported a thick network of markets. In areas that were suitable for the building of canals, particularly the Lower Yangtze and Pearl River deltas, regions were tied together by a highly developed system of water transport. The major rivers, particularly the Yangtze, provided links among regions, while the Grand Canal linked the food-surplus Lower Yangtze with the food-deficit North China Plain. Places on the water transport network could trade even heavy and bulky commodities. Local markets were joined into channels for interregional trade. Dense population and transport networks supported a highly commercialized premodern economy, including sophisticated institutions, competitive markets, and a small-scale, "bottom-heavy" economy (Zelin 1991; see also Brandt 1990; Naquin and Rawski 1987).

3.1.2.1 Sophisticated Institutions

Institutional support for the economy included the following:

• Widespread use of money. Paper money was one-third or more of total money in circulation as of 1820.

• Familiarity with large formal organizations. Clan or lineage organizations, particularly in south China, had extensive economic functions. Sometimes formal shares were issued to regulate an individual's membership in a corporate-lineage or local-place association.

• Advanced commercial procedures. Written contracts were ubiquitous. Contracts extended beyond business transactions to regulate obligations to family, the gods, and the afterlife. As early as the first century AD, "tomb contracts" proving the right of the dead to occupy a given plot of ground were buried with the dead. The use of middlemen in personal and commercial transactions was nearly universal.

• Supportive legal and customary institutions. Courts existed and were used for lawsuits. Interregional trade was often regulated by local-place and merchants' associations that helped resolve disputes and created support networks.

• Traditional banks that allowed merchants to transfer funds nationwide.

3.1.2.2 Competitive Markets

• Highly competitive markets for most products. Recent studies of such markets as coal and iron, textiles, and tea confirm that each of these was characterized by numerous suppliers, easy entry, and frequent exit.

• Competitive and efficient markets for land and labor.

• Few socially imposed barriers to mobility. There was no aristocracy or system of castes defined by birth. Individuals frequently migrated in search of economic opportunity. Although inequality was significant, potential social mobility was real.

3.1.2.3 Small-Scale, "Bottom-Heavy" Economy

Agriculture was based on individual, small-scale households. There were no plantations or large landed estates. Most nonagricultural production was also small scale and done by rural households. Textiles, leather goods, and iron tools, as well as food products such as wine, tea, sugar, noodles, and edible oils, were all produced by microenterprises in the countryside. Many households farmed, manufactured handicrafts, and marketed their own output. Thus traditional China had a vigorous household-based economy. Households were also directly linked to a number of different markets. In many cases, the consecutive stages of a production chain were handled by separate specialized households connected by markets. For instance, this kind of vertical segmentation characterized the manufacture of silk cloth. The raising of silkworms, care of silkworm cocoons, spinning of raw silk thread, and weaving of silk cloth were all carried out separately by specialized households or small firms that dealt with each other in the marketplace. Thus chains of small processors and middlemen linked household producers, merchants, and consumers.

One of the early successes of Chinese foreign trade was the rapid growth of the tea export industry after the 1880s. At its peak, more than a million households, mainly in Fujian Province, participated in the tea industry. The average farm household produced a couple of hundred pounds of tea per year, which in turn was processed by hundreds of small tea factories. This export industry grew rapidly around the turn of the twentieth century. But the Chinese system did not cope well with the rise of competition from Japan and India after the twentieth century began. Competitiveness required standardization and reliable high quality, which China's small-scale and dispersed producers were not organized to provide. As a result, Chinese exporters in the 1920s were pushed out of a world market they had created. As the export industry declined, households exited tea production as rapidly as they had entered it.

This was an economy with a fluid and flexible allocation of resources. On the positive side, resources and labor moved efficiently to the use with the highest rate of return and exited such activities just as rapidly when returns fell. On the other hand, economic activity was fragmented into small-scale businesses with little capital, which may have had negative consequences. For example, cotton fabric was woven in three-quarters of China's counties, but large-scale textile mills, the foundation of the Industrial Revolution elsewhere, did not emerge in China until the twentieth century. Accumulation of capital in large enterprises was either very difficult or inefficient compared with dispersed household-based production. Indeed, this fluidity may have been partially the result of a need to avoid risk, to prevent wealth from being too obvious to potential predators or rapacious officials. Nevertheless, it is impossible not to be impressed by the sophistication of the traditional Chinese economy. We would have expected the traditional Chinese economy to respond well to new challenges and opportunities presented by the impact of the West. And yet, as discussed below, this was not to be the case.

3.1.3   A High-Level Equilibrium

Premodern China had a population size and economic weight similar to that of pre-modern Europe. The important difference was that after AD 600 China was more often unified politically, whereas Europe never was. After political stability was established at the beginning of the Ming dynasty (1368–1644), the efficient farm economy was able to support a growing population for 400 years. Population more than quadrupled from 72 million in 1400 to around 310 million in 1794. China's population grew at a rate of almost 0.4% per year over this long period, faster than the rest of the world at this time, and quite fast for a premodern population (chapter 8). Thus throughout all of "late imperial China" (1368–1911), "massive population growth with stable long-run living standards [was] the defining feature of the Ming-Qing economy" (Brandt, Ma, and Rawski 2014, 52).

With its productive economy and about one-third of the global population, China was unquestionably the world's largest economy. How did the level of development compare between China and Europe? In his magisterial reconstruction of the global economy, Angus Maddison (1998) integrated China into the story by simply assuming that China's per capita GDP was equal to the global average ($600 in 1990 "international dollars") and unchanged from 1600 to 1820. Maddison's back-of-the-envelope calculation is a starting point but obviously not the last word in global economic history. As Pomeranz (2000) pointed out, it would be more meaningful to compare specific regions of China with countries or regions in Europe. Remarkably, economic historians have recently done just that. Allen et al. (2011) compared wages of unskilled workers in Chinese and European cities during the eighteenth and nineteenth centuries. Although wages in London and Amsterdam were much higher, wages in Beijing, Suzhou, and Canton were close to those in Milan and Leipzig. Li and Van Zanden (2012) found that Dutch GDP per capita was almost twice as high as that in the Yangtze delta in the 1820s, and that all the difference came from the larger high-productivity industry and service sectors in the Netherlands. These data imply that China's advanced regions were comparatively well off in a global context, but not as developed as England and the Netherlands, which were already the richest regions in the world and starting to accelerate.

3.1.4   The Role of Government: Qing-Dynasty Florescence and Decline

At the peak of its power in the eighteenth century, the Qing dynasty (1644–1911) was a remarkable multinational empire that brought together Han Chinese, Mongols, Tibetans, Uighurs, and other groups. It held them together in an intricate system that combined political, military, ceremonial, and even religious institutions. The Qing also provided a remarkable set of essential public goods: it operated granaries, repaired hydraulic works, and operated a justice system and a national courier network. It maintained the national examination system that integrated society through a shared Confucian ideology and a political hierarchy with a tradition of service. It permitted upward mobility and recruited talented people from the far corners of the empire. This system was remarkably "lean," providing a strictly limited basket of key public goods at the lowest possible cost. Most essential of all, of course, was internal and external security, which the Qing provided with great success for over a century.

During the "high" Qing, two capable emperors, Kangxi and Qianlong (Kangxi's grandson), between them ruled for an astonishing 122 years between 1661 and 1796. Qianlong pushed China's borders out to their greatest historical extent, basically establishing the modern boundaries of the People's Republic of China. In 1793, on his 82nd birthday, Qianlong received a delegation from the English king George III. What followed was one of the great episodes of cultural miscommunication in world history. Delegation leader George Macartney was sent to deliver gifts, seek trade concessions, and represent his country, which he considered the most powerful in the world and certainly the equal of China. Qianlong, on the other hand, saw Macartney as bringing tribute from a small and distant country without following proper protocol, and offering trade goods for which the self-sufficient "Celestial Empire" had no need. The aged emperor, soon to abdicate after decades of political and cultural achievement, can perhaps be forgiven for failing to see the full importance of the English visit. For us, the visit signals the end of an era of remarkable achievement and the beginning of a new century of weakening capabilities in the face of unprecedented challenges and external threats.

Even at its best, though, the Qing government was a very thin layer on a vast population and a big, bottom-heavy economy. It was much smaller, relative to the population and the economy, than were governments in Western Europe in the premodern period. Around 1800, there was only one government worker per 32,000 people in China, compared with one for every 600 to 800 in Europe at the same time (Perkins 1967). Revenues and expenditures per capita were also far less than in Europe. The Qing administrative system was in some respects extremely fragile, and the Qing emperors proved unable to increase their administrative capability as the economy and population increased. As Sng (2014) demonstrated, budgetary revenues fell from a peak of around 8% of GDP in the early 1700s to below 3% ultimately. This produced, in effect, a slow-motion, long-lasting fiscal crisis. Sng argued that given China's immense size, the tiny group of officials who made up the national Qing government were forced to delegate responsibility for taxation and justice to local officials in collaboration with local power holders. The volume of resources collected by local agents was substantial, but because of corruption and local favoritism, the revenue that reached the national government was low (and declining). National officials attempted to monitor their local agents but had limited capacity and were forced to accept the erosion in their budgetary revenues. For the same reasons, provision of justice at the local level was capricious and uncertain, and property rights, while widely recognized and understood, were almost impossible to protect against rapacious officials.

Perhaps because of this sustained fiscal crisis, there is evidence that each of the most important public goods provided by the Qing empire declined after the late 1700s. Food reserves in public granaries shrank. Large-scale irrigation networks and the system of dikes on the Yellow River were allowed to deteriorate, and the Grand Canal silted up. Domestic security worsened after the 1794 White Lotus rebellion in Sichuan and Hubei. Perhaps because the Qing emperors devoted so many resources to the inner Asian frontier, they were unprepared for the very different security threats that were building on the eastern coastal regions.

Less effective government provision of services may have contributed to a broader economic and environmental decline (Elvin and Liu 1998; Will and Wong 1991). Farmers encroached on wetlands and lakes that were essential parts of the complex river ecologies. The decline in domestic order made such encroachments on the public domain harder to prevent. As the population continued to grow, the rural population became increasingly vulnerable to any breakdown in the rural system, with the result that floods or droughts could cause terrible famines. For example, the Wei River valley, the site of the ancient city of Xi'an, had practiced sophisticated irrigation for over 2,000 years, but by the nineteenth century, this infrastructure had broken down and left the population vulnerable to droughts. Less effective government became apparent as China was straining the limits of economic possibility given traditional technologies. It is clear that ecological exhaustion deprived the economy of readily available materials, such as lumber and metal, and that environmental problems were becoming more severe. At the beginning of the nineteenth century, the Qing dynasty had clearly entered a broad period of dynastic decline just as the European countries, which were entering an unprecedented period of economic and population growth, were about to arrive on China's doorstep.

3.2   The Failed Response to the West and Japan

During the nineteenth century, foreign powers began to have an increasingly severe political, military, and economic impact on China. The economic stimulus from this contact could have been positive, but instead, China during the nineteenth century tumbled into a profound social crisis. This crisis was certainly aggravated by the political and military challenge from the West, but it went beyond anything we can explain by the direct impact of the West.

As we have seen, foreign encroachment on China began during a period of dynastic weakness. It started with economic disruption and then expanded to military confrontation. For centuries, China had run an export surplus with the outside world, preferring to import silver rather than foreign goods (indirectly confirming the Qianlong emperor's judgment that China did not need foreign manufactures). Traditional Chinese exports of silk, tea, and porcelain produced an inflow of silver that increased the money supply and contributed to economic expansion until the 1820s. However, British merchants were unhappy with the steady drain of silver into China and searched for a commodity that would appeal to Chinese consumers and could be imported into China and redress the trade imbalance. They finally located such a commodity in opium. Chests of opium, grown in India, were imported by British merchants into China. By the 1830s, China was importing more than it was exporting. China now faced both an economic problem—a slowdown caused by slow adjustment to a shrinking supply of monetary metals—and a new social problem, opium addiction.

Chinese attempts to stop the inflow of opium led to the Opium War with Britain in 1839. Britain's industrial revolution was still in its early stages, but Britain already had the ability to mobilize financial, commercial, and military resources of unprecedented scale. The British crushed the hopelessly outmoded Chinese defenses, and in the Treaty of Nanking (1842) forced China to cede Hong Kong to British rule and open the first five Treaty Ports to foreign control. Between 1839 and 1895, China fought and lost five wars against various foreign powers encroaching on its territory. After each loss, China was forced to pay reparations to the victors and open more Chinese cities to foreign residence and control. The Qing government, already enfeebled, was never able to develop an effective response, and each defeat intensified its fiscal crisis and reduced its options further.

The weakened Qing dynasty was increasingly unable to deal with domestic challenges. By far the most serious threat was the Taiping Rebellion (1850–1864). This uprising gained control of the rich Lower Yangtze, the economic heartland. The attacks of the rebels and their suppression by the Qing armies caused massive damage and casualties estimated at 20 to 30 million or more. The traditional Lower Yangtze center of Hangzhou was completely destroyed. The Qing dynasty might well have collapsed then, but it was propped up by the foreign powers, who thought that the Taiping rebels were worse than the enfeebled imperial regime. Instead, the Qing teetered from crisis to crisis until its ultimate collapse in 1911.

Other foreign powers piled on, winning concessions and spheres of influence in China. At their peak, there were more than 80 Treaty Ports, governed by foreign powers and not subject to Chinese jurisdiction. Shanghai was the most important, and emerged as the economic center of the Lower Yangtze region after it was protected from the destruction of the Taiping Rebellion by its foreign status. Extraterritoriality (foreign exemption from domestic law) and foreign control of Treaty Ports and customs revenues were politically controversial until their abolition in the mid-twentieth century. Because of this association between foreign contact and national humiliation, policies of economic and political opening to foreigners have remained a sensitive issue through the present day.

Japan gradually took over from Britain as the main foreign power encroaching on China economically, politically, and militarily. The Sino-Japanese War of 1895 led to the seizure of Taiwan and its incorporation into the Japanese empire. This defeat dealt a profound shock to the Chinese public, for the first time creating a broad-based realization of the need to reform and revitalize the political system. Since the 1868 Meiji Restoration, Japan had been actively reforming and trying to facilitate modernization, including military modernization, to stave off foreign intervention. Japan's earlier vigorous response contrasted sharply with the slow and uncertain response of the Qing government. The Japanese state was strengthened by a radical land reform that redistributed as much as 10% of GNP to the government and created a rising class of entrepreneurial landowners. The government then rapidly initiated a state-sponsored program of industrialization, technology transfer, and manpower training. By contrast, the Qing was actively trying to resist modernization, and with only minor exceptions, never did put together a serious package of reforms. The 1895 War showed the Chinese public how large the gap with Japan had become, and how dangerous it was.

To be sure, some progressive Chinese officials understood the type of measures required to meet the foreign challenge. After 1870, these officials sponsored industrial projects, including the China Merchants' Steam Navigation Company, an iron and steel mill in Wuhan, and shipyards and armories in the Shanghai area. These projects were called "official supervision and merchant management" (*guandu shangban*) because the projects were government sponsored but delegated management to experienced merchants. Some of these projects, like China Merchants' Steam, have survived to the present day, but most failed because of poor management or lack of commitment from the government. The Qing government, virtually bankrupt by this time, was incapable of mobilizing sustained support for these projects, and dynastic officials only rarely understood the urgency of doing so.

3.3   The Beginnings of Modernization, 1912–1937

After the collapse of the Qing dynasty and the 1911 Revolution, China entered a new phase of gradually accelerating institutional and economic change. Modern industrial development began, and modern transportation and communication links opened up new possibilities for other sectors. The period immediately after 1911 was troubled by warlord domination, political fragmentation, and civil war, but in 1927 the Nationalist (Guomindang) Party finally succeeded in unifying China again. For

10 years, until the Japanese invasion in 1937, China enjoyed relative peace, and the Nationalist government, from its capital in Nanjing, was able to begin building the institutional framework for development. During the "Nanjing decade," the government began tentatively to invest in such things as education and agricultural extension services. A national surveying project inventoried natural resources, and ambitious national development plans were drawn up. Few of these activities came to fruition during this period, but groundwork was laid for the future. Skilled individuals were trained, and new technologies were developed, such as the creation of new crop strains. A government developmental and modernizing program—similar to that of Japan under Meiji—finally seemed to be under way, and the seeds of future growth were sown.

3.3.1   Industry

From a tiny base, modern factory production grew at 8% to 9% annually between 1912 and 1936, quite a rapid pace of industrialization at this time (John Chang 1969). Ironically, modern industry began after 1895, when the Treaty of Shimonoseki, ending the Sino-Japanese War, compelled China to accept foreign investment. By 1933, modern factories produced 2% of GDP and employed a million workers, although this was only 0.4% of China's labor force. Two distinct patterns are apparent in this initial industrial growth: "Treaty-Port industrialization" and "Manchurian industrialization."

Modern industry began in enclaves in the Treaty Ports during the early twentieth century. This was the dominant pattern of industrialization in China proper (that is, China "inside the Great Wall," excluding Manchuria). Foreigners began to operate factories around the turn of the century, and Chinese businessmen, drawn by efficient transportation, available power, and the protection of a more predictable legal regime, quickly followed suit. Early enclave industrialization was concentrated in light, consumer-goods industries, that is, industries at the downstream end of the value chain (see chapter 4 for further discussion). According to the 1933 census of industry in China proper, textiles made up 42% of total industrial output, and 70% of textiles were produced in the three cities of Shanghai, Tianjin, and Qingdao. Shanghai alone accounted for 40% of total industrial output. Output from modern textile mills grew rapidly, replacing imports. By the 1930s, China had basically stopped importing textiles and was instead importing significant quantities of raw cotton to feed its own mills.

Enclave industrialization was started by foreigners and grew under the impetus of foreign example and competition. However, native Chinese capitalists quickly became major actors in this process. By the 1930s, some 78% of the value of factory output came from Chinese-owned firms, and they were gaining market share. Successful Chinese industrialists often had some foreign experience or contact with foreign

Table 3.1
Two patterns of industrialization.

	China proper	Manchuria
Market	Domestic China	Japanese industry
Ownership	Chinese, foreign	Foreign
Structure	Light, consumer goods	Heavy, mining, producer goods
Skill formation	Steady accumulation	Little transfer of skills
Linkages	Backward	Few or none

businesses that enabled their initial entry into modern industry. The skills necessary for modern industry spread rapidly, though, and helped form a basis for further industrialization, particularly in Shanghai. One example was the Shanghai Dalong Machinery Company. Initially set up as a ship repair station, it gradually diversified into repair of machinery for the textile industry. By the late 1920s, it began to produce its own models of textile machinery (Rawski 1989). Spillover of modern industrial skills had clearly begun in some parts of China.

A very different pattern of industrialization emerged in Manchuria (the Northeast; table 3.1). Investment in Manchuria was carried out primarily by the Japanese government and by quasi-official affiliates of the Japanese government, such as the Southern Manchurian Railroad. Japanese government-sponsored industrialization of Manchuria fulfilled a mixture of economic and strategic objectives. The Japanese developed railroads, actively exploited the rich deposits of coal and iron ore in the region, and focused on heavy industry. Construction began in 1917 on a huge steel mill at Anshan that today is still one of China's largest producers of steel. The Japanese poured investment into the mill for 15 years before production became profitable. Nowhere in China proper would an investor have been capable of mobilizing so much patient capital.

Most Manchurian industries produced materials for Japanese domestic industries. Japan was the most important market, and the main source of production machinery. Managers were discouraged from subcontracting with small Chinese firms, and skilled positions within industry were intentionally reserved for Japanese nationals. Thus there were few linkages and spillover effects from vigorous industrialization in Manchuria. In 1933, Manchurian industry accounted for more than one-quarter of industrial value added, and was poised for dramatic expansion during the subsequent wartime period. After 1949, it became the launchpad for China's heavy industrial push.

3.3.2   The Rural Economy

In the countryside, the agricultural economy was under enormous pressure. Steady population increase had caused the land-to-man ratio to decline by half over the previous century. Deterioration of agricultural infrastructure hobbled agricultural productivity. The impact of these social stresses fell disproportionately on the poor. The fact that this was a fluid, competitive, market-based economy should not obscure the grinding poverty that weighed on the vast majority. Income inequality was significant. Imperial degree–holding "gentry," who amounted to much less than 1% of the population, received about 20% of total national income (Zhang 1955). Land distribution was not extremely unequal: given the importance of intensive application of labor inputs, small farms were the most efficient organizational form. However, many farmers did not own the land they cultivated. Large-scale rural surveys that were carried out during the 1920s and 1930s showed substantial tenancy. According to a 1931–1936 survey conducted by the National Agricultural Research Bureau of the Republic of China, 46% of rural households were owners, 24% were owner-tenants, and 30% were tenants. Rents were high—about 45% of total output. Tenancy was much more common in the wet rice lands of the south, particularly in the richest delta lands of the Lower Yangtze and Guangdong. In the north, tenancy was uncommon, and the main problem was fragmentation into farms too small to support a family. Many farmers were in debt—various estimates collected by Feuerwerker (1969, 87) suggest that 40%–55% of households were in debt, paying annual interest rates of 20%–40%. For heavily indebted tenant farmers—indeed, for owners of small plots struggling to survive—life was very difficult. The poorest farmers were unable to marry or sustain households and helplessly experienced the extinguishing of their lineage. Sophisticated traditional agriculture allowed the growth of a huge population, but that population was highly vulnerable to any breakdown in the agricultural system that supported it. Two million perished in a catastrophic famine in the northwest after three years of consecutive drought in 1928–1931. More generally, as Tawney (1932, 77) said, "There are districts in which the position of the rural population is that of a man standing permanently up to the neck in water, so that even a ripple is sufficient to drown him."

3.3.3   Evaluation: How Broad Was Development in the 1912–1937 Period?

There is wide agreement that a small but significant modern sector grew in China during the 1920s and 1930s (John Chang 1969). Less clear is the impact that this modern sector had on traditional sectors. Rawski (1989) in particular stressed the potential positive impact on traditional sectors of growing demand from modern sectors, growing cities, and increasing trade. Ingeniously extracting information from limited data, Rawski estimated that agriculture, handicrafts, and traditional transport all experienced positive growth between 1914 and 1936. Combined with rapid growth of the small modern sector, this finding led him to conclude that GDP per capita rose modestly but significantly over this period. The complexity of the relationship between modern and traditional sectors can be seen by examining the single most important industrial sector, cotton textiles, on which extensive research has been done (Richardson 1999, 58). The textile industry has two main segments, spinning and weaving, and growing factory production had a very different impact on each. Factory spinning is so much more efficient than hand spinning that factories took over most of the market, and household spinning declined dramatically, even though the total market was growing. Regions where farm households had specialized in spinning experienced severe hardship. Factory weaving grew rapidly as well, but falling prices of cloth expanded the total market by more than enough to accommodate a significant increase in hand-weaving output as well. Household weaving turned out to be a cost-effective way to produce a blended fabric mixing homespun and machine-spun yarn, producing a warm and durable product much prized by rural people. Cheaper machine-spun yarn as an input enabled growth in regions where households already specialized in weaving (Grove 2006).

The cotton textile industry thus exemplifies the complexity of the impact of modern technologies. Some areas benefited, stimulated by new technologies and new sources of foreign and domestic demand. Other areas lost out because their products were unable to compete with new products. In agriculture, increased commercialization allowed intensification to continue without a technological revolution. Growing cities in eastern China increased the local demand for urban-oriented products, particularly cotton, peanuts, vegetables, fruit, rapeseed, and tung oil. In suburban areas, there were also increased opportunities for off-farm employment. Were the introduction of new crops and the attendant commercialization sufficiently widespread to keep rural incomes from declining or even lead to an increase? Clearly, there were a handful of regions that benefited from increased opportunities, particularly those around growing coastal cities or along railroad lines. Most farmers, however, especially those in the interior regions, continued to operate on the margin of subsistence as they had for centuries, and they probably noticed little impact. Industrialization had clearly made a start; a foundation had been laid for future progress, but industrialization had not begun to fundamentally change the overall structure of the Chinese economy.

In a broader sense, this was a vibrant society laying the basis for future development. Literacy gradually began to increase. Starting with individuals born after 1920, there was a gradual but steady improvement in literacy rates that even the subsequent war did not interrupt. Moreover, China was quite open to foreign influence during this period. Some 100,000 Chinese students went abroad for long-term study. The largest number went to Japan, but significant groups went to the United States and Europe as well. As of 1936, 370,000 foreigners were resident in China. This large interchange created substantial flows of technology, as well as an open and stimulating intellectual and cultural environment. New universities were founded that evolved into today's Tsinghua, Fudan, and Peking Universities. Shanghai became the center of a vigorous hybrid modern culture. Although society was divided by sharp political and social fissures, it seemed to be moving forward rapidly.

3.4   War and Civil War, 1937–1949

A steadily increasing Japanese presence loomed over the successes of the interwar period. Japan had already gained a toehold in Manchuria when it seized the Liaodong Peninsula from Russia in 1905. In 1931, Japan established the puppet state of Manchukuo, effectively extending control to all of Manchuria. In 1937, the Marco Polo Bridge incident outside Beijing marked the beginning of the Japanese invasion of China proper. For China, this initiated a nearly unbroken period of warfare that lasted more than a decade, until the Communist victory in 1949.

War brought mass suffering to the population and serious damage to the economy. The disruption of war created conditions that allowed China's civil war between Nationalists and Communists to fester. The Japanese invasion weakened the Nationalist government, and Communist guerrillas were able to gain a new legitimacy by fighting the Japanese. The end of the Pacific War in 1945 merely set the stage for a final showdown between Nationalist and Communist armies. The fog of war also obscures our understanding of the important changes that occurred during this decade. The wartime economy is often omitted from descriptions of China's development. In fact, however, five important changes occurred in this 12-year period.

3.4.1   The Rise and Fall of a Japan-Centered East Asian Economy

Japan's moves into China were part of a broader East Asian process. Through the 1940s, a Japan-centered East Asian economic system was coming into existence. Fostered in part by the explicit imperialist calculations of the Japanese government and in part by Japan's rising economic competitiveness, this regional system had a distinct structure. At the core of that system was Japan itself. Most manufacturing and services, as well as government, were reserved for Japan. Next came an inner circle of food producers, primarily Taiwan and Korea, which were incorporated into the empire. In both Taiwan and Korea, the Japanese combined political repression with efforts to foster economic development: They carried out land surveys and created an agricultural extension service, built transport infrastructure, and improved education and health care. Mortality declined in both colonies, and literacy—defined as the ability to read and write Japanese—increased.

Next came Manchuria, a captive supplier of semiprocessed goods (Ho 1984). Most of China proper was in an outer circle of regions with potential markets and sites for investment and future expansion. By the mid-1930s, Japan had surpassed Britain to become the largest foreign investor in Shanghai (at a time when two-thirds of foreign investment in China proper was in Shanghai). The various regions of the Japanese economic empire interacted in a reasonably well-functioning economic system. With the Japanese defeat in the Pacific War, this system collapsed. After 1949, China withdrew from the East Asian economy, and East Asian economic integration did not reemerge until many decades later.

3.4.2   The Rise of Manchuria

Even though the Japanese imperial project ultimately collapsed, it made a long-lasting contribution to the industrialization of Manchuria. The growth of Manchurian industry accelerated during the early war years, to 14% annually between 1936 and 1942. By contrast, industrial output in Shanghai and the rest of China proper peaked in 1936 and never regained prewar output levels until after 1949. By 1942, Manchuria produced the bulk of China's electric power, iron, and cement and more than half of industrial output value. By the end of the war, the majority of China's industrial capacity was in Manchuria.

3.4.3   Increased State Intervention

During the war, the Nationalist government retreated into the interior of China, setting up a temporary capital at Chongqing in Sichuan. Wartime pressures, as is always the case, led to an increase in state intervention in the economy. Before the war, there had been no significant public sector in Chinese industry. In order to move industry inland from Shanghai and build new inland military industrial capacity, the Guomindang government turned to a kind of planning commission, called the National Resources Commission (NRC), to run government-sponsored development (Kirby 1990, 1992). Originally focused on mineral development, the NRC was staffed primarily by engineers and gained a reputation as a relatively efficient and honest department of the government. By the early 1940s, the NRC was running factories with about 160,000 workers (compared with the 1 million total factory workers in 1933). Of all industry in unoccupied China, state-run firms accounted for 70% of the capital and 32% of the labor.

Meanwhile, in occupied Shanghai, the Japanese authorities were restructuring industry to support their war aims. Many Shanghai firms were converted to military production, and output of machinery and armaments increased, while consumer-goods output dropped. By the end of the war, the Japanese military authorities were running a large part of Shanghai industry. Already the largest foreign investor in Shanghai, Japan confiscated many factories during the war and forced some Chinese capitalists into collaboration. The Guomindang took over all these firms in 1945. The combination of NRC-developed industries and confiscated Japanese and collaborator factories gave the Nationalist government a huge industrial stake in the late 1940s, with the government controlling about two-thirds of modern industrial capital. By 1947, the Chinese government controlled 90% of iron and steel output, two-thirds of electricity, and 45% of cement output. In addition, most major banks and transportation companies were government controlled. The Communist government took over this state-run economy in embryo almost intact after 1949.

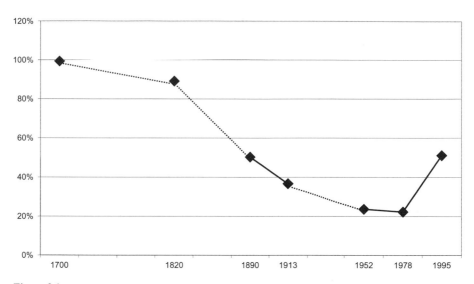

Figure 3.1
China per capita GDP as a percentage of world per capita GDP.
Source: Maddison (1998).

3.4.4   Inflation

Attempting to pay for the war, but separated from its economic base in the Lower Yangtze, the Nationalist government turned to printing money to finance operations. The result was accelerating inflation and ultimately hyperinflation. As the government collapsed, inflation became worse. If the Shanghai prewar price level is taken as 100, the price level in 1948 was 660 million. Severe macroeconomic imbalances threatened to cripple the economy.

3.4.5   Relative Standing

By the late 1940s, China's relative position in the world had eroded substantially over a century-long period. Figure 3.1 shows the changes in China's GDP per capita relative to the world average, as calculated by Maddison (1998). If we look at Maddison's benchmark years, China's GDP per capita went from being close to the global average to being below 40% in 1913 and about 20% in 1949–1952. As discussed earlier, Maddison's estimates were only preliminary, and we know much more now about relative incomes than Maddison did, but have not developed a new consensus on the best numbers. Liu Ti (2010) represents a school of Chinese economic historians who estimate that per capita GDP in China was already declining in the 1700s and by 1820 was 46% lower than Maddison's estimate. Maddison may have overestimated China's GDP in 1820 and therefore may have exaggerated the speed of China's relative decline, but the general picture is surely correct. Of course, while China was falling below world averages, Western Europe and the United States were accelerating well above world averages. From having been one of the centers of the civilized world, China had descended to a position of obvious underdevelopment and backwardness. Given the collapse in relative position, the aggressive and predatory attitude of Western colonialism, and the complete failure of the Chinese government to develop a coherent response to the West, it is understandable that the impact of the West turned out to be highly traumatic.

3.5   Legacies of the Pre-1949 Economy

3.5.1   Legacy for the Socialist Era (1949–1978)

The immediate legacy of the war years was extreme disruption and serious damage to the economic infrastructure. Destruction of industrial capital and deterioration of agricultural infrastructure (particularly irrigation networks) were serious and crippled the economy. Short-run output was well below potential. At the same time, financial chaos, manifested in hyperinflation, required immediate remedial action. War had derailed the economic growth that had begun in the 1920s and 1930s, so China was still very poor, probably slightly behind India at this time (table 3.2).

Several of the adverse economic experiences before 1949 may have contributed, ironically, to the relatively smooth adoption of socialist institutions after 1949. The Chinese experience with foreign aggression from 1839 through 1945—from the Opium War through the Anti-Japanese War—naturally caused China to be deeply suspicious of Western institutions and worldviews. The aversion to foreign dominance led to support for closed-door socialist development strategies. Moreover, the reputation of the

Table 3.2
A benchmark comparison: China 1952 and India 1950.

	China 1952	India 1950
GNP per capita (1952$)	50	60
Population (million)	573	358
Rice yields (ton/acre)	2.5	1.3
Wheat yields (ton/acre)	1.1	0.7
Industrial output per capita		
Coal (kg)	96	97
Steel (kg)	2	4
Electricity (kW)	0.005	0.04
Cotton spindles	0.01	0.03
Railroads (km; 1936)	20,746	72,000

Sources: Kumar (1992); length of Chinese railroads from Rawski (1989, 208–209).

Nationalist government—the primary opponent of the Communists—was seriously compromised by corruption and by hyperinflation, which reflected its inability to manage the economy between 1945 and 1949. More generally, the chaos, damage, and suffering of more than a decade of war made the Chinese population willing to accept a strong government if it could credibly promise peace and a degree of economic security.

More concretely, wartime changes in the economy aided the Communist government in the execution of its socialist industrialization strategy. The Japanese had begun the task of developing a core of heavy industry in Manchuria. Subsequently, those industries were seized by the Soviet army and then passed ultimately into Chinese government hands. In China proper, the combination of NRC-developed industries and companies confiscated by Japanese authorities created a foundation for the victorious Chinese Communist Party to establish direct control over the industrial sector. The Nationalist government had even created the nucleus of a planning apparatus, and many skilled officials from the Nationalist NRC stayed on to work under the new People's Republic of China. Thus the infant Communist government did not have to start from scratch, nor did it have to engage in politically sensitive nationalizations of industry for the first several years.

By 1949, China was still very poor, but development had nevertheless begun. China had a relatively good endowment of human capital. Literacy rates were reasonably high and had already begun increasing. A small university system had been created, and skilled individuals had been trained abroad. Some modern industrial and transport capital had been created that could serve as a nucleus for further development. The socialist development strategy followed between 1949 and 1978 turned its back on the vitality of the traditional economy, but ironically, the fruits of past success dropped into the lap of the new government, which received something like a mandate for its new approach to development.

3.5.2 Legacy for the Post-1978 Market Economy

Important as the legacy of the traditional economy was for the socialist era, it was equally important for the post-1978 market economy. As China began to open up, familiarity with the traditional household-based economic system provided a robust potential to adapt to new economic opportunities. China after 1978 everywhere saw the return of the traditional. Small-scale household businesses sprang up throughout China to meet market demand that had been neglected under socialism. Under the general rubric of "township and village enterprises," rural businesses grew rapidly in many areas and many different organizational forms, but nowhere more vigorously than in those parts of China where the densely populated, highly commercialized countryside had flourished (chapter 13). Traditional economic centers revived quickly and grew with astonishing speed. The Lower Yangtze macroregion began to reclaim its traditional economic primacy, while the Northeast (heartland of the planned economy) receded in importance. Outside the Lower Yangtze, districts that led the way in growth after 1978 have been shown to have deep roots in traditional economic activities (Eyferth 2009; Grove 2006). There was even a revival of traditional market-based organizational forms, in which large numbers of very small-scale specialized firms coordinated through markets with upstream and downstream producers. The intense entrepreneurial development of private business in Wenzhou, along the southeastern coast, exemplified this pattern. That China has been able to grow so rapidly since 1978 is due in no small part to the entrepreneurial and competitive behaviors that the traditional economy had nourished.

Traditional links with parts of maritime China outside the People's Republic of China also revived quickly (chapter 2). Indeed, the rapid economic growth of Hong Kong and Taiwan during the 1960s and 1970s could be considered a continuation and vindication of the traditional economy. After all, these were regions within the traditional Chinese economy that had followed a path of evolutionary growth from traditional beginnings and had relied primarily on small firms to jump-start economic development. After 1978, the capabilities that firms in Hong Kong and Taiwan had developed were reintegrated with the labor and other resources within the People's Republic, creating explosive growth of foreign trade. In this respect as well, the traditional economy laid down a highly positive legacy for development after 1978.

Finally, the traditional economy may have left a complex legacy shaping the nature of the transition from plan to market. Foreign intrusion into China was still a sensitive issue in the late 1970s. Deng Xiaoping promoted Special Economic Zones (SEZs) to jump-start the process of economic opening. The SEZs limited the scope of foreign incursion but simultaneously demonstrated that policy-makers were willing to overcome their traditional aversion to foreign domination. The resulting policy echoed some features of the Treaty Ports forced on China in the nineteenth century, but this time under Chinese sovereignty. These early experiments with SEZs may have contributed to the distinctive "dual-track" approach that became a defining feature of Chinese institutional transformation (chapter 5). The SEZs allowed a new set of market-friendly rules to operate in the interstices of the planned economy, foreshadowing the broader transformation of the Chinese economy. Indeed, China's approach to the transition overall, including a fiercely independent resolve to pursue a reform program "with Chinese characteristics," can plausibly be linked to the traumatic 100 years of encounter with the West.

In this and many other respects, China's contemporary economy includes a rediscovery of the traditional. Did China's traditional economy fail? It would be more accurate to say that the positive potential and achievements of China's traditional economy were repressed for years. War, civil war, and socialism hobbled the traditional economy and made it seem irrelevant. Today, the traditional economy has rebounded. Commercial and entrepreneurial networks and behaviors, rooted in the past, have a newfound relevance. They help power economic growth today and provide a positive legacy for the future.

Bibliography

Suggestions for Further Reading

The historical literature on China is vast and extremely accessible. To delve into the issues raised here, see Brandt, Ma, and Rawski (2014) or Richardson (1999). Von Glahn (2016) is a deep dive, going much further back while also drawing on the latest scholarship. Kallgren et al. (1991) is an interesting anthology that brings together related themes from different periods of China's modern history. Jung Chang's *Wild Swans* (1991) manages to capture an enormous sweep of Chinese history through a purely personal family memoir.

References

Allen, Robert C., Jean-Pascal Bassino, Debin Ma, Christine Moll-Murata, and Jan Luiten Van Zander (2011). "Wages, Prices, and Living Standards in China, 1738–1925: In Comparison with Europe, Japan, and India." *Economic History Review* 64 (S1): 8–38.

Brandt, Loren (1987). "Farm Household Behavior, Factor Markets, and the Distributive Consequences of Commercialization in Early Twentieth-Century China." *Journal of Economic History* 47 (3): 711–737.

Brandt, Loren (1990). *Commercialization and Agricultural Development: Central and Eastern China, 1870–1937.* Cambridge: Cambridge University Press.

Brandt, Loren, Debin Ma, and Thomas Rawski (2014). "From Divergence to Convergence: Reevaluating the History Behind China's Economic Boom." *Journal of Economic Literature* 52 (1): 45–123.

Chang, John K. (1969). *Industrial Development in Pre-Communist China: A Quantitative Analysis.* Chicago: Aldine.

Chang, Jung (1991). *Wild Swans: Three Daughters of China.* New York: Simon & Schuster.

Elvin, Mark, and Liu Ts'ui-jung, eds. (1998). *Sediments of Time: Environment and Society in Chinese History.* New York: Cambridge University Press.

Eyferth, Jacob (2009). *Eating Rice from Bamboo Roots: The Social History of a Community of Handicraft Papermakers in Rural Sichuan, 1920–2000.* Cambridge, MA: Harvard University Asia Center.

Feuerwerker, Albert (1969). *The Chinese Economy, ca. 1870–1911.* Ann Arbor: Center for Chinese Studies, University of Michigan.

Grove, Linda (2006). *A Chinese Economic Revolution: Rural Entrepreneurship in the Twentieth Century.* Lanham, MD: Rowman & Littlefield.

Ho, Samuel P. S. (1984). "Colonization and Development: Korea, Taiwan and Kwantung." In Ramon Myers and Mark Peattie, eds., *The Japanese Colonial Empire, 1845–1945*, 347–398. Princeton, NJ: Princeton University Press.

Kallgren, Joyce, K. Lieberthal, R. MacFarquhar, and F. Wakeman, eds. (1991). *Perspectives on Modern China: Four Anniversaries.* Armonk, NY: M. E. Sharpe.

King, Frank H. (1911). *Farmers of Forty Centuries.* Emmaus, PA: Rodale Press.

Kirby, William C. (1990). "Continuity and Change in Modern China: Economic Planning on the Mainland and on Taiwan, 1943–1958." *Australian Journal of Chinese Affairs* 24:121–141.

Kirby, William C. (1992). "The Chinese War Economy." In James C. Hsiung and Steven I. Levine, eds., *China's Bitter Victory: The War with Japan, 1937–1945*, 185–212. Armonk, NY: M. E. Sharpe.

Kumar, Dharma (1992). "The Chinese and Indian Economies from ca. 1914–1949." STICERD Research Program on the Chinese Economy, CP no. 22, London School of Economics, May.

Li, Bozhong, and Jan Luiten van Zanden (2012). "Before the Great Divergence? Comparing the Yangzi Delta and the Netherlands at the Beginning of the Nineteenth Century." *Journal of Economic History* 72 (4): 956–989.

Liu, Ti (2010). *Qianjindai Zhongguo Zongliang Jingji Yanjiu (1600–1840)* [An economic study of aggregate output in early modern China (1600–1840)]. Shanghai: Shanghai Shiji.

Maddison, Angus (1998). *Chinese Economic Performance in the Long Run*. Paris: Development Centre of the Organisation for Economic Co-operation and Development.

Naquin, Susan, and Evelyn Rawski (1987). *Chinese Society in the Eighteenth Century*. New Haven, CT: Yale University Press.

Perkins, Dwight (1967). "Government as an Obstacle to Industrialization: The Case of Nineteenth-Century China." *Journal of Economic History* 27 (4): 478–492.

Pomeranz, Kenneth (2000). *The Great Divergence: Europe, China, and the Making of the Modern World Economy*. Princeton, NJ: Princeton University Press.

Rawski, Thomas (1989). *Economic Growth in Prewar China*. Berkeley: University of California Press.

Richardson, Philip (1999). *Economic Change in China, c. 1800–1950*. Cambridge: Cambridge University Press.

Sng, Tuan-Hwee (2014). "Size and Dynastic Decline: The Principal-Agent Problem in Late Imperial China, 1700–1850." *Explorations in Economic History* 54:107–127.

Tawney, R. H. (1932). *Land and Labour in China*. London: George Allen and Unwin.

Vermeer, Eduard (1988). *Economic Development in Provincial China: The Central Shaanxi Since 1930*. Cambridge: Cambridge University Press.

Von Glahn, Richard (2016). *The Economic History of China: From Antiquity to the Nineteenth Century*. Cambridge: Cambridge University Press.

Will, Pierre-Etienne, and R. Bin Wong (1991). *Nourish the People: The State Civilian Granary System in China, 1650–1850*. Ann Arbor: Center for Chinese Studies, University of Michigan.

Zelin, Madeleine (1991). "The Structure of the Chinese Economy During the Qing Period." In Joyce Kallgren, K. Lieberthal, R. MacFarquhar, and F. Wakeman, eds., *Perspectives on Modern China: Four Anniversaries*. Armonk, NY: M. E. Sharpe.

Zhang, Zhongli (1955). *The Chinese Gentry: Studies on Their Role in Nineteenth-Century Chinese Society*. Seattle: University of Washington Press.

4   The Socialist Era, 1949–1978: Big Push Industrialization and Policy Instability

After the People's Republic of China (PRC) was established in October 1949, the Chinese economy was wrenched out of its traditional framework and completely reoriented. China's new leaders turned their backs on China's traditional household-based, "bottom-heavy" economy and set out to develop a massive socialist industrial complex through direct government control. Planners neglected labor-intensive sectors suitable to China's vast population and instead poured resources into capital-intensive factories producing metals, machinery, and chemicals. The early achievements of coastal-enclave industrialization oriented to the Pacific were discarded, and a new, inward-directed strategy was adopted. China turned to the Soviet Union as its primary model, as well as its chief trading partner and source of technology.

For 30 years, China pursued this vision of socialism. We use the term "economic strategy" to describe the overall pattern in which resources are allocated, and label this development strategy "Big Push industrialization" because it gave overwhelming priority to channeling the maximum feasible investment into heavy industry. This development strategy, in turn, shaped virtually every aspect of the Chinese economy. Today, no country systematically follows this type of development strategy, but at the time of the birth of the PRC, many people believed that this was the best approach to development. This belief was partly based on the apparent success of the Soviet Union in fostering industrialization and prevailing in the war with Nazi Germany. More broadly, the argument held that a developing country should "delink" from the capitalist world economy, and the government could then mobilize saving and investment, sacrificing consumption today in order to benefit future generations. Simultaneous development of many industrial sectors—the "Big Push"—would allow poor countries to break out of the vicious circle in which growth of any given sector was held back by the underdevelopment of other related industries.

To implement this strategy, a planned economic system was phased in between 1949 and 1956 (and then phased out after 1979). The term "economic system" describes the institutions that govern specific resource-allocation decisions; this is covered in the second section of this chapter. The type of system China adopted is often called a "command economy" because market forces were severely curtailed and government planners allocated resources directly through their commands, which were the crucial signals in the economy. The command economy was a very effective way to subordinate individual economic decision-making to the overall national development strategy. State-owned enterprises dominated the key industrial sectors and were unresponsive to market prices and profitability; instead, they were charged with carrying out the commands of their superiors and fulfilling planned targets.

The Big Push strategy and the command economic system dominated China's pursuit of socialist development throughout this period. However, under Mao Zedong development objectives were constantly being reinterpreted, and policy shifted in unpredictable ways that were disruptive to the economy. Economic instability and a pattern of policy oscillations marked the years through 1978. This chapter uses the framework of policy instability to describe some of the most important episodes during China's socialist period. A few distinctive and successful Chinese adaptations were made to the Big Push/command-economy model, and some catastrophic and misguided policies were followed. The Great Leap Forward (GLF) stands out as the most peculiar and the most terrible of all these episodes, overshadowing even the Cultural Revolution. Since 1979, China has gradually dismantled virtually all the institutions of the command economy. Nevertheless, the legacy to China's contemporary economy from the period of the socialist planned economy is large and complex. Indeed, no area of the contemporary economy has completely escaped the aftereffects of the command economy. We conclude with a brief assessment of the socialist period and its legacy.

4.1   The Big Push Development Strategy

After 1949, the PRC followed a socialist heavy-industry-priority development strategy, or Big Push strategy. Consumption was squeezed, as rapid industrialization was given the highest priority. The government controlled the bulk of the economy directly and used its control to pump resources into the construction of new factories. Investment, virtually all by the government, increased rapidly to over a quarter of national income. Investment rates worldwide have risen since the 1950s, but even today, poor countries on average invest 20% of GDP. China, by 1954, at a time when it was still a very poor country, had pushed its investment rate up to 26% of GDP (see figure 4.1, which shows gross capital formation—the sum of new investment in physical assets, replacement investment, and accumulation of inventories—as a share of GDP). Investment soared further during the GLF but then crashed in its

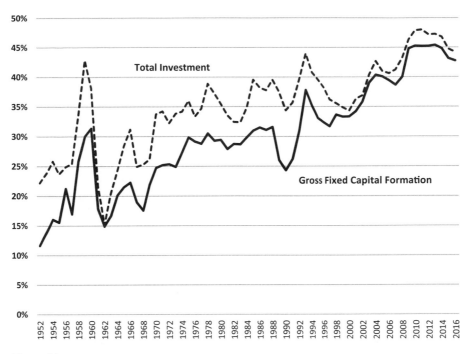

Figure 4.1
Investment as a share of GDP.
Sources: NBS (1999, 6–7); *SAC* (2017, 36).

catastrophic aftermath. Over the long term, as figure 4.1 shows, China's investment rates have been high and rising, though sometimes unstable. Figure 4.1 also displays a surprising feature of the contemporary Chinese economy: even though China abandoned the Big Push strategy after 1978, investment rates continued rising to the 2009–2014 plateau. There was no obvious interruption in the reform era, but rather a continuing pattern of mobilization of resources for investment.

Most investment went to industry, and more than 80% of industrial investment was in heavy industry. Because planners were pouring resources into industry, rapid industrial growth was not surprising. Between 1952 and 1978, industrial output grew at an average annual rate of 11.5%. Moreover, industry's share of total GDP climbed steadily over the same period from 18% to 44%, while agriculture's share declined from 51% to 28% (measured at current prices; see chapter 7 for further discussion). Entire new industries were created—for example, those producing electricity-generating equipment, chemical fertilizer, and motor vehicles. Most important, economic growth was jump-started after the stagnation and disruption of the depression and war years. The Chinese economy took off during the 1950s, and the Big Push strategy seemed to be working. The new government was able to mobilize the fiscal and other resources to finance a sustained investment effort.

Table 4.1
Two contrasting industrialization strategies.

	Heavy-industry-priority, PRC	Light-industry-priority, Taiwan, Hong Kong
Basic strategy	Strategic industries with most upstream and downstream linkages	Begin with downstream consumer-goods industries; gradually work upstream
Saving	Government, state-owned enterprises	Households, private business, government
Investment decisions	Government	Private business, government infrastructure
Source of demand growth	Domestic industries, government investment projects	Foreign and domestic consumer-goods markets
Household income	Slow growing	Moderate to fast growing
Coordination	Plan	Market, with some government "steerage"
Openness to world	Low	High

The PRC was not the only part of East Asia where growth accelerated in the 1950s. Hong Kong and Taiwan underwent rapid industrialization, largely by following the strategy of development that the PRC had abandoned. A direct comparison of strategies can provide further insight into growth in all these regions (table 4.1). It is possible to view the entire industrial economy as a series of "value chains" or streams that connect many different activities. At the top of the stream are natural-resource-extraction and materials industries; these feed into refining, processed-materials, and machinery industries; and ultimately, at the bottom of the stream are final products for businesses and consumers. China, with its heavy-industry-priority strategy, focused on industries in the upper and middle stages of the industrial economy. These industries can be considered "strategic," in the sense that they have the most linkages with other industries. For example, an industry such as steel has important linkages "downstream," because if it supplies high-quality, low-cost steel to machinery and equipment makers, it will lower their costs and stimulate their development. But steel also has important linkages "upstream," because its growth increases demand for coal, iron ore, and specialized machinery and stimulates the growth of those industries as well. (An input-output [I-O] table is a tool that shows all the direct supply relationships between sectors, and it can be used to quickly compute the full direct plus indirect implications of any change in output or demand.) Growth based on heavy investment in strategic sectors tends to create a self-reinforcing, but also self-contained, process. Heavy-industry sectors are developed that supply one another's demands, based on the government's investment decisions, but there are limited spillovers to market development and slow growth of consumption. Moreover, these heavy industries are technologically challenging and hard to master quickly. This approach fits easily with a strategy of national self-reliance and limited openness to the outside world.

Hong Kong and Taiwan, by contrast, specialized first in textiles, food products, and other light consumer goods. In other words, they concentrated on the downstream end of the industrial value chains. These are also the early industries in which most developing countries begin their industrialization process. Not accidentally, they were also the most important sectors in China's "enclave industrialization" during the 1920s and 1930s. Indeed, in some cases, the same people were running the factories: many Shanghai textile entrepreneurs moved to Hong Kong in the 1950s, and other Shanghai businessmen went to Taiwan. The markets for these industries were primarily abroad, particularly in developed countries. Openness to trade meant that industrialists could obtain their inputs—raw materials and equipment—on the world market. Only later, after successful light-industry development, did Taiwan and Hong Kong move upstream, developing industries that were more technologically demanding and capital intensive, sometimes with government help. It is striking that Hong Kong, Taiwan, Korea, and Singapore all made a relatively smooth transition from their early light-consumer-goods manufacturing to more technologically demanding sectors, and economic growth accelerated in all four of these economies in the 1960s and 1970s. In other words, despite the absence of domestic interindustry linkages in the initial phases of industrialization, Taiwan and Hong Kong were able to more than compensate through other advantages of openness. Cheaper production because of access to lowest-cost inputs from the world market, faster absorption of world technology, and faster learning about export markets led to more rapid growth of living standards and ultimately to a more rapid convergence to world best practice. Thus, although growth accelerated in the PRC under the impetus of the Big Push, growth accelerated even more in other parts of East Asia at the same time. By 1978, Taiwan and Hong Kong were far ahead of the PRC and served an important demonstration effect in persuading Chinese leaders to reform and open up the economy. When the PRC finally reoriented its development strategy and modified the Big Push strategy after 1979, it discovered that there were many unexploited opportunities in light manufacturing and export markets. China returned to those neglected opportunities, often in collaboration with businesses from Hong Kong or Taiwan. (See chapters 16 and 17 for a description of the interaction among the economies of the PRC, Hong Kong, and Taiwan in the contemporary period.)

4.2   The Command-Economy System in China

How did Chinese planners manage to channel resources into their Big Push industrialization strategy? What were the key institutions that shaped the way decisions were made? China adopted the command-economy system from the Soviet Union, and it had the following four fundamental characteristics:

• The government owned all large factories and transportation and communication enterprises. In the countryside, agricultural collectives took over ownership of the land and management of the farm economy.

• Planners issued commands that assigned production targets to firms and directly allocated resources and goods among different producers. Prices lost their significance as the primary signal that directed resource allocation in the economy. Finances were used to audit and monitor performance, not to drive investment decisions.

• Although the government neglected the microeconomic allocation role of prices, it nevertheless controlled the price system and set relative prices to channel resources into government hands and into Big Push industrialization.

• The government and the Communist Party reinforced their control of the economy through a hierarchical personnel system, in which the Communist Party controlled managerial career paths. All working adults were connected to the party and the government through their workplaces, either agricultural collectives or urban state or collective units.

These were the characteristic institutions of the system created initially in the Soviet Union under Stalin. China copied them during the 1950s. As we will discuss later, during the 1960s and 1970s, China altered these institutions to fit with Maoist ideology and to accommodate an economy that was much poorer than its Soviet mentor.

The government owned the factories and controlled the price system, and not surprisingly, factory products were expensive and farm products were cheap. That is, the socialist state intentionally assigned prices to the products of industry (owned by the government) that were relatively high and assigned prices to the products of agriculture (owned by peasant collectives) that were relatively low. The socialist state maintained terms of trade between the state-enterprise sector and the household sector that were highly favorable to state enterprises. In 1953, even before agricultural collectives were formed, the Chinese government established compulsory procurement of grain from farmers, creating a government monopoly over key agricultural goods that lasted more than 30 years. Farmers were forced to meet procurement quotas established by the state grain monopoly at low fixed prices. With cheap farm products, the "markup" on manufactured consumer goods was high (on cotton cloth, for example), while wages were kept low and stable. Given these systematic biases in price setting, agriculture seemed to be a low-return activity, while manufacturing appeared to be highly profitable. But not wanting too many farmers to leave the farm, the government imposed restrictions on mobility (see chapter 6).

The surpluses of government-controlled firms were the main source of government revenue. The distorted price system meant that state-owned industrial enterprises were extremely profitable even when they were not very efficient, and they served as a "cash cow" for the government and for the economy as a whole. This system gave the Chinese government the fiscal capacity to mobilize resources for Big Push industrialization and its other priorities. A modern tax system was not necessary: already by the mid-1950s, the government could raise more than a quarter of GDP as budgetary revenues, an impressive level for such a poor country and far higher than anything achieved by the Nationalist government before the war.

After the essential prerequisite of government control over the economy had been established, specific decisions were implemented through the planning system. "Material balance planning" was the main technique used to run the economy. The term "material balance" refers to the computation of sources and uses of an individual commodity that a planner "balances" in allocating all supplies. Planners simply assigned quantities and ignored prices. There were output plans for individual producers and supply plans that transferred resources among producers. In theory, a planner could use an input-output table to compute the interdependent needs of the whole economy. In practice, though, China was too big and its producers too diverse for planners ever to have been able to coordinate the economy through a single technical device. Instead, planners divided blocks of resources among different stakeholders, drew up their own wish lists of priority projects and the resources they needed, and then allocated anything left over to the numerous unmet needs. The foreign sector could be used as a last resort to make up for scarcities and sell surpluses.

Other types of control were used to reinforce control over materials. Control over personnel was exercised through the *nomenklatura* system. The *nomenklatura* is a list of urban jobs that are controlled by the Communist Party, which thereby manages personnel throughout the public sector. The Communist Party set up a strict hierarchy, in which each level supervises the performance and appointment of personnel at the next lower level. As a result, control of career paths, and thus of the ultimate incentive structure, rests with the Communist Party. Finally, control over financial flows and credit was also exerted from the top, typically through a state monopoly banking system (or "monobank") that audited compliance with state directives. Prices, profits, money, and banking all existed in this system, but the financial system was "passive." That is, financial flows were assigned to accommodate the plan (which was drawn up in terms of physical quantities) rather than to independently influence resource-allocation flows. The only exception was for household budgets: households could decide how to allocate their incomes among a limited supply of consumer goods. With all the plans, commands, and controls, the typical state-owned enterprise had very little authority. It could not adjust its labor force, did not retain any of its profits, and could do little other than scramble to find additional inputs and increase production. Yet at the same time, the core planning system in China was much less centralized and much less tightly controlled than it was in the Soviet Union. Small firms were more important in China's industrial structure than in the Soviet Union. Transportation and communication were less developed, so it is not surprising that central control was exercised less effectively. For example, central planners in Beijing allocated a maximum of 600 different varieties of industrial product, while the Soviet Union by the 1970s had allocated 60,000 separate commodities. In other ways, too, China's system was less centralized, especially in the 1970s, after financial decentralization reinforced decentralization of the planning system, providing local governments with substantial leeway in making economic development decisions. Arguably, there was less decision-making authority at the top (the central government) and bottom (enterprises) of the Chinese industrial economy. More authority, however, could be exercised by those in the middle, typically local-government officials.

But in one respect, China was substantially more controlled than the Soviet Union: ideological and social control was especially tight. Politics was in command during the Maoist years, and the Communist Party rigorously controlled speech and even thought. China maintained very strict controls over labor, including restrictions on movement and on remuneration. Migration to urban areas was tightly restricted, and during the Cultural Revolution, 17 million urban school-leavers were sent out to the countryside (see chapter 6). Employees in state enterprises stayed in a given enterprise for life, sometimes even passing jobs on to their children. Labor mobility was virtually nonexistent. It was illegal in principle and impossible in practice for firms to fire workers, and quits were also almost unknown. Despite decentralization, the system in many respects was extremely rigid.

4.3 Policy Instability

China's history since 1949 has been stormy. Even after the 1949 revolution, sharp turns in policy—including economic policy—marked nearly every period of China's development. Changes, and even reversals, of direction were common in many areas of economic policy. As a result, the legacy of the socialist period is especially complicated. In some periods the policy emphasis was so distinctive that it has been described as a unique Chinese or Maoist "model" of development. At other times policy stayed closer to an orthodox Soviet model or was driven by short-run pragmatism. These different periods had very different economic outcomes, ranging from highly successful to catastrophic.

Shifts in economic policy often came with sharp political conflict. Mao Zedong himself repeatedly changed economic policies in accordance with his own revolutionary ideals or personal wishes. He often portrayed the resulting policy changes as part of his own personal struggle against political opponents. Since 1949, major policy issues have often played out as internal power struggles dividing the Communist Party. Winners in factional fighting used policy advocacy to prevail over their opponents, and imposed policies they favored after winning power. For all these reasons, the twists and turns in policy in Maoist China are generally narrated from a political point of view (for a recent comprehensive account, see Walder 2015). While acknowledging the importance of politics, this section provides a brief narrative of the 1949–1978 period in which the emphasis is on economic changes and political factors are downplayed. This approach allows us to present a compact narrative that captures the diversity and instability of policy.

The conceptual framework for this approach is as follows: Because of the enormous information requirements, it was impossible for top leaders to coordinate or "plan" the vast and diverse economy of China. However, leaders recognized the enormous developmental potential of the Chinese people. As a result, they repeatedly launched mobilizations of resources, which led to sharp increases in the investment rate. Without good information or appropriate yardsticks to assess specific investments, each mobilization was achieved through a somewhat chaotic decentralization of authority to lower-level officials and managers. When these lower-level actors were given permission and access to resources, they responded to signals and opportunities and stepped up their investment activities. Each of these mobilization phases led to imbalances and difficulties that ranged from transitory to disastrous. After these problems emerged, a period of retrenchment followed that eventually restored favorable conditions. Since the stabilization of conditions also produced slower growth, leaders quickly became impatient to launch a new round of mobilization.

These patterns are clearly shown in figure 4.2, which depicts the percentage growth of investment in each year (using the same underlying data as figure 4.1). The data show clearly the successive periods of rapid investment growth, followed by slower growth or even decline. Average annual real growth of investment was 8.2% between 1952 and 1979, but there were only three years where the year-to-year growth rate was between 4% and 12% (1957, 1971, and 1977). Figure 4.2 gives labels to five successive waves of rapid investment growth. Each time the growth of investment in a single year surpassed 20%, it signaled a "leap forward." Each "leap" was a phase of more rapid investment growth but also corresponded with a period of political mobilization and institutional transformation. In most cases, leaps were associated with radical or leftist ideology, but this was not invariably the case. Often, retrenchment phases were characterized by a more moderate political climate, though again not always. After 1978, cyclical patterns were still discernible, but the extreme fluctuations were gradually eliminated.

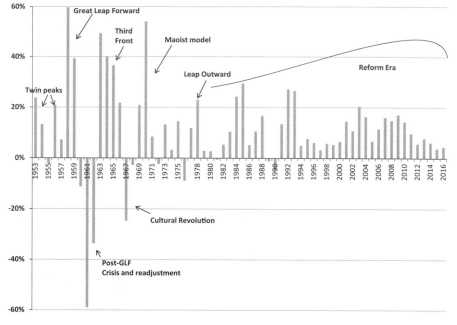

Figure 4.2
Total investment: Year-on-year growth.
Sources: NBS (1999, 6–7); *SAC* (2017, 34–35; and various years). Real-growth and fixed-investment deflators are not available before 1990; for consistency, the entire series is deflated by the implicit GDP deflator.

Investment cycles with a length of about five to seven years corresponded generally to policy cycles (and recurrent policy conflict). Policy swung like a pendulum from left to right and back again, driving and in turn being driven by economic developments. This approach can provide a simple framework to organize the complex history of socialist China, and it allows us to divide the era into subperiods that are quite different from the orthodox periodization used by the Chinese government.

4.3.1   Economic Recovery, 1949–1952

The new leaders of China came to power in 1949 committed to building socialism in China, a commitment that, to them, meant that they would re-create in China a version of the Soviet economic model. The Soviet Union had emerged victorious from World War II and was the leader of the "socialist camp." The Chinese Communist Party (CCP) officially adhered to Marxism as interpreted by the Soviet Union, and there is no evidence during the early years of a fundamental debate or disagreement among the leadership over the desirability of ultimately adopting the Soviet model. However, it was by no means certain how rapidly China should (or could) build a Soviet-style system, nor to what extent China would seek to precisely emulate Soviet practices. China faced immediate economic problems. Wartime damage to industry and agriculture had been substantial, and hyperinflation was raging. The invasion of South Korea by North Korea in June 1950 greatly intensified the hostility the capitalist powers felt toward the new Communist Party government. A trade boycott of China was instituted as Chinese intervention turned the Korean War into a protracted stalemate. These events pushed China into an especially close embrace with the Soviet Union while also keeping Chinese policy-makers focused on the need to be prudent and careful.

The Chinese government was able to move rapidly to restore the domestic economy and experienced remarkable successes in the first few years. Chen Yun took control of financial policy, and tight control of the budget and money supply brought inflation under control by the end of 1950. At the same time, both industry and agriculture were rehabilitated fairly smoothly. By 1952, industry and agriculture surpassed their highest prerevolutionary levels, and the stage was set for a new phase of development. The signing of an armistice in Korea in the summer of 1953 cleared the path for a new era. What is particularly striking during these early years is how effectively the new government adapted its ideology to the economic and political challenges of the day.

In the countryside, the party pushed through a radical land reform. Communist Party workers descended on rural areas throughout the country to distribute land to poor peasant households. Between 1950 and 1952—while the Korean War was raging—42% of China's arable land was redistributed, much of it in the south, where Communist guerrillas had not previously carried out land reforms. This stage of land reform maintained private property in land, but holdings were largely equalized among households. In this way, the Communist Party consolidated support among average and poor farmers and destroyed the economic and political power of landlords. At the same time, it deferred until later the question of how rapidly farmers would be organized into agricultural collectives.

In urban areas, the new government took over many factories, including those expropriated from the Japanese after the war and those belonging to the Guomindang or to capitalists who fled China after the revolution. But policy was generally welcoming to other social groups. Under the rubric of "New Democracy," the Communist Party welcomed non-Communists who were willing to work with the new government. Capitalists who were willing to stay in China—and there were many—were encouraged to expand production at their factories. Quite a few of the planners who had worked for the NRC in the Nationalist government were willing to continue working for the Communist government in the same capacity. Many intellectuals and scientists were persuaded to contribute their skills to the construction of the new China. By putting skilled entrepreneurs and technicians to work, the government was able to revive industry surprisingly quickly. The government's own investment was focused on the Northeast—the former Manchuria—which was critical to the Big Push development strategy since it contained the largest and most important heavy industries. Ironically, these factories had initially been created by Japanese investment as part of Japan's state-sponsored industrialization program and had been taken over by the Russians at the end of World War II. Now, the factories passed into Chinese government hands and were rehabilitated fairly quickly with Soviet aid. The heavy industries of the Northeast became a testing ground where the institutions of the command economy were introduced for the first time. By the end of 1952, economic recovery and rehabilitation had become a resounding success. This was the signal that the time had come to launch socialist industrialization nationwide.

4.3.2   1953 and 1956: The Twin Peaks of the First Five-Year Plan

The five years from 1953 through 1957 are officially designated as the period of the First Five-Year Plan. In fact, this was a period of nearly constant policy change and adjustment. Although the basic Soviet model was not in question, there were serious policy issues concerning the pace of transformation, the degree of centralization that was appropriate for China, and the proper policies on wages and incentives in urban areas, among other issues. Soviet-style institutions were put in place, especially during two periods of mobilization and rapid change that were followed by periods of retrenchment and consolidation. Ironically, even though the direction of change was consistently toward a Soviet system, the reality on the ground was one of a mixed and diverse economy through most of the period because the Soviet model had not yet been imposed in monolithic form. This point is important because the period was one of dramatic economic success.

During the 1950s, every aspect of Chinese society was subject to massive influence from the Soviet Union. The Soviet Big Push strategy and the command-economy system were copied wholesale. At the same time, Soviet industrial technology and organizational design were transplanted to China. The "twin peaks" of especially rapid change came in 1953 and 1956. In the first peak (1953), investment was ramped up quickly as part of the beginning of nationwide investment planning on the Soviet model. Compulsory agricultural procurement was adopted. The very first Five-Year Plan, nominally covering 1953 through 1957, was drawn up "half in Moscow, half in Peking." At the heart of the plan was the construction of 156 large industrial projects, all of them imported from the Soviet Union or Eastern Europe. Virtually all these projects were built in inland regions or in the Northeast. Thus the beginning of planning in China also meant the beginning of regional redistribution and the attempt to move the industrial center of gravity away from the coastal enclaves. The Russian machinery embodied fairly advanced industrial technology for this time, and blueprints and technical specifications were generally provided as well. The Soviet Union provided massive training and technical assistance across the board. Nearly every field was shaped by Soviet advice and training, ranging from architecture and sports training to industrial engineering and the organization of scientific research and educational institutions. Some 6,000 Soviet advisers came to China, typically for periods of a year or two, and more than 10,000 Chinese students studied in the USSR. Although China paid most of the ordinary costs of supporting advisers, there was a substantial aid component to this assistance, and it would have been impossible for a regime that had no experience with nationwide comprehensive planning to roll out a successful investment plan without assistance.

The initial investment surge of 1953 almost immediately threatened to reignite inflation and was curtailed. Moderate economic conditions prevailed in 1954–1955, and China was still a mixed economy. Household farms dominated agriculture, although the government had already established a monopoly over grain purchases and farmers were being encouraged to join cooperatives. In the cities, private businessmen were allowed to run factories and shops, although most capitalists were being pressured into signing contracts with the state-run wholesalers. But this balance was about to change.

During the second peak of transformation, the "High Tide of Socialism," in 1955–1956, the transformation to public ownership was abruptly pushed through. It began in mid-1955, as Mao Zedong criticized the slow pace at which farmers were joining agricultural cooperatives and accused the officials in charge of rural policy of timidity, likening them to old women "hobbling with bound feet." Mao's criticism touched off a mass campaign to push farmers into producers' cooperatives, a campaign that raged through the winter of 1955–1956. Mao's personal intervention at this time was of crucial importance. The shift of policy led immediately to the organization of virtually all farmers into agricultural cooperatives. At the end of 1954, only 2% of farm households had been enrolled in cooperatives or collectives; by 1955, 14% were enrolled; and by the end of 1956, 98%. Attention then turned to the cities, where during early 1956 private factories and shops were turned into cooperatives or "joint public-private" factories with substantial control exercised by the state. Private ownership, having survived and grown for six years since the establishment of the PRC, was virtually extinguished during six months in late 1955 and early 1956. Investment growth accelerated to a new peak as the government pumped resources into the newly established socialist organizations. Two waves of mobilization had produced dramatic social and economic change. The Soviet model was in place, and the year 1956 was thus the first year that China operated a fully "socialist" economy.

4.3.3   Retrenchment: The "Hundred Flowers" of 1956–1957

At the moment when China had just created the key features of the command economy, replicating those that Stalin had created in the Soviet Union, Nikita Khrushchev, standing before the 20th Congress of the Soviet Communist Party on February 25, 1956, denounced Stalin and revealed the crimes of Stalinism. Khrushchev set off global shock waves by declaring that all socialist countries had the right to determine their own path to build socialism. In China, leaders responded by relaxing the political environment while coping with increasingly serious economic problems caused by the stresses and strains associated with the overly rapid pace of change and industrial growth in 1955–1956. Nearly 5 million workers had been absorbed into the state sector in 1956, and while about half were urban dwellers previously employed in private businesses, the other half were rural dwellers migrating to the cities. Average wages had grown rapidly, and a flood of new bank credit was extended in rural areas to finance the infant agricultural cooperatives. At the same time, agricultural output stagnated. While rapid collectivization did not cause a dramatic decline in output, as it had in the Soviet Union in the 1930s, the countryside was buffeted by institutional change, and supplies completely failed to keep pace with the increase in demand. Both economic and international political factors were soon pressuring the Chinese leadership to moderate the pace of change.

By mid-1956, Chinese policy pronouncements had swung 180 degrees from those of a year earlier, stressing the importance of careful, gradual change and criticizing the earlier policy as "reckless advance." In September 1956, the Chinese Communist Party convened its Eighth Congress—actually the first congress since 1949—which charted a program of economic moderation. After the Eighth Congress, programs of economic reform were openly discussed that envisioned an economic system with a significant, though subsidiary, role for the market mechanism and even contemplated the revival and coexistence of different forms of ownership. This party congress thus touched off a period of liberalism that much later found echoes in many of the programs advanced after 1978. Economic liberalism spread gradually into the political domain, and by early 1957, party leaders were calling for open political discussion, a movement labeled the "Hundred Flowers." To some, these policies suggested an alternative path to a distinctive Chinese socialism, more moderate and market oriented than the Soviet model. However, the actual outcome of this complex period was far different from what anyone anticipated.

The Hundred Flowers seemed to promise an important new departure for China. Even though the shift to the Hundred Flowers was rooted in the stresses and strains of the overheating of the previous year, it seemed to herald a new era of self-confidence and social flexibility. Such a shift would have made perfect sense because overall, China was looking back at a record of remarkable success. Extraordinarily rapid economic growth had taken place, and industrial production had expanded 17% annually between 1952 and 1957. Virtually every sector of the economy had been rehabilitated, and the groundwork for sustained future growth had been laid by massive investments in education and training. It was a period of extraordinary social mobility as farmers moved into the city and young people entered college. Many Chinese old enough to remember this period of dramatic progress now look back at it with nostalgia. Having accumulated experience in its own economic construction, China now seemed well on the way to defining its own brand of socialism, one that was more flexible and market responsive than the Soviet model. But it was not to be. Within months Mao Zedong had taken the spirit of change so evident in 1957 and turned it in a dramatically new and ominous direction. From unprecedented success, China was about to plunge into unprecedented disaster. The Great Leap Forward was taking shape.

4.3.4 The Great Leap Forward, 1958–1960

The GLF was the most dramatic, peculiar, and ultimately tragic period in the history of the PRC. The turning point that signaled the emergence of the Leap actually came in mid-1957 when Mao suddenly attacked liberal critics who had spoken out in the Hundred Flowers. Within weeks Mao initiated the broad "Anti-Rightist Campaign" that targeted nonparty intellectuals and anyone with an independent mind. Over the next few months, some 800,000 intellectuals and others who had spoken out during the Hundred Flowers period were condemned, removed from their jobs, and, in many cases, sent to labor camps. The political atmosphere changed overnight. When economic-system reforms that decentralized power were finally readied in November 1957, they were implemented in a political atmosphere of renewed radicalism. Mao turned China in a new direction, shifted gears, and accelerated straight into a brick wall.

The GLF itself was dominated by a highly politicized intoxication with growth that envisaged a bold leap toward a fully communistic society within a few years. It is often seen as the period when China under Mao first developed a vision of socialism that was distinct from the Soviet model. Indeed, widespread enthusiasm for the Leap in its early years was fueled by dissatisfaction with the huge factories and bureaucratic organizations that had been implanted in China as part of the Soviet-style system. But at the same time, the GLF was also a simple intensification of the Big Push strategy. In fact, the most basic economic outcome of the GLF was a massive increase in the rate at which resources were transferred from agriculture to industry. The GLF was the product of a "vision, rather than a plan" (Schurmann 1966, 74), and logical consistency was not always maintained. Indeed, the essence of the GLF was the attempt to resolve contradictions by doing everything simultaneously, regardless of real resource constraints.

There were in fact several institutional innovations in the GLF as well:

1. "Communes" were established in the countryside. A commune was a large-scale (bigger than any collective) combination of governmental and economic functions. It was used to mobilize labor for construction projects, provide social services, and develop rural small-scale industries.

2. Material incentives and monetary rewards were rejected. Bonuses were eliminated in state industry, and free markets in the countryside were shut down.

3. Control over economic decision-making was decentralized.

4. A "walking on two legs" technology policy was established, in which simple technologies (appropriate to a poor nation) were to be combined with advanced industrial technology.

Throughout 1958, the ideological atmosphere became steadily more extreme, and at the same time, the leadership began to receive more and more good news about the economy. A spectacular autumn harvest in 1958 comfortably surpassed those of the previous two years. Output of steel increased rapidly. Growth was real, but reports were also inflated: in the overheated ideological environment, party officials competed to report ever more remarkable successes, with the result that the statistical reporting system became more and more inflated and ultimately collapsed. The leaders convinced themselves that unprecedented political mobilization had enabled the Chinese economy to break through the resource constraints that had held it back (and had seemed so overwhelming at the beginning of 1957). Blinded by their ideological fervor and the breakdown of their statistical eyes and ears, the top leaders made two fateful decisions. First, they sponsored the movement of labor (and even land) out of agriculture, particularly food production. Second, they increased grain procurement, that is, the compulsory deliveries of food to the state. The first decision implied that less food would be produced in the countryside; the second decision implied that the state would take more out. Inevitably, the food available in the countryside would decline. At first, the impact of these policy measures was obscured by an apparently inexhaustible growth surge. Nearly 30 million new workers were absorbed into the state sector during 1958. In rural China, more millions of able-bodied workers were drawn out of agriculture to work in rural factories, including highly publicized "backyard steel mills." Workers who remained in agriculture were instructed to reduce the acreage sown to grain after the 1958 harvest. Top leaders had allowed themselves to be convinced by crackpot science, which claimed that deep plowing and superdense compact planting of seedlings could double or triple crop yields. This would allow farmers to allocate more land to commercial crops, particularly cotton, needed to feed industry's voracious appetite. Laborers at all levels were pushed to work overtime, seven days a week, in a frenzied attempt to do everything at once. In industry, large- and small-scale facto-ries grew simultaneously ("walking on two legs"); educational and cultural enter-prises expanded almost as rapidly as industrial enterprises. In the communes, new social services, including communal dining halls and child-care facilities, were ini-tiated on a large scale; mass poetry-writing sessions were held. Industrial output targets were repeatedly revised upward, especially the target for steel production. Workers were exhorted to surpass Britain within three years and to catch up with the United States. In fact, industry grew rapidly. Although much of the output was unusable junk, the fundamental problem was not the poor quality of industrial out-put but rather the drain of resources and manpower away from agriculture that was entirely unsustainable.

The insanity of the Leap would have been impossible if the party had not silenced critical voices during the Anti-Rightist Campaign or if the voices of farmers warn-ing of disaster could have been heard. For a brief period, it seemed that the party might see the danger and correct its policies. In the summer of 1959, the party con-vened a work conference at Lushan to decide on measures to address serious imbal-ances that were already emerging, including local food shortages. But after several days of discussion, Mao Zedong suddenly seized on the comments of the minister of defense, Peng Dehuai, to launch a bitter attack on the critics of the GLF. A new Anti-Rightist Campaign was launched, this time targeting those within the Commu-nist Party and the government who had dared to make realistic criticisms of the Leap. Both core policies of GLF were resumed: state-sector employment surged again during 1960, and grain procurement reached new heights. But by this time there were few reserves of food or human energy for the system to draw on. Harvests were declining, and food stocks were being exhausted. As the system careened into 1960, local food shortages were ballooning into regional shortages, and China was facing a massive subsistence crisis.

External factors exacerbated the situation during 1960, but it is clear that the fun-damental problem was the willful blindness of China's leaders, beginning with Mao Zedong. Relatively poor weather in 1960 exacerbated the food crisis but did not cause it. In the summer of 1960, Nikita Khrushchev, alarmed by the increasingly erratic and dangerous tilt of Chinese policy, suddenly recalled all Soviet advisers from China. The move was doubtless intended to pressure China to abandon its profoundly misguided policies, but the result was a permanent rift between the two countries. In 1960, full-blown famine burst on China. The famine was fundamentally rural and was most severe in inland provinces. Several inland provinces were absolutely dev-astated. Cumulative excess mortality reached 11% of the population of Sichuan and nearly 6% of the populations of Guizhou and Anhui (figure 4.3). Throughout the worst times, the state continued to extract grain from the countryside and supply urban areas, maintaining an appearance of normality in the main coastal cities.

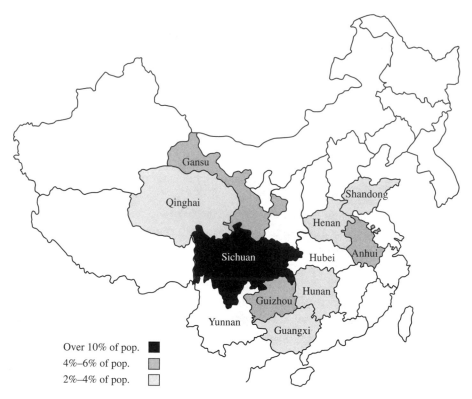

Figure 4.3
The post-GLF famine.
Sources: Lin and Yang (2000); NBS (1999).

Chinese official population data fully reflect the magnitude of the famine. There are different ways to use the data to compute the full extent of the catastrophe, but they agree that through the end of 1961, about 25 to 30 million excess deaths occurred due to the great Chinese famine. In addition, another roughly 30 million births were postponed because of malnutrition and shortages. The worst effects of the famine began to recede during 1962, although mortality remained significantly above normal. By the end of 1962, the worst of this immense catastrophe was over. It was the largest famine of the twentieth century anywhere in the world. Although the catastrophe is acknowledged officially in China, there are no photographs, or memorials to the dead.

4.3.5   Retrenchment: Crisis and "Readjustment," 1961–1963

Finally, in early 1961, the Chinese leadership recognized the necessity of drastic action. Liu Shaoqi and Chen Yun, in particular, pushed through a new set of policies. Investment was chopped back, and some 20 million workers were sent back to the countryside. Within the rural sector, the communes were retained but drastically restructured to place responsibility for agricultural production on smaller groups of households. Bonuses and other material incentives in industry were revived. Nationwide, small factories were shut down by the thousands in an attempt to concentrate production in a smaller number of relatively efficient plants; rural industry in particular was cut back. Control over the economy was recentralized in an attempt to restore order. Virtually all basic necessities were rationed to minimize the impact of shortages. Existing production was reoriented, to the extent possible, to provide greater inputs into agriculture. China, which had been exporting food during the 1950s, entered the world grain market for the first time and became a net importer of food.

Crisis-control policies continued and were extended through 1964. Free markets—closed during the Leap—were reopened to provide an additional channel for peasants to supply food to cities and soak up purchasing power. Imports of consumer goods and market liberalization gradually stabilized prices at a new, higher level. During 1963, attention shifted from crisis management to the elaboration of a new set of long-term policies. Initial drafts of a new five-year plan implied a turn away from Big Push policies and an attempt to restore living standards. These policies were simple common sense at that time. Agriculture had been seriously weakened by misguided policies that had destroyed valuable land in an attempt to build water-control projects, construct mines and factories, and cut down forests. Living standards in both cities and the countryside had been eroded by shortages and inflation. And China could no longer rely on assistance from the Soviet Union. The new draft plans envisaged rehabilitating existing industrial bases in the coastal regions and concentrating new investment in industries (especially chemical industries) that could support and bypass agriculture by producing fertilizer and chemical fibers.

4.3.6   Launch of the Third Front, 1964–1966: Expansion Hijacked by Radicalism

The moderate policies developed between 1961 and 1964 were abruptly discontinued in the summer of 1964. Alarmed by China's isolation in the world and threatened by the increasing American involvement in Vietnam, Mao Zedong shifted China's development strategy again during 1964. As the worst of the post-GLF crisis ended, Mao pushed for the construction of the "Third Front." The Third Front was a massive construction program focused on China's inland provinces (figure 4.4). The objective was to create an entire industrial base that would provide China with strategic independence. By building factories in remote and mountainous interior regions, Mao hoped to ensure that China's industrial base would not be vulnerable to American or Soviet military pressure. In late 1964, a new "high tide" of production was begun that focused on the construction of factories and railroad lines in China's southwestern provinces, particularly Sichuan and Guizhou. With this program, the Big Push strategy was firmly reestablished as the basis of China's development

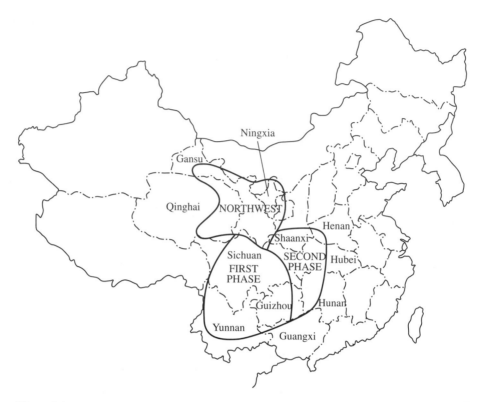

Figure 4.4
The Third Front, 1964–1975.
Source: Naughton (1988).

policy, this time with a militarized and regionally redistributive cast. During 1965 and 1966, investment and industrial production surged as the first stages of inland construction were completed. The Third Front dominated economic construction from late 1964 onward. However, the rapid expansion of which it was a part was brought to an abrupt halt by the eruption of the Cultural Revolution.

4.3.7   Retrenchment: The Cultural Revolution, 1967–1969

In August 1966, Mao launched the so-called Cultural Revolution. The Cultural Revolution has many definitions and even more explanations. The term "Cultural Revolution Era" is often used in China to refer to the entire 10-year period between 1966 and Mao's death in 1976, a usage in which it becomes synonymous with an entire era dominated by a particular kind of leftist political rhetoric. A more precise terminology, however, uses the term to describe a shorter period of political disruption and unrest between 1966 and 1969. During this period, Mao encouraged groups of students, called Red Guards, to overthrow the entrenched Communist Party leadership, except for Mao himself. The Communist leaders of China, including Deng Xiaoping, were suddenly subjected to criticism, dismissal, and sometimes worse at the hands of gangs of students and "revolutionary workers." The Cultural Revolution is far too complex and peculiar a phenomenon to be dealt with here; it is usually seen either as an attempt by Mao to use young people to revive the revolutionary spirit and cleanse China of bureaucratic tendencies, or else as a Machiavellian plot by Mao to purge his opponents in the power structure. In either case, the result was substantial disruption and a gradual descent into unrestrained factional conflict.

From an economic standpoint, the Cultural Revolution (in the narrower definition) was, surprisingly, not a particularly important event. It produced much dramatic new political imagery but had relatively little effect on the economy. This result clearly occurred because of the unusual coincidence between a phase of radical politics and a phase of economic retrenchment. In contrast to the GLF, the disruption of the Cultural Revolution was "managed" quite effectively: investment was curtailed in a relatively orderly fashion; agricultural production was only slightly affected; and although industrial production declined, the fall was moderate, and production of vital necessities and priority projects continued. The guiding economic policies before the Cultural Revolution were quickly reinstated after the worst disruption was over, beginning in 1969. As in 1965–1966, the focus of economic construction continued to be the Third Front. One difference was that by 1969 the threat from the United States in Southeast Asia was deemed to have decreased, while relations between China and the Soviet Union had continued to deteriorate and had reached the point of open military clashes at disputed points on the border and ominous Soviet saber rattling.

4.3.8   The Maoist Model: A New Leap in 1970

Between 1969 and 1971, as China emerged from the "narrow" Cultural Revolution, a new "leap forward," focused on the Third Front, unfolded. This time there was no massive diversion of resources from agriculture, but investment surged and consumption was restrained as all efforts went to industrial construction. During this period, China was operating under something approaching martial law. The army had been called in to quell the factional fighting into which the Cultural Revolution had deteriorated, and the direct involvement of the army in civil affairs was now reinforced by the perception of a military threat from the Soviet Union. Along with the militarization of society came a systematic attempt to revive some of the ideals of the GLF. Once again, material incentives were criticized and bonuses were eliminated, control over economic decision-making was decentralized, and an attempt was made to develop rural and urban industry simultaneously. The difference from the

GLF was that austerity was built into the program from the beginning. Rather than trying to do everything simultaneously, the Chinese people were urged to tighten their belts and give everything for construction. For a while, these policies seemed to bear fruit, and production quickly surpassed pre–Cultural Revolution peaks.

In what way was this Maoist model a distinctive variant of the overall Soviet system? We can identify five elements:

1. Pervasive militarization of the economy. Priority was given to the national defense–related investment program of the Third Front. In addition, the People's Liberation Army had been called in to resolve Cultural Revolution factionalism. As a result, uniformed army officers were often managing production facilities. Austerity was encouraged.

2. Decentralized operation of the economy. Rural industries were encouraged, particularly the "Five Small Industries" that directly served agriculture (see chapter 13).

3. Relative autarky was practiced. Economic links with the outside world were minimized, and regions within China were expected to achieve as much self-sufficiency as possible.

4. There was an almost complete absence of material incentives (bonuses or piece rates). There were few markets of any kind for farmers, and no market for grain.

5. Market-driven labor mobility virtually ceased. Urban school-leavers were sent to the countryside, and the government directed manpower and resources to remote inland areas, but migration and urbanization were halted.

4.3.9   Retrenchment: Consolidation and Drift, 1972–1976

During 1971, economic problems began to emerge once again. Despite the general mood of austerity, industrial growth was again outpacing agricultural growth by too wide a margin. The steadily swelling ranks of industrial workers were putting pressure on the food supply. In the decentralized and generally disorganized process of investment, too many new projects had been started that could not be expected to begin producing for many years. An increasingly large amount of manpower and other resources was being tied up in construction, while the output necessary to support these people and projects was not forthcoming. Economic pressures were suddenly reinforced by dramatic political events. In late 1971, Lin Biao, a key Cultural Revolution leader and the head of the military, was suddenly purged, and almost immediately thereafter a rapprochement was engineered between China and the United States, marked by the visit to China of President Richard M. Nixon in 1972. With the sudden relaxation of the international environment and the purge of China's most powerful military figure, the leadership was in a position to address the emerging economic problems.

Premier Zhou Enlai took the lead in introducing a new, more moderate course. Investment was cut back, and the priority given to the Third Front was dramatically reduced. Some investment was shifted to coastal regions, where projects could be completed more efficiently. Economic relations with the capitalist world were re-established, and a decision was made to spend US$4.3 billion to import industrial equipment. One of the largest items was a set of 11 very large scale fertilizer plants from a U.S.-Dutch consortium. During 1972–1973, a major restructuring of Chinese economic policy in a more moderate direction was emerging. As Zhou Enlai's health deteriorated, Mao brought the moderate Deng Xiaoping, a prominent victim of the Cultural Revolution, back to power at the end of 1974. During 1975, Deng presided over a "rectification" of policy, trying to overcome some of the worst Cultural Revolution problems. However, Deng had not fully won Mao's confidence and was again deposed in 1976.

Political struggles thus prevented a thorough reorientation of Chinese policy. Figure 4.2 shows the annual pattern of fluctuating investment: It was impossible to get follow-through on any systematic economic policy. The aging Mao refused to allow any criticism of policies associated with the Cultural Revolution and encouraged a group of radicals (subsequently dubbed the "Gang of Four") to obstruct trends toward economic rationalization. Although the Gang of Four succeeded in radicalizing culture and ideology, they never had control of economic policy-making. Nevertheless, their political power led to a period of deadlock in the top leadership, which increasingly turned into an open power struggle as it became clear that the succession to Mao was near. Between 1974 and 1976, economic policy-making was paralyzed.

4.3.10   The Leap Outward: 1978 and the End of Maoism

This deadlock was finally broken by the death of Mao Zedong in September 1976. Within days a new leadership threw the Gang of Four in prison and quickly turned its attention to economic matters. Through 1977, conscious of the chaos that had come to dominate economic administration, the post-Mao leadership concentrated on a series of rectification and data-collection exercises. Investment was maintained at modest levels while a program of moderate recentralization was put in place. Systematic rehabilitation of key sectors, such as railroads, was carried out. While it was rehabilitating the economy, the leadership was making big plans. The new leader, Hua Guofeng, staked his power and prestige on a massive investment push, framed as a 10-year plan for the 1975–1985 period. This plan envisaged the creation of 120 major projects, all large in scale and most in heavy industry. Ten huge integrated steel mills were envisioned, as well as 10 new oil fields, 30 large power plants, and 5 new ports. Lying behind this grandiose plan was a belief that the Chinese economy was capable of rapid growth: if only China could purge leftist politicians, focus attention on economics, and rebuild economic institutions, it could experience a major economic takeoff.

Yet it was not to be, for China was not yet ready for economic acceleration. The plan was based on faulty calculations. Between the early 1960s and 1977, China's petroleum production had grown by 15% annually, and the 10-year plan was based on the idea that China would export oil to pay for high-quality industrial capital goods embodying the latest Western technology; for this reason, it was dubbed in Chinese a "great leap outward." Given the decimation of the planning apparatus during the Cultural Revolution years, planners were in no position to address the difficult problems of absorption of new technologies and massive resource flows, selection of sites and detailed project planning, and coordination of multiple new projects. Instead, the "leap outward" collapsed under its own weight for two reasons. First, as policy enthusiasm spread, investment plans kept being raised, just as they had been in the GLF, 20 years earlier. Given permission to import foreign technology, numerous Chinese agencies scrambled to sign contracts with foreign suppliers. By late 1978, China was negotiating at least US$40 billion worth of projects, and contracts worth about US$7 billion were actually signed. This would have been a massive commitment for an economy only barely open to the outside world. Second, China's effort to expand oil production and export ran into unexpected obstacles. All along, half of China's oil production had come from the one field, Daqing in the Northeast, which was showing signs of depletion. During 1977 and 1978, China drilled nearly 15 million meters of new oil wells (which would have cost several billion dollars in the West) and struck oil only once, at a remote site in Xinjiang. It became clear that China did not have the oil to pay for these expensive contracts, and the entire leap-outward strategy began to collapse.

4.3.11   A Final Turning Point: The Third Plenum and the Beginning of Economic Reform

Finally, at the end of 1978, political factors came together in a way that allowed a fundamental departure from the economic and other policies of the Cultural Revolution era. The December 1978 Third Plenum (i.e., meeting of all members) of the 11th Central Committee initiated a new era in the Chinese economy and Chinese politics. This plenum marked an unmistakable break with the past. Politically, Deng Xiaoping, in alliance with other veteran CCP leaders such as Chen Yun and Li Xiannian, assumed the position of paramount leader. These veteran leaders terminated the unsustainable leap outward. Ideologically, the way was opened to free discussion of a number of previously taboo topics. In the economic realm, a host of new policies were adopted, and from 1979 onward, the discussion of specific economic policies belongs with that of the contemporary period of economic reform (chapter 5).

4.4   Legacies of the Socialist Period

4.4.1   The Legacy of Growth and Policy Instability

The details of the political conflicts that repeatedly split Maoist China are exhausting, sometimes bewildering, and ultimately dispiriting. By the end, the aged Mao was an enormous obstacle to China's development, confusing his own personal power and self-justifications with China's realities and needs. Yet from the economic standpoint, a rather simple picture emerges. Here was a system that created all the strategic and systemic settings to maximize the flow of resources into industrialization. It concentrated discretionary power at the top, so that leaders could throw resources at whatever their priorities were. The system, in other words, was set up to maximize the potential to "leap." But every time the system really began to accelerate, it ran into fundamental problems. The economy would overshoot and hit its head on the ceiling. What was this "ceiling"? The ceiling was the inability of agriculture to rapidly generate adequate food surpluses, combined with the weak capacity of the system to generate productive employment for its abundant labor. Every time the economy began to accelerate, it was forced into a retrenchment after a few years.

This legacy had important consequences after 1978. First, it generated profound dissatisfaction with the standard socialist system, even among CCP leaders. Although there was no fundamental rejection of the socialist system in the late 1970s, there was a remarkably deep willingness to experiment and revise, founded on deep misgivings about the existing system. Second, the sharp political divisions meant that CCP leaders could disassociate themselves from the failures of the past by blaming mistakes on Mao, who, after all, richly deserved the blame. Finally, China's leaders could find in the past, in periods of experimentation or economic recovery, policy models that might be appropriate in an era of economic transition. The most significant sources of inspiration were the 1956–1957 Hundred Flowers, at least its economic policy components, and the agricultural policy experiments in the early 1960s, immediately after the GLF famine. Indeed, the policy of contracting farm output to households, which was the critical reform breakthrough in the early 1980s, had its roots in Anhui Province in 1962–1963. Even the decentralization of the early 1970s had some demonstration value to reformers in the 1980s. Reformers at the end of the 1970s had learned how deep rooted the problems of the planned economy were, and they were aware of potential alternatives.

4.4.2   Achievements and Shortcomings of the Development Strategy

Overall, the Big Push strategy "worked," in the sense that it achieved a high and rising investment rate and initiated a self-sustained process of industrialization. China built a heavy industrial base and successfully weaned itself from its initial dependence on Soviet technology and assistance. This created an important basis for the later acceleration of the Chinese economy. But China at the end of this period was still an underdeveloped economy: After 25 years of taking steel as the "key link" of development strategy, China produced 22 million metric tons of finished steel in 1978, only 50 pounds per capita. For comparison, most developed economies produce 1,000 pounds or more per capita, and China in 2015 produced 1,800 pounds per capita. The Chinese development strategy was successful in beginning the process of structural transformation necessary for growth, but it seriously underperformed China's potential once development was under way.

Official Chinese data show an annual GDP growth of 6% between 1952 and 1978, which is comparatively rapid. However, this growth rate certainly exaggerates the Chinese achievement and is clearly overstated because the price system assigned relatively high prices to fast-growing industrial sectors and correspondingly low prices to slow-growing agricultural staples (section 4.2). That means that fast-growing sectors are overweighted in the aggregate GDP calculation. More fundamentally, there were several adverse factors associated with the Big Push development strategy. First, the single-minded pursuit of industrial development meant that consumption was neglected. During the entire 1952–1978 period, gross capital formation grew at an average annual rate of 8.4% and was eight times as large in 1978 as in 1952, but household consumption grew at a rate of only 4.3% and was triple the 1952 level by 1978. After allowing for population growth, per capita household consumption grew only 2.3% annually by official statistics, which somewhat overstate real growth. Moreover, the urban-rural growth differential was significant: urban growth at 3% was significantly above rural growth of 1.8%. Thus by 1978, per capita consumption in urban areas had slightly more than doubled, but rural per capita consumption was only 58% higher than in 1952. Consumption growth of this magnitude would be perceptible but slow and certainly not exceptional by comparative standards.

Growth in services was neglected. Normally, as an economy develops, agriculture shrinks in relative importance, while industry and services expand (this relationship is discussed in more detail in chapter 7). However, this generalization was not true for China between 1952 and 1978. Services declined from 29% of GDP to 24% of GDP over this period, mostly because of a declining contribution from commerce. The government was hostile toward the marketplace and independent businessmen. In 1952, there was one retail salesperson for every 81 people, but by 1978 there was one for every 214 people. There was one restaurant for every 676 people in 1952, but only one for every 8,189 people in 1978. Social services like science, education, and health together increased their share of GDP, but by less than one percentage point.

The relative shrinkage of the retail sector reflected the fact that there was no real competition in consumer markets. There was thus little quality improvement, and few new products were introduced. Moreover, pricing policy further discriminated against consumption. Any consumer good that could vaguely be considered a luxury was priced with a high markup, satisfying egalitarian impulses and also conveniently soaking up excess purchasing power. Such goods—including relatively mundane items such as wristwatches and electric fans—were often not affordable by average households even when they were available. But even given slow income growth and high prices for luxuries, rationing was imposed to limit demand and distribute goods in scarce supply. From 1955 until well into the 1980s, ration coupons were always required for the purchase of grain and cotton cloth. Although the scope of rationing fluctuated with the degree of shortage, as of 1978, there was some type of rationing in place for more than 20 items, including such items as soap, tofu, and good-quality bicycles. The degree of shortage of basic consumer goods was much greater than in the Soviet Union, which abolished most rationing after World War II.

A second major shortcoming of the development strategy was that employment creation was relatively slow. Because most industry was capital intensive and services were neglected, requirements for new labor were modest. Between 1952 and 1978, the total labor force grew by 191 million (from 207 to 398 million), but growth of the modern industrial and service sectors absorbed only 37% of the increase in the labor force. The agricultural workforce grew by 2% per year over the entire period. By 1978, the agricultural labor force was 70% larger than it had been in 1952, notwithstanding a virtually zero increase in cultivated land and rapid ongoing industrialization. As a result, underemployment, particularly in rural areas, became an increasingly serious problem.

Third, much of the industrial investment was not only capital intensive but also relatively demanding technologically. Plants were often large, complex, multistage commitments that took years or even decades to construct and put in operation. This fact had immediate implications: the economic return was often low in the sense that capital was tied up for many years without producing output. Indeed, there were numerous cases of Chinese factories that never fully ramped up mass production of complex processes, steel mills, for example, that encountered problems with difficult ores and complex processes. Perhaps as a result, the industrial growth rate showed a tendency to decelerate: growth was highest during the 1950s (17% per year between 1952 and 1957) and slowed to 8% per year during the 1970–1979 period. In a sense, the Chinese industrialization strategy was overambitious. By concentrating on capital- and technology-intensive heavy industries and neglecting labor-intensive consumer-goods industries, the Chinese were pouring scarce resources into difficult undertakings while ignoring opportunities to exploit relatively "easy" projects. This strategy created an important heavy industrial base, but those assets were being used at very low efficiency.

4.4.3 Human Capital Base

One area where a qualified positive appraisal of China's policies in the 1952–1978 period is possible is the investment in basic human capital. The flow of resources into basic health and education was significant throughout the socialist period, and Chinese people were healthier and better educated at the end of the socialist era. Individual consumption growth was restrained, but socialized consumption such as education and health grew rapidly. Moreover, these outlays were often made in ways that benefited lower-income members of society. Thus, even though the Cultural Revolution shut down the university system for years, primary education spread significantly during that period and illiteracy declined rapidly. Strong entry-level health-care institutions in the countryside were built up during the same period. The result was that life expectancy at birth climbed to 60 for the overall period 1964–1982 according to our best estimates. This was quite high for a country at China's income level and was up from about 50 in 1957 and perhaps as low as 30 in the early years of the twentieth century (Banister and Hill 2004). According to the 1982 census, two-thirds of the population was literate, again a fairly good comparative performance. Basic industrial skills were widespread in the population.

One is tempted to claim that the socialist system did a good job of providing for basic needs and putting a subsistence floor under its poorest citizens. The problem is that the famine of 1959–1961 makes a mockery of this statement. What good does it do to provide for your citizens' basic needs for 27 years if you force on them policies of starvation in the other 3 years? The profound irrationality of the GLF undermined what could and should have been the proudest achievement of the socialist system. It is terrible to have to weigh unnecessary deaths against the additional life years provided to the population by gradually lengthening life spans.

After 1978, China's leaders struggled to transform a system that they themselves had built over the preceding 30 years. As a result of the twists and turns of the preceding decades, the system they confronted was more decentralized, more contested, and less entrenched than that of the Soviet Union. Chinese leaders perceived more options and flexibility, and they were determined not to be left behind by their dynamic East Asian neighbors.

Bibliography

Suggestions for Further Reading

For a good recent overview and discussion, see Walder (2015). On the economics of the socialist era, see Riskin (1991), Lardy (1987), and Lin, Cai, and Li (1996). There is now an extensive literature on the GLF and the subsequent famine. Becker (1996) is a moving account. The data were first seriously analyzed by Ashton et al. (1984). Since then, important contributions have been made by Chang and Wen (1997), Peng (1987), Lin and Yang (2000), and many others. There is now an extensive Chinese literature on the Third Front, but Naughton (1988) is still the main English-language contribution. Joseph, Wong, and Zweig (1991) is a good reassessment of the Cultural Revolution period.

References

Ashton, Basil, Kenneth Hill, Alan Piazza, and Robin Zeitz (1984). "Famine in China, 1958–61." *Population and Development Review* 10 (December): 613–645.

Banister, Judith, and Kenneth Hill (2004). "Mortality in China, 1964–2000." *Population Studies* 58 (1): 55–75.

Becker, Jasper (1996). *Hungry Ghosts: Mao's Secret Famine*. New York: Free Press.

Chang, Gene Hsin, and Guanzhong James Wen (1997). "Communal Dining and the Chinese Famine of 1958–1961." *Economic Development and Cultural Change* 46 (October): 1–34.

Joseph, William, Christine Wong, and David Zweig, eds. (1991). *New Perspectives on the Cultural Revolution*. Cambridge, MA: Harvard University Press. Includes reassessments of rural industry, the Third Front, and central-local relations during the Cultural Revolution.

Lardy, Nicholas (1987). "The First Five Year Plan, 1953–1957," and "The Great Leap Forward and After." In Roderick MacFarquhar and John K. Fairbank, eds., *The Cambridge History of China*, vol. 14, *The People's Republic*, pt. 1, *The Emergence of Revolutionary China, 1949–1965*, 144–184, 360–397. New York: Cambridge University Press.

Lin, Justin Yifu, Fang Cai, and Zhou Li (1996). *The China Miracle: Development Strategy and Economic Reform*. Hong Kong: Chinese University Press. The section on the socialist development strategy is especially good.

Lin, Justin Yifu, and Dennis Tao Yang (2000). "Food Availability, Entitlements and the Chinese Famine of 1959–61." *Economic Journal* 110 (January): 136–158.

Naughton, Barry (1988). "The Third Front: Defense Industrialization in the Chinese Interior." *China Quarterly*, no. 115 (Autumn): 351–386.

NBS (National Bureau of Statistics, Department of Comprehensive Statistics) (1999). *Xiandai Zhongguo 50 Nian Tongji Ziliao Huibian* [Comprehensive statistical data and materials on 50 years of new China]. Beijing: China Statistics Press. Easily accessible source of official data, with headings in Chinese and English.

Peng, Xizhe (1987). "Demographic Consequences of the Great Leap Forward in China's Provinces." *Population and Development Review* 13 (December): 639–670.

Riskin, Carl (1991). *China's Political Economy: The Quest for Development Since 1949*. New York: Oxford University Press.

Schurmann, Franz (1966). *Ideology and Organization in Communist China*. Berkeley: University of California Press.

SYC (Annual). *Zhongguo Tongji Nianjian* [Statistical yearbook of China]. Beijing: Zhongguo Tongji.

Walder, Andrew (2015). *China Under Mao: A Revolution Derailed*. Cambridge, MA: Harvard University Press.

Market Transition: Strategy and Process

Since 1978 China's economy has been transformed by successive waves of economic reform. In one of the most dramatic policy shifts in modern world history, China's leaders in 1978 abandoned their commitment to the command-economy model of socialism and headed off in a new and unfamiliar direction. In the following years, China successfully dismantled the command-economy system and built a functioning market economy. It did so with an obvious acceleration of growth and development, completely avoiding the economic collapse that marred transition in the former Soviet Union. China's spectacular economic growth and ascent to the world's second-largest economy would be inconceivable without successful market-oriented reforms.

China's market transition coincided with its miracle-growth phase (chapters 1 and 7). The extraordinary growth potential inherent in the structural potential of the miracle-growth phase undoubtedly made market reform easier. But the dysfunctional system China inherited was an obstacle to growth and China's experience was unique in the sense that it could achieve miracle growth only through a thorough program of institutional change and reform.

Over the years, the content of the reform process has adapted to new challenges and circumstances and has been continuously reformulated. China has already spent substantially more time building a market economy than was spent "building socialism" under Mao. Change was especially rapid in 1979–1989 and in 1993–1999, during which policy-making and institutional changes were truly extraordinary. There have also been reverses and periods of reform stagnation, but the reform process has maintained its relevance as the challenges the economy faces have changed. In contemporary China, the Xi Jinping–Li Keqiang administration has, since November 2013, attempted to breathe life into a broad program of renewed reform. While it is too early to declare success with these efforts, it is clear that market-oriented reform will be central to the policy agenda for the foreseeable future.

The process of market transition is certainly not complete. Many of the institutions necessary for a market economy are still rudimentary, and further market building and economic opening are possible. Yet today there is no obvious leadership consensus on the ultimate goal of transition and reform. It is even possible that China is no longer in transition at all, but simply involved in ordinary policy-making in an unusually dynamic economic context. However, the broad issues related to market transition show up in every aspect and sector of today's economy. The most important issues are being raised, debated, and resolved in a problem-specific and sector-by-sector manner, and not in a discussion of a society-wide model. Market transition is still relevant, but it plays out in an increasingly complex and fragmented playing field.

This chapter provides a chronological and policy framework for the post-1978 transitional economy. It provides an overview, interpretation, and periodization. Section 5.1 establishes the analytic framework, defines market-oriented reform, and explains its difficulty. Sections 5.2 through 5.5 are chronological and show how market transition formed successive, highly distinctive phases and an initial breakthrough followed by two phases of accelerated, top-down market-reform policy. Section 5.6 introduces a simplified sketch of the political economy of the current system, and then sections 5.7 and 5.8 bring the story up through the Hu Jintao-Wen Jiabao and Xi Jinping-Li Keqiang administrations. Section 5.9 concludes.

5.1   The Challenge of Reform

In attempting to transform a command economy, Chinese reformers faced a nearly overwhelming challenge. Market forces had been banished from the Chinese economy for decades. There were virtually no private businesses. Most significant urban enterprises were state owned, had little decision-making authority, and were more like government departments than business firms. Farmers were organized into rural collectives that owned all the land; they were forced to farm in teams and sell their output to the government at low, state-fixed prices. Individual prices were meaningless, and profit was therefore meaningless as well; and companies had no stake in their own profitability. The economy was completely insulated from world markets, sealed off from their impact and the opportunities they provided.

The intrinsic insularity of the command economy was reinforced in China by the strong moral element added to the abolition of markets during the Cultural Revolution. People had routinely been exhorted to sacrifice their personal interests for the good of the collective. Material incentives of all kinds were abolished and frowned on. Wages of workers in state-owned firms had been frozen for over a decade. "Profit" was a dirty word. Society was making the "transition to socialism through poverty" (*qiong guodu*) rather than waiting until production forces were more developed. Despite widespread disillusionment with these ideas, movement toward a market economy immediately faced a myriad of practical, political, economic, and ethical questions and obstacles. Today there are no command economies left in the world, but in 1978 a third of the world's population lived under command-economy systems. How to change this system, much less reform or abolish it, was a question with no obvious answers.

5.1.1   Defining Market-Oriented Reform

China's leaders began the reform process without a road map or even a clear destination. Their initial steps were in a consistent direction: they reduced the power of planners (especially their monopoly powers), lowered entry barriers, and gave ordinary people some decision-making authority. The success of these initial steps touched off a complex and generally successful reform process. In subsequent decades, though, numerous policies have been adopted and rather indiscriminately labeled "reform." A more precise definition of reform is required. A reform is a type of deliberate policy measure that changes the rules under which economic actors operate. "Market-oriented reform" is a policy measure that increases the scope for fair competition, either by enabling more participants in a given sector or market or by making the rules governing market competition more transparent and fair. Measures that reduce the advantages enjoyed by privileged incumbents are clearly market-oriented reforms. Reforms that make competition more fair can include price reforms that provide equal access to goods at a uniform price and regulatory reforms that provide rules and procedures that are known, predictable, and applied equally to all market participants.[1]

Reforms are intrinsically difficult to carry out for both economic and political reasons. Economically, reforms cause immediate disruption and deliver benefits only with a lag. Market-oriented reforms can be expected to improve economy-wide efficiency, but the benefits of improved efficiency will be diffused gradually throughout the economy. Therefore, it is difficult for individuals to identify the benefits of reform beforehand, and they might forget to credit reforms by the time they are enjoying its benefits. The time structure of the reform process also creates risks. Modest, partial reforms may be rolled back when initial costs appear; radical, comprehensive reforms may lead to economic collapse. Politically, there is a fundamental asymmetry between the position of current incumbents (the winners in the status quo) and that of potential beneficiaries of reform. Each incumbent enjoys a large personal return to his or her privileged position, whereas each of the potential

---

1. It should be clear that governments adopt many important and positive policy measures that are not market-oriented reforms, for example, redistribution to the sick or elderly and provision of national security. Market-oriented reforms should not necessarily enjoy priority over other policy objectives except in special circumstances.

beneficiaries, by definition, will earn only the ordinary competitive market-based rate of return if reforms succeed. Moreover, the privileged incumbents have full information about the benefits they stand to lose, while the reform winners are uncertain about what future benefits, if any, they will receive from the reform process. Reforms benefit the young, who have less political influence. In short, the potential losers from reform have better information and stronger incentives to oppose reform than the potential winners have to support reform, and they are more accustomed to exerting political influence (to protect their rents). Thus it is difficult to assemble a sufficient coalition in support of reform in any political system. Market-oriented reforms must be both politically feasible and economically coherent.

5.1.2   The Chinese Approach to Transition

China's approach to economic transition was quite different from that of most of the other socialist command economies. In the first place, China's transition was initiated from the top by an incumbent group of Communist Party leaders. Elders such as Deng Xiaoping and Chen Yun were part of the founding revolutionary generation who had been instrumental in the creation of the command-economy system. That gave them enormous credibility, legitimized the introduction of markets, and reduced opposition to the reform process. These leaders understood their own system well; they were aware of its flaws and the tremendous challenge they faced, but they also had little incentive to overturn the system altogether. China carried out a strategy of gradualist reform because Communist Party leaders wanted to remain in control and limit the scope of disruptive change.

China's leaders viewed China, quite correctly, as a low-income developing country, and the imperative of economic development was constantly on their minds. It was never conceivable to Chinese policy-makers that economic development would be postponed until an interlude of system transformation was completed. It was always assumed that system transformation would have to take place concurrently with economic development, and that the process of economic development would drive market transition forward and guarantee its eventual success. Individual reform policies were frequently judged on the basis of their contribution to economic growth rather than to market transition as such. In the beginning, this was true because reformers literally did not know where they were going; they were reforming "without a blueprint" and merely seeking ways to ameliorate the obvious serious problems of the command economy. But even after the goal of a market economy gradually gained ascendance in the minds of reformers, it was not anticipated that market transition would be completed until the economy reached at least middle-income status.

The approach to transition differed starkly in Eastern Europe and Boris Yeltsin's Russia. In those countries, the predominant objective of reformers was to move as rapidly as feasible to a modern market economy. Reformers had a model to emulate, the prosperous social democracies of their Western European neighbors, such as [West] Germany. They wanted to shed the legacy of communism as quickly as possible to begin a rapid convergence to this model. These basic considerations framed their view of the economy. Reformers did not believe that their governments could correct distortions in their economy. Reformers had come to power through mainly democratic processes, displacing the previous Communist Party leaders, and they distrusted the bureaucrats and planners that were supposed to follow their instructions. Moreover, there were just too many distortions that were too deeply interrelated. It was better to smash the entire edifice, eliminating as many distortions, privileges, and rent-seeking opportunities as possible, and start over from the bottom up, even if there was some short-term loss of output in the process. The strategy they followed has often been called the "Big Bang." For these reformers, it was of critical importance to free prices as quickly as possible in order to let the price system begin to work, and then to move rapidly to property rights reform, that is, privatization. If there were costs to be borne, it was better to face them early and in a concentrated form in order to get on the path to healthy long-term growth as soon as possible.

The Chinese approach to transition could not have been more different. Chinese reformers were driven by a profound sense of crisis in the wake of the Cultural Revolution. They wanted to rehabilitate the economy and avoid further disruptions. The survival of the post–Cultural Revolution system was in question, and China's leaders were consciously trying to mend and strengthen the economic and political systems in order to ward off collapse. Moreover, Chinese leaders saw unmet needs everywhere in their economies. Some needs were unmet because China was poor and underdeveloped, while others were unmet because the command economy was wasteful; reformers did not make a fundamental distinction between these two types. The command economy had lavished resources on expensive industrial projects and had neglected simple and easily satisfied demands of consumers. Chinese reformers, in essence, decreed that individuals and organizations should be allowed to satisfy unmet needs and earn some additional income; if this new activity tended to erode the command economy and had to be exempted from some of its rules, so be it. Chinese reformers lowered barriers and gradually opened up their system; they gave individuals and groups the opportunity to act entrepreneurially and meet market demands. Early reforms created pockets of unregulated and lightly taxed activity within the system. The reformers allowed such pockets to grow because they were seen as contributing to developmental objectives. For example, rural communities were permitted to run township and village enterprises outside the plan because that would contribute to local investment and economic growth. Foreign businesses were allowed to operate freely in Special Economic Zones (SEZs) because that would increase investment in China and might persuade foreign corporations to transfer technology to China. Such policies were seen as contributing to growth while not initially threatening the overall ability of the government to manage and direct the economy.

As a result, these reforms almost never reduced or eliminated distortions; instead, they loosened control over resources so that those distortions encouraged resources (people, money, initiative) to flow into these less regulated pockets. Gradually, the process of attracting new entrants began to shift the balance between plan and market. The plan, from having been the solid material out of which a few pockets were excavated by pioneering entrepreneurs, became more like a sponge floating in a sea of predominantly market activity. As markets developed, the focus of reform shifted to providing the institutional framework that markets needed to function effectively.

This approach developed into a multidecade "gradualist" transition strategy. Gradualism in this sense involves conserving institutions when possible, repurposing those that have concentrations of expertise, and trying to minimize opposition to change. However, "gradualism" is a broad characterization that—as this chapter demonstrates—covers many different policy configurations. The genius of China's transition process was not that it was gradual—after all, walking slowly is not better than walking fast if you know where you're going—but rather that specific policy packages were well suited to the specific requirements of rapidly changing situations.

5.2   Reforms Begin: Political Relaxation and the Rural Breakthrough

China's market transition began at the end of 1978 with a wide-ranging reassessment of nearly every aspect of the command economy. Simultaneously, a broad social relaxation took place in which the political restraints that had been imposed during the Cultural Revolution were thrown off. In this environment, experimental reforms were launched everywhere, but it was in the countryside that reforms succeeded first, and the dramatic success of rural reforms cleared the way for more profound change (chapter 11). Subsequently, after 1984, policy-makers took advantage of this momentum and crafted a coherent policy framework for a period of accelerated transition.

The rural reforms began with a simple policy decision: the government should reduce the pressure under which farmers had operated for the previous 30 years. For years, China had been locked into a losing cycle with its farmers in which the government pressed to collect more grain from farmers, keeping procurement targets high and procurement prices low. But farmers had resisted this unattractive bargain: grain production had grown slowly; farmer marketing had increased slowly; and farmers were unenthusiastic about investing more time and money in agriculture.

At the end of 1978, at the landmark Third Plenum, China's leaders decided to ease the terms of trade with agriculture and "give farmers a chance to catch their breath." Procurement targets were reduced; procurement prices were raised; and, most important, prices for farm deliveries above the procurement target were raised dramatically. These were not initially systemic decisions; they did not alter any of the fundamental institutions affecting farmers but simply adjusted some of the most important parameters. Nevertheless, these tough choices involved costly trade-offs: in order to reduce grain procurements, planners in 1979 had to double grain imports and chop back the ambitious technology import program of the leap outward (chapter 4). China was already desperately short of foreign exchange, so this difficult choice was palatable to China's leaders only because they believed that the rural economy desperately needed a period of recuperation.

Reformers did not initially envision changing the system of agricultural collectives, just a period of experimentation to let farmers find better ways of organizing work and marketing output. Collectives responded with a wide range of innovative approaches but eventually gravitated toward a radical solution: contracting specific parcels of land to individual farm households. Farm households took over management of the agricultural production cycle on a specific plot of land, subject to an agreement to turn over a contracted amount of low-price grain after the harvest. Because it implied such a dramatic reduction in the role of the collectives—now essentially serving as a landlord—this policy was extremely controversial. But Chinese leaders did not block it and, after 1980, gradually gave it de facto support.

The result was astonishing. The practice of contracting land to households spread rapidly throughout rural China and had become nearly universal by the end of 1983. As it spread, agricultural production surged. Helped by higher prices and the increased availability of modern inputs, such as chemical fertilizers, production climbed rapidly through 1984 (chapter 12). By 1984, staple grain output was a third higher than in 1978, and there was enough grain for everybody. The decades in which China's industrialization had been repeatedly held back by agricultural weakness were over, and the centuries of a food-short China were over as well. But the increase in grain output was only half the story. Freed to allocate their own labor in the way they wanted, farmers boosted output while reducing the number of days spent in the grain fields. They sharply increased their labor input into sideline crops and nonagricultural businesses. The number of workers in township and village enterprises (TVEs)—locally run factories—increased rapidly, and output from this sector surged (chapter 13). These TVEs were not incorporated into state plans, so their output met heretofore-unmet market demands and created new competition for the existing state-owned enterprises. TVE activity was disruptive and set off profound changes.

Successful farm and TVE reforms emboldened reformers in at least four ways. First, a gigantic supply-side experiment had just been performed, and it had proved that improved market incentives could dramatically increase the output of China's farmers. China's reformers gained confidence to persist in the reform project and push forward in other sectors where initial efforts had been less successful. Second, rural reforms supplied ideas that could be used in further reforms, notably the practice of signing contracts to stabilize essential relationships while liberalizing "above-quota" transactions. This was arguably the origin of the "dual-track" approach to reform described in section 5.3.2.1. Third, rural success relaxed the constraints imposed on policy-makers by scarcity, most immediately by easing access to foreign-exchange. Fourth, since farmers were now much better off, reforms had gained the support of the majority of the population. The way was clear to forge ahead with market transition.

5.3   Accelerated Transition, 1984–1989

Rural changes had run ahead of policy-makers, dragging them along. Now, successful rural policies emboldened reformers and touched off a search for concrete policies that could transform the core economic system, consisting of the urban state-owned enterprises and the command organizations that managed industrialization. Could rural reforms be brought into the city? Over the next few years, policy-makers gradually developed a coherent package of reforms.

5.3.1   Economic Decision-Making (Political Economy Interlude No. 1)

China's political system is structured around two parallel, overlapping hierarchies: the Communist Party and the government. At each level, there is both a Communist Party organization and a government organization, and almost all important individuals have both a party position and a government job. The party organization is superior to the government, holding ultimate political power and also the final say in the decision-making process at each level. In the field of economic policy, the party generally delegates substantial decision-making and implementation authority to the government. This arrangement grew out of the early reform period and has shaped the evolution of policy ever since.

After 1978, it was clear that top authority within the Communist Party was exercised by a small group of elders. Deng Xiaoping was the most prominent and is sometimes called the "paramount leader," but Chen Yun exercised nearly equal influence, particularly in economic policy. These elders were intent on preventing a recurrence of the disasters that had occurred because of the concentration of absolute power in the hands of Mao Zedong. Deng Xiaoping intentionally devised a new division of responsibility between the party and the government, on one hand, and among individuals within a collective leadership, on the other hand.

This vision was effectively realized in economic policy. Deng brought Zhao Ziyang from Sichuan and made him premier in order to take charge of economic policy.[2]

As a result, for most of the 1980s, the key economic policy-maker was Zhao Ziyang, premier from 1980 to 1987 and then first party secretary until the Tiananmen Square demonstrations in 1989. Although Zhao was always subordinate to Deng Xiaoping, he was responsible for the day-to-day policy-making that steered the Chinese transition through this first period. Zhao had to defer to both Deng Xiaoping and to Chen Yun, whose influence was greatest in economic affairs. Partially because of this political environment, Zhao's policy-making was cautious and gradual, and he had to create at least a passive consensus behind each policy he wished to push forward. Zhao's key economic challenge was to extricate the economy from the grip of command-economy institutions. His key political challenge was to mobilize support for these policies without alarming or antagonizing his superiors, the elders. Zhao was able to avoid a Soviet-style collapse by disentangling China gradually from the institutions of the planned economy, but in the end he fell afoul of the elders, who removed him during the turbulence around the 1989 demonstrations in Tiananmen Square.

The policy environment in the 1980s was thus highly personalized and characterized by multiple powerful players who possessed potential veto power over many policies (Naughton 2008). At the same time, Deng Xiaoping established an institutional principle that outlived the specific individuals: economic policy-making would henceforth be delegated to the premier and implemented by government agencies. This was one important element of a process by which the party gradually adopted institutionalized procedures while maintaining ultimate power.

5.3.2 Features of Accelerated Transition, 1984–1989

The period of intensified reform, 1984–1989, over which Zhao Ziyang presided had several distinctive features. Some of these features came from the rural economic reform; others emerged from the government's limited administrative capabilities. The features of this period can be seen most clearly by comparing them with the subsequent period of intensified reform during 1993 to 1999. Table 5.1 displays these features and illustrates a surprising point: the features of these two highly productive periods were in many respects opposites. Zhao Ziyang presided over a cautious,

---

2. In addition, both Deng Xiaoping and Chen Yun paid enormous attention to personnel and promoted younger politicians who would carry on their policies and serve as successors. They brought in Hu Yaobang (age 65) as general secretary and Zhao Ziyang (age 61) as premier and head of government. After 1980–1981, Hu and Zhao had the top formal positions, but both men acknowledged that they served at the discretion of Deng and Chen.

Table 5.1
Contrasting styles of economic reform.

1980s reform	1990s reform
Zhao Ziyang: cautious, consensual decision-making	Zhu Rongji: rapid, personalized decision-making
Introduce markets where feasible; focus on agriculture and industry	Strengthen institutions of market economy; focus on finance and regulation
Dual-track strategy; growing out of the plan	Market unification; unite dual tracks
Particularistic contracts with powerful incentives	Competition governed by uniform rules; "level playing field"
Competition created by entry; no privatization	State-sector downsizing; beginnings of privatization
Decentralize authority and resources	Recentralize resources; macroeconomic control
Inflationary economy with shortages	Price stability, goods in surplus
"Reform without losers"	Reform with losers

decentralizing approach, while Zhu Rongji launched a bolder and more comprehensive process that was, on balance, recentralizing.

By building on rural reforms, policy-makers created a transition strategy that characterized the entire period from 1978 to 1989, both the rural reforms of 1979–1982 and the accelerated transition of 1984–1989. Reform overall was decentralizing, shifting power and resources from the hands of central planners to local actors, while core state interests were protected, often through contracts. This allowed entry barriers to be reduced and market forces to grow. The nature of China's policy in the 1980s as a strategy of transition can be shown by focusing on two main characteristics, the dual-track system and the approach to macrostabilization Each was a complex bundle, but put together they added up to a simple package: introduce markets and then use your remaining capabilities to keep the macroeconomy on track.

5.3.2.1   Dual-Track System

Perhaps the most characteristic feature of China's initial departure from the planned economy was the dual-track system. The core meaning is the coexistence of a traditional plan and a market channel for the allocation of a given good. Rather than dismantling the plan, reformers acquiesced to a continuing role for the plan in order to ensure stability and guarantee the attainment of some key government priorities. The system had seven key elements:

Entry. The whole process was kicked off by "entry," when the protected industrial sector was effectively opened to new entrants beginning in 1979. Large numbers of start-up firms, especially rural industries, rushed to take advantage of large potential profits in the industrial sector, and their entry sharply increased competition and changed overall market conditions in the industrial sector. Most of these firms were collectively owned, and some were private or foreign owned. These firms were never part of the planned economy. They operated at "negotiated prices" that reflected whatever bargain the firm could strike. Facilitated by China's diversity and the attraction of its huge market, as well as by the important role that local governments played in economic management, entry was a key driver of change throughout the reform period.

Dual track inside state firms. The dual track was also introduced into state-owned enterprises (SOEs) that were the core of the planned economy. Indeed, this is the fundamental meaning of the term "dual-track system": it refers to the coexistence of two coordination mechanisms (plan and market) rather than to the coexistence of two ownership systems. State-owned firms that were still assigned a compulsory plan for output were almost all allowed, by the mid-1980s, to use additional capacity for production of above-plan, market goods. The dual track operated within each state-run factory. This had two immediate practical consequences: SOEs began adapting to the market, collecting information and earning profits on the basis of market prices. Perhaps even more important, SOEs were allowed to do business with nonstate firms. Nonstate firms could legitimately procure resources, including scarce natural resources and complex machinery, and begin to upgrade their operations. SOEs reduced costs by subcontracting with rural nonstate firms with cheap labor and land. A unified marketplace outside the plan came into existence.

Market prices. From the beginning, prices outside the plan were flexible and equated supply and demand. Beginning in 1985, market prices were given legal sanction for exchange of producer goods outside the plan. Gradual decontrol of consumer-goods prices—initially cautious—steadily brought most consumer goods under market-price regimes.

Growing out of the plan. Chinese planners in 1984 made a commitment to keep the overall size of the central government's materials-allocation plan fixed in absolute terms. Since the economy was growing, this commitment implied a gradual process in which the plan would become proportionately less and less important until the economy grew out of the plan. Figure 5.1 shows how this process worked concretely with sales and allocation of finished steel, the archetypical planned commodity. Until 1984, the quantity of steel allocated by central-government planners increased in step with production. Unusually in a planned economy, a substantial share of output in China was allocated by local-government planners. A tiny share of output was sold independently by enterprises in the early years. After 1984, though, the quantity allocated by the central government leveled off, and nearly all the increment in output was channeled into the market; that is, it was left to the control of enterprises to sell at the best price they could obtain. Subsequently, in the early 1990s, quantities allocated began to decline in absolute terms and then dropped off

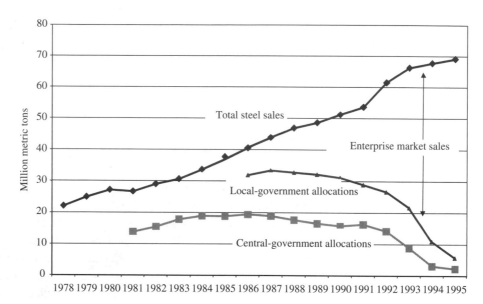

Figure 5.1
Steel production and planned allocation.
Source: Naughton (1995, 224).

precipitously after 1992; the economy had grown out of the plan. A generally credible commitment to freeze the compulsory plan set in motion a dynamic process that gradually increased the share of nonplan, market transactions in the economy and made the dual-track system into an unabashed transitional device.

Once the plan was fixed in absolute terms, the incentives of individual enterprises changed dramatically. Enterprises now faced "market prices on the margin" (Byrd 1991). Even those firms with compulsory plans covering, say, 90% of capacity understood that future growth and development of profitable opportunities would take place at market prices. The plan served as a kind of lump-sum tax on (or subsidy to) the enterprise. So long as the commitment not to change the plan was credible, it had no real impact on the enterprise's decision-making, which was based on market prices. In that sense, the plan became irrelevant.

Particularistic contracts. In order to make the dual-track system work, planners signed individual contracts with every state-owned enterprise. These contracts specified the tax payments and deliveries of planned commodities the firm was required to make. There was no longer a regular corporate income tax system; the de facto tax rate was specific to an individual enterprise. These contracts were typically drawn up on the basis of the firm's performance in a previous base year, so that each existing enterprise was grandfathered into the transitional system.

Incremental managerial reforms. Policy-makers experimented with ways to improve incentives and management capabilities of SOEs. Incentives increasingly rewarded profitability (and deemphasized plan fulfillment) for SOEs. The combination of increased competition, improved incentives, and more effective monitoring of performance improved performance of SOEs over the 1980s. This was an alternative to the more radical policy of privatization. Urgent privatization tends to follow from a belief that state-sector performance cannot be improved, and it often leads to a short-run "abandonment of the enterprise" as the attention of reformers shifts from short-run performance to the difficult task of privatization. Conversely, the sense that privatization was not imminent lent urgency to China's attempt to improve monitoring, control, and incentives in the state sector.

Disarticulation. Reforms followed a strategy of "disarticulation," in which successive sections of the economy were separated from the planned core. Reformers understood that their actual control of the economy was tenuous, but they wanted to move forward while retaining stability. For example, the early establishment of SEZs was done precisely to ensure that these export-oriented enclaves would have almost no links to the remainder of the economy (see chapter 17). In the countryside, policy-makers realized that the poorest areas could be cut loose from the planned economy because they had no surpluses to sell in any case. Poor areas reformed quickly, while the state fulfilled its procurement goals from the richer areas, which reformed more cautiously.

With these seven elements in place, the dual track became not just a feature of the economy but a transition strategy. Many economies have dual tracks in the sense that they have core parts of the economy subject to government control or regulation and less regulated market fringes (sometimes "gray" or "black" markets). What was distinctive about the Chinese dual-track strategy was that it drove marketization progressively and systematically. An individual SOE, for example, facing stronger incentives to increase profit in the context of a fixed plan and a growing market, naturally began to transform to a market-oriented actor. Growth, disarticulation, and a credible commitment to freeze the plan ensured that this trajectory would take root economy-wide.

In retrospect, the dual-track policies had economy-wide coherence. Reduction of the state's monopoly led to rapid entry of new firms. Entry of new firms, combined with adoption of market prices on the margin, led to enhanced competition and began to accustom state-sector managers to the market. Competition eroded initially high profit margins for state firms and induced the government, as owner of the firms, to become more concerned with profitability. The government experimented with better incentive and monitoring devices, which improved state-sector performance. Nonetheless, the state sector grew more slowly than the nonstate firms that were entering new markets. The economy gradually grew out of the plan as both the plan and the state sector as a whole became less dominant elements in the economy.

5.3.2.2 · Macroeconomic Stabilization

Transition inevitably causes inflation and macroeconomic distress. China's approach to this challenge was distinctive.

Traditional "planned" instruments used to stabilize the economy. When China's reformers first faced serious macroeconomic imbalances in 1979 through 1981, they used the institutions of the planned economy to cut back investment and relieve pressure on the economy. Rather than combining stabilization and reform into a single rapid but traumatic episode, as in a "big-bang" transition, the Chinese used the instruments of the planned economy to shift resources toward the household sector and relieve macroeconomic stresses at the very beginning of reform. This dramatic shift in development strategy created favorable conditions for the gradual development of markets. Inflationary pressures were vented off as supplies grew rather than being resolved in a quick transition from suppressed to open inflation. In a related fashion, the planning structure was used to provide an initial impetus away from the capital-intensive Big Push strategy and toward more sustainable labor-intensive sectors, generally consumer-goods sectors. This initial shift toward a more labor-intensive strategy was given urgency by the need to provide jobs for a large group of unemployed young people, including many who had returned to the cities from the countryside. The temporary use of planning to reduce unemployment and increase the supply of consumer goods tended to preserve stability and solidify support for the reform orientation. In subsequent episodes, policy-makers used all the instruments at their disposal—including those inherited from the planned economy—to make short-run structural adjustments and stabilize the macroeconomy.

Continued high saving and investment. With relative economic stability, households gradually took over national saving from the government (chapter 18). The Chinese government relinquished control of some of GDP during the early stages of reform in order to allow rural and urban households more resources and better incentives. In order to accommodate this readjustment of the economy, government investment was reduced, and the overall investment rate declined and then stabilized (figure 4.1: 1978–1983). This gave space for a steady increase in household income and enabled households to increase their saving. Since household financial assets were deemed reasonably secure, households were willing to increase voluntary saving. In turn, increased household saving offset the reduction in government saving that took place due to increased competition.

Macroeconomic cycles. Macroeconomic policy was far from perfect, though, and macroeconomic cycles recurred throughout the early reform era. Inflation spiked in

1980, 1985, and 1988–1989, with consumer price inflation peaking at 28% in 1988–1989 (figure 18.1). Inflation at this level caused significant hardship to workers on relatively fixed incomes and introduced bouts of uncertainty. In retrospect, such episodes never lasted more than a couple of quarters and overall inflation was much less than in the transitional economies of Eastern Europe and the former Soviet Union. At the time, however, these inflationary episodes caused significant popular discontent and provoked opposition among the more conservative elders, such as Chen Yun. Inflation triggered harsh scrutiny from conservatives who were skeptical of reform.

Macroeconomic cycles were also reform-policy cycles. Reforms advanced strongly in certain years (1979–1980, 1984, 1987–1988) but in each case were accompanied by increased imbalances and inflation. Decentralization of decision-making empowered firms and local governments to make new investments, while price decontrol allowed suppressed inflation to emerge. Reacting against adverse developments, policy-makers would swing toward caution and suspend reforms (1981–1982, 1986, 1989–1990). Only after stabilization achieved some success were new reform measures pursued again. These "political business cycles" were similar to those in the socialist economy, except that the expansionary phases corresponded to accelerated reform rather than to political mobilization.

As a result of these dynamics, macroeconomic outcomes frequently determined the success or failure of specific reform initiatives. By far the most serious challenge to the reform process came in the wake of one such cycle, when macroeconomic conditions in 1988–1989 fed an upsurge of urban discontent. Inflation surged as policy-makers gave firms more authority and resources, then considered a radical price decontrol in the face of intensifying macroeconomic imbalances, and then hesitated. Economic imbalances turned into a short-run economic policy crisis. Policy-makers then changed course and tried to stabilize the economy through traditional instruments, cutting investment and reimposing price controls during the winter of 1988–1989. Contractionary policies were already starting to bite into economic growth, while inflation had not yet been brought under control. Economic crisis suddenly turned into political crisis with the unexpected death of Hu Yaobang on April 15, 1989. Hu had been Deng Xiaoping's designated successor and an important reformer. Even though he was widely admired because of his steadfastness in rehabilitating millions of victims of political persecution, conservative elders had deposed Hu at the end of 1986. Now students poured into Tiananmen Square in central Beijing to mourn him. A volatile mixture of expectations and grievances fueled extravagant hopes and massive disillusionment and led to months of demonstrations in China's main square. Ultimately the demonstrations were suppressed with military force, many of the most influential reformists in the government were sidelined or exiled, and the course of China's reform was forever altered. These dramatic events marked the end of the first period of accelerated reform.

5.4   Interlude, 1989–1992

After the Tiananmen Square political crisis, a period of conservative ascendancy followed between 1989 and 1991. The conservatives greatly overestimated the economic costs of the inflation and disorder of 1988–1989 and underestimated the achievements of reform. They carried out severe economic retrenchment and attempted to roll back reforms across the board. These efforts were a complete failure, today either forgotten or passed over in embarassed silence. Urban inflation, which had seemed so corrosive in 1988, was quickly controlled, and other imbalances in the economy were soon corrected. The market track adapted much more quickly and effectively than the plan track. Conservatives were surprised, and planners were left far behind. Without a viable economic program, conservative support among the Communist Party elite crumbled.

Economic reform survived the traumatic post-Tiananmen period because of the broader dynamics unleashed by reform. Once immediate problems were addressed, it became clear that the benefits of reform had been widely shared. Even more striking, almost no major social group had suffered significant economic losses during the 1980s. This pattern has been called "reform without losers" (Lau, Qian, and Roland 2000). The dual-track strategy meant that the position of workers in SOEs had generally been protected. Rural residents were much better off, having gained from the dissolution of collectives, improved agricultural prices, and the rapid growth of nonagricultural production in the countryside. Urban residents who were able to exploit new niches in the economy certainly gained. Bureaucrats and intellectuals suffered some relative erosion, but they were partially compensated by a much richer cultural and intellectual environment. The broad enjoyment of the benefits of reform—and the absence of a group clearly disadvantaged by reform—meant that reform was still widely popular despite the debacle at Tiananmen Square.

After the conservative ascendancy began to fade in 1991, economic reform resumed with astonishing speed in 1992–1993. In early 1992, Deng Xiaoping emerged to give the latest pendulum swing a forceful push. Deng took a "Southern Tour" in which he visited and endorsed the SEZs created a decade earlier. Deng (1992) reemphasized the need for accelerated economic reform and an experimental, nonideological approach. "Development is the only hard truth," Deng declared, emphasizing that the contribution to growth was the ultimate policy criterion. Reformers prevailed at the October 1992 Communist Party Congress, which for the first time endorsed a "socialist market economy." Zhu Rongji joined Jiang Zemin in the Party Standing Committee, and a year later, the Third Plenum of this congress approved a broad reform program. It is often said that China reformed without a blueprint, but this was not true in 1993. The Third Plenum Resolution contained almost all the key measures carried out by Zhu Rongji over the subsequent six years. The reform blueprint was not tightly sequenced—it was more like a menu than a road map—but the most important reform measures were clearly laid out in an interdependent and coherent package. Of course, there was always uncertainty about what reforms would actually be adopted, but in the end, most were, and all the major reforms that were actually implemented can be traced back to this reform document.

5.5   Accelerated Transition, 1993–1999

Reforms moved quickly from the drawing board to reality. Policy-makers were driven by a sense of great urgency, indeed, of crisis, and in Zhu Rongji found a forceful leader committed to reform. China's economic gains were threatened by renewed macroeconomic turbulence. In the wake of Deng Xiaoping's Southern Tour, the discipline exerted by the central government over local officials—and over local bank credit—collapsed. Short-run and long-run challenges demanded a response.

5.5.1   Renewed Inflation and Macroeconomic Austerity

Inflation, previously tamed, came roaring back, accelerating through 1993 and remaining above 20% throughout 1995. The political system exhibited nothing like the sensitivity to inflation that had hobbled Zhao Ziyang's policy-making in 1988, so Zhu Rongji's objective was a gradual "soft landing" in which inflation was controlled without seriously compromising growth. Still, the collapse of monetary control made it obvious that China's monetary institutions were utterly inadequate. To break the momentum of accelerating inflation, Zhu Rongji was given authority over economic policy in mid-1993 and assumed the position of governor of the central bank as well. As a stopgap, direct political control was used in the absence of effective institutions. It took a prolonged period of monetary restraint to put an end to the inflationary surge, and price stability was not achieved until 1997 (see chapter 18).

The shift to a restrictive macroeconomic policy was an essential prerequisite for further reforms. The control of aggregate demand increased competition, creating "buyer's markets." Holding the line on monetary policy allowed a "hard budget constraint" to be imposed on banks and, through banks, on enterprises. Public enterprises were increasingly made responsible for their own profits and losses, a move that was meaningful only in the presence of competitive markets and hard budget constraints. Tough macroeconomic policies created conditions under which corporate governance reforms could support restructuring driven primarily by market forces.

5.5.2   Crisis of State Capacity

The Chinese economy faced a grave new challenge: a crisis of state capacity. The "reform without losers" approach of the 1980s had required the central government to steadily surrender control over resources in the economy. The most direct evidence of this declining control was the dramatic erosion of the Chinese government's fiscal position. Figure 5.2 shows that during 15 years of reform, budgetary revenues as a share of GDP dropped from 33.3% of GDP in 1978 to only 10.7% at its low point in 1995. It was feared that this decline threatened the government's ability to achieve its most basic goals; worse, that the decline was simply out of control. A new impetus for reform was provided, since even the most conservative official could see that something needed to be done.

Reforms also had a new requirement: to provide adequate resources for the central government to carry out its essential functions. The central government needed to strengthen its regulatory and macroeconomic management functions, which meant it needed an adequate revenue base. By the end of 1994, fundamental

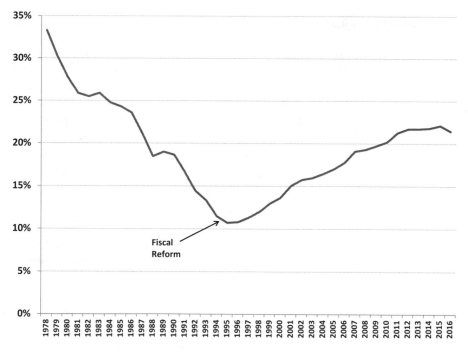

Figure 5.2
Budgetary revenue share of GDP.
Source: *SYC* (various years).

fiscal reforms were implemented that provided a new, broader tax base for the economy and led to a steady revival of government budgetary collections. The reforms restored robust growth to fiscal revenues, which increased every year until 2015, when they reached 22.1% of GDP (figure 5.2). They also greatly increased the central government's share of revenues (chapter 20). Control of inflation and restoration of budgetary soundness created the indispensable foundation for the overall reform package.

5.5.3   Regulatory and Institutional Restructuring

Zhu Rongji presided over a massive institutional reconstruction that embodied a new approach to economic reform. The new reforms were regulatory in the sense that they introduced new rules that at least in principle applied equally to all economic actors. Movement in the direction of a regulatory state, with a focus on regulating competition, reduced government intervention and direction management of enterprises. By the 1990s, when the economy had "grown out of the plan," the most important tasks were to improve the legal and regulatory environment, create a "level playing field" and reduce some of the most obvious distortions in the economy. At the core of this program were dramatic institutional reforms in four core areas of the economy: the fiscal and tax system, the banking and financial system, ownership and corporate governance, and the external sector. Each of these is discussed in more detail in a separate chapter. The commitment to this new direction was strongly signaled at the end of 1993, when three important measures were adopted that became effective during 1994: a new fiscal system, a new foreign-trade system, and a new Company Law. These took time to implement, but there was now no going back.

5.5.3.1   Market Unification

By the early 1990s, the dual-track system had served its function. Figure 5.1 shows that allocation of materials (in this case, steel) dropped off rapidly after 1991 and was abolished altogether by the end of 1993. The orthodox planning system disappeared with barely a whimper, scarcely noticed. Particularistic contracts with individual enterprises were also allowed to lapse. Those contracts had always involved a two-sided agreement covering supply and financial relations. The plan side of the contracts had become obsolete, while the financial side was in conflict with the impending fiscal and tax reforms, which were high on the reform agenda and necessary in order to restructure macroeconomic fundamentals.

5.5.3.2   Fiscal and Tax System

Fiscal reforms in 1994 were designed to arrest the slide in budgetary revenues but also to transition to a broader tax base by implementing a 17% value-added tax and other business taxes. These taxes had relatively low rates, compared with the old system, but they were uniform and applied to all economic actors. The strong performance of tax revenues after 1995 showed that broadening the tax base was successful. Fiscal reforms were also designed to put fiscal relations of the central and local governments on a sounder and more stable basis. They did so by increasing the share of total taxes initially collected by the center and establishing a set of rules for sharing revenues between central and provincial governments (chapter 20).

5.5.3.3   Banking and Financial System

The banking system underwent fundamental restructuring during the second half of the 1990s. The People's Bank of China (PBC) had been nominally established as a central bank in 1983, but at that time it remained beholden to government officials at both central and provincial levels. The bank was given a formal charter in March 1995 that made it responsible for monetary policy, under the "guidance" of the State Council. It was finally given a workable organizational structure in late 1998, when a restructuring plan abolished the provincial-level branches and set up nine regional branches along the lines of the U.S. Federal Reserve Board. With its new mandate to conduct monetary policy and with a monetary policy board established as a governance and advisory body, the central bank began to play an active role in determining and implementing monetary policy. This administrative restructuring took place in tandem with the adoption of macroeconomic austerity: state-run commercial banks soon found themselves facing a much harder budget constraint as their access to easy government money was curtailed. In turn, they began to impose tougher standards on their clients in state-owned enterprises.

Shortly after the constitution of a central-bank system, banking authorities began to tackle the enormous problem of lax financial supervision and nonperforming loans in all the state banks. In 1999, four asset-management corporations were established to take over some of the nonperforming loans of the four big state commercial banks and begin to liquidate them for as much residual value as possible. Clearly, these were essential steps on the long and difficult road to a stable banking system. Eventually, in April 2003, the PBC supervisory functions were spun off to the newly created China Bank Regulatory Commission (chapter 19).

5.5.3.4   Corporate Governance

A large-scale effort to restructure the state-owned corporate sector was begun with the adoption of the Company Law, effective July 1, 1994. The Company Law provided for all state-owned enterprises to gradually reorganize as limited-liability corporations, with clarified corporate governance institutions. These provisions have been implemented only gradually but have slowly transformed the organizational structure of the Chinese public sector (chapter 14). Systematic restructuring of corporate governance was combined with selective listing of state-owned companies on China's newly opened stock markets, which grew significantly during the late 1990s (chapter 19). Together, these measures changed the structure of China's large state-owned companies and created a demand for new types of financial regulation. With implementation of the Securities Law in July 1999, the China Securities Regulatory Commission's branches became operational nationwide, thus forming a centralized network of securities supervisors. At the same time, a host of new central-government agencies were established to deal with other types of regulatory oversight, including, for example, the State Intellectual Property Office and the State Administration of Technical and Quality Supervision. China took the first steps toward becoming a regulatory state.

5.5.3.5 External Sector: Opening Capped by Entry into the World Trade Organization

Extraordinary steps were taken to open the economy in 1993. Foreign firms were allowed access to China's market through foreign direct investment, touching off a surge of incoming investment. At the end of 1993, reforms unified China's foreign-exchange regime (eliminating the dual track in foreign exchange), devalued the currency, and established current-account convertibility. These important steps laid the basis for membership in the World Trade Organization (WTO), although the deal was concluded only after six more years of arduous negotiations. WTO accession involved Chinese acceptance of an extraordinarily broad range of regulatory undertakings, designed to allow China to harmonize with international standards. At the same time, and even more fundamentally, WTO accession implied an important further step in the degree of openness of the Chinese economy and the extent to which foreign goods and companies could compete in China (chapter 16).

5.5.4 Outcomes

5.5.4.1 From Inflation to Price Stability

After 1996, inflation was tamed in China, and the overall macroeconomic context swung sharply toward price stability (chapter 18). Price stability and increased competition greatly intensified product-market pressure on Chinese firms and drove further restructuring.

5.5.4.2 State-Enterprise Restructuring and Downsizing

From the mid-1990s, Chinese authorities began to cut the formerly close ties that bound the government and SOEs. Public firms faced increased product-market competition and pressure, on the one hand, and reduced access to funding from government banks, on the other. Gradually, SOEs moved toward significant restructuring

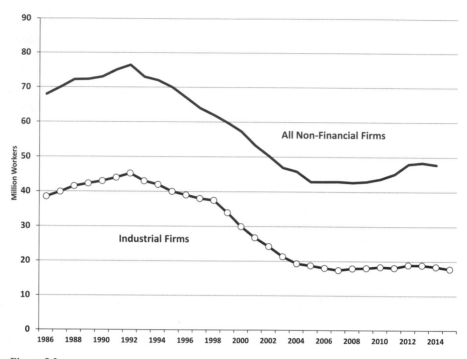

Figure 5.3
Workers in state-owned enterprises and state-controlled corporations.
Sources: *SYC* (various years); and Labor Yearbook (various years). A slightly different series in SASAC (Annual) shows the same basic trends.

and downsizing, encouraged by the government. SOE restructuring has meant converting vaguely defined public ownership into more explicit, legally defined ownership categories, sometimes involving privatization. After the Fifteenth Communist Party Congress in September 1997, local-government officials were given an almost free hand to proceed with state-sector reforms that included bankruptcy, sales and auctions, and mergers and acquisitions. SOE employment had been declining in relative terms since 1978, as new firms entered and the economy blossomed, but as figure 5.3 shows, SOE employment had grown in absolute numbers through the first 15 years of reform (through 1993), though its share of total employment had declined. After 1993, SOE employment began to decline dramatically in absolute terms, from 76 million in 1992 to 43 million in 2005; the new figure included workers in state-controlled corporations as well as traditional SOEs. Thus employment in all government-controlled enterprises declined by 33 million (or 43%) over 10 years. Industrial SOEs downsized even more drastically, declining 61% from 45 million in 1992 to their low point of 17.4 million in 2007.

Given the decentralized nature of the Chinese economy, the progress of SOE restructuring depended on the incentives facing local governments, which "owned" the majority of SOEs. In fact, SOEs had already ceased to be "cash cows" on which local government officials could draw: industrial SOE profits were 15% of GDP in 1978 but fell below 2% of GDP in 1996–1997. Local governments began to rethink the value of possessing their own SOEs and increasingly concluded that they derived few advantages from local state ownership that could not be achieved just as well from a generally prosperous local economy.

5.5.4.3   Growth of the Private Sector and Privatization

The Chinese government has never unambiguously embraced privatization and continues to avoid the term in favor of vague circumlocutions such as "restructuring." However, privatization, often in the form of management buyouts, became common in the TVE, collective, and SOE sectors. More generally, a series of policy shifts have given gradually increasing recognition and legitimacy to private business. Indeed, the rise of private business is perhaps an inevitable consequence of a policy shift toward a level playing field.

5.5.4.4   Reform with Losers

These momentous changes in transition strategy have broken sharply with one of the key characteristics of reform in the early period. Reform after 1993 clearly imposed significant losses on substantial social groups. Most directly affected were SOE workers, who had been a relatively privileged group in the past. Millions were laid off, and further millions abandoned failing firms. At its peak, the true urban unemployment rate reached 10% (see chapter 9). Deprived of job security for the first time since the establishment of the PRC, some state workers suffered precipitous losses in income and social standing. Groups and individuals emerged from this phase of reform less sheltered from competition than in the past, and the shortcomings in China's social safety net were now glaringly obvious. The benefits of transition were more unequally spread among the Chinese population than had been the case in the 1980s, and inequality soared.

5.5.5   Conclusion to the Second Period of Accelerated Transition

The second reform period was a fundamental turning point in China's development. The institutional framework that governs the Chinese economy today was established during the second reform period. China made the transition to what is fundamentally a market economy. Many of the subsequent chapters in this book describe and analyze institutions that were created during this period. Moreover, this reform period laid the foundation for the astonishing surge of growth that transformed China in the subsequent decade. By 2003, GDP growth had rebounded to 10%, and it stayed above 10% for the next five years. This astonishing performance, which few people anticipated, was in large part the delayed impact of the radical reforms of the Zhu Rongji era.

The transition strategy employed between 1993 and 1999 was more orthodox and less distinctively Chinese than the approach taken in the 1980s. There was a less stark opposition between "big-bang" and "gradualist" transitions. In both types of transition, there was a cost for change. Growth slowed to below 8% in 1998 and 1999, and unemployment soared. To be sure, China's "growth recession" was very small compared with the huge "transition recessions" experienced in the former Soviet republics. Since China had already created a much larger, more diverse, and more resilient nonstate sector, it was possible for China to absorb these costs much more easily. However, in both cases, the downsizing of the state sector imposed serious short-run costs that were repaid only later with long-run efficiency gains and growth acceleration.

5.6   A New Institutional Framework (Political Economy Interlude No. 2)

It might seem from the description of accelerated reforms in the 1990s that China's reform effort was designed and implemented top-down by the Jiang Zemin-Zhu Rongji administration. This was not the case. Rather, a new division of roles and resources was bargained out between the central government and local governments, and this bargain led to a new kind of political economy. While this system had its roots in the 1980s, a more regularized and fully-formed system emerged during the 1990s. Thus, although Zhu certainly shaped the reform program, the actual outcomes reflected this new political economy system. A full description of this system is beyond the scope of this book, but a few key crucial features should be mentioned.

Zhu Rongji centralized resources but also permitted local governments significant retained resources and new areas of autonomy. Although local governments lost control of some fiscal revenues, they had greater clarity in their decision-making rights over remaining revenues. Local governments had a great deal of voice in determining the outcome of reform policies in their regions. Local governments restructured and privatized local SOEs and learned to use land as a resource in their development strategies. Thus a relatively stable division of labor between central and local, especially municipal, governments was created. While the central government made policy, local governments were expected to be entrepreneurial and drive economic development.

Entrepreneurial governments initially emerged in the 1980s in the wake of the explosion of TVEs. The most successful local governments had aggressively fostered their local firms. Now this system was moved into the city and formalized as part of the overall political system. Formal "target responsibility systems" established targets, or success indicators, for bureaucrats at all levels and gave them explicit weight in an evaluation function. These targets were predominantly economic, with GDP growth and increase in fiscal revenues the most important (Whiting 2001; Chan and Gao 2008). Good performance in meeting these targets brings cash awards and an increased chance of promotion. An extensive political economy literature has developed on the operation and impact of these incentives (among others, see Li and Zhou 2005; Shih, Adolph, and Liu 2012; and Landry and Lü 2014).

These formal incentives reinforced the normal desire of local officials to foster local economic development. They were also quite compatible with the deal-making incentives of local officials. Land development and support for businesses are excellent ways to enrich cronies and relatives as well as contributing to investment and, perhaps, growth. The alignment between local economic incentives and national institutional incentives created an extremely powerful pro-growth coalition. This needs to be stressed, because it is extremely unusual for such high-powered incentives to be introduced into government bureaucracies. Normally, high-powered incentives are avoided for publicly accountable officials because incentives for one or two main targets draw effort away from other objectives (Acemoglu, Kremer, and Mian 2008). Such an incentive system can make sense only when a single objective—such as economic development—is seen as an overwhelming priority. In China, this system may be regarded as a reasonable adaptation to the imperatives and opportunities of the miracle-growth phase. This system helped power the high investment rate and activist government policies that contributed to China's extreme high growth period.

China's bureaucratic system is a vast hierarchical pyramid, and during the 1990s, the norms and rules that govern promotion, including these incentives, were increasingly regularized. New norms established term limits and rotation of power at the top. This system gave local officials very strong incentives. All bureaucrats want to move up, but the number of slots for promotion is limited. Besides delivering growth, local officials had to get noticed, preferably by developing innovative approaches to reform. Interactions between the central government and local governments sometimes contributed to good economic policy-making (Heilmann 2008). Ambitious local officials would pioneer new approaches to common problems. If the pilot projects were promising, central officials might champion them and spread them nationwide. For example, Shandong Province piloted a new form of worker-owned corporation; Jiangsu developed special zones in collaboration with foreign investors. This relationship allowed for flexibility and innovation in the development and application of national policy.

5.7   Reform Slowdown After 2003

In 2002/2003, the new Hu Jintao–Wen Jiabao administration took over in China. It quickly became clear that the new administration had new policy priorities in addition to economic reform. These policies are discussed in subsequent chapters, but certainly included rebuilding social services, such as health insurance (chapters 6, 11, and 20); bolstering agriculture by cutting taxes and providing protection (chapter 12); developing robust industrial policies (chapter 15); and initiating steps to reverse increasing environmental degradation (chapter 21). These policies do not contradict economic reform and are potentially complementary to well-designed market-oriented reform. Moreover, economic reform remained high on the formal policy agenda. Nevertheless, it slowly became apparent that the political commitment to introducing new market-oriented reforms and implementing reforms already adopted had weakened dramatically.

This policy shift implied a step away from the overwhelming priority that economic growth and market reform had held over the previous 25 years. Policy-makers sought a broader definition of development (Hu Jintao's "scientific developmentalism") and showed a willingness to displace the unquestioned priority of GDP growth as a policy-making objective. This was in principle a momentous break, but it had a modest practical impact on the development trajectory in the short run. First, the strongly pro-growth institutional framework described in section 5.6 was still in place. Local governments had strong formal and informal incentives to pursue traditional policies of maximizing investment and GDP growth and to improve profits and budgetary revenues. This powerful and self-reinforcing system could not be expected to change quickly. Second, Zhu Rongji's reforms had succeeded, and economic growth had begun to accelerate. As economic growth accelerated and budgetary revenues climbed rapidly, policy-makers had resources to do more without imposing undue distortions on the economy.

These same factors inevitably implied a lower priority for further market-oriented reform. Unlike the case in the 1980s and 1990s, no immediate crisis required market-reforms to resolve. Even the state sector, which had been bleeding red ink during the 1990s, returned to profitability in the new century. With policy-makers' attention elsewhere, and reform seemingly having little urgency, progress slowed to a crawl. There was a general sense that China's accession to the World Trade Organization—agreed in November 1999 but phasing in gradually after 2001—would serve as a capstone locking in the substantial reforms already achieved. Chinese policy-makers were complacent about the progress already made and nervous about the impact of WTO, so policy-makers began to look for ways to blunt the WTO impact. The urgency of market-oriented reform evaporated.

In addition, it was clear that market reforms had intensified very real social problems that now cried out for solutions. China's social safety net—traditionally provided by state-owned enterprises and agricultural collectives—was in tatters. Whole new populations were emerging, such as rural-to-urban migrants and new small-scale businesses, that were not covered at all. Other social services, notably education and health, had been underfunded for years and demanded attention now that budgetary revenues were increasing. Wen Jiabao in particular seemed intent on addressing these problems.

It is thus not surprising that market-oriented reform received lower priority after 2003, but it is surprising how far the reform agenda was pushed to the background. According to the definition of market-oriented reform presented at the beginning of this chapter, there were no major market-oriented reforms during the Wen Jiabao administration. One apparent exception was the bank recapitalization carried out in 2005–2006, but this was the exception that proves the rule. This large-scale program was designed under Zhu Rongji but executed in the Wen Jiabao administration. The actions under the Wen administration were the culmination of an almost decade-long effort to clear a crippling burden of bad debt off the books of China's banks and to prepare the ground for a fundamental restructuring of the banking system (chapter 19). In some cases, reforms simply stalled out for unclear reasons. For example, the State Council published an ambitious "Nine Articles" on capital-market reform in January 2004 that called for rapid, market-driven expansion in the quantity and variety of equity and debt (bonds) instruments, but none of these changes were implemented. In 2005, Wen Jiabao touted the Tianjin Binhai district as a comprehensive reform zone, including financial liberalization, but the experiment went nowhere. Economic bureaucracies such as the National Development and Reform Commission became more powerful and adopted more conservative positions.

Subsequently, in 2008–2009, the impact of the global financial crisis elicited a vigorous response from the Chinese government (chapter 18). As in other major economies, the response involved a major short-run expansion of the state's role in the economy. The Chinese central bank pumped credit into the economy, which, given the need for rapid disbursement of funds, went predominantly to state-linked corporations. Corporate bailouts, justified by crisis conditions, tended to merge into industrial policy initiatives. Budget constraints of local governments were dramatically softened as banks were encouraged to lend to local-government funding vehicles set up to quickly ramp up new infrastructure investment programs.

The absence of major reform initiatives does not imply that marketization stopped in its tracks. In many arenas, marketization had its own momentum. For example, figure 5.3 shows that the decline in the absolute number of state workers stopped in 2005–2006. Nonetheless, the relative share of state workers continued to decline because with robust growth, the number of workers in all ownership formers grew.

In industry, state employment declined from 37% of employment in 2003 to just 19% in 2010 (excluding very small firms). Money flowed into the stock market, which boomed until 2007. In many areas markets grew and deepened, but without the impetus of a firm push from government policy. Without clear guidance from government policy, unresolved issues built up. The reform slowdown after 2003 is understandable but nonetheless surprising. China's market-oriented reforms brought stunning economic growth, dramatically improved productivity and performance, and extraordinary increases in living standards. How could China's leadership have valued so lightly something so overwhelmingly beneficial? This question deserves further scrutiny.

5.8   Renewed Reform Initiative After 2013

The new Xi Jinping–Li Keqiang administration that came to power in 2012/2013 clearly acknowledged the stagnation of market-oriented reform during the previous administration. Premier Li Keqiang characterized the previous decade when he declared, "Reform is like sailing a boat against the current; if you don't move forward, you will be pushed backwards" (Xinhua 2012). In November 2013, the new administration convened the Third Plenum of the 18th Party Congress that had brought it to power. They seized on the obvious opportunity to roll out a renewed program of economic reforms at a Third Plenum, echoing those of 1978, 1984, and 1993. The "Resolution" of the 2013 Third Plenum (CCP 2013) was both a call for a re-commitment to the principles of market reform and a remarkably broad and wide-ranging to-do list of issues to tackle. In the following months, a special top-level Leadership Small Group was established to oversee implementation, and it assigned literally hundreds of reform initiatives to lead agencies in different sectors.

Ambitious as it was, the "Resolution" of 2013 did not have the high level of structure and interconnectedness that one can observe in its most immediate precursor, the reform document of 1993. The 2013 document reads like a list of problem areas. All deserve attention, but it is somewhat difficult to discern priorities and sequencing. Work went forward in almost all areas in 2014, but 2015 was a difficult year. In the face of worries about slowing growth and potential instability, many reforms stalled out. Extreme volatility in the stock market undercut promising reforms there (chapter 19). A bold program of fiscal reform laid out in 2014 was modified and postponed in 2015 (chapter 20). The household registration (*hukou*) system was loosened but not fundamentally changed or abolished (chapter 6). At the end of 2015, policy-makers introduced a new initiative "supply-side structural reform" that drew some of the attention away from the Third Plenum reform agenda. The most prominent item of "supply-side structural reform" was a government-led effort to reduce excess capacity in heavy industries, including steel and coal, which had been caught out by the structural slowdown in the economy. It is easy to see the rationale for this policy, which is to facilitate and accelerate the process of structural change. However, it does not fit the definition of market-oriented reform used here, because it relies on direct government action to achieve its goals, rather than market forces. The fate of the market-oriented reforms of the Third Plenum is still undetermined.

The Xi Jinping administration has advanced an extremely broad agenda, centered on the idea of the "China dream." Xi's emphasis on national rejuvenation leaves unresolved the relation between national power and prosperity, on the one hand, and market-oriented reform and opening, on the other. Moreover, Xi seems willing to countenance relatively large changes in the institutional framework described in section 5.6. With so many elements apparently in flux, it is more than usually difficult to divine the future of market-oriented reform. The Nineteenth Communist Party Congress in the fall of 2017 awarded Xi Jinping a second term as Party Secretary, while most other top leaders retired. After that Congress, the newly constituted leadership group forms a new government and will likely give high priority to determining the next step of "reform and opening." In the fall of 2018, another Third Plenum will convene, giving policy-makers an opportunity to flesh out their vision and write a new chapter in China's long-running reform process.

5.9   Market Transition: Conclusion

Chinese policy-makers used the first phase of accelerated transition effectively to build support for further reforms. During the 1980s "reform without losers," Chinese policy-makers deferred difficult and costly measures as long as possible but enabled the economy to reap the benefits of new kinds of producers and organizations as early as possible. This is a good strategy, but logically it cannot continue indefinitely. In the second phase of accelerated transition, the strategy based on a level playing field inevitably signaled the end of the "reform without losers" approach. By driving forward equal competition—particularly under conditions of relative macroeconomic austerity—policy-makers guaranteed that there would be a group of "losers." The social problems created were not seriously addressed until years later.

China's market transition is still a work in progress and continues to face multiple challenges. These challenges have changed in content over the years as China has developed a market economy, but they have not necessarily become less serious. In the background is the fact that the unified system of governance seems increasingly in conflict with the multiple independent centers of authority that are the norm in a modern mixed-market economy. The development of independent regulatory institutions, for example, has lagged far behind the need. As China's market economy has become established and much more sophisticated, this shortcoming seems increasingly problematic. China's reformers have made numerous efforts to strengthen checks and oversight within the system, but they all ultimately rely on a kind of internal accountability within the administrative system.

The Chinese experience has many valuable lessons. Those lessons come from a broad view of China's transition, however, and not from specific policies that can be identified and transplanted to other economic environments. After all, the Chinese policy-making process has been extremely complex and has produced dramatically different outcomes in different periods of "gradualist" transition. There is no single "Chinese model" of economic transition. The caution and gradualism captured in the phrase "crossing the river by groping for stepping-stones" reflect an approach to the problem of change rather than a strategy of change. The first stages of accelerated reforms were successful precisely because they were effectively adapted to the specific challenges and opportunities provided by China's situation at that time. Second-stage reforms were then dramatically recast and adapted to a completely different set of challenges and opportunities. As McMillan (2004) pointed out, the lesson is not that a particular policy prescription is the right one, but rather that careful policy-making, firmly grounded in local conditions, has a much better chance of success than prepackaged policy prescriptions. Moreover, policies that give weight to development of social and economic capabilities will be more successful than policies that single-mindedly emphasize institutional change. As Deng Xiaoping (1992) said in the midst of China's transition process, "Development is the only hard truth."

Bibliography

Suggestions for Further Reading

Wu (2014) has the best comprehensive coverage of China's transition. Qian (2017) combines a theoretician's insight with an intimate knowledge of the Chinese institutional environment to create an account that is absorbing and thought provoking. Wu Jinglian (2013) collects some of this important adviser and analyst's most important policy essays written from the 1980s to the twenty-first century, with introductory essays that provide context. Lau, Qian, and Roland (2000) introduced the analytic concept of "reform without losers" that serves as the basis for the two periods of reform used in this text.

References

Acemoglu, Daren, Michael Kremer, and Atif Mian (2008). "Incentives in Markets, Firms and Governments." *Journal of Law, Economics and Organizations* 24 (2): 273–306.

Byrd, William (1991). *The Market Mechanism and Economic Reforms in China.* Armonk, NY: M. E. Sharpe.

CCP (Chinese Communist Party) (2013). "Decision of the Central Committee of the Communist Party of China on Some Major Issues Concerning Comprehensively Deepening the Reform." November 12. Accessed at http://www.china.org.cn/china/third_plenary_session/2014-01/16/content_31212602.htm.

Chan, Hon S., and Jie Gao (2008). "Performance Measurement in Chinese Local Governments" (with translated documents). *Chinese Law and Government* 41 (2–3): 4–111.

Deng, Xiaoping (1992). *Nanxun Jianghua* [Talks on the southern journey]. Sohu Materials. Accessed at http://business.sohu.com/20120113/n332115956.shtml.

Heilmann, Sebastian (2008). "Policy Experimentation in China's Economic Rise." *Studies in Comparative International Development* 43 (8): 1–26.

Labor Yearbook (various years). National Bureau of Statistics, Department of Population, Social, Science, and Technology Statistics, and Ministry of Labor and Social Security, Department of Planning and Finance, eds. *Zhongguo Laodong Tongji Nianjian* [Yearbook of labor statistics of China]. Beijing: Zhongguo Laodong.

Landry, Pierre, and Xiaobuo Lü (2014). "Show Me the Money: Interjurisdiction Political Competition and Fiscal Extraction in China." *American Political Science Review* 108 (3): 706–722.

Lau, Lawrence, Yingyi Qian, and Gérard Roland (2000). "Reform Without Losers: An Interpretation of China's Dual-Track Approach to Transition." *Journal of Political Economy* 108 (1): 120–143.

Li Hongbin and Li-An Zhou (2005). "Political Turnover and Economic Performance: The Incentive Role of Personnel Control in China." *Journal of Public Economics* 89 (9–10): 1743–1762.

McMillan, John (2004). "Avoid Hubris, and Other Lessons for Reformers." *Finance & Development*, September 2004, 34–37.

Naughton, Barry (1995). *Growing Out of the Plan: Chinese Economic Reform, 1978–1993.* New York: Cambridge University Press.

Naughton, Barry (2008). "A Political Economy of China's Economic Transition." In Loren Brandt and Thomas Rawski, eds., *China's Great Economic Transformation*, 91–135. New York: Cambridge University Press.

Qian, Yingyi (2017). *How Reform Worked in China: The Transition from Plan to Market.* Cambridge, MA: MIT Press.

Qian, Yingyi, and Jinglian Wu (2003). "China's Transition to a Market Economy: How Far Across the River?" In Nicholas C. Hope, Dennis Tao Yang, and Mu Yang Li, eds., *How Far Across the River?*, 31–64. Stanford, CA: Stanford University Press.

SASAC (Annual). State Asset Supervision and Administration Commission. *Zhongguo Guoyou Zichan Jiandu Guanli Nianjian* [China state-owned assets supervision and management yearbook]. Beijing: Zhongguo Jingji.

Shih, Victor, Christopher Adolph, and Mingxing Liu (2012). "Getting Ahead in the Communist Party: Explaining the Advancement of Central Committee Members in China." *American Political Science Review* 106 (1): 166–187.

SYC (Annual). *Zhongguo Tongji Nianjian* [Statistical yearbook of China]. Beijing: Zhongguo Tongji.

Whiting, Susan H. (2001). *Power and Wealth in Rural China: The Political Economy of Institutional Change.* New York: Cambridge University Press.

Wu, Jinglian (2013). *Wu Jinglian: Voice of Reform in China.* Cambridge, MA: MIT Press.

Wu, Jinglian (2014). *Understanding and Interpreting Chinese Economic Reform.* 2nd ed. Singapore: Gale Asia.

Xinhua News Agency (2012). "Reform Is Like Sailing a Boat Against the Current; If You Don't Move Forward, You Will Be Pushed Backwards." *Xinhua*, November 23. Accessed at http://whb.news365.com.cn/yw/201211/t20121123_796468.html.

6 The Urban-Rural Divide and Chinese-style Urbanization

The difference between urban and rural society is especially pronounced in China. While some urban-rural gap is inevitable in a developing economy, the urban-rural gap in China is unusually large. Extensive administrative barriers were set in place during the 1950s as part of the command economy. For 60 years, urban and rural areas have had different governance structures and different systems of property rights. Most important, because of the systemic differences, China has what amounts to two different forms of citizenship, one rural and one urban. Rural dwellers have fewer privileges than urban dwellers and rarely receive the entitlements that accompany urban citizenship. In China, city and countryside often seem like two different worlds, running on different technologies, organized in different ways, and having a different standard of living. These differences have been maintained for decades by strict controls on mobility. From the 1960s into the 1990s, it was extremely difficult for rural people to move to the city. During the 1990s, the system was relaxed but not abolished, and mass rural-to-urban migration began. Migration has since reshaped Chinese society, driving urbanization, social change, and economic growth, but the institutional system has never caught up. Reforms of the institutional regime have begun, and the invisible walls separating urban and rural society have begun to break down. China has become a majority urban society. Nevertheless, the basic institutional features that separate urban and rural are still intact.

This system of separate rural and urban institutional structures has important consequences. It leads to an unusually large urban-rural income gap that is the largest cause of inequality in Chinese society. It discourages rural migrants from putting down roots in the city and bringing their families with them. It distorts the pattern of urbanization, which is an essential part of development and growth. It obstructs the development of efficient local-government budgets and social services, as well as the development of national social security programs. For all these reasons, reforms of the *hukou* system and the twin systems of urban and rural land management have been part of the economic reform agenda for decades, yet the system has remained stubbornly resistant to fundamental change.

One of the peculiar aspects of the Chinese system is the way in which institutions that govern land and those that govern people are intertwined. Urbanization is fundamentally the redistribution of people on the land, so both institutional systems are immediately relevant. Moreover, they interact in complicated ways and both are different in China from related systems in other countries. To get to the bottom of these processes, this chapter first delves into the origin and nature of the separate organizational forms of citizenship and the property rights regimes that characterize the rural and urban economies. These help explain the depth of the divide between urban and rural society. Barriers to mobility and different kinds of citizenship complete the institutional divide. Section 6.2 discusses the process of urbanization. Urbanization is an indispensable part of economic development, but China's urbanization has swung from highly controlled during the Cultural Revolution to encouraged and proceeding robustly today. Migration is an important part of that story, and section 6.3 discusses the reemergence of large-scale migration in the 1990s and its rapid increase since. The chapter discusses the economic consequences of the urban-rural divide in section 6.4, stressing the widening of the already large urban-rural income gap through 2009 and showing that it has begun to shrink in the years since. After 2003, Chinese policy-makers made a sustained effort to reduce the degree of urban bias and move to a single integrated system of national citizenship. Important steps have been taken and are discussed in section 6.6. Despite these efforts, the urban-rural gap remains large in China, and an integrated institutional framework has not yet been created. Moreover, new urban-rural inequalities are being created in domains that are much more important in today's economy than in the past, such as education and housing.

6.1   A Dualistic System: The Division Between Urban and Rural

6.1.1   Origin and Evolution of the Urban-Rural Divide

Today's large urban-rural gap has its roots in the socialist period. Chapter 4 noted that during the 1950s, every Chinese citizen was connected through his or her workplace to the socialist state. Virtually every business and productive enterprise was converted to public ownership and subjected to government control. This massive change was implemented in systematically different ways in urban and rural areas. Urban residents were organized by their place of employment, that is, by their "work unit," or *danwei*. Almost all urban work units were nationalized—converted to state ownership—and state ownership became predominant in urban areas, with two consequences. First, urban work units were knit into a formal hierarchy, directly subject to planning, command, and control; the work unit was part of a "top-down" system. Second, the work unit was put in charge of a comprehensive system of social benefits and welfare entitlements, which was gradually built up and extended more or less uniformly to urban workers. Urban residents became a relatively privileged group in Chinese society, and the work unit became the basic building block of urban society.

Rural institutions were altogether different. Private property in land was eliminated in 1955, and the land in every village was pooled and became the property of the village as a whole, the "collective." Collective ownership became the predominant form of ownership. Village residents automatically became members of the new agricultural collectives, and access to land and village resources was therefore equalized within the collective. Rural residents were organized into a "bottom-up" system. Collectives were encouraged to support social services out of their own local resources, but farmers had no entitlements in the eyes of the national government. There was no mechanism to redistribute resources across collectives, and there were no standards or entitlements that applied to all rural residents.[1] The agricultural collective's primary function was to produce and sell farm goods, and it could provide social services and public goods only if it generated a large-enough surplus from the sale of agricultural produce. As a result, the average level of benefits and public goods provided was much lower than in the city. Rural residents both were poorer than urban residents and had a cheaper and less comprehensive set of social institutions to serve them.

The different urban and rural administrative systems grew up in the context of the socialist "Big Push" strategy. The two systems were used to carry out two drastically different functions: the rural system was used to extract low-cost food and fibers from the farmers, while the urban system was used to build industry. Cheap grain was provided to urban workers—the vanguard class of socialism—through their work unit, which was enabled to keep wages low and stay profitable. Ration coupons were introduced in 1955 as a short-run expedient but then stayed in place for over 30 years. The whole dualistic system worked as an implicit tax on farmers, who had lower incomes because they were compelled to sell grain to the government at artificially low prices. The system was relaxed after 1978 but survived until after the turn of the twenty-first century.

To keep the system functioning, farmers had to be tied to the land. It was impossible to make money by farming—especially growing grain—and during the 1950s, farmers began to migrate to the cities to take up new factory jobs. However, everything changed after the Great Leap Forward. During the GLF, as grain harvests declined, the government at first kept supplying urban dwellers with at least some of

---

1. One partial exception was that in most years, the national government would "loan" grain to poor collectives whose members did not have enough to eat. Most of these loans were never repaid, so this was a kind of subsistence guarantee.

their grain ration. As the economy tipped into crisis, it became impossible to support so many city dwellers with meal tickets. Six million urban residents, mostly recently arrived from the countryside, were cajoled into returning to their native villages in 1961–1962, and the household registration system became a tool for restricting rural-to-urban migration. All household registrations were strictly divided into urban (or "nonagricultural") *hukou* that entitled holders to grain rations and "agricultural" *hukou* that did not. It became virtually impossible for a rural household to get an urban *hukou* after the early 1960s. Without an urban residence permit, a farmer could not go to work in the city, and even short trips to the city required him to bring his own grain with him. Rural-to-urban migration dwindled practically to zero. The basic system of "internal passports" was taken over from the Soviet Union, but the extreme rigidity of the system in China grew out of the trauma of the GLF (Census Office 2014, 256–257; Cheng and Selden 1994).

Only much later, after successful rural reforms in the early 1980s, did the Chinese government begin to soften this rigid institutional dualism. Successful rural reforms eased concern over basic food supplies and increased the availability of grain in free markets. Grain rationing was gradually phased out, and an urban residence permit was no longer required to eat in the cities. The government began to ease restrictions on migration to the cities, at first for smaller cities and for temporary migrants. Broad economic changes have increased opportunities for rural workers in the city and, since the 1990s, have resulted in huge migration flows. However, the urban residence permit still exists, and possession of an urban *hukou* still marks a fundamental divide in Chinese society. It has become much easier to live and work in a city without a *hukou*, but it has not become that much easier to obtain an urban *hukou* registration. Without an urban residence permit, a rural migrant still has only limited access to the benefits of urban citizenship, including health care, social security, and education for accompanying children.

6.1.2   The Urban Economic System

6.1.2.1   The Urban *Danwei*

Through the mid-1990s, urban life in China was defined by the privileges associated with an urban residence permit (*hukou*) and by membership in a work unit (*danwei*). The urban residence permit was a form of entitlement that guaranteed the holder membership in a *danwei* and thus a job. When a city dweller graduated from middle school—or university, if smart and lucky—he or she was assigned employment as a matter of course. Thereafter, the work unit became responsible for providing services and benefits to the urban resident. During the peak period of the urban *danwei*, from the mid-1960s until well into the 1990s, urban residence conveyed the following benefits:

- Job security
- Guaranteed low-price access to food grains, as well as other scarce commodities
- Health care (about 40% of all general hospital beds were in the state-owned industrial system)
- A pension and other benefits, including health care, upon retirement
- Primary- and middle-school education for the children (70% of state enterprises ran schools of some kind)
- Low-cost housing, supplied by the work unit

These extensive subsidies added significantly to the privilege of urban residence: many services were provided free, and staple foods were priced well below cost. Of course, incomes at this time were low, and services and housing were provided in limited amounts and were generally of low quality. A distinctive feature of the Chinese system was permanent employment. After the restrictions on migration were put in place, job mobility between urban work units disappeared as well. In this sense, the Chinese work unit was quite different from the Soviet model from which it otherwise derived (chapter 9). Once a worker entered a *danwei*, he or she expected to remain a member of that *danwei* for life (Lü and Perry 1997).

The system reached its maximum size in 1993, when 109 million workers were in the state-run *danwei* system: 76 million in SOEs that produced goods and services for a profit; 23 million in nonprofit public service units such as hospitals and universities; and 10 million in the government bureaucracies and party and mass organizations. Despite their different primary functions, these work units had many features in common. First, each was state owned and integrated into a national administrative hierarchy, with managers appointed by the Communist Party. Furthermore, the benefits each work unit provided to its workers were explicitly defined as entitlements, specified by statute or regulation. The benefits were thus part of an implicit urban social compact that the government has consistently acknowledged and tried to uphold. Finally, each unit had responsibility for social and cultural activities and even for political coordination. The work unit was the fundamental building block, or cell, of urban society. Many work units even had the physical form of a cell, with a perimeter brick wall enclosing a nucleus of productive activity. The *danwei* was a microcosm of urban society, into which individuals were born, and in which they lived, worked, and died.

6.1.2.2 Urban Property Rights

All urban land was nationalized, and all urban property was incorporated into the national, hierarchical system of state ownership. Municipal governments were treated as divisions of the national government, and municipal receipts and expenditures were incorporated each year into the integrated national budget. That meant that, in effect, the government assumed responsibility for water, sewage, transportation, police protection, and schools—the entire panoply of ordinary services. As Judith Banister (1987, 328) described the classic system: "Urban areas are essentially owned and administered by the state."

State-owned enterprises (SOEs) were usually controlled by local and municipal governments. It was obviously impossible for the national government to exercise effective oversight of hundreds of thousands of often small-scale enterprises. The authority to manage state firms was delegated to local governments through successive rounds of decentralization, especially in the early 1970s, creating de facto property rights for local governments. With day-to-day control over decision-making, local government leaders had significant authority over both cash flow and decisions on use of land and other assets. However, these rights were always seen as delegated to local governments by the national government, and local officials were formally agents of the central government and the Communist Party, part of a chain of authority leading to the highest political officials in Beijing. As a result, economic reforms after the 1980s consisted of repeated, careful renegotiations of the lines of authority within the state-run hierarchy.

Urban land markets developed in this hierarchical context. All urban land is owned by the state, at least in theory, even today. But a system has evolved in which rights to use land for up to 50 years are bought and sold. A market for transferable urban leaseholds emerged during the 1990s. Under this system, the use rights of existing occupants are usually, but not always, recognized—there are—"squatter's rights"— and with the permission of local government they can be bought and sold. Urban land has become an important source of wealth, both for state-run enterprises and for the individuals who control the land conversion process. Land transactions are taxed, but most of the value is captured by the occupying enterprise, the local government, or private parties. China's housing boom is built on this property rights system: apartment owners do not "own" the land on which their building sits, enjoying instead a 50-year lease on the land rights.

6.1.3   The Rural Economic System

6.1.3.1   Rural Collectives

No attempt was ever made to integrate rural areas into the hierarchical system of national state ownership that prevailed in the cities. In the countryside, villages were organized into collectives, but the agricultural collectives were never part of the formal government hierarchy. Even today, villages, which have their own village councils and elect village leaders, are not formally part of the government hierarchy. Rather, they are theoretically autonomous organizations. (In practice, important decisions must be approved by government and party officials at the township and county levels.) Thus, even during the period of agricultural collectives, from 1955 through about 1982, most rural residents were organized into local bodies with a primarily economic function. The organization was all-encompassing and subject to political control, but it was still relatively looser than organization in the city. The rural resident had membership in a local collective rather than—like the urban resident—a compact with the state. This organization is described further in chapter 11. Rural collectives could decide to tax themselves and provide services, but since few collectives had the financial resources to subsidize a large range of goods and services, rural residents were much more likely to pay full cost for the public services they received.

6.1.3.2   Rural Property Rights

Just as rural collectives were never incorporated into the national administrative hierarchy, so, in similar fashion, rural property, including land, was never integrated into the system of national state ownership. The agricultural collective in principle owned the land within its boundaries, as well as nonagricultural rural enterprises. Thus ownership rights in the countryside were held at the local level and were never as centralized—as concentrated in the hands of bureaucrats—as was the case with urban ownership systems. Rural households always had access to the land, but households had direct ownership only of their own houses, plus guaranteed free access to the land the house and outbuildings were built on.

During the rural reforms of 1978–1984, collective farming ended in almost all of China, and family farms returned as the dominant agricultural form. Each collective divided the land among its individual household members according to formulas negotiated within the collectives. Historical ownership (before collectives) was ignored in favor of formulas based on the number of workers and the number of mouths to feed in a household. By all accounts, this process went smoothly, and it has been called "the most egalitarian land reform in history" (Walder 2000). But even after the land was divided, the land system did not change over to a simple private property system. Although the land is *worked* by individual households, the formal ownership still remains with the "collective." Farmers sign contracts with the collective giving them land-use rights for periods that have gradually been lengthened and now often extend up to 50 years. Even today peasants do not own the land free and clear (but see section 6.5.3). This system has a number of unusual side effects:

• Collectives in many areas of China can and do redistribute land periodically. According to one large-scale study, farmland had been redistributed at least once in 66% of villages and three or more times in 25% of them (Rozelle and Li 1998). Usually, redistribution is carried out in order to accommodate natural population growth.

• There is very little landlessness. Because almost all peasants have access to some land, there is little of the crushing poverty caused by absolute landlessness found in many developing economies. Indeed, a rough guarantee of access to land is the most important form of social insurance in the countryside.

• The lack of completely secure land tenure affects farmers' incentives. The rewards for investment in the land's long-term productivity are diluted (since there is a possibility that land may be redistributed). Land cannot be used as collateral for borrowing, and land use-right markets have been slow to develop. Although private households have (agricultural) use-rights and cash-flow rights, they do not have the right to alienate (sell) their property. Moreover, there is an additional cost to permanent out-migration. Families that move away permanently may have to surrender their land to the collective, which would distribute it to a more "needy," permanently resident family. In other words, a de facto policy of "use it or lose it" prevails in many villages. To avoid this outcome, a rural family has a strong incentive to leave some family members on the land while sending others out for temporary jobs outside agriculture. This approach to migration is a familiar risk-minimizing family strategy in many countries, but the land system in China causes families to cling to it long after they would otherwise have been ready to move permanently into urban jobs.

From the standpoint of the village (or "collective"), land is an important resource that has only become more valuable as the economy has grown and cities have sprawled beyond their original boundaries. However, for the village to monetize the value of its land, it must persuade the municipal government to reclassify the land as "nonagricultural." Therefore, the village head or township officials, representing the collective, must negotiate with the city government. In this negotiation, the city government has almost all the bargaining power. It is in a monopoly position and can easily play different villages off against each other. The outcome is that the city purchases the land from the collective—which has to settle for a lower price—and then reclassifies it and develops it or sells to a developer. Ordinary farmers are not formally part of the negotiation process at all, but when it is over, the collective must move farmers off the land and compensate them appropriately. Honest and effective local leaders will represent the interests of all the collective members in these commercial transactions, but selfish, disinterested, or corrupt officials fail to share the benefits of land transactions with local citizens. Rural collectives and individual farmers often disagree over the appropriate level and form of compensation for land transfers. When the land is sold or leased out from under them, rural people react with anger. The largest cause of social conflict in China today is almost certainly disputes over land deals (Yu 2005). The rural land property system is an issue of central importance in China today, both for reasons of fairness and because it distorts urbanization and migration patterns.

6.2   Urbanization

Urbanization is a vital part of the development process. As development occurs, workers move out of agriculture and into modern industrial and service jobs that are much more productive. Moreover, the clustering of these jobs in cities unleashes additional productivity. "Agglomeration economies" arise from the lower costs of exchanging goods and ideas when people locate near one another. China today is in the midst of rapid urbanization, and China's population was 57% urban at the end of 2016. For millennia, China was a predominantly rural civilization, tied to the soil by work, poverty, and tradition. That is history now, and China's present and future are unmistakably urban. China's level of urbanization today is within the normal range for a developing country, but China arrived at the current level through a trajectory that is unique and even bizarre. In most developing countries, the pace of urbanization is determined by the decisions of millions of separate individuals, who assess their life chances and decide to leave the countryside and go to the city. Moreover, urbanization is closely linked to industrialization, which provides the new urban jobs. But China's past process of urbanization was determined primarily by government policies that, until recently, tightly constrained the scope for individual choice. These policies also resulted in a de-coupling of urbanization and industrialization through the 1970s.

6.2.1   Urbanization: Historical Trends

The data that describe the process of urbanization in China are shown in figure 6.1. The lower series shows the percentages of Chinese citizens classified as "non-agricultural," that is, those with urban residence permits (*hukou*), discussed earlier in this chapter. This definition is unique to China. The upper series shows the proportion of the Chinese population resident in urban settlements of a minimum size. These numbers are conceptually consistent with definitions of urbanization in other countries and can be used to make comparisons. Together, the series reveal China's bizarre history of urbanization. Both series show that China deurbanized between the end of the 1950s and 1978. This remarkable 20-year period of de-urbanization had two phases. First, after 1960, China was forced to wind down the unsustainable surge of urbanization during the Great Leap Forward. Millions were forced to leave the cities, and millions more left of their own volition in search of food; the urban population dropped by 14 million by 1963. Even more remarkable is what happened after the economy stabilized in 1964. The urban share of population declined again by more than a percentage point and then stabilized through 1978. Over those 14 years, official GDP growth clocked in at 7% per year, industrial employment grew, and the size of the urban economy tripled, but the urban share of the population shrank. How did this unparalleled de-urbanization take place?

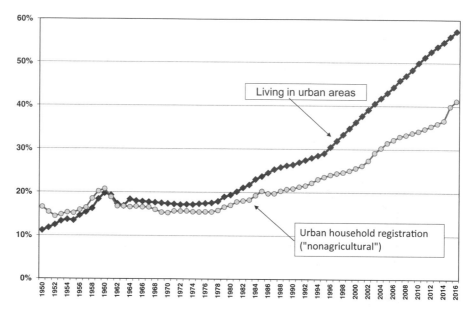

Figure 6.1
Urban share of population.
Sources: NBS Department of Comprehensive Statistics (1999, 1) for series by residence permit; updated from *SAC* (various years); and *Population Statistics Yearbook* (2005, 266). *SYC* for standard urbanization series. New procedure for calculating urban household registration population adopted in 2015.

Throughout the 1964–1978 period, China maintained draconian restrictions on population movement. Access to urban residence permits was jealously guarded, and almost no farmers were allowed to move to the city. Instead, there was even forced out-migration from urban areas. From the mid-1960s to the mid-1970s, millions of urban dwellers were sent out to the countryside. The largest group, around 17 million, consisted of young middle-school graduates who were "sent down" to the countryside in the wake of the Cultural Revolution. "Sent-down youth" remained in the countryside for periods ranging from two years to a lifetime and were told to learn from (and teach) the poor and middle peasants. Workers were also mobilized to leave big cities to build factories in western China. Between 1955 and 1976, China's largest city, Shanghai, experienced a net out-migration of 1.86 million people, and its total population did not grow at all. That such unusual population dynamics could occur is a testament to the extreme degree of political control and mobilization in Maoist China. As Ma Hong said, "Every time there was a political movement, one of the after-effects was that another big batch of urban people were sent to the country-side" (Zhang Shanyu 2003, 362, 367, 376). Given that the rest of the world was steadily urbanizing, China became more and more unusual through the late 1970s. China's urbanization rate declined from 18.4% in 1964 to 17.9% in 1978, while developing countries as a whole increased from 26% to 31% in the same period (WDI).

China's urbanization lagged less than 8 percentage points behind in 1964 but more than 13 percentage points in 1978.

It was not until 1978 that China began to urbanize rapidly, but since then cities have grown rapidly for more than 30 years. China's urbanization rate—shown as the top line in figure 6.1—surpassed the global average after 2012. The broad social relaxation that accompanied the beginnings of reform in 1978 ended the most extreme forms of population control. Sent-down youth and mobilized workers began to return to their native cities, and urban population growth surged above 5% per year in the nine years from 1978 through 1987. At first, government officials were cautious, trying to restrict growth to the smaller cities while maintaining tight restrictions on migration to the largest cities. After the mid-1990s, planners grudgingly accepted the need for the largest cities to grow as well, but they still monitored the growth of megacities closely. Urban population growth again surged above 5% per year from 1996 to 2000. More recently, in the face of dramatically different demographic conditions (chapter 8), annual urban population growth has slowed to slightly below 3% since 2010.

Figure 6.1 shows that total urban residents have increased much more rapidly than urban residence permit holders. As of the end of 2016, there were 793 million urban residents, only 570 million of whom had an urban *hukou*. Therefore, 223 million people, almost one-third of China's urban population, are there without an urban residence permit. Although it is much easier to live in the city without a residence permit than it used to be, it is still extremely difficult to get an urban residence permit in China, particularly in a large city.

6.2.2   Patterns of Urbanization

Growth in the urban population can come from three sources, and all have been important in China over the past 40 years. Migration to cities has resumed; cities have sprawled into the countryside; and natural growth of the urban population has continued until very recently. Chen and Song (2014) analyzed the rapid urbanization between 2000 and 2010 and concluded that migration from rural areas accounted for 40.6% of urban population growth; reclassification of population that lives in formerly rural and suburban land (sprawl) accounted for almost exactly 40% of urban growth; and natural growth of the urban population was almost 20% of urban growth.

Physical spread of urban areas, like many other features of the urbanization process, takes on a distinctive form in China. When China was trying to limit urbanization, the boundaries of Chinese cities were sharply defined. One could walk out from the densely packed urban areas and suddenly cross into farmland. As policy changed, the number of places designated urban soared from 2,860 to 21,000, and the amount of urban land approved for development also jumped, as individual cities sprawled into the countryside (Zhang Shanyu 2003, 321; Census Office 2014, 269).

All Chinese cities are now surrounded by suburban belts comprising a mix of high-rise and low-rise housing, industrial and commercial spaces, and farmland. Many cities have engulfed former farming villages, creating islands of rural property rights land completely surrounded by the city. These "urban villages" (discussed later) are built on the land that farmers occupy for their family's housing. They exist largely because municipal governments prefer to requisition only farmland for development, avoiding the expense of resettling displaced villagers, who often prefer to stay in their traditional homes in any case. Market forces powerfully drive this aspect of urbanization.

Perhaps the most remarkable urban transformation has occurred in the Pearl River delta in Guangdong Province. On the eastern side of the Pearl River, a 120-kilometer stretch of land changed from entirely rural to predominantly urban within 25 years. Between Hong Kong and the provincial capital of Guangzhou, two entirely new cities have grown up—Shenzhen and Dongguan—creating a chain of four large cities, each of which has a population over 6 million. The areas between these cities still have many farms but are never entirely rural; instead, a pattern of "urbanized countryside" has emerged. As China's transportation network improves, new possibilities are opening up for creating urban clusters in which medium-sized urban centers are linked by high-speed connections.

Many policies in China restrict the development of the largest cities, such as Shanghai and Beijing. It is much harder to get permanent residence in those cities, and land-use and other policies constrain their physical expansion, despite substantial evidence that very large cities play a special efficiency-enhancing role in market economies. The extreme concentration of certain types of services, especially financial services, in New York, London, and Tokyo is associated with their extraordinary size and leads to extremely high productivity. Au and Henderson (2006) found that most Chinese cities are too small, and that the costs of forgone GDP are significant. Relative to its enormous population, China has fewer of the world's biggest cities than expected. National policies overall tend to limit growth of the biggest cities. The air-pollution crisis in Beijing has led to a determination to keep that city's population capped at 23 million for 2020. An ambitious plan to disperse population through the broader Beijing-Tianjin-Hebei region is being promoted, including reducing the population of the central districts by 15% and creating new secondary centers linked by high-speed transit. In 2017, an ambitious plan was announced to relieve population pressure on Beijing by creating the Xiongan New District, an entirely new city for more than 2 million residents only 100 km. southwest of Beijing. However, urban planning schemes that try to go against market forces have a poor record in many cities outside China, so caution is in order. The Yangtze River delta region—already a network of medium-sized cities around Shanghai—may develop into a new kind of networked urbanized countryside without such massive intervention by national planners.

6.3   Rural-to-Urban Migration

Rural-to-urban migration grew rapidly in China after the 1990s and turned into a flood during the first decade of the twenty-first century. Between 2005 and 2010, each year more than 10 million people crossed provincial boundaries to take up a new life in the city. This has been the largest peaceful mass movement of people in history. Since 2010, migration has leveled off and begun to decline. Migration surged when the government relaxed the restrictions that tied farmers to their land. Although the administrative system has been substantially relaxed, it still exists, and migrants face discrimination and limitations on their ability to integrate into urban society. Most migrants remain on the fringes of urban society, sleeping in substandard housing, typically on the outskirts of the city, working long hours, and planning a return to the countryside. Indeed, in many respects, Chinese rural migrants in the city resemble undocumented Mexican migrants working in U.S. cities. By migrating, they substantially increase their income-generating potential and begin to work their way upward. Moreover, they contribute both to the economy in which they are working and to that of their home villages, largely by remitting funds home. However, they lack effective channels to integrate into urban society, including access to the education, housing, and social services that go with full urban citizenship.

6.3.1   Overview of Migration

How large is migration in China today? The sudden emergence and growth of large-scale migration in China produced initial confusion about the scale of the phenomenon. Chinese migrants had become unfamiliar visitors in China's cities during the long period of population immobility. Their reappearance evoked complex and sometimes negative reactions from city dwellers. The widely used Chinese term "floating population" (*liudong renkou*) only gradually took on a precise definition. Now, the national population censuses count individuals who live in a place away from their household registration and have been there for more than six months. These are considered "floating population" (unless they are crosstown migrants with residence and registration in the same city). Using this definition, figure 6.2 shows the remarkable growth of this population to a peak of 253 million in 2014. In 1982, less than 1% of China's population was "floating"; by 2014, it was 18.5%. The floating population declined slightly in 2015 and 2016, for the first time since records have been kept. The decline reflects the slowdown in rural-to-urban migration that has been evident since 2010, but it may also reflect an increase in the number of migrants permanently changing their registration to the urban areas in which they live.

We can get a sense of the flow of migration that created this stock of migrants by looking at a consistent series of net interprovincial migrants compiled by Kam Wing Chan, the top U.S. expert on urbanization and migration in China. Chan (2012)

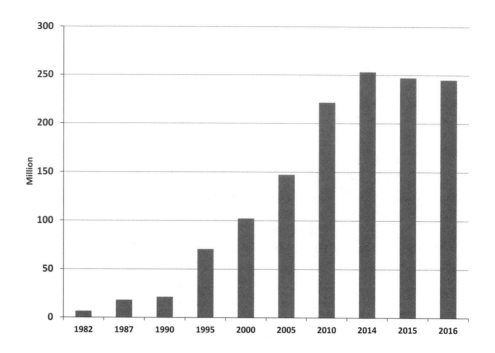

Figure 6.2
"Floating population" (resident more than six months in a place away from household registration).
Sources: Census Office (2014, 231); NBS (2017).

tracked a total of 136 million of these long-distance migrants over 20 years and showed that interprovincial migration started in the early 1990s and increased steadily thereafter (table 6.1). Between 2005 and 2010, 11 million people moved across provincial boundaries annually (netting out return migration). We do not have comparable numbers after 2010, but interprovincial migration certainly slowed after 2010.

Migration is a complex, multidimensional, and mostly individual phenomenon that is analyzed further in chapter 9. Here we are primarily concerned with migration as one of the determinants of urbanization and the changing composition of Chinese society. Long-distance migrants have naturally been attracted to the booming southern coastal regions. From 1990 to 2010, 36.4 million people moved to Guangdong Province, and 28 million to the three Lower Yangtze provinces of Shanghai, Jiangsu, and Zhejiang. Together, these two regions attracted about half of all long-distance migrants. The largest out-migration provinces were Sichuan, Anhui, Henan, and Hunan. Since 2010, long-distance migration has declined as a share of total migration. Farmers in central and western China are finding more opportunities closer to home, both in the growing cities of the interior and in small towns near their farms. As described in chapter 16, some labor-intensive exporters have moved large

Table 6.1
Interprovincial migration.

	Average annual net migration (millions)
1990–1995	2.14
1995–2000	4.66
2000–2005	7.60
2005–2010	11.04

Source: Chan (2012).

factories inland to access cheaper labor. For example, electronics assembler Foxconn now has gigantic factories in Zhengzhou, Henan, and Chengdu, Sichuan, which allow many local farmers who would otherwise have migrated to the coast to move to cities closer to home. Population aging is also changing the supply and composition of migrants.

6.3.2   Characteristics of Migrants

Migration in China is broadly similar to migration in other developing countries that are undergoing rapid urbanization. Migrants are predominantly young people in search of better jobs. Research in China has consistently found that migrants are attracted to regions with higher wages and greater job opportunities. People move in search of economic opportunity. For rural residents, the probability of migration is by far the highest for those aged 16 to 20 and declines by about half for every 10 years of age thereafter. When large-scale migration began in the 1990s, a male was three times as likely to migrate as a female with the same characteristics. However, by 2000, female migrants had closed the gap, and the floating population was equally balanced by gender. Women are concentrated in service occupations and light manufacturing, attracted in particular to the many jobs in the export-oriented factories in southeastern coastal areas. Male migrants are more widely scattered across the construction sites, factories, and businesses of urban China.

Single males and females pioneer migration, and their family ties to the native village encourage them to think of migration as temporary. The institutional divide between rural and urban encourages this "temporary" mental orientation, since it is difficult to gain permanent urban status and to transform land into other types of assets. Nevertheless, migrants gradually bring their families and seek to settle in the city on a long-term basis. Of the 102 million urban "floating population" counted in 2000, exactly one-third were still in the city in 2010. As migrants stay longer and establish themselves, migrant households are gradually becoming larger and more complex. In the 2010 census, only 27% of the floating population consisted of solo individuals; 30% had a spouse or sibling; 38% had children with them; and 5% had a parent (Census Office 2014, 233, 238). Migrants are already long-term residents in the city, so their integration into urban life has become a topic of pressing importance.

Inside the city, migrants do different kinds of work (chapter 9) and live in different physical conditions than do urban *hukou* holders. Only 1.3% had purchased homes in 2015, compared with the more than 85% of urban *hukou* holders who own their own homes. Migrants traditionally lived on the job, and although the proportions have been falling, almost half still do (in 2015, 16% of migrants still lived at their work sites, and 29% in dormitories provided by the production unit, almost always "for free," that is, as part of the employment contract). Most of the rest (37%) rent rooms, often with a roommate, and frequently in the urban villages described in section 6.2.2 (NBS 2016). For example, in Beijing, there are 867 identified urban villages. Migrants live there in cramped quarters (8.2 square meters per person, less than one-third of the average in the formal housing sector). They have electricity but almost never their own kitchens or bathrooms (Zheng et al. 2009).[2] These crowded spaces are like shantytowns but are tucked away almost invisibly in China's major cities (Hsing 2009).

6.4   Economic Consequences of the Urban-Rural Divide

Urban-rural income gaps inevitably open up during the development process. Industrialization begins in cities during the early stages of development, and at first, virtually all of the modern economy is located in cities. In comparison with urban residents, rural people have lower educational levels, are equipped with less capital, and suffer the economic impact of remoteness and incomplete markets for many needed resources. Not surprisingly, participants in the modern economy, namely, urban residents, earn higher incomes, while rural dwellers, remaining within the traditional economy, have much lower incomes for a long time. In addition to these general factors, China's special institutions create an even wider urban-rural gap, as discussed in the following sections.

6.4.1   Surplus Labor Penned Up in the Countryside

In the decades before the 1990s, given the restrictions on mobility imposed on the rural population, surplus labor built up in the countryside. Between 1957 and 1977, average rural incomes stagnated. The rural labor force increased while the amount of land farmed was roughly constant; under these conditions, the marginal physical product of workers fell, despite technological progress. Since government agricultural

---

2. Zheng et al. (2009) found that the price per unit of space is about the same in formal urban housing and in the "urban village," but the average migrant consumes much less of it than the average urban *hukou* holder.

procurement prices were basically unchanged, the marginal value product fell as well. The population was bottled up in the countryside, but membership in the agricultural collective assured every rural resident access to the land. The new worker was still put to work, even though his or her marginal productivity was low (chapter 11). Under these circumstances, it is obvious that labor could be "surplus," in the sense that a worker's marginal product could be well below his income. Individual migration decisions did not serve as an escape valve to rebalance the economy; migration was not available to limit the growth of income differentials between urban and rural.

6.4.2   Full Employment in the Cities

The situation in cities was the mirror image of that in the countryside. Growing industry in the cities in the 1960s and 1970s created a demand for more labor. As a result, expanding urban employment gradually incorporated virtually all young women. Urban female labor-force participation became nearly universal during the 1960s and 1970s. Almost all urban households came to have more than one bread-winner. Moreover, strict birth-control policies, implemented first in the big cities, reduced the number of dependent children. The result was that the urban dependency ratio (total population/employed population) decreased steadily, from 3.4 to only 2.0 from 1957 to 1977. Thus, even though urban residents suffered under a wage freeze, the real per capita income of urban households increased significantly.

6.4.3   Relative Incomes

The size and evolution of the urban-rural gap depends on the preexisting institutions described in previous sections, as well as the impact of migration and the pace of economic growth in the city and countryside. To track this evolution, we use the ratio between per capita money incomes for urban households and those of rural house-holds, shown in figure 6.3. This information is recorded in the large-sample household surveys conducted by the Chinese National Bureau of Statistics (NBS). The NBS carried out separate rural and urban surveys for decades, with households rotating out of the sample after five years. Sampled households maintain diaries of income and expenditures, and rural households record income in kind as well as cash income.[3] The data show a very strong pattern: At the beginning of the reform era in 1978, the urban-rural divide was already rather wide. The average per capita income of urban residents was 2.6 times that of rural residents, at the top of the range of

---

3. As described earlier, urban dwellers not only have higher money incomes than rural dwellers but also enjoy a range of subsidies that they receive in addition to their higher money incomes. However, it is difficult to quantify the monetary value of these subsidies, and this can only be done for a few bench-mark years. (This topic is covered further in chapter 10.) The fact that consumer prices are higher in the city partially offsets these subsidies.

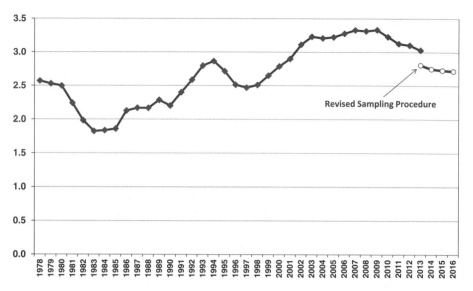

Figure 6.3
Ratio of urban to rural per capita incomes (1978–2016).
Source: *SYC* (various years).

comparable developing countries. In the early years of reform, the urban-rural gap declined as the success of rural reforms sharply boosted farmers' income. The ratio shrank below 2 for the years 1983–1985.

Starting from 1984, however, the gap widened steadily, reaching a peak at 3.3 in 2007–2009. This increase in the urban-rural income differential between the 1980s and the first decade of the twenty-first century is the outcome of two contrasting forces pulling in opposite directions. On one hand, the rapid growth of urban economies drove up urban wages faster than incomes from farming were growing. Urban growth increased the "skill premium," rewarding well-educated urban dwellers (chapter 9), while the explosive growth of exports (chapter 16) pushed up wages of industrial workers. On the other hand, the lowering of barriers to immigration would have tended to equalize wages, at least of unskilled workers. In the earlier periods, this liberalization was not enough to narrow the urban-rural gap. Instead, when rural incomes grew slowly from 1998 to 2003, the gap widened, exceeding three for the first time. This very large gap fueled the rapid increase in migration after 2000. Administrative barriers were reduced, but income differentials stayed high, continuously generating strong "pull" factors that drew rural residents to the cities. Only after the massive increase in migration in the 2005–2010 period did the urban-rural gap finally begin to decrease after 2009.

Exactly how much the urban-rural gap has declined since 2009 is hard to tell because the NBS switched to a new method of integrated sampling in 2013, which lowered the measured differential significantly.[4] There is little doubt that the decline is real, though, and the adjusted measure for 2016 measures the rural/urban differential at 2.72, the lowest since the mid-1990s, when migration was just getting under way. To be sure, migration is not the only cause of a moderating urban-rural divided. Fundamental changes in demographics and labor conditions, discussed in chapter 9, play a role. Moreover, many aspects of policy have shifted since about 2003 in an effort to reduce the urban-rural gap. These are described in the next section, and their effectiveness discussed in the following section.

6.5   Policy Efforts to Close the Urban-Rural Divide Since 2003

The economic conditions that had led to the creation of dualistic urban-rural institutions in the 1950s are now long past. Famines and food shortages are history. Since about 2003, Chinese policy-makers have begun to make efforts to abolish the dualistic system, create national institutions that span urban and rural, and shrink the urban-rural divide. Policy-makers began with modest steps to eliminate abuses and relax constraints on migration. The ultimate goal, though, is much more ambitious, since it requires the abolition of the old system and the creation of a qualitatively new set of institutions. This effort has been underway for more than a decade, and many important steps have been taken, but overall progress has been halting and incomplete. Three areas of policy initiative are most significant: raising rural incomes by eliminating the "urban bias" in economic policy; reducing the salience of the urban *hukou* in order to create a single unified form of citizenship; and the strengthening of farmer property rights in land in order to create a functional and competitive land market.

6.5.1   Raising Rural Incomes by Reducing "Urban Bias"

Since the turn of the century, central-government policies designed to extract resources from the countryside have gradually been abandoned. Especially during the Wen Jiabao administration (2003–2013), increasing rural incomes and shrinking the urban-rural gap became a major focus of policy attention. Motivated by the widening of the urban-rural income gap, the desire to rebuild social services, and anxiety about the anticipated impact of World Trade Organization (WTO) membership on farmer income, policy-makers shifted gears dramatically on rural policy.

---

4. The new integrated sampling method is superior in principle, replacing the decades-old method of having completely separate urban and rural surveys. The urban survey had initially included only urban *hukou* households but had been augmented to include resident migrants in 2001 (although migrants were still underrepresented). In 2013, procedures for imputing owner-occupied housing services to income were also changed. The 2013 methodological changes by themselves caused measured urban incomes to decrease by 2% and rural incomes to increase by 6% on average.

• Rural taxes were dramatically reduced in the years after 2003. The new policy package began in the fiscal realm with a campaign against the miscellaneous fees that local governments charged farmers. However the campaign was soon expanded to cover the main agricultural tax, which was ultimately abolished at the end of 2005. With overall budgetary revenues growing strongly, the government had no need to continue to extract the rural surplus (see section 11.5.1).

• Concern about the impact of freer agricultural trade under WTO membership after 2001 led to direct subsidies for grain farmers, carefully designed to be compliant with WTO regulations. Since that time, agricultural policy has steadily swung toward price supports and direct subsidies to farmers (section 12.5.3).

• A substantial increase in budgetary expenditures for education and health and an expansion of government provision of social services in the countryside followed. The absence of government programs for health insurance or social security in the countryside began to change in 2005 with the national rollout of the New Cooperative Medical System (NCMS). As its name implies, this system was still organized around cooperatives, but for the first time the national government made a specific budgetary commitment for each participant (initially only 5 RMB per head but steadily raised to 60 RMB in 2016). Rural education outlays expanded considerably, and a rudimentary retirement program for rural residents was introduced. These social insurance schemes are covered in section 20.4.

With these steps, the economic factors that were the drivers of the initial creation of the dualistic system have been eliminated. Nevertheless, the institutional features themselves persist.

6.5.2 Encouraging Migration and Relaxation of the Urban Residence Permit System

Policy-makers have discarded the ambivalence with which they once viewed rural-to-urban migration. During 2003, the government rolled out a "Sunshine Policy," designed to provide prospective migrants with rudimentary job training and information about conditions in destination cities. Shortly thereafter, the government publicized a strong affirmation of the right of rural people to migrate to cities and reside there without harassment. Gradually, government policy began to affirm the right of migrants to get education for their children—at least up through lower middle school—and participate in social protection and welfare programs. For the first time, the government began to support migration instead of trying to stop it.

A government effort to make these initiatives more systematic was incorporated in the 2014 program for "New-Style Urbanization." As described earlier, mass migration had already eliminated the necessity for an urban *hukou*. In 2014, the national government committed in principle to a gradual phaseout of the urban *hukou* system.

The qualitative distinction in residence permits between urban and rural is to be gradually eliminated, and the government also set a quantitative target of transferring the residence permits of 100 million migrants to their permanent urban dwellings by 2020. This would raise the formally permitted urban population to about 45% of the total population by 2020, and correspondingly reduce the floating population (compare figure 6.1). Obviously, this goal envisioned a substantial liberalization—but not yet the abolition—of the urban residence permit system (New-Style Urbanization 2014).

6.5.3   Strengthening Farmer Property Rights in Land

Individual farm households have gradually been given stronger property rights in land. The term of individual land contracts has been steadily extended, and now is generally 30 years, or even more. Since the late 1990s, redistribution of land by the village collective has been officially discouraged, and while it still occurs, the frequency has declined (Whiting and Wang forthcoming). However, these policy measures still left migrants subject to fears that they would be vulnerable to "use it or lose it" norms if their families left the village. At the same time, national policymakers have been hesitant to move to full private property in land because they worry that commercial capital would buy up land on the urban periphery, depriving farmers of their subsistence fallback, and potentially threatening national food security.

The compromise policy devised after 2013 has been to strengthen farmers' property rights further while hardening existing distinctions between different kinds of rural land. An ongoing national cadastral survey is nearing completion, establishing property records and a national land registration system for the first time. In these land records, much rural land is classified as "permanent agricultural land," which can never be sold or leased for nonagricultural uses. On this basis, farmer land property rights have been expanded in two ways.

First, private contractual rights to farmland are to become permanent and use-rights fully tradable. This is being done by creating a third layer of landownership between ultimate collective ownership and private land-use rights. According to the new law, the original household contract rights are to become permanent and inalienable, but contractors can now lease land-use rights to other households or corporations. In theory, holders of contractual rights would no longer be subject to the risks of redistribution by the collective or forfeiture because of emigration. Farmers can rent out their contracted land, but can only rent permanent agricultural land to other farmers.

Nonfarm rural land comprises land set aside for houses, as well as that for rural township and village enterprises. The land for rural housing is surprisingly large because each farm household has the right to use such a plot for free, and it typically includes not just houses but also outbuildings, vegetable plots, and work yards. In total, there are about 9 million hectares of such land—about 7% of the area of arable land, substantially larger than all the urban land already developed. Rural enterprise land—which in aggregate is about twice as big as housing land—can now be transferred by the collective without first being requisitioned by the municipal government (Wang et al. 2012; Xu and Jia 2015). Thus, these policies seek to increase the revenue that farmers and their collectives can reap from rural land, and free them from their dependence on municipal governments for permission to change land use. As such, they constitute a small but important step forward to a better functioning land market.

6.6   Conclusion: The Urban-Rural Divide Today

The policy initiatives described in the previous section, following on the impact of mass migration, have knocked large holes in the walls that once separated urban and rural in China. Nevertheless, the fundamental features of the separate urban and rural institutional systems are all still in place. While the urban-rural divide has begun to shrink because of policy changes and fundamental structural changes, it still exists and it is still large.

6.6.1   Restrictions on Big City Access Have Replaced the Old Urban-Rural Divide

Relaxation of urban *hukou* requirements has been much more complete in small cities than in large ones. The new residence permit policies incorporate and strengthen the policy bias against very large cities. Small towns and cities under 1 million population are to eliminate restrictions completely and promptly; cities of one to 5 million are to eliminate restrictions, but "carefully and appropriately." The 16 cities with populations over 5 million are to strictly control the pace of overall population growth and may adopt "points systems" to control the type of migrants and pace of immigration. These points systems, already in place in Beijing, Shanghai, and Guangzhou, allow migrants to qualify for a permanent residence permit after several years of steady work and residence. They are more transparent than previous regulations and provide a clear pathway to urban status. However, in order to qualify for residence in a city like Shanghai, a migrant must work for at least five years, pay into social security, and rent a home throughout that time; be able to document these actions; and then visit and satisfy numerous, sometimes capricious, bureaucratic agencies. Even then, permits are quota-limited, so permanent status may be denied to qualified candidates if the year's quota has already been reached.

6.6.2   Reproduction of the Urban-Rural Divide in the Segmented Urban Labor Market

The flow of migrants into the city has transformed urban labor markets, since migrants account for well over half of the urban labor force. But the types of work—predominantly manual, unskilled labor—and the nature of employment for migrants are very different from those for permanent city residents. Migrants participate in segmented labor markets that reproduce much of the underlying urban-rural inequality that they sought to escape. Migrants in the city typically work much longer hours for lower pay. They are less likely to be rewarded for investments in education and job skills because many high-skilled jobs are effectively barred to them, and they are rarely covered by any social insurance programs (chapter 9).

6.6.3   Second-Generation Inequalities

Today's persistent urban-rural divide is manifested in so-called second-generation inequalities, especially education. Rural schools are of much lower quality than urban schools to begin with, and there is some evidence that the education gap between urban and rural people is widening (chapter 9). Migrants to the city, despite central-government policies that encourage migrant enrollment in urban schools, still find it difficult and costly to enroll their children, especially in the largest cities. Additional fees are charged, and quantitative quotas are enforced. Even if migrants succeed in enrolling their children in primary and lower-middle schools in the city, they almost always send them back to the countryside for upper-middle school. This is because national government policy does not articulate any right of migrant children to enroll in urban upper-middle school, and college entrance procedures and exams are tied to a students' permanent residence, which is still in the countryside.

Many migrants leave their children at home. This in turn creates a serious problem of "left-behind children," typically cared for by their grandparents. Many grandparents doubtless provide emotional sustenance and loving care to these children, but they are less well equipped to introduce children to the types of knowledge increasingly required for China's modern economy. There is evidence that educational and health outcomes are worse for left-behind children (Li, Liu, and Zang 2015). Moreover, as grandparents age, there is a danger that they will also become a left-behind generation that increasingly needs care. The significant effort to roll out nationwide programs of health insurance and pensions for which rural people and migrants qualify will be discussed in section 20.4. These new programs still provide much lower levels of coverage to migrants than those enjoyed by permanent urban residents.

6.6.4   Misallocation of Land

Land in China is scarce and valuable, but the property rights system creates incentives to use land wastefully. Municipal governments have an incentive to requisition as much land as possible and sell it to the highest bidder or use it to attract new investment to their locality. Between 2000 and 2010, the amount of built-up urban land increased by 76%, while the urban population increased by 50.5% (New-style Urbanization 2014). Su and Tao (2017, 242) showed that Chinese city governments allocate about three times as much land to industry proportionately as other countries. The total amount of land included in the plans of "development zones" is 7 million hectares, almost as much as the total of rural residential land (Xu and Jia 2015). In the villages, many homes are vacant: migrants hold on to their houses for security and leave them vacant because there is no way to easily monetize them.

6.6.5   Urban Governance and Urbanization

City governments, especially those in the largest cities, strongly resist *hukou* reform, even as they show great enthusiasm for land development schemes. In fact, both are symptoms of the basic structures of urban governance (cf. section 5.6). Mayors of cities are appointed by higher government and party authorities, so they have only limited accountability to city residents. Instead, they are given aggressive targets for economic growth, budgetary revenues, and attraction of outside investors; their careers depend on meeting these targets. In this situation, giving migrants formal residence only brings new burdens, since migrants already contribute their labor and will require costly additional social services if they become citizens. Land, on the other hand, brings new resources, which can be leveraged to bring in new investment and growth. Municipal leaders have a strong incentive to maintain their control over land and little incentive to integrate migrants into the local economy and society. Local-government land dependence and resistance to *hukou* reform both create a need for more profound reform of the fiscal system, particularly the system of central-local relations (chapter 20). Current national policy suggests linking land conversion quotas to the number of new residents a city accepts—a logical step, but little more than a stopgap.

Despite substantial reforms, the basic features of the urban-rural divide are still in place. The remaining features of the urban-rural divide tend to be self-reproducing. Economic reforms have begun a process of dismantling the barriers between the urban and rural economies, but they remain fundamental in understanding the functioning of the Chinese economy, as well as in determining the different life outcomes of Chinese households.

Bibliography

Suggestions for Further Reading

Hsing (2009) and Fan Zhang (2014) provide good overviews of urbanization in China, combining political and economic insights, respectively.

References

Au, Chun-Chung, and J. Vernon Henderson (2006). "Are Chinese Cities Too Small?" *Review of Economic Studies* 73 (3): 549–576.

Banister, Judith (1987). *China's Changing Population*. Stanford, CA: Stanford University Press.

Census Office, State Council, and Population and Employment Division, National Bureau of Statistics (2014). *Maixiang Xiaokang Shehui de Zhongguo Renkou* [China's population on the way to a moderately prosperous society]. National vol. Beijing: Zhongguo Tongji.

Chan, Kam Wing (2012). "Migration and Development in China: Trends, Geography and Current Issues." *Migration and Development* 1 (2): 187–205.

Chan, Kam Wing (forthcoming). "Introduction: China's Hukou System, Migration, and Urbanization." In Kam Wing Chan, ed., *Urbanization with Chinese Characteristics: The Hukou System and Migration*. Abingdon: Taylor and Francis.

Chen, Qin, and Zheng Song (2014). "Accounting for China's Urbanization." *China Economic Review* 30:485–494.

Cheng, Tiejun, and Mark Selden (1994). "The Origins and Social Consequences of China's Hukou System." *China Quarterly*, no. 139 (September): 644–668.

Henderson, J. Vernon (2009). "Urbanization in China: Policy Issues and Options." Report prepared for the China Economic Research and Advisory Programme, November 14. Accessed at http://www.econ.brown.edu/faculty/henderson/Final%20Report%20format1109summary.doc.

Hsing, You-tien (2009). *The Great Urban Transformation: Politics and Property in China*. Oxford: Oxford University Press, 2009.

Knight, John, and Lina Song (1999). *The Rural-Urban Divide: Economic Disparities and Interactions in China*. Oxford: Oxford University Press.

Li, Qiang, Gordon Liu, and Wenbin Zang (2015). "The Health of Left-Behind Children in Rural China." *China Economic Review* 36:367–376.

Liang, Zai, and Zhongdong Ma. 2004. "China's Floating Population: New Evidence from the 2000 Census." *Population and Development Review* 30 (3): 467–488.

Lu, Ming, and Guanghua Wan (2014). "Urbanization and Urban Systems in the People's Republic of China: Research Findings and Policy Recommendations." *Journal of Economic Surveys* 28 (4): 671–685.

Lü, Xiaobo, and Elizabeth Perry, eds. (1997). *Danwei: The Changing Chinese Workplace in Historical and Comparative Perspective*. Armonk, NY: M. E. Sharpe.

NBS (National Bureau of Statistics) (Annual). "Nongmingong Jiance Diaocha Baogao" [Annual monitor and survey report on nonagricultural workers]. Accessed at http://www.stats.gov.cn/tjsj/zxfb/201704/t20170428_1489334.html.

NBS Department of Comprehensive Statistics (1999). *Xiandai Zhongguo 50 Nian Tongji Ziliao Huibian* [Comprehensive statistical data and materias on 50 years of new China]. Beijing: China Statistics Press.

New-type Urbanization (2014). "Guojia Xinxing Chengzhenhua Guihua (2014–2020)" [National new-type urbanization program, 2014–2020]. March 17. http://politics.people.com.cn/n/2014/0317/c1001-24649809.html.

Population Statistics Yearbook (various years). National Bureau of Statistics, Department of Population and Employment Statistics, ed., *Zhongguo Renkou Tongji Nianjian* [Population statistics yearbook of China]. Beijing: Zhongguo Tongji.

Qin, Bo, and Yu Zhang (2014). "Note on Urbanization in China: Urban Definitions and Census Data." *China Economic Review* 30:495–502.

Rozelle, Scott, and Guo Li (1998). "Village Leaders and Land-Rights Formation in China." *American Economic Review (Papers and Proceedings)* 88 (2): 433–438.

SAC (Annual). *Zhongguo Tongji Zhaiyao* [Statistical abstract of China]. Beijing: Zhongguo Tongji.

Su, Fubing, and Ran Tao (2017). "The China Model Withering? Institutional Roots of China's Local Developmentalism." *Urban Studies* 54 (1): 230–250.

SYC (Annual). *Zhongguo Tongji Nianjian* [Statistical yearbook of China]. Beijing: Zhongguo Tongji.

Walder, Andrew (2000). "Chinese Society." Public lecture, Institute for International Studies Conference, "China at the Crossroads," Stanford University, May 19.

Wang, Hui, Lanlan Wang, Fubing Su, and Ran Tao (2012). "Rural Residential Properties in China: Land Use Patterns, Efficiency and Prospects for Reform." *Habitat International* 36:201–209.

WDI (World Development Indicators), World Bank. Accessed at http://databank.worldbank.org/data/home.aspx.

Whiting, Susan, and Dan Wang (forthcoming). "The Rural Economy." In Weiping Wu and Mark Frazier, eds., *The Sage Handbook of Contemporary China*. Vol. 1. London and Thousand Oaks, CA: Sage Publications.

Wu, Xiaogang, and Donald J. Treiman (2004). "The Household Registration System and Social Stratification in China: 1955–1996." *Demography* 41 (2): 363–384.

Xu Dianqing and Jia Shuaishuai (2015). "The 1.8 Billion Mou Cultivated Land Red Line." In Qiu Dong, Xu Dianqing, and Zhao Nan, eds., *Guomin Hesuan Yanjiu Baogao* [National accounts research report 2014], 1–98. Beijing: Zhongguo Caizheng Jingji.

Yu Jianrong (2005). "Social Conflict in Rural China Today: Observations and Analysis on Farmers' Struggles to Safeguard Their Rights." *Social Sciences in China*, March, 125–136.

Zhang, Fan (2014). *China's Urbanization and the World Economy*. Cheltenham: Edward Elgar.

Zhang Shanyu (2003). *Zhongguo Renkou Dili* [China population geography]. Beijing: Kexue Publishing House.

Zheng, Siqi, Fenjie Long, C. Cindy Fan, and Yichen Gu (2009). "Urban Villages in China: A 2008 Survey of Migrant Settlements in Beijing." *Eurasian Geography and Economics* 50 (4): 425–446.

Beijing 1985: The form and scale of cities reshaped by structural change.

Economic growth, in the simplest meaning of the term, is an increase in the total amount of goods and services available. This is measured by the growth of gross domestic product (GDP), which is the total of all the value added in an economy. Dividing by population gives the amount of goods and services available per individual, that is, GDP per capita. The development process is a gradual but steady and sustained increase in output per capita. Output increases because society accumulates physical capital to equip workers to become more productive, and because households boost the productivity of their family members by investing more in human capital, especially health and education. Technology becomes more sophisticated as better-educated, better-equipped workers become more adept at their work. This chapter begins with a brief characterization of China's long-run growth experience, followed by a short discussion of the data on which it is based.

Growth is not just expansion in the quantity of output; many structural changes occur in regular patterns as the economy is reshaped by the actions of many individuals. The second part of this chapter emphasizes the common processes that drive structural change and growth in all developing economies. Chapter 6 set the stage for this discussion because urbanization is a core driver of structural change. However, we here broaden the discussion to structural change in GDP, in which China shares common features with most other developing countries. There are still distinctive Chinese features, but they are not as unusual as those that shape urbanization. The structural perspective thus provides benchmarks that show how far China has come along a common development path and where it diverges from that common path.

All developing countries go through common structural changes, but only a select few become growth miracles. In this, China's extremely rapid growth phase resembles those of earlier East Asian growth superstars. To approach that story, this chapter first addresses perhaps the most distinctive feature of China's economic structure, its extraordinarily high and sustained rate of investment. Although investment has long been high, many analysts had expected it to become less extreme after economic reforms at the turn of the century, but it did not. Instead, from 2006 to about 2010, China's investment rate and the share of industry increased again, a development pattern generally described as "unbalanced." Government policy accounts for much of China's high investment rate, which, in turn, explains a great deal of China's rapid growth.

Although investment is of particular importance, all factors of production must be considered to explain growth. A general production function approach is introduced that shows that growth is the outcome of the growth of factor inputs into production and also an unexplained component or "residual." This framework allows us to perform a "growth accounting" analysis that helps us understand China's growth-miracle phase.[1] Growth miracles are the result of rapid growth of inputs plus productivity improvement; China's experience is no exception to this general rule. The structural-change and growth-accounting approaches provide a more concrete understanding of the end of the growth miracle and a basis for projecting China's future development. The growth of factor inputs will slow: labor-force growth has slowed to zero, and the potential of rural-to-urban migration to offset the otherwise shrinking urban workforce is also shifting down. The contribution of the productivity-enhancing residual is uncertain. It is likely that China's long-run growth rate will ratchet down but still be robust by international standards.

Because structural change occurs in regular patterns, we can expect that China will repeat many of the changes undergone by earlier developing East Asian economies, especially miracle-growth economies. The comparative perspective suggests that the transition to a slower-growing economy can be difficult. The transition to slower growth is not inherently bad—quite the contrary, since slower growth partially reflects slower population growth and can be accompanied by continued rapid increases in living standards. However, many forerunner economies have had difficulty making the shift to a lower growth rate, and China may also experience turbulence as it moves to a different growth model. These changes are easy to understand but hard to predict because structural changes are associated with many other dramatic social changes. The outlook for these intersecting changes is briefly discussed in the final section.

7.1   Long-Run Growth

China grew rapidly between 1949 and 1978, but growth really took off after the beginning of reform in 1978. Moreover, the acceleration of economic growth coincided with the slowing of population growth, so per capita growth accelerated even

---

1. The growth-accounting framework will be used later in this book in discussing agriculture (chapter 12), technology (chapter 15), and macroeconomics (chapter 20).

Table 7.1
Growth of per capita GDP (average annual growth rates, percentage).

	GDP	Population	GDP per capita
1952–1978	6.0	1.9	4.1
1978–2000	9.7	1.3	8.3
2000–2010	10.5	0.6	9.9
2010–2016	7.7	0.5	7.1

Source: *SAC* (2017, 16, 21–37).

more dramatically. According to the most recent (2017) official data, shown in table 7.1, average annual GDP growth accelerated from 6% in the pre-1978 period to almost 10% in the 1978–2000 period. At the same time, population growth decelerated from 1.9% per year before 1978 to only 1.3% after 1978. As a result, per capita GDP growth doubled, jumping from 4.1% to 8.3% annually.

As impressive as the performance was until 2000, the subsequent decade was even more remarkable. China was an integral part of the global economic boom during the 2003–2007 period and then managed to sidestep the worst of the global financial crisis in 2008–2009. By 2010, China had already returned to growth rates comparable to those it had enjoyed before the crisis. As a result, China's growth rate for the decade after 2000 actually accelerated compared with the previous 22 years. China emerged as the world's second-largest economy during 2010, much earlier than had previously been expected. Moreover, since population growth continued to slow, growth of GDP per capita accelerated noticeably, from 8.3% per year before 2001 to 9.9% per year through 2010. The achievement of a decade of per capita growth at almost 10% annually is an astonishing achievement that may be unprecedented. Since 2010, growth has unambiguously slowed, with per capita GDP growth dropping to 7.1% annually between 2010 and 2016. Overall, between 1978 and 2010, per capita growth proceeded at an annual average rate of 8.8%, and per capita GDP was 15 times in 2010 what it was in 1978. China is a certified growth miracle.

7.1.1 Data and the Measurement of Growth

However, the data shown in table 7.1 and those used throughout this text are official Chinese data. How reliable are these data? First, we must acknowledge that the official data are more reliable than any others. That is, there is no plausible alternative set of data for China, and no one has ever demonstrated that the extensive Chinese numbers published are mutually contradictory or inconsistent with externally verifiable facts. The truth is that we have no choice but to use official data, which, after all, are the product of an enormous data-collection network systematically analyzed by a large group of conscientious government statisticians. That said, there are many reasons to emphasize that the data are neither as precise nor as reliable as we would like. Even in the best of circumstances, we would expect Chinese data to suffer from the same data collection shortfalls as other developing countries, and from some of the issues of statistical interpretation encountered by other transitional economies because the magnitude of change in output and prices is so large.

Since the mid-1990s, Chinese statisticians have made important changes in the way they collect and analyze data in an attempt to keep up with changes in the economy. Unfortunately, these changes have not always led to better data quality overall. In 1998, just as the composition of Chinese output was going through a period of dramatic change, China adopted a new data-collection system based on sample surveys to estimate of the size of small-scale industry and services. The resulting GDP numbers not only were arguably less reliable than before but also were difficult to corroborate with other time series. In subsequent economic censuses, in 2004, 2008, and 2013, the NBS has "discovered" additional small-scale production and revised GDP upward. Most dramatic was the 16% upward revision in 2005, but smaller upward adjustments were also made in 2009 and 2015. When current year GDP is revised, earlier years are adjusted through rough, and not always consistent, estimates (see discussion in Holz 2014).[2]

Three sets of serious problems must be acknowledged:

1. Deflation: Official statistics do not adequately correct for the effects of inflation. The GDP deflator, the measure of inflation that official government statisticians use to convert nominal (current-price) GDP growth to real (constant-price) growth, grew more slowly than almost every other measure of inflation in the 1980s. Ren (1997) and Young (2003) presented good accounts of the data and argued for alternative price indexes. Since 1996, prices have been stable, and the problem is less serious in the aggregate. However, measuring inflation in the service sector is still extremely difficult and current procedures are inadequate.

2. New products: Statisticians have a very hard time accounting for the expanding scope of the economy. In 1978, China did not produce color televisions, to say nothing of computers. Chinese statisticians tend to count fast-growing items like computers by valuing them at their early, very high, prices, which overweights them and therefore overstates growth. But there were also many low-priced items, such as health care and housing, that were rationed at the beginning of the period but are now available at near-market prices and have grown rapidly. Counting these items

2. The most recent round of adjustments also brought China closer to recent international practice by counting research and development as investment rather than as an intermediate input and by imputing a value for the service of owner-occupied housing. Put together, these adjustments raised 2013 GDP by 4.6%. The most recent revised series is used throughout this book.

at their beginning-of-period prices tends to understate growth and creates an offsetting bias.

3. Politics: Many crucial data series, including GDP, are used as success indicators in evaluating local officials, who therefore have incentives to inflate or otherwise distort the numbers that are reported. Moreover, the NBS has a monopoly on the collection of economic data, while the Communist Party monopoly over the press affects the way economic news is reported.

These are serious problems and we should use caution with Chinese data and accept them only within a fairly large margin of error. China's national accounts are certainly less accurate than developed-country accounts. This does not mean, however, that Chinese economic growth is somehow illusory. Quite the contrary: some key elements of the economy are fully verifiable. For example, exports have grown much more rapidly than GDP and are fully corroborated by the independent statistics of importing countries. If China's GDP were actually growing significantly more slowly than official figures indicate, exports would have increased their share of GDP through 2006 even more dramatically, and it would be difficult to explain how exports had grown so much more rapidly than GDP. China's dramatic export boom makes sense only in the context of a rapidly growing GDP. There are several similar cases of readily verified series (fiscal revenues, for example). As noted earlier, no alternate procedure for assessing China's growth meets basic consistency checks; and finally, rapid growth and transformation correspond to the commonsense evidence of personal experience. Overall, then, there is likely to be some upward bias in the official recorded growth rates, but it will not change the fundamental picture of rapid growth. If we allow for inadequate deflation during the 1980s and early 1990s and perhaps for an undercount of GDP in 1978, the maximum plausible adjustment of Chinese GDP growth would lower it 1 to 2 percentage points per year. If China's actual per capita GDP growth was 1.5 percentage points lower than the official rate every year between 1978 and 2010, the long-run annual average growth rate would still be 7.3% over 32 years. This would still be the most sustained period of rapid economic growth in human history.

Growth of per capita GDP above 6% for more than 15 years, one definition of a growth miracle, has occurred in three episodes in East Asia. First, Japan led the way with growth of GDP per capita slightly above 8% per year for 18 years, from 1955 to 1973. After 1973, Japanese growth moderated but remained healthy until the end of the 1980s. Second, during the 14 years from 1982 through 1996, several East Asian economies grew at very high rates. During this period, annual growth of GDP per capita in Korea was 7.4%; in Taiwan, 7.1%; and in Thailand, 7.8%. However, these economies experienced a fairly dramatic economic shock after 1996 and slower growth thereafter. The third episode is China since 1978. If we accept the maximum possible correction for statistical overstatement, China's growth has not necessarily been more rapid than the other two. However, China's miracle-growth period is still unique because it has extended over 35 years, far longer than the other two episodes. In addition, China's growth miracle has affected many more people than the two previous episodes.

7.1.2   Growth Cycles

Figure 7.1 shows that there has been a pronounced cyclical pattern of GDP growth since 1978. Three times growth peaked at over 12% per year: in 1984–1985, 1992–1994, and 2006–2007. Each of those peaks came after a period of policy-induced slowdown. Each peak-growth period corresponded to a period of accelerated restructuring triggered by institutional changes, but also to a bounce back from the policies in place in the earlier period. Thus the 1984–1985 growth surge was the result not only of successful rural reforms but also of the end of the "readjustment" of the national economy that had cut back investment in 1981–1982. The 1992–1994 surge was the result not only of accelerated opening and liberalization after Deng Xiaoping's "Southern Tour" but also of the end of the period of retrenchment that followed the Tiananmen disorder. The 2006–2007 surge was the result not only of World Trade Organization (WTO) membership and harvesting the results of SOE restructuring but also of the end of the slowdown caused by that same SOE restructuring and the

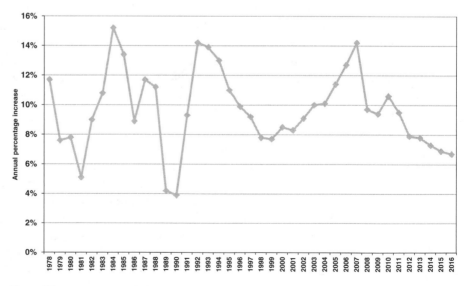

Figure 7.1
Annual GDP growth, 1978–2016.
Source: *SAC* (2017, 21–37).

Asian financial crisis of 1998–1999. The post-2013 slowdown is quite different from earlier policy-based slowdowns. As we will see, it is the result of deep long-term structural factors in the economy.

7.2   Structural Change

All countries are predominantly agricultural when they begin development. In the early stages of development, farmers make up the bulk of the labor force, and most value added is in agriculture. As development proceeds, certain common patterns of structural change are observed that are associated with growth away from a predominantly agricultural economy and to an industrialized and diversified economy. The simplest way to track these changes is to classify all economic activity into three sectors: primary (agriculture, including fisheries, forestry, and animal husbandry); secondary (including mining, manufacturing, construction, and utilities); and tertiary or service (including transportation, communications, household and business services, social services, and technology and education). This corresponds to the "production approach" to GDP (see box 7.1).

The first obvious change during the development process is that the share of the labor force in the primary sector declines. Then, as economies move into the middle-income ranks, the absolute number (not just the share) of workers in the primary sector, agriculture, begins to decline. The remaining farm laborers boost their productivity and

Box 7.1
Calculating GDP.

The basic idea of GDP is simple: it is the total "value added," the sum of all the market-priced, value-adding activity carried out in a given geographic territory in a certain time period. Calculating GDP involves getting rid of the double counting that would be involved if we simply added output from different sectors. There are three different ways to calculate GDP, each of which provides a different kind of insight into the economy. In principle, each approach should produce the same number. Each is based on very different types of data, so the calculation methods serve as a check on one another. (In practice, of course, there are differences because there are errors and the different sources cannot precisely match up, but hopefully these are small.)

Production: The production approach builds up GDP by looking at the net value added in each sector. Double counting is avoided by excluding the value of purchased inputs from the value of output, of steel (for example), from the value of automobiles produced.

Expenditure: The expenditure approach looks at broad categories of expenditure to determine what goods and services are actually used for. Consumption, investment, government consumption, and net exports are the most common way to classify expenditure-side GDP.

Income: The income approach aggregates the net income of different categories of the population. Households, businesses, and governments all receive income.

This chapter presents analyses based on the production and expenditure side. The income side is discussed in chapter 19 on the financial system.

are able to feed the entire country. This process continues indefinitely: a high-income country like the United States has only 3% of its labor force in agriculture. Rozelle (2004, 60) called the decline in agriculture's share the "iron law of development." It may seem initially that agriculture plays an entirely passive role, shrinking steadily as the economy modernizes, but successful developing economies typically experience modernization of the agricultural sector as an early and integral part of overall development. As will be discussed in chapter 12, agricultural development supports the broader process of economic growth in a number of fundamental ways: providing food at low cost, which keeps wages economy-wide at reasonable levels; releasing workers for growing modern sectors; and providing a source of finance and markets for growing modern sectors. Healthy agricultural development leads to more rapid development overall.

Industrialization gradually changes the structure of the economy. The secondary sector, starting from a low base, grows through the initial stages of development, increasing the number and share of workers and the share of GDP. Industry does not grow forever, though. At a certain point, the industrial share of GDP levels off. Moreover, as industrial productivity continues to rise, the share of the workforce in industry declines. Economies vary substantially in the relative size of their industrial sectors. However, there is a strong common pattern that for many countries, the industrial share of GDP tends to increase until a country reaches an income level of around $15,000 GDP per capita, evaluated at purchasing power parities (PPP; see box 7.2). At this income level, the industrial share plateaus and then begins to decline (Herrendorf, Rogerson, and Valentinyi 2014). Manufacturing—the most important part of the secondary sector—typically peaks at about 20%–25% of GDP, but there is considerable variation.

The tertiary or service sector tends to increase share throughout the development process. During the early phase of development, the share of the service (tertiary) sector increases only gradually. Many underdeveloped economies have large proportions of their labor force engaged in services, predominantly low-value jobs: small-scale retail and repair, hauling goods, and personal services. Early development in these economies may result in a declining agricultural share and an increasing industrial share without a large change in tertiary employment. However, above the $15,000 per capita PPP GDP threshold, the increase in the service sector's share accelerates. The shares of both primary and secondary sectors are declining, and modern, high-value services such as finance and medical care expand. As an economy reaches high-income status, the service sector dominates. For example, in the United States, with a GDP per capita over $50,000, more than 70% of employment is in the service sector, and services account for two-thirds of private consumption. Let us now see how well these patterns apply to China.

Box 7.2
Purchasing power parities.

GDP for each country is initially calculated in that country's currency, so China's GDP is calculated first in RMB. However, in order to make comparisons among countries, we need to convert GDP or GDP per capita into some common benchmark currency, most often the U.S. dollar. The simplest way to do so is to use the prevailing exchange rate. However, conversion using exchange rates is often unsatisfactory because the price structures of different countries can be extremely different, varying according to relative scarcities, and exchange rates can sometimes fluctuate dramatically. An alternative is to calculate purchasing power parities (PPPs). For China, this means first calculating how many RMB it takes to purchase a given basket of goods and services and then comparing this figure to the U.S. dollar cost of an equivalent basket in the U.S. economy. This ratio is then used to value the "purchasing power" of the RMB, which allows us to express Chinese GDP per capita in comparable PPP-adjusted dollars. This procedure is especially useful for evaluating living standards or the incidence of poverty, and we will use it extensively in chapter 10 to discuss those topics.

When a PPP calculation is done for many different countries, it gives us a common benchmark to evaluate the development process. The computation is complex: the bundles of goods and services produced and consumed in different economies vary significantly, so a great deal of data is required, and more than one procedure for calculation is defensible. However, the recent comparison project carried out by the World Bank in collaboration with other organizations has produced PPP estimates according to a consistent methodology for a large number of economies. All the PPP figures in this book use this World Bank series of PPP-adjustments based on constant 2011 U.S. dollars. By this standard, China's PPP-adjusted GDP per capita in 2015 was $13,572.

7.2.1   Structural Change in China: Labor

For the first 25 years of transition in China, roughly from 1978–2003, structural change of the labor force took place in the context of unrelenting pressure on the employment-generating capability of the economy. The ability of the growing modern sector to absorb labor was the key determinant of the economy's ability to transform itself. As figure 7.2 shows, at the end of the planned-economy era in 1978, the Chinese labor force reflected both the fact of underdevelopment and the distortions imposed by the administrative regime that divided urban and rural areas. At that time, 71% of the workforce was engaged in agriculture, a number that is very high in comparative terms. (The overall rural share of the labor force, including rural industry and service along with agriculture, was 76% at this time.) Following common patterns of structural change, the share of the labor force in agriculture has declined steadily since 1978. In absolute terms, the number of farmers was highest in 1991 (391 million) and fell steadily to 215 million at the end of 2016. Two rapid bursts of structural change took place in 1983 through 1987 and from 1991 through 1996; and then after 2003, the agricultural labor force resumed rapid decline through the present. The first burst followed the early success of rural reforms: as collectives were disbanded and farm output surged in the early 1980s, millions of farmers left to take up new nonagricultural jobs, especially those in township and village

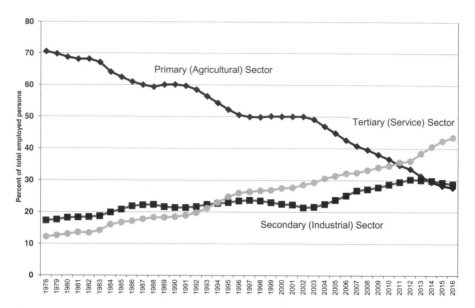

Figure 7.2
Structural change in employment.
Sources: *SYC* (2016, table 4-3); *SAC* (2017, 12).

enterprises (chapter 13). The second burst occurred in the early 1990s, when a new round of economic reforms kicked off a growth surge and restrictions on rural-to-urban migration were reduced. The third burst corresponded with the 2003 acceleration of the economy, attributable to investment acceleration and rapid growth of exports. At the same time, as shown in chapter 6, migration increased substantially. The share of agricultural workers fell below 50% after 2002 and continued to fall steadily to only 28% in 2016. China is thus no longer a predominantly agricultural economy.

As workers left agriculture, the share of industrial and service workers increased steadily until 2012. Figure 7.2 shows the slow, gradual growth of China's late-developing service sector. The share of workers in services in 1978—only 12%—was among the lowest ever recorded. There is some undercount involved here, since statisticians are unlikely to have captured all the employees of urban industrial work units who were providing services to other work-unit employees. But it is undoubtedly true that, as noted in chapter 4, socialist development involved neglect of investment in the service sector and discrimination against individual service providers. Given that background, it would be expected that market transition should create a dramatic expansion in service-sector employment. In fact, as figure 7.2 shows, service-sector employment grew steadily, but not especially rapidly, through 2012, when it was still only 36% of total employment. After 2012, service employment growth accelerated and reached 43.5% in 2016. This was still low in comparative perspective. Most middle-income developing countries have more than half of their labor force in services.

In the employment data, 2012 stands out as a turning point. Industrial employment growth abruptly halted, and between 2012 and 2016 industry shed some 9 million jobs, while service sector employment accelerated. China fits well with common developmental patterns. China grew out of the distortions of its planned economy legacy, and underwent a process of urbanization and industrialization. After 2012, the focus of urban job growth shifted to the service sector from industry. The one anomalous feature is the relatively small size of service-sector employment, which we return to later.

7.2.2   Structural Change in China: GDP

Structural change can be viewed through the changing shares of total GDP produced by the primary, secondary, and tertiary sectors. Unlike labor, which we can measure simply by counting bodies, GDP must be measured in value. Therefore, we must choose an appropriate price standard for comparison and properly treat changing prices over time. These issues are particularly important in the case of China because the "Big Push" socialist development strategy imposed distortions both on the price system and on the real structure of the economy. These issues can best be discussed in the light of two phenomena generally observed in the process of economic growth. First, faster growth is associated with more rapid productivity increase in any given sector. Second, productivity increase is associated with reductions in relative prices. These two fit together in a virtuous cycle that can be modeled in different ways (Matsuyama 2008). From the output side, productivity growth causes prices to fall, causing demand to shift to the cheaper goods and services being produced by that sector. From the demand side, goods and services with higher income elasticities (luxury goods) are more in demand as incomes rise, and the increase in quantities demanded fuels investment and stronger productivity growth. The relationship among growth, productivity, and demand shapes structural change.

For China, prices of industrial goods were unusually high at the end of the command economy period. China then began explosive industrialization: industry grew much faster than other sectors while industrial prices dropped dramatically. As a result, if we look at the structure of GDP in current prices, we see hardly any change: industry produced 48% of output in 1978 and after 30 years of rapid industrialization, industry in 2008 produced 47% of output. Relative price reductions for industry had offset all of industry's more rapid quantitative growth. Price changes and real growth rates were thus negatively correlated in China, even more strongly than in other growing economies.

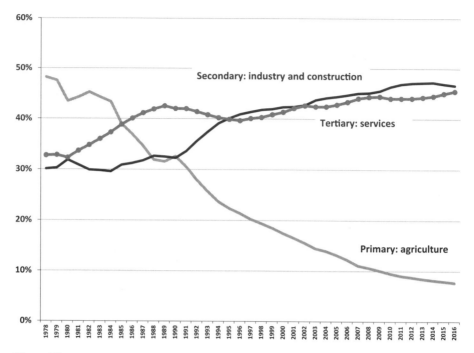

Figure 7.3
Composition of GDP: Production side (2010 constant prices).
Source: *SAC* (2017, 21–37).

The negative correlation between price and real growth means that we must use constant prices to examine China's output composition. A recent year is best because it will be closer to world prices and so provide a better benchmark than early, highly distorted prices. In figure 7.3, we use the implicit sectoral GDP deflators to revalue sectoral output to a constant 2010 price basis, and the long-run pattern of structural change emerges clearly. This provides a more accurate picture of the structure of the economy in 1978. In current prices, a 1978 industrial worker produced 7 times as much value as an agricultural worker, but measured in 2010 prices, the industrial worker produced 2.5 times as much as a farmer. Overall, agriculture produced 48% of GDP, while industry produced 30%. Service-sector workers, however, produced 4 times as much as farmers, again suggesting an undercount of service workers.

Figure 7.3 displays a clear picture of structural change after 1978. Generally speaking, three periods are discernible. During a "recovery period," from 1978 through 1991, structural change was moderate because agriculture and services both grew rapidly. Agriculture maintained its share during the first six years as reforms succeeded first in the countryside, and the service sector showed strong recovery from its suppression during the command-economy period. The second period, one of "rapid industrialization," began after the renewal of economic reform in 1991 and extended through 2012. Driven by linkage to the global market, the share of GDP originating in industry moved steadily upward from 32% in 1990 to 47% of GDP in 2012. Indeed, the industrial boom was so overwhelming that the share of services, which we would normally expect to be increasing in a rapidly growing economy at China's income level, actually declined almost three percentage points between 1989 and 1996 before resuming moderate growth. Agriculture's share of GDP, as one would expect, has resumed its rapid decline, slipping from 31% of GDP in 1991 to 9% in 2012 (as measured in constant 2010 prices).

Figure 7.3 clearly shows a third "post-industrial" period after 2012, but it does not show the unambiguous change evident in the labor force data in figure 7.2. Industry's share of value added plateaued around 47% between 2012 and 2016, but did not significantly decline, and the service sector increased its share by only 1.5 percentage points. Although this is a big change from the previous rapid industrialization period, it does not yet qualify as a clear period of service-sector–led growth. China's service sector is still relatively underdeveloped in comparative terms, whether measured in employment or value added. One possible explanation is that market-oriented reforms have had a much bigger impact on the goods-producing (primary and secondary) sectors of the Chinese economy. Agriculture and industry are both highly marketized and dominated by private producers. By contrast, the government has maintained near-monopoly controls over many higher-skill service sectors, including finance, education, and health care. Since these sectors have generally not been opened up, market-driven restructuring and productivity gains have been less obvious than in industry and agriculture. In this interpretation, if the acceleration of service-sector employment growth after 2012 reflects the gradual lowering of domestic entry barriers to service sectors, it may be a sign that service-sector growth can be sustained and may accelerate.[3]

China's industrial share is extremely high. Industry includes mining, petroleum extraction, and utilities, which vary substantially across countries, so a more precise comparison is thus with the share of manufacturing value added in GDP. Manufacturing was 32% of GDP in 2010, significantly higher than other upper-middle-income economies in that year (22%). Only a few countries have reached China's level of manufacturing in GDP, and these usually for a short time. Although

---

3. The normal negative correlation between growth and price changes did not hold in 2013–2016. Industrial prices dropped dramatically, even as industrial growth slowed below service sector growth. The abrupt shift in relative prices may obscure the structural changes under way.

China's level of manufacturing is unusual in comparative context, the pattern of change appears quite normal. As China's per capita PPP GDP approaches $15,000, which it will slightly surpass in 2017, the share of manufacturing has leveled off and begun to decline.

7.2.3   Structural Change and Globalization: Comparison

It is clear that China's high manufacturing share is closely related to its emergence as "the world's factory." Globalization changes some of the patterns of structural change. As China emerges as a favored site for certain types of manufacturing worldwide, and as it clusters certain stages of Asia-wide manufacturing networks, it clearly can continue to expand its manufacturing sector for a longer period than if it were not so integrated into world industry (chapter 16). South Korea is a comparable case. Korea's manufacturing share was 31% of GDP from 2010 through 2013; not only was this very high, it came when Korea's per capita GDP was $29,000, almost twice the $15,000 PPP benchmark. Korea is one of the few economies that continued to increase manufacturing share well after the usual $15,000 turning point. This evolutionary path is clearly related to Korea's strong competitiveness in manufacturing exports, some of which traces to its close links to China's manufacturing (chapters 16 and 17).

India provides an instructive contrast, touching on globalization and also on economic development patterns. Like China, India shows a steady decline in the share of agriculture in its overall GDP, but the relationship between change in industry and services is reversed in the two economies. Compared to China, India's service sector has always been relatively more important and its industrial sector much smaller. Each country established a comparative advantage in one broad sector and then developed in a pattern that expanded that sector, using globalization and international trade to create additional opportunities for specialization. Today, the economies are growing more structurally similar, as China shifts toward service-sector growth and India fosters catch-up industrialization.

Rodrik (2016) points out that economies are experiencing the turning point to postindustrial growth at a lower level of per capita income in the twenty-first century than they were in the 1970s–1990s. Competition from China may be a factor, but profound technological changes may also be a driver. Rodrik reminds us that manufacturing has been the traditional avenue for catch-up development because technological borrowing and rapid productivity growth are more attainable in manufacturing. This holds lessons for China as well, since the postindustrial growth period will need to generate unprecedented productivity growth from the service sector if growth is to be sustained.

7.3   Investment

7.3.1   Overall Patterns of Investment

Closely related to China's rapid growth is the enormous investment effort China has made over the past 35 years. Indeed, ironically, since China has abandoned the "Big Push" socialist development strategy, its investment rate has actually risen. The output of this investment effort is what most strikes the visitor to China: the pace at which new buildings, airports, power lines, and other infrastructure appear provides striking visual testimony to China's elevated investment rate.

The high rate of investment is the most immediate explanation for China's rapid growth. The basic facts are shown in figure 7.4, which exhibits total investment and its most important component, fixed capital formation (shown in the solid line), which corresponds to new factories, roads, and housing and is fundamental to economic growth. Gross fixed capital formation was already around 30% of GDP at the end of the 1970s and stayed in that range through most of the 1980s. It increased through

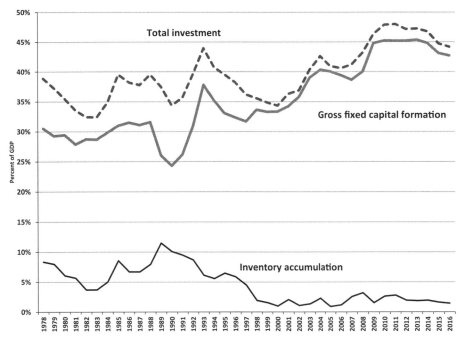

Figure 7.4
Investment share of GDP.
Source: *SAC* (2017, 21–37).

the 1990s and then jumped upward after 2002. Between 2003 and 2008, fixed investment stayed in a tight range between 39% and 40% of GDP. Then, something remarkable happened: in 2009, in the face of the global financial crisis, China launched a government stimulus program. This pushed fixed investment up to 45% of GDP, where it remained through 2014.

In international experience, investment rates as high as the 39–40% China experienced through 2008 have occurred only in exceptional circumstances. The two previous episodes of rapid growth in East Asia described in section 7.1.1 were also characterized by high investment. Japan invested 35% to 37% of GDP in gross fixed capital formation during 1970–1973 at the very end of its long boom. Korea sustained a very high fixed investment rate from 1990 through 1997, peaking at 39% in 1991. For brief periods in the mid-1990s, boosted by large inflows of foreign direct investment, Thailand and Malaysia invested over 40% of their GDPs in fixed capital. The only previous economy that came close to Chinese investment levels was tiny, highly open Singapore, which enjoyed massive foreign investment inflows to reach a total investment share averaging 42% over 15 years from 1971 to 1985. There was no precedent for the investment levels of 45% of GDP that China sustained for six years from 2009 to 2014.

Why is Chinese investment so high? To be sure, many of the reasons are rooted in market fundamentals. Chinese saving is high: households, businesses foreign and domestic, and government all contribute to the supply of saving, making high investment possible (chapter 19). Moreover, investment opportunities are abundant. However, it should also be said that investment is high because the Chinese government has long seen investment as the key to growth, and growth as its most important objective. As a result, the Chinese government has adopted a series of policies designed to keep investment high. These include the following:

1. Keeping the cost of investible funds low through subsidies and "financial repression" (chapter 19). A series of credit, tax, and financial policies have been used to steer funds toward entities (usually government linked) with high investment propensities.

2. Cost deferral. The government has encouraged productive investment by shielding investors from environmental, land, and energy costs. In essence, the cost of factors of production is held down by conscious government policy.

3. Target responsibility systems. Local-government leaders have been given growth targets to which their promotion possibilities and short-run bonuses are linked. In practice, they only way for local officials to maximize these success indicators is to increase investment (see section 5.6 and chapter 18).

China has created a growth-oriented political system and it has produced high investment and growth.

7.3.2 The Relationship Between Investment and Growth

High investment is a major explanatory factor and precondition for rapid growth in China, as it has been in previous episodes of rapid East Asian growth. Clearly, a big part of the answer to the question "Why is China growing so fast?" is simply "Because the investment rate is so high." Particularly from the 1940s through the 1960s, economists examining development and growth tended to see investment as the key to growth. Development economists argued that the first task of development was to increase investment from, say, 5% of national income to 15% of national income or more. (Today, most economies already invest more than 15% of national income, and China, obviously, invests much more than this.) The simplest possible growth model, called a Harrod-Domar model, is one that includes only fixed capital as a source of growth. This simple model can make sense if (and only if) labor is so abundant that labor to work the new capital is always available without significantly increasing costs. For example, if there is a pool of surplus labor in the countryside (see section 9.8), eager for the opportunity to work at jobs in the modern sector, then investment can be increased without running into diminishing returns. In such an environment, the investment rate is the sole determinant of the growth rate.

If we suppose that these conditions hold, we can create a simple model based on a constant capital/output ratio. That is, set a parameter, $k = K/Y$, where lowercase k represents the number of units of capital (K) required to produce each unit of GDP or income (Y). In a reasonably well-functioning economy, we might expect this capital/output ratio to be a number between roughly three and six. Assume that in a given economy, such as China, this ratio is fixed in the short term and is equal to four. In that case, once we know the capital stock, we know the level of output. Output (GDP) is given by the capital stock:

$Y = 1/k \cdot K$.

Growth of output is then given by the increment in the capital stock:

$dY = 1/k \cdot dK$.

The growth rate is then derived by dividing both sides by Y:

$dY/Y = 1/k \cdot dK/Y$.

Since (ignoring depreciation), $dK/Y = $ investment/Y, it is convenient to relabel it i, for the investment rate. Finally, dY/Y is the growth rate, which we can call g. That gives us growth as a linear function of investment:

$g = i/k$.

Suppose that in China, the value of k on average was 4 (a fairly typical middle-income value). That means that as the investment rate was pushed up to 40% of GDP, the growth rate of the economy as a whole approached 10% (10% = 40%/4). Clearly, this simple relationship captures something important about the Chinese growth experience.

Although this perspective is illuminating, it is too limited. International experience shows that the relationship between investment and growth is not so straightforward and cannot explain very much of the variation in growth experience across countries. A significant investment effort is a prerequisite to growth, but although today virtually all economies invest more than 15% of GDP, some are growing robustly, while others are not growing at all. Even for a single economy, the investment rate tends to be relatively persistent over the long term, but countries' growth rates can fluctuate dramatically (as China's experience demonstrates). Although there is definitely an association between investment and growth, the relationship is not as strong as we might expect, nor is the causality as clear as is predicted (Blomstrom, Lipsey, and Zejan 1996; Easterly and Levine 2001). In East Asia, China or Korea have very high investment rates, but the economy of Taiwan has achieved rapid growth with fixed capital formation only occasionally pushed above 30% (and the last time was in 1980).

An alternative is that rather than treat the capital/output ratio as a fixed parameter that explains growth, we can convert it to a variable that expresses the productivity with which capital is used. That is, we keep the simple expressions developed earlier but turn them around to provide empirical information about the economy's performance. Multiplying our previous expression by k/g, we derive:

$k = i/g$.

In this expression, k is no longer a constant capital/output ratio but rather an empirical observation about the number of units of capital it took to provide an additional unit of output. Called an "incremental capital/output ratio" (ICOR), this measure provides a "quick and dirty" assessment of how much investment is required to "grow" the economy. The lower the number, the better. The long-run average ICOR was 4.1 for India and 4.3 for all lower-middle-income countries. ICORs for developed countries are typically much higher.[4] For the United States between 2002 and 2012, private investment in structures and equipment was 10.8% of GDP, and growth was only 1.8%, so the average ICOR was 6. The results for China are displayed in table 7.2.

---

4. For a developed country, a larger share of investment is needed simply to maintain the existing capital stock (that is, to offset depreciation); a larger share of investment goes for nonproductive assets like housing; and there are fewer opportunities for catch-up or copycat investment. For these reasons, the ICOR is expected to be higher.

Table 7.2
Incremental capital/output ratio (ICOR).

	Fixed investment (percentage of GDP)	GDP growth	ICOR (annual average)
1979–2000	30.8	9.7%	3.2
2001–2010	39.2	10.5%	3.7
2011–2016	44.0	7.7%	5.7

Source: *SAC* (2017, 21–37).

Table 7.2 shows that over the long run, China has used investment relatively efficiently. The average ICOR between 1979 and 2000 was only 3.2, significantly lower than the middle-income average. As China stepped up investment in the 2000–2010 decade, the ICOR rose, but only slightly, and China was still below the international average, despite having a very high investment rate. As a result, growth accelerated slightly from already high levels. After 2010, China's ICORs increased, approaching 6 for the 2010–2016 period.

An ICOR is affected by short-run fluctuations in the GDP growth rate. If GDP growth drops in a single year, the ICOR for that year will spike. To control for this effect, table 7.2 displays long-run ICORs comparing average growth rates over at least five years with long-run investment rates. However, the short-run fluctuations in ICORs also provide information. Figure 7.5 exhibits ICORs averaged over only three years (of growth and investment). The figure shows clearly the three periods of peak growth described in section 7.1.2: 1984–1985, 1993–1994, and 2007–2008 when, because of extraordinary circumstances, resources previously bottled up in the countryside or state-owned enterprises were released, growth surged, and ICORs dropped to 3 or below. Conversely, the figure shows that the increase in ICOR after 2010 has been steep and without precedent in the reform period. Although gradual increase in ICORs is an unavoidable result of the maturing of an economy, this rapid increase is due to the change in economic conditions in China, the end of the growth-miracle phase, and the difficulty of adapting a new growth strategy. One benefit of the ICOR is that it gives a quick and simple indicator of investment productivity. As soon as aggregate data are available, the reader can quickly update with 2017 data and beyond, and see if investment productivity has stabilized.

7.4   Production Functions, Productivity, and Growth Decomposition

In examining the relationship between investment and growth, we have been examining productivity in terms of a single input, capital. In a parallel fashion, discussions of productivity in the United States often focus on labor productivity, in which

Figure 7.5
Incremental capital/output ratio (three-year moving average).
Source: *SAC* (2017, 21–37).

output is compared to a single input, labor. To pursue the analysis further, we need to take into account the obvious fact that output is produced by several different factor inputs. Including all these inputs gives an aggregate production function:

$$Y = f(K, L, H, \ldots).$$

This says that output (Y, or GDP) is a function of inputs of capital (K), labor (L), and human capital (H). Capital, labor, and human capital are the most important factors of production that are inputs into the production process.[5] By explicitly setting up a production function, we can quickly achieve two analytic objectives:

1. Growth decomposition: We can use the production function to investigate how much of past growth can be attributed to measurable increases in factor inputs. That is, how much growth came from the increase in labor? How much from human capital? And so on.

---

5. Land is also an essential factor of production, but we set it aside here because it typically changes so slowly. See chapter 9 for further discussion of human capital.

2. Total factor productivity: When we have calculated the total amount of growth that can be attributed to factor inputs, we will still be left with an unexplained component or "residual." This tells us how much of growth we cannot explain by measurable increases in factor inputs. We call this "total factor productivity growth" or TFP growth. It tells us how much more output was produced by more productive use of factor inputs over and above that produced by increased quantity of inputs.

In order to achieve these objectives, we need to give the production function a specific form. The specific form we adopt should have at least two essential characteristics: it should display overall constant returns to scale, and it should display diminishing returns to scale for any single input. The most straightforward way to accomplish this is through a Cobb-Douglas production function:

$$Y = A \cdot K^{\alpha} \cdot L^{\beta} \cdot H^{\gamma},$$

in which $\alpha + \beta + \gamma = 1$, and α, β, and γ are each less than 1. The restrictions fulfill our requirements of overall constant returns to scale and diminishing returns to each factor, respectively. The coefficients show the marginal productivity of each input.[6] Even within the Cobb-Douglas form, several different specifications are possible. In a competitive market economy, we can assume that businesses will employ each factor of production up to the point where its marginal productivity is exactly equal to its cost. At the aggregate level, that would imply that the share of the wage bill in the overall economy would equal β plus γ, and the share of capital would equal α (otherwise, entrepreneurs would shift a dollar's worth of input from wages to capital or vice versa). These values provide plausible ranges but cannot really be applied in the Chinese economy, given the huge government role and the multiple distortions in factor markets. The marginal products could be estimated directly from the historic data, but given limited numbers of observations and large institutional changes, this is also not very promising. The best recourse is probably just to assign plausible and reasonable values to the coefficients. This was the procedure followed by Perkins and Rawski (2008) to obtain the results displayed below.

Once the decision has been made on what values of the coefficients to use, and all the data have been collected and properly processed, it is straightforward to calculate the growth of inputs ("total factor inputs," as it were) and then the residual. To do this smoothly, first convert the production function into logs:

$$\ln Y = \ln A + \alpha \ln K + \beta \ln L + \gamma \ln H.$$

---

6. Constant returns can be demonstrated by multiplying all inputs by a common integer and then rearranging terms. Plugging plausible coefficient values into a spreadsheet and manipulating results can show diminishing returns.

We can then express any subsequent value of Y and the inputs K, L, and H in terms of their growth rates, in which a capital G denotes a percentage growth rate:[7]

$$G_y = G_A + \alpha\, G_K + \beta\, G_L + \gamma\, G_H.$$

Rearranging terms, we have

$$G_A = G_y - (\alpha G_K + \beta G_L + \gamma G_H).$$

The last of these expressions says that we can define a "residual" term, G_A, which is the growth of output minus the growth of a weighted basket of inputs. That is, the residual G_A refers to the unexplained growth of output after we have accounted for measured factor inputs.

What is this residual? We label it "total factor" productivity (and G_A as total factor productivity growth) because it measures the change in the productivity of all the factors put together. It is common to equate TFP with technological progress, but this is too simple. Although technological progress is an important part of TFP, the reality is that TFP is a residual and thus a measure of things that we cannot fully explain or account for. Nevertheless, we can immediately identify at least three important components of TFP:

1. Technological progress: when new "blueprints" are available, such that new production techniques or processes can be introduced that use fewer inputs per unit of output.

2. Institutional or organizational progress: when new incentive systems and coordination techniques are implemented that make people work smarter or harder.

3. Reallocation of factors: when workers move from one sector to another or from one firm to another where their productivity is higher. In a market economy, lower-productivity firms go bankrupt and release factors to higher-productivity firms. In a developing economy, workers leave low-productivity agriculture and move to higher-productivity industries or services.

If we keep in mind these multiple causes of TFP growth, it is meaningful to track the performance of China's economy in terms of TFP growth. Table 7.3 shows one version.[8] Perkins and Rawski's (2008) calculations tell a story about China's entire

---

7. We can be comfortable dropping the log notation because of an important "shortcut": if X is a number near 1, then the approximation $\ln(X) \approx X - 1$ is roughly correct. Therefore, the log of 1.05 is roughly 0.05, and the log of 1.1 is roughly 0.1. Of course, we can retain the precise log computation when appropriate but use the shortcut in quick calculations. We will use this shortcut again in chapter 18.

8. Note that there are many variants of an aggregate production function calculation. Each analyst must decide which price deflators are most appropriate, how to handle index-number problems, and the appropriate size of the individual coefficients.

Table 7.3
China GDP growth and TFP (1952–2005).

Period	GDP growth	Fixed capital	Labor	Human capital	TFP
1952–1978	**4.4%**	**5.8%**	**1.9%**	**2.5%**	**0.5%**
During which:					
1952–1957	6.5%	1.9%	1.2%	1.7%	4.7%
1957–1978	3.9%	6.7%	2.0%	2.7%	−0.5%
1978–2005	**9.5%**	**9.6%**	**1.9%**	**2.7%**	**3.8%**
During which:					
1978–1995	10.2%	8.9%	2.3%	3.2%	4.0%
1995–2005	9.1%	11.5%	1.0%	1.7%	3.2%

Source: Perkins and Rawski (2008).

post-1949 growth experience. Between 1952 and 1978, growth of inputs was fairly rapid, but after 1957, productivity performance was terrible. TFP declined by 0.5% annually, such that output in 1978 was 10% lower for any given total factor input than it had been in 1957. After the beginning of the reform era, TFP growth rebounded to 4% annually, making up about a third of total growth. Moreover, capital accumulation accelerated at the same time.

Table 7.3 shows that each of the major components of growth of the aggregate production function were growing robustly after 1978: capital grew at almost 10% annually, while labor and human capital grew at almost 2% and 2.7%, respectively. The calculation shows that TFP growth was positive and significant for China during the 1978–2005 period.

7.5   What Is a Growth Miracle?

We earlier defined a "growth miracle" as a period of rapid, sustained growth for 20 years or more. Such growth miracles display a common feature: rapid growth of all factor inputs, that is, rapid increase in labor (L), capital (K), and human capital (H), along with positive TFP growth. What is most remarkable is that such economies sustain a set of economic conditions that allow for sustained growth of factor inputs for decades. As Krugman (1997, 11) wrote, "Productivity isn't everything, but in the long run it is almost everything." This is well put, but it should also be turned around. In the early stages of growth, productivity is not nothing, but it is almost nothing. That is, no poor country ever escaped from poverty by relying on productivity improvement. This is not even really conceivable; only by mobilizing labor and new fixed capital can a country begin the development process. No economy can get near the frontier—the ability to function at the highest possible productivity levels—without a prior sustained period of accumulating capital and human capital and building institutions that work. Growth miracles occur when this process of accumulation continues at remarkable speed and over a sustained period; therefore, productivity is not the main thing in a growth miracle. Productivity growth must be positive to sustain this process, but it is not the main driver. In this, China resembles earlier growth miracles.

The rapid growth of all three of the main factor inputs in a growth miracle occurs precisely because growth creates a virtuous cycle in which rapid growth supports further rapid input growth. The process begins with the "demographic dividend," described in chapter 8. The population at working age increases rapidly, and dependency ratios drop, so growth of output per capita accelerates. With this acceleration, incentives and opportunities for households to invest in physical and human capital increase. With fewer dependents, households invest more in education for each child, and saving rates rise, permitting more financial and physical investment. Migration from agriculture provides a seemingly infinite supply of labor, and the high investment rate drives the overall growth of the economy. Thus, labor, human capital, and capital all grow rapidly.

To sustain this process, it is essential that governments adopt an open economic policy. An export-oriented policy permits output to grow essentially without limits and enables the inflow of foreign technologies, hard and soft, and new business models. In this accommodating environment, government actions to increase investment in productive capital and infrastructure are generally successful. Productivity (TFP) grows as well. These features have been the common experience of all growth-miracle economies.

It is clear that China's high-growth era, from 1978 to 2010, fully fit these conditions. First, China enjoyed the demographic dividend of having a large and increasing share of the population of working age and a low dependency burden. Moreover, the demographic dividend was in place just as the structural transformation from agriculture to industry gained steam. Under these circumstances, the amount of new capital provided by investment was the key driver of growth: as the machines and structures were put in place, there were plenty of farmers ready to move to factory jobs, and as they did so, productivity and total output grew. Investment was the key facilitator of this process of structural change. As rural-to-urban migration became large, China's economy shifted into overdrive.

Second, in China's "follower" economy, there were myriad opportunities for transplanting business models, technologies, and infrastructure patterns from developed countries. Businesses were rewarded for moving fast, and planners could adapt infrastructure solutions from developed countries. China built grids of highways and electric power and, later, airports and high-speed rail. The basic pattern and scale of these infrastructure solutions were copied wholesale from developed countries.

Chinese policy-makers argued that it was more important to build these networks quickly than it was to have each node in the network appropriately adapted to local demand. They were right: China built out infrastructure ahead of demand and drove the growth process. Moreover, during the 1990s, the institutional setup was adapted in myriad ways to support the high investment imperative. The system delivered investment, and investment delivered growth.

Third, these processes were already well under way when two dramatic changes in the structure of demand took over in the twenty-first century: the housing boom and the restructuring of China's export economy. Both of these changes in the structure of demand should be recognized as imperfectly foreseen outcomes of the reform process China undertook in the 1990s. The housing boom developed after the privatization of urban housing at the end of the 1990s. Capital-intensive steel, cement, and aluminum industries expanded enormously to meet the demands of the housing boom. The housing boom affected both saving behavior and investment. Chinese households increasingly began saving in order to afford housing; investment in construction soared, and derivative investment in supporting heavy industries increased as well. China's foreign trade changed dramatically after membership in the WTO began to phase in after 2001. WTO membership brought a wholesale reorganization of China's traded-goods sectors. Liberalization produced not so much a flood of imports as it did a flood of new ways to produce industrial goods cheaply and efficiently. With imported parts and components, China's industry cut costs dramatically, unlocking new international and domestic markets.

7.6   The End of the Growth Miracle

The multiple favorable conditions that supported China's growth-miracle phase logically cannot last forever. This is clearest with respect to the growth of labor inputs. Changes in birth rates and the age composition of the population inevitably affect the size and growth of the labor force (chapters 8 and 9). China's working-age population has now plateaued and has begun a slow, steady decline. Can growth of other factor inputs compensate for zero growth of labor inputs? This is an important question. It is unlikely that more investment can compensate for less labor. We have already noted that China's investment rate over the past several years has been the highest the world has ever experienced, and the investment rate has declined annually between 2013 and 2016 (figure 7.4). This decline seems likely to continue, since changing structure and slowing growth ought to imply that previously profitable investments will become less attractive, and businesses will reduce their investments. For example, as wages climb rapidly, labor-intensive manufactured exports attract less investment. The ease with which planners can build infrastructure ahead of demand may also decline, as the highways, airports, and high-speed rail networks are completed. Finally, a larger existing capital stock implies that depreciation is bigger and proportional increases in net capital are harder to achieve. Thus the prospects that increased investment will compensate for slower labor growth seem dim indeed. It is much more likely that investment will also make a smaller contribution to China's growth in the future.

This leaves two additional sources of future growth. One is human capital. China's educational levels are increasing rapidly as the proportion of high-school- leavers, especially in urban areas, going on for additional education increases. However, human capital is spread over the entire labor force, so there are limits to how rapidly it can increase. Moreover, rural children have not yet experienced the same educational advances. So although human capital can increase its contribution to growth, it is unlikely to be able to substitute for slower growth of labor and capital. This leaves TFP growth. Here the potential is still great. China's PPP-adjusted GDP per capita in 2016 was only 27% of that of the United States. This means that a great deal of catch-up is still possible. As China's economy moves toward the frontier of highest-productivity workers, it still has the possibility to experience rapid TFP growth.

However, this kind of TFP catch-up is by no means guaranteed. As discussed earlier, TFP is a residual, not an automatic pass-through of technological sophistication. Institutions, structural change, and economic policy choices all affect the size of this residual. The most common effect of sudden growth slowdowns is a sharp drop in TFP as existing allocations of capital and labor turn out to be less appropriate for new conditions. Moreover, policy-makers often resist adapting policy appropriately to new, slower-growth conditions. Since 2009, Chinese policy-makers have tried hard to resist the tendency of the economy toward slower growth. In the face of the global financial crisis (2008–2009), growth was maintained by large increases in investment. Presumably the ultimate efficiency of these investments will be comparatively low. The increasing ICOR shown in figure 7.5 suggests that the efficiency of investment has declined rapidly since 2010. Calculations of TFP growth require more time and data, but it would not be surprising to find that TFP growth has slowed during this period of rapidly rising ICORs. If this occurs, it will take significant changes in policy to restore rapid long-run TFP growth.

The difficulties associated with the transition to slower economic growth (discussed in chapters 18 and 19) are evidenced in the past experience of earlier growth-miracle economies. When Japan, Korea, and Taiwan reached the end of their periods of rapid growth, they experienced substantial economic turbulence—and sometimes serious economic crises—as they transitioned to a slower-growth, lower-investment development path. China may also run into such difficulties. The end of the high-growth phase is complicated because many things change at once. Most immediately, the long-standing comparative advantage based on cheap labor suddenly starts to diminish, while other changes occur, more or less by chance, at approximately the same time. Urban growth creates new urban social groups with higher incomes, different consumption patterns, and new skills. New markets and new social possibilities emerge along with these groups, and they make new demands on society and the political system, as well as on consumer markets. In China, the end of surplus labor and rapid increase in wages has coincided with the beginning of absolute decline in labor supply. This was not the case in earlier growth miracles, and the difficulty of adjustment may well be intensified by the simultaneity of these two structural shifts.

7.7   Conclusion

China's transition to a post-growth-miracle new normal is bound up with the question of how quickly its economy will "rebalance." A key focus of uncertainty is the investment rate. Investment is, of course, a good thing. Growth and development cannot occur without it. But the fact that investment is a good thing does not mean that a higher investment rate is always better. China today needs to rebalance by reducing its investment rate and releasing more resources for consumption. In the long term, rebalancing will ultimately be part of China's evolution into a middle-income society. It is difficult to see how China can assume technological leadership, support a more prosperous and diverse society, and develop a healthy and sustainable environment without substantial economic rebalancing. In the short term, if China does not take steps to rebalance the economy—that is, if it tries too hard to keep the growth rate high—the economy risks the creation and continuous re-creation of numerous asset bubbles, flimsy financial structures, and investment projects of declining quality. Such policies increase the risk of a significant financial shock in the future.

The growth decomposition described earlier shows that future growth depends on the extent to which TFP growth substitutes for slower growth of labor and capital inputs. In a simple mechanical sense, future TFP growth will determine future growth, since "in the long run, productivity is almost everything." But TFP is a simple number, a residual, which captures indiscriminately the net impact of a large number of complex factors that are impossible to predict: How thoroughly will technological changes alter the relationship between services and industry? How rapidly will China be able to move toward the technological frontier, given its massive investment in human resources and technology? Will the size of the domestic market insulate China from some of the rough parts of the transition? Will the speed and abruptness of the demographic changes China faces make the transition more difficult? How flexible is the future development model? The answer to these questions will influence how smoothly China moves into a "new-normal" economy with sustainable—but no longer miraculous—growth.

Bibliography

Suggestions for Further Reading

For a good discussion of the regularities of structural change in development, see Perkins et al. (2001) and Herrendorf, Rogerson, and Valentinyi (2014). The World Bank (1997) has a very accessible discussion of structural change and productivity growth in China. For those interested in a deeper exploration of growth potential, Holz (2008) lays out the main issues, and Holz (2014) assesses the data limitations.

Sources for Data and Figures

Comparative data on investment rates, growth rates, and structure are from World Bank, World Development Indicators, at http://devdata.worldbank.org/dataonline/. Taiwan data are from Council for Economic Planning and Development, Republic of China, *Taiwan Statistical Data Book 2005*, http://www.cepd.gov.tw/upload/Statis /TSDB/2005DataBook@774477.875041538@.pdf. All figures for China are based on official Chinese data, as published in *SAC* (2017, 21–37); except manufacturing value-added *SYC* (2016, table 3-6). Historic GDP data are based on the revised estimates in NBS (2006).

References

Blomstrom, Magnus, R. Lipsey, and M. Zejan (1996). "Is Fixed Investment the Key to Economic Growth?" *Quarterly Journal of Economics* 111 (1): 269–276.

Easterly, William, and Ross Levine (2001). "It's Not Factor Accumulation: Stylized Facts and Growth Models." *World Bank Economic Review* 15 (2): 177–219.

Herrendorf, Berthold, Richard Rogerson, and Akos Valentinyi (2014). "Growth and Structural Transformation." In Philippe Aghion and Steven Durlauf, eds., *Handbook of Economic Growth*, vol. 2B, 855–941. Amsterdam: Elsevier.

Holz, Carsten (2008). "China's Economic Growth, 1978–2025: What We Know Today About China's Economic Growth Tomorrow." *World Development* 36 (10): 1665–1691.

Holz, Carsten (2014). "The Quality of China's GDP Statistics." *China Economic Review* 30:309–338.

Krugman, Paul (1997). *The Age of Diminished Expectations: U.S. Economic Policy in the 1990s.* Cambridge, MA: MIT Press.

Matsuyama, Kiminori (2008). "Structural Change." In Steven Durlauf and Lawrence Blume, eds., *The New Palgrave Dictionary of Economics*, 2nd ed., 6408–6411. Basingstoke: Palgrave Macmillan.

NBS (National Bureau of Statistics) (2006). "Woguo Guoneishengchan Zongzhi Lishi Shuju Xiuding Jieguo" [The results of revision of China's historical GDP figures]. January 9. Accessed at http://www.stats.gov.cn/tjdt/zygg/t20060109_402300176.htm.

Perkins, Dwight, Steven Radelet, Donald Snodgrass, Malcolm Gillis, and Michael Roemer (2001). *Economic Development*. 5th ed. New York: W. W. Norton

Perkins, Dwight, and Thomas Rawski (2008). "Forecasting China's Economic Growth to 2025." In Loren Brandt and Thomas Rawski, eds., *China's Great Economic Transformation*, 829–864. New York: Cambridge University Press.

Ren Ruoen (1997). *China's Economic Performance in an International Perspective.* Paris: Development Centre of the Organisation for Economic Co-operation and Development.

Rodrik, Dani (2016). "Premature Deindustrialization.*" Journal of Economic Growth* 21:1–33.

Rozelle, Scott (2004). "The Rural Economy" and discussion. In *Hearing Before the US-China Economic and Security Review Commission, China as an Emerging Regional and Technology Power: Implications for US Economic and Security Interests*, 36–61. Washington, DC: U.S. Government Printing Office.

SAC (Annual). *Zhongguo Tongji Zhaiyao* [Statistical abstract of China]. Beijing: Zhongguo Tongji.

SYC (Annual). *Zhongguo Tongji Nianjian* [Statistical yearbook of China]. Beijing: Zhongguo Tongji.

World Bank (1997). *China 2020: Development Challenges in the New Century*. Washington, DC: World Bank.

Young, Alwyn (2003). "Gold into Base Metals: Productivity Growth in the People's Republic of China During the Reform Period." *Journal of Political Economy* 111 (6): 1220–61.

8 Population: Demographic Transition, the Demographic Dividend, and the One-Child Policy

Population dynamics are a crucial part of economic change and growth. Rapid demographic change has important effects, both positive and negative, on the economy. China reaped a powerful "demographic dividend" during the 1980s and 1990s that contributed to its high-growth period. Today, that dividend has been exhausted, and China faces the long-run challenge of an aging society. The magnitude of these effects is particularly large because the speed of China's demographic changes has been unusually rapid.

China has long been the world's most populous nation, and the pressure of population on resources and the environment has been a constant of China's economic condition. China's population of 1.38 billion in 2015 accounted for about 19% of world population. China's share of global population has been declining gradually for four decades, from 22.5% of world population in 1974. This recent period is in fact a chapter in a long-run story. Back in the early 1800s, China accounted for around a third of world population. The shocks of the nineteenth and early twentieth centuries slowed population growth, and it was not until after 1950 that the population stabilized and grew again.

Even then, the demographic shock did not end, for the famine that followed the Great Leap Forward was the largest famine of the post–World War II era and the biggest population disaster of our time.

In the contemporary period, the most extraordinary phenomenon has been direct government intervention into household reproductive behavior. The "One-Child Policy," announced in 1980 and in effect until the end of 2015, has been judged "one of the most draconian examples of government social engineering ever seen" (Wang, Cai, and Gu 2012, 116). Government policy contributed to a fertility decline that was faster than similar fertility declines that have occurred elsewhere in the world. Rapid fertility decline produced a demographic dividend, resulting in a population today that is young and has a remarkably low dependency rate, which is favorable for growth. However, in retrospect, it is clear that most of this decline in fertility would have occurred anyway, since rapid social change created the same forces that have lowered fertility everywhere. Today, the favorable aspects of the demographic dividend have already been enjoyed, and going forward, China will cede its place as the world's most populous country to India around 2028, and about the same time, China's population will begin a long-term decline. These long-term demographic realities will have profound implications for China's future growth trajectory. China faces three significant challenges: an unbalanced sex ratio, a reversal of the demographic dividend, and ultimately a shrinking and aging population. These forces will slow China's economic growth, and may create significant social burdens.

8.1   The Demographic Transition and the Demographic Dividend

8.1.1   Demographics in Traditional Societies

In traditional societies, population growth rates are typically low. As noted in chapter 3, China's premodern population grew for over 400 years at about 0.4% per year, which appears to be near the maximum that premodern societies can sustain. Despite the fact that birthrates are high in traditional societies, population growth is slow because death rates are also high. It is common for traditional societies to have birthrates in the range of 30 to 40 per 1,000 and death rates fluctuating from 20 to over 40 per 1,000.[1] Population is in a precarious balance. When harvests are poor or diseases strike, population shrinks. Although each adult woman has many children, many die in infancy. The total fertility rate (TFR), a measure of the total number of children a typical woman bears during her lifetime, typically hovers around six (see box 8.1). China remained in a premodern demographic pattern until after 1949. Death rates were high, and disease, crop failure, and civil war undoubtedly caused population to decline in the worst years. Between 1850 and 1950, estimated population growth was 0.3% per year, which, because of the social and economic setbacks China experienced, was lower than in the preceding four centuries. Population growth resumed after 1949, and China's first modern census, in 1953, counted 594 million people.

8.1.2   The Demographic Transition

During the modernization process, population vital rates change in fairly regular ways. First, nutrition and sanitation improve, and as a result, population health improves and death rates decline. Infant mortality rates drop fairly quickly as simple

---

1. Demographers commonly express population changes as a rate per 1,000. A birthrate of 40 per 1,000 and a death rate of 20 per 1,000 imply a population growth rate of 20 per 1,000, or 2%.

Box 8.1
Birthrates and total fertility rates.

There are two rates most often used to describe fertility. The simplest is the birthrate, which expresses the number of births as a percentage of the total population. This statistic has the advantage that it is easy to obtain and provides information about current population growth. Population growth equals the crude birthrate minus the crude death rate. However, birthrates are sensitive to the age composition of the population: the birthrate will be temporarily higher when there is a larger proportion of women at childbearing ages. The second rate is the total fertility rate (TFR), which is calculated in order to describe the underlying behavior of the population and understand long-run trends. The TFR is computed by first calculating the age-specific birthrate for women in a given year. That is, the birthrate is calculated separately for 18-year-old women, 19-year-old women, and so on. These age-specific rates are then aggregated to form a total birth, or fertility, rate of a representative woman as if she were passing through the successive years of her life according to the average pattern of all women in that year. Alternately stated, the TFR expresses the number of children a woman would have during the course of her life if her fertility in each year of her life were equal to the average fertility of all the women in the population of that age during the reference year. Total fertility rates are not affected by the age structure of the population, but they are affected by changes in the timing of births. If, on average, women begin to delay births, the TFR will be temporarily lowered for a period. When the TFR falls below 2.1, fertility is below the replacement level, and population growth will eventually fall to zero or turn negative.

improvements in maternal care and nutrition take place, and a handful of deadly communicable diseases are controlled. Initially, this decline in death rates takes place without any corresponding change in birthrates. Birthrates stay high and may even increase at first because better-fed, healthier women are more fertile. As a result, population growth accelerates. Many babies are born to each woman, and the majority now survive into adulthood and have children of their own. Population growth rates accelerate from under 10 per 1,000 to as high as 30 per 1,000 or more, resulting in a population explosion. This type of population explosion occurred in Europe during the nineteenth century. In most parts of the developing world, however, declining death rates and the associated population explosion did not occur until after World War II. In China, death rates began to decline soon after the Communist government took control in 1949. In the early 1950s, rapid improvements in sanitation, more equal distribution of available food, and control of the most important communicable diseases began to drive death rates down. Birthrates remained high, and by the mid-1950s the population was growing more than 2% per year. China began its own population explosion.

The population explosion does not continue indefinitely. Birthrates begin to decline gradually in nearly all populations we observe. What causes birthrates to decline? One factor is that families require fewer births to reach their preferred number of children, or "target family size," because infant survival rates increase, and because birth-control technology improves. However, the more important factor is that social changes associated with modernization lead families to prefer smaller families, which translates into a smaller target family size. Social changes redefine the costs and benefits of children to parents. As families leave agriculture and move to cities, they have less use for child labor and find that space for a large family is more expensive. As women enter the (paid) labor force, the opportunity cost of the mother's time becomes greater. The mother can contribute more to the family's income by working outside the home, so it is more expensive for her to stay home and take care of children. An especially important role in declining birthrates is played by increasing levels of education, both for the mother and the children. As children's education becomes more highly valued, families increase their target levels of education for their children. Families begin to think of children as beings who need to be supported in school, at first for 5 or 6 years and then, later in the development process, for 10 or even 20 years. As a result, the costs of supporting children through the end of the educational process become much greater. Families decide to have fewer "more expensive" children but invest more resources in each child. An increase in the mother's level of education has a major impact, because it affects fertility through several different channels simultaneously. Better-educated mothers have a higher outside wage, and the opportunity cost of their time is higher. In addition, better-educated mothers value the child's education more and have a better understanding of health and contraceptive issues. For all these reasons, as development proceeds, families tend to have fewer children and then try to invest more scarce time and resources in each individual child. Some say that they "trade quantity for quality."

As a result of falling birthrates, population growth slows, but this process can take a long time. In the European countries that experienced clearly falling death rates by the second half of the nineteenth century, birthrates fell slowly but steadily for about a century. This process—from low through high to low population growth—is called the demographic transition. While the demographic transition took about a century in Europe, it has proceeded more rapidly in other countries since World War II. In East Asia, the demographic transition has proceeded particularly fast. The populations of Japan, Korea, and Taiwan have already completed a rapid transition to a low birth and death rate and a low-population-growth equilibrium. China has experienced rapid fertility decline and has now basically completed its demographic transition.

8.1.3   The Demographic Dividend

The demographic transition has its most direct economic effect through the creation of a "demographic dividend." The demographic dividend occurs because at a certain stage of the demographic transition, the number of people of working age increases more rapidly than the population as a whole. When this happens, the dependency rate declines; that is, the share of the population that is too young or too old to work decreases, and the economy becomes more productive. The impact of the demographic dividend is especially significant in East Asia because the declines in mortality and fertility on which it is based came early and quickly in East Asia compared with other developing regions (Mason and Kinugasa 2005). Indeed, the demographic dividend has a close relation to the economic-miracle phase of accelerated growth. The demographic dividend has three distinct effects on economic growth: a mechanical effect (increased share of producers in the population), a savings effect, and a human capital effect.

The mechanical effect is the most predictable way in which the demographic transition produces a demographic dividend. Because mortality reductions precede fertility reductions, a baby boom occurs, and when this group enters the workforce about 20 years later, it has fewer children (lower fertility). A bigger working-age group with fewer children spells a lower dependency rate. The decline in dependency rates at first affects the growth of GDP per capita through a purely mechanical relationship. Since GDP, the numerator, is produced by workers, and the denominator is total population, GDP per capita increases when the share of workers in the total population increases. When the increase in the share of workers (the decrease in the dependency ratio) is spread over two or three decades, growth of GDP per capita is higher across that entire period. To get a sense of the potential magnitude of this effect, consider a simple numerical example. If a traditional economy consists of households with one paid worker earning 100, plus a spouse and four children, GDP per capita is 100/6, about 17. If this household instead has only two dependent children, GDP per capita is 100/4, or 25. If the spouse enters the labor force and also earns 100, GDP per capita increases to 200/4, or 50. GDP per capita triples simply because of changes in family structure and (paid) labor-force participation. If this shift were spread out over 25 years, annual growth of GDP per capita would be 4.5% without any increase in average worker productivity or wages. Clearly, the mechanical effect of the demographic dividend on economic growth can be large. More generally, lower dependency rates imply higher income per capita for any given level of worker productivity.

The demographic dividend increases household saving. In general, individuals save while they are working and dissave (draw on accumulated savings) after they retire. This creates a general "life-cycle" pattern of saving. If a society is composed of life-cycle saving households, then a society with a higher proportion of working-age adults will have higher aggregate household savings, which contribute to higher investment economy-wide (chapter 7). The specific pattern in China is more complex because so far, older people in China have kept their saving rate stubbornly high, but China certainly combines a large demographic dividend with a high household saving rate (Choukhmane, Coeurdacier, and Jin 2013).

The human capital effect works primarily because families invest more in their children. The smaller total number of children (the trade-off of quality for quantity) leads to longer education and higher lifetime expected incomes. Moreover, as the baby boomers move into their 30s, they accumulate enough on-the-job experience to reach their peak productivity. Zhang, Zhang, and Zhang (2015) found that age-composition factors accounted for about 20% of China's rapid growth from 1990 to 2005, equally divided between the mechanical dependency effect and the (human capital–related) share of prime-age workers, 35 to 54.

The demographic dividend thus acts as a powerful accelerator of the growth process, leading at first to an acceleration of labor-force growth and then to an acceleration of the growth of physical capital and human capital inputs. Indeed, only countries that have reaped demographic dividends have been able to launch full-fledged growth miracles. It should be stressed that the benefits of the demographic dividend are not automatic. The existence of a demographic dividend depends on complementary economic policy and development outcomes. If the economy is not growing and generating jobs, the demographic dividend can become a demographic nightmare as unemployment increases and social stability declines. But with good policy and economic opportunity, the demographic dividend contributes to a virtuous circle of changes that support growth.

8.2   China's Demographic Transition

China's demographic experience is shown graphically in figure 8.1. Before we can examine the long-range trends shown by the figure, our attention is immediately drawn to the most striking feature in the graph, the crisis that peaked in 1960, the final year of the Great Leap Forward (GLF). The graph shows clearly the surge in deaths in 1960 (above the otherwise clear trend of a declining death rate) and the collapse in births. As death rates soared and birthrates plummeted, China's population declined (see chapter 4 for description). Demographers estimate the excess deaths from the GLF by first interpolating a normal mortality curve, in which death rates would have declined smoothly between 1957 and 1962 in line with long-term trends. Excess deaths equal the area under the actual mortality curve and above the normal one; by this estimate, the crisis caused about 30 million excess deaths from starvation or aggravated disease conditions. In addition, many millions of births were deferred because of the famine conditions. The massive quantities of demographic data published by the Chinese government since the 1982 census all clearly show the large impact of the GLF.

The long-run trends start with a sustained decline in death rates that is quite impressive despite the interruption during the GLF. This rapid sustained reduction

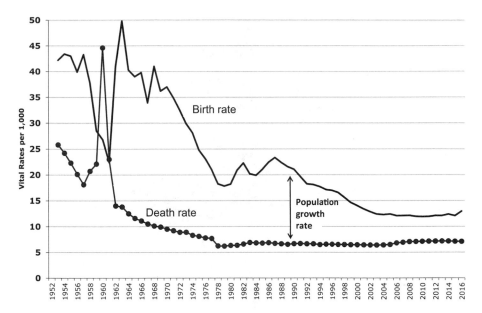

Figure 8.1
Vital rates.
Source: Banister (1987), updated from *SYC*.

in death rates is unusual because it occurred in a very large population that was still at a relatively low level of income. Life expectancy at birth increased substantially from 42 for men in 1950 to 66 (in the 1982 census) and from 46 to 69 for women over the same period. The causes were typical of sustained improvements in population health anywhere in the world: improved sanitation, water supplies, and pest-control and vaccination programs, combined with improved nutrition, particularly for the poorest groups. In China, the governmental emphasis on public health and preventive medicine, combined with a large network of basic-level health-care workers, that is, midwives and "barefoot doctors," made possible this substantial achievement.

As figure 8.1 shows, birthrates stayed high from the early 1950s through 1970, fluctuating in the range of 35 to 45 per 1,000 (except for 1959 to 1961). The peak in 1963 reflects the phenomenon of "replacement births" as households that had postponed births or lost family members during the famine years now had children to make up their desired family size. Through 1970, China resembled most developing countries of that time: consistently high birthrates combined with steadily declining death rates meant that the population was growing extremely rapidly. Population growth peaked in the mid-1960s at nearly 3% per year.

Until 1970, the trends that China experienced with respect to vital rates were rather typical, but there are few precedents for the extremely rapid decline in birthrates that started around 1970. Between 1968 and 1980, China's birthrate declined

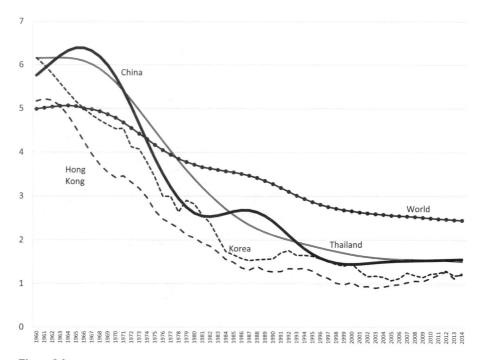

Figure 8.2
Total fertility rate: China in context.
Source: World Bank, World Development Indicators, http://databank.worldbank.org/data/reports.aspx
?source=world-development-indicators, accessed November 30, 2016.

more than half, from 41 to 18. As figure 8.2 shows, total fertility rates dropped
at a similar rate, from over 6 in the 1960s to just 2.6 in 1980. We can recognize
this decline as the ordinary process of the demographic transition, except that it
occurred at a compressed and accelerated rate. The decline was sustained through
the end of the 1990s after which total fertility rates stabilized well below the replacement rate.

Figure 8.2 shows the evolution of China's TFR in comparative context. The period
in the 1970s still looks remarkable because China's TFR dropped from well above
world average rates to well below them in the course of a decade. However, in the
long term and placed in the East Asian context, the Chinese experience looks less
extraordinary. Rapid fertility decline has been a feature of all the successful East
Asian developing countries, and China's decline is quite similar to that of Thailand.
Korea and Hong Kong have even lower rates of fertility than China, but they have
higher income and higher levels of urbanization. From figure 8.2, China is distinctive primarily in that its fertility declined suddenly and at a much lower level of
income than its East Asian neighbors.

The gap between fertility in rural and urban societies is a feature of almost all countries. The low fertility rate in Hong Kong reflects its entirely urban population. Urban areas are crowded, and raising children is costly; in rural areas, space is abundant, and children can contribute to agricultural household income at quite a young age. Farm children as young as six or seven care for pigs, goats, and chickens and start to earn their keep. Rural households have higher target family sizes. Urban society in China has many features that are associated with smaller target family size (cf. chapter 6): relatively high female labor-force participation, high female educational attainment, high educational aspirations for children, good access to health and contraceptive services, and a relatively good social security system. Rural China displays none of these features. Moreover, social controls that enforce prohibitions against multiple births are much stronger in urban areas. China's social and institutional features strongly accentuate the basic urban-rural difference in target family size. The demographic transition in China's cities was correspondingly rapid.

8.3   The Role of Government Policy

Shortly after China's first modern census in 1953, the government initiated modest voluntary family-planning programs, providing contraceptive information and services. However, Mao Zedong was ambivalent about family planning, sometimes arguing that China's big population was an advantage, and family-planning policies were not vigorously pursued. The disaster that followed the Great Leap Forward convinced many in China's leadership that there was a need for birth limitation, and Mao eventually allowed such policies to proceed. The Chinese government launched its first all-out family-planning initiative in 1971. This policy was known as *wan-xi-shao*, or later-longer-fewer, meaning "later marriages, longer spacing between children, and fewer children in total." The legal minimum age of marriage was increased, and couples were urged to wait before having a second or third child. The policy lasted through 1978 and was directed at both urban and rural couples. The introduction of this policy was the key tuning point after which both birthrates and total fertility rates fell dramatically, as shown in figures 8.1 and 8.2. Virtually all the reduction in fertility was the result of fewer births of third and higher order. Through 1979, the probability of a couple having a second child, given that they had already given birth to a first child, was 95% (Feeney and Yu 1987). This could be characterized as a "two-child, but wait" policy.

The success of the later-longer-fewer policy was not sufficient to allay fears of a population crisis. Even with reduced fertility rates, population growth was set to accelerate as China's baby boomers—the large cohorts born between 1962 and 1971—reached marriage age. China's leaders worried that continued population growth would outstrip the nation's population-carrying capacity and obstruct economic development. Moreover, this was the time of greatest international anxiety about population because global population growth peaked in the 1970s. Population "hawks" argued that it was necessary to reduce fertility rates below replacement levels, at least temporarily, in order to break the inexorable momentum of continued population growth and prevent another wave of births. In September 1980, the "One-Child Policy" was adopted with a population target of 1.2 billion in the year 2000.

The One-Child Policy sought to convince Chinese families that the most desirable number of children was one, and it provided an array of sanctions and penalties for women who had two or (especially) more than two children. Implementation of the One-Child Policy was delegated to local governments, and officials at the provincial level and below were evaluated, in part, on their success in lowering population growth rates in their locality (part of the system described in section 5.6). As a result, local officials were under substantial top-down pressure to control births.

The One-Child Policy was immediately controversial, particularly since implementation was extraordinarily strict during the first several years. In 1983, for example, the policy called for mandatory insertion of intrauterine devices (IUDs) for women with one child, sterilization for couples with two or more children, and abortion for unauthorized conceptions. By 1984, domestic resistance and international controversy led the Chinese government to substantially relax the policy, making it what could be more aptly described as a "one-and-a-half-child" policy after 1984. Provincial governments developed implementing legislation that allowed second children to rural couples if their first child was a girl or if hardship factors were involved. The government officially renounced forced sterilization and forced abortion. Local implementation allowed significant regional variations in the One-Child Policy as provincial governments developed implementing legislation that recognized regional differences. In order to avoid charges that China was seeking to control the populations of non-Han ethnic minorities, the One-Child Policy was not applied to minority groups; birthrates for ethnic minorities are about double the rate for Han Chinese. The policy varied between urban and rural areas and across different provinces. After 1991, the policy was again tightened by increasing the salience of birth targets in the local-government evaluation systems and raising penalties.

The One-Child Policy subjected all Chinese households to monitoring of fertility and births. This monitoring was much more intense in urban areas, where work units routinely tracked their female workers' fertility cycles, but it also existed in rural areas. In urban areas, work units might be assigned birth quotas, and couples might sometimes have to wait their turn before being allowed to have even their first child. Couples who pledged to have a single child received a "one-child certificate" that entitled them to various privileges, including preferential access to day care and schooling. Compliance was high in urban areas: more than 86% of urban families had only one child. In rural areas, if a couple became pregnant after their allotted one or two children, they might be subject to pressure from local family-planning workers to abort the fetus. Family-planning workers would visit the couple repeatedly, perhaps daily, trying to persuade them to submit to an abortion. If the couple went ahead with an unauthorized birth, they would incur various penalties. In most provinces, substantial financial penalties, equal to a household's annual income or even more, were levied on families that had a third or fourth child. If families were unable to pay, their belongings might be confiscated or their house might even be knocked down. At the same time, farmers in many areas resisted the One-Child Policy. Births were sometimes hidden, and newborn children were spirited away to be raised by relatives.

The One-Child Policy lasted for 35 years. By the early years of the twenty-first century, a consensus had formed among demographers that the One-Child policy was unnecessarily draconian and was creating long-term problems for Chinese society. Nevertheless, the government delayed action for almost a decade. Finally, in December 2013, couples in which either the father or the mother were only children were allowed to have a second child (couples where both partners were singletons had long been able to have two children). Two years later, this right was extended to all Chinese couples: from January 1, 2016, all Chinese families were allowed to have two children. A historical era had come to an end.

8.4   The Impact of the One-Child Policy and Declining Fertility

The One-Child Policy was controversial from its inception. Proponents described it as a necessary emergency response to a surge in the population at peak childbearing ages. Critics argued that the policy was neither necessary nor appropriate and claimed that the unanticipated consequences of the policy were too severe. Despite the strictness of the One-Child Policy, it was never fully successful. Even during 1983, the year of maximum strictness, 19% of total births were third order and above, and through the mid-1990s, over half of all births were second- or higher-order births. Partially for this reason, China's population exceeded the original target of 1.2 billion in 2000, reaching 1.266 billion in the census that year. Some demographers have argued that a more moderate policy might have been more effective by continuing to provide positive incentives for families to delay births and increasing overall compliance (Bongaarts and Greenhalgh 1985). Indeed, the success of the "later-longer-fewer" policy from 1971 to 1979 demonstrates exactly this point.

8.4.1 Impact on Fertility

The One-Child Policy involved a substantial level of coercion applied by the government against the Chinese population, but the level of coercion varied substantially from region to region. In large cities, the average voluntary target family size probably dropped below the birth limits set by government policy. Chinese demographers have computed an implied policy-permitted total fertility rate for each province, which tells us what the TFR would be in that province if there was perfect compliance with the policy. The lowest is in Shanghai (1.28), and the highest is in Xinjiang (2.4). Around 2000, 13 provinces already had actual TFRs significantly below their policy-permitted TFR, and nearly all of them were in urban and coastal areas where the policy was strictest (Zhang 2003, 68–71). Thus there were significant parts of China where little coercion was required to implement the policy, and other areas where there was substantial resistance. In other provinces—especially poor, rural provinces like Guizhou and Jiangxi—fertility was significantly above what was theoretically permitted by the policy. This regional variation makes clear that the One-Child Policy is not the sole, or even the main, force driving changes in fertility in China today.

Indeed, there are substantial reasons to expect that fertility would be low in today's China even without the One-Child Policy. Other parts of East Asia have experienced extremely rapid fertility decline, and the TFR is below replacement levels in Korea, Taiwan, and Hong Kong. Since the 1980s, China has experienced rapid urbanization and increases in the education levels of both sexes, along with continued high female labor-force participation. These societal trends are associated with low and declining fertility everywhere in the world, and China is unlikely to be different. There are even "experimental zones" within China where the One-Child Policy was never applied; those zones have also experienced rapid reductions in fertility. Reflecting on a regional comparison and other data, Cai (2010, 434) concluded:

China's drive to below-replacement fertility might have been jump-started and accelerated by a heavy-handed government policy, but policy is not the key factor behind the very low fertility that has emerged. … Socioeconomic development plays the decisive role in the transition to below-replacement fertility in China as it does in other societies.

Further confirmation comes from the relatively restrained response to the initial relaxation of the One-Child Policy. It is estimated that in 2014–2015, 11 million couples became newly eligible to have a second child, but only 16% registered their intention to do so. This relatively slow uptake was followed both by the universalization of the two-child policy in 2016 and by a modest policy effort to encourage additional births (Attané 2016). Births did increase by more than a million in 2016, to just below 18 million—about an 8% increase—and are likely to remain at this higher level. Zeng and Hesketh (2016) predict localized surges in some rural areas plus a somewhat higher long-term urban fertility rate, and they project China's peak population will be 46 million greater (and six years later) than it would have been if the One-Child Policy had been retained. Still, the low fertility regime will continue and population will decline after 2029. It is unlikely that China's policy relaxation will trigger a flood of new births.

8.4.2   Underreporting of Births Due to the One-Child Policy

The coercive element of the One-Child Policy evoked a defensive response from Chinese families, especially in rural areas: they underreported births, especially births of baby girls. Rural families and rural officials had no incentive to report births accurately and strong incentives to delay reporting or not to report at all. Children could sometimes be gradually streamed into society, bending the rules and evading punishment. This was especially true for girl births. The most striking evidence for incomplete birth recording is that successive censuses routinely discovered more children aged 10–12 than there were children reported born in the previous census, 10 years before. The result is that all official demographic statistics are made inaccurate by the underreporting of births. According to Wang Feng (2005, 1), the One-Child Policy led to "the collapse of a credible government birth reporting system."

One example of the problems caused has been the difficulty understanding the rapid decline in Chinese fertility during the 1990s. In the 2000 census, the initial calculation of TFR was only 1.22, implying a reduction in fertility that was so fast as to be unbelievable. Officials in the birth-planning agency and the National Bureau of Statistics decided that this result was due to an increase in the number of hidden births and overcorrected to 1.7. Independent demographers in turn criticized the corrected figure for being too high. Ironically, in this debate, the official agencies had the least faith in the official census numbers, perhaps because their interest in defending their official mission and continuing the One-Child Policy. Subsequently, sufficient data have accumulated to support a consensus figure of around 1.5; consensus revisions are shown in figure 8.2. The uncertainty about the true fertility figure doubtless contributed to the delay in ending the One-Child policy.

Use of the official birth numbers leads to inaccurate and understated figures for infant and child mortality (since there are even stronger incentives not to report stillbirths or the birth of sickly children). Thus unadjusted official data on infant mortality and life expectancy at birth are not at all credible or useful. The adjustments necessary to correct life expectancy data for underreporting are quite complex, but efforts have been made by independent demographers to do so. These indicate that life expectancy at birth in China, after increasing rather slowly between the 1982 and 2000 censuses, increased briskly in the first decade of the twenty-first century. Cai

(2013) showed life expectancy at birth increasing from 69.7 to 74.1 for men and from 72.8 to 77.4 for women between 2000 and 2010. This increase of 4 to 5 years within a decade, while not completely unprecedented in international experience, is a strongly positive result. Thus the One Child-Policy distorted the data on which good policy-making should be based and obscured an important public health achievement.

8.4.3   Unbalanced Sex Ratio: Missing Girls

The most important unanticipated impact of the One-Child Policy has been the unbalanced sex ratio due to the Chinese preference for sons. The traditional cultural preference for boys is sustained by the marriage system. Girls "marry out," leaving their home village, while boys remain in the village and often stay in the family homestead. Boys are thus more likely to contribute to the household's income and support their parents in old age. Girls, while they may be willing to help, are at the very least some distance away, are bound to a new family, and have fewer resources and less ability to assist aged parents. Thus boys are culturally and materially more valuable to many peasant households than girls. When this preference for boys collides with government-enforced birth limitations in China, the result is an extremely unbalanced sex ratio.

In most populations, more boys than girls are born. The average ratio is 105–106 boys for every 100 girls, with some normal variation, such that anything between 103 and 110 might be considered within the normal range. In traditional China, female infanticide dramatically skewed this ratio. In the late 1930s, there were more than 120 boys for every 100 girls. Economic and social progress after 1949 brought this imbalance steadily down, so that during the 1960s and 1970s, the sex ratio was well within the normal range (Coale and Banister 1994). Table 8.1 shows the sex ratio at birth as reported in each of China's national censuses. The ratio was normal in 1953 and 1964, but since the early 1980s, the sex ratio has risen steadily and steeply and is clearly outside the normal range.

The sex-ratio data also suffer from the underreporting of births discussed in the previous section. Some of the "missing" girls are in fact "hidden" girls. Demographic

Table 8.1
Reported sex ratio at birth (males per 100 females).

1953	104.9
1964	103.8
1982	107.6
1990	111.8
2000	117.8
2010	118.6

Source: Census Office (2014, 94).

detective work has been stimulated by the discovery that the 2000 and 2010 censuses counted more 10-year-olds than the previous decennial census recorded as births. A majority of these reappearing children are girls, although there are substantial numbers of reappearing boys as well. The 2010 census upset calculations again, though, by showing a larger number of 20-year-olds than had been counted as 10-year-olds in the 2000 census, mostly girls. Provisionally, the explanation seems to be that families defer registering children until they enter middle school. Not reporting higher-order births avoids penalties, and even first or second births might not be reported in order to keep later options open. Local officials turn a blind eye since they are also penalized for excess births, and primary school is typically in the village, while children usually go to the township headquarters for middle school. The 2010 census data seem to show that many families defer registering girls until marriage, when they often leave the village. The raw numbers show almost a million missing girls every year since about 1990; various estimates are that at least one-quarter and perhaps one-third or even half of the unbalanced sex ratio at birth can be explained by selective underreporting of female births (Cai 2013). This still means that half a million girls a year are missing. Sex ratios have also risen in urban areas where surveillance is much tighter and under-reporting unlikely. The most important factor probably is the availability of sex-selective abortion. Since the early 1980s, ultrasound machines, which can determine the sex of the baby in utero, have become widely available in both city and countryside. Although it is illegal for ultrasound technicians to reveal the gender of the fetus, such regulations are easily evaded. Diffusion of ultrasound machines has been associated with worsening gender imbalances in many Asian societies. Under pressure to limit the total number of births per family, many Chinese families appear to make the choice to limit those births to more highly valued male children. Adding to the problem is the fact that child mortality rates for girls are higher than those for boys, a pattern in contrast to that observed in most other societies. Discrimination against female children is a serious problem.

8.4.4   Unbalanced Sex Ratio: Excess Males

Gender imbalance also creates hardship for males, specifically through the operation of the "marriage market." Traditionally, virtually all Chinese women eventually married. Even today, more than 99.5% of women aged 45–49 currently are or previously have been married, and 97% of males (Census 2010, 1862; this cohort was born in the early 1960s, before the unbalanced sex ratio developed). With a norm of nearly universal marriage, the unbalanced sex ratio implies by simple arithmetic that millions of males will be unable to marry. Since the early 1990s, if there have been half a million more males than females born every year, there are well over 10 million excess males in the marriage market. These men will probably never marry (Tucker and Van Hook 2013).

Since women marry "out," and aspire to marry "up," the imbalance implies that men with the lowest income and social status will be unable to find wives. Since women can migrate to make a better marriage, surplus males will be concentrated in rural areas, especially those that are poverty stricken. Poor villages with disproportionate numbers of unmarried males—"bare branch villages"—have already been publicized in the Chinese media. It is argued that discontented males in this position may be more prone to criminality and other social problems. This problem will be exacerbated by the onset of zero population growth. Since males typically marry females a few years younger than themselves, the problem of surplus males will be worse because the pool of marriageable females has been shrinking since 1990. According to Jiang et al. (2011), the imbalance in marriage markets will become much more severe until 2025 as this "shrinking-pool" effect comes into play at the prime marriage ages. The evolution after that depends on whether the imbalanced sex ratio at birth can be corrected.

8.4.5   Further Consequences of the Unbalanced Marriage Market

The unbalanced marriage market has further economic and social implications beyond the frustration of underprivileged males unable to marry. There is intense competition among males for the most eligible females. Wei and Zhang (2009) showed a correlation between household saving rates and the sex imbalance across different regions in China. They argued that sex imbalance pressures males to accumulate savings and often to purchase an apartment in order to demonstrate their value in the marriage market. Parents and other family members may also contribute to this accumulation of assets. In this argument, sex-ratio imbalance is one of the drivers of China's extremely high household saving ratio (cf. chapter 7). A similar effect may be at work in another unusual phenomenon observed in China's marriage market. A country undergoing the kind of social changes China is experiencing typically experiences a narrowing of the age differential between male and female in first marriages. Indeed, this was the Chinese experience through the 1990s. However, since the mid-1990s, the age gap at first marriage has increased again, which is quite unusual. Some argue that the need to demonstrate financial stability in a highly competitive marriage market favors older husbands and drives this social change.

8.5   Changing Age Composition

Changes in birth and death rates have regular and predictable effects on the age composition of the population. These are most immediately visible in a population age pyramid. Figure 8.3 shows the age pyramid of China in 1953. The pyramid is stacked

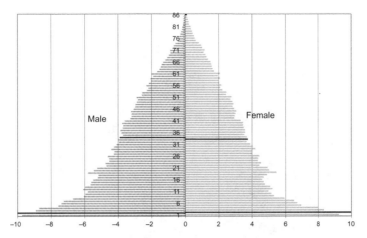

Figure 8.3
1953 population age pyramid.
Source: China 1953 National Census, given in Yao and Yin (1994, table 2-3).

from youngest to oldest, and the width of the horizontal line shows the size of the age cohort of that year. China's 1953 age pyramid is typical of a population in a poor economy: both birthrates and death rates are high, and many babies are born (relative to population size), so the base is broad. Because death rates are high at all ages, the pyramid narrows steadily toward the top.

Figure 8.4 shows China's age pyramid in 2015. The shape is very different from that of a traditional age pyramid and shows clear evidence of the dramatic events that have shaped China's population history. The indent at age 55 shows the impact of the Great Leap Forward, reducing births and raising infant mortality around 1960. Even more striking is the sharp decline in cohort sizes below the age of 25, that is, starting from 1990. The narrowing of the base sharply displays the impact of declining fertility. (Note that these are official data, not adjusted for underreporting, so the bottom layers may actually be 5% broader.) Currently, both of the two bulges are in the workforce, a "baby-boom" generation in its late 40s and early 50s and a "baby-boom-echo" generation in its 20s.

The age pyramid can be thought of as moving upward year by year. Change in the size of the labor force depends on the size of the young age cohorts entering the labor force and the older cohorts retiring from labor. From figure 8.4, it can be seen that China is poised for a prolonged period of declining labor-force size. As the baby-boom generation begins to retire, it will be replaced by young cohorts that are much smaller. Since 2012, the absolute size of the population between the ages of 15 and 64 has plateaued and is now beginning to decline. These shifts will ultimately have a large effect on Chinese society and the Chinese economy.

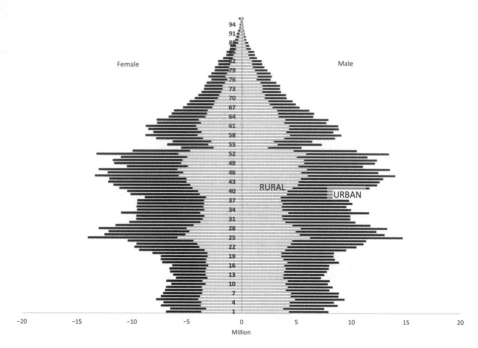

Figure 8.4
2015 population age pyramid: Urban and rural.
Source: National Bureau of Statistics (2016, table 3-1). Data are grossed up from this 1.55% sample of national population.

8.6   Long-Run Trends and Population Aging

Fertility and mortality rates are known and behave in ways that are generally predictable and rule driven, as shown in previous sections. This assumption, combined with the existing structure of the population, allows us to predict long-run changes in the population and labor force with reasonable confidence. For the next 20 to 30 years, that confidence is enhanced because the number of new workers and parents 25 years from now has basically already been determined by the births recorded today. To be sure, there is uncertainty due to imprecise data and lack of clear understanding of what the impact of relaxing the One-Child policy will be, but population is still one of the more predictable aspects of the future.

The rapid growth of the working-age population is already over, and in the future, the working-age population will shrink. During the 1980s and 1990s, the working-age population grew extremely rapidly and significantly more rapidly than the population as a whole. During the 1980s, the working-age population grew 2.5% annually. Moreover, population growth combined with rural-to-urban migration to fuel an

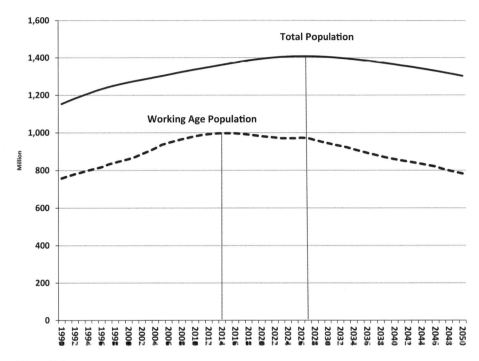

Figure 8.5
Total and working-age population projections.
Source: U.S. Census Bureau International Database, http://www.census.gov/population/international
/data/idb/informationGateway.php, accessed December 15, 2016.

even more rapid growth of the urban labor force, which grew 4.1% per year between 1978 and 2010.

Figure 8.5 shows the evolution of China's total and working-age populations from 1990 through the present and on to 2050. Two obvious turning points stand out. Total population will peak around 2027—slightly later if the response to policy relaxation is bigger—and then begin a long steady decline. The working-age population has already peaked, around 2014, but the decline in available workers will be gradual for another decade. In essence, the working-age population plateaus from about 2010 through 2027, and will then begin to decline fairly quickly, at a rate of a little over 0.5% per year.

Later, an aging population will create substantial strains on China's social system, requiring an effective policy response. It is estimated that the number of Chinese over 65 years old will more than triple from 115 million in 2010 to around 350 million in 2050. By 2030 the elderly will make up approximately 20% of China's population. Rapid population aging essentially echoes the earlier declines in fertility and mortality. In China's case, the impact of the rapid decline in fertility is amplified

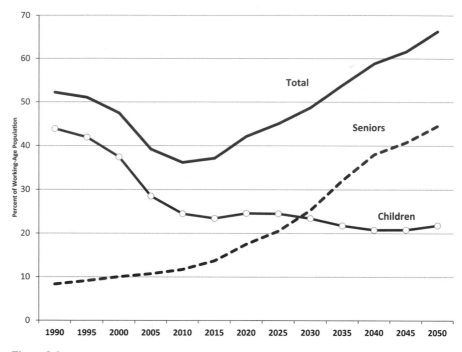

Figure 8.6
Dependency rates.
Source: U.S. Census Bureau International Database, http://www.census.gov/population/international
/data/idb/informationGateway.php, accessed December 15, 2016.

by the mandatory retirement (beginning at age 60 in many sectors) of the eldest baby boomers, which began around 2015.

The current age structure provides a window of opportunity for China's economy. China has the advantage of a young population with low dependency rates; that is, both young and old dependents represent a relatively small share of the population. In 2015, 73% of the population was between the ages of 15 and 64, and 27% was below 15 or over 65. Expressed as a dependency rate, that means each 100 persons of working age supported 37 dependents, young and old. Figure 8.6 shows the dependency rate between 1990 and 2050. China has just reached the end of the extraordinarily trough between 2005 and 2015, during which China's dependency rate was more than 10 points below that of the middle-income average. As shown in figure 8.4, this is because both of the large baby booms are now mainly in the workforce. The youth dependency rate (number of children) has already declined sharply because of the fertility transition described in this chapter, while older dependents (65 and up) are not yet a large segment of the population. The decline in death rates that began in the 1950s is only now leading to an increased share of the elderly.

Table 8.2
Percentage of population age 65 or older.

	2015	2030	2050
China	10.0	17.0	26.7
Hong Kong	15.3	27.4	35.3
Japan	26.6	32.2	40.1
Korea	13.2	24.0	34.7
Taiwan	12.5	23.1	34.9
Vietnam	5.8	11.3	20.7

Source: U.S. Census Bureau International Database, http://www.census.gov/population/international/data/idb/informationGateway.php, accessed December 15, 2016.

Coming changes in dependency rates will lead to lower growth of GDP per capita. This is most obvious for the mechanical effect. From now on, the number of producers in China will stabilize and start to decline. Population growth will continue, but most of the growth will be concentrated in the elderly population. The ratio of producers to total population will decline.

China's aging is similar to that of other East Asian populations. Table 8.2 shows that all major East Asian economies are heading for a sharp increase in their elderly dependency ratios. Indeed, there is a clear succession. Japan is already an elderly society, with 26.6% of its population over 65. Hong Kong, Taiwan, and South Korea are clustered together as societies with very low fertility rates that are beginning the population aging process. China's future looks like a third wave of aging, about 35 years after Japan and 20 years after Hong Kong, Taiwan, and Korea. China's problem is not more severe than that of the others, and China has more time to prepare for the coming changes. At the same time, it is likely that China's per capita income in 2030 will be below that of Hong Kong, Taiwan, and Korea today, so the burden of supporting the elderly may be relatively heavier. Not all countries share the demographic dilemmas of the East Asian miracle economies. Vietnam, for one, is 15 years behind China; the United States is undergoing a more gradual aging process than many societies, and by 2050, its senior share, at 21.6%, is projected to be significantly below that of China.

Currently, most elderly in rural areas primarily rely on their children for financial support, as do a significant minority of urban elderly. Males are much less likely to be dependent on their children than are females, reflecting higher (formal) labor-force participation, more generous pensions (in cities), and greater female longevity. Whether or not the elderly are financially dependent on their children, most live in the same household with them. In rural areas, only 9% of those aged 60 and over do not live in multigenerational households, while in urban areas the figure is 26%. Indeed, children are legally obligated to care for their parents in their old age. This traditional reliance on children will face severe strains as a result of China's declining birthrate. By 2030, the average 65-year-old urban dweller will have only one living child, and the average rural resident of that age will have only 2.3 living children.

Rural and urban areas both face different challenges in dealing with future aging. Rural areas are arguably at a disadvantage. Rural elders are usually not covered by the pension plans that are commonplace in urban areas, have a lower overall income, and face the reality that most of their working-age children have left for urban areas. These three factors result in the rural elderly being more dependent than urban elderly on their own income and financial transfers from their children. In the cities, most workers enjoy some kind of promised pension after they retire. The Chinese government has struggled to set up a functioning and funded pension system, and reforming the pension system has become an important issue. China's pension liabilities are unfunded, meaning that the pensions of currently retired persons are paid from the tax payments of current workers, and almost nothing has been set aside for future retirees (chapter 20). In this respect, China resembles many other countries that are struggling with the implications of population aging for social security and pension programs. However, there is one important difference: Most developed countries grew rich first and then grew old, but China will grow old before it has had the opportunity to grow rich.

8.7   Conclusion

The One-Child Policy has shaped China in many important ways and has had important impacts on its economic development. The policy forced China through the demographic transition at an accelerated pace and created an exceptional demographic window of opportunity for growth during the reform era. At the same time, the policy is responsible for the exceptional severity of problems that will challenge policymakers in the immediate future. It will cause the number of retirees and the future elderly dependent ratio to increase particularly quickly, exacerbating future demographic strains. The One-Child Policy has led to serious gender imbalances that may ultimately cause discontent and further problems

Overall, demographic conditions in China are shifting dramatically just as this book goes to press. Chapter 9 will explore some of the labor-force implications of these changes. What is clear, however, is that the demographic advantages China has enjoyed over the past 20 years are now over; slower labor-force growth and an aging society are the prospects for the foreseeable future. However, these changes have finally brought about the end of the One-Child Policy, so Chinese citizens will have greater scope to choose family arrangements that are more personally satisfying. Individual actions, supported by new institutions and growing affluence, will allow the economy to adapt to these changing conditions.

Bibliography

Suggestions for Further Reading

Wang, Cai, and Gu (2012) is a sharp but fair appraisal of China's policy by three of China's top demographers. Attané and Gu (2014) collects a broad range of interesting articles. Many articles in *Population and Development Review* contain accessible discussions of Chinese demography.

References

Attané, Isabelle (2016). "Second Child Decisions in China." *Population and Development Review* 42:519–536.

Attané, Isabelle, and Baochang Gu, eds. (2014). *Analysing China's Population: Social Change in a New Demographic Era*. Dordrecht: Springer.

Banister, Judith (1987). *China's Changing Population*. Stanford, CA: Stanford University Press.

Bongaarts, John, and Susan Greenhalgh (1985). "An Alternative to the One-Child Policy in China." *Population and Development Review* 11 (4): 585–617.

Cai, Yong (2010). "China's Below-Replacement Fertility: Government Policy or Socioeconomic Development?" *Population and Development Review* 36 (3): 419–440.

Cai, Yong (2013). "China's New Demographic Reality: Learning from the 2010 Census." *Population and Development Review* 39 (3): 371–396.

Census 2010 (2012). Census Office, State Council and Population and Employment Division, National Bureau of Statistics. *Zhongguo 2010 Nian Renkou Pucha Ziliao* [China 2010 census statistics]. 3 vols. Beijing: Zhongguo Tongji.

Census Office, State Council, and Population and Employment Division, National Bureau of Statistics (2014). *Maixiang Xiaokang Shehui de Zhongguo Renkou* [China's population on the way to a moderately prosperous society]. National vol. Beijing: Zhongguo Tongji.

Choukhmane, Taha, Nicolas Coeurdacier, and Keyu Jin (2013). "The One-Child Policy and Household Savings in China." Accessed at http://econ.sciences-po.fr/sites/default/files/file/draft_ocp_130213.pdf.

Coale, A. J., and J. Banister (1994). "Five Decades of Missing Females in China." *Demography* 31 (3): 459–479.

Feeney, G., and Jingyuan Yu (1987). "Period Parity Progression Measures of Fertility in China." *Population Studies* 41 (1): 77–102.

Jiang, Quanbao, J. J. Sanchez-Barricarte, Shuzhuo Li, and Marcus Feldman (2011). "Marriage Squeeze in China's Future." *Asian Population Studies* 7 (3): 177–193.

Mason, Andrew, and Tomoko Kinugasa (2005). "East Asian Economic Development: Two Demographic Dividends." East-West Center Working Papers: Economics Series, no. 83 (June). East-West Center, Honolulu.

National Bureau of Statistics (2016). National Bureau of Statistics Division of Population and Employment. *2015 Nian Quanguo 1% Renkou Chouxiang Diaocha Ziliao* [2015 national 1% population sample survey materials]. Beijing: Zhongguo Tongji.

SYC (Annual). *Zhongguo Tongji Nianjian* [Statistical yearbook of China]. Beijing: Zhongguo Tongji.

Tucker, Catherine, and Jennifer Van Hook (2013). "Surplus Chinese Men: Demographic Determinants of the Sex Ratio at Marriageable Ages in China." *Population and Development Review* 39 (2): 209–229.

Wang, Feng (2005). "Can China Afford to Continue Its One-Child Policy?" *AsiaPacific Issues*, no. 77 (March). Honolulu: East-West Center. Accessed at http://www.eastwestcenter.org/publications/can-china-afford-continue-its-one-child-policy.

Wang, Feng (2010). "The Future of a Demographic Overachiever: Long-Term Implications of the Demographic Transition in China." *Population and Development Review* 37 (Supplement): 173–190.

Wang, Feng, Yong Cai, and Baochang Gu (2012). "Population, Policy, and Politics: How Will History Judge China's One-Child Policy?" *Population and Development Review* 38 (Supplement): 115–129.

Wei, Shang-Jin, and Xiaobo Zhang (2009). "The Competitive Saving Motive: Evidence from Rising Sex Ratios and Savings Rates in China." NBER Working Paper no. 15093, National Bureau of Economic Research, Cambridge, MA, June 18.

Yao Xinwu and Yin Hu, eds. (1994). *Zhongguo Changyong Renkou Shuju* [Frequently used data on China's population]. Beijing: Zhongguo Renkou.

Yi Fuxian (2012). *Daguo Kongchao: Fansi Zhongguo Jihua Shengyu Zhengce* [Big country with an empty nest]. Beijing: Zhongguo fazhan.

Zeng, Yi, and Therese Hesketh (2016). "The Effects of China's Universal Two-Child Policy." *Lancet* 388:1930–1938.

Zhang, Haifeng, Hongliang Zhang, and Junsen Zhang (2015). "Demographic Age Structure and Economic Development: Evidence from Chinese Provinces." *Journal of Comparative Economics* 43:170–185.

Zhang, Shanyu (2003). *Zhongguo Renkou Dili* [China population geography]. Beijing: Kexue Publishing House.

9   Labor and Human Capital

China's 770 million workers make up the world's largest labor force, more workers than in all developed countries put together. As China grows and undergoes massive structural change, the nature of work has changed—and is changing—dramatically. Just 10 or 20 years ago, workers were often engaged in heavy physical labor, especially in the countryside. It was common to see labor power used for tasks better accomplished by machines, such as breaking up rocks and digging ditches, and men and women carrying 70- or 80-pound loads up and down steep hillsides. These sights have by no means disappeared, and most workers are still engaged in repetitious manual labor, but machinery has taken over many of the backbreaking tasks, and labor is less physically wearing than before. Now this workforce is beginning another wave of rapid change as automation is increasing, education levels are rising, and white-collar and service occupations are growing.

China has also gone through one of the most colossal social experiments in history: the all-encompassing *danwei* (work-unit) system was dissolved, and a comprehensive set of labor markets was created. The old system was loosened slightly in the 1980s and then broke down completely in the 1990s under the combined onslaught of two historic events. First, the state enterprise system, staggering under the weight of increasing competition and low productivity, finally crumpled and was rebuilt on a much smaller scale. Between 1996 and 2003, China laid off almost 50 million workers, 40% of the public enterprise workforce. Second, the massive influx of less skilled migrant workers into the cities drove the creation of a completely new set of market institutions. China's contemporary labor economy is founded on these two events.

However costly it was, the creation of functioning labor markets was an essential prerequisite for a prosperous economy. When China entered the reform period, its fundamental comparative advantage was its abundant, low-cost labor. This advantage could be brought into play only if labor could be deployed to new firms and used efficiently; China's return to world markets depended on its ability to quickly scale up labor-intensive manufacturing. Once that was accomplished, the most urgent task was to upskill that labor and move into more sophisticated production tasks. When labor markets work well, they drive this transformation: functional labor markets create jobs that require and reward specific skills and education. Workers have an incentive to get training and education, and businesses have an incentive to seek out and reward workers with greater talent or training.

Today, a further wave of fundamental change is again reshaping labor markets. Rapid growth of the economy—and of the demand for labor—has begun to push up wages for unskilled workers across the board, just as the growth in the supply of unskilled workers has now begun to taper off. Labor markets, having facilitated the emergence of "cheap China," are now signaling its end. This chapter begins with a snapshot of the Chinese labor force. It then covers the institutional transformation of the labor system over the past decades. Subsequently, the question is posed: How well do Chinese labor markets reward productive attributes like education and experience? We examine evidence on returns to human capital and migration. The chapter concludes by directly addressing recent changes in supply and demand and discusses whether the concept of a "Lewis turning point" is a good framework for understanding current changes.

9.1   The Chinese Labor Force Today

China's dynamic workforce is a major source of comparative advantage. China's labor force is young, with a low dependency rate and a high labor-force participation rate for both genders (chapter 8). Moreover, today, China's workers are employed in a diverse set of institutional arrangements, imparting substantial flexibility to the labor economy. As a following section will show, segments of the labor force are also rapidly upskilling. Since much attention has been given to China's future aging problem, it is worth stressing that China's workforce today is quite young, particularly in urban areas. The average age of all urban and rural employed people has been creeping up but was just 39 in 2010, compared with 42 in the United States. The average urban worker is considerably younger than this, only 36, because the urban workforce is continuously replenished by predominantly young migrants from the countryside, and because urban workers retire early. Moreover, urban workers have fewer dependents than do rural workers (31 per 100 urban workers, compared with 52 per 100 rural workers) (Census 2010). This makes for an extremely adaptable urban labor force and reminds us that although China has already reaped most of the gains from the demographic dividend, there is no sudden loss of the benefits of a young, adaptable workforce with a low dependency ratio. Instead, the workforce ages only gradually, and, then, as workers retire, the dependency rate increases.

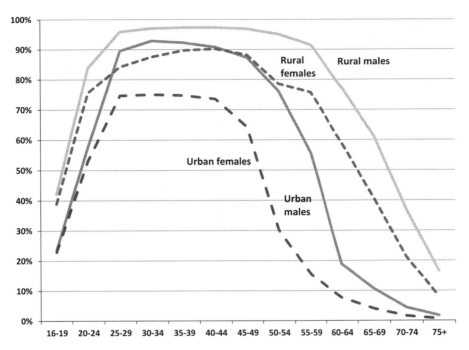

Figure 9.1
Labor-force participation by age.
Source: Census 2010 (2012, 839–841, 847–849).

Figure 9.1 shows employed persons as a share of population at that age. Both men and women have high labor-force participation rates during their peak working years, ranging from 97% for rural men to 75% for urban women. Urban female labor-force participation was substantially higher in the socialist period, but women suffered disproportionately from layoffs from the state sector and now are reducing labor-force participation to take on new roles in the household (Hare 2016). However, labor-force participation by college-educated women is as high as that of men. The expansion of higher education means that urban males and females now enter the labor force on average at age 22, while most rural people are in the labor force by age 19.

Particularly striking is the relatively young age at which urban workers leave the labor market, especially women. During the downsizing of state enterprises at the end of the 1990s, many redundant state firm workers took early retirement, and a norm of early retirement became established in the cities. Most urban women leave the labor force in their early 50s, even before the statutory retirement age of 55. Few urban males work much past 60. In the countryside, there is still essentially no retirement, and most men are still at work in their late 60s. Long working hours should be taken into consideration alongside early retirement: the average workweek was

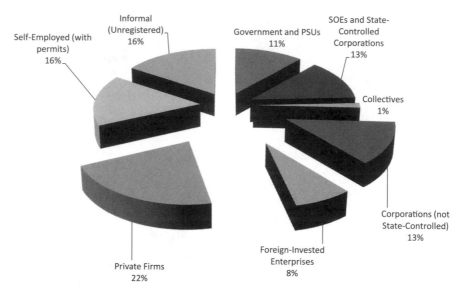

Figure 9.2
Urban employment by ownership, 2013.
Sources: *SYC* (2014) and *Labor Yearbook* (2014).

45 hours in 2010, and 38% of workers put in more than 48 hours a week. Not surprisingly, these workers generally feel that they have earned early retirement.

In 1978, 99% of China's workers were in publicly owned undertakings, and three-quarters of them were still on the farm in agricultural collectives and their associated enterprises. In urban areas, 78% of workers worked for the state and 22% for collective firms. A tiny handful of self-employed tradespeople (150,000), mostly elderly traders or repairmen, had somehow managed to stay independent through 30 years of socialist mobilization. Today, urban employment is diversified among ownership forms and types of occupation. Figure 9.2 shows the main components of 2013 urban employment. These can be grouped into three large categories: the public sector, the formal private sector, and the informal sector. The public sector accounts for exactly one-quarter of urban employment (but a much larger share of permanent residents with urban *hukou*) and has three main components: government, nonprofit public service units (PSUs), and state-owned enterprises (SOEs), including corporations in which the government has a controlling interest. It also includes urban collectives, although they have shrunk to only 1.5% of total employment. The formal, large-scale private business sector accounts for 43% of employment. This includes foreign and domestic corporations (excluding government-controlled firms) and private firms in a variety of legal forms (chapter 14). Finally, there is a substantial small-scale and informal sector, accounting for 32% of total employment.

Houschold businesses registered as "self-employed" are in principle limited to seven employees other than family members. The informal unregistered sector is a residual but corresponds to small businesses that have not bothered to register. Household and unregistered businesses are "informal" in the sense that they are extremely unlikely to participate in social insurance programs, and they pay lower and irregular wages.

9.2   The Institutional Transformation of Chinese Labor

The Maoist system had unusually tight controls over labor. Chapter 6 described how rural-to-urban migration basically stopped after the 1960s, and urban residence became a privileged status. In fact, mobility of all kinds, including job mobility within urban areas, declined sharply. The government assumed direct control over all urban hiring: from the early 1960s onward, the government assigned 95% of high-school or college graduates to work and did not allow enterprises to make hire or fire decisions on their own (Bian 1994). The state decided a worker's job, and a job was for life. Workers could not be fired, but they couldn't quit either. In 1978, 37,000 workers (0.05% of all permanent workers) in all of urban China quit or were fired. This was a very different system from Soviet socialism. In the Soviet Union, manual workers were rarely fired but were free to quit and often did so. The rate of voluntary job turnover in the USSR was more than 200 times that in China (Granick 1987, 109). When economic transition began after 1978, the extreme rigidity of the Chinese system was seen as a severe handicap that slowed the progress of gradualist reforms and hampered the introduction of market forces. After all, the entire urban social system was built around the workplace, so loss of a job meant loss of almost all services and access to the social safety net. In this sense, firing workers would undermine the implicit social contract that tied urban dwellers to the political system and make a mockery of the Communist Party's claim to speak for the working class. Thus the creation of labor markets was one of the most important tasks of reformers, but also one of the most sensitive.

As a result, change initially was slow. Some flexibility was built in on the margins of the system through a system of renewable five-year contracts, but hardly anyone was actually terminated. In fact, total state employment—including state enterprises, public service units, and government jobs—actually increased from 75 million in 1978 to 112 million in 1996. In 1996, 18 years after reforms began, state employment still accounted for the bulk of urban employment, and the features of the first phase of China's gradualist transition strategy were very much in evidence: publicly owned enterprises generated much of the increased employment and output in the economy; reform was "without losers" because state jobs were protected; and marketization began with product markets and only slowly extended to labor markets. Then, starting in the mid-1990s, this whole institutional setup changed dramatically. State-owned enterprises, under increasing competitive pressure, began laying off redundant workers. Figure 5.3 in chapter 5 showed the dramatic decline in state enterprise workers after 1996. If anything in China's transition counts as a "big bang," this was it: the rapid increase in involuntary layoffs and the dramatic downsizing of the state sector.

9.2.1   The Turning Point: State-Sector Downsizing

The broad policy governing state-sector downsizing was "focus on the large, let go of the small" (*zhuada fangxiao*; see chapter 14). In practice, that meant that the central government directly managed the restructuring of several hundred large state firms but left decision-making about the tens of thousands of medium- and small-sized firms at the local level. Local decision-makers, comprising enterprise managers, immediate government supervisors, and local mayors and governors, responded to competitive pressures, massive losses, and (potentially) the opportunities for privatization. Not surprisingly, the process was decentralized, uncoordinated, and sometimes chaotic. Yet at the same time, the handling of the large number of laid-off SOE workers was a massive attempt at social engineering. Substantial cost and effort were expended to buffer SOE workers from the immediate shock of unemployment; "surplus workers" were designated "laid off" (*xiagang*) and were then transferred to the jurisdiction of newly created reemployment centers (RECs), designed to provide retraining and job-search assistance. Perhaps more crucially, the REC became a substitute work unit that paid into the worker's social security and welfare funds and typically provided a stipend to the worker for a maximum of three years. In a prosperous city like Shanghai or Beijing, this system meant that a redundant worker could receive as much as five years of transitional assistance and support as he or she was gradually eased out of state employment. Less prosperous cities, however, were not usually able to maintain a high standard of support. Actual outcomes varied, and overall, laid-off workers experienced dramatic reductions in their income and standard of living (Appleton et al. 2002).

Figure 9.3 lays out the broad patterns of change that led to almost 50 million people losing jobs in state and urban collective enterprises. The vertical bars show the number of enterprise workers laid off during each year (official data from 1997; estimated data through 1996). Layoffs averaged 7.2 million per year for the peak four years, 1996 through 1999. In total, just shy of 50 million workers were laid off between 1993 and 2003 from SOEs, urban collective enterprises, and public service undertakings. The year 2003 was the final year of mass layoffs, and after that, public enterprise employment stabilized.

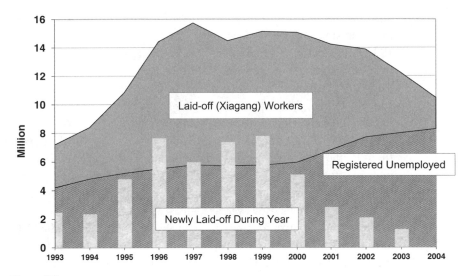

Figure 9.3
Laid-off and unemployed workers.
Sources: *Labor Yearbook* (1996–2004); *Labor and Social Security Yearbook* (2004, 478); Yang Yiyong
(1997); Mo Rong (1998).

9.2.2   Unemployment

The layoffs in the years 1993–2003 led to a serious problem of open unemployment.
It was the third episode of unemployment in the People's Republic, after the 1950s,
when China had struggled to find work for all, and in 1978–1980, when sent-down
youths returned to the city and needed work. Outside these episodes, China had been
able to essentially export the employment problem to the countryside by preventing
migration to the cities despite a steadily growing urban economy that created new
jobs. It was easy to assign all urban school-leavers, male and female, to a job. Rapid
labor-force growth in the 1980s, combined with liberalization of labor and product
markets, gradually changed this setup by the mid-1990s. The shaded areas in Figure 9.3 show the stock of unemployed workers during the years 1993–2004 in two
categories. Formally, "laid-off" workers were in a different category from "unemployed" workers. Only when these two categories are combined do we get a reasonably accurate count of China's urban unemployed. This measure of urban unemployed
peaked at almost 16 million in 1997 and stayed elevated for five years, slipping just
below 14 million in 2002. Thus China's urban unemployment rate peaked at 10% of
urban workers (with urban residence permits) and stayed above 8% for about five
years. For an urban population accustomed to full employment, this was a big shock.
In some regions of China, unemployment became a major social issue. In the far
northeastern province of Heilongjiang, with a stagnant economy and a legacy of huge

and uncompetitive heavy industrial plants, unemployment was high, and the RECs provided stipends to laid-off workers equal to only 6% of the average SOE wage in 1997, compared with 43% in Shanghai. Heilongjiang was not able to meet its existing pension obligations, and half a million SOE retirees went unpaid in 1997 (Mo Rong 1998). Large-scale protests forced the central government to step in and assume some of Heilongjiang's pension obligations. Other cities in China were in between the Shanghai and Heilongjiang extremes.

After 2003, China's accelerating economy began to mop up the urban unemployed. In 2005, those laid-off workers who still had not found work were streamed back into the official unemployed category. To be sure, millions of workers who took early retirement either stayed out of the workforce altogether or moved into the informal sector for casual jobs. However, as China's export boom took off after entry into the World Trade Organization, the economy absorbed most of the idled labor, as well as millions of rural-to-urban migrants. On the eve of the global financial crisis in 2009, the economy was back to full employment, and the shock to labor demand from the crisis in the end was moderate. In fact, it appears that the influx of migrant workers has provided urban labor markets with a new adjustment mechanism—when the economy slows, migrant workers are the first to feel the brunt and may be sent (or choose to go) back to their home villages. In this way, the jobs of formal urban employees again have a degree of stability they appeared to have lost in the 1990s. Slower growth of the labor supply has also helped keep registered urban unemployment low.

9.2.3   Migrant Workers

As described in chapter 6, rural migrants began to stream into the cities in the 1990s at a pace that accelerated in the twenty-first century. Migrants have filled an increasingly broad spectrum of jobs. At first, migrant workers filled a few niches in the urban economy, working on construction gangs and as peddlers and food sellers. However, as the urban economy grew and restructured, demand for migrant labor grew as well. It is common to characterize migrant jobs as "unskilled," but we must be careful. By "unskilled." we increasingly mean "without much formal education." Today, young rural-to-urban migrants in China are universally literate, almost all have lower-middle-school education, and a substantial proportion have high-school and even some college education. These are "unskilled" workers with computers and smartphones. Moreover, they have aspirations that are completely different from the "unskilled migrants" of 20 or 30 years ago.

Migrants find employment through an enormous range of occupational arrangements. However, 94% of those outside their home township work for wages; only 6% run their own businesses. Manufacturing is the biggest employer (35%), especially in the export-oriented regions of the coast. Labor-intensive factories ranging from tiny to enormous rely on migrant labor. One extreme case is the Foxconn complex in Longhua, Shenzhen, with 230,000 workers, 90% of whom are young female migrants from the countryside. Construction is the second-biggest migrant employer (23.5%), employing mainly men. Retail, food services, and household services together account for another 24.5% (NBS Migrant).

Migrant workers have gradually become important in most sectors of the urban economy. Many of these jobs have in common the fact that it is possible to show up one day and be working the next day. There are vigorous spot markets for workers. This does not mean that workers in the informal sector always find work on their own; there are important market intermediaries who facilitate employment. These include government-run employment centers, labor "gang" leaders who recruit construction teams, and roving employment agents for big factories. These markets are characterized by a great diversity of forms, high fluidity, and rapid turnover.

9.2.4 Evolution of Urban Labor Markets: Segmented Markets

Thus there is now a division within the urban labor force that, to some extent, mirrors and replaces the old division between urban and rural workers. The overall contours of this development can be seen from the aggregate urban employment numbers. Although those numbers are not very accurate in their coverage of the informal sector, they still provide a clear picture of the emerging reality.

Figure 9.4 shows the evolution of urban employment according to official data. Quite a few striking trends emerge: The absolute number of government employees and workers in public service units (*shiye danwei*) has hardly changed, growing slowly but steadily over the last decade. State and collective enterprises have shrunk dramatically, while a group here labeled "new corporate" has increased. These new corporate forms include modern limited-liability and joint-stock companies, as well as a few other idiosyncratic transitional forms. The government has a controlling stake in many of the larger "new corporate" firms. Thus in 2011, of a total of 46 million workers in this category, 20 million worked in firms controlled by the government (chapter 14).

As a first approximation, it makes sense to group all these new corporate forms, along with state and collective enterprises, government employees, and urban foreign-invested firms (FIEs), into a single large-scale government and corporate sector, which for convenience we call the urban formal sector. In this sector, almost all workers are covered by social security and other welfare provisions, and most have urban *hukou*. (This category excludes registered private firms, most of which are small. Some privately owned firms are large, but these are most likely registered as limited-liability corporations, in which case they are included in "new corporate" employment.) The urban formal sector, in this definition, declined from 152 million

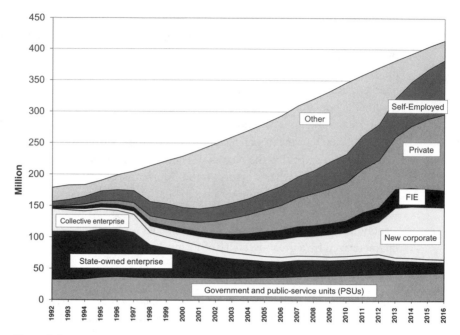

Figure 9.4
Urban labor force by ownership and registration.
Source: *SYC* (2016).

in 1996 to only 105.5 million in 2003, in the wake of the state-sector downsizing described earlier. However, since 2003, employment in this sector has rebounded, at first gradually and then jumping to 180 million in 2012–2015.

The bulk of the growth in the urban labor market—which doubled from 200 to 400 million between 1996 and 2015—has occurred in the private, self-employed, and "other" categories. These three categories make up the informal (or "semiformal") sector, where most workers are not covered by social security and do not have urban *hukou*. "Other" employment simply represents workers who are known to exist because surveys and census investigations reveal the size of the overall urban workforce, but who are not enumerated in any of the registered organizational forms. The total size of the informal sector—private, self-employed, and other—surpassed that of the urban formal sector in 2000 and by 2015 had grown to 226 million. Since 2009, the National Bureau of Statistics has published data on wages that break down the aggregate into two categories, which it calls "private" and "nonprivate." In the private category—which includes mostly people in the informal sector, but also a few private limited-liability corporations—the average annual wage in 2015 was just under 40,000 yuan. In the nonprivate category, which includes publicly held corporations as well as government, PSUs, and SOEs—the annual wage was 62,000 yuan (this is the same number regularly reported as the "urban wage"). The private wage has been inching up as a share of the nonprivate wage, from 55.6% in 2009 to 64% in 2015. This may reflect a compression of skilled/unskilled wage ratios (see section 9.7), but may simply be a classification effect, since a larger share of private employment is now in the organized corporate sector. Manufacturing and construction make up 45% of the sampled private labor force (NBS Private 2015).

Migrants and urban dwellers generally exist in separate labor markets, with migrants in the informal and urban permanent residents in the formal sector. Migrants dominate certain job sectors, such as construction and textile mills, where labor is particularly tiring or boring and urban workers lack interest. In these areas, firms prefer to hire rural migrants, who are much cheaper and have a reputation as harder workers. In general, urban residents with urban household registrations prefer white-collar occupations where the work is less tiring and dirty, and where they can use their educational skills. Meng, Shen, and Xue (2013) document dramatic change in the occupational distribution of urban workers with urban household registration. In 1988, 40% of urban *hukou* holders were production workers, but this had declined to 27% by 2009; the proportion of clerical or service workers increased from under 30% to almost 45% over the same period. Thus, urban *hukou* workers moved out of the jobs that migrants took on. A segmented labor market emerged in cities that reproduced some of the features of the old urban-rural divide.

The Chinese government has been pushing to incorporate more of the urban economy, especially urban labor markets, into the formal regulatory system. The 2008 Labor Law required all employers to provide labor contracts, limited arbitrary layoffs, and required employees to participate in social insurance. Implementation of the provisions has been slow, however. Many businessmen argue that they push up labor costs too much just at the time when wages are rising rapidly. Since 2013, the government has made registration requirements for businesses less burdensome and thus has increased the incentives for new and existing businesses to register. As a result, the line between formal and informal may be changing. Figure 9.4 shows a sharp spike in both new corporate and private firm employment in 2013. Despite dramatic change in labor markets, many permanent urban residents have continued to have somewhat protected jobs in the formal sector, while a massive flood of new migrants has populated the informal sector.

9.3   How Well Do Labor Markets Function in China Today?

Labor-market institutions have changed dramatically in China. How well do they function today? What attributes do they reward? Labor markets are a very particular type of market because they must match not just individuals and job slots but also specific skills and capabilities with the needs of specific positions. "Friction" is uniquely high in this market because people make decisions about acquiring skills, gaining experience, and bearing risk that are based on very incomplete information and have long time lags. Over time, some formal skills are honed by practice and become even more valuable, while other skills obsolesce quickly in the face of changing circumstances. Moreover, changing jobs is very costly because it is risky and involves abandoning job-specific human capital, so transaction costs in the market are high. Labor markets thus violate the simplifying assumption that economists often make about market transactions, namely, that market decisions are made with full information and zero transaction costs.

But if labor markets are uniquely noisy, they are also uniquely powerful. Labor-market decisions affect an individual throughout life and directly affect quality of life. Moreover, because careers are cumulative, building on early achievements, labor-market conditions early in a person's career have an impact on progress and income throughout that person's working life. Even when their operation is less than transparent; even when we are unaware of them, labor markets are usually at work and have a powerful impact on our lives. In this context, China presents a remarkable test case. China went from having essentially no labor market to having robust labor markets within about 25 years. How did this dramatic institutional change affect labor-market outcomes?

9.3.1   Mincer Wage Models

An efficient labor market rewards a more productive worker. However, productivity is almost never directly observable. An individual will be more productive to the extent that he or she is adaptive, clever, and cooperative, qualities that cannot be directly measured and sometimes cannot even be clearly perceived by outsiders. However, even allowing for the importance of these unobservable traits, we can gain a great deal of understanding about labor markets by measuring the importance of various observable traits. The most important analytic tool for doing this is Mincerian wage regression, named for the economist Jacob Mincer, who pioneered the approach. For a large cross section of individuals, Mincer regressed wages on a set of explanatory variables, including years of education. The Mincerian return to education was the coefficient on the worker's years of education. (Using data from the 1950 and 1960 censuses, Mincer found that an additional year of education increased the wage of a U.S. worker by between 5% and 10%.) The same approach can be used to investigate the value of other attributes, including seniority, gender, and on-the-job training.

The Mincerian model has simplicity and explanatory power. Large data sets can be brought to bear relatively easily. Moreover, data from various sources, including household surveys, can be used, so issues of selection bias and possibilities of intentional distortion of official data can be identified and avoided. This is particularly important in the Chinese context. Finally, Mincerian models have been estimated for many economies, with stable and consistent results. In this chapter, the Mincerian relationship will be used for three purposes: (1) to provide information about market institutions and their outcomes; (2) to shed light on the incentives labor markets provide to individuals, particularly in regard to their decision to invest in those attributes with the highest return; and (3) to analyze the determinants of income distribution and inequality.

The biggest challenge in using a Mincerian model is interpreting coefficients, given that the observable attribute may often signal the presence of some unobservable individual characteristics. For example, in the case of education, we may be estimating the value of a signal that indicates innate intelligence rather than the return to investing in education. These issues need to be kept in mind in the subsequent discussion. However, the approach retains its value even if one allows for some variability in interpretation. In the following sections, we examine the evidence with respect to returns to education and then briefly examine three other attributes that might be related to worker productivity: experience, Communist Party membership, and gender.

9.3.2   Returns to Education: The Knowledge Premium

The socialist system provided basic education to the population at public expense and spread literacy and basic industrial skills. However, that system did a very poor job of rewarding individuals who had attained higher levels of skills or education. When researchers began to study the determinants of urban incomes in China at the end of the planned-economy period (in the late 1970s and early 1980s), they found that incomes were not consistently higher among individuals with more education. Other correlates of higher income were significant: Communist Party membership, being male, and having more seniority on the job were all associated with higher incomes. But education did not significantly increase income. The private return to education was very close to zero.

This result revealed how inconsistent China's system was at that time with a fully functioning market economy. Perhaps the most fundamental requirement of a well-functioning market economy is that a person be able to feel secure that she will be able to reap the income created by an investment she makes, so long as that investment succeeds in creating new output and income. Investment in education—in human capital—increases the overall productivity of the economy. For a market economy to function, an investment that a person makes that increases social productivity must also provide an individual reward to that person. Only in that case will people have an incentive to make socially productive investments. Since education is expensive, it is unlikely that the government could bear the whole cost, even if it wanted

to; individual households will inevitably bear a substantial part of the cost of education. Thus a positive and significant private return to education is essential for the
continued healthy investment necessary for a more productive economy. The return
to education is also a useful index of the extent to which labor markets have developed and are able to provide adequate rewards to those who invest in human capital.

An extensive literature has examined the changing returns to education in urban
China. A consistent result from this literature is that the rate of return to education
began to climb in the early 1990s and sustained an important increase during the
next decade. Zhang et al. (2005) traced the return to education in urban China from
1988 through 2001, using annual data; and Ge and Yang (2011; figure 9.5) updated
the results through 2007. Ge and Yang showed that in the late 1980s and early 1990s,
an urban worker would improve his income by less than 4% per year for each additional year of schooling he completed. This was far below the U.S. level of 9% at
that time. In the early 1990s, the measured return to education began a sustained
rise to slightly over 11% per year, converging with the U.S. level (which also increased,
but much more modestly, to 11% by the turn of the century). Note that returns to
education are not necessarily higher in developed countries; in poor countries,

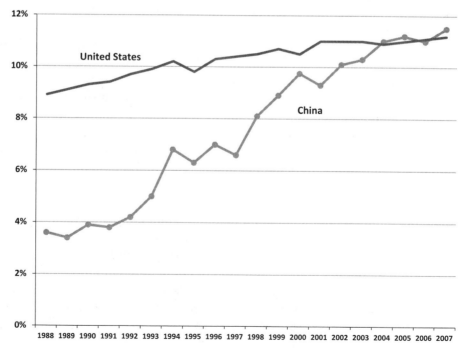

Figure 9.5
Rate of return to additional year of education, urban China and the United States, 1988–2007.
Source: Ge and Yang (2011).

education is scarcer, so there are reasons to expect it to be more valuable. In their survey of many country studies, Psacharopoulos and Patrinos (2002) found that the average return to a year of schooling was 9.7%, but the rate was systematically higher in low-income countries (10.9%). In any case, from about 2000, China's measured rate of return was close to 10%, near world averages. Meng (2012) reported a decline in the rate of return in 2008–2009, which may have been due to the large number of new college graduates entering labor markets. However, Hu and Hibel (2014) found that returns to a college degree were higher in 2010 than in 2003.

In China, as in other economies, some of the estimated return to education is in fact a function of signaling of innate abilities. Appleton, Song, and Xia (2005) exploited an especially rich data set that covered urban incomes in four benchmark years from 1988 to 2002. They found that the return to education estimated in cross section increased from 3.6% in 1988 to 7.5% in 2002, roughly consistent with the results of Zhang et al. With their (panel) data set, they were able to control for unobserved individual attributes (fixed effects) and occupational effects, which lower the measured return to education. Li, Liu, and Zhang (2012) went further by using a data set of several hundred sets of twins to control for unobserved attributes (since twins share family background and their native intelligence is highly correlated). They found that if they accounted for common fixed effects between twin pairs, the return to a year of education declined—roughly as expected—from 8.4% to 3.8%. They argued that in China, secondary education in particular has a rote-learning, exam orientation that serves to select individuals for college rather than improve productivity. By contrast, university and vocational education both appear to serve a productivity-enhancing purpose.

These results are consistent with increasingly competitive labor markets. They show Chinese labor markets overcoming an obvious distortion in their functioning that the planned-economy era bequeathed to them. How did this dramatic change take place? During the 1990s, new higher-income jobs became available for the most educated workers. For example, it is widely accepted that foreign-invested firms have bid up the wages of educated urban workers. Foreign-invested firms consider a wide range of skills valuable, including management and English proficiency, and their bids put upward pressure on the wages of more educated workers (Guo and Sun 2014). During the same period, the "iron rice bowl" was broken; the secure and stable income previously available to everyone was lost, and less educated workers were significantly more likely to be laid off and experience drastic reductions in income. In one important study, each year of education was found to reduce the likelihood of being laid off by one percentage point (Appleton et al. 2002). Thus layoffs put downward pressure on the income of less educated workers.

The increase in the return to education provides incentives for individuals to invest in their own human capital and contributes substantially to the accumulation of skills necessary to the economy. Note that the increase in the return to education in itself does not indicate that the supply of educated workers is increasing; in the market for skill, as in any other market, an increase in supply would be expected to reduce the equilibrium price. The increasing knowledge premium thus either indicates an increase in the demand for skill as China moves toward an increasingly skill-intensive economy or, more fundamentally, a development of market institutions that allows specific skills to be matched to the needs for them, and the owners of these skills to be appropriately compensated.

9.4   Human Capital and Educational Attainment

Labor markets now reward workers for having more education. What is the evidence on the accumulation of human capital in China? Have workers in fact increased their educational attainment? Table 9.1 shows the educational attainment of the Chinese population in benchmark years.[1] When China emerged from the Cultural Revolution, it was a low-income country with an unusual pattern of educational attainment. The 1982 census, conducted at the beginning of the reform era (see column 1 of table 9.1), showed that basic education was fairly widespread for a low-income country, with two-thirds of the adult population having received some formal schooling. One-third of the population was illiterate or semiliterate, but this was significantly less than India, for example, where more than half the population at this time was illiterate. However, less than 11% of the Chinese population had attended upper-middle school, and less than 1% had any college education at all. India at this time had three times as many college graduates per capita as China. Thus, although China's percentage of illiterates was significantly below that of India, so was the percentage of college graduates.

During the reform era, investment in education has grown rapidly, particularly in higher education. In reaction to the egalitarianism of the Cultural Revolution, educational resources in primary education, particularly in rural areas, were neglected during the 1980s and 1990s. This resulted in some regression in rural areas until the government began to place more effective emphasis on basic education in the late 1990s. A program was adopted to make nine years of education compulsory and to eliminate illiteracy among young people, initially in those counties with sufficient economic development and budgetary resources to support the effort on their own. After about 2005, the program was dramatically expanded in an attempt to achieve truly universal coverage. These programs have reduced the proportion of adults with

---

1. The categories in table 9.1 are defined in an inclusive manner that tends to overstate overall educational attainment. Each category includes partial attainment, so attendance for a year or two is sufficient to be placed in a category: graduation is not required. Moreover, a large part of tertiary education consists of three-year junior colleges and technical schools. China also has extensive degree-granting adult education programs that are included.

Table 9.1
Educational attainment of the Chinese population (percent).

Population, 15 and above	1982	1990	2000	2010	2015
Tertiary (above grade 12)	0.9	1.7	4.7	11.0	14.9
Upper-middle (up to grade 12)	10.0	9.4	14.4	16.1	18.2
Lower-middle (up to grade 9)	23.8	27.2	39.1	42.4	39.9
Primary (up to grade 6)	30.8	43.2	32.9	24.1	21.0
No formal schooling	34.5	18.5	9.0	6.4	6.0

Urban employed, 2015				
Tertiary (above grade 12)	32.2		Postgraduate education	1.9
		OF WHICH:	Four-year university	14.4
			Technical school	15.9
Upper-middle (up to grade 12)	25.6			
Lower-middle (up to grade 9)	34.0			
Primary (up to grade 6)	7.5			
No formal schooling	0.6			

Sources: Census 2010; Census 2015.

no schooling or just a few years of elementary school. In related fashion, illiteracy has declined to 2.9% of males and 8.0% of females by 2015 (Census 2015).

At the top of the educational pyramid, progress has been extremely rapid since the end of the 1990s. From 2001 through 2011, the total number graduating from college jumped from 1 million to 6 million, and continued to grow more slowly thereafter. The census results in table 9.1 show the dramatic increase in the share of the population with some college education, which increased fifteenfold in the 33 years from 1982 to 2015. With about 15% of its population now with some higher education, China has surged past India, even though that country is also rapidly expanding its higher education.

Nevertheless, people with skills and education remain in comparatively short supply. The figures for "college" include many with a few years of training at technical schools, and the gap with developed countries is still very large. In the United States, 84% of the population above 25 years old are high-school graduates, 52% have some college, and 26.7% have completed four or more years of college (U.S. Census Bureau). In China's large cities, though, the gap with the United States is much smaller. The bottom panel of table 9.1 shows the educational attainment of workers in China's cities: 32% of urban workers have some college. Because of China's huge population, it is able to provide adequate numbers of skilled individuals to support rapidly growing high-skill sectors in urban areas (see chapter 15).

The average level of skills in China is still low. Even in 2015, two-thirds of China's workers have a ninth-grade education or less. China is a middle-income country and still has a shortage of a broad range of productive skills, even though it is building those skills at a rapid pace. More worrisome is the increasing educational gap between urban and rural. In urban areas today, almost all students graduate from high school ("upper middle"), and almost half of these go on to some kind of post-secondary education; in rural areas, even today, only half of students graduate from upper middle school, and a very small share of those go on to college (Khor et al. 2016 discussed the issue and showed that Ministry of Education figures overestimate rural secondary-school attendance). The modal attainment of a junior high school ("lower middle") education in China's rural areas is adequate to equip a migrant for unskilled work in the city today, but it is utterly inadequate for China's future high-skilled economy. Because 70% of China's school-age children are rural, this is a pressing issue for Chinese policy-makers.

In a broader sense, economic development depends on the accumulation of human capital just as surely as it depends on the construction of physical capital. As a government planning document put it, "Accelerating the development of education is the basic path to converting the enormous pressure of population in our country into the comparative advantage of abundant human resources" (Eleventh Plan Suggestions 2005, section 30). China has already taken the first big step in this direction by dramatically increasing the human capital with which new urban labor-force entrants are equipped, creating a large stream of high-quality human resources. The second big step is to upgrade the human capital that rural labor-force entrants possess in equally dramatic fashion, thereby raising the skill level of the entire young workforce. To ensure this occurring, the national government will probably need to fund universal primary—and perhaps secondary—education. The third step—which inevitably takes more time—is the diffusion of skills through the entire workforce as young workers gain experience and maturity, as older less-educated workers retire, and as adult education and on-the-job training raise the skill of middle-aged workers. In this sense, human capital is a crucial input into development, but the effort to increase the human capital of every single worker is one that extends over an extraordinarily long time. Indeed, it is coterminous with the entire development process, transforming a population and a workforce over a period of more than a hundred years.

9.5   Returns to Other Attributes

Education is prima facie productive, but the impact of other worker characteristics on productivity is more ambiguous. Work experience—virtually identical to age in China—was amply rewarded in socialist China in what was essentially a seniority wage system. During the reform era, the returns to experience have declined moderately but have not disappeared (Appleton, Song, and Xia 2005; Zhang et al. 2005;

Zhou 2000). This change seems consistent with greater market competition: on the one hand, skills acquired by young people have become more valuable, and some of the on-the-job experience of older people has become obsolete; on the other hand, expertise and productivity do still increase with years on the job. Meng (2012) showed that the returns to job tenure were declining in absolute size and peaking earlier (at 20 years of experience rather than 30). Age and experience are less rewarded in a dynamic and changing technological and market environment.

In socialist China, membership in the Communist Party was rewarded with a significant income differential. Just as it was natural to anticipate that marketization would bring an increase in the return to education, it also seemed natural to most analysts that marketization would bring about a decrease in the return to Communist Party membership. In fact, this has not happened. Both Appleton, Song, and Xia (2005) and Zhou (2000) found that returns to party membership increased during the reform era. According to Appleton, Song, and Xia, the premium increased from 7% to 20% between 1988 and 1999 before falling back slightly in 2002. Does this result indicate that Communist Party members have all along had knowledge and skills that have become more valuable during the era of marketization? Or does it mean that Communist Party members today enjoy opportunities to intervene in the market economy for personal profit? Another interpretation relies on the information signaled to the marked by party membership. Li et al. (2007) point out that the Communist Party carries out a demanding selection process and intentionally tries to select elite individuals (the "Three Represents"). They found that the return to party membership was around 10%, but that this return disappeared entirely when they used a twin study to control for unobserved attributes (such as intelligence or diligence). The simplest explanation for this pattern is that the party selects members based on intrinsic characteristics that are correlated with superior income-earning capability. In any case, party membership helps signal those characteristics to the market, so Communist Party membership continues to have positive economic benefits for individuals.

During the socialist period, gender gaps in wages were relatively modest. Although women were underrepresented in management, the system was one of "equal pay for equal work." Appleton, Song, and Xia (2005) found that the gender gap—the difference of male and female wages for comparable levels of experience and education—increased from 12% in 1988 to 22% in 1999 before falling back to 19% in 2002 (compared with 25% in the United States in 2000). Numerous studies have shown variations on this pattern. Meng (2012) found that the gender gap increased from 8% in 1988 to 23% in 2007. To the extent that the gender gap results from discrimination, it represents a failure of the competitive marketplace. The widening of the gender gap presumably explains some of the reduction in female labor-force participation described earlier. Women were more likely than men to be laid off from state firms during their restructuring. On the other hand, women enjoy a slightly higher skill premium than men. This means that gender discrimination is stronger in low-skill occupations and diminishes in relative terms as workers move into higher-skill occupations. Since about 2007, women have made up slightly more than half of all college students, hopefully indicating that female graduates are well positioned to become better-educated workers and reduce the persistent gender gap in the future.

9.6   Labor-Market Segmentation: A Deeper Look

The Mincerian framework introduced earlier can be used to take a closer look at the segmentation of urban labor markets. In general, two populations can be compared in terms of both the attributes they possess and the return they receive for those attributes. Rural-to-urban migrants face barriers and restrictions on their occupation choice. As a result, the return to attributes in migrants' particular segments of the urban labor market may be different from that of workers with a *hukou* (urban residence permit). For example, migrants are less educated, but they also experience a lower return to education (a lower skill premium) than permanent urban residents. Xue, Gao, and Guo (2014) estimated a model of migrant wages based on a large survey for 2005 and 2010. They found that participation in the informal sector resulted in a 23% lower hourly wage; in addition, even within the informal sector, those without an urban residence permit had 7.6% lower wages. Migrants have lower education levels and this explains over a third (37%) of the earnings differential. In addition, however, migrants earn a lower skill premium for the education they do have: a year of education increased wages only 4.6% in the informal sector but 9.6% in the formal sector in 2010. Thus, the lower return to skill and the residence permit penalty explain more of the earnings gap than the education differential. Not all estimates agree with this striking conclusion, and work is ongoing in the search for consensus. The potential policy implications are significant: if the return to education for migrants is lower, they have less incentive to invest in education, and policies designed to encourage education may be ineffective. Conversely, policies to reduce the degree of discrimination in labor markets have a wider scope to succeed.

9.7   The Migration Decision

Having examined the return to different worker characteristics or attributes, we are now in a position to return to the phenomenon of rural-to-urban migration, described in chapter 6, and examine the individual decision-making process more closely. Migrants move in search of opportunity, seeking higher incomes. Thus we expect the income differential between urban wages and rural incomes to be the most important factor explaining migration. In addition, a basic premise is that households rather than individuals make the decision to migrate. Migration is initially costly, and households must subsidize the start-up costs of out-migration, typically of a young adult household member. They do so because they expect that migration will bring long-run benefits to the household. Thus, although the individual income gap between the urban wage and the return to farming is the right starting point for understanding rural-to-urban migration, it is only the beginning. For example, Taylor, Rozelle, and de Brauw (2003) found that an additional family worker increased the chance that an individual would migrate in the 1990s by 28% because a larger family was able to support the migrant's initial costs and could more easily sustain agricultural production.

Unique institutional features in China also shape the migration decision. At the place of origin, ties to the land continue to be strong because landownership is to some degree contingent on farmers using the land. Migrants worry about de facto "use it or lose it" policies over collective land (chapter 6). At the place of destination, the household registration system in China raises the costs and risks of living in the city, making it much more expensive to settle down. Moreover, as discussed earlier, the urban labor market is strongly segmented, and some occupations are still not open to migrants. For these reasons, we might expect Chinese migration to take the form of "sojourning," that is, medium-term residence in the city, followed by a return to the native place. Migration everywhere is characterized by a significant share of sojourning, but if this phenomenon turns out to be even more important in China, it may have a significant impact on urban and rural development patterns.

In fact, we observe that migrants often return to their place of origin, in part to fulfill long-term life goals, such as marriage and raising children (Hare 1999). How should we understand these returned migrants? Do they represent those who have failed in the city and now retreat to their native place? Or do they represent relatively well-educated residents who return with new experiences and entrepreneurial ideas, and who can provide benefit to their places of origin? Zhao (2002) studied return migrants in six provinces. She found that older and married persons were more likely to return, and that the probability of return declined as the migrant's stay in an urban location lengthened. Perhaps surprisingly, more education significantly raised the probability a migrant would return. These features seem to suggest that returnees may be those who have positive skills and experiences they can bring to bear in their place of origin.

The interaction between education and out-migration is particularly worth attention. In most studies of migration, education is found to encourage migration. Indeed, a large part of the economic value of education in rural areas comes from the fact that it increases the chance that a worker will relocate and find a higher income outside his place of origin. However, several of the initial studies of migration in China found a very weak relationship between education and migration. Zhao (1999) studied a large sample in Sichuan Province and found that although schooling raised the probability that an individual would take a nonagricultural job in his or her place of origin, it had an insignificant effect on raising the probability of out-migration. Hare (1999) found similar results in an intensive study of Xiayi County in Henan Province. De Brauw and Giles (2005) studied the interaction between rural high school and migration and found that high school did little to increase the income of migrants, and that, perhaps as a result, out-migration was an alternative to attending high school. These studies suggest that the positive benefit of migration might be limited by the institutional rigidities of China's system. If education does not increase the benefits of migration, it may be that the full range of opportunities potentially created by migration is still restricted in the Chinese context.

Younger workers are increasingly specializing in off-farm work, either through migration or through local nonfarm employment, and this may be changing the migration calculus. Many of these younger workers have little or no direct experience with farming. They are more likely to stay in the city long term and have generally foreclosed the option of farming in their place of origin. The share of female migrants, while still below that of males, has also been increasing rapidly. This suggests a shift in the pattern of migration in China away from the temporary sojourning of the previous generation and toward a new mass movement as young people leave the land. For this shift to be sustained, though, China's urban labor markets must prove capable of absorbing the increased inflows and expanding the opportunities available to migrants.

9.8   Labor Supply and the Lewis Turning Point

China is going through profound changes in its labor markets that point to substantially slower growth. For decades, the abundant supply of labor in the countryside, high natural growth rates, and (most important) rapidly increasing rural-to-urban migration meant that the supply of unskilled labor seemed inexhaustible, and unskilled wages grew very slowly. But around 2004, demand for unskilled labor began to increase more rapidly than supply, with the result that the wages of unskilled, and especially migrant, workers began to increase rapidly. Feng Lu of Peking University has compiled available studies into a consolidated series for migrant worker wages; he found that migrant wages increased very slowly from at least the mid-1990s to 2002. This period of slow growth seems to go back earlier, but the data are sparse and unreliable. Between 2003 and 2007, migrant real wage growth (corrected for inflation) accelerated to 7.8% annual growth. As figure 9.6 shows, wages then accelerated further after 2007, and grew at an average annual rate of 12.4% over the next eight years, through 2015. Wage growth decelerated in 2016, but by that time wages were almost four times what they had been in 2002. Between 2008 and 2014, migrant

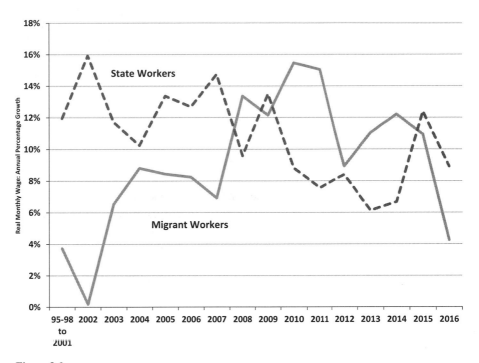

Figure 9.6
Wage growth: Migrant and state workers.
Sources: Lu (2012); NBS Migrant (2017).

wage growth sensibly outpaced that of state workers, shrinking the differential between them. The extraordinary rise of Chinese exports in the middle of the first decade of the twenty-first century pushed up migrant wages after a decade of very slow growth, and growth accelerated after 2007. In turn, this quadrupling of wages eroded the profitability of traditional labor-intensive exports, such as garments and toys. Li et al. (2012) referred to this change as the "end of cheap Chinese labor."

The pattern of unskilled wages passing from a phase of long-term relative stagnation to a phase of rapid growth suggests to many Chinese economists that China has passed through a so-called "Lewis turning point." The Lewis turning point is based on the idea that in a poor, underdeveloped economy, there is a substantial pool of underutilized, surplus labor in the countryside. Through the early stages of development, modern industry and urban services can draw from this pool of rural labor at a constant wage. However, there comes a point in the development process when abundant supplies of "surplus" labor are exhausted, and wage increases are necessary to draw workers out of the agricultural sector (that is, the supply of labor becomes less than perfectly elastic). According to the original Lewis model, these changes primarily reflect changing conditions in the rural economy: as agriculture becomes

more productive, while more young workers leave the countryside, there is no longer a pool of surplus labor willing to move to the cities or export zones. Changes of
this sort occur in all successful developing economies. Clearly, they have occurred
in China: in many accessible rural areas, all the young people have left; nonagricultural jobs are available nearby; and older people are not willing to leave the farm.
These labor-force changes force broader structural changes in the economy.

The concept of the Lewis turning point is controversial. Three arguments are
made against the concept. First, some deny that China has reached the Lewis turning
point on the grounds that there is still substantial underemployed labor in the countryside willing to leave (see the 80 million estimate from Knight, Deng, and Li
2011). Relatedly, some argue that the wage trends are a reflection of cyclical phenomena (the big trade boom in 2005–2007) and the improvement of terms of trade for
agriculture (Yao and Zhang 2010). Finally, some reject the concept in principle
because they believe that it contradicts the observed income-maximizing behavior
of farmers (Ge and Yang 2011). These are important arguments. However, the
essence of the idea of the Lewis turning point in China is that labor supply has
passed from a period of near-perfectly elastic supply to one of relatively inelastic
supply. In figure 9.7, as labor demand increases (shifts to the right) it eventually

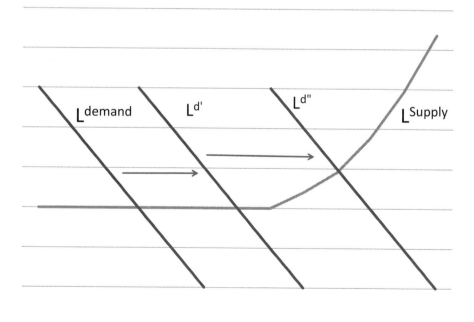

Figure 9.7
Labor supply: From elastic to inelastic.

moves from the horizontal to the upward-sloping section of the labor supply curve. This seems to fit the situation in China, in which the lowering of barriers between rural and urban areas unleashed an enormous flow of laborers previously prevented from moving. The under-utilized workers in the countryside today are typically older, more settled, less willing to move, and less located in accessible regions near the coast. Thus the real wage necessary to attract them to leave the farm is rising systematically.

9.9   Conclusion

Labor markets in China appear to be increasingly competitive and more effective at rewarding the productive characteristics of workers. In both urban and rural areas, there is evidence that the returns to education are increasing. Nevertheless, China's labor markets are still distorted by institutional barriers and incomplete markets. The initial absolute separation between urban and rural work has been eliminated, but it has been replaced by a segmented urban labor market in which rural migrants over-whelmingly work in the informal sector. Further stages of labor-market integration are urgently called for and can be expected to significantly improve the productivity of the Chinese economy.

In the broader perspective, China's labor market is now facing dramatic changes. These portend large changes in cost conditions and undoubtedly will lead to a more slowly growing China in the years ahead. The demographic factors discussed in the previous chapter are logically separate from the Lewis turning point but will rein-force and intensify the labor-force impacts. The Lewis turning point fundamentally derives from the productivity of marginal workers in agriculture versus their wage in the nonagricultural economy, while labor-force growth depends on birth decisions made decades ago. It is simply a coincidence that the growth of the population at working age is ending just as the Lewis turning point is being reached. This was not true in earlier Asian growth economies, where labor-force growth ended 20 years or so after the widespread increase in unskilled wages. In China, the two are occurring at the same time, which will increase the magnitude of the adjustment required.

Bibliography

Suggestions for Further Reading

Li et al. (2017) are easily accessible while pushing the discussion forward several steps. Li et al. (2012) and Meng (2012) lucidly present more advanced labor-related material. A debate on the Lewis turning point, starting with Cai and Du (2011), the leading proponents of this interpretation, makes up a special issue of *China Economic Review*, with strong contributions on all sides.

References

Appleton, Simon, John Knight, Lina Song, and Qingjie Xia (2002). "Labour Retrenchment in China: Determinants and Consequences." *China Economic Review* 13 (2–3): 252–276.

Appleton, Simon, Lina Song, and Qingjie Xia (2005). "Has China Crossed the River? The Evolution of Wage Structure in Urban China During Reform and Retrenchment." *Journal of Comparative Economics* 33:644–663.

Bian, Yanjie (1994). "Guanxi and the Allocation of Urban Jobs in China." *China Quarterly*, no. 140 (December): 973.

Cai Fang and Du Yang (2011). "Wage Increases, Wage Convergence, and the Lewis Turning Point in China." *China Economic Review* 21:601–610.

Census 2010 (2012). Census Office, State Council, and Population and Employment Division, National Bureau of Statistics. *Zhongguo 2010 Nian Renkou Pucha Ziliao* [China 2010 census statistics]. 3 vols. Beijing: Zhongguo Tongji.

Census 2015 (2016). Population and Employment Division, National Bureau of Statistics. *2015 Nian Quanguo 1% Renkou Chouyang Diaocha Ziliao* [Materials on the 2015 1% sample population survey]. Beijing: Zhongguo Tongji.

de Brauw, Alan, and John Giles (2005). "Migrant Opportunity and the Educational Attainment of Youth in Rural China." July 6. Accessed at http://www.msu.edu/~gilesj/adjg1final.pdf.

de Brauw, Alan, Jikun Huang, Scott Rozelle, Linxiu Zhang, and Yigang Zhang (2002). "The Evolution of China's Rural Labor Markets During the Reforms." *Journal of Comparative Economics* 30:329–353.

Eleventh Plan Suggestions (2005). Chinese Communist Party Central Committee. "CP Center Suggestions on Setting the 11th Five Year Plan for National Economic and Social Development." October 11.

Ge, Suqin, and Dennis Tao Yang (2011). "Labor Market Developments in China: A Neoclassical View." *China Economic Review* 22 (4): 611–625.

Granick, David (1987). "The Industrial Environment in China and the CMEA Countries." In Gene Tidrick and Chen Jiyuan, eds., *China's Industrial Reform*, New York: Oxford University Press.

Guo, Qian, and Wenkai Sun (2014). "Economic Returns to English Proficiency for College Graduates in Mainland China." *China Economic Review* 30:290–300.

Hare, Denise (1999). "'Push' and 'Pull' Factors in Migration Outflows and Returns: Determinants of Migration Status and Spell Duration Among China's Rural Population." *Journal of Development Studies* 35 (3): 45–72.

Hare, Denise (2016). "What Accounts for the Decline in Labor Force Participation Among Married Women in Urban China, 1991–2011?" *China Economic Review* 38:251–266.

Hu, Anning, and Jacob Hibel (2014). "Changes in College Attainment and the Economic Returns to a College Degree in Urban China, 2003–2010: Implications for Social Equality." *Social Science Research* 44:173–186.

Khor, N., L. Pang, C. Liu, F. Chang, D. Mo, P. Loyalka, and S. Rozelle (2016). "China's Looming Human Capital Crisis: Upper Secondary Educational Attainment Rates and the Middle-Income Trap." *China Quarterly* 228:905–926.

Knight, John, Quheng Deng, and Shi Li (2011). "The Puzzle of Migrant Labour Shortage and Rural Labour Surplus in China." *China Economic Review* 22:585–600.

Labor and Social Security Yearbook (various years). Ministry of Labor and Social Security, ed. *Zhongguo Laodong he Shehui Baozhan Nianjian*. Beijing: Zhongguo Laodong Shehui Baozhang.

Labor Yearbook (various years). National Bureau of Statistics, Department of Population, Social, Science, and Technology Statistics, and Ministry of Labor and Social Security, Department of Planning and Finance, eds. *Zhongguo Laodong Tongji Nianjian* [Yearbook of labor statistics of China]. Beijing: Zhongguo Laodong.

Li, Hongbin, Lei Li, Binzhen Wu, and Yanyan Xiong (2012). "The End of Cheap Chinese Labor." *Journal of Economic Perspectives* 26 (4): 57–74.

Li, Hongbin, Pak Wai Liu, and Junsen Zhang (2012). "Estimating Returns to Education Using Twins in Urban China." *Journal of Development Economics* 97 (2): 494–504.

Li, Hongbin, Pak Wai Liu, Junsen Zhang, and Ning Ma (2007). "Economic Returns to Communist Party Membership: Evidence from Urban Chinese Twins." *Economic Journal* 117 (523): 1504–1520.

Li, Hongbin, Prashant Loyalka, Scott Rozelle, and Binzhen Wu (2017). "Human Capital and China's Future Growth." *Journal of Economic Perspectives* 31 (1): 25–48.

Lu, Feng (2012). "Trends in Wages of Migrant Workers in China, 1979–2010." *Zhongguo Shehui Kexue* [Social sciences in China], no. 7, 45–65.

Meng, Xin (2012). "Labor Market Outcomes and Reforms in China." *Journal of Economic Perspectives* 26 (4): 75–102.

Meng, Xin, Kailing Shen, and Sen Xue (2013). "Economic Reform, Education Expansion, and Earnings Inequality for Urban Males in China, 1988–2009." *Journal of Comparative Economics* 41 (1): 227–244.

Mo Rong, Jiuye (1998). *Zhongguo de Shiji Nanti* [Employment: China's problem of the century]. Beijing: Jingji Kexue.

NBS Migrant (Annual). "2015 Nian Nongmingong Jiance Diaocha Baogao" [2015 migrant monitor and survey report]. April 28, 2016. Accessed at http://www.stats.gov.cn/tjsj/zxfb/201604/t20160428_1349713.html.

NBS Private (Annual). "2015 Nian Chengzhen Siying Danwei Jiuye Renyuan Pingjun Gongzi 39589 Yuan" [2015 urban private employment average wage 38,589 RMB]. May 13, 2016. Accessed at http://www.stats.gov.cn/tjsj/zxfb/201605/t20160513_1356093.html.

Psacharopoulos, George, and Harry Anthony Patrinos (2002). "Returns to Investment in Education: A Further Update." World Bank Policy Research Working Paper no. 2881, September.

SYC (Annual). *Zhongguo Tongji Nianjian* [Statistical yearbook of China]. Beijing: Zhongguo Tongji.

Taylor, J. Edward, Scott Rozelle, and Alan de Brauw (2003). "Migration and Incomes in Source Communities: A New Economics of Migration Perspective from China." *Economic Development and Cultural Changes* 52 (1): 75–101.

Xue, Jinjun, Wenshu Gao, and Lin Guo (2014). "Informal Employment and Its Effect on the Income Distribution in Urban China." *China Economic Review* 31:84–93.

Yang Yiyong (1997). "China's Unemployment Problem: Current Conditions, Trends, and Appropriate Measures." In Liu Guoguang, Wang Luolin, and Li Jingwen, eds., *1998 Nian Zhongguo Jingji Xingshi Fenxi yu Yuce: Jingji Lanpi Shu* [1998 China economic conditions, analysis, and projections: Economic blue book]. Beijing: Shehui Kexue Wenxian.

Yao, Yang, and Ke Zhang (2010). "Has China Passed the Lewis Turning Point? A Structural Estimation Based on Provincial Data." *China Economic Journal* 3 (2): 155–162.

Zhang, Junsen, Zhao Yaohui, Albert Park, and Xiaoqing Song (2005). "Economic Returns to Schooling in Urban China, 1988 to 2001." *Journal of Comparative Economics* 33:730–752.

Zhao Yaohui (1999). "Labor Migration and Earnings Differences: The Case of Rural China." *Economic Development and Cultural Change* 47 (4): 767–782.

Zhao Yaohui (2002). "Causes and Consequences of Return Migration: Recent Evidence from China." *Journal of Comparative Economics* 30:376–396.

Zhou Xueguang (2000). "Economic Transformation and Income Inequality in Urban China: Evidence from Panel Data." *American Journal of Sociology* 105 (4): 1135–1174.

10 Living Standards: Incomes, Inequality, and Poverty

The ultimate objective of economic growth is to improve the quality of life. Income growth provides a society the wherewithal to reduce poverty and risk and increase consumption and leisure. But growth does not automatically spread these benefits throughout the population. Instead, the relationships among income, inequality, and poverty are complex, and the notion of quality of life can be difficult to define precisely. China exemplifies the complex relationship among these concepts. Household income has grown extremely rapidly in China since 1978, and individual Chinese are vastly better off than they were 35 years ago. Moreover, the number of people in extreme poverty has declined dramatically. But over the same period, the distribution of income has become much more unequal. Income growth has been fastest among the best-positioned urban households in coastal regions and slowest among rural households in the western and northern regions. Thus Chinese society has become much better off and much less poor but much more unequal. The deterioration in income equality implies that the living standards of tens of millions of low-income households improved less than they would have if the same growth had been spread more equally.

Since 2009, inequality (by official measures) has leveled off and begun to decline. The change is due to dramatic structural changes in the economy and provides indirect evidence of the Lewis turning point occurring about that time. Government policy has also been a significant contributor. Government policy not only has shifted to support agricultural prices and rural incomes in general but also has increased outlays for social services. Although that social welfare component is still small by comparative standards, it has already improved living standards of the less well-off.

The basic trends in Chinese income, described in the previous paragraph, emerge clearly from nearly all the data available from China. There is no debate about these basic trends. However, more precise and more fundamental characterization of household income in China is challenging, because in any country, the data needed to accurately measure poverty, inequality, and well-being are hard to collect. But even more important is the fact that some of the distinctive features of the Chinese economy—the large urban-rural gap, peculiarities in the nature of income, and changes in the composition of household income over the reform period—present challenges in both collection and interpretation of data. The assessment of Chinese living standards in comparative perspective is particularly complex. This chapter introduces the main issues and presents the current state of our knowledge.

10.1   Income Growth

Household income has grown rapidly in China. A repeat visitor to China can easily see the striking evidence of improved standards of clothing and housing and more diverse and better prepared food. The best source of statistical data on this dramatic transformation is a large household survey that Chinese statisticians have carried out annually since the late 1970s. Statisticians surveyed two separate large samples, one rural and one urban, until 2013, when they began to merge the samples to create a unified frame and also began reporting a higher disposable income for rural households.[1] This chapter begins with an overview of what this source tells us about the growth of household income; its data are the basis of much of what we know and are embedded in virtually all analyses of the Chinese economy. Table 10.1 shows data from the urban and rural household income series, converted into 2015 constant prices with the official consumer price index. According to these data, both rural and urban household incomes have grown extremely rapidly: incomes in both urban and rural households in 2015 were more than ten times what they were in 1978. The general picture of rapid income growth in both rural and urban areas is surely accurate.

If we examine the data more closely, we see that urban incomes have grown consistently and robustly throughout the reform period, but that rural incomes have experienced three rather different periods.

• During the early years of reform, from 1978 to 1985, rural incomes grew exceptionally rapidly, at about 15% per year. This extraordinary achievement was the result of the success of early agricultural reforms, which increased agricultural incomes and also freed family members to engage in nonagricultural occupations. Urban incomes grew at the respectable rate of 7% per year, so rural households achieved substantial catch-up. However, it must be acknowledged that household income data for the late 1970s are much weaker than the data for later years (discussed below).

1. See chapter 6; this chapter retains the former definition of "household income" for intertemporal comparisons, such as those in table 10.1.

Table 10.1
Growth of real per capita household income.

	1978	1985	2009	2015
Rural real per capita net household income				
1. Constant 2013 prices	(About 750)	1,918	6,139	10,772
2. Average annual growth rate		14.4%	5.0%	9.8%
Urban real per capita disposable income				
1. Constant 2013 prices	2,276	3,650	20,377	31,790
2. Average annual growth rate		7.0%	7.4%	7.7%

Source: *SYC* (various years).

• The long following period, from 1985 through 2009, was one of significantly slower growth of rural incomes. Annual average growth fell to 5%. Urban incomes grew significantly more rapidly (7.4%), although urban income growth was slower in the middle of this period as urban households felt the brunt of state-sector downsizing at the end of the 1990s. Rapid recovery after that downsizing was complete brought urban income growth back to its long-term trend.

• From 2009 through 2015, rural household income growth has accelerated dramatically and has significantly exceeded that of urban households. While the urban growth trend showed a very slight tendency to accelerate, rural income growth jumped to almost 10%.

Thus, after the urban-rural gap reached its minimum in the mid-1980s, it widened again for about 20 years. Only during the past decade has the gap stabilized and begun to shrink. This corresponds with the discussion in chapter 6 and is clearly evident in the data.

Unfortunately, these calculations of real income growth cannot be relied on for a precise accounting of the growth of living standards. There is no acceptable rural consumer price index in the 1978–1985 period, when change was most rapid. There are other limitations of the official data. The household survey covered only rural residents and urban people with residence permits, so migrants and others with intermediate status were not covered at all until 2013. There are also significant differences between urban and rural areas in the way income is measured, and differences over time in how in-kind incomes and imputed rents from owner-occupied housing are evaluated. These problems limit comparability, overstate the growth rate of rural incomes in the earlier period, and may also somewhat overstate the growth of urban and rural incomes in other periods. Despite these shortcomings, the picture of rapid income growth is robust. Moreover, the household surveys provide an extremely rich body of data that can be used to support further analysis and diverse efforts to go beyond the simple headline number of average income growth. In the following, efforts that further develop the data from and beyond the household survey will be discussed in the course of examining trends in poverty and inequality.

10.2   Poverty

10.2.1   Rural Poverty

Growth reduces poverty, and one of the great successes of China's economic reform has been a dramatic reduction in the number of people in poverty. Only a tiny share of urban dwellers are in poverty, so poverty is fundamentally a rural phenomenon.

10.2.2   The Official Poverty Line

China first set an official poverty line in 1985 and has since raised it twice. This experience shows how conceptions of poverty change as a country develops. The initial poverty line—only 200 RMB per year in 1985—was draconian, capturing those who were completely destitute. By contrast, the second revision, after 2010, raised the official poverty line from 1,274 to 2,300 RMB (in 2010 prices, to be adjusted annually). Even after a quadrupling of prices between 1985 and 2010 is accounted for, the new poverty line is almost three times the initial one. Where the poverty line is set makes a huge difference because a large proportion of the Chinese rural population is near these poverty lines. In 2011, the government established an ambitious target of the elimination of poverty by 2020. This target may seem unrealistic. However, so far, China's performance in reducing poverty has been exceptional, and a good start has been made toward reaching the long-term target.

10.2.3   The World Bank Internationally Comparable Poverty Line

To provide a common standard to evaluate poverty, the World Bank introduced the concept of the "dollar-a-day" poverty line. The underlying idea was that if 50% of expenditure was used for food, this level of income could purchase—but just barely—sufficient calories for subsistence. The World Bank has since expended enormous effort to collect prices on the goods that poor people purchase (especially food) along with large household surveys to account for income. In this way, they have been able to meaningfully compare the incidence of poverty across countries. With worldwide inflation, the dollar-a-day standard has also been revised, most recently to $1.90 per day (based on 2011 purchasing power parity [PPP] calculations; see box 7.2 in chapter 7 for a discussion of PPP). Ravallion and Chen (2007) broadly revised Chinese data to correct problems and make Chinese measures comparable to the World Bank standards. Ravallion and Chen's calculations of poverty in the

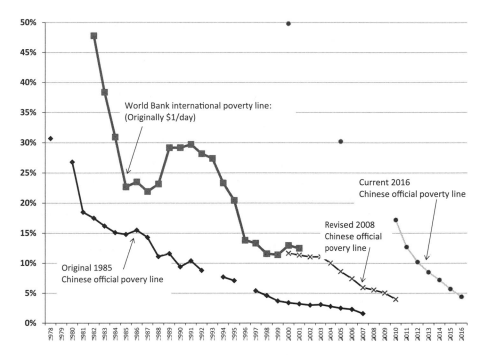

Figure 10.1
Share of rural population in poverty (different poverty lines).
Sources: *SAC* (2016, 70); Ravallion and Chen (2007).

Chinese countryside, compared with the various official calculations, are shown in figure 10.1. The dramatic reduction in rural poverty is plainly obvious. Poverty was serious and pervasive in China at the end of the 1970s and has not been eliminated today. Moreover, the vulnerability of low-income households increased through much of the reform period as greater economic insecurity and reduced access to health care made the position of the poor more precarious. Only after 2005 was this trend toward increased vulnerability arrested. Even with these qualifications, China's record in poverty reduction has been exceptional.

Figure 10.1 puts the different data series into a consistent framework, showing the relation among the four different poverty lines that have been adopted over the years. As Chinese incomes have grown, the official Chinese poverty line has evolved from one much lower than the World Bank dollar-a-day line, to an intermediate (2008) poverty line, to a more generous (2010) standard. These lines tell a consistent story of poverty reduction, but each provides a slightly different picture of the incidence of poverty at any given time. Official Chinese data now record the number (headcount) and proportion of rural people in poverty (headcount index), which provides a fairly complete statistical picture.

There was a dramatic reduction in rural poverty between 1978 and 1985, in the wake of the early rural economic reforms. According to the austere Chinese official poverty line, 31% of farmers were poor in 1978, but only 15% in 1985. By the World Bank dollar-a-day standard, the number of poor was larger, but the achievement of poverty reduction was proportionately even greater. By the Ravallion and Chen (World Bank) calculation, 48% of the rural population was poor in 1982 and only 23% in 1985. Moreover, making backward projections from the 1985 data, Raval- lion and Chen calculate that 70% of the rural population was poor in 1978. It is not clear that the data Ravallion and Chen use are sufficient to support a credible purchasing-power calculation for 1978, but the more fundamental issue is the differ- ence in the nature of poverty. Most of the poor in 1978 were "socialist poor," which we can divide into two conceptually distinct groups (although in practice there was no sharp dividing line). One group had a low material standard of living, but were part of a functioning collective system. As a result, they had access to the land, rudi- mentary income guarantees, and even some access to basic health care (chapter 11). Their measured incomes were low, but they were not destitute in the same sense as a landless laborer in other economies, with low income *and* an extremely precari- ous existence. The other group lived in extreme poverty and their collective institu- tions had failed; farmers had no income guarantees or health care at all. This group not only had low income, they were also constantly vulnerable to health shocks or crop failures, like those in "below-dollar-a-day" poverty in other countries. There are no good data on the relative size of these two groups of socialist poor, but an informed guess is that the group in extreme poverty might well have been around a third of the rural population in 1978 (as implied by the early Chinese official pov- erty line).

Ravallion and Chen then documented a bounce-back of poverty after 1985, as inflation eroded the gains many farmers had made. This bounce-back could be severe in a short time because there were large numbers of Chinese households above, but close to, the dollar-a-day poverty line. This large group of "near-poor" fell back below the poverty line when conditions deteriorated moderately. The number of poor increased, and from 1989 through 1993, there were on average just over 250 million rural people below the dollar-a-day poverty line in each year. From the 1990s, better household survey and price data, combined with a slow-down in institutional change, give us more confidence that intertemporal comparisons are valid. The 2008 official Chinese poverty line is almost identical to the World Bank dollar-a-day standard, which allows us to make consistent intertemporal comparisons. By 2010, the num- ber of rural people under the poverty line had declined to 27 million. This almost 90% reduction in poverty over a 20-year period is a remarkable achievement.

The success in poverty reduction through 2010 triggered two important policy changes. A new and much more generous official poverty line was adopted, and an ambitious commitment was made to eliminate poverty by 2020. The new poverty line, described earlier, caused the poverty headcount in 2010 to soar from 27 million to 166 million. The large increase in the poverty headcount again highlights how many rural Chinese live near the poverty line. A near-doubling of the poverty line caused a six-fold increase in the number of poor. Chinese statisticians also calculated what this poverty line would have meant if applied to benchmark years in the past: in 1978, 97% of the rural population would have been below this line, and 60% as late as 1995. For the reasons given above, these should be taken as rough approximations.

The objective of eliminating poverty was given more concrete form in the 13th Five Year Plan (2016, 9, 105–108). The plan set a binding target of moving all 55 million people designated poor in 2015 out of poverty by 2020. About 30 million people in designated poor counties were to be brought out of poverty mainly through increased investment in infrastructure and businesses; about 10 million would emigrate to take jobs in the city; and about 10 million would be relocated to more productive natural environments. National welfare dossiers are to be set up for those who cannot be brought out of poverty through economic development. This is an extraordinarily ambitious objective. As of 2016, China still had 43 million rural people under the poverty line. According to the official data shown in figure 10.1, this is 4.4% of the rural population. However, Chinese statisticians use the largest possible definition of the rural population as the denominator in this ratio, comprising all those with rural household registrations plus recently changed registrations. If instead of this artificial denominator of 980 million we use instead the 599 million people actually resident in rural areas in 2016, the 43 million poor are 7.4% of the rural population. Despite China's remarkable success in poverty alleviation, there is still a substantial poor population in the countryside, and elimination of poverty will be difficult indeed.

10.2.4   Explaining Poverty Trends

What economic causes explain the rapid reduction in rural poverty? Rural poverty declined rapidly in the early 1980s because several one-time factors came together in dramatic fashion. The terms of trade of agriculture improved dramatically as ultralow procurement prices that had discriminated severely against farmers were raised; the supply of modern inputs to farmers increased dramatically; and the dissolution of collectives allowed farmers to work harder and allocate inputs into agriculture more efficiently. Land was initially distributed to households on a highly egalitarian basis, and virtually everyone got a share. Periodic redistribution of land in many areas of China means that there is a floor for intravillage poverty, and there are few landless laborers. Moreover, because poverty had been so pervasive in the prereform countryside, general economic growth was quite efficient in reducing poverty. The huge rapid reduction in poverty in this initial period indirectly shows that the previous command-economy system had created poverty on a massive scale. Each of the individual steps taken to ameliorate the worst features of that system reduced poverty. Once those steps had been taken, by the mid-1980s, the speed with which poverty could be further reduced inevitably slowed.

As poverty alleviation became more difficult, the government launched a more activist policy. A State Council Leading Group for Poverty Reduction was set up in 1986. It began a program of geographic targeting of designated poor counties that has been the focus of China's antipoverty strategy ever since. From 1993, almost 20% of China's counties have been designated "poor counties" and made eligible for special assistance. These 592 counties received three kinds of assistance. Subsidized development loans were made available for households and enterprises. Cheap credit, administered by the Agriculture Bank, was designed to encourage investment in moneymaking activities. Food-for-work programs supported local infrastructure projects. In this program, the government provides material and food for workers, while the village provides labor. Finally, earmarked budgetary grants were provided to local governments to finance public investment projects (Ang 2016). Funding for these programs has been sustained for 30 years, fluctuating but averaging about 0.2% of GDP. The objective of eliminating poverty by 2020 includes graduating each of these poor counties—systematically, but one by one—and phasing out the program.

Appraisals of this program have been mixed. To a certain extent, geographic targeting makes sense because China's poor counties are especially common in a belt around the Aihui–Tengchong line (see chapter 2), where dense population runs up against the limit of environmental sustainability. However, targeting is rather imprecise because many of the residents of poor counties are not poor, and there are significant numbers of poor people outside poor counties. Moreover, many of the resources sent to poor counties ended up expanding local-government bureaucracies and were spent on nonessentials. Nevertheless, rigorous evaluation indicates that designation did raise economic growth in poor counties by around 1% annually (Park, Wang, and Wu 2003; Meng 2013). Government antipoverty programs had a positive impact but cannot account for the dramatic reduction in rural poverty. Instead, overall rapid economic growth has clearly been the main driver of the fall in poverty. Three important policy-related factors facilitated the positive impact of economic growth on reducing poverty.

First, the dramatic increase in off-farm jobs and out-migration helped poor families. Policies eliminating restrictions on migration had a strongly favorable impact. This was by no means a guaranteed outcome. In some countries, impoverished regions serve as "poverty traps" because local residents without resources find it impossible to escape and take advantage of outside opportunities. In China, although migration began from relatively well-off accessible regions, after the turn of the century, rural residents from poor regions were only slightly less likely to emigrate than those from rich regions. Poor farmers were able to exit agriculture, and emigration had a powerful impact on reducing poverty. The bottom quintile of the rural population increased the share of wages and salaries in their total income from 26% to 43% in the decade from 2002 to 2012 (Wu 2016). Under these conditions, the benefits of rapid growth trickled down to the rural poor.

Second, poor farmers have benefited from the shift in government agricultural policies since 2003 (chapter 11). Since, as mentioned, the distribution of agricultural land is extremely equal, and there are almost no landless farmworkers, the poor have benefited from the abolition of agricultural taxes and now receive significant subsidies for growing grain. The canceling of rural taxes and fees between 2003 and 2006 alone increased rural incomes by about 5%, and the impact on the lowest 20% of the income distribution was proportionately greater. The incidence of those fees had been erratic and often regressive. According to one calculation, the lowest quintile paid a 6.5% tax rate in 1988 and a 12% tax rate in 1995. By 2007, though, the tax rate had fallen to 0.3%, almost nothing (Li and Sicular 2014). Agricultural terms of trade have a significant effect on poverty. A dramatic reduction in poverty came during the 1993–1996 period, when farm prices were high. Since 2003, government policy has aimed to keep farm prices high and stable, sometimes at substantial cost, and this has reduced poverty.

Third, government welfare spending reaches the poor to a certain extent. A program of basic minimum income support has been rolled out in rural areas over the past decade. Fifty-three million people receive minimum income grants that average 1,250 RMB, about half of the official poverty line. However, because the program is poorly targeted, studies have found that it reduces poverty by only a few percent (Li and Sicular 2014). Other government social spending programs also benefit the poor. Rural cooperative medical assistance and free elementary education are available to all but have a disproportionate impact on the poor.

10.2.5   Urban Poverty

Unlike most of the developing world, poverty in China has been largely a rural phenomenon. In the past, policy kept urban population low by restricting immigration and then guaranteed everyone a public-sector job (see chapters 6 and 9). Since China's opening, most economic growth has occurred in the cities. Traditionally, urban inhabitants enjoyed stable social welfare conditions and extensive government subsidies of basic needs. Today, this cushion of assured benefits is eroding, but there are still very few permanent urban residents (those with urban residence permits) with incomes below the poverty line. Ravallion and Chen found that the cost of living in the city was 41% higher than in the countryside (in 2002) and so used a higher poverty threshold but still found that only 0.5% of the urban population was in poverty in 2001. Li and Sicular (2014, 21), using the World Bank's then $1.25/day poverty line, found 0.44% of urban residents in poverty in 2007. Although cities are becoming less equal, and unemployment and disability can result in serious economic hardship, very few permanent urban residents are in absolute poverty. Surprisingly, the share of migrants under the poverty line is actually lower, only 0.17%. This is probably because migrants are in the city to work, are overwhelmingly of working age and physically healthy enough to work, and have few dependents. Because almost all migrants are working, almost none are in poverty. By comparison, some urban dwellers are elderly or infirm and, in the absence of state support, fall into poverty.

10.3   Inequality

Under the socialist economy, Chinese society was dualistic but egalitarian. That is, although the gap between urban and rural residents was large (society was dualistic), incomes were fairly equal within each of the urban and rural sectors (egalitarian). At first, rural reforms in the late 1970s and early 1980s narrowed the urban-rural gap. The result was that China became less dualistic at a time when it was still highly egalitarian in both urban and rural sectors. The result was that around 1983–1984, China was probably the most equal that it has ever been, even more equal than under socialism. As figure 10.2 shows, China's overall Gini coefficient in 1983, measured on income, was 0.28, which made China one of the most equal countries in the world, comparable to Japan (0.25 in 1993) and Germany (0.28 in 2000). China's urban society was especially equal, with an intraurban Gini of only 0.166.

It is worth emphasizing how unusual it was that China at that time had a low Gini coefficient. Generally speaking, large countries have higher Gini coefficients (since they contain a greater diversity of natural endowments), and China is certainly large. Moreover, lower- and middle-income economies typically have higher Gini coefficients than developed, high-income countries, and China was certainly a lower-income economy in 1983. Comparable levels of equality are seen in the small former socialist states, but most of those are very small and had much higher income than China in 1983. For a big, developing country, China had an exceptionally equal society. The figure for urban China was especially unusual since in most developing countries, cities are more unequal than the countryside.

Since the early 1980s, though, inequality in China has increased steadily and inexorably. As figure 10.2 shows, inequality has climbed steadily within both rural and urban areas. Total national inequality is higher than either rural or urban inequality in every year because the urban-rural gap is large. Moreover, total inequality has increased even more than urban or rural inequality because the urban-rural gap widened again until 2008–2009. China's overall Gini coefficient reached 0.49 in 2009

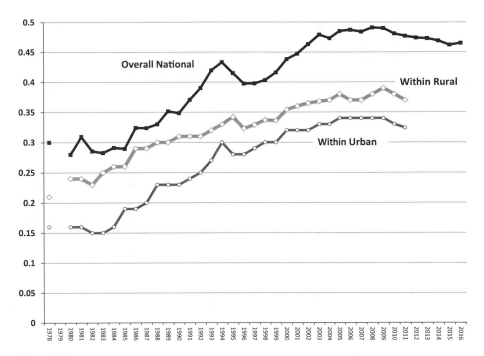

Figure 10.2
Evolution of China Gini coefficient: Urban, rural, and national overall.
Sources: UNDP China (2016); UNDP (2016); update to 2016 from Ning (2017).

before beginning to moderate. The speed and size of China's increase in inequality are unprecedented. Moreover, these Gini coefficients are calculated from the large household survey described earlier, which means that they undoubtedly omit many of the highest-earning households and thus understate actual inequality (this is a feature of measures based on household surveys in every country). China is now more unequal than the average middle-income country. China does not yet approach the extreme inequality characteristic of, say, Brazil (0.547, although this has been declining because of aggressive welfare programs). However, China is now significantly more unequal than some of the most important Asian developing countries, such as India (0.339) or Indonesia (0.381), or even countries traditionally considered fairly unequal, such as Thailand (0.430) or even Mexico (0.472) (all Ginis except those of China are from World Development Indicators). Current Chinese levels of inequality are in the upper half of the range of developing economies. In light of China's size and geographic diversity, this might be expected, but it is a dramatic change from China's past record, and there may be no other case where a society's income distribution has deteriorated so much so fast. As a side note, China's Gini coefficient has surpassed that of the United States, which has also been rising and equaled 0.408 in 2010. Thus, in the course of two decades, China has gone from being one of the most egalitarian societies, about as equal as Japan, to being more unequal than the United States. However, as figure 10.2 shows, since 2008–2009, the trend has reversed, and official data show China's Gini declining, a welcome development. Although the decline was not large, it was sustained for seven years, reaching 0.462 in 2015 before ticking up slightly to 0.465 in 2016.

10.3.1   Causes of Inequality Trends

What economic causes lie behind the dramatic changes in income distribution in China? Many factors have contributed. The most important single factor in Chinese inequality is the urban-rural gap. As we have seen in chapter 6, socialist institutions reinforced the urban-rural divide and in this respect contributed to inequality. Market reforms at first shrank this gap because they benefited rural residents first. But ultimately, market reforms contributed to inequality because they led to the acceleration of urban economic growth.

It is sometimes argued that the economic development process inevitably leads to a medium-term increase in inequality. Simon Kuznets, a pioneering scholar of economic development, argued that inequality would increase during the initial stage of development but decrease in subsequent stages. Kuznets's logic was that pockets of modern economic growth would first generate high incomes in a few limited areas, while most of the traditional economy remained low income, but that later growth would ripple out to most of the economy. The first phase of this prediction certainly seems to be true in China, amplified by three factors: China's huge size and geographic diversity, which limit spillovers; the catalytic role played by foreign trade and investment, which naturally concentrate in coastal cities; and the legacy of socialist institutions. The result has been increased inequality as high incomes are concentrated in fast-growing coastal cities.

Inequality has also increased within each of the urban and rural sectors. In the urban economy, returns to various kinds of capital have increased dramatically. Before reform, nobody possessed any income-generating capital, the only income was labor income, and so equality was high. After reform, urban residents have increasingly been differentiated between those who possess the capital, skills, and opportunities to benefit from the new economy and those who don't. Asset income has increased as a share of total income and is much more unequally distributed. Returns to human capital, as discussed in chapter 9, have increased substantially, and human capital is relatively unequally distributed. The ability of well-positioned individuals to take advantage of opportunities generated by market distortions, either through luck or through corruption, must also contribute to urban inequality. Within rural areas, the most disequalizing part of income has been the wage and profit opportunities created by township and village enterprises and by individual entrepreneurship. As such opportunities spread through the countryside, they were at first highly concentrated in suburban areas (chapter 11) and thus made the overall countryside more unequal.

China imposes an individual income tax, but it does almost nothing to reduce inequality (Xu and Yue 2012). This is in contrast to most developed countries, including the United States, where progressive income taxes reduce inequality substantially, lowering Gini coefficients by around 10 points. For example, the United States' pretax Gini coefficient is 0.51, but for taxable income, after income tax and transfers, it is 0.40 (OECD 2016). The Chinese household income tax affects a small proportion of urban wage earners; it is assessed on individuals, not households; and administration is inefficient. Many high-income households escape the income tax. So far, China has missed an opportunity to moderate the high level of inequality by using the power of progressive income taxation.

Has China turned a corner, and will inequality in China now start to decline? From a broad structural economic viewpoint, it is certainly plausible that China is reaching a stage at which inequality will decline. The model of the Lewis turning point implies that structural changes will begin to reduce inequality. According to the Lewis model, wages for unskilled labor do not improve much in the early stages of development, indeed, not until the initial labor surplus is absorbed. Only after gradually expanding industrial and urban sectors absorb the rural surplus will wages for unskilled workers begin to increase rapidly. Fei and Ranis (1964), formalizing the Lewis model based on study of Taiwan, showed that inequality should decline after the Lewis turning point. In China, the rapid growth of migrant wages, especially between 2008 and 2014 (chapter 9) contributed to the plateauing of the Gini coefficient. If the Lewis model is correct, the trend toward reduced inequality will continue in the future.

At the same time, Chinese government policies have become much more concerned with population well-being. New programs of medical insurance and modest retirement funds have been rolled out in the countryside. Government policy seeks to raise rural incomes by (1) lowering taxes, (2) directly subsidizing grain farmers, (3) increasing welfare payments, and (4) keeping farm prices high. Cumulatively, these policies may have an effect in lowering inequality. If economic structural forces and government policy continue in this direction, there is some hope that China's inequality may have plateaued around 2008–2009 and will head downward in the future.

10.3.2 Accounting for All Income

The preceding discussion of income inequality still suffers from some important limitations. Based on household surveys, the measures are limited by the standard definition of income and by survey coverage. In terms of the definition of income, urban dwellers received substantial additional income as benefits or subsidized services that are not well captured by the existing measures of income (mostly cash). Rural residents also receive noncash income, but the forms of this income are completely different from those in urban areas, and both were different under the planned economy than we would expect in a market economy. The China Household Income Project (CHIP), an ambitious collaboration between Western scholars and the Chinese National Bureau of Statistics has made an effort over many years to account more broadly for all important sources of income for urban and rural residents. This international team carried out a series of supplemental surveys in conjunction with the normal household survey in five benchmark years—1988, 1995, 2002, 2007, and 2013—in a large and fairly representative subsample of China's provinces.

In the analysis of Khan and Riskin (2005), China started out in the 1980s considerably less egalitarian than it was portrayed by the conventional statistics, primarily because urban dwellers received substantial benefits. Complete accounting for urban incomes raised them by 55%. Urban dwellers enjoyed a large subsidy income, especially for the implicit value of ration coupons that were provided them free of charge. They also benefited from significant housing subsidies because most paid extremely low rents while living in work-unit-supplied housing. Surprisingly, though, a complete accounting of rural incomes raised them, too, by almost 40%, mostly because of the imputed value of owner-occupied housing, and because of the revaluation of home-grown food at market prices (instead of procurement prices). KR computed an overall national Gini coefficient of 0.38 in 1988, significantly above the Ravallion and Chen (RC) estimate of 0.33. Subsequently, however, Khan and Riskin's (KR's) national Gini climbed less quickly than RC's Gini, because by 1995, most hidden urban subsidies had either been eliminated or converted into explicit form. Ration coupons had been abolished, and subsidized housing had been privatized. By 2002, urban comprehensive income was just 29% higher than money income, while the estimate for rural households was that comprehensive income was now 33% above money income. Since the difference between urban and rural households was practically unchanged by the inclusion of noncash income, KR's method of calculation now yielded a result very similar to CR's more standard computation. Both methods produced an identical Gini coefficient of 0.45 (in 2001 for RC's terminal year and in 2002, for KR's benchmark year).

Household surveys in China, as in other countries, likely miss extremely rich and extremely poor people at the tail ends of the income distribution. Wealthy people in particular have little incentive to subject their higher incomes to scrutiny by outsiders. Li Gan et al. (2014) report an interesting effort to overcome this obstacle. They also use a representative sample household survey, but one that is centered on wealth management. Surveyors were unusually persistent in soliciting survey participation and arguably provided an incentive for wealthier households to participate (feedback on wealth management practices). Li and his colleagues find a higher share of business income in overall income and, not surprisingly, compute a significantly higher income Gini: 0.61 in 2011. This alarmingly high number cannot be considered the "true" Gini in China, and it is also difficult to compare it with other countries that might also undercount wealthy households in their regular household survey-based inequality measures. However, Li's survey certainly indicates the potential magnitude of gray and entrepreneurial incomes that may be omitted from the calculation of the official inequality measure. Li and his team also confirm that tax and welfare policies make a negligible contribution to reducing China's Gini coefficient.

10.4   Physical Quality of Life Indicators

Given some of the complexities with the income data discussed in this chapter, it is worthwhile to look at other indicators of living standards, in particular, those that directly reflect the health, physical security, and well-being of the population. Physical Quality of Life Indicators (PQLIs) provide another look at living standards and a way to compare China with other countries. Economic growth, particularly in the early stages of development, is strongly correlated with improvement in PQLIs. Moreover, PQLIs arguably provide a more direct measure of improvements in the quality of life.

10.4.1   Life Expectancy at Birth

Of the various constituents of PQLI, perhaps the most important is life expectancy at birth. Life expectancy summarizes the impact of health and nutrition on the human organism and provides information about the net impact of environmental hazards (usually by-products of an industrializing society) compared with other kinds of health hazards more characteristic of underdevelopment.[2] China's life expectancy is relatively high. Although China's population censuses provide abundant data, they need to be carefully adjusted to properly account for underreporting of births (chapter 8). UNDP China (2016) and Cai (2013) both made adjustments to the 2000 and 2010 censuses and showed comparable increases in life expectancy at birth and an identical 77.4 for women in 2010. UNDP China showed a larger female-male gap, at five years, with an estimate of male life expectancy of 72.4, compared with Cai's

---

2. Moreover, in the calculation of average life expectancy, each individual counts equally as a single unit. When we track changes in income, using them as a proxy for changes in well-being, the welfare of high-income individuals is implicitly being counted more than that of low-income individuals.

74.1. These life expectancies are about the same as in Latin America as a whole, which has a much higher income per capita, but less than those of developed countries, where life expectancy averages 78.

The steady improvement in life expectancy is encouraging because during the period of rapid economic growth up through the early twenty-first century, there had been an erosion of institutions supporting health, nutrition of the poorest, and the social role of women. The life-expectancy statistics indicate that, on balance, the positive impact of economic growth has been larger than these negative effects. Life spans have grown virtually everywhere in the world—except in the countries affected most severely by AIDS—and the improvement in China's life expectancy is not exceptional. Indeed, 35 years ago, China had unusually impressive life-expectancy data compared with its low income. More recently, income has "caught up" with life expectancy, and China looks more like a normal country, albeit one that still has relatively good life expectancy.

10.4.2   Other Health-Related Indicators

Closely related to life expectancy are other health-related indicators. Infant mortality (death of a child during the first year of life) is relatively low in China, having declined from 50 per 1,000 in 1991 to only 8.9 per 1,000 in 2014. This number is close to OECD levels (6.5 in 2013), but it is uncertain whether it has been adequately corrected for underreporting of births, as discussed in chapter 8. However, the percentage of infants with low birth weight is reported as only 6%, which is near developed-country levels and supports the picture of a relatively healthy birth environment. Also important are changes in the nature of mortality. In the early stages of development, infectious diseases take a heavy toll on children and adults alike and account for the majority of deaths. However, these sources of mortality can be relatively easily reduced by moderate investments in sanitation and preventive health care. China has already passed this initial hurdle: 85% of children are immunized against the main childhood diseases. Today, China faces challenges relating to the "second health revolution." The primary causes of death are similar to those in developed countries. The most important are heart disease, cancer, and lung diseases. These are not simple communicable diseases but are instead often chronic diseases related to population aging and weight and lifestyle issues. Environmental pollution plays a role, as does cigarette smoking. Sexually transmitted diseases, including AIDS, have emerged as significant health-care problems.

10.4.3   Education

Another important PQLI is education. Literacy rates in China are quite high, calculated at 94.6% of the adult population in 2015. This is significantly above the Latin America average of 92%. Rates of illiteracy are closely related to age, which means that it cannot be quickly eliminated. According to the 2015 census, illiteracy was under 2% for every age group under 45 but sharply higher among those older. The literacy data tell us something about China's relatively strong performance on PQLIs. For three decades under the socialist system, China followed a development strategy that included substantial attention to so-called basic needs. This stress on provision of basic health and education services to the population meant that as of 20 years ago, basic-level indicators already looked good. Basic health care, control of infectious diseases, literacy, and basic education had already achieved strong results in comparative context. In the past 20 years, good performance has gradually expanded to more advanced-level indicators in education and health.

10.4.4   Human Development Index

One important effort to summarize a large number of PQLIs is represented by the United Nations Development Programme's (UNDP) Human Development Index (HDI). The HDI has been computed for many countries and reflects a weighted average of life expectancy, literacy and school enrollment, and price-adjusted purchasing power parity (PPP) GDP per capita. The UNDP has also sponsored a series of China Human Development Reports, which give the same information for China's provinces (table 10.2). This is convenient because it provides us with a way to compare China's provinces with one another and also with other developing countries. The right-hand column shows a number of comparison countries in 2014, plus data in bold for China in five benchmark years from 1980 through 2014, which show China moving up steadily from "low human development" to "high human development." To be sure, almost all countries have moved up, but China is the only country to have moved all the way from low to high. Ironically, China's success in improving its HDI tells us less than we would prefer about PQLI improvement. China in 1980, as mentioned earlier, was an unusually healthy society with a long life expectancy given its low level of income. Thus most of the initial improvement in relative position has come from China's income catching up with its already good PQLIs.[3] However, the improvement in education's contribution has increased since 2000. At the same time, China's HDI ranking has improved rapidly since 1980. By this comparison, between 1980 and 2014, China moved from a level of human development below that of Pakistan or Haiti to a level just barely below the middle-income economies of Brazil, Thailand, and Turkey.

Table 10.2 also shows that there is significant variation among China's provinces. The bulk of China's provinces and the national average fall in the middle of the "high

3. The UNDP has revised the indexes for earlier years. UNDP China (2016, 29) provides a helpful decomposition of the improvement of China's HDI from 1980 to 2010: income growth accounted for 56%, education improvement accounted for 35%, and health accounted for 10%.

Table 10.2
Comparison of Human Development Index, 2014.

Chinese provinces		Nations	
Very high human development			
		Norway	0.94
		United States	0.92
		Hong Kong	0.91
		Korea	0.90
Beijing	0.87		
Shanghai	0.85		
Tianjin	0.84	Poland	0.84
		Chile	0.83
High human development			
Liaoning, Zhejiang, Jiangsu	0.80	Malaysia	0.79
Guangdong, Inner Mongolia, Shandong, Jilin	0.77	Turkey, Mexico, Brazil	0.76
Fujian, Heilongjiang	0.76		
Hubei, Shaanxi, Chongqing	0.75		
Shanxi, Hebei, Hunan, Hainan	0.74	**China, 2014**	0.73
Henan, Ningxia, Jiangxi	0.73	Thailand	0.73
Xinjiang, Sichuan, Anhui	0.72	Colombia	0.72
Guangxi	0.71		
Medium human development			
		China, 2010	**0.70**
Qinghai, Gansu	0.69	Egypt	0.69
		Indonesia	0.68
Yunnan, Guizhou	0.67	Philippines, Vietnam	0.67
		India, Honduras	0.61
Tibet	0.60		
		China, 2000	**0.59**
		Pakistan	0.54
		China, 1990	**0.50**
Low human development			
		Haiti	0.48
		China, 1980	**0.42**

Sources: UNDP China (2016); UNDP (2015, 212–215).

human development" range, about the same as Mexico and Brazil. The municipalities of Beijing, Shanghai, and Tianjin have very high human development, comparable to that of Poland or Chile and almost as high as that of Korea. The richest coastal provinces of Liaoning, Zhejiang, and Jiangsu fall at the boundary between "high" and very high" human development. Four provinces—Qinghai, Gansu, Yunnan, and Guizhou—have "medium" human development, comparable to that of Egypt, Indonesia, or Vietnam. The least well-off is Tibet, which has a slightly lower score than India. To be sure, much of the relative ranking reflects the urban-rural gap (see chapter 6) and the proportion of urban residents in each province.

10.5   Conclusion

No single indicator can tell us how much economic growth in China has contributed to well-being. However, the combination of many indicators allows us to draw a reasonably accurate picture and to place China in the context of other developing countries. China's GDP per capita (at exchange rates) ranks China right in the middle of the middle-income countries at just over $8,000 in 2016. Shifting to PPP-evaluated GDP per capita at $14,000 in 2016 moves China up a little in comparative terms. In fact, measures of well-being in China look considerably better than we would expect from either GDP per capita calculation. China's HDI is similar to those of middle-income countries—Turkey, Mexico, and Brazil—that had about 50% higher PPP GDP levels in 2011. Undoubtedly, some of this difference reflects the legacy of China's relatively egalitarian, socialist past. Basic health and education diffused through the countryside 30 years ago continue to affect population well-being today. Trends in inequality over the past 20 years, though, tell us that China will no longer reap benefits from these past policies. Future improvements in the quality of life will depend more on the way in which growth policies are crafted to spread the benefits of growth as widely as possible to the whole society.

Bibliography

Suggestions for Further Reading

Li and Sicular (2014) greatly broaden the discussion here, and the edited volumes that come out of CHIP go into more depth. See, most recently, Li, Sato, and Sicular (2013). The UNDP China webpage is an excellent resource that allows exploration in many directions: http://hdr.undp.org/en/countries/profiles/CHN.

References

13th Five Year Plan (2016). National People's Congress. *Zhonghua Renming Gongheguo Guomin Jingji he Shehui Fazhan Dishisange Wunian Guihua Gangyao* [People's Republic of China outline 13th Five Year Plan for economic and social development]. March 17. Accessed at http://news.xinhuanet.com /politics/2016lh/2016-03/17/c_1118366322.htm.

Ang, Yuen Yuen (2016). *How China Escaped the Poverty Trap.* Ithaca, NY: Cornell University Press.

Cai, Yong (2013). "China's New Demographic Reality: Learning from the 2010 Census." *Population and Development Review* 39 (3): 371–396.

Fei, John, and Gus Ranis (1964). *Development of the Labor Surplus Economy.* Homewood, IL: Irwin.

Khan, Azizur, and Carl Riskin (2005). "China's Household Income and Its Distribution, 1995 and 2002." *China Quarterly*, no. 182, 356–384.

Li, Gan, Zhichao Yin, Nan Jia, Shoo Xu, Shang Ma, and Lu Zheng (2014). *Data You Need to Know About China: Research Report of China Household Finance Survey 2012.* Berlin: Springer.

Li, Shi, Hiroshi Sato, and Terry Sicular, eds. (2013). *Rising Inequality in China: Challenges to a Harmonious Society.* New York: Cambridge University Press.

Li, Shi, and Terry Sicular (2014). "The Distribution of Household Income in China: Inequality, Poverty and Policies." *China Quarterly*, no. 217, 1–41.

Meng, Lingsheng (2013). "Evaluating China's Poverty Alleviation Program: A Regression Discontinuity Approach." *Journal of Public Economics* 101:1–11.

Ning, Jizhe (2017). "Press Conference, Statistical Bureau Director Responds on 2016 Economic Results." January 20. Accessed at www.stats.gov.cn/tjsj/sjjd/201702/t20170120_1456268.html.

OECD (2016). "Dataset: Income Distribution and Poverty." Data extracted on November 22, 2016 from http://stats.oecd.org/.

Park, Albert, Sangui Wang, and Guobao Wu (2002). "Regional Poverty Targeting in China." *Journal of Public Economics* 86 (1): 123–153.

Ravallion, Martin, and Shaohua Chen (2007). "China's (Uneven) Progress Against Poverty." *Journal of Development Economics* 82:1–42.

SAC (Annual). *Zhongguo Tongji Zhaiyao* [Statistical abstract of China]. Beijing: Zhongguo Tongji.

SYC (Annual). *Zhongguo Tongji Nianjian* [Statistical yearbook of China]. Beijing: Zhongguo Tongji.

UNDP (United Nations Development Programme) (2015). *Human Development Report 2015: Work for Human Development.* New York: UNDP. Accessed at hdr.undp.org/sites/default/files/2015_human _development_report.pdf.

UNDP China and Development Research Center of the State Council (2016). *China National Human Development Report 2016: Social Innovation for Inclusive Human Development.* Beijing: China Translation & Publishing House. Accessed at http://www.cn.undp.org/content/china/en/home/library /human_development/china-human-development-report-2016.html.

Wu, Guobao (2016). "Four Factors That Have Driven Poverty Reduction in China." Blogpost, October 21. Accessed at https://www.weforum.org/agenda/2016/10/four-factors-that-have-driven-poverty-reduction -in-china.

Xu, Jing, and Ximing Yue (2012). "Redistributive Impacts of the Personal Income Tax in Urban China." In Shi Li, Hiroshi Sato, and Terry Sicular, eds., *Rising Inequality in China: Challenges to a Harmonious Society*, 362–383. New York: Cambridge University Press.

III THE RURAL ECONOMY

The contemporary Chinese countryside, Yangshuo 2005. (Courtesy of Chuck Morrow.)

11 Rural Organization

The Chinese village—the fundamental unit of rural society—was swept by two dramatic revolutions during the second half of the twentieth century. The first revolution, during the 1950s, converted every village into an agricultural collective and mobilized hundreds of millions of farmers to build a socialist countryside. The second revolution, just as dramatic and consequential as the first, dissolved the collectives and vaulted much of the countryside into a modernizing and marketizing economy after 1979. Both these revolutions imprinted their features on the Chinese countryside and left pervasive legacies superimposed on the traditional village. Today, a third wave of change is taking place in the Chinese countryside. On the one hand, massive out-migration has drained the countryside of many of its young people; on the other hand, an unprecedented level of attention from the national government has led to a substantial infusion of resources, designed to build a "New Socialist Countryside." While not as revolutionary as the two previous changes—and not as socialist as the name would indicate—the current set of policy changes are reshaping rural society from top to bottom.

In this chapter, we examine the dramatic changes in rural organization that have helped make the Chinese countryside what it is today. Section 11.1 surveys the traditional, organic organization of Chinese rural life. Section 11.2 looks at the rural collectives: their nature and distinctive features; the process of organizational change; and their dissolution. Section 11.3 examines the second revolution in the Chinese countryside. It stresses the fact that the impact on agricultural production was unambiguously positive, but that the failure to find alternatives to the provision of services by the collectives led to a decline in the supply of public goods, with effects on rural health and education. Section 11.4 looks at the mostly top-down innovations that over the past 10 years have sought to reconstruct the rural public goods regime and redirected resources to agriculture and rural communities. Section 11.5 concludes the chapter.

11.1   The Chinese Village

There are 3.3 million natural villages in China, and nearly every Chinese farmer lives in one (Agricultural Census 2008, 24). In the developed areas around large cities, what were originally separate villages now merge into a dense landscape of suburban industrialization and urban sprawl. In remote areas, village size dwindles, and settlements may consist of only five or six houses; farmers live in individual farmsteads in a few areas. Especially in the south, some villages are composed entirely of households with the same surname, known as single-lineage villages. The national government promotes the idea of the administrative village, which should have a "village committee" to serve as a rudimentary institution of self-governance and to carry on some of the functions of the agricultural collectives that were dismantled in the early 1980s. At year-end 2012, there were 588,000 of these administrative villages. Administrative villages usually incorporate several natural villages or hamlets, and there are also villages where no village committee functions.

Villages vary enormously in their level of modernization and connection to the outside world. In more prosperous areas, houses of reinforced concrete, usually two stories high, have become the norm and now account for half of all rural housing. The remainder are predominantly wood and brick, and about 10% are still built of clay or rammed earth. The countryside has been connected rapidly to modern communication networks: almost all villages now have landlines and cell-phone coverage and average two mobile phones per household. However, outside the prosperous coastal deltas, many villages still have limited modern infrastructure. Running water and improved household cooking facilities (gas or electric stoves) are available only to a minority, and the majority cook either with coal or with straw or twigs gathered from the fields or forests. Interiors are dark and smoky, and indoor air is polluted. Every part of rural China has been affected by modern technologies and the modernizing Chinese state, but traditional technologies have not disappeared.

The dominant activity in the village is farming. When villagers need to carry out other tasks, they generally go to nearby market towns. The market town holds a regular market once or twice a week, or perhaps every 10 days. Villagers come into town to sell produce, buy and sell livestock, and purchase other producer or consumer goods. The entire Chinese countryside has long been loosely organized into "standard market areas," consisting of a market town and the surrounding villages from which the market is easily accessible within a day's walk (Skinner 1964–1965). The market town is the primary interface between the villager and the larger world and most market towns were the seat of one of the 31,775 township governments at the end of 2016. Before mass emigration and cell phones, the standard market area was the average villager's entire world, home to virtually all the individuals with whom he or she had regular face-to-face contact.

11.2 Agricultural Collectives

After 1949, the government of the People's Republic superimposed a new organizational structure on traditional rural society. The socialist organizations did not do away with the traditional rural organizations, but the existing institutions were gradually forced into new molds and given new functions by the Chinese state. The most fundamental change was the organization of farmers into collectives, which took over responsibility for agricultural production from individual households. From the mid-1950s to the early 1980s, the collectives were the dominant rural institution. Until the state suddenly changed course and allowed the collectives to disband in the early 1980s, the collectives were the main instrument for the state's intrusive and transformative approach to rural life.

During the heyday of the socialist economy, planners required rural institutions that could facilitate the procurement of a steady supply of agricultural produce at a low price, relative to industrial prices and wages. The entire socialist development strategy was predicated on the state's ability to mobilize resources for industrial investment, so the state had to be able to extract resources from the countryside. The state imposed a direct agricultural tax on cropland, but much more important was the implicit tax the state imposed in the form of compulsory delivery of agricultural produce, especially grain, at low, state-set prices. Already in the early 1950s, the state required farmers to sell grain and cotton, the two most important marketed crops, to the government at fixed prices. Thus, although the primary role of the rural collectives was to organize agricultural production, they were also designed to facilitate the extraction of agricultural surpluses from the countryside. At the same time, the Chinese leadership was committed to using rural organizations to transform the character of rural life. Mao Zedong famously said that Chinese peasants were "poor and blank," meaning that they could be remade into exemplary socialist citizens. Rural collectives were seen as a cheap and effective way to provide new social services and improved production inputs. Thus the rural institutions created by collectivization were multifunctional. In addition to their purely economic functions, they were inevitably instruments for the extension of state political control into the countryside. After 1970, the government birth-control policies extended the reach of political control into formerly private family realms. Collectives helped the government maintain tabs on rural residents and provided a convenient conduit for economic and political innovations that the government was promoting in the countryside.

11.2.1   Features of the Agricultural Collectives

The primary function of the collectives was agricultural production, however, and there were three basic definitional characteristics of the collectives:

1. The land was pooled and worked in common. Collectives differed from farmers' co-ops in other economies because of this basic characteristic: cooperation was not restricted to marketing or service delivery but included farming itself. Ownership of the land was transferred to "the collective," meaning the residents of a given village. Individual farm households kept ownership of their homes and a few farm animals and retained control of "private plots" (which ranged from 3% to 10% of cultivated area). The collective owned all other productive assets.

2. The collective served as the basic accounting unit. The collective purchased agricultural inputs (often on credit), coordinated farm tasks, and sold output after the harvest. Each able-bodied worker was assigned a daily job by the collective, and labor was coordinated. With the income derived from sale of the harvest, the collective paid off debts incurred to buy inputs and set aside money in several collectively controlled funds. Only after these costs were paid and set-asides were deducted did the collective calculate the available net income and distribute it to households. Households received income both in kind (as food grain) and in cash. The most important collective funds that were set aside were the accumulation (or investment) fund and the public welfare fund.

The size of this basic accounting unit fluctuated over time, as the collectives were gradually adapted to the traditional social structures of the Chinese countryside. In the 1950s, especially in the winter of 1955–1956, farmers were organized into Agricultural Producers Cooperatives (APCs), which were generally the size of a large village. During the Great Leap Forward, in 1958, the accounting unit jumped to a new, much larger unit, the commune, which often had 5,000 or more households (see table 11.1). This huge and unwieldy organization tried to do too much without proper incentives and led the countryside to disaster. In the immediate wake of the Great Leap Forward, three important changes were made. First, the commune was adjusted so that it typically coincided with a traditional market town and a standard marketing area. This is generally the same as today's township. Second, the accounting unit was dropped all the way down to a group even smaller than the old APCs. This was the "team," a relatively small group of about 30 to 40 households that corresponded to a small village or hamlet, or a neighborhood of a larger village. The team became the primary accounting unit between 1962 and 1981. Finally, this whole structure was organized into a three-level hierarchy, consisting of commune, brigade (large village), and team. The commune and the brigade carried out most nonagricultural functions, including the development of industry and quasi-governmental

Table 11.1
Changes in the organization of agriculture.

Natural units	1956–1958	1958–1959	1962–1981	1982–present
Standard marketing area—market town		Commune* (over 5,000 households)	Commune (2,000 households)	Township (3,000 households) government and economic corporation
Large village	Agricultural producers Cooperative* (100–250 households)		Brigade (200 households)	Village
Small village or neighborhood	Team		Team* (c. 30 households)	
Household	Household	Household	Household	Household*

*Basic accounting unit.
Source: Author, based on Skinner (1964–1965).

responsibilities such as health and welfare, education, and public safety. This basic configuration lasted until the early 1980s.

3. Net income was distributed to households on the basis of work points. Individuals earned work points for the tasks or days of work done. These work points were entered in ledgers over the course of the year. At the end of the year, after the harvest was in, the total net income of the collective was computed and divided by the total number of work points earned during the year. Only then did the collective members learn the value of a work point. In 1978, according to the newly revived household surveys, average annual distributed collective income amounted to 88.5 yuan per person (a little over $50 at the prevailing exchange rate). However, more than 70% of this (63 yuan) was received in the form of distributed grain. In addition, households earned money income from the sale of crops and animals raised on their private plots (36 yuan), as well as "other income" (9 yuan), including remittances from relatives. Combined with the 25.5 yuan distributed by the collectives in cash, total household money income was 70.5 yuan, just over half of total household income (133.5 yuan). In other words, the collectives were partially demonetized. Households received most of their money income from household activities but relied on the collectives for their supplies of staple foods (NBS 1985).

The work-point system gave the collective enormous control over the distribution of income. Some collectives experimented with different methods of assigning work points, searching for methods that would effectively motivate workers, minimize monitoring costs, and still be consistent with socialist ideals. During the Cultural Revolution, collectives were pressured to use the "Dazhai system," under which each worker evaluated his work contribution in front of village meetings and then invited public comment and criticism. In most places, most of the time, though, work points were assigned more routinely for tasks or days of labor. Most collectives were too close to subsistence levels and too aware of their economic vulnerability to be willing to indulge in much utopian experimentation. Work points were not awarded just for farm labor; they could be awarded for any activity the collective deemed worthwhile, such as teaching or serving as a medic. In this way, the collective could erase the distinction between moneymaking and nonmoneymaking activities.

11.2.2   The Collectives in Practice

In principle, the collectives could have been market-oriented cooperatives, responding to price and other economic signals. In practice, though, the decision-making autonomy of the collectives was severely restricted. Collectives were required to deliver grain to the state and were used to attain three types of objectives: economic, social, and political.

The primary economic objective, not surprisingly, was organizing agricultural production. In this task, the collectives clearly failed. They created incentives for farmers to show up for work every morning (otherwise no work points would be received), but it was more difficult to motivate farmers to work hard throughout the day. It was difficult for collectives to coordinate tasks among 40 or 50 households, especially since tasks were spatially separate and had to be expertly performed throughout the seasons. Long-term face-to-face relations could ensure that the most important tasks got done reasonably effectively, but they did not provide incentives to work harder or develop more efficient forms of work organization. There are no economies of scale in most types of agricultural production in China, so collectives were unable to improve efficiency by organizing larger units.

However, the collectives could mobilize resources and so increase the total inputs available for production. In the early years, traditional graves that had taken up farmland were plowed under, and scattered fields were consolidated. In this way, the collectives augmented the effective land supply. The collectives mobilized and rewarded labor during the agricultural off-season. Construction projects, large and small, were undertaken during the winter. During the 1970s, 100 million workers (30% of the rural labor force) were mobilized for a few weeks of slack-season construction each year, primarily building and repairing irrigation systems. During the 1920s, the average farmer had worked only 160 days per year, but by the late 1970s the average farmer was working 200 to 275 days per year (Vermeer 1988, 157).

Collectives were also a convenient way to organize commercial activities to support agriculture. Producer services were provided by rural credit cooperatives (RCCs) and supply and marketing cooperatives (SMCs), which were nominally independent but integrated into the collective organization. Each would have a branch in the commune headquarters (the market town or township), forming a cluster of affiliated institutions. The RCCs collected household savings and provided liquidity to agricultural trade. The SMCs supplied most of the modern agricultural inputs that were required as agriculture developed, and they purchased most of the farmers' marketed surplus. Even more important was the role of collectives in developing rural industries, especially after 1970 (chapter 13). The social functions of the collectives included the provision of social services, especially education and health, as well as insurance against risk. The work-point system made it extremely convenient for the collective to tax its own members to provide social services. All that was required was a decision to award work points to the local teacher or medic. By the mid-1970s, this system had created a network of rudimentary social services (discussed later). The system paid for 1.2 million rural teachers, for example, and pushed the number of children in schools up to unprecedented levels. The collectives were also a mechanism to buffer risk. Within a given collective, households were less subject to risk because the collective guaranteed access to land and provided modest welfare payments in the event of extreme need. In 1979, some 15 million households received some kind of relief, either from the state or the collective, although the collective contribution averaged only 3 RMB per household (NBS 1985, 129, 132). Many other households "owed" the collective for staple foods distributed, and many poor collectives were in arrears to the government: these "debts" would never be repaid. A basic safety net had been cobbled together at a very low level of income.

Finally, the collectives inevitably had political functions as well. The collectives were a channel for education and indoctrination. Collective registration was used to control migration and prevent population movements that were not approved by the government. After 1970, the collective system was used to implement controls on fertility and restrict births in the countryside. Although it was part of the three-level collective structure, the commune also functioned part-time as the lowest level of government in the countryside.

The collectives were an inefficient way to organize agricultural production. However, they proved to be adequate for organizing much of the rest of rural social and economic life. Particularly after the harsh lessons of the Great Leap Forward, the rural collective system between about 1962 and 1982 settled into a reasonably stable configuration. The three-level collective system of commune, brigade, and team was adapted reasonably well to traditional social structures. The commune headquarters was built in the market town, and the commune corresponded roughly to the standard marketing area. The brigade corresponded to the large village. The production team was transformed into a moderate size subvillage unit, consisting of individuals who knew each other well and interacted face-to-face. In 1978, the average team had 167 men, women, and children. This basic accounting unit was much smaller, for example, than a Soviet collective farm or the APCs or communes of the 1950s. The team specialized in agriculture; most of the nonagricultural functions, both economic and noneconomic, were taken over by the brigade and the commune. Thus the three-level collective system also represented a reasonably effective division of labor among organizational forms. It persisted in this form for about 20 years, until the dramatic changes of the early 1980s.

11.2.3   The Agricultural Policy Environment of the Collectives: "Grain First"

In practice, agricultural collectives were under constant pressure to produce grain. "Grain First" policies were exemplified by the prominent Cultural Revolution slogan "take grain as the key link" (*yiliang weigang*). The political emphasis on grain production can be seen as a necessary component of the overall development strategy. Compulsory procurement of grain from the peasantry at a low price served as an implicit tax, making farmers indirectly pay much of the cost of the industrialization drive. However, precisely because grain prices were low, peasants had no incentive to grow grain for sale. Once their own subsistence needs were met, peasant households would have preferred to pursue more lucrative undertakings (economic crops or household sideline activities) on which the state did not impose such onerous hidden taxes. To prevent this, the Chinese government used the collective system to apply extraeconomic pressure on peasant households to meet or exceed their grain procurement targets. The effect of this pressure in retarding agricultural growth was significant, and, as Lardy (1983) showed, the costs were large.

• Procurement quotas served as quantitative targets and were often supplemented with acreage targets. Farmers did not have the freedom to decide how much land would be used for each crop, and so were unable to devise their own income maximization strategies.

• Many collectives were forced to increase grain output even when this decreased income. Even in the rich Yangtze delta, well suited to rice cultivation, collectives were forced to grow three crops per year to maximize output. They used increasingly labor-intensive production strategies, transplanting seedlings, and increasing fertilizer and irrigation inputs. The additional inputs cost more than the value of the additional grain produced (Wiens 1982).

• Regional grain self-sufficiency was stressed everywhere during the Cultural Revolution. Areas not well suited to grain grew grain anyway. The result was a loss of opportunities for regional specialization and a decline in interregional shipments of grain.

• Nongrain crops suffered comparative neglect. While total grain output grew at 2.2% annually between 1955–1957 and 1977–1979. Cotton output grew 1.5% and oilseed output only 0.5% annually over this period (averaging over three years to reduce the impact of weather). Since population grew 2% annually over this period, output of grain per capita increased 0.2% per year, while per capita output of cotton and oilseeds declined (section 12.1 and figure 12.1). Grain availability increased somewhat more because China began importing grain after the Great Leap Forward, slightly reducing the procurement burden and allowing farmers to retain and consume more grain.

• The uniform national Grain First policy led to a paradoxically wide range of local outcomes. Some regions did well, particularly in the one-fifth of counties designated "high and stable yield areas," which accounted for about half of grain procurements. They received priority access to scarce modern inputs, such as fertilizer, machinery, and electricity and were able to reap the benefits of the agricultural "green revolution" (discussed in chapter 12) and experienced substantially improved living standards. Areas that did not have a comparative advantage in grain production were forced to strive for grain self-sufficiency anyway. To achieve this objective, they had to devote essentially all their land to grain, and abandoned their previous specialty crops. Regions that initially had a comparative advantage in grain production, on the other hand, were able to meet their quotas with green revolution techniques and then divert some of their land to cash crops to raise incomes. These effects sometimes produced a perverse "reverse specialization" under which localities were growing more of the crops in which they had the least comparative advantage.

11.3 The Second Revolution in the Countryside: Rural Reforms, 1979–1984

After 1978, the relaxation of policy in the countryside led to explosive changes, as described in chapter 5. The Third Plenum in December 1978 made relatively modest adjustments to rural policy that touched off major changes in rural society. Indeed, only two new policies were adopted at first: (1) an across-the-board increase in agricultural procurement prices, and (2) a reaffirmation of the theoretical right to self-management of collectives. Individual farming was explicitly condemned. With higher grain-procurement prices, it became less necessary to coerce grain surpluses from the peasantry by extraeconomic means. Policy-makers gradually reduced their emphasis on the Grain First policy and even stepped up grain imports for a few years in order to allow new patterns of specialization to emerge in the countryside. With higher prices and less extraeconomic compulsion, decision-making autonomy for the collectives came closer to being a reality.

An unanticipated consequence of the expanded autonomy of collectives soon emerged, however. In some areas, collectives began experimenting with more radical changes in the way work points were allocated. Instead of allocating work points for inputs (for labor days, reputation, or effort), some collectives began allocating work points for output, linking the remuneration of a given work group or household to the output of a specific plot of land. Some went even further and simply contracted pieces of collective land to individual households to cultivate. Such experiments clearly tested the limits of the collective system as it had been practiced up to that time. During 1978 and 1979, peasant experiments with individual household agriculture were tolerated and protected in Sichuan and Anhui Provinces. These provinces had suffered greatly during the Great Leap Forward and by the late 1970s were governed by close associates of Deng Xiaoping—Zhao Ziyang and Wan Li, respectively. After successful experiments, the provincial leader Zhao Ziyang was promoted to national premier and, not surprisingly, expanded the boundaries of permissible local policy and experimentation. The most radical policies were initially limited to relatively poor and remote areas, and grain surplus areas were kept on a tight leash to stabilize all-important government procurements. As success emerged in poor areas, the scope of permissive policies was steadily increased.

By 1981–1982, a nationally defined program of contracting land to households, known as "household contracting" or the "household responsibility system," emerged as the clearly preferred organizational system. By the end of 1982, more than 90% of China's agricultural households had returned to some form of household farming. Initially, land was contracted to households for one year or even just for a single harvest. Quickly, however, it was seen that contracts should be longer to be more effective, and most collectives moved to 3-year contracts. These were soon succeeded by 5-, 15-, and even, in some areas, 50-year contracts to the land. What happened next was quite dramatic.

11.3.1   Production Surged in the Wake of Rural Organizational Change

Three spectacular shifts in trend occurred simultaneously. First, growth of grain production accelerated dramatically. This was particularly striking since the Grain First policy had been abandoned, and households had more freedom to find an efficient mix of crops to plant and sell. Despite the reduced emphasis, grain output growth between 1977–1979 and 1983–1985 jumped to 4.1% annually from the previous 2.2%. From previous peaks of just over 300 million tons per year, the annual harvest surged to a remarkable bumper harvest in 1984 of 407 million tons. For the first time in years, there was enough grain to go around, and given the centrality of grain to the Chinese diet at this time, this achievement was key. Second, output growth accelerated even more in virtually every other sector of agriculture. Cotton and oilseed production grew at 15% and 16% per year, respectively. Meat production surged, growing at just below 10% per year.

Third, perhaps most remarkably, these output gains occurred while farmers were reducing their labor inputs into farming. Left to themselves, farm households showed that they valued their labor time more highly than collective planners had. With greater freedom to allocate labor, farmers worked harder but for fewer hours. Labor

Table 11.2
Labor days per hectare.

	1953	1978	1985	2004	2015
Rice	250	421	328	178	93
Cotton	300	908	643	n.a.	256
Wheat	120	461	218	122	70

Sources: Taylor (1988, 740, 747); Li (2013); NBS Rural Department (2016, 275, 276, 279).

inputs to the main staple crops declined, after having increased steadily for 20 years under the collectives (see the decline from 1978 to 1985 in table 11.2). People were simply working harder on their own farms. Farmers also shifted cultivation toward crops with lower labor requirements, even though these were sometimes of lower value per unit of land. Sorghum, millet, and sugar beets all increased their share in output; all are slow-growing, relatively low-value crops that require modest labor inputs. These changes then allowed farmers to free up family members to move into nonagricultural activities (chapter 13). Rural reforms showed that it was possible to produce more with less input, once the incentive and policy environment was set straight. (Much later, in the twenty-first century, as migration and scientific advances changed agricultural technology more fundamentally, further dramatic reductions in labor inputs per unit of land took place; see table 11.2 and discussion in chapter 12.)

Rural change was rapid because the household responsibility system was adopted quickly. But other aspects of the rural system changed more slowly. The state continued to procure most of the grain crop. There was a movement toward use of multitier prices, with the state paying a near-market-price premium for procurements above the minimum compulsory quota. Meanwhile, free markets grew outside the state apparatus. But the government maintained systematic control over key elements of the marketing system, particularly over cotton, staple grains, and fertilizer, well into the 1990s. It was not until 2000 that the government finally freed up the price of cotton and allowed textile mills to purchase cotton directly from farmers.

11.3.2   Administrative Villages and Village Self-Government

In the wake of successful rural reforms, the role of the collective changed dramatically. In some places, the agricultural collective collapsed: village officials suddenly found there was a great deal that needed to be done on the family farm. With the land leased to individual households, collectives had lost their core functional element and their main justification. The commune had always had some governmental functions, so it was straightforward to transform communes into townships, and they became the local, bottom level of the formal governmental hierarchy. Those communes that had set up profitable enterprises typically spun them off into a local government-supervised corporation. The village, by contrast, is not, and has never been, part of the government structure in China. However, villages still faced a range of important decisions. Should land contracting procedures change as circumstances changed? Should the village redistribute land as out-migration occurred and family sizes changed? How much should be invested in local public goods? How should the village pay for local public goods?

The Chinese government, since the 1980s, has supported the creation of administrative villages to allow farmers to address these issues. Larger and more institutionalized than natural villages, administrative villages speak for village residents and represent the "collective" that still owns all rural land. A 1987 law permitted villages to select their committees through general election, and the 1998 Organic Law of Villagers' Committees made this a general rule nationwide. Village committees should be elected by all resident members of the village over 18. This experiment has been quite successful. Economists have used the gradual diffusion of open elections to examine the impact of direct election of village leaders on village provision of public goods. There is abundant evidence that village elections have had a positive economic impact, increasing the level of public spending and increasing local public goods provision (Wang and Yang 2007; Luo et al. 2010; Martinez-Bravo et al. 2011). Moreover, villages in which leaders are directly elected provide better quality public goods, such as roads, since leaders depend on the approval of users for reelection (Wong et al. 2017). There is also some evidence that direct elections lead to younger and better-educated leaders. Village elections were sufficiently successful that pilot programs to extend elections to townships were tried in some provinces, but such experiments have been discontinued.

Despite the success of village self-government, few villages had resources to provide an adequate level of public goods. Although the government stopped using compulsory procurement as a tool to extract resources from farmers in the 1980s, until around 2005, villagers still paid taxes without receiving much in the way of government expenditures. As a result, village committees worked in a very underresourced environment. In particular, they had to make difficult decisions about taxes and fees required to provide public services but much resented by local farmers. Through most of the 1990s, the villages were left alone to fend for themselves.

11.3.3   The Side Effect of Reform: Decline of Rural Public Services

The success of reforms in agricultural production demonstrated conclusively that rural collectives were less efficient in agriculture than household farms. But in the provision of social services, the collapse of collectives left a void in the countryside. Rural collectives had been important in providing health care and education, and after their elimination, the supply of both declined. Here we concentrate on the rural health-care system, but the process was similar, though less dire, with respect to primary education and even physical infrastructure, such as irrigation networks (chapter 12). The rural collectives were key components in the creation of an impressive system of basic-level health-care delivery in rural areas. The capacity to improve life expectancy and basic health conditions, as described in chapter 10, depended on the system of rural organization that provided basic health services. The level of care provided was primitive, but the system had a large impact on overall health because it provided three critical components: first, an efficient way to invest in preventive (as opposed to curative) health care; second, basic treatment for simple illnesses and injuries; third, at least in some regions, a system of referrals to higher-level medical services. Thus basic health care, sanitation, and preventive care were brought to most villages for the first time. The collectives also mobilized large numbers in campaigns against public health threats, such as schistosomiasis, a debilitating disease spread by the snails that infested flooded rice fields.

The Cultural Revolution increased the attention given to rural health care. Mao Zedong had proclaimed in June 1965 that "the focus of health-care work should shift to rural areas," and this was one of the few Maoist slogans that led to genuine positive outcomes. By the mid-1970s, a network of medical services had been created in the countryside. Paramedics, part-time medical workers who continued to farm, comprised two groups: brigade-level "barefoot doctors" who had typically participated in a six-week training course in the county town, their only medical training, and even more lightly trained team paramedics, who might have taken only a simple first-aid and sanitation course. By the mid-1970s, 1.5 million barefoot doctors and 3.5 million team paramedics were on the job, enough for the average village to have one or two of its own resident, part-time paramedics available year-round.

These paramedics, at both the brigade and team levels, were paid in work points. In practice, therefore, they were compensated by a tax on the output of the local community, since assigning work points to paramedics meant that the value of the work points assigned for farm work was reduced. In turn, their services were generally provided free to community residents. Most Chinese farmers were thus covered by a rudimentary system of medical insurance, called "cooperative health services." For simple complaints, they could turn to their local paramedic. If the ailment was more serious, they could be referred to the hospital in the commune or county town. By rough estimates, some 70%–80% of the rural population was covered by cooperative health services at the end of the 1970s.

Decollectivization in the 1980s cut off the flow of resources into this system, and it collapsed. The production teams were no longer assigning work points, so there was no method to compensate health workers. Some communities had established township and village enterprises (TVEs, see chapter 13), and it was easy to spin these off into stand-alone firms. If they had profitable TVEs, the local community could use these revenues or set aside "rent" paid to the community as part of household contracting to support social services. However, only a small proportion of communities had the resources and chose to fund health services in this way. The number of paramedics dropped dramatically, to less than a quarter of the 1970s peak. The number of hospital beds per thousand rural residents, after reaching a peak of 1.5 in 1985, began a long, steady decline to 0.72 in 2003 (Zhang and Kanbur 2005). Without resources, the coverage of cooperative health services declined to less than 10% of the population by the mid-1990s. In 1998, rural residents paid for 87% of their health-care expenses out of pocket, compared with urban residents, who paid for only 44% of their health-care expenses (Zhang and Kanbur 2005, 193).

The central government considered different models for rebuilding rural health care during the 1980s and 1990s, but efforts were inconsistent and funding was inadequate. Then, in 2003, a previously unknown, highly infectious, and often fatal disease, severe acute respiratory syndrome (SARS), spread rapidly through China. Rural migrants left the cities by the millions, in some cases bringing the disease with them. As these fleeing migrants melted back into their home villages, China's leaders faced the reality that there was no rural health-care system to take care of them. If the disease were to take root in the Chinese countryside, there were no health-care facilities adequate to administer care, institute quarantines, or even track the spread of the infection. As it turned out, the new disease suddenly lost potency in the summer season and for unknown reasons faded away as quickly as it had come. However, this near miss strengthened the resolve of policy-makers to rebuild China's shattered rural health system.

11.4   The New Socialist Countryside: Establishing Supportive Government Policy

Around 2005, important changes took place in Chinese government policy toward the countryside. Since that time, a series of major policy changes toward agriculture have been adopted, encapsulated in the slogan "Give more, take less, and enliven." Overall, the slogan means that government should give more support to agriculture and rural villages, lower the direct and indirect tax burden on farming, and carry out policies to improve rural markets, including markets for land. The abolition of the agricultural tax, completed during 2005, directly increased agricultural incomes by about 5%. These policy changes were multistranded: they were discussed in chapter 6 because of their impact on immigration; and chapter 12 will take up their impact on agriculture as a production sector. Here we consider their impact on village life and the organization of rural society. The concept of the "New Socialist Countryside" was incorporated in the 11th Five-Year Plan (2006–2010), and provides a convenient label for the complex set of policies, especially insofar as they affect village life. A central component from the beginning has been the decision to rebuild public services in the Chinese countryside.

11.4.1   Reconstructing the Rural Public Goods Regime

When the Chinese government began to build a new rural public goods regime, it marked the end of more than 20 years when the post-collective countryside had operated with little or no assistance from the national government. New institutional arrangements were introduced for health care, education, and pensions. Change has been most evident in health care and education (see chapter 20). Trial implementation of the rural New Cooperative Medical System (NCMS) began in 2003 and expanded nationwide in 2005. The NCMS is an insurance program that provides coverage for serious diseases or injuries and is subsidized by upper levels of government. Initially, the program was very modest: the government contributed just 20 RMB, and participants contributed 10 yuan per family member. However, the ramp-up has been sustained and rapid: by 2016, the government contribution had increased to 420 RMB per participant, compared with an average of 150 per person from the household. The achievement has been remarkable. The national health survey of 2013 found that 97% of rural residents were covered by some form of health insurance (74% by NCMS). Coverage is not generous: NCMS members were actually reimbursed 50.1% of the cost of their hospital stays, and the out-of-pocket average expense for a single hospital stay (3,309 RMB) was still a significant burden, 33% of per capita household income. As a result, 8.2% of NCMS members reported not seeking medical care because of the cost (Center for Health Statistics 2016). Yet the proportion not seeking medical care, measured with the same methodology, has declined dramatically from 26.6% a decade earlier.

The rapid expansion of the NCMS program brought other shortcomings to light. First, the supply of basic-level health facilities has not increased rapidly, so patients often must go to larger hospitals in bigger towns or cities. Salaries of medical professionals continue to lag, so skilled doctors and nurses are in short supply. Moreover, the insurance features of the NCMS are limited: a serious illness or injury is much less devastating, but there are caps on total payments that limit the insurance impact and catastrophic events still have a huge economic impact. If care requires less than a threshold amount, it is also not reimbursed. These problems indicate clear directions for improvement and investment in public health.

Availability of elementary and middle-school education has also expanded rapidly. For decades, policies called for universal elementary education but did not provide the resources or the organizational commitment to achieve it. As the New Socialist Countryside policy has rolled out, though, money has finally become available for expanding educational coverage. After 2006, local governments were expected to provide compulsory education free in the countryside. Governmental funding increased from around 100 RMB per student in 2006 to 500 (for elementary) and 700 (for middle-school) students. Enrollment rates have increased substantially (but see section 9.4). Students from poor families are encouraged to attend boarding schools in townships or county towns, and their living expenses are partly or fully paid by the government. Leaving home for full-time boarding school can be a hardship for young children, but is effective in increasing enrollments, especially in remote areas.

11.4.2   Rebuilding the Village

The support given to boarding schools in township or county towns illustrates another characteristic of the New Socialist Countryside program: it is designed to concentrate activities in a smaller number of modernized towns. Careful management of land to develop denser, more compact villages is an integral part of the New Socialist Countryside program. Local officials have strong incentives to concentrate population to free up land for development and to generate revenues (see chapter 6). Even remote villages may be induced by provincial leaders to free up some agricultural land so that land near cities can be converted to nonagricultural uses within the provincial quota. The New Socialist Countryside program often involves construction of dense blocks of multistory homes. These can be seen anywhere in China today through the window of the high-speed trains speeding through the countryside.

Although they provide more physical amenities, these new housing schemes are not always welcomed by village residents, who consider them ugly and overly uniform. The program is especially controversial in Tibet and other areas on China's periphery, where rural people are used to combining agriculture and herding and do not like being cooped up in dense concrete villages. These features illustrate the fact that the New Socialist Countryside program is a top-down program, imposed on rural people for their benefit as defined by the government.

The policy of concentrating residential land is in part a response to out-migration. The absolute size of the agricultural labor force has declined by half since the early 1990s, and many have left the village. In some places, village life has been "hollowed out." Young adults have left, leaving higher proportions of children and elderly persons. When this happens, houses and household plots are generally kept within the family, even when rooms or whole houses are empty. As discussed in chapter 6, the property rights system encourages this behavior and has been only partially adapted to accommodate the new realities. The New Socialist Countryside is an effort to compress the settlement pattern. Close to cities it facilitates the overall urbanization process and in more remote areas it represents a kind of small-scale urbanization imposed on the traditional Chinese village.

11.4.3   Government Adaptation to a New Budgetary System

In order to accommodate the new rural policies, China's fiscal system has been quite fundamentally restructured (chapter 20). The central government stepped in to provide funding for the new network of rural social services and at the same time abolished both the agricultural tax and the fees and surcharges that had funded local public goods and initiatives. As a result, local governments have become much more dependent on budgetary transfers from higher levels. County governments now receive most of their funding from upper levels, and township budgets are increasingly being integrated into county-level budgets. Departments like education—previously the poor stepchildren of local government—have become relatively well resourced because of the steady flow of top-down subsidies. Counties and townships, with mandates from the national government, increasingly have the money and the power. Villages, on the other hand, have rarely received any of the new government revenues. As self-governing bodies that are not part of the formal governmental hierarchy, villages have no automatic claim on fiscal resources distributed through inter-governmental transfers.

As a result, since 2005, the village has become a less central player in rural policy. Decisions on policy and personnel are more directly influenced by township and even county governments, which control the resources necessary for implementation. Inevitably, the salience of village elections has declined. Elections are still regularly held and often competitive. Villagers may feel that the important decisions are no longer being made at the village level; the county and township are where the resources are and the decisions are made. Rural people are much better off but may feel that they have less control over their own lives.

11.4.4   Land Consolidation and the Business of Agriculture

Almost as soon as land was contracted to households, some policy-makers began to worry that farms were too fragmented. There is little evidence that the prevalence of very small farms has blocked productivity improvement in the Chinese countryside, but as workers leave agriculture, it is obvious that some kind of land consolidation must take place. Migrants can lease their contracted land to other families, allowing the most efficient farmers to stay and cultivate larger farms.

Land markets emerged quickly in the 1990s, but have developed slowly since. According to the Agricultural Census (2008, 199) only 10.8% of China's cultivated land was rented or leased. That is, almost 90% of farmland was either being cultivated by the family that contracted it directly from the village, or else was part of that family's "private plot." There is substantial regional variation: in Hebei, Henan, and Shandong—almost the entire North China plain—less than 5% of cultivated land is rented or leased; in northeastern Heilongjiang where mechanized grain farming is feasible the figure is 27.9%; and in highly commercialized Zhejiang, 24.3%. It seems clear that land markets have not yet developed their nationwide potential.

As discussed in chapter 6, a number of institutional obstacles impede the development of land markets. Households have not had secure tenure to the land and may find their land taken away if they leave permanently (Deininger et al. 2014). Outsiders are formally and informally limited in their ability to lease local village land. The Chinese government has moved steadily, but slowly, to survey and title land and strengthen land property rights. At the beginning of 2013, the Chinese government undertook to survey, register, and provide titles to all rural land. Subsequently, it was announced that all farmers would be able to register their permanent contractual use-rights (from the village), and could rent out or lease those fields without losing their contractual rights. Use of land as collateral for bank loans was explicitly permitted in 2016.

For all that, the Chinese government has also increasingly displayed a preferred format for managing village land. In this model, the village establishes a joint-stock corporation to own the land (with the original villagers as shareholders). It then leases land to farmers—usually local—who are seeking to create larger and more efficient farms. This corporate form has spread through the Chinese countryside. From the village's perspective, these corporations have numerous advantages. They often allow village leaders to skirt rules on converting rural land to nonagricultural uses. Government policy favors agri-business combines, so village corporations that combine cropping and agricultural processing often have more leeway. The corporations therefore allow the village and its members to capture the gains from shifting land to higher-value uses. The corporate structure allows village leaders to bring in village residents while still providing profitable commercial activities.

Economic forces and institutional changes may be accelerating the consolidation process. One of China's top agricultural economists, Jikun Huang (2016) argues that in the years between 2008 and 2013, about 25% of the land in the North and Northeast was consolidated into farms of over 7 hectares (17 acres). Much of this consolidation is being managed by village-owned corporations, with many of the benefits retained for locals. The traditional village community, though less populated than before, retains meaning and identity.

11.5   Conclusion

The Chinese village has undergone successive revolutionary changes over many decades. Today, the village faces a new era in a predominantly urban China. The village is no longer under pressure from an extractive state but rather sees its foundations undermined by the steady outflow of its members. The next stage will likely see the further decline of traditional village independence and the steady penetration of the countryside by the forces of urbanization and commercialization.

Bibliography

Suggestions for Further Reading

Chan, Madsen, and Unger (2009) is an excellent account of a village in Guangdong that updates the original 1984 edition through decades of change, covering Maoism, reform, and globalization. Skinner (1964–1965) is still worth reading. Cao Jinqing (2000) combines firsthand observation with grounded analysis.

References

Agricultural Census (2008). *Zhongguo Dierci Quanguo Nongye Pucha Ziliao Zonghe Tiyao* [Comprehensive abstract of materials from the Second National Agricultural Census]. Beijing: Zhongguo Tongji.

Cao Jinqing (2000). *China Along the Yellow River*. Trans. Nicky Harman and Huang Ruhua. London and New York: Routledge Curzon.

Center for Health Statistics (2016). [Quinquennial Report]. *2013 Nian Diwuci Guojia Weisheng Fuwu Diaocha* [2013 fifth analysis report of National Health Services survey in China]. Accessed at www.nhfpc.gov.cn/mohwsbwstjxxzx/s8211/201610/9f109ff40e9346fca76dd82cecf419ce.shtml.

Chan, Anita, Richard Madsen, and Jonathan Unger (2009). *Chen Village: Revolution to Globalization*. Berkeley: University of California Press.

Deininger, Klaus, Songqing Jin, Fang Xia, and Jikun Huang (2014). "Moving Off the Farm: Land Institutions to Facilitate Structural Transformation and Agricultural Productivity Growth in China." *World Development* 59:505–520.

Huang, Jikun (2016). "China's Agriculture and Policies: Challenges and Implications for Global Trade." Presentation at the 60th AARES Annual Conference, Canberra, ACT, February 2–5.

Lardy, Nicholas (1983). *Agriculture in China's Modern Economic Development*. New York: Cambridge University Press.

Li, Zhou (2013). "China's Agricultural Development." In Ross Garnaut, Cai Fang, and Ligang Song, eds., *China: A New Model for Growth and Development*, 147–178. Canberra: ANU E-Press.

Luo, Renfu, Linxiu Zhang, Jikun Huang, and Scott Rozelle (2010). "Village Elections, Public Goods Investments and Pork Barrel Politics, Chinese Style." *Journal of Development Studies* 46 (4): 662–684.

Martinez-Bravo, Monica, Gerard Padró i Miquel, Nancy Qian, and Yang Yao (2011). "Do Local Elections in Non-democracies Increase Accountability? Evidence from Rural China." NBER Working Paper no. 16948, National Bureau of Economic Research, Cambridge, MA, April.

NBS (1985). *Zhongguo Sheui Tongji Ziliao* [China social statistical materials]. Beijing: Zhongguo Tongji.

NBS Rural Department (Annual). *Zhongguo Nongcun Tongji Nianjian* [China rural statistical yearbook]. Beijing: Zhongguo Tongji.

Skinner, G. W. (1964–1965). "Marketing and Social Structure in Rural China." 3 parts. *Journal of Asian Studies* 24:3–43, 195–228, 363–399.

Taylor, Jeffrey (1988). "Rural Employment Trends and the Legacy of Surplus Labour, 1978–86." *China Quarterly*, no. 116 (December): 736–766.

Vermeer, Eduard (1988). *Economic Development in Provincial China: The Central Shaanxi Since 1930*. Cambridge: Cambridge University Press.

Wang, Shuna, and Yang Yao (2007). "Grassroots Democracy and Local Governance: Evidence from Rural China." *World Development* 35 (10): 1635–1649.

Whiting, Susan, and Dan Wang (forthcoming). "The Rural Economy." In Weiping Wu and Mark Frazier, eds., *The Sage Handbook of Contemporary China*. Vol. 1. London and Thousand Oaks, CA: Sage Publications.

Wiens, Thomas (1982). "The Limits to Agricultural Intensification: The Suzhou Experience." In U.S. Congress Joint Economic Committee, ed., *China Under the Four Modernizations*, 462–474. Washington, DC: U.S. Government Printing Office.

Wong, Ho Lun, Yu Wang, Renfu Luo, Linxiu Zhang, and Scott Rozelle (2017). "Local Governance and the Quality of Local Infrastructure: Evidence from Village Road Projects in Rural China." *Journal of Public Economics*. doi: 10.1016/j.jpubeco.2017.06.006.

Zhang, Xiaobo, and Ravi Kanbur (2005). "Spatial Inequality in Education and Health Care in China." *China Economic Review* 16:189–204. See the sources cited therein as well.

For years, food availability was the gravest challenge that faced China. From the failure of the Great Leap Forward (GLF) until well into the 1980s, the basic question whether Chinese agriculture would be able to feed China's growing population remained unsettled. Today that question has been definitively answered: in the past 35 years, China's agriculture has displayed the productivity and resilience necessary to feed China while also releasing hundreds of millions of workers from agricultural production.

Behind the abundance of China's food economy today lies a technological revolution that has transformed Chinese agriculture. It is a mistake to think of agriculture merely as the traditional sector of the economy, constrained by a limited endowment of fertile land, dependent on the weather, and bound to the rhythms of the past. It is true that agriculture must release labor to the dynamic urban economy, but this can happen only if agriculture itself is healthy and growing. One of the most paradoxical—but also most universal—patterns of successful development is that agriculture shrinks as a share of the overall economy even as it grows and increases productivity.

The key to resolving this apparent paradox is to see how technological change adapts production to the availability of different inputs, and how technological change itself is shaped by the relative abundance of inputs. In China's case, the relative scarcity of land, rather than obstructing the development of agriculture, has shaped the trajectory of technological change that has allowed agriculture to develop. The first part of this chapter looks at the supply side of the agricultural economy, first reviewing production trends (section 12.1) and then showing how the process of technological change has reshaped Chinese agriculture, particularly through the impact of the "green revolution" (sections 12.2–3). These changes have allowed China to escape from food scarcity even as the agricultural labor force has fallen by half. Not only has overall productivity increased rapidly, but also the agricultural sector has had the flexibility to adapt to very different combinations of factor inputs.

Section 12.4 discusses the demand side. As incomes rise throughout the economy, the products that households demand from agriculture change. Through the early 1980s, the Chinese diet was overwhelmingly based on grain. As households have grown richer, they have demanded a more diverse diet, including more convenient processed foods and more meat. Consumers strongly prefer a higher-quality and more diverse diet, and these demands affect every aspect of the agricultural economy, from the crops grown to the production, processing, and marketing chains involved.

Agricultural policy is the subject of section 12.5. Every country intervenes in agricultural markets to some extent, if only to smooth out fluctuations in agricultural prices and protect basic food security. However, countries make very different choices about how much to tax or support agriculture, and how open to trade their agricultural sector will be. China's policy toward agriculture has shifted dramatically since the early twenty-first century; it has drastically cut taxes on agriculture and has adopted a series of policies to subsidize and protect agriculture. Moreover, China has adhered to a "grain self-sufficiency" policy even while somewhat reinterpreting what that policy means. These policies have achieved their goals, but they have also been costly and raise challenging issues for the future. The final section, 12.6, looks briefly at the relationship among prices, technology, and the sustainability of agricultural practices. The concentration of large amounts of chemical fertilizers and pesticides on limited cultivated acreage increases production but at the cost of greater long-term environmental stress.

12.1   Output Growth in Agriculture

Chinese traditional agriculture was extremely sophisticated, adapted to wring the highest possible yields out of a piece of land through intensive application of human labor and organic fertilizers. It was also prescientific in that it relied on traditional techniques (albeit refined through centuries of experimentation) without significant application of modern inputs. After about 1970, new technologies and industrial inputs began to flow to the Chinese countryside for the first time, and at the end of the 1970s—simultaneously with China's economic reforms—a true technological transformation of Chinese agriculture began that in the years since has only accelerated.

Grain is by far the most important product of Chinese agriculture. Production of grain in 1956–1957 was nearly 200 million metric tons, just enough to feed the population, and more than tripled to 620 million tons in 2015, while China's population slightly more than doubled over the same period. Figure 12.1 expresses these data in per capita terms, enabling us to clearly distinguish several different periods in China's post-1949 agricultural development. A horizontal line has been placed at the level of 300 kilograms of grain per person. For a diet based predominantly on grain, this is

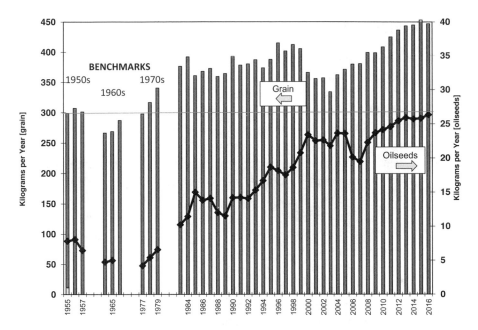

Figure 12.1
Per capita agricultural output.
Source: *SYC* (1991, 357; 2015, 407–408).

roughly equal to the level of food sufficiency. After setting aside some of the harvest for seeds and reserves and accounting for losses in milling, this is enough to provide a sufficient number of calories per day per person—approximately 2,000 calories—if food is distributed equally. The first benchmark period was 1955–1957. The newly formed agricultural collectives, discussed in chapter 11, were used to increase inputs by expanding the irrigated area and increasing the number of days farmers put into land improvement. Distribution of grain was equalized. The result was probably close to what the traditional technology could achieve: production at 300 kilograms per capita, enough to feed the population.

In the event, this level was not sustained. The misguided policies of the GLF led to a sharp drop in output, and remarkably, even after the recovery, per capita output in the benchmark 1964–1966 period was still well below the 1955–1957 level. Given the still very low levels of consumption of fats and calories from oilseeds (shown in figure 12.1) and meat, this implies that tens, probably hundreds, of millions of people were undernourished. China imposed strict grain rationing and began to import grain. It was not until 1978, over a decade later, that per capita production returned to the level of 300 kilograms per capita that had been attained in the 1950s. During the later 1960s and 1970s, China's agriculture grew primarily by intensification of land use, that is, applying more labor to a given plot of land, and developing new patterns of grain cropping, including triple cropping and intercropping of different varieties, to facilitate this intensification. As described in chapter 11, the Grain First agricultural policy gave absolute priority to grain at the expense of other crops. Even the slow increase in per capita grain output was achieved at the cost of offsetting reductions in output of some important nongrain crops. For example, as figure 12.1 shows, production of oilseeds per capita was significantly lower in the 1970s than in the 1950s. Average availability was less than a tablespoon of vegetable oil per person per day, and oil was strictly rationed. Considering that Chinese cuisine is dependent on vegetable oil for deep-frying and stir-frying, and that a tablespoon of oil is hardly adequate for a single dish, one can see that Chinese households were limited to a monotonous and austere diet even when there were adequate calories.

Beginning in 1979, policy shifted drastically, and output surged. Farmers were given much greater control over their economic activity, and this resulted in very large one-time-only gains as peasants responded to better incentives, not only to work harder but also to meet market demands more effectively. Per capita output soared in the bumper harvest in 1984 and then grew more moderately, reaching the historically unprecedented level of 400 kilograms per capita in 1996–1999. At this level, there is more than enough grain for direct human consumption, and after 1999, farmers retrenched in response to market signals, shifting land from grain to non-grain crops, including oilseeds. Indeed, the increase in non-grain products is even more striking than the increase in grain.

After the modest harvest of 2003, a new period of growth began. Grain acreage and output increased annually for 12 straight years, through 2015. This phase of growth is discussed later, in the context of two trends that explain it: the shift toward grain grown as fodder to feed animals and the policy shift toward agricultural support after 2003. Overall, since the reform era, Chinese output has been comfortably above the subsistence level and has grown strongly, diversified, and increased productivity. Behind these changes lies a profound change in agricultural systems and incentives (discussed in chapter 11), but also a technological transformation, the "green revolution."

12.2   The Green Revolution

The term "green revolution" refers to an integrated package of modern inputs that dramatically increases agricultural output. The three key elements of the green revolution are improved seeds, chemical fertilizer, and irrigation. The scientific breakthroughs that created the green revolution were achieved by international teams of scientists in the 1960s and 1970s, working at international centers, especially the International Rice Research Institute (IRRI) in the Philippines and the International

Maize and Wheat Improvement Center in Mexico. At the same time, but separately, Chinese agronomists began to produce new seed varieties that also had the potential to substantially raise agricultural production. Since 1978, Chinese scientists have cooperated closely with international centers, and many similarities in the separate early research programs have become evident. In fact, the three elements of the green revolution are the same as those on which traditional Chinese rice cultivation was based (chapter 3): improved seeds, fertilizers, and irrigation. The green revolution transforms each element by the systematic application of the scientific method: farmer seed selection is transformed into systematic breeding programs and, eventually, genetic modification; organic fertilizers are supplemented and eventually replaced by chemical fertilizers; and irrigation is mechanized by the installation of pumps.

12.2.1 Complementary Inputs

A crucial feature of green revolution technologies is that they form a complementary package of inputs: the productivity of each input is significantly increased by the presence of the other technologies. There is thus a triad of green revolution techniques that must be implemented together in order to achieve maximum efficiency. A simple way to display this complementarity is to look at the output response of different crop varieties to fertilizer application. Figure 12.2 shows that application of chemical fertilizers increases yields of traditional varieties up to a point. Green revolution crops—so-called high-yield varieties (HYVs)—are not necessarily any

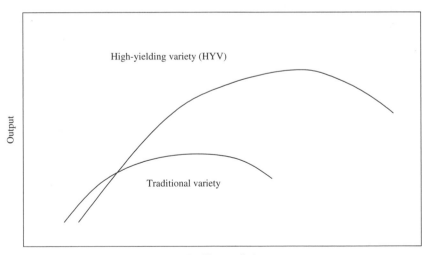

Figure 12.2
Choice of technology.
Source: Author.

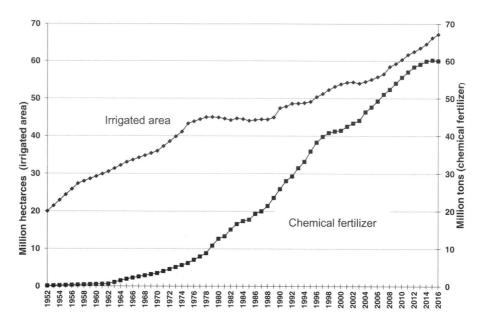

Figure 12.3
Fertilizer and irrigated area.
Source: *SYC* (1991, 323, 331, 356; 2015, 400).

more productive in the absence of fertilizer. However, HYVs are superior because they enable the farmer to increase the application of fertilizer through a much larger range and continue to get a significant positive output response. The result is much higher output per unit of land, combined with much larger total fertilizer application.

12.2.2 Irrigation

After 1949, the first part of the green revolution triad to be developed in China was improved irrigation and drainage. Starting in the early 1950s, traditional irrigation networks were repaired, and new projects were built. Figure 12.3 shows the development of irrigated area. Construction of irrigation projects was carried out by labor from the collective farms, mobilized during the winter slack season. Irrigated area grew rapidly throughout the 1960s and 1970s, but the expansion of irrigated area stopped abruptly in the 1980s, another manifestation of the collapse of public goods provision after the dissolution of the collectives (chapter 11). However, growth resumed in the 1990s as new organizational forms were worked out for irrigation districts that allowed them to charge farmers for water delivered.

The expansion of irrigated area was facilitated by the introduction of power machinery, especially electric pumps, which also improve the efficiency of water control. In the 1950s, water was lifted by human power or animal traction. Today, two-thirds of the irrigated area is serviced by machine pumping, facilitating the more precise water control necessary to support production of HYVs. Tens of millions of electric and diesel pumps now drive China's irrigation systems. This had an enormous impact in allowing the green revolution to be extended to China's wheat region, especially the North China Plain. As chapter 2 recounted, the whole Yellow River area is chronically short of water, with much competition among urban, industrial, and agricultural water users. Although the region has rich soil and abundant sun, the innovations of the green revolution could not be applied without irrigation. During the 1970s, a submersible pump was introduced that could bring up fresh water from aquifers 30 meters underground, and since then literally millions of pumps have been installed. Wheat yields grew rapidly, almost catching up with traditionally high rice yields. Today, however, overexploitation of these aquifers is leading to a water crisis that may eventually curtail wheat production on the North China Plain (chapter 21).

12.2.3   Improved Seeds

The second leg of the green revolution tripod is improved seeds. There are two indispensable steps to improved seeds: the first is developing appropriate and productive strains through research, and the second is getting the seeds into the hands of farmers through agricultural extension services. During the 1950s, the People's Republic founded a multilevel research system with the Chinese Academy of Agricultural Sciences (CAAS) at the apex. Farmers have long recognized the value of diverse genetic material for breeding improved varieties, and the CAAS imported seeds from abroad and collected varieties from remote parts of China. Plant-breeding programs included components of conventional plant breeding like selection and hybridization, as well as a gradual move into advanced genetic engineering techniques that are prominent today. Along with provincial-level academies and an agricultural extension service in every county, China built a seed-production and distribution system that is today the largest in the world. The GLF and the Cultural Revolution disrupted the growth of this system, but even in the middle of the Cultural Revolution, there was some progress as agricultural technology, research, and extension organizations were created at the county, commune, and brigade levels (see table 11.1). The focus was put on adaptation of cultivars to local conditions and dissemination of new varieties, while basic research suffered from relative neglect. After 1979, the institutes were reconstituted, and basic research revived. Provincial- and even lower-level institutes focus on local conditions, and the overall system is unusually decentralized compared with other countries.

The most important output of agricultural research has been improved seeds for HYVs. Among HYVs, dwarf varieties were a critical breakthrough in the green revolution. Dwarf varieties have short and stubby stalks, so when they are given fertilizer, they channel more of the plant's energy into the grain instead of producing tall, spindly stalks that are in danger of toppling over ("lodging"). As a result, dwarf varieties can absorb enormous amounts of nutrients from fertilizer, producing the pattern shown in figure 12.2. The beginning of the global green revolution is frequently taken to have been in 1966, when the IRRI in the Philippines released its revolutionary high-yielding dwarf, IR-8. In fact, Chinese scientists independently developed a true high-yielding dwarf variety of rice in 1964. These parallel independent discoveries show scientists working on the research frontier coming up with similar solutions to identical problems.

Another successful experience was the introduction and extension of hybrid varieties. When a hybrid is bred from very different parent strains, it often displays greater productivity ("hybrid vigor") but with sterile offspring, so it cannot be used as seed for the next generation of crop. Hybrid maize was introduced in 1961, but rice was more difficult because rice crops typically self-pollinate. In the 1970s, Yuan Longping—who has since become a celebrity scientist in China—developed a hybrid rice that was released commercially in 1976, spread quickly, and is today sown to more than half of rice area. China was able to disseminate hybrid varieties largely because the agricultural extension service was quite reliable in supplying new generations of seeds to farmers. Here is an example of institutional infrastructure created during the socialist period—indeed, strengthened during the Cultural Revolution—that contributed to rapid technological change and robust output growth later, during the market reforms.

Today, Chinese plant scientists are at the frontier of genetic research, especially on rice and cotton. At the turn of the twenty-first century, multiple teams around the world raced to sequence the rice genome. Today, a complete mapping of rice's chromosomes, produced by collaborative efforts in more than 10 countries, is publicly available and is already transforming the way plant research is carried out. Rice is the world's most important food crop, and 90% of the world's rice is produced and consumed in Asia. In China, rice is the most important single source of calories. Now, new strains of rice with added vitamins and protein are emerging from the pipeline. Genetically modified Bt cotton has an inserted gene that makes the plant less susceptible to insect pests. Cotton receives an especially heavy dose of pesticides, potentially creating a downward spiral of insect resistance and toxic, multipesticide cocktails. Bt cotton was developed by the CAAS in the mid-1990s and released in 1997. It enables a reduction of almost two-thirds in the amount of pesticides applied to cotton and has revitalized the northern China cotton crop (Pray et al. 2002; Huang et al. 2003). China spends more on agricultural research and development than any other country, and its broad effort in biotechnology will have important applications to many other crops as well. So far, however, China has been extremely cautious in commercializing genetically modified plants. Although more than 90% of the cotton planted in 2015 was Bt cotton, this accounted for virtually all of the acreage used to grow genetically modified plants.

12.2.4   Fertilizers and Agricultural Chemicals

The third leg of the green revolution tripod is agricultural chemicals, including chemical fertilizer and pesticides. In the traditional system, Chinese farmers applied large amounts of organic fertilizer to the soil, up to six tons per hectare. Organic fertilizer provides sufficient nutrients for traditional varieties, but it is very labor intensive, is unpleasant to handle, and does not give the boost in yield that modern HYVs are capable of. Chemical fertilizer was initially used to augment traditional labor-intensive organic fertilizers, but in the 1960s and 1970s, the government began a big push to improve fertilizer availability. At first, small-scale local factories producing low-quality nitrogen fertilizers were promoted (the first township and village enterprises [TVEs]). In 1973–1974, the central government made a huge commitment of scarce foreign exchange by importing 13 large synthetic ammonia and urea factories, which eventually served as the foundation for a large domestic nitrogen fertilizer industry. As figure 12.3 shows, fertilizer supply really took off after 1978, and quadrupled by 1996; paused, and then took off again in 2003. Since the turn of the century, inputs of traditional organic fertilizer have begun to fall off rapidly (Liu, Huang, and Zikhali 2014). This is unfortunate since organic fertilizer, for all its drawbacks, contributes to maintaining long-term soil fertility and structure. Moreover, the end of the traditional system of recycling human wastes means that another pollutant must be disposed of properly.

12.2.5   Putting the Pieces Together

During the 1980s, all the elements of the green revolution finally fell into place. China by this time had extensive irrigated fields; HYVs, including dwarf rice and hybrid varieties; and a large agricultural extension service that could bring advanced technologies to hundreds of thousands of villages. All that was missing was chemical fertilizer. There were, therefore, latent technological gains that could be realized only when all three elements were present simultaneously. The addition of chemical fertilizers ensured that the surge in output created by new incentives in the early 1980s could be transformed into steady, sustained growth over the next 20 years.

The completion of this technological revolution took place at almost exactly the same time as the institutional revolution led by rural reforms. Technological change was crucial, especially given the complementarity of chemical fertilizer, the last element to arrive, with the rest of the green revolution triad (Stone 1990). The incentive properties of rural reforms were also essential for productivity increases (McMillan, Whalley, and Zhu 1989; Lin 1992). It is important to recognize that both reformed incentives and technological change have driven China's agricultural development. Indeed, the two cannot be completely separated. Farmers with improved incentives make much better decisions about which crops to grow and which inputs to purchase. For example, farmers during the mid-1970s had latent, unsatisfied demand for fertilizer, but the subsequent reforms gave farmers stronger incentives to locate fertilizer and direct it to the highest-value use. In turn, improved incentives drove market development and ultimately the search for appropriate new technologies.

12.3   Technology Choice and Innovation in Agriculture

The preceding discussion of the complementarity of the green revolution inputs might lead to the impression that agricultural inputs are pulled out of the box and used in fixed proportions, predetermined by the technology. Nothing could be further from the truth. Agriculture in China, as anywhere else, adapts to the availability of production factors, such as land and labor. Farmer use of inputs and their relative proportions in the agricultural production process are determined by their relative scarcity and hence their relative prices. This is true even when green revolution technologies are available.

Figure 12.4 shows the standard way in which economists analyze the choice of technology in agricultural production (or any kind of production, for that matter).

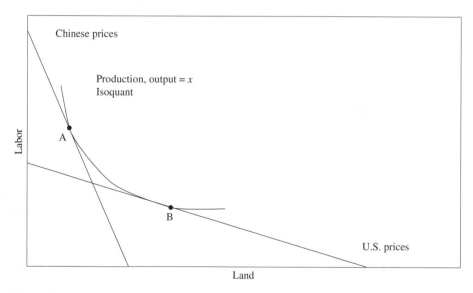

Figure 12.4
The green revolution: Fertilizer responsiveness.
Source: Author.

The horizontal axis shows the quantity of land, and the vertical axis shows the quantity of labor used in the production process. The curved line is an isoquant: at any point on the isoquant, a given output x can be produced with the use of the quantities of land and labor corresponding to that point on the graph. (Isoquants further from the origin represent larger output quantities.) Different points on the isoquant display varying factor (input) proportions; the isoquant is curved because a continuous range of varying input combinations can be used to produce output x. In a land-abundant, labor-scarce economy like that of the United States, the shallow straight line expresses U.S. relative prices: land is abundant and therefore cheap, and one worker's wage equals the rental value of a large area of land. Minimizing cost, a U.S. farmer will produce output x at point B. In China's labor-abundant economy, land is scarce and therefore expensive: the much steeper straight line displays Chinese relative prices, in which one worker's wage equals the rental value of only a small plot of land. Minimizing cost, a Chinese farmer will produce output x at point A. A Chinese farmer will use a labor-intensive production process, applying large amounts of labor to a small amount of land, relative to, for example, a U.S. farmer. This much is a straightforward application of relative prices and cost minimization.

12.3.1 Induced Innovation

This simple analysis can be extended to the more challenging area of technological change. The "induced-innovation" hypothesis states that technical change is also derived from the demands of cost-minimizing agents to save on relatively scarce resources and to use relatively plentiful ones. Chinese farmers will especially value new technologies that allow them to economize on scarce land—that is, to use existing land resources more intensively. They will thus seek out and adopt new technologies that allow them to apply more (relatively cheap) labor to their land. Hayami and Ruttan (1985) originally demonstrated this by comparing agricultural development in the United States and Japan over the period from 1880 to 1980. The growth paths of the two countries differed greatly. In the United States, with plentiful land and relatively scarce labor, power machinery was developed to substitute for relatively scarce labor. In Japan, with plentiful labor and relatively scarce land, a package of high-yielding seeds, fertilizer, and water control was developed to substitute for relatively scarce land. Although the paths of development were different, the rates of growth and levels of output were commensurate. The different paths implied by these North American and East Asian experiences are shown in figure 12.5 (note that the axes are different from those in figure 12.4). We might label the initial part of the two paths "tractorization" and "chemicalization," respectively.

China, like Japan, followed a process during most of the twentieth century in which the fundamental objective of technological development was improvement in yield per unit of land, that is, the "East Asian pattern." From the 1950s through the end of

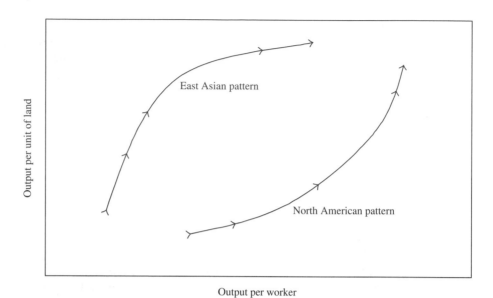

Figure 12.5
Induced-innovation paths.
Source: Derived from Hayami and Ruttan (1985).

the 1970s, China moved primarily "up" (north) as output per unit of land increased while output per agricultural laborer increased relatively little. Labor was particularly cheap in China because workers were penned up in the countryside and had limited alternative earning possibilities. After the 1980s, economic reform opened up new opportunities for workers outside agriculture and empowered households to determine the opportunity cost of their workers. Workers began to leave agriculture in large numbers during the 1990s, while output continued to increase. By 2016, the total number of workers in agriculture had declined by 45% (about 175 million) from its peak of 390 million in 1991. As workers left agriculture, output per remaining worker increased much more rapidly. China reached the point in figure 12.5 where the East Asian pattern turned "right" (east). Table 11.2 (page 269) shows the continued rapid reduction in labor inputs per unit of land since 1985.

A concrete example of these processes can be found in the high-productivity rice-growing areas of Zhejiang Province in the south. With abundant water and a long growing season, but with a hilly topography that severely limited the availability of arable land, Zhejiang had sophisticated irrigation networks that made it easy to adopt green revolution technologies. At first, collective leaders mobilized labor to plant multiple crops per year, relying on complicated crop rotations, intercropping, and relay cropping. While one crop was ripening, a different crop was planted in alternating rows, with a different harvest schedule. During the busy season, one crop would be transplanted while another was being harvested, and every able body in the village would be working in the fields. Collective farms carried out these extremely labor-intensive technologies because they were under pressure from the Grain First policy to maximize grain output, and because even in the absence of labor markets they understood that labor was their abundant (cheap) factor. Later, farmers in these relatively rich and highly commercialized areas were the first to have abundant off-farm employment opportunities. The opportunity cost of farm labor increased dramatically. When farmers regained authority over their own decision-making, multicropping declined substantially, but increased application of chemical fertilizers and pesticides kept per area yields high and rising. Output per worker increased dramatically in Zhejiang, and technological change facilitated this increase

12.3.2   Factor Proportions and Motive Power in the Countryside

As late as 1977, animal power was more important than mechanical power in the Chinese countryside (figure 12.6). Since that date, however, the mechanical power available to Chinese farmers has increased tenfold, to a billion kilowatts. China's countryside is now electrified and mechanized. Draft animals—oxen, horses, mules, and camels—were attractive in the 1950s because animals not only could pull the plough but also could produce organic fertilizers, provide transport, and be an

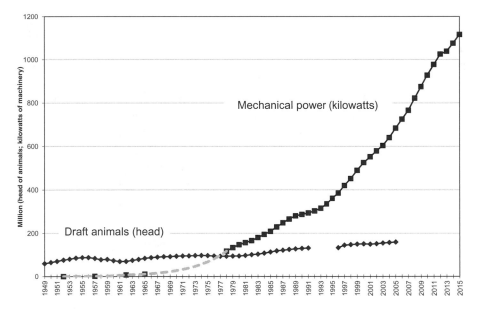

Figure 12.6
Rural motive power.
Source: *SYC* (2016 and earlier editions).

emergency food supply. With falling prices and increased availability, machines have steadily taken over from animals, and mechanization now complements chemicalization in the transformation in Chinese agriculture.

China's mechanization path has had some peculiar characteristics. Labor-augmenting technology, particularly tractorization, was a traditional feature of the "Big Push" industrialization strategy in the Soviet Union that China initially borrowed rather uncritically. During the socialist period, whenever China was in a "left" phase, policy-makers would stress consolidating fields in large collectives and providing large tractors to plow them. However, farmers refused to use these unsuitable large tractors in the field and instead transformed them into trucks to haul bricks and fertilizer around the countryside. After reforms began, peasant households ditched large tractors altogether. However, the stock of small "walking" tractors grew rapidly since they were maneuverable, affordable, and suited to the small Chinese fields. The share of large tractors in the total fell from 38% in 1978 to only 7% in 2000. Subsequently, as labor left agriculture and farms began to consolidate (section 11.4.4), farmers have begun to reassess their need for labor-saving technology. As labor became more valuable (after the "eastward" turn of the East Asian pattern in figure 12.5), demand for large tractors revived. By 2015, there were 6 million large tractors working, over one-quarter of the total stock. Changing relative factor prices induced a resurgence in demand for large tractors, a classic labor-saving innovation.

12.3.3   Output, Yields, and Total Factor Productivity

The preceding discussion prepares us to consider technical change and production growth in Chinese agriculture today. Technological change has facilitated dramatic change in the combination of factor inputs, while still supporting dramatic growth in output. Most obviously, the agricultural labor force in 2016 was 215 million, which was back down to what it had been in 1963, after peaking in 1991. Table 11.2 showed that by 2015 labor inputs per hectare for major crops had declined by 60%–70% from 1985, which was after the withdrawal of the artificially induced inputs of the collective era. In the same period, agricultural value-added has tripled, growing 4% annually. Cultivated land has increased only modestly. Cao and Birchenall (2013) argued that when labor inputs are properly measured, total factor productivity in Chinese agriculture grew at the rate of 6.5% annually between 1991 and 2009, a truly remarkable record.

Chinese agriculture has achieved these results by continuing its movement to a very intensive, chemicalized agriculture. Chinese yields in wheat, rice, and fiber crops were just over 50% higher than global averages in 2010 (FAO 2013). China still has about twice as many workers per hectare as the world average, even after recent dramatic declines. Most important, Chinese farmers apply almost five times as much nitrogen fertilizer per hectare of crop as the global average. Applications of phosphates and potash are also three to four times global averages and pesticide application proportionally even greater. Chinese agriculture is still high-input, high-output per unit of land. The contrast with the United States is particularly telling. U.S. yields of wheat and plant fibers are close to global averages (rice in the United States is a niche crop and has very high yields). U.S. fertilizer inputs per hectare are also near global averages. The difference is that the United States has less than 2% as many workers per hectare as does China. Despite recent changes, starkly different factor endowments mean that the differences between the land-augmenting technology bundle in China and the labor-augmenting technology bundle in the United States are still plainly evident.

12.4   Diversification and Structural Change

In addition to the process of intensification described in the previous section, Chinese agriculture has also been going through a process of diversification. Diversification also increases productive efficiency, since different crops are suited to different types of terrain. A large economy like that of China can achieve efficiency gains by having different localities specialize in crops to which they are especially well suited and then trade with other locales.

12.4.1   Demand Diversification

Higher income creates a demand for more diverse food products. When a person does not have enough to eat, a bowl of rice is everything. As income increases, households feel more secure about their food choices and naturally seek diversity, novelty, and convenience. Figure 12.7, an overview of consumption trends from 1961 to 2013, shows the steady increase from chronic malnourishment in the mid-1960s, through the adequate but monotonous diet of the 1970s and 1980s, to abundance and diversification in food consumption today.

The traditional Chinese diet was dominated by grain consumption (in the Chinese definition, grain includes cereals, soybeans, and potatoes). As late as 1978, 94% of the calories in the average Chinese diet came from plant products (and 86% from grain). Even more surprising, 90% of protein came from plant products (83% from grain) and only 10% from all animal products. The year 1978 is also when average consumption finally recovered to 2,000 calories per day. Above this level, diversification began. As of 2013, the average Chinese derived 77% of calories from plants and 54% from grain.

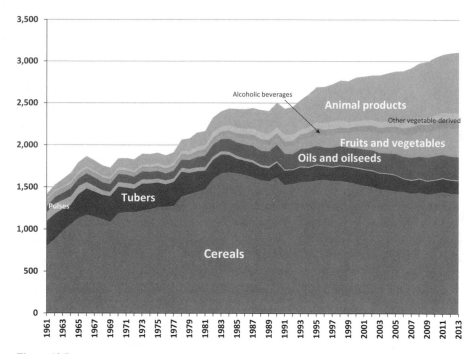

Figure 12.7
Average consumption (total calories per person per day).
Source: Food and Agriculture Organization, *Food Balances*, accessed at http://faostat3.fao.org/download /FB/FBS/E.

As household incomes move into the middle-income range, demand for a variety of food products, including meat, fresh fruit and vegetables, poultry, and eggs increases more than proportionately (income elasticity is greater than one). A dietary transition shifts consumption from carbohydrates to higher levels of protein, fat, and sugar. This transition is initially positive for health: a more diverse diet provides more vitamins and minerals. Dairy consumption early in life reduces stunting and produces taller and more solid frames. Increased protein from initially low levels is positive. As the transition continues, though, it also brings negative health effects. Obesity and related chronic illnesses, including type II diabetes, which were previously almost nonexistent, start to become significant problems. These shifts are all under way in China today.

12.4.2   Derived Shift in Output Composition

Dietary improvement places new demands on the agricultural system. Demand for millet and sorghum disappears as better-off households shift to better-tasting rice and wheat. Despite this shift, demand for rice and wheat, the dominant staples, stabilizes and then begins to inch downward. Per capita rice and wheat consumption plateaued after 1983 and 1993, respectively, and 2013 consumption was down by 8% and 21%. Despite the decline in household consumption of grain, overall demand for grain has continued to increase because demand for meat and meat products creates derived demand for feed grains, or fodder. Meat production is a relatively inefficient way of conveying calories to the human consumer. Animals convert vegetable calories into a more highly valued food, but they do so through a relatively expensive conversion process that loses calories along the way. The continuing increase in China's grain production has been driven by those varieties most readily converted into meat. Maize (corn) output surpassed that of rice in 2012, making maize China's largest crop for the first time in history. Soybeans—predominantly imported—have also become much more important. These changes are fully explained by the different ratios of direct consumption of rice and wheat (83%–87% goes directly to the table) versus soy and corn (only 8%–12% of which is consumed directly, the remainder going to animal feed or further processing) (Xu and Jia 2015).

A new animal-feed industry is developing that mixes grain with oilseed meal (especially from soybeans) and vitamin and protein supplements. These modern feed systems go primarily to new businesses that raise pigs on a large scale. Pork is by far the largest source of animal protein in China, which raises more than half of the world's pigs. New specialized household producers and large-scale commercial producers have developed to meet this demand. After the turn of the century, these producers began to rapidly replace the traditional households that had for generations raised a few pigs in their farmyard, feeding them primarily from kitchen scraps and green roughage. New systems of feedlots, slaughterhouses, and marketing networks have also developed alongside new feeding systems. "Agribusiness" is developing rapidly in China (Schneider and Sharma 2014).

12.4.3   Modern Food-Supply Chains

A more sophisticated transport and storage system has developed as well. A crucial link is cold storage. Refrigerated trucks and warehouses make up a "cold chain" to supply supermarkets with fresh, frozen, and prepared food (Twilley 2014). Today, almost all Chinese urban households and even most rural households have refrigerators and spend an increasing share of their food money in supermarkets. This stimulates the creation of new food-processing industries while also putting new demands on the traditional agricultural sector. Alongside these developments, China's traditional household-based, bottom-heavy economy continues to show remarkable vitality and staying power. Every Chinese city has numerous farmers' markets where diverse fresh produce and meat—none of it frozen or refrigerated—are abundantly supplied. This testifies to the resilience of the familiar small-scale model of trade.

12.5   Agricultural Policy

Although the amount of land in the world is limited, there is no immediate practical limit to the amount of food that can be produced from that land. As long as farmers are willing to put in more labor, energy, and technological resources, they can draw more agricultural product out of the land. Unless climate change leads to a dramatic disruption of the ecosystem's productivity, agriculture is subject to the law of diminishing returns but is nowhere close to the point of no returns. The amount of food actually produced is determined by the price of agricultural output, which the farmer receives, compared with the price of inputs, which the farmer must pay. In the short run, agricultural prices are strongly influenced by government agricultural policy. Governments affect the profitability of agriculture through a broad range of policies: taxation or subsidization of farming, land policy, agricultural price policy, and foreign-trade policy (manipulating rules and taxes at the nation's border).

12.5.1   The Agricultural Policy Life Cycle

Agricultural policy follows a common trajectory in many countries. When the economy is poor, the government taxes agriculture, which is the only readily available source of tax revenue or surplus for investment. As the economy develops, the government begins to take less out of agriculture in the form of taxes and puts more government expenditure into agriculture. Government policy becomes neutral in the sense that it taxes agriculture at about the same rate as other sectors. However, in most cases, things do not rest here. As development continues, governments may shift to an across-the-board regime of support for farmers. This was true in East Asia for Japan and South Korea, which enacted regimes with very high subsidies, especially for rice farmers. The European Union and the United States also built formidable policy regimes to protect their farmers. In other words, countries do not merely stop imposing punishing taxes on agriculture; they "overshoot," moving right through a policy of neutrality and to a regime of subsidy and protection. Decades later, many developed countries swing back toward neutrality as they seek to reduce the volume of subsidies going to an agricultural sector that has become proportionally very small.

The agricultural policy life cycle applies to China, at least partially. During the mid-1990s, China began to abandon the aspects of the state procurement system that were most punitive to farmers. Figure 12.8 shows three different studies that summarize the net impact of government policies on farm prices. They compare the domestic price to the farmer with the international price (at the border, including cost, insurance, and freight to deliver importable goods). Throughout the 1980s, prices to

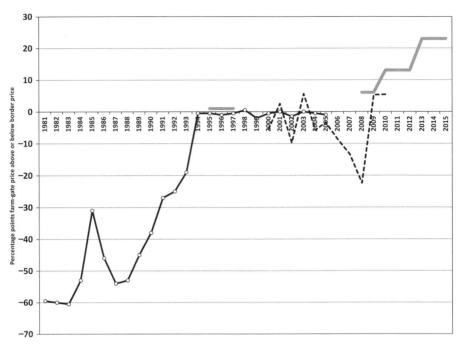

Figure 12.8
Farm-gate price relative to border price.
Sources: 1981 through 2005, aggregate of 11 commodities from Huang et al. (2009, figure 80); 2000–2010, simple average of 4 commodities from Huang, Yang, and Rozelle (2015); three-year averages for 1995–1997 and 2008 through 2015 from OECD (2011, 2013, 2015, 2016).

farmers were half or less of international prices.[1] The data shown in figure 12.8 aggregate prices of 11 commodities, but prices varied substantially across commodities, and the price penalty was largest for rice. This price differential disappeared by 1994. For a decade, from 1994 through 2005, China's agricultural price policy was basically neutral. This policy stance was compatible with China's effort to join the World Trade Organization (WTO). China's WTO entry commitments seemed to foreclose its option to set up a subsidy regime, since the WTO imposes limits on how much a country can protect agriculture (although specific limits are negotiated for each country).

China was dislodged from this neutral policy stance by the surge in global food (and energy) prices during 2007–2008. Rather than let domestic food prices rise along with global prices—which would have contributed to a significant inflation problem

1. This implies that it would have profitable for farmers to export their grain, but they were not allowed to do so.

at that time—policy-makers took a number of measures. They sold rice, wheat, and maize from government stockpiles and taxed and ultimately prohibited the export of food grains (Huang, Yang, and Rozelle 2015). Thus, for a brief period of very high global food prices, China resumed indirect taxation of its farmers. When global prices came abruptly back down with the global financial crisis, Chinese policy-makers seemed to have been converted to the view that they needed to put more resources into agriculture to guard against potential future shocks. Chinese policy-makers began to steadily raise domestic support prices. When, in 2014, global food and energy prices again dropped sharply, Chinese domestic support prices were maintained significantly above world prices (figure 12.8). This policy stance is completely unprecedented in the People's Republic of China.

China, like other forerunner economies, overshot the neutral position for agricultural price policy and has erected a broadly protectionist policy regime for its farmers. To be sure, some portion of the overshooting reflects the unexpected drop in world prices in 2014–2015 and might be attributed to policy-makers smoothing out the shocks from world prices. Indeed, the steady increase in farm support prices finally stopped in late 2015 and 2016 and some prices were even lowered slightly as policy-makers worried about growing costs and stockpiles. Policy-makers today show little appetite for moving back to a neutral regime, though. The price trends shown in figure 12.8 are just one part of the agricultural policy regime that includes taxation and a broad range of subsidies designed to support and protect agriculture.

12.5.2   Price, Tax, and Subsidy: "Take Less, Put in More"

As discussed in chapter 11, China shifted to a new rural policy regime in the early twenty-first century. In 2005, China abolished the agricultural tax, which had taken 5%–7% of agricultural value added in recent preceding years. At almost the same time, a range of new subsidies, particularly targeted at grain producers, was introduced. From 2008, those subsidies began to increase rapidly. According to Gale (2013), the most important types of subsidies were the following:

• Direct payments and "general input" subsidies for grain producers. These two subsidies are payments made from the government budget directly to farmers, based on the acreage traditionally allocated to grain production. They increased quickly after 2008 to about 2.4% of agricultural value-added in 2012.

• Specific input or project subsidies. More than 20 items supporting, for example, improved seeds or agricultural machinery are funded, usually by local governments. In the aggregate, these amounted to about 4% of agricultural value-added in 2011.

• Support prices for major commodities. China introduced support prices in 2004 when it pledged to purchase high-quality rice at a premium price if market prices fell below that level. In subsequent years, support prices were introduced for wheat, corn, soybeans, rapeseed, and cotton and were raised or maintained annually until the end of 2015.

These programs add up to a major regime of agricultural support and protection.

12.5.3   Land Use Policy: The 120 Million Hectare "Red Line"

In the 11th Five-Year Plan, produced in 2006, China committed itself to maintaining 120 million hectares of cultivated land; this was to be a "hard target," incorporated into local land-use decisions and enforced by the central government. The adoption of this target was prompted by fears that China's farmland was being lost to development since government planners believed numbers that said that cultivated land had declined to about 122 million hectares. They determined to hold the line at 120 million hectares, and this bright "red line" was incorporated into subsequent five-year plans (Xu and Jia 2015). The red line was essentially a commitment to no net loss of cultivated land. The national target of 120 million hectares was disaggregated to each province, which became responsible for maintaining its own red line of cultivated land.

Driven by this sense of urgency, the government commissioned a new land survey in 2009, deploying substantial resources and integrating remote sensing and field studies. Certainly the most accurate China has ever had, the survey found that China had 135.4 million hectares of cultivated land (cf. table 1.1). Suddenly the urgency of maintaining 120 million hectares did not seem so great, and the government delayed reporting the results for four years while it decided how to respond. Previous data had missed the significant new acreage that Chinese farmers had put under cultivation over the years. The shift to feed grain encouraged this already substantial activity: maize can be grown on steeper, rain-irrigated hillslopes that could never support rice or wheat. Moreover, the survey took place after the Chinese government had shifted from taxing to subsidizing agricultural land, and during a period when new contractual use-rights were being assigned to individual farmers (section 11.4.4). Instead of having an incentive to hide land from the tax man, farmers now had an incentive to make sure that land was declared so that use rights could be registered.[2]

Government policy-makers eventually realized that the new figures did not require them to change the no-net-loss policy, and have continued strict enforcement at the local-government level. This policy keeps land bottled up in agriculture and lowers the value of land to the farmers who own it. Some policy to control urban land

---

2. See Xu and Jia (2015) for an account of the complicated history of the land numbers. They showed that China's land data were a kind of compromise reflecting the political and institutional relationship between farmers and the state.

conversion is necessary, since local-government officials who control the process have demonstrated a strong tendency to convert excessive amounts of land to industrial and public projects, including development zones (chapter 6). Unlimited speculation and land conversion could certainly cause serious problems. However, the draconian "red-line" approach is a costly way to prevent such speculation.

12.5.4   Agricultural Trade and Grain Self-Sufficiency

China has a policy of "grain self-sufficiency." Self-sufficiency was originally defined as meaning that 95% of all grain would be produced domestically. Since 2012, self-sufficiency has been redefined: China should maintain "absolute" self-sufficiency in staple cereals (wheat, rice, and corn), but not in nonfood grains. Overall grain self-sufficiency (in the broad definition) could fall to 85%. In fact, as table 12.1 shows, this is already the situation. China still maintains self-sufficiency above 98% in each of the three key food grains, rice, corn, and wheat, but 85% of soybeans are imported. Most corn is used as animal feed, but production has grown rapidly, in part because of the support it receives.

China's agricultural support and self-sufficiency policies imply that domestic grain prices are substantially above world prices. Domestic grain output has grown rapidly, and total net grain imports have been modest. Many expected WTO membership to preclude this outcome. In fact, Chinese agricultural support policies have been specifically crafted to be compliant with WTO regulations. WTO rules prohibit certain types of subsidies ("red box") and allow "green box" subsidies that are fixed in the short term to subsidize long-term ecosystem productivity or research. Subsidies in the "amber box," including price support payments, are limited to 8.5% of agricultural value-added. This means that China was generally in compliance, although since about 2013 the total subsidies must be very close to the amber box limit and may even surpass it. As part of WTO membership negotiations, China also agreed to allow

Table 12.1
Grain production, imports, and exports (2014) (million metric tons; percent).

	Production	Imports	Exports	Net imports	Total supply	Self-sufficiency
Rice	178.0	3.9	0.5	3.4	181.4	98.1%
Corn	218.5	3.1	0.0	3.1	221.6	98.6%
Wheat	112.5	1.9	0.0	1.9	114.4	98.3%
3 key grains (KGs)	509.0	8.9	0.5	8.4	517.4	98.4%
Soybeans	13.8	75.0	0.2	74.8	88.7	15.6%
3 KGs + soybeans	522.8	83.9	0.7	83.2	606.0	86.3%

Source: Lockett (2015), from National Bureau of Statistics and Customs Administration.

up to a fixed limit of low tariff grain imports, so-called tariff rate quotas (TRQs). The TRQs for rice, corn, and wheat were 5.3, 7.2, and 9.6 million tons, respectively, above which much higher tariffs would be triggered. Given that domestic prices are significantly above world prices, one would expect these TRQs to be fully used, but as table 12.1 shows, they have not been. This has not been explained.[3]

Every country must take food security into account. This is especially true for China because of its large size. The total amount of wheat, rice, and corn sold on world markets is about 320 million metric tons (MMT), just over half of China's domestic production (550 MMT). If China were to derive 40% of its demand from international grain markets, as Japan and Taiwan long have done, huge market adjustments and major price increases would probably be necessary. Still, China's self-sufficiency policy involves substantial economic costs. Considering its limited land endowment, China imports surprisingly little food directly. Instead, China imports an enormous amount of agricultural raw materials that feed its manufacturing sector (paper pulp, cotton, rubber, and lumber), as well as feed products for animals (soybeans in particular). Looked at in this way, China depends on the world market for a very substantial quantity of land-replacing commodities. Moreover, although it is a net importer of agricultural products, China exports a substantial amount of labor-intensive agricultural products (aquatic products, followed by vegetables, flowers, and tea). Less grain self-sufficiency would allow China to adapt further to the opportunities of globalization, accepting greater dependence on world markets for grain but perhaps importing less agricultural raw materials or exporting more labor-intensive agricultural products, achieving a similar balance of trade but with greater efficiency.

12.5.5   Implications of the Agricultural Policy Regime

It should be clear that the three policies of subsidy, land maintenance, and grain self-sufficiency fit together and reinforce one another. The cultivated-land red line keeps land bottled up in agriculture and effectively suppresses the opportunity cost of land. Price supports raise agricultural product prices, and restrictions on imports are necessary to maintain those prices when they are above world prices. Finally, direct subsidies go directly to the farmers' bottom line, with ambiguous effects on output prices. These policies greatly increase the profitability of growing grain. Through their effect on prices, they encourage intensification of agriculture, greater production of grain, and more use of fertilizers and machinery. It is not surprising

---

3. Half of the TRQs were to be given to state-owned firms and half to private firms. State firms might respond to pressure to limit imports, but imports of wheat are less than half the TRQ. Note that the limit on amber-box payments is calculated according to a fixed reference year for prices (1996–1998), so they are not affected by the fall in current world prices.

that since the policies were introduced, grain production has increased annually for 12 years.

The policies are costly. Not only are significant budgetary outlays needed to support the subsidies, but also, in the price-maintenance scheme, the government must buy up large quantities of grain. China now has extremely large stocks of grain and cotton. These are expensive to maintain, and a substantial amount of grain is lost to insect pests and rot. China will probably continue to be a net importer of agricultural commodities, but there are many different ways to do this, and reliance on the market would be the most effective way to discover the most efficient arrangements.

On the positive side, the policy regime protects against two dangers: mass encroachment on agricultural land by speculators and government officials and a sudden disruption in international supplies of food grains. Moreover, these policies provide income support for agricultural households, long the poorest class of Chinese society. It is not an accident that China's Gini coefficient began to decline modestly at about the time these large subsidy programs were rolled out. The combination of tax remission, subsidies, and price supports could easily be responsible for a 20%–30% increase in average agricultural incomes. This would make a major contribution to a more equal society.

12.6   Conclusion: Toward Sustainable Agriculture

Chinese agriculture has achieved remarkable success in the past 40 years, enabling the dramatic growth and transformation of the Chinese economy as a whole. Food is abundant today. At the same time, China has paid a substantial price for the performance it has elicited from its agricultural sector, and it is legitimate to raise questions about the sustainability of China's current agricultural practice. Three problems stand out.

First, environmental sustainability is not guaranteed. It is not clear that intensification of agriculture can or should be pursued much further than it has been already. The Chinese and nearby coastal environment is overburdened by the excessive amounts of nutrients from chemical fertilizers in the water, which are leading to eutrophication of important bodies of water (chapter 21). Agricultural chemicals have left residues of heavy metals that are known to be harmful to human health. A special survey of the problem in 2015 discovered millions of hectares of farmland polluted by toxins, including cadmium, nickel, copper, arsenic, mercury, lead, DDT, and polycyclic aromatic hydrocarbons (PAHs). Toxic pesticides are hurting bird and animal life. China is by far the world's largest user of pesticide, using 4.8 times as much pesticide per hectare as the United States, the second largest aggregate user.

The depletion of aquifers in the North China Plain was mentioned earlier. Groundwater and surface-water sources are both showing signs of severe overexploitation. Groundwater levels in some places in Hebei Province are falling more than one meter per year. This problem has been aggravated by the shift to double-cropping patterns on the North China plain in which farmers rotate wheat and corn (Lohmar et al. 2003; Yang et al. 2017). The policy of "grain for green," under which farmers were compensated for returning steep or arid farmland to forest or grassland, was dramatically scaled back in 2007 (NBS Rural 2016, 61). All these environmental problems are aggravated by agricultural policies that raise output prices while suppressing input costs. The result is that high levels of water, land, fertilizer, and pesticide are used to sustain high output. Only since 2016 has there been some moderation of these policies: as figure 12.3 shows, fertilizer application in 2016 fell for the first time ever, albeit by only 0.3%.

Second, China's food-grain self-sufficiency policy imposes significant costs on the Chinese economy. The direct financial cost of subsidies is probably bearable, but the network of tariffs and nontariff barriers that is required to support the policy diverts demand in different directions in many interlinked markets and retards progress toward marketization. As China's economy grows richer and more sophisticated, and as the share of the labor force in agriculture continues to shrink, there will come a time when it is economically more effective to dial down the pro-production impact of current policies. A transition to a more sustainable agriculture with slower-growing grain output would not preclude continued growth in higher-value products and continued increases in rural incomes.

Finally, China's agricultural labor force is shrinking and aging. The median age of a farm worker (as measured by the Second Agriculture Census in 2006) was 42 years and increasing rapidly. The possibilities and challenges of China's agriculture are both changing rapidly. It is certain that agriculture has the capacity to adapt and continue to grow. If China's policy-makers follow a common life cycle of agricultural policy, they will gradually (but slowly) begin to shift toward a more neutral policy. This would contribute to a more sustainable agricultural economy.

Bibliography

Suggestions for Further Reading

Lohmar et al. (2009) is an overview of the rural economy, touching on virtually the entire range of issues. Lin (1992) is a classic article that is an eminently clear and effective argument based on estimation of the agricultural production function.

References

Cao, Kang Hua, and Javier A. Birchenall (2013). "Agricultural Productivity, Structural Change, and Economic Growth in Post-reform China." *Journal of Development Economics* 104:165–180.

FAO (Food and Agriculture Organization) (2013). *FAO Statistical Yearbook 2013: World Food and Agriculture*. Rome: Food and Agriculture Organization. Accessed at http://www.fao.org/docrep/018/i3107e/i3107e00.htm.

Gale, Fred (2013). *Growth and Evolution in China's Agricultural Support Policies*. Economic Research Report no. 153. Washington, DC: U.S. Department of Agriculture.

Hayami, Yujiro, and Vernon W. Ruttan (1985). *Agricultural Development: An International Perspective*. Baltimore: Johns Hopkins University Press.

Huang, Jikun, Ruifa Hu, Carl Pray, Fangbin Qiao, and Scott Rozelle (2003). "Biotechnology as an Alternative to Chemical Pesticides: A Case Study of Bt Cotton in China." *Agricultural Economics* 29:55–67.

Huang, Jikun, Yu Liu, Will Martin, and Scott Rozelle (2009). "Changes in Trade and Domestic Distortions Affecting China's Agriculture." *Food Policy* 34:407–416.

Huang, Jikun, and Scott Rozelle (1996). "Technological Change: Rediscovering the Engine of Productivity Growth in China's Rural Economy." *Journal of Development Economics* 49:337–369.

Huang, Jikun, Jun Yang, and Scott Rozelle (2015). "The Political Economy of Food Price Policy in China." In Per Pinstrup-Andersen, ed., *Food Price Policy in an Era of Market Instability: A Political Economy Analysis*, 362–383. New York: Oxford University Press for the United Nations University—World Institute for Development Economics Research (UNU-WIDER).

Lin, Justin Y. (1992). "Rural Reform and Agricultural Growth in China." *American Economic Review* 82:34–51.

Liu, Ying, Jikun Huang, and Precious Zikhali (2014). "Use of Human Excreta as Manure in Rural China." *Journal of Integrative Agriculture* 13 (2): 434–442.

Lockett, Hudson (2015). "Cereal Dysfunction: China's Grain Self-Sufficiency Policy Lives On After Its Official Demise." April 7. Accessed at http://www.chinaeconomicreview.com/cereal-dysfunction.

Lohmar, Bryan, Fred Gale, Francis Tuan, and Jim Hansen (2009). *China's Ongoing Agricultural Modernization: Challenges Remain After 30 Years of Reform*. Economic Information Bulletin no. 51. Washington, DC: U.S. Department of Agriculture.

Lohmar, Bryan, Jinxia Wang, Scott Rozelle, Jikun Huang, and David Dawe (2003). *China's Agricultural Water Policy Reforms: Increasing Investment, Resolving Conflicts, and Revising Incentives*. Agriculture Information Bulletin no. 782. Washington, DC: U.S. Department of Agriculture, Economic Research Service. http://www.ers.usda.gov/publications/aib782.

McMillan, John, John Whalley, and Lijing Zhu (1989). "The Impact of China's Economic Reforms on Agricultural Productivity Growth." *Journal of Political Economy* 97 (4): 781–807.

NBS Rural Department (Annual). *Zhongguo Nongcun Tongji Nianjian* [China rural statistical yearbook]. Beijing: Zhongguo Tongji.

Nyberg, Albert, and Scott Rozelle (1999). *Accelerating China's Rural Transformation*. Washington, DC: World Bank.

OECD (Annual). *Agricultural Policy Monitoring and Evaluation*. Accessed at http://www.oecd-ilibrary.org/agriculture-and-food/agricultural-policy-monitoring-and-evaluation_22217371.

Ray, Carl, Jikun Huang, Ruifa Hu, and Scott Rozelle (2002). "Five Years of Bt Cotton in China: The Benefits Continue." *Plant Journal* 31 (4): 423–430.

Schneider, Mindi, with Shefali Sharma (2014). *China's Pork Miracle? Agribusiness and Development in China's Pork Industry*. Washington, DC: Institute for Agriculture and Trade Policy. February. Accessed at http://www.iatp.org/documents/china%E2%80%99s-pork-miracle-agribusiness-and-development-in-china%E2%80%99s-pork-industry.

Stone, Bruce (1990). "Evolution and Diffusion of Agricultural Technology in China." In Neil G. Kotler, ed., *Sharing Innovation: Global Perspectives on Food, Agriculture, and Rural Development*, 35–93. Washington, DC: Smithsonian Institution.

SYC (Annual). *Zhongguo Tongji Nianjian* [Statistical yearbook of China]. Beijing: Zhongguo Tongji.

Twilley, Nicola (2014). "What Do Chinese Dumplings Have to Do with Global Warming?" *New York Times*, July 25. http://www.nytimes.com/2014/07/27/magazine/what-do-chinese-dumplings-have-to-do-with-global-warming.html.

Xu Dianqing and Jia Shuaishuai (2015). "The 1.8 Billion *Mou* Red Line for Cultivated Area." In Qiu Dong, Xu Dianqing, and Zhao Nan, eds., *2014 Guomin Hesuan Yanjiu Baogao* [National accounts research report], 1–98. Beijing: Zhongguo Caizheng Jingji.

Yang, Xiao-Lin, Yuan-Quan Chen, Tammo S. Steenhuis, Steven Pacenka, Wang-Sheng Gao, Li Ma, Min Zhang, and Peng Sui (2017). "Mitigating Groundwater Depletion in North China Plain with Cropping System That Alternate Deep and Shallow Rooted Crops." *Frontiers of Plant Science* 8:980. doi: 10.3389/fpls.2017.00980 PMCID: PMC5463059.

13 Rural Industrialization: From Township and Village Enterprises to Taobao Villages

Rural industry has been an important part of China's economy for centuries, but it played an especially important role during the golden age of township and village enterprises (TVEs), from 1978 through 1996. During this period TVEs played the catalytic role in transforming the Chinese economy from a command economy to a market economy. Springing up in the rural areas, which were much less rigidly controlled than the cities, the entry of TVEs provided competition to state-run industrial enterprises and drove the process of marketization forward in the entire economy. TVEs increased rural incomes, absorbed rural labor released from farms, and helped narrow the urban–rural gap. TVEs had a special distinction during this period because of their unusual ownership and corporate governance setup. Originating under the rural communes, initially most TVEs were collectively owned. TVEs thus presented the unusual spectacle of publicly owned enterprises growing rapidly and providing the competitive challenge that dissolved the monopoly previously held by a different set of publicly owned (state-run) enterprises. A diverse set of TVE models adapted to a range of different conditions emerged and ended up fundamentally changing nearly every part of the Chinese economy.

Rural enterprises have been a locus of institutional experimentation, and since 1949 have experienced four successive transformations:

• When agriculture was collectivized in the 1950s, traditional rural businesses were swept away. The collectives were told to focus on growing grain, and supply and marketing cooperatives took over remaining nonagricultural activities. During the Cultural Revolution (1966–1976) the government supported "commune and brigade industries" that would "serve agriculture" instead of the market.

• After 1978, during the golden age, rural enterprises were set free to respond to market demand and make money. Commune and brigade enterprises were rebranded as TVEs, and they transformed the Chinese rural economy and, eventually, China.

• During the 1990s, TVEs privatized themselves. Facing more intense competition and a level playing field, and with a more permissive ideological environment, nearly all collectively owned TVEs became private firms.

• Since 2000, TVEs have developed organically into new forms exemplified by industrial clusters. These clusters usually involved a few large firms cooperating with hundreds or even thousands of tiny household-based enterprises. After the arrival of the Internet in the Chinese countryside around 2009, hundreds of these villages began to use it to reach a national and even global market.

The flexibility and institutional creativity of China's rural entrepreneurs continues to find new forms.

13.1   Origins of the TVEs

As described in chapter 3, the preponderance of small household-based rural businesses led China's traditional economy to be called "bottom heavy." Rural households spun and wove cotton, raised silkworms, and reeled silk thread; they made noodles and mud bricks, carted goods to market, and ran shops and businesses. The most important nonagricultural undertakings were handicraft operations processing agricultural goods and converting them into market goods.

The organic link between growing and processing agricultural products in the countryside was broken under the command economy. When the state established its monopoly control over agricultural goods during the 1950s, as described in chapter 4, rural processing businesses were inevitably cut off from their supplies. Grain, cotton, silk, peanuts, and soybeans—the staple supplies of nonagricultural businesses—were taken by the state immediately after the harvest. During the 1950s, the countryside became deindustrialized. As the rural population was organized into agricultural collectives, nonagricultural production declined, and the state took over virtually all manufacturing production (Fei Xiaotong 1957 [1989]). These policies were an integral part of the creation of the command-economy system, but the harmful effects were soon evident. Household income declined in commercialized rural areas where a high proportion of income previously had come from sideline activities. Some formerly prosperous, densely populated regions found it difficult to support their large populations on the tiny amount of agricultural land available per capita. Many specialized handicrafts fell into decay as state factories moved into mass production.

One among the many strands of policy during the Great Leap Forward (GLF, 1958–1960) was an effort to change the overwhelming dependence on agriculture in rural areas by creating communes and encouraging them to start construction teams and run factories, including the notorious "backyard steel mills." However, as described in chapter 4, the drain of manpower from agriculture proved to be disastrous, and the GLF collapsed. Virtually all these commune-sponsored enterprises were shut down during the terrible post-GLF crisis in 1961–1962.

A second attempt to develop rural industry occurred during the Cultural Revolution era. After 1970, during the Maoist "new leap forward," the government encouraged a new wave of state-sponsored rural industrialization under the rubric of "commune and brigade enterprises."[1] This time, care was taken to avoid the problems that crippled the GLF. Movement of workers out of agriculture was carefully controlled, rural industries were tied to the agricultural collectives, and rural industries were constantly exhorted to "serve agriculture." Rural industry began to revive rapidly during the 1970s under Cultural Revolution era policies.

This 1970s rural industrialization was very different from traditional rural industry, which had primarily processed agricultural products. The new exhortation to "serve agriculture" was interpreted narrowly to mean supplying producers' goods to agriculture. Policy during the 1970s stressed the rural "Five Small Industries" that included iron and steel, cement, chemical fertilizer, hydroelectric power, and farm implements. Rural industries were expected to replicate the heavy-industry-based Big Push development strategy: the factories were small relative to urban factories, but compared with the traditional rural handicrafts or rural workshops in most countries, they were large and capital intensive (Wong 1982). They did not generate much employment per unit of investment or in the aggregate. By 1978, only 6% of the total rural labor force worked in commune and brigade enterprises (today's township and village enterprises), and another 2% of the labor force was engaged in nonagricultural activities (perhaps petty trading or hauling) outside commune or brigade enterprises. (Usually, these were "team enterprises," run collectively under the village, but occasionally they were run by private individuals.) Some sectors required government subsidies to survive. Rural industries in the 1970s were a peculiar offshoot of the command economy. Since they were mainly small firms serving local customers, it was impractical to incorporate them into central planning. Instead, they were integrated into the existing collective organization of the countryside. Profits from commune and brigade industries went to the collective, which used them for community infrastructure and welfare programs and also to raise the value of work points for all the collective workers. Sometimes workers in brigade industries were paid in work points (Wong 1988, 18–21). In a sense, rural collectives were being made junior partners in the state's monopoly over industry and shared some of the

---

1. As noted in chapter 11, the communes were renamed townships in 1982, and brigades returned to being villages, so commune and brigade enterprises became township and village enterprises. For consistency, I will refer to them as township and village enterprises, or TVEs, throughout.

revenue created. Maoist China was well known for its promotion of rural industry, but the type of industry fostered was a poor substitute for the dense network of small-scale, nonagricultural activities that had been suppressed in the 1950s.

13.2   The Golden Age of TVE Development

During 1979, the central government dramatically shifted its policy toward rural enterprises. The broad liberalization of rural economic policy included a relaxation of the state monopoly on purchase of agricultural products, allowing more to remain on rural markets and thus available to rural enterprises for processing. The new policy was "Whenever it is economically rational for agricultural products to be processed in rural areas, rural enterprises should gradually take over the processing work" (SRC 1984, 97–104). Since TVEs were collective firms, they were still ideologically safe. Once the monopoly on farm procurement was broken and rural industries were allowed to perform agricultural processing, they were essentially free to engage in any profitable activity. Urban firms were also encouraged to subcontract work to TVEs. Of course, state firms and state procurement monopolies fought to maintain their monopolies, and there were policy twists and turns and slow progress in the sensitive areas. Nevertheless, local-government officials quickly recognized the economic implications of TVE development and became vigorous advocates and defenders of TVEs. A new form of close government cooperation with TVEs, sometimes called "local-government corporatism," emerged in the countryside (Oi 1992). Indeed, for many localities, TVEs were the only available path out of poverty.

TVEs responded with explosive growth. Between 1978 and the mid-1990s, TVEs were clearly the most dynamic part of the Chinese economy. TVE employment grew from 28 million in 1978 to a peak of 135 million in 1996, a 9% annual growth rate. TVE value added, which accounted for less than 6% of GDP in 1978, increased to 26% of GDP in 1996, despite the fact that GDP was growing very rapidly as well. The growth of nonagricultural income raised rural incomes and contributed to shrinking the urban-rural gap. Not only has TVE growth been rapid, but also that growth has played an important role in the transformation of the Chinese economy because TVEs have created competition for existing state-owned enterprises (SOEs) and have served as a "motor" for the entire transition process. In industry, TVEs presented mounting competition for SOEs throughout the 1980s and early 1990s. SOE monopoly profits were eroded as aggressive TVEs drove price relationships into line with underlying costs. SOEs had to implement new incentive programs and improve efficiency in order to survive in the face of the TVE competitive onslaught. In foreign trade, TVEs provided opportunities for Chinese exporters to move into new labor-intensive manufactures. In the end, TVEs transformed virtually every aspect of the Chinese economy.

13.3   Causes of Rapid Growth

Why were rural industries able to grow so rapidly? There is no single answer; rather, a confluence of five favorable factors contributed to rural industrial success: favorable fundamentals, ability to tap into monopoly rents, a favorable institutional environment, revival of traditional locational patterns, and organizational flexibility.

1. TVEs faced factor-price ratios that reflected China's true factor endowment. China's basic economic endowment in 1978 was that it possessed abundant labor, limited land, and scarce capital. One of the greatest irrationalities of the Big Push strategy was that it gave priority to capital-intensive industries. Urban factories faced highly distorted prices: labor was expensive since total worker compensation was quite generous (chapters 6 and 9), while capital was cheap because it was often allocated without charge or provided at highly subsidized interest rates. TVEs, by contrast, faced factor prices much more in line with China's real factor endowment. Through the 1980s, rural-enterprise worker salaries were less than 60% of those of state-enterprise workers, and total compensation was much less than half that of urban workers. Once TVEs were cut loose from the Maoist Five Small Industries straitjacket, they adapted quickly to the underlying availability of production factors. TVEs rarely had access to subsidized capital. The bulk of TVE capital was provided at near-market interest rates or came from internally generated funds with a high opportunity cost. As a result, the ratio of labor to fixed capital in TVEs was nine times that in state-run industries. Figure 13.1 shows that TVEs (in this case, village firms) specialized in sectors with low capital-labor ratios, where the competitive advantage of their low wages was biggest. Facing realistic factor-price relationships, TVEs had the right incentives to find lines of profitable business that were most appropriate in the Chinese economy and that, over the long run, gave them an advantageous competitive position. Economic fundamentals were on the side of the TVEs.

2. TVEs were able to share in the monopoly rents created for state firms, and so were extremely profitable. In 1978, the average rate of profit on capital was 32%. If we include taxes—because TVEs were often created by local governments that could claim a share of the tax revenues generated—the total rate of profit and tax per unit of capital was 40% (capital is here defined as the value of depreciated fixed capital plus all inventories). The high rate of profitability was not merely the result of better and more realistic use of production factors and consequent lower costs,

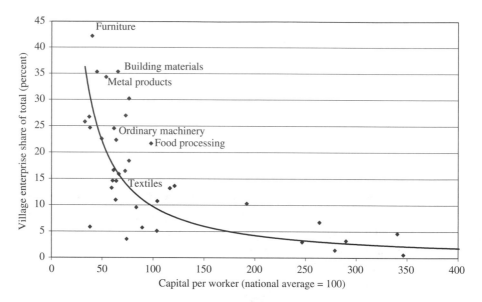

Figure 13.1
Village-enterprise share of total output × capital intensity, 1995.
Source: Third Census Office (1997, 5, 46–197, 198–233) provides village-level and total national capital and labor, respectively.

described in the previous paragraph. Indeed, in subsequent years, even as TVEs grew, achieved economies of scale, and developed a broader network of supporting services, profitability declined steadily and steeply.

What can explain this pattern of rapid growth combined with steadily declining profitability? Early TVEs were in a position to benefit from the protected market created for state-run factories. By easing the state monopoly over industry, the Chinese government allowed TVEs to enter this previously protected market and share in a portion of the monopoly profits. First-mover advantages were large enough to reward early entrants with windfall profits. State firms scarcely noticed the competition at first because they were protected by a cushion of high profits. As long as they could gain access to low-price raw materials, they were indifferent to a few TVEs producing similar products. But gradually, as entry continued, competition among TVEs and between TVEs and state firms began to erode monopoly profits and profit margins.

TVEs sprang up to provide goods in empty market niches. These empty niches existed for two reasons. The inefficient command economy had simply not provided certain commodities, particularly miscellaneous consumer goods, and TVEs jumped in to meet needs that until then had largely been unmet. The early success of Wenzhou businesses came from small-scale firms specialized in such items as buttons, ribbons, and elastic bands in a variety of colors and specifications; producing these items for a market of one billion people led to explosive growth. In addition, the sudden growth of rural incomes and the relaxation of rural economic policy created a whole series of new markets. For example, rural housing construction took off, and new rural industries developed to supply building materials to this new market. In both situations, early entrants could to reap windfall profits, and the presence of potential windfalls naturally induced extremely rapid entry. Gradually entrants create competition that eroded the early exceptional profits.

3. The institutional framework surrounding TVEs was favorable to development. Local governments became enthusiastic partisans of TVE development. Indeed, the distinctive political economy described in section 5.6 first emerged alongside TVE growth. Initially, local governments were also owners of many TVEs. Although TVEs were classified as "collectives," this did not mean that the firm was a worker-owned cooperative, but rather that it belonged to the rural collective or village as a whole, which in practice was usually represented by the local village or township government. Later, from the 1980s onward, the ownership of TVEs diversified to include many private firms, but local officials still had powerful incentives to develop TVEs. TVEs provided employment and money to local economies and were often the only realistic source of both. Local-government support contributed to the formation of a favorable environment for TVEs in at least three ways:

a. Formal taxes were low on rural industry, so money stayed local. Rural enterprises enjoyed very low tax rates in general and particularly low tax rates on profits. By contrast, state-run industrial firms benefited from government price policy, but they also paid the price in a very high tax rate—sometimes 100%—on profits. Rural enterprises enjoyed the benefits of price policy without the corresponding high tax burden. The average rate of profit tax collected from TVEs was only 6% in 1980, and only gradually climbed to around 20% by 1986, before stabilizing. Firms at the township and village levels paid about 30% of their total profits to local governments to support agriculture or local social services. Local governments welcomed these funds because they were classified as "extrabudgetary" and therefore did not have to be shared with higher-level governments. In turn, most local governments recycled this money into new and expanded TVEs, since they perceived a high return for their funds in these investments.

b. Local governments acted as guarantors for TVEs, so bank capital was available. Local-government sponsorship of China's TVEs greatly enhanced access of these new businesses to capital. By contrast, the experience of other transforming socialist economies has been that new start-up businesses proliferate, but that these businesses have difficulty getting access to capital and as a result remain small and undercapitalized. Local-government officials in China acted as intermediaries and guarantors, reassuring local agents of the banking system that their loans would ultimately be repaid.

Despite local-government actions supporting and serving as guarantors of TVEs, those TVEs had mostly, but not completely, hard budget constraints. That is, government sponsorship served to spread the risks incurred by these new start-ups, essentially by having the entire local community absorb the cost of failure. Soft budget constraints—implying no responsibility for failed or misguided investments—would have been disastrous in China's rural economy. But it is unlikely that perfectly hard budget constraints for start-up businesses would have been optimal either; a certain amount of "insurance" provided to start-ups by local governments almost certainly enhanced welfare. By underwriting a portion of the risk of entry, local governments enabled start-up firms to enter production with a larger size, to start with some mechanization, and to exploit the economies of scale that came from moving away from the smallest form of household production.

c. Existing credit institutions were easily adapted to support TVEs. With local governments facilitating the flow of capital to rural enterprises, those firms were able to take advantage of China's relatively abundant household saving. Chinese traditional credit clubs and other forms of informal credit markets were put to good use. As Chinese rural household saving skyrocketed during the 1980s, the supply of funds to the local rural credit cooperatives (RCCs) expanded quickly. The RCCs, nominally independent, locally controlled financial co-ops, had in fact been used before reform primarily to transfer the modest rural savings to urban uses. With the onset of reform, the RCCs had more money, and also were allowed to lend a much greater proportion of it locally. The result was that the RCCs emerged as the main source of financial resources for the TVEs. Local money stayed local, and those areas that enjoyed successful TVE development early, when profits were high, were able to plow money back into production and snowball rapidly.

4. Revival of traditional economic ties meant that proximity to urban areas fostered rural industry growth. The growth of China's rural industries occurred first in regions that might more properly be termed suburban. Rural industries were highly concentrated regionally, with a disproportionate share in coastal areas. In 1988, three coastal provinces—Jiangsu, Zhejiang, and Shandong—accounted for 17% of China's rural population but 43% of total rural industry and exactly half of all township- and village-level industrial output. This geographic concentration was entirely natural. These areas were better located to begin with, having more of the locational assets required for city growth. In turn, because cities had developed, they could also provide transport networks, communications, markets, technology, and other conditions that boost productivity throughout the cities' hinterlands, as well as in the cities themselves. Therefore, it is not surprising to find that "rural" enterprises thrived in regions where they benefited from the spillover effects of the urban economies.

Rather, what is striking is that these organic linkages between city and countryside had been so thoroughly cut off during the command economy. As a result, even a modest recovery of urban-rural linkages, beginning in the 1970s, resulted in rapid growth of suburban industry, given the low base from which it was starting. The growth of rural enterprises in periurban areas was facilitated by direct cooperation between urban state-run firms and rural factories, primarily in the form of subcontracting. In the three province-level municipalities of Beijing, Shanghai, and Tianjin, an estimated 60%–80% of rural industrial output was produced by firms subcontracting with large urban factories. The proportions were only slightly lower in nearby provinces: linkages with Shanghai firms "played a decisive role in the development of TVEs in southern Jiangsu" (Tao Youzhi 1988, 100). Such arrangements were facilitated by family relations; rural people who had migrated to the cities and urban youth sent from Shanghai to the countryside during the Cultural Revolution helped rural firms get started. Later on, rural firms purchased talent from the cities, especially by paying high salaries to technicians and retired urban workers. Urban SOEs were willing to cooperate: as state firms gained a greater interest in profit, they sought to reduce costs, and subcontracting operations to rural enterprises became increasingly attractive, particularly in the garment industry. Such relationships also allowed urban firms to escape from some of the tight constraints of the state-run industrial system. By entering into relations with rural firms, state firms could gain access to land and labor at low cost, and operate with more flexibility than in the rigidly controlled state sector.

5. Organizational diversity accommodated growth. A simple but important aspect of TVE development was that there was no single organizational model that TVEs had to follow. TVEs were sometimes government run, but often and increasingly they were private. TVEs were sometimes bureaucratic but often were highly adaptable. In this respect, they were very different from SOEs, which were compelled to adopt a uniform organizational form. As a result of this flexibility, TVEs were able to adapt to a broad range of opportunities. As we will see in section 13.4, a variety of different regional models of rural industrialization grew up, each plausibly suited to a different set of economic conditions.

A steadily increasing share of TVEs were privately run. During the 1980s, entrepreneurs started new small-scale firms, and many firms started under collective auspices became de facto private firms. Sometimes these firms continued to register enterprises as collectives because this practice was safe politically. Local officials formed alliances with entrepreneurs—sometimes for mutual benefit, sometimes more predatory—as rural industrialization spread. After the late 1990s, as the stigma on private business dissipated, TVEs became predominantly private. In all periods, because TVEs were not constrained to a single organizational form, localities were able to adapt as the advantages and disadvantages of various options became evident.

Conclusion: Causes of rapid growth. Rural enterprises grew up in the interstices of the command-economy system. It should be clear that their successful growth cannot be understood in isolation from that system. The command economy, having destroyed the traditional diversified rural economy in the 1950s, then created the distinctive conditions for the emergence of a new diversified rural economy during the 1980s. The influence of the command economy is particularly clear in the profitability of early rural enterprises, the differential tax treatment accorded rural enterprises, and the close links between emerging rural enterprises and the existing state-run urban economy. Moreover, the unique semipublic character of rural enterprises assisted in the supply of capital to these firms. These "artificial" conditions were the most powerful proximate causes of the explosive growth of rural industry in the 1980s.

Yet rural-enterprise growth would not have taken root had it not been favored by additional, more fundamental considerations. Of these, the basic fit between rural enterprises and China's underlying factor endowment is the most important. China's huge size played a crucial role. The simple fact that China has some 2,000 counties, and more than a million villages was crucial to the success of rural industry. Even when a township tried to operate a miniature command economy, it was ultimately subject to competition from thousands of other townships and villages. When firms could not make money, there was no one from outside the village to bail them out, and they had little choice but to go bankrupt. In this fundamentally competitive environment, each township or village found that it faced a relatively hard budget constraint and had to make its own enterprise economically successful. Rural enterprises created competition for state firms, but they themselves were shaped by the competitive process as well. Ultimately, this competitive climate may have been adequate to overcome some of the disadvantages under which rural enterprises labored due to local-government control and the distortions of the economic system as a whole.

13.4   Diverse Regional Models of TVE Development

Responding to different regional conditions, TVEs developed in different patterns in different parts of China.

13.4.1   The Southern Jiangsu (Sunan) Model

Southern Jiangsu, or "Sunan" for short, is the prosperous and developed area of the Yangtze delta around Shanghai, for centuries among the most economically advanced regions of China. Here the dominant model of TVE development was one in which the township and village governments maintained the leading role. TVEs here flourished early, beginning in the early 1970s, while the collective system was still firmly in place in the countryside. Subcontracting and technical-assistance ties with urban SOEs were often important. Because of the longer history and greater capital resources in these areas, TVEs tended to be much bigger, more capital intensive, and more technologically sophisticated than TVEs in other parts of the country. Moreover, as TVEs expanded, the village governments maintained control and retained "collective" ownership, even when private businesses were springing up elsewhere.

Elements of the southern Jiangsu model appeared wherever TVEs grew up early, close to cities. Suburban areas with locational advantages and entrepreneurial village leaderships developed TVEs early under the collectives, and village leaders subsequently had the resources to maintain control for a decade or more. These villages tended to develop a kind of "corporate village" in which village leaders ran an entire business complex. At the same time, these corporate villages maintained government social services and continued to provide public goods formerly provided by collectives. These corporate villages did not usually welcome outsiders, since they wished to protect the lucrative jobs, benefits, and opportunities of locals.

13.4.2   The Wenzhou Model

The town of Wenzhou is only about 300 kilometers south of southern Jiangsu, on the coast of the neighboring province of Zhejiang, but it has a very different geographic setting and evolved a very different model of TVE development. Rugged and fairly remote despite its coastal location, Wenzhou was quite removed from the urban influences so important in southern Jiangsu. From the beginning of its explosive growth, Wenzhou's economy has been based on private ownership. Firms in Wenzhou were initially tiny, based on individual households, and specialized in modest articles of daily use. Wenzhou businesses first flourished by selling buttons, ribbons, plastic ID-card holders, and other ordinary items. Wenzhou peddlers then took these items throughout China, filling a market need for diverse, inexpensive items that state firms had filled either very poorly or not at all.

Wenzhou is a very special place with a long cultural tradition of entrepreneurship and spectacular economic growth since the 1970s. But elements of the Wenzhou model appeared in any place where farmers were willing to seize entrepreneurial opportunities despite the lack of advantageous suburban locations. In these areas, the collectives had not developed TVEs into moneymaking propositions, so collectives were weak and often disappeared early in the reform process. Individually owned firms sprang up in response to opportunity, and they naturally tended toward labor-intensive activities oriented toward the market. Indeed, perhaps the most striking feature of development in Wenzhou itself is the intense reliance on the market to coordinate all aspects of production. The Wenzhou button industry, for example, developed around individual households that specialized in individual stages of the button-production process. Households that milled plastic blocks into button rounds sold these rounds in a specialized marketplace to households that drilled holes in the rounds and finished the buttons. In turn, a different group of households that specialized in mounting buttons on button cards would purchase the finished buttons at another specialized marketplace. Button cards would be sold to peddlers at still another market. In this fashion, production chains linked by markets sprang into existence. This pattern appeared repeatedly for different commodities. Many private businesses—even private banks—developed in the Wenzhou model.

13.4.3   The Pearl River Delta Model

In the Pearl River delta (PRD)—the region between Hong Kong and Guangzhou that is the core of the Southeast Coast macroregion—TVEs developed rapidly under the stimulus of foreign investment. This model was pioneered by Hong Kong businessmen who had grown up in the delta and returned to their home villages to start cooperative businesses. In these transactions, village leaders acted as managers of village assets, leasing land, signing contracts for export processing, and coordinating labor and social issues. As in the southern Jiangsu model, nearby urban (Hong Kong) businesses and local governments both played important roles. Production grew rapidly in large factories. In the Pearl River delta, however, factories were usually export-oriented manufacturers of light, labor-intensive products.

The big difference between the PRD model and the southern Jiangsu model is that the Pearl River delta is much more open both domestically and internationally. Of course, the prosperity of the model depends on openness to foreign trade and investment. The TVEs were often partly foreign (or Hong Kong) owned, but these villages tended to be quite open to workers from other parts of China as well. The PRD needed workers for its large, labor-intensive export factories, and it became by far the largest destination in China for migrant workers. Villagers in the Pearl River delta earned locational "rents" by being open to both foreign and domestic agents.

13.4.4   Failed or Absent TVE Development

As item 4 of section 13.3 indicated, TVE development was highly concentrated in areas with strong economic potential. Conversely, there were many areas of China where TVE development was weak or nonexistent. Large swaths of rural China have had little TVE development. In remote areas, where transportation is costly and difficult, there are few business opportunities for TVEs to exploit. Without TVEs to contribute to the local economy, incomes were much lower, village governments had few resources, and public services were weak to nonexistent. In these areas, outmigration was one of the few ways for households to increase income, and not until national policies changed after 2005 did villages have better options for community services and development.

13.5   The Transformation of TVEs in the New Century

The entire TVE sector underwent dramatic transformation after the mid-1990s. First, TVEs faced a more challenging external environment, and their overall growth rate slowed significantly. Second, faced with this external pressure, TVEs restructured and transformed into predominantly privately owned businesses. Finally, new forms of economic cooperation and competition grew up as TVEs adapted to the new challenges and opportunities.

13.5.1   The Changing Economic Environment of TVEs

During the mid-1990s, fundamental changes occurred in the economic environment in China. These changes were associated with a shift in economic reform strategy, discussed in chapter 5. National-government policy shifted toward building markets and regulatory institutions, just as macroeconomic policy shifted to a tighter, inflation-fighting stance. Bank credit was restricted and banks made more accountable. These changes created a tougher competitive environment for TVEs, and the very rapid growth of TVEs came to an abrupt end.

Figure 13.2 shows employment of all TVEs. In the 1980s and early 1990s, TVEs created millions of new jobs for rural residents, but the pace of TVE job creation dropped off abruptly after 1996. TVE employment declined for two years before resuming moderate growth. Tougher macroeconomic conditions forced both rural and urban firms to cope with a more competitive market economy, and they responded either by closing up shop or by developing more effective market strategies. These often put firms into head-to-head competition with TVEs, as consumer goods market shifted from one of chronic shortage to one in which virtually all goods were regularly available.

With increased market integration and competition, TVEs lost their protected position. There were few, if any, empty niches for TVEs to exploit. Moreover, as incomes, especially urban incomes, rose, consumers increasingly demanded higher-quality products than traditional TVEs, with their outdated technologies, could provide. TVEs seemed to lose their special role in the economy. TVEs continued to grow after 1996, but at rates closer to overall GDP growth than in the past. TVEs in general became less special but also led the rest of the economy in becoming more private.

13.5.2   TVE Restructuring: The Great Privatization

Figure 13.2 shows the dramatic change in the ownership composition of TVEs. Collectively owned TVEs initially dominated the TVE sector. After the 1980s, private firms grew rapidly, but collective TVE employment increased as well through 1995, at which time collectives still accounted for almost half of TVE employment. But the situation changed dramatically in the following 10 years, and by 2005 collective

Figure 13.2
TVE employment.
Sources: TVE Bureau (2003); *TVE Yearbook* (2011).

firms represented a tiny proportion of total TVE employment. Ownership figures are not precise. Early on, there were private firms that operated under the polite fiction of being collectives. As national policy has accepted private businesses, these firms have come out of the closet and acknowledged their true identity. On the other hand, figures for collectively owned TVEs exclude many firms with local government minority stakes. Still, the basic picture is clear: TVEs began as an offshoot of the rural collectives, but today they are predominantly private businesses.

The unique position of TVEs as publicly owned enterprises was thus a defining characteristic of the "golden age," from 1978 to 1996. In no other transitional economy did public enterprises play the pivotal role that TVEs played in China (not even in Vietnam, which had no publicly owned TVEs despite having a similarly large rural economy). A broad spectrum of interpretation has been put forward to explain public ownership of TVEs. At one extreme, public ownership of TVEs has been interpreted as the result of a uniquely cooperative Chinese culture, which enabled local actors to resolve incentive problems without explicit contracts (Weitzman and Xu 1994). This explanation is most plausible in the early phase of TVE development, when the absence of population mobility meant that local actors were forced to deal with each other repeatedly and face-to-face. At the other extreme, publicly owned TVEs are seen, at best, as adequate adaptations to the political constraints and insecure private property rights that the central government imposed (Chang and Wang

1994). Between these extremes, some have argued that in an environment in which many markets were missing or underdeveloped, local governments were able to leverage their access to credit, land, and relationships in the service of local economic development. Local governments could operate like diversified corporations with relatively hard budget constraints at the community level, combined with operational flexibility at the firm level. Qian and Jin (1998) explained the variation in public ownership across provinces by variations in the level of product and credit-market development. Publicly owned TVEs are sometimes also seen as striking the right balance in motivating local government officials. Public ownership protected local interests against expropriation by higher-level governments, while local-government officials were given strong incentives and hard budget constraints.

Changes in the economic environment gradually reduced the benefits of public ownership and increased its costs. As market competition and population mobility increased, the local-government owners adopted more powerful incentive systems to reward TVE managers (Chen 2000; Chang, McCall, and Wang 2003). Latent shortcomings of public ownership became more evident. As markets developed, a friendly local government official was no longer indispensable. Privatization was the increasingly widespread response of local governments to these changing conditions (Dong, Bowles, and Ho 2002; Li and Rozelle 2003). At the same time, national ideological constraints were being relaxed. Many external factors thus changed simultaneously.

13.5.2.1   National Policy and Local Control

The national government gradually lifted taboos against private businesses in the mid-1990s, and local governments were empowered to privatize their public firms at this time. While the shift in national-government policy was a necessary prerequisite, the process of TVE privatization was controlled by local governments. As a result, we can track a process of experimentation with incentive mechanisms that culminated in privatization, and we can observe a broad range of privatization outcomes and mechanisms.

13.5.2.2   Market Conditions and Privatization

In section 13.5.1, the general argument was made that an intensification of product market competition was an important driver of institutional change in the TVE sector after 1996. Heightened competition also affects factor markets with specific links to privatization:

Labor markets. Although TVEs never had the lifetime employment system that SOEs adopted, publicly owned TVEs were often pressured by local governments to keep local employment as high as possible. Moreover, publicly owned firms can find it difficult to lay off workers in times of adversity. Almost certainly, the slowing of labor absorption by TVEs was related to the transition to increased private ownership.

Moreover, as the Chinese economy became increasingly marketized, managers of TVEs saw dramatic changes in their opportunity costs. TVE managers had long enjoyed relatively high incomes and privileges, but their point of comparison had been the local community, and few managers became personally wealthy. As the private sector grew and private wealth became more conspicuous in the 1990s, managers saw lucrative opportunities outside the village. It is likely that the best managers were unwilling to settle for the moderate compensation offered by public firms, and without a privatization option, they would have left the TVE sector altogether.

Capital markets. Banks faced a new incentive environment in the 1990s, as policy-makers carried out reforms that induced them to focus on risk and profitability. Banks began to vet lending projects more carefully and discriminate among profitable and unprofitable firms instead of automatically lending to firms with government backing. Some banks even preferred to lend to private firms, which had collateral that could be seized if necessary (seizure of assets from public firms was significantly more difficult). A more "businesslike" banking sector eroded some of the benefits of public ownership and tended to push TVEs in the direction of privatization. Since TVE profitability had declined substantially from the heights in the 1980s, local governments were less likely to indiscriminately support any local government TVE.

These channels of influence through various types of markets combined with the most fundamental channel, the intensification of punishing product-market competition. Driven both by judgments about the relative efficiency of different ownership types and by market pressures, local governments increasingly voted for private ownership and converted their TVEs. It became impossible for managers to wear two or three hats and successfully run a business while also managing the village's political affairs.

13.5.2.3   Insider Privatization

Because TVE privatization was locally initiated and controlled, the forms and process varied from place to place. Still, different case studies have shown that "insider privatization" was a common form of privatization, probably the most common. That is, TVE privatization has generally ended up with incumbent managers or closely related government officials owning significant shares of the privatized firms. Table 13.1 shows the results from one careful study of three sites in Shandong and Jiangsu. The level of insider privatization evident in the TVEs is comparatively rare in government-managed privatization processes. Governments often try to

Table 13.1
Distribution of shares in privatized TVEs (three sites in Shandong and Jiangsu, 2000).

Shareholders	Percent
Managers	53
Other board members	25
Workers (nonmanagerial)	18
Local government	3
Others	2

Source: Dong, Bowles, and Ho (2002, 421).

discourage insider privatization and make an effort to attract outside bidders in the hopes of driving up the price of the firm. Insiders have a great deal of local knowledge about the firm and probably have a better idea about the value of the firm than the government officials who are selling it have. As a result, there is a clear moral hazard problem: privatization presents opportunities for corruption and plundering of public assets. Incumbent managers are in a position to manipulate the preprivatization performance of the firm, making the firm look worse so that it can be purchased at a lower price. Because of the difficulty in monitoring the price at which privatization takes place, insider privatization represents a clear risk to public wealth.

Insider privatization has advantages as well. Incumbent managers are experienced, and their familiarity with the firm should help them run it after privatization. TVE managers, even under collective ownership, were often observed to have exceptionally close and enduring relationships with the firm. In some cases, they were the entrepreneurs who founded the firms under collective auspices. In those cases, managers may have a legitimate claim to own part of the privatized firm. Ironically, the fact that China has never officially embraced "privatization" as such, preferring imprecise euphemisms like "restructuring," made it impossible for the central government to give guidance to localities on the institutional framework appropriate for an open and transparent privatization process. At the same time, TVEs have always been a local phenomenon, embedded in the ongoing face-to-face relationships among members of a rural community. In that sense, TVE management and TVE privatization were everybody's business. Privatization and restructuring took place under the eyes of the local community.

13.5.2.4 Institutional Experimentation in the Privatization Process

Local control of TVE privatization has resulted in a natural laboratory of experimentation with incentive mechanisms. In general, these experiments were pathways to private ownership, which ended up as the overwhelmingly dominant form of TVE ownership (table 13.2). Many of these experiments should therefore be seen as efforts to control moral hazard and protect the communities' interest during the privatization process. Three experiments were especially noteworthy:

• Some public TVEs were converted into worker-owned joint-stock companies, usually called "shareholding cooperatives." In the most important local program, Zhucheng in Shandong Province, workers were allocated purchase rights for shares. Allocations were not equal: managers could receive allocations as much as 20 times as large as those of ordinary workers, although the average was around 4 times. A single share cost about 5,000 RMB, roughly a worker's annual wage, but time payment and favorable financing were available. After one year, workers could sell their shares to other workers. The objective was to enfranchise workers while also creating the unambiguous property rights structure of a joint-stock company. The Zhucheng experience was publicized nationwide as a pilot program, and in 2010, there were 2.5 million workers in joint-stock cooperatives (table 13.2).

• In many localities, the government retained a stake in the firm, essentially creating a joint venture with the new private manager. (In these cases, the local government retained a much larger stake than in the cases shown in table 13.1.) Indeed, it can be hard to determine what constitutes a privatized firm today among China's TVEs: local governments may retain stakes ranging from 20% to 50%.

• "Privatization with a tail" was a common practice. In many places, local governments confronted incumbent managers with a choice: purchase the TVE free and clear at a "high price" (above book value) or purchase it at a "low price" (at or below

Table 13.2
TVE employment by ownership, 2010.

	Million	Percent
Domestic capital enterprises	149.2	93.9
Individual/family business	60.8	38.3
Private firms	56.5	35.6
Limited liability	21.0	13.2
Collective	3.9	2.5
Joint stock corporations	3.6	2.3
Shareholding cooperatives	2.5	1.6
Jointly operated	1.0	0.6
Hong Kong/Taiwan invested	5.6	3.5
Foreign invested	4.1	2.6
Total	158.9	100.0

Source: *TVE Yearbook* (2011, 137).

book value) and agree to pay the local government a share of profits over the next 5 to 10 years. In this case, the "tail" is the future profit share. This is essentially an information-elicitation device. If managers believe that the firm will increase profits, it will be in their interest to offer a higher price today; if they are skeptical or uncertain about the firm's future prospects, they will prefer to pay a lower price today. Such a mechanism can help overcome the problems of insider knowledge that we would expect to be severe in the Chinese context (Li and Rozelle 2003).

Privatization proceeded rapidly even in those areas, such as southern Jiangsu, where collective ownership was formerly dominant. That region is still distinctive in many ways, but it gradually lost its distinctive Sunan model of TVE development under collective ownership.

13.6   Emergence of Rural Industrial Clusters in the Twenty-First Century

After the great privatization wave of the 1990s, TVE's continued to evolve and grow, and changes in the Chinese economy have increasingly blurred the boundaries that once separated TVEs from other kinds of firms. Some TVEs have become successful private multinational corporations. For example, Wanxiang Auto has become one of the world's largest auto-parts suppliers, with $20 billion in annual revenues and large investments in the United States. Many of the seedbed areas of TVE growth have been transformed from rural regions into cities. After about 2010, it no longer makes sense to treat TVEs as a distinctive category of enterprises. Evolutionary changes continue to remake rural industries.

The most important development has been the emergence of highly competitive "industrial clusters" in rural and suburban areas. The key feature of an industrial cluster is the large number of firms that contribute to a single specialized product. Typical industrial clusters include scores—perhaps hundreds—of small firms that compete with one another but cooperate to form a link in a relatively complete industrial chain. Clusters may have three or four large firms cooperating with scores of small firms. Typical, though, is an exceptionally fine division of labor among different stages of the production process. Small, competitive firms specialize in extremely narrow activities. Relationships among firms can be quite complex, but they are generally mediated by efficient markets, in which a balance is struck between flexibility and long-term cooperation. Clusters generally produce light consumer goods. Industrial clusters emerged earliest in Zhejiang Province (with 519 distinct recognized industrial clusters by the turn of the century; Qian 2003), and we can certainly see elements of the Wenzhou model in these Zhejiang clusters. Ground zero for the Chinese industrial-cluster phenomenon today is certainly Yiwu, also in

Zhejiang Province. Famous for its "Small Commodity Market," Yiwu is at the center of hundreds of specialized industrial clusters. The Commodity Market is not an industrial cluster but rather the world's largest wholesale market, the point of coordination and sales for thousands of specialized clusters to which merchants come from all over the world (Yiwu Market Guide 2017). For example, the sock industry cluster is centered in Zhuji Municipality, about an hour from Yiwu, which, along with Yiwu itself, claims to produce more than 50% of the world's socks. Other industrial clusters produce toothbrushes and Christmas ornaments, power tools and low-voltage electrical equipment, promotional items, and copies of oil paintings.

Industrial clusters are not unique to China but are emerging in many places around the world. The shoe industry in Brazil and the garment and luxury-goods industries in Italy display many of the same characteristics. Yet we can also identify some typically Chinese elements characteristic of the traditional economy, as well as in the early Wenzhou model of TVE development. The clustering of numerous small producers, linked to a larger marketplace by a series of smaller intermediate-goods markets, is a form of industrial organization with a long tradition in China. Today, there are a number of industries where a resurgence of this type of organization has been accompanied by a surge in the competitiveness of Chinese goods on the world marketplace. Indeed, as the Yiwu example shows, TVE export orientation has remained strong. TVEs continue to change and restructure in response to market challenges and opportunities.

13.7   Epilogue: Taobao Villages

As the Internet spread across China after 2009, observers began to notice a new phenomenon: villages where many households produced similar items and the whole village was selling directly to consumers through Taobao. Taobao is a unit of the Chinese e-commerce giant Alibaba; it is a website similar to eBay in the United States, or to that part of Amazon that sells third-party merchandise. "Taobao villages" have all the characteristics of the traditional industrial cluster, combined with Internet connectivity and B2C (business-to-consumer) business models. Like other industrial clusters, Taobao villages tend to specialize in a single inexpensive product type with a mass market but with specific requirements in different market niches. The Taobao village then makes the most of its flexibility to provide specific features and variations valued in different market segments. Top products are clothing, furniture, shoes, and leather bags. Like traditional industrial clusters, a Taobao village typically specializes in a single main product that accounts for more than half of sales. They may need other specialized villages nearby to supply certain inputs: the Taobao village is the upfront B2C shop, behind which may lie a network of B2B (business-to-business) relationships. The largest cluster of Taobao villages in China—no surprise—is in Yiwu, Zhejiang. Thirty-seven Yiwu villages have reorganized around their Internet sales businesses. Besides location, households need only an Internet connection and a bit of familiarity with digital technology, which can often be provided by a returning rural-to-urban migrant.

Since 2009, Taobao villages have spread rapidly, and as of August 2016, the Ali Research Center (a subsidiary of Alibaba), had located 1,311 such villages. These villages operate over 300,000 websites, and the researchers calculate they employ about 840,000 workers full- or part-time (Ali Research Center 2017). Although this accounts for only 0.5% of China's rural nonagricultural workforce, Taobao villages can nonetheless tell us a great deal about the present and future of China's rural industry.

First, institutional innovation is still thriving in China's countryside, particularly those semirural areas close to cities. Moreover, the reasons are the same as in the past: institutional flexibility built on relatively low factor costs (land and labor) combined with proximity to urban markets and infrastructure. Of course, the definition of infrastructure has changed dramatically: in the case of Taobao villages, the key piece of infrastructure is a broadband Internet connection, which is typically available only near cities. Taobao villages are extraordinarily well placed, it turns out, to benefit from the combination of low transaction costs enabled by the Internet and low production costs.

Second, while it might appear that the Internet allows Taobao villages to set up anywhere, the reality is that location still matters: the distribution of Taobao villages in 2016 was eerily similar to that of TVEs in the 1980s. Fully 97% are in six provinces: Zhejiang, Guangdong, Jiangsu, Fujian, Shandong, and Hebei (in that order), the same provinces that led the development of TVEs in the 1980s.

Taobao villages often receive vigorous support from local-government officials. As was the case for TVEs in the golden era, local officials are likely to be fiercely supportive of enterprise development, seeing it as one of the few feasible routes to bring economic development and income growth to their communities. The researchers from Alibaba highlighted 10 Taobao villages they discovered in designated "poor counties" (four of them in Pingxiang, Hebei). After the development of two Taobao villages in Daji Township in Shandong, local officials launched a campaign to persuade rural-to-urban migrants from the township to stay home after the Chinese New Year and brought fiber-optic cable to more than 1,200 homes (Ali Research Center 2016, 19–20).

China's rural industry shows that many economic features from the past are still in effect today. It demonstrates that China's legacy of a densely populated, commercialized countryside is still working in its favor. It shows that the unique Chinese configuration of entrepreneurial local government officials and local businesses still operates. It exemplifies the general economic principle that the benefits from economic exchange are especially great when it can take place between agents facing very different costs. Finally, it shows that China can still reap substantial economic gains as long as it permits continued institutional flexibility and the continued expansion of markets.

Bibliography

Suggestions for Further Reading

The literature on TVEs is especially rich. First, there is a rich body of descriptive and case-study material that provides a good introduction to the topic. For example, Byrd and Lin (1990) assembled a team of Chinese and international scholars for mixed case-study and analytic work. Second, there is a stimulating literature on the institutional underpinnings of the TVE phenomenon. Chang and Wang (1994), Che and Qian (1998), and Weitzman and Xu (1994) are important milestones in this literature. The Yiwu Market Guide English language website is well worth a quick visit.

References

Ali Research Center (Annual). *Zhongguo Taobaocun Yanjiu Baogao* [Research report on China Taobao villages]. Hangzhou: Ali Research Center. (Year of publication is one year after year in title). Accessed at http://i.aliresearch.com/file/20170125/20170125164026.pdf.

Byrd, William, and Qingsong Lin, eds. (1990). *China's Rural Industry: Structure, Development, and Reform.* New York: Oxford University Press.

Chang, Chun, Brian P. McCall, and Yijiang Wang (2003). "Incentive Contracting Versus Ownership Reforms: Evidence from China's Township and Village Enterprises." *Journal of Comparative Economics* 31:414–428.

Chang, Chun, and Yijiang Wang (1994). "The Nature of Township-Village Enterprises." *Journal of Comparative Economics* 19 (3): 434–452.

Che, J., and Qian Yingyi (1998). "Insecure Property Rights and Government Ownership of Firms." *Quarterly Journal of Economics* 113 (2): 467–496.

Chen, Hongyi (2000). *The Institutional Transition of China's Township and Village Enterprises: Market Liberalization, Contractual Form Innovation and Privatization.* Aldershot: Ashgate.

Dong, Xiao-yuan, Paul Bowles, and Samuel P. S. Ho (2002). "The Determinants of Employee Ownership in China's Privatized Rural Industry: Evidence from Jiangsu and Shandong." *Journal of Comparative Economics* 30:415–437.

Fei Xiaotong (1957 [1989]). *Rural Development in China: Prospect and Retrospect.* Chicago: University of Chicago Press.

Li, Hongbin, and Scott Rozelle (2003). "Privatizing Rural China: Insider Privatization, Innovative Contracts and the Performance of Township Enterprises." *China Quarterly*, no. 176 (December): 981–1005.

Oi, J. (1992). "Fiscal Reform and the Economic Foundations of Local State Corporatism in China." *World Politics* 45 (1): 99–126.

Qian, Pingfan (2003). "Development of China's Industrial Clusters: Features and Problems." *China Development Review* 5 (4): 44–51.

Qian, Yingyi, and Hehui Jin (1998). "Public Versus Private Ownership of Firms: Evidence from Rural China." *Quarterly Journal of Economics* 113 (3): 773–808.

SAC (Annual). *Zhongguo Tongji Zhaiyao* [Statistical abstract of China]. Beijing: Zhongguo Tongji.

SRC (System Reform Commission) (1984). *Jingji Tizhi Gaige Wenjian Huibian, 1977–1983* [Collected economic system reform documents, 1977–1983]. Beijing: Zhongguo Caizheng Jingji.

Tao Youzhi (1988). *Sunan Moshi yu Zhifu zhi Dao* [The southern Jiangsu model and the road to prosperity]. Shanghai: Shanghai Shehui Kexue Yuan.

Third Census Office (1997). Disanci Quanguo Gongye Pucha Bangongshi, ed. *Zhonghua Renming Gongheguo 1995 Nian Disancia Quanguo Gongye Pucha Ziliao Huibian* [The data of the Third National Industrial Census of the People's Republic of China in 1995]. Vol. 1, *Zonghe, Hangyezhuan* [Overall, sectoral]. Beijing: Zhongguo Tongji.

TVE Bureau (2003). TVE Bureau, Ministry of Agriculture. *Zhongguo Xiangzhen Qiye Tongji Ziliao, 1978–2002* [China township and village enterprise statistical materials, 1978–2002]. Beijing: Zhongguo Nongye.

TVE Yearbook (Annual). Zhongguo Xiangzhen Qiye Nianjian Biaji Weiyuanhui [China Township and Village Enterprise Yearbook Editorial Commission], ed. *Zhongguo Xiangzhen Qiye Nianjian* [China township and village enterprise yearbook]. Beijing: Zhongguo Nongye.

Weitzman, Martin, and Chenggang Xu (1994). "Chinese Township-Village Enterprises as Vaguely Defined Cooperatives." *Journal of Comparative Economics* 18 (2): 121–145.

Wong, Christine (1982). "Rural Industrialization in the People's Republic of China: Lessons from the Cultural Revolution Decade." In Joint Economic Committee, U.S. Congress, *China Under the Four Modernizations*, 394–418. Washington, DC: U.S. Government Printing Office.

Wong, Christine (1988). "Interpreting Rural Industrial Growth in the Post-Mao Period." *Modern China* 14 (1): 3–30.

Yiwu Market Guide (2017). "Yiwu Market Guide." Accessed at http://www.yiwu-market-guide.com /yiwu-market.html.

Urban commercial exuberance: Red lanterns in Shanghai's Ganghui Mall. (Courtesy of Micah Fisher-Kirshner.)

Since 1978, China has gone through multiple industrial revolutions. Nearly every aspect of the technological and institutional foundations of Chinese industry has been transformed. Industrial output was about 50 times in 2016 what it had been in 1978, and industrial growth has driven the transformation of the Chinese economy (chapter 7). Whole new industries have been created; structural change has been enormous; and China has emerged as the industrial workshop of the world. These achievements would have been impossible had China not shrugged off the institutions of the command economy and shifted to a market basis. Institutional change in industry was central to the transition from a planned to a market economy, particularly in state-owned industry, which had been the core of the command economy. China today has achieved a successful transition from a state monopoly to a diverse mix of ownership types. As figure 14.1 shows, state firms in 2015 account for 23% of large-firm industrial revenues, substantially less than domestic private corporations (34%) and about the same as foreign-invested firms (22%). Moreover, these various firm types compete vigorously in most industrial product markets. Probably the single most important fact about China's institutional transformation over the past 35 years is that the industrial economy has become a market economy in which domestic and foreign private firms play a predominant role (Lardy 2014).

However, Chinese industry has not simply converged to a standard market model. On the contrary, the Chinese industrial economy remains distinctive because of the strong role of state-owned firms and of government at both central and local levels. In addition, after breakthroughs in the late 1990s, the progress of market-oriented institutional reforms clearly slowed around 2005. Finally, while the institutional changes China carried out from the 1980s into the twenty-first century were clearly adequate to support China's industrialization during the miracle-growth phase, the next stage of growth, in which innovation and steadily increasing efficiency will be required to offset the effects of steadily rising costs, presents qualitatively different

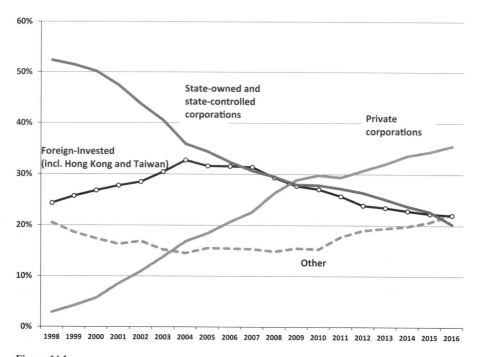

Figure 14.1
Ownership composition of industrial sales revenue.
Source: *SYC* (2016, tables 13-1 through 13-4). Data are for revenue from principal lines of business.

challenges. China's industrial institutions will need to be increasingly robust and sophisticated to meet these challenges.

Some insight into the current situation can be gained by taking a closer look at one of the most striking recent achievements. In the Fortune Global 500 rankings based on 2015 sales revenues, there were 93 firms from the People's Republic of China among the world's biggest 500 firms, an outcome much celebrated in the Chinese press. Of these, 76 were nonfinancial companies, almost all industrial. A closer look reveals that almost all of these firms—68 out of 76—are state-owned enterprises (SOEs). Even more striking, 47 of them are owned by the central government's State Asset Supervision and Administration Commission (SASAC), which is surely the world's largest controlling shareholder. (Indeed, it is probably the richest organization in the world that almost nobody has heard of.) Especially striking is the fact that most of these giant SOEs depend on protected domestic markets for their supersized revenue. For this reason, Nolan (2014, 763) concluded that "China's SOEs are far from catching up with the world's leading firms. Chinese [state] firms have a negligible share of the world's most competitive markets in high-income countries." These firms have grown big and improved their efficiency but are still a long way from the global frontier.

There are eight private Chinese firms in the Fortune Global 500, also a substantial number. Nevertheless, it is telling that 20 years after the massive downsizing of the state sector initiated in 1996, the sector of very large firms is still almost entirely dominated by state-owned enterprises. An external observer is left with the suspicion that, given the rapid, transformative growth of China's industry in the past 40 years, there may have been promising private firms that did not grow to be dynamic global firms because of subtle and not-so-subtle barriers in the domestic environment. In China, private firms are encouraged to grow, but not necessarily to grow big and powerful.

This chapter is divided into three parts linked to different ownership systems. The first part describes the dynamic small-scale, hybrid, and private firms that created China's current diverse and competitive industrial landscape (section 14.1). It describes the dynamic process through which an extraordinarily wide range of actors displaced the old state-run monopoly and the vibrant competitive environment that emerged (section 14.2). The second part shifts focus to state-owned enterprise and uses this perspective to discuss a range of issues related to corporate governance. It begins with the dilemmas that face public ownership (section 14.3), governance institutions at the firm level (section 14.4), agencies that exercise public ownership (section 14.5), and corporate finance (section 14.6). Section 14.7 examines the sectoral composition and concentration of state-run industry. All the issues raised in these sections extend beyond the state sector, and comparisons are made with private corporations inside and outside China. The final part of the chapter (section 14.8) puts the most distinctive feature of China's ownership system in an international context. China went through transition without mass privatization, a decision that—at least initially—served it well. However, as a result, the state sector today plays a prominent role in the Chinese economy in a way that raises a number of corporate governance challenges.

14.1   Entry of Small-scale, Hybrid, and Private Firms

The most important factor that drove institutional change in Chinese industry was the entry of new firms that steadily created an intensely competitive product market. A competitive product market is one of the most important external forces that disciplines a firm and forces it to become more efficient. Entrants were an extraordinarily diverse group. The township and village enterprises, described in chapter 13, played the catalytic early role, and because of the backing of local governments could often raise capital and enter with significant scale. Foreign-invested firms, which were crucial drivers in the 1990s and brought high-level skills as well as experience with global markets and suppliers, will be described in chapter 17. They reached their peak share of industrial output in 2004–2006 (figure 14.1). The sections following describe entry process first from the standpoint of size—the revival of small-scale industry—and then in terms of two domestic ownership types: hybrid firms and private family businesses.

14.1.1 Entry and the (Re-)Creation of Small-Scale Industry

The diverse ownership structure of China's industry today was created through a multidecade process of entry and market change. On the eve of economic transition, in 1978, China's industry was made up of thousands of similar, publicly owned organizations. The traditional state-owned enterprise (SOE) dominated the scene, and since each SOE typically consisted of just one factory (multiplant corporations did not exist), most industry was urban and middle sized. China had very few small firms under the planned economy, and the potential was huge. As a result, growth of small-scale firms was the dominant story of the first decade and a half of reform. Almost all developing economies have a substantial small-scale sector that plays a vital role. Even in an economy like that of Japan, where most attention has been paid to large firms and industrial groups, small firms were crucial to development during the high-growth era; the dense network of small-scale machinery firms in Ota Ward of Tokyo, for example, "provided the crucial underpinning for Japan's machinery industry" (Seki 1994, 61). China reaped huge productivity gains by permitting such sectors to emerge, reviving patterns from the traditional economy (section 13.6). Microenterprises of various kinds emerged to take advantage of underserved markets. The Wenzhou model, described in the previous chapter, is an example of this entrepreneurial response.

By 1997, Chinese authorities had adopted a policy of "focus on the large, let go of the small" (*zhuada fangxiao*), essentially ceding the small-scale sector to start-ups and private firms. They were content to let the small-scale sector revive with relatively little interference, showing benign neglect toward private firms as long as they remained small. Yet 1998 may have been the peak relative importance of small-scale firms, as they accounted for 43% of total industrial output. Intense market competition emerged after 1997 and deprived many small firms of the sheltered niches in which they were operating, forcing many small firms to shut down. TVE employment growth slowed dramatically around this time (figure 13.2). Successful start-ups, of course, left their origins as small firms behind and became medium or large corporations. Consistent comparative data are not available to track the small-scale sector over time, but the most recent economic census, in 2013, revealed that there were over 2 million small-scale industrial firms that employed 42 million workers, or 30% of the industrial workforce.[1] Small firms are still an important part of China's industrial economy, especially in garments, mining of building materials, and metal products and repair.

14.1.2 Hybrid Firms

During the 1980s, the reformist government adopted a welcoming attitude toward many kinds of entrepreneurship, including the creation of firms as spin-offs from existing organizations. This was especially evident in the high-tech sector, where the government—always eager to foster a high-tech industry—was especially supportive of institutional innovation and entrepreneurship. While small start-ups brought competition to low-tech sectors, hybrid firms were often pioneers of new high-tech sectors.

There is no precise definition of the Chinese hybrid firm, but rather a pattern of hybrid firm development with three main characteristics. First, there is often a dominant manager or managerial group, usually with a significant ownership stake. The manager is often the individual who first proposes spinning a profitable enterprise off from a bureaucratic organization. These firms move quickly because they have personalized decisive leadership; they are not bureaucratic companies. Second, ownership is divided. These firms are usually not 100% privately owned. Local governments or other government agencies often hold minority stakes, either directly or through intermediaries. These firms sometimes are listed on the stock markets, in which case a minority of shares are typically sold. Companies from Hong Kong, Taiwan, and overseas often hold stakes as well. Shared ownership is commonly used to align interests between entrepreneurs and other stakeholders, including local governments. Third, multiple forms of integration—not limited to equity stakes—link these firms to overseas actors through global production and innovation networks. Contract manufacturing (in both directions), research partnerships, licensing, and many other forms connect domestic and foreign firms.

A classic early example of such a hybrid firm is Legend Computer, later called Lenovo. Created in 1984 as a spin-off from the Computer Science Institute of the Chinese Academy of Sciences, Legend began as a reseller of foreign computers and gradually moved into assembly. Legend never really became a manufacturing powerhouse, but it developed a strong domestic China brand, a domestic design and distribution network, and a good supply network. Legend outsourced 100% of its laptop assembly to Taiwanese contract manufacturers, thus creatively integrating into global production networks. Building on this step, Legend moved audaciously at the end of

---

1. Our ability to track the small-scale sector declines sharply after 1998, when statisticians began to collect complete information only on "above-scale" firms.

2004 to acquire IBM's personal computer division. As part of its acquisition, Lenovo received substantial investment from U.S. private equity firms, and these investors became strategic partners. The new consolidated firm was then listed on the Hong Kong Stock Exchange. The shares are 36% owned by the original Beijing Legend Company (enough to maintain control), and the Chinese Academy of Sciences (the original state "parent") maintains its one-third stake in Beijing Legend. Legend/ Lenovo is an extreme example since it internationalized in fundamental ways, keeping substantial headquarters and design functions in North Carolina (the original headquarters of IBM's personal computer division). However, the features it displays are present in most hybrid forms to a greater or lesser extent.

Like Lenovo, many leading Chinese information technology firms—TCL, Founder, ZTE, Datang, and SMIC—can be characterized as hybrid firms. They have substantial public and private ownership stakes, complex histories, and foreign connections. It is not accidental that hybrid firms are most prominent in the high-tech sector. State permissiveness, derived from the desire to foster technologically sophisticated industry, led to innovations in corporate governance designed to support an entrepreneurial, start-up economy, looking distantly to the Silicon Valley model. This unique confluence of opportunities attracted visionary owner-managers who somehow found a way to bring these elements together to create successful companies.

Hybrid firms can be observed in many sectors of the Chinese economy today. In many cases, the hybrid form is a remnant of the firm's creation by its founder, originally working for a government agency. His employer may have initially provided him capital and given him time and space to start a business. As the environment liberalized during the 1990s, many managers took managerial control of firms, while governments maintained a minority ownership stake. For example, Wahaha Beverage is a large consumer-products company—said to be China's largest beverage producer—based in Hangzhou and dominated by a charismatic owner-entrepreneur, Zong Qinghou. But the city district government where the firm originated maintains a 46% ownership stake in the company, reflecting its origin as a spin-off from a district school.[2] Such companies are sometimes categorized as "privately run" (*minying*) companies, a term that implies that they are privately owned but is noncommittal about formal ownership structures. The largest industrial *minying* firm is Huawei, which is more precisely an employee-owned company.

2. Zong maintains control through a complex system of holding companies, including offshore holding companies. Wahaha was engaged in a bitter dispute with its international joint-venture partner Danone in the mid-2000s, which led to the disclosure of many details of its ownership and corporate structure.

14.1.3   Private Businesses

Most start-up microenterprises were household businesses, and many TVEs were de facto private firms, sometimes with a thin veneer of village or township supervision. Thus private businesses have been important from the beginning. China initially allowed "household businesses" (*getihu*), typically with eight or fewer employees, and only gradually permitted "private businesses," which can be much larger. Thus formally registered private businesses were relative latecomers to the urban business scene in China. It was not until 2004 that employment in businesses registered as private corporations reached 10% of the urban workforce; by 2015 that number reached 28%.

Today, private business is the predominant ownership form in Chinese industry, but there has been relatively little systematic work on private corporate governance. What we do know seems to suggest that Chinese private firms share some characteristics with other Asian private businesses. They tend to be family run, diversified, organized into closely held companies, and dependent on internal finance.

14.1.3.1   Dominance of Family Firms

Almost all of China's private business firms, even the largest ones, are dominated by a founding individual and his or her immediate family. In a review of the top 500 nonstate enterprises in 2010, a natural person was found to hold a controlling interest in 307, and this list included some firms, such as Legend, better designated "hybrid" (Feng, Ljungwall, and He 2015). Other surveys have found that over 85% of private corporations are family controlled. Naturally, family control is even more likely in the smallest businesses, including household and unregistered businesses in the vast small-scale fringe.

Many of China's private businesses fall into the category of diversified family businesses (DFBs). DFBs have been well described in the business and sociology literature outside China (Hamilton and Biggart 1988; Wong 1985). Some of the world's wealthiest men are the heads of DFBs located in Hong Kong and Southeast Asia. However, in China, private business people are required to keep a much lower profile. They must cultivate good relations with local officeholders and emphasize their commitment to the common goal of economic development. In 2012, about one-third of private business owners in a large survey were members of the Communist Party. Li et al. (2008) found that private firms whose CEOs were party members were better able to access bank credit and expressed greater confidence in the legal system. Moreover, these effects were stronger in provinces where market and legal institutions were weaker. Family firms have obvious benefits in the strong trust and loyalty among family members. However, they can also be less effective in accessing and deploying capital and in using professional managers in formal arrangements.

14.1.3.2   Diversified Businesses

Above a certain size, private firms have a strong tendency to diversify. They deploy productive assets in a wide range of seemingly unrelated sectors. Du, Lu, and Tao (2015) argued that private firms diversify because of their need for political protection. Private businesses incur substantial setup costs and must nurture close relations with government officials. Once they do so, they have political protection that is valuable within a geographic jurisdiction; this geographically specific relationship capital is more valuable than the sector-specific expertise they have developed in their initial line of business. As a result, Du, Lu, and Tao found empirically that firms are highly diversified across sectors and are more likely to expand within jurisdictions. Moreover, these effects are more likely where measured political interventions are greater and have greater economic cost, and they are stronger when entrepreneurs are former government officials or SOE managers and SOE cadres. Private firms need regulatory forbearance to prosper and need to minimize informal levies exacted under the pretext of providing local public goods. These findings are consistent with the cross-national literature on DFBs.

The introduction of international business into China increased the complexity of private business organization. Taiwan and Hong Kong businesses set up many subsidiaries in mainland China, and they often cooperated with local family members in these businesses. Simultaneously, Chinese businesses learned that it could be advantageous to have overseas subsidiaries, especially in Hong Kong. Sometimes Chinese firms set up simple Hong Kong subsidiaries; in other cases, complex chains of subsidiaries and holding companies have been created that weave across international boundaries.

14.1.3.3   Legal Status

The World Bank Enterprise Survey project interviewed 2,700 private firms in China in 2012 (World Bank and IFC 2014). It found that Chinese firms were much less likely to be organized as public shareholding companies (either "open" or "closed," that is, with equity publicly traded or not) than firms in East Asia or globally. Only 5.3% of the firms in its sample were organized as one of those two types of limited-liability corporations, as opposed to 21.6% in East Asia generally. In China, 50.8% were sole proprietorships, and 39.7% were various kinds of partnerships.

14.1.3.4   Finance

Private firms in China regularly report difficulty in accessing external finance, particularly from the banking system. Since most private firms are small and new, this is hardly surprising. Chinese banks are known to require substantial collateral from private firms before they are willing to lend. The World Bank survey cited in the previous section found that private firms raised 90% of their investment finance internally and only 4.5% from banks and 3% from equity. The proportion of funds raised internally is higher, and the proportion from banks lower, than for private firms in other East Asian countries (72% and 15%) and from upper-middle-income economies in general (62% and 23%). It is also a huge contrast with SOEs, with their heavy reliance on bank financing. When private firms in the survey were asked to identify their "main obstacle," the top reply was "access to finance" (22%), followed by "practices of the informal sector" (20%) and "tax rates" (15%). The picture that emerges is one of private firms in a financially constrained environment, in which access to—or protection from—influential officials can be an important determinant of success.

14.2   A Diverse and Competitive Industrial Economy

The business environment in today's China is intensely competitive, and in many sectors there is head-to-head competition between different types of firms. For example, consumers can choose among cell phones made by top quality multinationals (Apple, Samsung), high-quality domestic hybrids (Lenovo, Xiaomi), mass-market private firms (Oppo) or manufacturers of cheap, no-brand knockoffs. The gray-market off-brand (*shanzhai*) phones have now developed substantial markets in Africa and south Asia as well. Brandt and Thun (2010) have written about competition in the construction machinery industry. Foreign firms, such as Caterpillar and Komatsu, initially entered in the premium market segment, selling expensive top-quality machinery. Gradually, hybrid Chinese firms, such as Sany and Zoomlion, have expanded into the medium-quality segment, selling machinery that is not premium quality but is substantially cheaper. A fringe of smaller, local firms, selling low-quality but inexpensive equipment, survives. This pattern of intense competition helps explain the extraordinary vitality of Chinese industry.

We can establish benchmarks for the institutional environment from the World Bank Group (2016) survey in the "Doing Business" database, which covers many countries and benchmarks their main economic centers (Shanghai and Beijing, for China). Examining 45 indicators, such as days needed to achieve permits, costs of enforcing contracts, and protection of minority shareholders, the measure in June 2016 ranked China 78th out of 190 countries. This is almost exactly what one would expect given China's level of development—far above the less developed countries but well below most developed economies. The survey ranked Beijing and Shanghai high in contract enforcement, property registry, availability of credit, and insolvency procedures. The scores were poor for ease of starting a business, taxes, and protection of minority investors. By far the most difficult task was getting permits for construction.

14.3   Ownership and the Public Interest

Chinese policy-makers have been bold about allowing entry, but cautious about transforming existing state-owned firms. China has never embraced an explicit program of privatization of state firms, and many official statements describe public ownership—and state ownership in particular—as a long-run feature of the economy that should be "consolidated and developed" (Ji 2014). As a result, state ownership of industry has persisted and has continued to be controversial and widely debated almost forty years after market-oriented reforms began. State ownership is important in its own right and in addition, state ownership can serve as an important prism to view issues relating to ownership and corporate governance.

Why do governments own firms? As box 14.1 describes, ownership can be defined as the right to dispose of residual income and residual control rights (after contractual obligations are fulfilled). Although income and control rights are bundled together in ownership, for the public owner there is an irreconcilable tension between these two aspects of ownership. The public owner needs to make substantive choices between emphasizing control rights (to achieve public objectives) and emphasizing income rights (to earn revenues). Cross-national research on state-owned enterprises has consistently found that there is an efficiency penalty to public ownership, but that it can be quite small when state enterprises are properly incentivized to maximize profit and cut costs. In other words, state-owned enterprises can be nearly as efficient as privately-owned firms if the government keeps a hands-off attitude and rewards efficiency and profit maximization. This achievement is greatly facilitated if state-owned firms operate in an environment of transparency, competition, and hard budget constraints.

This characterization suggests an important question: If SOEs are to behave exactly like private firms, why bother to have state-owned firms at all? Qian (1995) pointed out that if the government gives the firm a great deal of autonomy, without close monitoring or market discipline, it is inevitable that "slack" will grow, and corruption and asset stripping will become serious.[3] On the other hand, if the government monitors firms closely, political interference is inevitable. "Political interference" refers to any non-profit-maximizing task: maintaining employment, investing in impressive show projects or new technologies, or distributing investment across regions in an "equal" way, up to and including actions that benefit government monitors personally or politically. In public ownership, both managers and politicians have

---

3. "Slack" is here defined as any diversion of enterprise resources to the personal advantage of the manager, including the benefit of an easy life, cushy benefits, or out-and-out corruption. "Asset stripping" refers to conversion of public assets to private ownership through some kind of transaction that allows private parties to underpay for the asset.

Box 14.1
Ownership and governance.

> Ownership can be defined as the residual rights over an asset or organization. Rights are residual in the sense that they are those rights over assets or resources that have not already been explicitly promised or allocated by contract. In other words, the owner has the right to decide what happens to an asset after all contractual obligations are fulfilled.
>
> There are two main types of residual rights: the right to income produced by the asset and the right to physically control the asset. An asset produces income, and the owner enjoys the net income left over after contractual payments to bankers and bondholders are made. Of course, the owner also bears the risk of losses. Similarly, physical control may also be shared or limited by contract or public regulation, but the owner enjoys the residual right to any aspect of control that is not otherwise specified by contract or prohibited by law.
>
> Corporate governance refers to the institutions that are used to make decisions that have not been specified by contract. That is, they are the means through which the residual rights of the owners are exercised. The corporate governance system specifies the distribution of rights and responsibilities among different participants in the corporation, paying special attention to the way in which shareholders delegate responsibility to managers. The corporate governance system spells out the rules and procedures for making decisions on corporate affairs. In so doing, it provides the structure through which company objectives are established and the means to monitor performance and attain company objectives (OECD 2004).

incentives to pursue extraeconomic objectives. Public owners have three competing objectives: to provide public firms autonomy and incentives to improve efficiency; to increase oversight to control managerial slack and especially corruption; and to justify public ownership by assigning firms developmental or public interest objectives. To a certain extent, this is an "impossible trinity," and the contradictions among these objectives make it difficult to design a coherent policy toward SOEs.

These issues are important today, but in the early stages of industrial reform, there was no need to address them. In 1978, China's industry was essentially 100% publicly owned (SOEs produced 77% of output, urban collectives 14%, and rural TVEs the remaining 9%). The urgent issue was whether the efficiency of this public sector could be improved by incremental reforms, or whether it was better to radically alter the setup through a bold and disruptive program of privatization. Incremental reforms were difficult because of the vast distance that separated the enterprise under the planned economy from the modern, market-oriented corporation. Under the planned economy, what was called the "enterprise" was really a constituent part of a vast bureaucracy. The enterprise was like a branch plant of the single vast undertaking that was Socialism, Incorporated. It did not possess any of the strategic-planning, marketing, logistics, or personnel capabilities that we associate with a market business. The government took all of the enterprise's profit and kept the managers busy fulfilling myriad tasks assigned by ministries and local governments and running the affairs of the multifunctional social unit, the *danwei* (chapter 6). The most fundamental issues were to provide firm managers with autonomy and incentives.

To transform a socialist enterprise into a profit-oriented company required change in multiple dimensions. As described in chapter 5, during the first period of intensified reform (1984–1989), reformers experimented with a variety of incentive devices, strongly increasing the rewards given to managers and tying incentives closely to profitability. Reformers adopted contract systems, where SOEs committed to turning over a fixed amount of profit (typically tied to the size of their output and supply plans, which were also frozen). Under this approach, SOE managers faced high-powered incentives and access to market prices at the margin. This "incentivization" approach helped dismantle the bureaucratic economy and reorient firms to respond to market competition. By 1993, the industrial economy had grown out of the plan, and a new stage of reform could be prepared.

During the 1990s, a de facto policy consensus emerged in China that public firms had to focus on profit, and that radical SOE reforms were necessary. Faced with a crisis of declining state revenues, policy-makers readily agreed that profit maximization and income rights were more important than control rights, and few if any extra tasks were assigned to SOEs. After the mid-1990s, competition increased and Chinese reformers significantly hardened the budget constraints faced by enterprises, at the cost of a painful, medium-term spike in unemployment. Chronic loss-making enterprises were finally closed down or sold off, quietly but on a large scale. The total number of industrial SOEs dropped from 120,000 in the mid-1990s to only 34,000 by 2003, including all state-controlled corporations. With stronger competition and harder budget constraints, the state sector was dramatically downsized. Under these conditions, policy-makers could set about addressing the questions that confronted the remaining state firms. Those questions included most prominently: What firm-level corporate governance institutions were appropriate? How should the government's ownership interest in state firms be exercised in practice? How should state firms be financed? In what sectors should state firms remain active? Each of these questions is discussed in the following sections.

14.4   Corporate Governance: Firm-Level Institutions

The essential prerequisite for establishing corporate governance institutions for all firms, state or private, is a company law. China's Company Law of 1994 provided the legal framework for corporations and ultimately for the entire regulatory and ownership system. Before this, China had only ad hoc laws to cover specific types of enterprises (for example, the Law on Foreign Joint Ventures, 1979, and the State Enterprise Law, 1988). The early entrants and start-ups described in section 14.1 lacked any kind of legal charter whatsoever. The Company Law, by contrast, provided a uniform legal framework for different ownership forms. It tried to create a level playing field for competition among enterprises by providing for a range of legal forms that could be applicable to any ownership form. Most important were joint-stock corporations, for large firms, and simpler limited-liability companies, intended for a smaller and more close-knit group of owners. Subsequent statutes fleshed out the system with rules for partnerships and individual businesses.

14.4.1   Corporatization

In addition, the Company Law provided a framework for "corporatizing" SOEs, that is, converting traditional SOEs into the legal form of the corporation, more appropriate in a market economy. The Company Law meant that there was now a distinction between government ownership and company legal status: state firms could be either traditional SOEs organized under the old State Enterprise Law, or new corporations in which the state had a controlling interest.[4] A state-owned corporation should have shareholders and a board of directors even if the government owned 100% of the shares. Reorganizing under the Company Law was thus the first step for a traditional SOE in improving and modernizing its corporate governance procedures. Individual SOEs were to reorganize into corporations gradually, one by one, and the intention was that traditional SOEs would gradually disappear as each was converted either into a joint-stock corporation or a simpler limited-liability company.

The corporate form helps align the interests of a firm's management with those of its owners. The crucial institution is the firm's board of directors, which the Company Law specifies is the supreme authority in the corporation. The state appoints the members of the board in its capacity as a shareholder in the firm, thus redefining its role as that of a pure shareholder. In turn, this gives the firm greater autonomy since the firm's managers are now accountable only to the board of directors.

14.4.2   A Legal Basis for Mixed Ownership

Finally, the Company Law created a new legal framework for mixed ownership. As the discussion of hybrid firms showed, mixed ownership has always been a feature of the Chinese corporate environment. However, the corporate form allows much more complex development of mixed ownership forms. Now, if several parties share ownership, their interests are reduced to a common denominator, equity, and they voice their interests through voting their shares. The shareholders now share a common interest—distributable profits—which encourages the owners to focus on the single target of profitability and to incentivize managers accordingly (Clarke 2010). If desired, the new corporate forms can even be vehicles for privatization, since

---

4. As a result, accurately describing the state sector requires including both these categories, as is done throughout this volume. Some categories of data are still not available in the more inclusive definition of "state and state-controlled companies."

successive tranches of equity can be sold to the public, drawing down the government stake, potentially even to zero.

The corporate form permitted reorganized SOEs to be listed on the stock market, which diversified ownership and substantially improved transparency. It also created a strong incentive to create attractive listings quickly, since listing can raise a large amount of money. In 1998, the three state-run oil companies were restructured into partially competing, potentially integrated oil companies: Sinopec, CNPC (Petrochina), and China National Overseas Oil Corporation (CNOOC). Each firm packaged its highest-quality assets into a fully corporatized subsidiary and, between April 2000 and February 2001, listed them on the New York and Hong Kong Stock Exchanges. Sinopec sold a minority stake for $3.5 billion, and BP, ExxonMobil, and Shell took significant stakes in each of the companies. These were among the biggest stock-market listings anywhere in the world at that time, and they made the Chinese oil majors some of the most highly valued firms in the world.

However, to move quickly, the government put virtually all the valuable oil- and gas-producing and refining properties in the listed vehicles, while most of the money-losing services and welfare firms were put into "successor" (*cunxu*) or "left-behind" firms. For example, after CNOOC was listed, it had 1,000 employees in its listed firm but 16,000 employees in left-behind firms. The listed firm was highly profitable, and the dividends were used to offset the significant losses of the left-behind firms. To make the new listed companies attractive, severe overstaffing had to be addressed. Some 360,000 workers were laid off from CNPC by 2000, leading to unrest in the famous oil city at Daqing in northeastern China (Downs 2008). Virtually all SOEs followed this path to listing firms.

14.4.3   Uneven Progress

Implementation of the Company Law was slow. Data on the process of corporatization are fragmentary, but it appears that about 30% of state firms were corporatized by 2004 and 64% by 2008. As of 2013, the date of the landmark Third Plenum that decreed an acceleration of reform, some 80% of state firms had been corporatized, but this usually did not include the biggest most powerful firms at the top of the hierarchy (Ji 2010; SASAC 2009, 57–58; 2014, 685). Thus, almost 20 years after passage of the Company Law a substantial portion of state firm had not taken the first step toward corporatization, and traditional SOEs were still common. Moreover, many state corporations either had no boards of directors or had purely nominal boards. The state sector settled into a pattern of partial reform: fully corporatized and listed firms reported to state entities that were little transformed. At the 2013 Third Plenum (chapter 5), policy-makers vowed to accelerate the pace of transformation, and declared that by the end of 2017, all SOEs should be reorganized under the

Company Law and establish boards of directors. In related fashion, the partial listing of state-owned firms on the stock market was potentially the beginning of a progressively deeper transformation of ownership and governance. Large firms rushed to create profitable subsidiaries and list them on the stock market, since this was extremely lucrative. However, when it came to converting the parent companies into corporations, appointing boards of directors, and exposing the firm to greater transparency, progress was much slower. The result was the widespread creation of nontransparent, nonreformed left-behind firms with significant employees and assets. This provided enormous scope for related-party transactions between firms and their listed subsidiaries. Similarly, listing firms has the potential to be the first step of a process of gradually selling down the state share, converting firms to publicly held companies with dispersed shareholding (very different from a publicly owned or government-owned firms). This has generally not happened. Instead, the government has typically retained a majority or large controlling minority of the big SOE subsidiaries listed on the stock market.

14.4.4   Mixed Ownership: Post-2013 Revival

The post-2013 reform program put a great deal of stress on developing "mixed-ownership systems." The reform document revived the term and gave it new emphasis, even though, as we have seen, mixed ownership has been a feature of Chinese enterprise reform since the 1980s. Mixed ownership gives officials more flexibility, and so can be interpreted in diverse ways. In some cases, mixed ownership has served as a framework to allow local governments to sell majority ownership stakes in troubled SOEs to private owners. Employee ownership plans have been promoted as part of mixed ownership and, after a long delay, began trial implementation in late 2016 and 2017. On the other hand, mixed ownership has also been interpreted to mean that SOEs can take stakes in private firms when the government wishes to provide support for their development.

Mixed ownership shows the most promise today when state firms are classified as operating in "fully competitive" sectors. Such firms are instructed to accelerate corporatization; they may take in outside investors, even with majority stakes, and can be listed on stock markets where possible. Moreover, an effort is being made to break out potentially competitive operations within sectors that have been considered natural monopolies: for example the big petroleum companies are opening up their gasoline service stations to private participation. Shanghai has gone further by classifying all its firms as competitive, "functional," or public service. These initiatives all have the potential to improve incentives, accelerate marketization, and facilitate a process of privatization, especially on the local level. What remains unclear is how to handle firms in the subgroup of commercial enterprises that are not in fully competitive sectors. Moreover, many large central government firms now have hundreds of subsidiaries in different markets: classification of those firms has hardly begun and it is still unclear what principles will be used. The post-2013 reform program contains important elements that could play a positive role, but a great deal depends on how the implementation process is interpreted.

14.5   Public Ownership Agencies and Their Missions

The agencies that exercise ownership rights in practice determine the objectives to which public ownership is devoted. Those agencies establish the reward systems that motivate enterprise managers and effectively shape their behavior. Under the command economy, industrial ministries and the industrial bureau of local government in practice exercised the key ownership functions through bureaucratic subordination. Most of the central government industrial ministries were abolished in 1998, as part of Zhu Rongji's program of bureaucratic consolidation, and central SOEs actually functioned for five years without any formal owners, carrying on as before, embedded in a web of interests and traditional bureaucratic relationships.[5] Not until 2003 did China set up an organization specifically designed to exercise public ownership.

14.5.1 Ownership Agency: The Emergence of SASAC

The State Asset Supervision and Administration Commission (SASAC) was established in 2003 as an "ownership agency," empowered to exercise the government's ownership rights over government firms. SASAC was an evolutionary creation, cobbled together from the bureaucracies with oversight responsibility within the state government. Nevertheless, its creation marked a clear step in defining government control primarily as "ownership" rather than bureaucratic subordination or regulation. Upon creation, central SASAC was given ownership of a specified list of 196 corporations. However, these 196 were the largest SOEs, in fact gigantic corporations with thousands of subsidiaries. As of the end of 2013, central SASAC controlled 9.3 trillion RMB of state assets in a total of more than 38,000 firms, including subsidiaries (figure 14.2). Central SASAC had no ownership claim on the thousands of other state-owned companies that were now, for the first time, fully "owned" by local governments (which gradually set up their own "local SASACs"). After central SASAC was created, local governments had more leeway to restructure their own firms and sometimes to privatize or close them down. Local government-run factories were smaller than those of the central government, operated in a wider range of

---

5. Accounting-style oversight was exercised by a weak "State Assets Management Bureau."

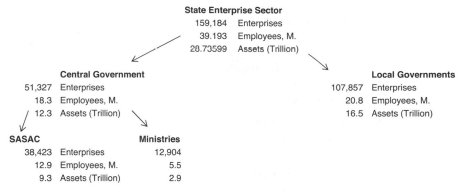

Figure 14.2
Map of the state sector.
Source: SASAC (2014, 685–697). Includes all nonfinancial enterprises.

sectors, were more exposed to competition, and consequently were less profitable. As table 14.1 shows, the central SASAC's share of state industrial workers increased from 23.7% in 2002 to 43% in 2013, and even with the massive expansion of the Chinese labor force, SASAC industrial workers still accounted for 8.1% of the total in 2013. Central SASAC's large firms are an increasingly important part of the state sector.

Central SASAC began life with an ambitious two-strand agenda: to improve corporate governance (discussed here) and to restructure state-owned firms so that they were concentrated in sectors in which there was a justification for continued state ownership (section 14.7). Both strands of this agenda were initially subordinate to the consensus objective of returning the state sector to profitability.

14.5.2   SASAC's Corporate Governance Agenda

SASAC's corporate governance agenda has been to carry through the corporatization process. The objective was to develop a complete set of corporate governance institutions, including boards of directors. These boards should be authoritative and have a significant number of outside, independent directors. In many cases, SASAC would also aim for a corporation that would be "100% listed." This meant that all the assets of the company—not just a portion of the most attractive assets—should be rolled into a single corporation that would then be publicly listed on the stock market. This would give better transparency and oversight and would prepare the way for boards of directors that might represent diverse ownership stakes.

SASAC also promulgated a uniform model of incentive contracts for the CEOs of its companies. Nearly all SASAC firms sign three-year performance contracts in which profit plays the dominant role. A 100-point scale is established: about one-third of

Table 14.1
Central SASAC share of state-enterprise workers.

	2002	2008	2013
All state-enterprise employees (millions)	**50.3**	**36.7**	**39.193**
Central SASAC employees	8.6	11.4	12.876
Central SASAC proportion	17.1%	31.0%	32.9%
State industrial enterprise employees (millions)	**24.9**	**18.6**	**18.3**
Central SASAC employees	5.9	7.7	7.9
Central SASAC proportion	23.7%	41.2%	43.0%
All above-scale industrial employees (millions)	**54.7**	**88.4**	**97.2**
Central SASAC proportion	10.8%	8.7%	8.1%

Sources: SASAC (2014, 685–697; and earlier volumes); *SYC* (2016, tables 13-1 through 13-4).

the points go for annual profit (relative to an agreed-on target); one-third is delayed for long-term return on equity or increase in assets; and the final third is for firm- or sector-specific targets. These targets do a reasonable job of striking the balance among efficiency and growth, profit, and value. Of course they have evolved over the years. On the basis of performance on the 100-point scale, managers receive grades of A through E, on which incentive payments depend, ranging up to three times base salary for managers who receive an A.

14.5.3   Limitations on SASAC's Authority

The creation of SASAC was certainly an improvement: some of the biggest problems with public ownership come from the lack of a specialized "ownership agency" designed to aggressively advocate the public interest. From the beginning, SASAC was vested with the power of ownership over assets of great value. However, there were also important limitations on SASAC's authority that affected both its residual control and residual income rights. Three limitations are most important.

First, the largest central SOEs that SASAC nominally owns are in fact powerful autonomous actors. The largest SASAC firms were carved out of industrial ministries, can rely on strong networks of cooperating bureaucrats and officials, and may have powerful political patrons. For example, after the powerful politician and Politburo Standing Committee member Zhou Yongkang fell because of corruption charges, it was revealed that he had used his control of the China National Petroleum Company to enrich his family and build a powerful and dangerous political faction. Zhou's fall brought into sharp relief the fact that oversight of managers of the largest SOEs was inadequate. SASAC has a small staff and little independent political influence, so its oversight is limited.

Second, SASAC is supposed to possess appointment power, since that is the means by which its control rights ought to be realized. But the reality of the Communist Party system is that the party makes the ultimate decision about all key personnel matters. The top manager and chairman of the board of the 53 largest SASAC enterprises—those of vice-ministerial rank—are appointed directly by the Communist Central Committee Organization Bureau. These positions are viewed as important patronage jobs that control substantial resources and so remain in the hands of the party. As a result, true SASAC personnel power begins with the smaller firms and at the vice-manager level for the largest firms.

Third, until 2007, SASAC had no direct control over the stream of net income—the profits—that SASAC firms earn. In the mid-1990s, when SOEs were earning scarcely any profits (see below), the government relinquished its claim on after-tax profits. Only gradually, after SOEs returned to profitability, was SASAC able to claim a proportion of profits as government "dividends." These dividends began in 2007 as 5% of SOE profits and were subsequently increased to the 15%–20% range. SASAC's collection of funds is overseen by the Ministry of Finance, and the SOEs still retain the bulk of after-tax profits.

14.5.4 New Ownership Agencies

The post-2013 reform program called for the transfer of front-line ownership authority to a new group of investment funds, to be called "state capital investment and operations companies" (SCIOs). This was a logical development: SASAC was established in an incremental and provisional way, without clear specification of its objectives or success indicators. A more consciously designed set of ownership funds could be a key step in moving ownership reform forward. However, policy-makers quickly found that it was difficult to agree on the nature of these SCIOs. Two competing conceptions arose. In one version, SCIOs should be like sovereign wealth funds (SWFs), exemplified by the Temasek SWF set up by the Singaporean government. It should be clear that this is the logical extension of treating SOEs as a component of national wealth and managing them to maximize profit. An SWF rarely (or never) exercises direct control rights, instead seeking to manage a wealth portfolio in a way that maximizes long-run returns. The SWF emphasis on wealth management may be especially appropriate in a society like China's, which will soon undergo rapid aging.

The competing conception advocated SCIOs that would exercise control rights more effectively in pursuit of developmental and restructuring objectives. SCIOs of this type would not necessarily maximize investment returns but would instead try to balance a mixture of objectives assigned to them by higher levels. This conception, which calls for the creation of SCIOs under the auspices of the existing ownership agencies (central and local SASACs) ultimately prevailed. These pilot SCIOs have very clear developmental objectives. According to the 2015 implementation document, they should "push state capital into important industries and key sectors that affect national security [and] the commanding heights of the national economy ... concentrate on outstanding enterprises with core competitive strength ... fully bring into play the core and exemplary function of SOEs in realizing the strategy of innovation-driven development and become a manufacturing power; strengthen the predominant position of enterprises in technological innovation; and attach great importance to training scientific personnel" (CCP and State Council 2015, article 14). These SCIOs clearly represent an effort to assert government control rights and assign new objectives to the SOEs.

The choice of an institutional form for the new SCIOs can thus be seen as a response to the tension between income and control rights and, more broadly, to the existence of an "impossible trinity" for public ownership. Policy-makers have shown their preference for both types of control rights. Increased oversight is sought to control managerial slack and especially corruption, particularly important given the ongoing campaign against corruption that has marked the Xi Jinping administration. Policy-makers have strengthened oversight institutions, importantly including the direct role of the Communist Party in the enterprise. At the same time, policy-makers have sought to justify public ownership by assigning firms more developmental objectives. The contradictions and tensions among these objectives make it difficult to design a coherent SOE reform policy, and create the risk that enhanced oversight and multiple objectives might lead to a decline in managerial autonomy and incentives, offsetting improvements made elsewhere in corporate governance institutions.

14.6   Profitability and Finance of the State Industrial Sector

SOE profitability has been on a roller-coaster ride since 1978. Under the command economy, SOEs operated in protected markets and generated ample profits. In 1978, at the beginning of reforms, SOE profits were huge, totaling 14% of GDP, all of which were turned over to the government budget. Entry of new firms created increased competition, and the excess profits of SOEs were gradually eroded. By 1996, profits were almost zero, and policy-makers faced a crisis. The downsizing of SOEs and the layoffs and ending of lifetime employment in SOEs, described in chapter 9, can be seen as an inescapable response to the impact of market competition on SOEs. The decline in protected monopoly profits inevitably affected every aspect of industrial finance. As SOEs turned over less money to the government, the government provided much less money to SOEs for investment. SOEs turned to banks, which had not financed long-term investments under the command economy. Policy-makers gradually shifted to a heavy reliance on bank loans to finance the industrial sector, a decision that had important consequences economy-wide. Fortuitously, households were rapidly increasing their saving rates, and banks began to channel those savings ("intermediate") to the corporate sector (chapter 19).

SOEs turned increasingly to bank credit without too much concern about their future ability to repay, and the indebtedness of SOEs steadily increased. By the mid-1990s, SOEs faced a combination of declining profit and increasing debt. One commonly used measure of the relationship between firms and banks is the ratio of total bank debt to shareholder equity, or the debt-equity ratio (sometimes called the leverage ratio). Table 14.2 shows that under the command economy, the debt-equity ratio was very low, at 12%. "As the government gradually abandoned its direct financing of industrial activity through the budget," Holz (2003, 140) pointed out, "the ratio had nowhere to go but up." By 1994, the debt-equity ratio had climbed steadily and reached a peak of 211%. This high ratio was similar to that of Japan or Korea in the 1990s, economies that were well known for the predominant role banks played in financing industry. The rapid sustained increase and the comparatively high level, in conjunction with low profits, were enough to alarm Chinese policy-makers. By the mid-1990s, Chinese firms had gone from being nearly debt free to being among the more indebted firms in the world in less than 20 years. With cash flow evaporating and debt accumulating, China's SOEs were virtually insolvent. The Asian financial crisis erupted in 1997 and hit Korea especially hard, where the highly leveraged corporate groups, the *chaebol*, were vulnerable, and many went bankrupt. Chinese policy-makers were alarmed, and responded with decisive policies to restructure the state sector.

From about 1998, the program of reform and restructuring began to change the financial position of SOEs in fundamental ways. As figure 14.3 shows, state industry profitability (normalized by total assets) increased steadily from 1998 through 2007. State firms benefited from successful reforms and, of course, from the closure of many inefficient and highly indebted SOEs. Moreover, the largest remaining SOEs were protected by various kinds of entry barriers the government put up to protect a new system of oligopolistic competition; SOEs would compete with each other but would not necessarily face new entrants (section 14.7). Last but not least, the government injected billions into the banking system to allow banks to write off bad loans to SOEs (chapter 19). The increase in SOE profitability closely mirrored the increase in profitability of the nonstate sector through 2007, and total central SASAC profits hit the psychological milestone of 1 trillion RMB.

However, 2008 marked a turning point after which state and nonstate profitability diverged. State firm profitability dropped under the impact of the global financial crisis, doubtless because state firms were required to pump money into investment projects as part of government stimulus policies (chapter 18). While state profitability stabilized in 2010–2011, the gap with nonstate has remained large, and state profitability continued to decline. Partly as a result, debt-equity ratios began to creep

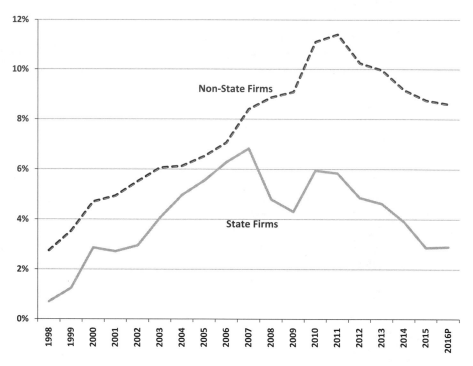

Figure 14.3
Rate of return on industrial assets.
Source: Calculated from *SYC* (2016, tables 13-3 and 13-5; and earlier volumes). Updated from http://data.stats.cov.cn.

up again after 2006, reaching 163% by 2015, in between Japanese and U.S. levels (table 14.2). Industrial corporation debt levels are not the highest in China: debt for real estate and infrastructure is proportionately much higher. Nevertheless, rising industrial SOE debt has contributed to a rise in China's overall debt level, which has raised concerns (chapter 19). More generally, the large gap in profitability between SOEs and non-SOEs, which had almost disappeared in the mid-2000s, now appears entrenched. This may be related to the choice policy-makers have made between exercising control rights and exercising income rights over SOEs.

14.7   Sectoral Composition of the State Sector

Today's state sector emerged from the massive downsizing of the state sector, beginning in 1996 (chapter 9). Tens of thousands of SOEs and urban collective firms were shut down, and millions of workers were laid off. As figure 5.3 showed, the number of SOE industrial workers declined from 46 million in 1992 to 18 million in 2007

Table 14.2
Debt-equity ratios.

China: state-owned industry, 1978	12%
China: state-owned industry, 1994	211%
China: state-owned industry, 1998	180%
China: state-owned industry, 2006	129%
China: state-owned industry, 2015	163%
Comparison economies: 1988–1996 average	
Korea	347%
Japan	230%
United States	103%

Sources: *SYC* (table 13-5), for state-controlled corporations; comparisons from Claessens, Djankov, and Lang (1999, 9).

before stabilizing. That level is essentially the same today; the 2013 Economic Census counted 18.9 million SOE industrial workers, only 13.5% of the 140 million total. Today's state sector has been shaped both by the force of entry and competition and by the policies of SASAC, the ownership agency.

14.7.1   Competitive Processes

As figure 14.4 shows, SOEs have a systematically larger presence in capital-intensive sectors (here measured by capital/labor ratios). In sectors where capital requirements are modest—textiles, garments, and plastic and metal products—there were few impediments to entry, and TVEs (first) and private firms (later) entered and gradually established dominant positions. Where capital requirements are larger, SOEs have been able to maintain significant positions. This is consistent with a large literature showing that SOEs have easier access to cheaper capital than private firms. Cheap capital has served as a competitive advantage for state firms and an entry barrier to private firms. In addition, administrative entry barriers protect state firms in several sectors. Formal barriers to private ownership of natural resources, for example, effectively make oil and gas the preserve of state firms. In some parts of the machinery industry, particularly those that are defense related, state firms are also largely sheltered from competition. State firms have generally maintained a dominant role in utilities, like electric power, where government regulation plays a crucial role. At the other extreme, some state firms are active in nearly every industry, although their impact is tiny in many cases. A few remnant state firms still make clothing and plastic flowers, even though private firms have long since dominated those industries.

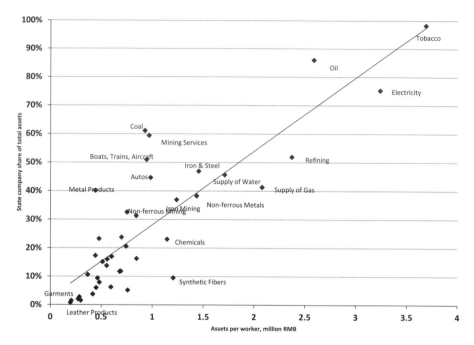

Figure 14.4
Share of sectoral assets in state-controlled companies.
Source: Economic Census (2013).

14.7.2   SASAC's Restructuring Agenda

Faced with a competitive onslaught, SASAC has sought to restructure and rational-
ize central-government assets while never abandoning the idea that state ownership
could expand in some areas. The post-1997 policy of "focus on the large, let go of
the small" already displays a desire to bolster certain elements of the state sector
that were deemed most competitive. However, while SASAC envisaged pulling back
from many sectors, it never laid out a policy of completely withdrawing from any
sector. Instead, SASAC in practice pursued three objectives:

a. Create oligopolistic competition. Under Zhu Rongji, central government
monopolies were typically split into two or three competing firms, a model followed in
petroleum, telecommunications, and even crucial military industrial firms. Big SOEs
were protected from non-SOE entrants in strategic sectors but were made to compete
with one another.

b. Concentrate assets in a few sectors. SASAC has tried to concentrate assets in
sectors with national security, natural resource, or natural monopoly characteristics. In 2005, the head of SASAC declared the state should maintain "full control"

in seven sectors: military industry, electricity, oil, telecommunications, coal, civil aviation, and transport. In nine other sectors—including steel, electronics, machine building, and automobiles—the center should maintain ownership of a number of technologically advanced enterprises.

c. Focus on core business. SASAC firms should pull out of or spin off their "non-core" enterprises. The total number of central SASAC firms should shrink to below 100.

These guidelines were pragmatic and pointed SASAC in the right direction. The creation of oligopolistic competition certainly served the interests of policy-makers: a few large state firms competed vigorously with each other, improving operations and productivity, while entry barriers kept overall profits high.

14.7.3   The Restructuring Agenda Today

In practice, SASAC's restructuring agenda ran into many obstacles. SASAC was never able to articulate clear principles about which sectors state firms should occupy and, crucially, which sectors they should leave. As a result, firms in every sector have had to deal with the possibility of potentially unfair competition from state firms (to the extent that SOEs have cheaper access to capital or receive regulatory preference). The objective of large SASAC firms sticking to their "core business" has not been effectively realized. SASAC firms have formed large diversified conglomerates, and the pace of this diversification seems to have picked up after 2009. Pressured to invest large sums of money quickly, SOEs understandably pushed into many new realms. The numbers in figure 14.2 imply that the average top-level SASAC firm has more than 450 subsidiaries, sometimes organized in four, five, or even six layers of companies. The central-state sector is a gigantic pyramid that has been mostly transformed from a bureaucratic edifice into a network of businesses. However, the largest firms at the top of the pyramid, with their near monopolies giving them a privileged position, are the least transformed. At the bottom of the pyramid, many of the best enterprises have been thoroughly restructured into market-oriented corporations, and quite a few thrive in the face of vigorous competition. However, the transformation process is still incomplete, particularly at the top, in the gigantic corporations just below central SASAC, where a tangle of competing interests mixes bureaucratic recalcitrance, agency loss, lack of transparency, and stubborn problems that have been swept under the rug.

Finally, the commitment to oligopolistic competition seems also to have weakened around 2006–2008, as the drive to create large, internationally competitive firms overwhelmed the desire to preserve domestic competitiveness. SASAC began to merge firms in a few strategic sectors, starting with civil aircraft production and railroad equipment. By 2016, more than 10 mergers of large central SASAC firms had taken place. This policy runs the risk of weakening the force of the competitive pressures state firms face, and increasing the temptation of protective policies and entry barriers. The post-2013 reform drive seeks to locate and expand competitive sectors. However, it does little to change the principles under which competitive or noncompetitive sectors are designated. In that sense, there has been no replacement for the initial pragmatic policies of restructuring that SASAC put forward after 2003.

14.8   Conclusion

Over more than 35 years, China has created a remarkably vibrant and competitive system of diverse ownership in industry. In some respects, the transformation in industry has been more thorough than that in any other sectors, since industry has gone from being the focus of government control under the Big Push strategy to being a sector dominated by privately owned firms. This transformation lies behind the extraordinary growth of China's industry and its emergence as the workshop of the world.

Strikingly, state firms still play an important role. However, crucial questions about the role of SOEs and the most appropriate institutions to run them efficiently remain unanswered, and no clear consensus has emerged on the future evolution of the state sector. As a result, the profitability of SOEs has declined, and they are unable to make a satisfactory contribution to China's national wealth and well-being. Looking back on the transformation process, one is struck both by the huge successes and by the persistent failures. The first period of accelerated reform must be judged an unambiguous success in the industrial sector, despite the limits that circumscribed reform strategy during that period. The overall command structure was eroded and dismantled without an abandonment of the state-run enterprise and without, perhaps as a result, a catastrophic economic decline. The second phase of transformation has gone far beyond the first stage, but in comparative terms, the achievements are less impressive.

The Chinese industrial economy is intensely marketized and competitive, so it is inconceivable that firm-level governance institutions that are not themselves fully marketized will be successful. In other market economies, large corporations have long since institutionalized a substantial separation between ownership and managerial control. Managers' incentives are brought into line with the objectives of the owners either through the operation of capital markets or through direct oversight by owners or by banks. In China, firm-level corporate governance institutions have not developed their full potential in either private firms or in state-owned firms. There is scope for the share of modern, transparent corporations to grow both in the private and state-run industrial sectors.

Within the state sector, the limitations on development of both firm-level corporate governance and authoritative ownership agencies have led to a serious lack of oversight on managerial discretion. Managers owe some accountability to their boards of directors, to the Communist Party committee that appointed them, to the ownership agency that establishes their incentive contract, to the banks that finance them, and to external markets. However, none of these bodies has the capabilities and incentive to closely monitor the CEO of a large and powerful state firm. The extremely broad scope of managerial discretion inevitably leads to abuses in some cases. Although the penalties for corruption are severe, the overall institutional environment makes it relatively difficult to detect and punish unless it is particularly blatant. Managers have wide discretion to establish subsidiaries and joint ventures, so the scope for related-party transactions is wide. It is relatively easy to sell public resources for a price slightly under the true market price to a privileged company with which the manager has a private relationship. The anticorruption campaign launched by Xi Jinping after 2013 has turned up many examples of such abuses. In some respects it is not surprising that the Communist Party and the related disciplinary system are stepping up oversight of managers.

China's current system can be placed in comparative context by considering the two most common systems of corporate oversight. In the first, equity-market-based system, there are relatively strong requirements for disclosure of public information and relatively strong emphasis on the protection of minority shareholders in law and regulation. Dissatisfied "owners" exit the company by selling their shares, so share price is a sensitive indicator of performance, and low share price often leads to a replacement of management. The second main method of oversight is sometimes called "control based." In practice, banks or founding families typically monitor managerial performance. This system is sometimes called the "Continental" or "Japanese" system because in continental European and Japanese economies, banks play a much more important role in monitoring corporate behavior. In this system, oversight is exercised by groups that have access to insider information about the firm, either through the banking relationship or through supplier and customer relationships. The system accommodates the interests of a wider range of stakeholder groups, including worker interests, than does the Anglo-American system.

China today does not fit into either of these systems. Stock markets do not have adequate disclosure or contestability of ownership and control. Chinese SOEs strongly rely on banks as providers of capital, but because of their long tradition of state ownership, banks have neither the capability nor a clear mandate to aggressively monitor enterprise performance. In China, then, the question of corporate governance is still unresolved. For this reason, the post-2013 reform program highlighted improvements in state firm corporate governance. The good news is that there are substantial efficiency gains that can be realized from improvement in the corporate governance system. However, the tendency to entrust SOEs with additional developmental missions may undermine these potential gains. Since 2013, state firms have been called on to take the lead in, for example, technological development and environmental improvement, alongside existing missions to improve profitability, become large and internationally visible, and maintain high levels of investment in order to sustain overall economic growth. The tendency to use SOEs as instruments to achieve multiple objectives may detract from their focus on improving productivity and profitability, which are the essential prerequisites for these firms to contribute to national development and well-being.

Bibliography

Suggestions for Further Reading

Brandt and Thun (2010) do an excellent job of conveying the nature of competition in China, and Nolan (2014) is a balanced assessment. To go deeper, see Hsieh and Klenow (2009).

A Note on Sources for Data

The most consistent data are for large industrial firms. These include state-owned firms and nonstate firms with an annual output value of more than 5 million RMB (about $600,000 at that time)—raised in 2011 to 20 million RMB ($3 million in 2016 dollars). After 1998, annual data do not include small firms. State firms include traditional state-owned enterprises and joint-stock and limited-liability corporations in which the state has a controlling interest. In figure 14.4, the denominator is gross assets at purchase price, so this is a noisy measure of profitability.

References

Brandt, Loren, and Eric Thun (2010). "The Fight for the Middle: Upgrading, Competition, and Industrial Development in China." *World Development* 38 (11): 1555–1574.

CCP (Chinese Communist Party) and State Council (2015). "Guiding Opinions on Deepening Reform of State-Owned Enterprise." August 24. Accessed at http://news.xinhuanet.com/politics/2015-09/13/c_1116547305.htm.

Claessens, Stijn, Simeon Djankov, and Larry Lang (1998). "East Asian Corporations: Growth, Financing and Risks over the Last Decade." *Malaysian Journal of Economics* 35 (1/2): 137–156.

Clarke, Donald C. (2010). "Law Without Order in Chinese Corporate Governance Institutions." *Northwestern Journal of International Law and Business* 30:131–199.

Du, Julan, Yi Lu, and Zhigang Tao (2015). "Government Expropriation and Chinese-Style Firm Diversification." *Journal of Comparative Economics* 43:155–169.

Economic Census (2013). *Zhongguo Jingji Pucha Nianjian 2013* [China economic census yearbook]. 4 vols. Beijing: Zhongguo Tongji.

Feng, Xingyuan, Charister Ljungwall, and Guangwen He (2015). *The Ecology of Chinese Private Enterprises.* Singapore: World.

Hamilton, Gary, and Nicole Biggart (1988). "Market, Culture, and Authority: A Comparative Analysis of Management and Organization in the Far East." *American Journal of Sociology* 94 (Supplement): S52–S94.

Holz, Carsten A. (2003). *China's Industrial State-Owned Enterprises: Between Profitability and Bankruptcy.* Singapore: World Scientific.

Hsieh, Chang-Tai, and Peter J. Klenow (2009). "Misallocation and Manufacturing TFP in China and India." *Quarterly Journal of Economics* 124 (4): 1403–1448.

Ji, Xiaonan (2010). "Correctly Understand the Debate About the State Advancing While Private Capital Retreats." *New State Capital*, August 9. Accessed at http://www.xinguozi.com.cn/article/show/130/0/1.

Ji, Xiaonan (2014). *Jianchi he Wanshan Jiben Jingji Zhidu Shilun* [Ten essays on adhering to and improving the basic economic system]. Beijing: Shehui Kexue Wenxian.

Lardy, Nicholas (2014). *Markets over Mao: The Rise of Private Business in China.* Washington, DC: Peterson Institute.

Li, Hongbin, Lingsheng Meng, Qian Wang, and Li-An Zhou (2008). "Political Connections, Financing and Firm Performance: Evidence from Chinese Private Firms." *Journal of Development Economics* 87 (2): 283–299.

Nolan, Peter (2014). "Globalisation and Industrial Policy: The Case of China." *World Economy*, 747–764.

OECD (Organisation for Economic Co-operation and Development) (2004). "OECD Principles of Corporate Governance." Accessed at www.oecd.org/dataoecd/32/18/31557724.pdf.

Qian, Yingyi (1995). "Reforming Corporate Governance in China." In Masahiko Aoki and Hyung-ki Kim, eds., *Corporate Governance in Transitional Economies: Insider Control and the Role of Banks*, 215–252. Washington, DC: World Bank.

SASAC (Annual). State Asset Supervision and Administration Commission. *Zhongguo Guoyou Zichan Jiandu Guanli Nianjian* [China state-owned assets supervision and management yearbook]. Beijing: Zhongguo Jingji.

Seki Mitsuhiro (1994). *Beyond the Full-Set Industrial Structure: Japanese Industry in the New Age of East Asia.* Tokyo: LTCB International Library Foundation.

Shanghai Stock Exchange (2003). *Corporate Governance Report.* Shanghai: Shanghai Stock Exchange.

SYC (Annual). *Zhongguo Tongji Nianjian* [Statistical yearbook of China]. Beijing: Zhongguo Tongji.

Wong, Siu-lin (1985). "The Chinese Family Firm: A Model." *British Journal of Sociology* 36 (1): 58–72.

World Bank and IFC (2014). *Enterprise Surveys: China Country Profile.* Accessed at http://www.enterprisesurveys.org/data/exploreeconomies/2012/china.

World Bank Group (2016). "Doing Business: Ease of Doing Business in China." Accessed at www.doingbusiness.org/data/exploreeconomies/china/.

As China grows into upper-middle-income status, its capabilities mature and extend into new areas; at the same time, as the high-growth era ends, China seeks new drivers of growth. These imperatives lead Chinese policy-makers to seek an "innovation-driven" economy, in which technology and productivity advances make an increasing contribution to growth. China's technology challenge is often implicitly or explicitly framed within the context of a "middle-income trap." This holds that economies can grow out of low-income status in a straightforward way, but after an economy reaches middle-income status, growth requires a different mix of less common skills, including the ability to innovate and to compete in market segments that demand high quality and constant innovation. Whether there is a middle-income "trap" is contested, but there certainly is a middle-income "challenge." Will China pass through the ranks of middle-income economies and vault into the select group of high income economies? The most important factor deciding this question will be the pace at which China adopts, adapts, transforms, and contributes to the world's body of science and technology.

Since 2005, Chinese government policy has been strongly committed to direct government support of technology development. Perhaps no issue more effectively unites policy-makers, executives, and the urban public in China than the need to propel China into a high-technology future. This commitment has led to a strong technology effort and has also led the government to develop a series of industrial—or "techno-industrial"—policies that include a direct government role in fostering specific industrial sectors. Thus, although the overall trend since 1978 has been for the reduction of direct government intervention as the market economy grows, in high-technology sectors government intervention has increased steadily since 2003. High-tech sectors are the most important areas in which the government attempts to steer the economy today. The reality is that the People's Republic of China has been committed to technology development from its inception, but the effectiveness of the strategies followed in the pursuit of technological advance has varied enormously. The effectiveness of current policy has yet to be determined and is discussed at the end of this chapter.

This chapter first presents a general framework for analyzing technical progress and shows how China today fits into a comparative context. This includes an examination of China's technology effort and human resource base. From this, we turn to discussion of China's technology policy. We show how it has changed over the years—while maintaining a strong commitment to technology development—and its dramatic turning point after 2003–2006. A preliminary assessment of technology outcomes is presented, followed by a discussion of several important issues related to technology development.

15.1   Framework

How does technology contribute to the economy and economic development? Chapter 7 discussed the aggregate production function, in which factors of production—land, labor, human capital, and capital—are combined to produce output and income. Technology does not enter directly as an argument in the aggregate production function; it is in the background, and can be thought of as a set of blueprints that determine what combinations of production factors are possible. Technological improvements, in turn, can be likened to a superior set of blueprints that instruct producers on ways they can get more out of a given combination of inputs. But where do technological improvements come from? Only in very rare instances does technology appear as an unprompted flash of insight; much more often, new technologies emerge from a purposeful process of search for better solutions, such as that described in chapter 12 for agricultural productivity improvements. This search requires resources of time and money.

This suggests that one approach to analyzing technology in an economic context is to consider the triad of technology effort, human resource base, and the incentives that determine what ideas and technologies are applied to the production process (Cliff 1998). Technology effort describes the volume of resources used in research and development (R&D). The human resource base is the capability of the labor force to discover, improve, and implement more sophisticated technologies. Incentives should be interpreted here in the broadest sense to cover the whole range of institutions that provide rewards for people to make changes in their way of doing things. Together these make up a knowledge-production function, analogous to the aggregate production function but completely separate:

Technological knowledge = f(R&D, human resources, incentives).

Knowledge—the output of the knowledge-production function—is intangible and cannot be directly measured. Various proxies are available: for example, patents or publications in scientific journals. These have obvious value but must be analyzed carefully because they have obvious pitfalls as well (discussed later).

From the economic perspective, the major importance of technological knowledge is that it enables capital, labor, and human capital to be combined in new ways that yield higher overall productivity. The technological knowledge that is the output of the knowledge-production function provides better ways to combine inputs in the aggregate production function. Thus, increased technological knowledge should show up as an increase in total factor productivity, which can be measured either at the enterprise level or at the aggregate economy level. However, we expect the impact of technological knowledge to be diffuse and apparent only after substantial time lags. Moreover, the effect of technological knowledge will be confounded with other long-term factors, such as quality of institutions and appropriateness of incentives. Thus, although we are convinced that technological knowledge can be produced by appropriate investments in research and human resources, and that technological knowledge makes an economy more productive, we should be modest about our ability to demonstrate the precise magnitude and nature of these linkages.

This modesty is especially appropriate because research on innovation and technology over many years has consistently found that the impact of science and technology on productivity is extremely gradual. That is, only a very small portion of the economic productivity gains from major innovations are experienced when the invention is created; the vast majority of the productivity gain comes during the "Beta" phase, in which multiple incremental changes drive down costs and improve efficiency. From the steam engine to the microprocessor, breakthrough ideas at first produce ingenious products or processes that have only a modest impact on overall productivity. However, successive generations of the same basic technology continuously produce incremental productivity gains for decades. One classic example is the diesel engine, "invented" and produced in the mid-1890s. Today's diesel engines use the same fundamental technology but are a hundred times as efficient and astonishingly reliable. This pattern is true of many technological advances (and especially for the 30 or so "general-purpose technologies," such as electricity, that have transformed virtually every sector of the economy). These general considerations frame the following discussion of China's technology effort.

15.2   Technology Effort

How much effort does a country need to put into technology development? Technology has public goods characteristics: no innovator can capture the total social gain from innovation. Therefore, it is not optimal to let pure market forces determine the level of inputs into technology development, and there is clearly a role for government intervention. In general, the higher a country's GDP per capita, the larger the proportion of GDP it spends on research and development. How should we interpret this regularity? Today's modern technologies come almost entirely from the rich countries, and developing countries are marginal to most global innovation. Since developed countries spend a larger proportion of their larger economies on research, a continuous stream of innovation emerges from them, basically ensuring that most of tomorrow's technologies will also come from developed economies. On the one hand, this situation tends to reinforce the advantageous position of developed countries already at the technology frontier; but on the other hand, it opens up sources of potential advantage for late developers. Since there is a substantial technology gap, there is an enormous backlog of modern technologies that developing countries can adopt. Rather than expending resources on risky and uncertain research, developing countries can concentrate on selecting, transferring, and adapting the best existing technologies, combining them with their inexpensive production factors to build competitive advantage for their companies. This catch-up strategy should work for a long time.

However, developing countries face enormous difficulties exploiting these potential advantages. It takes time and skills to identify the technologies that are available and appropriate. When new technologies are purchased, it can take substantial effort and resources to get them working on the factory floor, and productivity and profitability are typically low for a prolonged period as various bugs are worked out. Moreover, companies in developed countries increasingly view their technologies as income sources and fence off their intellectual property rights (IPR) with patents or secrecy. Developing economies have found it difficult to develop their technological capabilities and almost impossible to catch up with the technology leaders. Indeed, after Japan, only the East Asian economies of Korea, Taiwan, and Singapore stand out as unambiguous success stories of technology catch-up.

Because of the difficulty in managing successful technology development programs, developing countries have increasingly welcomed foreign direct investment (FDI) as an alternative. Most developing countries today hope that foreign investors will help build capable industries, from which knowledge and technological capabilities will gradually spill over to the rest of the domestic economy. Such a strategy can substitute for and stretch scarce research and development resources. In the 1990s, China fit into this category. With limited R&D resources, China opened widely to FDI and integrated rapidly with global production and innovation networks (chapter 17). During this period, policy in China was quite different from what it had been in Japan and Korea during their national industrial-policy period in the 1950s to the 1970s, when they had restricted incoming FDI while promoting domestic investment. Today, though, China has unmistakably reduced its reliance on multinational corporations and increased its domestic technology effort. This increase of domestic resources has raised the stakes in the choice among different technology policies: there is potentially more to gain, but the costs of failed or misdirected policies will be correspondingly higher.

15.2.1   International Context: The Common Pattern of Technology Effort

The general pattern of spending on R&D by successful developing countries is quite clear. Low- and lower-middle-income countries spend relatively little on R&D, typically less than 1% of GDP. Since it makes no sense for them to reinvent the wheel, they spend modest sums on the identification and adaptation of foreign science. As economies approach middle-income status, their indigenous technology effort increases; they make more profound adaptations of existing technologies, absorb technologies that are closer to the developed-economy frontier, and engage in some limited basic research. Expenditures on R&D begin to rise. For example, both Taiwan and South Korea pushed expenditures on R&D as a percentage of GDP above 1% in the early 1980s as they reached middle-income status, and then above 2% in the 1990s. The situation today is shown in figure 15.1: Taiwan's rate is above 3%, and Korea's is the highest in the world, at 4.3%. More generally, developed countries like the United States and Germany have rates of 2.8%–2.9%, while the Scandinavian countries and Japan are above 3%.

Figure 15.2 shows that China is now increasing its technological effort rapidly. China's R&D first exceeded 1% of GDP in 2002 and it pushed above 2% in 2014. In the mid-1990s, China was slightly below the expected rate (based on GDP per capita), but it has now risen above the expected rate. China's current technology effort

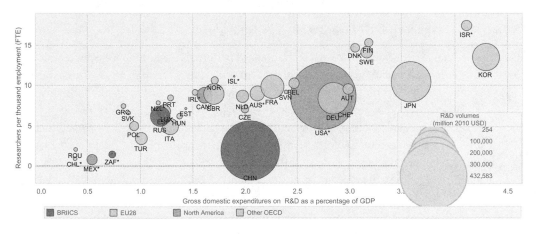

Figure 15.1
Human and financial resources devoted to R&D, 2014.
Source: OECD, accessed at http://www.oecd.org/innovation/inno/researchanddevelopmentstatisticsrds.htm.
*Latest available data before 2014.

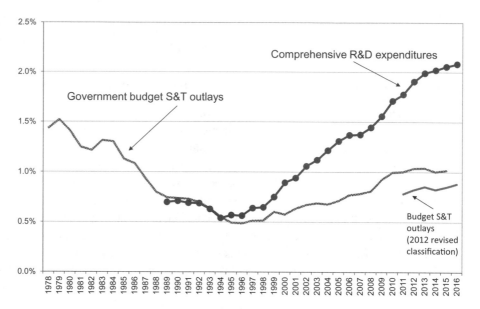

Figure 15.2
R&D expenditures (percent of GDP).
Sources: *SAC* (2017, 21, 71, 173); *SYC* (2016, table 20-1; and earlier volumes); Technology Statistics Office (1990). Classification of budgetary outlays was changed in a 2012 regulation; figure shows both series for available years.

is slightly above the 28-country EU average and is about where Korea and Taiwan were 20 years ago. In aggregate totals, China now devotes the world's second-largest volume of resources to R&D, after the United States and ahead of Japan.

15.2.2   The Trajectory of China's Technology Effort

In fact, China never followed the standard pattern of steadily increasing technology with economic development. Instead, from the 1950s through 1978, China, despite being a low-income country, pursued a high-technology strategy. It mobilized available intellectual resources for defense purposes and created elite research institutes, particularly in the Chinese Academy of Sciences (CAS). Government outlays for science- and technology-related purposes (a proxy for R&D, data for which only become available in 1989) actually peaked at 1.7% of GDP in 1964, the year China exploded its first atomic bomb, and averaged 1.4% of GDP from the late 1950s through 1978. Despite the apparent anti-intellectualism of the Cultural Revolution, China mobilized its scarcest intellectual resources for its critical technologies effort. There were successes, especially military ones: atomic and hydrogen bombs and intercontinental missiles. This big effort was an integral part of the command economy and the Big Push strategy described in chapter 4.

The Soviet Union was China's technology patron during the 1950s. The Soviet Union transferred not only the technologies, which had a profound impact on every aspect of Chinese industrial and military technology, but also the key institutions that shape incentives to adopt technology. The organizational structure of the entire national system of research and innovation came from the Soviet model, beginning with the elite research institutes of the CAS. Roy Grow (1984, 262) called the Soviet actions "the largest coordinated international transfer of technology in the history of the world." When China and the Soviet Union abruptly split in the early 1960s, China was cut off from its primary technology source at a time when it had no alternative partners and very little market access to technology. China went abruptly from dependence on the Soviet Union to technology autarky. For a decade, from the mid-1960s through the mid-1970s, China forged ahead with its military effort and also imported a handful of factories that embodied specific industrial technologies. The objective was to reverse engineer and replicate these technologies, specifically in metallurgy and synthetic fibers. Incremental improvements were also made in some Soviet-legacy technologies, such as electricity generation, where equipment was scaled up to larger units. Overall, though, the gap between China and the world increased. Cut off from world technical progress, China had to fend for itself. In some cases, China was unable to ramp up half-finished Soviet supplied plants to efficient scale (automobiles), and several ambitious development programs failed (airliners). Isolated from the vital sources of science and technological progress, China fell further behind despite its large technology effort.

During the reform era, China at first tried to keep government R&D outlays high while beginning marketization in other areas. As figure 15.2 shows, government budget outlays for science and technology (S&T) stayed above 1% of GDP through 1986. But this level of government effort was not sustainable, with SOE revenues eroding and the budget's share of GDP declining. Moreover, the existing approach of "mission-oriented" and often military-related R&D was under fire for its low economic effectiveness. R&D was scaled back as policy-makers searched for a viable model. When the first R&D statistics became available in 1989, they showed China investing only about 0.7% of GDP in R&D, and the effort slipped further to below 0.6% in 1994. By this time, China was beginning to look more like a normal country, with R&D outlays at or even below the level the standard pattern of R&D development would dictate. But Chinese policy-makers had no desire to be normal; they actively sought to raise the R&D/GDP rate above 1%.

After 2000, R&D outlays began to increase and diversify. As figure 15.2 shows, total R&D has climbed much more rapidly than government outlays for science and technology (a reclassification of budgetary outlays carried out in 2012 reduced these outlays by about 0.2% of GDP). A much bigger R&D effort at the enterprise level was partly responsible for the rapid increase in R&D: according to Chinese data, business firms carried out 75% of R&D spending. This percentage jumped when the government reclassified hundreds of government-run research institutes as enterprises in the late 1990s and promulgated a set of complementary policies that strongly incentivized R&D effort and sales.

As one would expect from an economy engaged in the catch-up process, the bulk of China's R&D goes toward development, and relatively little is devoted to basic research. The proportions of development, applied research, and basic research are 84%, 11%, and 5%, respectively, in China, compared with 63%, 19%, and 18% in the United States. The much higher U.S. effort in basic research is due primarily to government funding for university-based research, a channel that is much less important in China.

15.3   Human Resources

Human resources can be likened to a pyramid, with elite scientists and intellectuals at the apex and workers with broad literacy, numeracy, and mechanical skills at the base. Coming out of the planned-economy era, China already had a broad base of basic manufacturing skills, such as forging, welding, and machining. In addition, there were many programs of vocational training and accreditation that spread and upgraded these skills. At the turn of the century, half of the 56 million state workers in SOEs and public service undertakings possessed some kind of technical certification, including 12 million teachers (*SAC* 2005, 184). At the top, the CAS and the Chinese Academy of Engineering (CAE) contained pockets of excellence in scientific and technological research that were at or near the world frontier. In the middle, however, China was weaker. The efficiency of mass production and integrated production complexes lagged far behind, and China had few first-class firms with significant leading-edge technologies. To strengthen these capabilities, China has engaged in a massive effort to upgrade technological skills through the education system.

China's effort to build human resources reached an inflection point in the late 1990s. The annual number of graduates of tertiary education (colleges and technical schools) had been growing relatively slowly and was below a million. Driven by the need to accelerate technological development—and also by worry about unemployment, which spiked in the late 1990s (chapter 9)—the intake of new college students jumped dramatically. In 2001, 1 million graduated from college; by 2008, the number had jumped to 5 million. Thereafter, it grew more gradually to 7 million in 2016. Science and engineering majors make up about 45% of graduates, while economics, management, and law account for another 25%.

To put these numbers into comparative perspective, we must first divide tertiary education into its two main components. Students graduate from four-year colleges

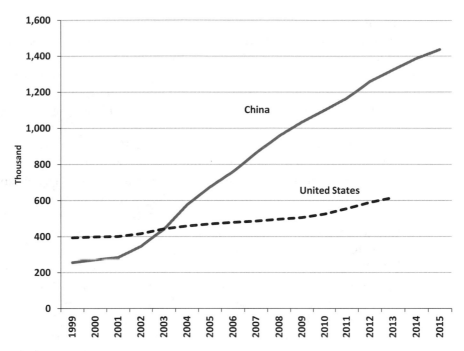

Figure 15.3
Science and engineering graduates (four-year colleges).
Source: *SYC* (2016, table 21-13; and earlier volumes).

and three-year technical schools in about equal proportions. Three-year technical schools provide training roughly equivalent to that of community colleges in the United States. Taking just four-year colleges and universities, China graduated 1.4 million students in 2015 with bachelor-level credentials in engineering and science, compared with 600,000 in the United States. Figure 15.3 shows trends for both countries over the past 15 years. The flow of engineers and scientists into the labor force is much greater in China than in the United States. To be sure, there is still a quality differential, and the rapid expansion of Chinese tertiary education may have temporarily lowered the average quality of graduates. Moreover, the average level of the current U.S. labor force is still significantly higher. More than half the U.S. labor force has a community college degree or higher, while as table 9.1 showed, only 14.9% of Chinese workers have any tertiary education. However, in Chinese cities, 32% of workers have some tertiary education, so the gap in the urban workforce is much narrower and closing fast.

At the very top of the skills pyramid, Chinese who have studied abroad play an important role. Through 2016, a cumulative total of 4.5 million Chinese students had gone to study abroad. The United States is the most common host country by a large margin. So far, 2.6 million (58%) have returned to China. Since 1999, China's government has made strenuous efforts to encourage students to return voluntarily, and a booming economy has helped attract larger numbers home; the proportion of returnees increased substantially after 2009. Chinese scientists and engineers with advanced degrees overseas have contributed enormously to the growth of China's human resources. Many return with work experience in the United States or other foreign countries, which increases their value. Returnees are highly educated: 41% had PhDs in an earlier survey reported in Wang and Bao (2015, 13). The proportion of today's returnees with PhDs is certainly lower because more go abroad at an early age, but this is still overall the most highly educated group in Chinese society. Returnees have played a disproportionately large role in fostering new high-tech start-ups and upgrading educational institutions. Even when students do not return, they play a role in connecting domestic scientists and engineers to international networks of research and innovation (Zweig and Wang 2013).

In 2008, the government introduced a program to encourage the return of middle-aged scholars who were successful abroad. Usually called the "1,000 Talents Program," this program brings outstanding scholars under age 55 with the equivalent of 5 to 10 years of work experience at the full-professor level back to China. Since 2011, a Youth 1,000 Talents Program has been under way that brought 2,000 scholars and engineers under age 40 back to China through 2015. In addition to the national program, all provinces and several industries now have similar programs.

These overseas recruitment programs are sometimes controversial because they provide salary supplements and special research funding worth hundreds of thousands of dollars. This creates jealousy, implicitly undervalues domestic Chinese educational credentials, and may be especially attractive to scholars who have already completed their most productive research periods (this was one of the motivations for creating the Youth program). But these senior scholars can mentor junior scholars, and they lobby for modern laboratories and policies favorable to science. It would be misguided to rely solely on such a program as a technology strategy, but as one part of a strategy aimed at the entire pyramid of technological skills, it can play a positive role.

In fact, this is just what we see in China: a large pyramid of human resources that is being strengthened at every level. Because of its enormous size, China would in any case have an impressive total stock of technical personnel. The number of individuals engaged in R&D (full-time equivalent) jumped to 3.85 million in 2016. China has more scientists and engineers engaged in research than any other country. Average standards are still relatively low for this large group of scientists and technicians, but this corresponds to China's factor endowments: manpower is still relatively cheap, and high-quality human capital required to train technical personnel to a high level are still relatively scarce and therefore expensive. China is following a labor-intensive pathway to increasing the technology effort, and there may be additional opportunities for upgrading personnel quality at relatively low cost.

15.4   Strategies of Technology Development

Chinese policy-makers have maintained a high degree of consensus around the need to invest in new technology and improve China's technological standing. Now that both the technology effort and the human capital base are expanding rapidly, the choice of technology development strategies has become more important than ever. But whereas the objective of fostering technological development has been constant, the policies adopted to reach this objective have been subject to dramatic ongoing changes. In broad terms, over the past 40 years the pendulum has swung first toward greater openness, and then after 2003–2006, toward a more interventionist set of industrial and technology policies. Even within this broad trajectory, there has been a restless alternation among different specific policies. Moreover, China remains deeply integrated into the global economy, so the openness of the 1990s and the interventionism of the post-2006 period are combined in a complex balancing act.

15.4.1   From Autarchy to Openness, 1978–2003

China entered the reform era in 1978 with an inherited strategy of technological autarchy. It then moved step by step along a policy continuum from autarchy to openness:

Autarchy. China's high R&D effort in the socialist period was in the classic "mission-push" mode of R&D. Leaders in China set a few key tasks, and planners then coordinated flexible multidisciplinary and multiskilled research groups with plenty of money to pursue those key goals. This approach can work well when there is broad agreement on priorities, and it has been judged successful in developing nuclear weapons and strategic missiles in China (Feigenbaum 1999). However, this approach is bad at transferring technology to the civilian economy. Security obsessions create secrecy barriers around the most talented scientists and engineers even today. When planners fund research with the avowed intent of aiding the civilian economy, they are not efficient at transferring technologies. Planners do not have the technical capabilities to evaluate the technology they have funded, so scientists are free to pursue their own research with little oversight on the economic importance of their work. Scientists and engineers have no incentives to commercialize their discoveries, and factory managers have few incentives to seek out and implement innovations in the laboratories. Isolation from world science made these drawbacks especially debilitating, and Chinese policy-makers were very aware of the shortcomings.

Centralized purchase of foreign technology. To break out of technological isolation, policy-makers made massive purchases of industrial machinery from global technology leaders. The first wave of contracts collapsed when China's oil revenues failed to materialize after 1978, but government outlays of foreign exchange for technology embodied in plants and equipment remained high. During the 1980s, US$46.8 billion was spent on imports of technology embodied in plants and equipment, big money for the time (Gu 1996). This approach is expensive, and as China's budgetary revenues skidded during the 1980s (see chapter 20), it was clear that China could not afford the luxury of prestige technology purchases.

Conditional foreign direct investment (FDI). The next step was to seek out top multinational corporations (MNCs) as technology partners who would be rewarded with privileged access to China's market for their willingness to share technology. During the 1980s, ambitious negotiations between the two sides, each with some monopoly power, often dragged on for years. MNCs were not eager to give away their most advanced technologies, and China sought highly restrictive and comprehensive deals. Very few successful projects produced the large-scale technology transfers that Chinese policy-makers had hoped for.

There were individual successes, though. Mu and Lee (2005) argued that the joint venture Shanghai Bell Alcatel was a successful example of the policy of "trading market access for technology." The foreign partner, a Belgian Bell affiliate, was not a global technology leader and was willing to agree to generous terms for technology transfer of fairly sophisticated digital telecom switches. The Ministry of Post and Telecom became the project champion and rotated many Chinese engineers through the facility, in a way that was critical to developing the expertise for domestic telecom equipment manufacturers, including some very successful firms, such as Huawei and ZTE Telecom. Chinese policy-makers today have moved away from this model of restrictive, bilateral grand bargains, but they continue to drive tough technology bargains that "trade market access for technology" when they think that they have sufficient bargaining power.

Opening up to FDI. After 1992, China accepted a more general approach in which a number of competitive foreign technology suppliers would be allowed in the Chinese market. FDI immediately took off and became the predominant source of new technology in China for the next decade. MNCs became increasingly important technology actors in China, not only through their attempts to access the domestic market but also because of the speed with which they knit China into global production networks of high-technology items. By the turn of the century, China had established a broadly permissive regime for foreign investors.

15.4.2   Broadening the Domestic Base

Research and development funding. Even as China became more open to the outside technologically, it took steps to broaden its domestic technology base and make government support of technology more efficient. Although budget allocations to research institutes were cut, they were partially replaced with a system of competitive grants. For basic science and research, institutes now submit applications to the National Natural Sciences Foundation and other funding agencies. A new "86-3 Program" named after the year and month of launch, funded goal-dedicated research teams in 10 priority areas. The program involved modest amounts of what was essentially seed funding, which sometimes limited its effectiveness, but it transformed the research funding process and was succeeded 11 years later by the 97-3 Program. A new "Torch" program provides bank loans for technology adoption by enterprises, in order to support technology diffusion, and the "Spark" plan funds technological upgrading for township and village enterprises. With the commitment of modest amounts of funding blended with bank credit, these programs made the Chinese government more strategic and more effective in supporting research and technology diffusion.

Encouraging spin-offs. During the 1980s, policy-makers gave research institutes stronger incentives to diffuse technologies into the civilian economy. Institutes and universities were allowed to earn money providing technical services to businesses and were allowed to establish their own commercial subsidiaries. This permissive stance led to the creation of the "hybrid firms" described in section 14.1.2, many of which became important high-technology firms. The successful, Legend/Lenovo, became an important presence in the burgeoning Zhongguancun high-technology district in northwestern Beijing (Segal 2003; Xie and White 2004). Both Peking University and Tsinghua University set up subsidiary high-tech commercial enterprises and business parks. Not many spin-offs were as successful as Lenovo, but the creation of civilian spin-off firms marked a crucial stage of liberalization in China because it showed the extra latitude planners were willing to give high-technology firms, and it set the stage for broader reforms

Supporting domestic entrepreneurship. After 1999, private Chinese firms began to receive across-the-board support to enter high-technology fields. Instead of favoring only large SOEs, the government began to support virtually all technologically advanced enterprises, including small, private start-ups and technology-intensive spin-offs from schools and research institutes, viewing these firms as "national" enterprises. Private firms could also be the national champions that competed with foreign firms for technological advantage. At the beginning of the new century, the environment for domestic firms had been sufficiently liberalized to allow all ownership forms to play dynamic roles in technology development.

15.4.3   Integrating into Global Production Networks

During the 1980s and 1990s, China rapidly integrated into world trade. Investment from Taiwan, Hong Kong, and Korea allowed firms in Taiwan and Korea to upgrade rapidly into more technologically demanding products, while China took over low-tech, labor-intensive products (chapter 17). After the turn of the century, a remarkable transformation occurred. Firms in Taiwan and Korea began to move the labor-intensive stages of high-technology products to China as well. The most striking example was the laptop computer: after 2001, virtually the entire assembly of laptops moved over to China. Moreover, this reorganization of production created a hypercompetitive industry: to this day, laptops assembled by Taiwan firms in China account for more than 90% of world laptop production. Nobody else can compete.

This rapid restructuring of global production networks seemed to catapult China into the ranks of high-technology powers. As figure 15.4 shows, China was a minor player in high-tech exports in 2000, but by 2005 it had surpassed the United States to be the world's largest high-tech exporter. High-tech exports continued to grow rapidly through 2012, when they surpassed $500 billion. This sudden emergence provoked some inflated rhetoric about China's high-tech success, but of course, this

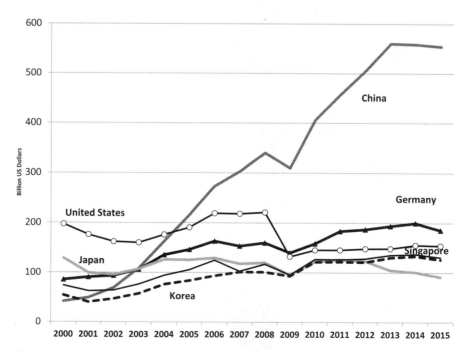

Figure 15.4
High-technology exports.
Source: OECD data via World Development Indicators.

was not the essence of what happened. Precisely because China specialized in the least technologically demanding stages of production, these linkages initially had few implications for technological development. Even when China was exporting finished goods that embodied high-technology components, such as iPhones or laptop computers, the spillovers into indigenous technological capabilities were modest.

15.4.4   Regional Innovation Systems

By the turn of the century, China had developed distinctive regional innovation clusters with different capabilities and diverse policy environments. This diversity was a source of strength. Local governments tried out pilot projects and other experimental methods, invested in different sectors and technologies, and developed different relationships with foreign investors. Even when the central government emphasized control over "core technologies," local governments often invested in incremental, "fast follower" strategies that had a big economic payoff. A rich literature has described the emergence and different characteristics of regional systems and the way their interaction with central policy-makers contributed to better policy outcomes (Breznitz and Murphee 2011; Liu Xielin 2009; Segal 2003).

The three most important regional systems were those in Beijing, Guangdong, and the greater Shanghai region. The Beijing cluster benefited from the extraordinary concentration of high-quality scientific manpower in northwestern Beijing, around the top universities (Peking, Tsinghua) and the two academies, CAS and CAE. The neighborhood of Zhongguancun quickly became home to the spin-off firms from these elite institutions, like Lenovo. This cluster became an incubator of China's Internet economy and attracted many other participants in a high-tech economy. After the turn of the century, Zhongguancun developed a complete ecology of innovation-related institutions, including venture-capital firms, new-firm incubators, and even angel investors. In later years, many multinational corporations set up research facilities in the Zhongguancun area to tap into the abundant high-quality talent.

In southern China, a vibrant high-tech cluster grew up in the Shenzhen special economic zone. Perhaps most striking was the growth of a comprehensive set of manufacturers producing telecommunications equipment. At one extreme, the most technologically sophisticated firm was the Huawei Company, perhaps the single most innovative company in China today and the global company that has been, in most years, the largest recipient of international patents. At the other extreme, the complex contains a large number of so-called *shanzhai* phone producers. The term *shanzhai* is sometimes translated as "counterfeit," but properly it refers to any operation producing cheap knockoffs or variants of established products. In general, these are small companies producing off-brand handsets typically by sticking inexpensive two-steps-behind-the-frontier telecom chip sets from companies such as

Taiwan's Mediatek or Shanghai's Zhangxun (Spreadtrum) into their own homemade housings. The resulting inexpensive phones were sometimes innovative and attractive, and they found substantial markets in rural China and throughout many developing countries. A few *shanzhai* producers have grown to become large manufacturers and exporters. The watchwords of the Shenzhen cluster were very different from those in Zhongguancun: openness, flexibility, and a preference for quick and dirty solutions at a low price. Shenzhen's telecom cluster has some similarities to the TVE-based industrial clusters described in section 13.6. Government and university research played little role.

The entire Yangtze River delta (YRD), with Shanghai at the core, became a cluster of innovative activity as well. Foreign firms—including Taiwan computer firms—played an important but by no means dominant role in the YRD. Most Taiwan laptop assembly located here, centered at Kunshan in Jiangsu. The large complexes of factories related to the automobile industry also became important drivers of incremental industrial innovation. Massive industrial capability and relative openness made the region into an innovation powerhouse. The rise of Alibaba, headquartered in Hangzhou, helped make the YRD a center of China's Internet economy, equal to Beijing. China's size enabled the creation of different clusters with their own capabilities; at the same time, policy diversity was a source of strength in its own right.

15.4.5   Achievement and Dissatisfaction

As of 2003, the environment for innovative business in China had improved dramatically. Investments in human resources were paying off, new Chinese firms were emerging, and cooperative relations with foreign investors had been established. Moreover, nearly all the movement in technology policy had been in the direction of greater marketization, liberalization, and opening. Direct government intervention had been cut back. For example, big flagship government technology projects like integrated circuit fabrication, next-generation nuclear power plants, and civilian airliners had all been quietly wound down. Policy had focused on building human resources, strengthening universities and research institutes, and encouraging enterprises to develop their own technological capabilities through favorable tax and other types of policies. There had been a restless and ongoing search for institutions and policies that could effectively support the technology drive, and although many policies had not succeeded, failing policies had been pruned and discarded, and the resulting technology effort was diverse, multistranded, and seemingly successful. China had moved out of self-imposed backwardness, was playing a crucial role in the global technological present, and had found a policy complex that was propelling it rapidly forward.

However, the new administration of Hu Jintao and Wen Jiabao (2003–2013) was not satisfied. They wanted to do more, and as budgetary resources were recovering, the government had the means to "accomplish big things." Policy had always been ambitious, but now that it was less constrained by limited budgetary resources (chapters 5 and 20), it became even more ambitious. Chinese policy-makers expressed dissatisfaction with certain aspects of China's situation. First, they were unhappy with the large role of foreign-invested firms in China. The electronics hardware sector had grown rapidly, but most of the firms were foreign. In the auto industry, the dominant foreign firms were all in joint ventures with domestic state-owned companies, but were thought to have done little to help their domestic partners to upgrade technologically. Second, the mode of integration into global production networks provoked dissatisfaction. Policy-makers and technology intellectuals tended to see China as stuck in the low-return links of global production networks. In the prevailing interpretation, a production network is characterized by high profitability at two places: at the beginning (upstream) section, companies engage in research and design and produce valuable intellectual property with high return; at the end (downstream) section, companies manage brands and sales and marketing networks that can generate high returns as well. China, by contrast, was stuck in the middle, in activities dominated by ordinary manufacturing and assembly, with low entry barriers, many similar competitors, and low profitability. Chinese policy-makers saw themselves as mired in a low-profit "ghetto," contributing poorly remunerated low-skill labor, even though the output was valuable and high technology.

In addition, World Trade Organization membership, which phased in between 2001 and 2005, placed new restrictions on policy-makers. Certain traditional tools for dealing with foreign MNCs, such as local-content requirements, were now off-limits. Policy-makers began to search for new tools to foster high-tech industry and ended up becoming much more interventionist. Finally, technology policy is everywhere intertwined with national security. As Chinese policy-makers saw information technology transforming traditional defense industries, they sought to control technologies they saw as essential to national security.

15.5   The Turn to Techno-Industrial Policy After 2006

China's policy toward technology development and innovation began to shift almost immediately after the beginning of the Wen Jiabao administration in 2003, and the concrete manifestations of the new policy approach appeared in 2006. From that time on, successive waves of techno-industrial policy have emerged from Chinese policy-makers. These policies have steadily grown in size and sophistication. They represent a substantial shift of direction, compared to the previous two decades. All these major policy initiatives involve government interventions that target specific industries for promotion, reversing the previous trend to reduce targeted interventions. In addition, all of the policies are nationalistic, in the sense that they strongly empha-size the creation of independent technological capabilities within China as well as the creation of "national champion" firms. The commitment to these policies, in terms of rhetoric and in terms of resources, has increased consistently since 2006.

15.5.1   The Medium-Long Range Plan for Science and Technology (2006).

The Medium-Long Range Plan for Science and Technology (MLP) was the outcome of a multiyear planning process. It envisaged many steps to improve the overall environment for innovation in China, and specifically to improve domestic innovative capabilities (Chen and Naughton 2016). The MLP introduced the term "indigenous innovation" (*zizhu chuangxin*) to describe one of its objectives: to develop the separate and independent innovation capacity of Chinese actors, particularly firms but including universities and research institutes. In the years since, this objective—if not always the specific slogan—has remained central in Chinese techno-industrial policy.

The MLP designated 16 "Megaprojects" (table 15.1). These were large-scale government-funded projects, but they were selected for their specific industrial applications: they were not primarily science policy but rather primarily industrial policy. The purpose was to have the government fund R&D arenas where the spillovers to the economy would be largest and most immediate. The megaprojects ramped up gradually, with funding commitment accelerated during the global financial crisis of 2008–2009.

15.5.2   Strategic Emerging Industries (2010)

A new set of industrial policies emerged out of the 2008–2009 economic crisis, and were formalized in a central government plan in 2010: the strategic emerging industries (SEIs). SEIs comprised 20 industrial sectors grouped into 7 large groups. As table 15.1 shows, there was significant sectoral overlap between the megaprojects and the subsequent SEI program: some SEI initiatives were direct continuations of individual megaprojects, and most megaprojects had some relation to a subsequent SEI. However, there were important differences. Whereas the megaprojects were fully government funded projects, SEIs were industrial policies. A broad range of instruments were to be deployed, inducing business actors to invest in these sectors, while some government funding would be used to "make the market," creating favorable conditions for enterprises to develop and grow.

The SEI program was motivated by a new intellectual justification that had emerged in the years 2008–2010. Sectors were included in the SEI initiative not only because they were expected to be large and important in the future, but also because they had qualitatively new elements that had not been fully mastered anywhere in the world. Because of the absence of entrenched incumbent firms or countries, these

Table 15.1
Sectoral targets of industrial policy.

16 megaprojects (2006–2015)		20 strategic emerging industries (2010–2020)
		Energy conservation and environmental protection
		a. Energy-efficient machinery
1	Water-pollution control and treatment	⟶ b. Environmental protection
		c. Recycling and reutilization
		Next-generation information technology
2	ULSI semiconductor manufacturing	⟶ d. Next-generation Internet
3	Next-generation broadband wireless	e. Core electronic components
4	Core electronics and high-end software	⟶ f. High-end software and information services
		Biotechnology
5	Major new drug initiative	⟶ g. Biopharmaceuticals
6	Major infectious disease initiative	h. Biomedical engineering
7	Genetic transformation and plant breeding	⟶ i. Biological agriculture
		j. Biomanufacturing industry
		Precision and high-end machinery
8	Large passenger aircraft	⟶ k. Commercial aircraft
9	High-resolution earth observation system	⟶ l. Satellites and applications
10	Manned space flight and lunar landing	m. Railroad and transport machinery
		n. Marine engineering equipment
11	High-end numerically controlled machine tools	⟶ o. Intelligent manufacturing equipment
		New energy
12	Large-bed oil and gas; coal gasification	p. Wind power
13	Large high-pressure nuclear reactor technology	q. Solar power
		r. Biomass energy
14–16	Three undisclosed military projects	**New materials**
		s. New materials
		New energy vehicles
		t. Electric vehicles and plug-in hybrids

Source: Chen and Naughton (2016).

industries were seen as providing competitive opportunities. The SEI strategy thus echoed the insight of Perez and Soete (1988) that new industries present an opportunity for leapfrog development by latecomers. The SEI program was a response to a high degree of technological opportunity, combined with confidence that the returns to innovation would be appropriable, given China's ongoing manufacturing cost advantages. The SEI approach is often encapsulated in the slogan "Seize the commanding heights of the new technological revolution" (Wan 2009, 1). China was undoubtedly influenced by the fact that during the global crisis of 2008–2009, many developed-country governments, including that of the United States, selected certain emerging industries for government promotion from mixed stimulus and industrial policy motives. These factors are particularly evident in renewable energy (solar and wind) and electric vehicles, which are prominent in the SEIs as well. The SEI approach thus put Chinese industry into direct competition with companies in the developed market economies to develop new industrial sectors.

15.5.3   Made in China 2025 (2015)

A new wave of industrial policies was rolled out in 2015. Most prominently, these included "Made in China 2025" and "Internet Plus." What these two programs have in common is that they are primarily directed toward the use of information technology in other production sectors, including traditional industries. Made in China 2025 has the objective of upgrading China's manufacturing industry in order that China continue to be the world's dominant manufacturer, despite the impact of rising labor, land, and environmental costs. In a sense, Made in China 2025 is an initiative designed to avoid the middle-income trap, and make sure that industry continues to be a prominent part of China's development going forward.

More specifically, Made in China 2025 envisages the creation of "smart factories," with industrial robots, high-end computerized machine tools integrated with networks of sensors, and customized, service-oriented production (Wubbeke et al. 2016). Made in China 2025 bears many similarities to Germany's "Industry 4.0" program, in that both envisage government assistance to foster the integration of information technologies into "traditional" mechanical industries.[1] China's program is more ambitious, in two senses. First, China's current industrial technology is generally at the "Industry 2.0" level, so China's program involves leaping over a much bigger gap. Second, China will spend much more money than the comparatively modest outlays budgeted by the German government (less than $1 billion). The objective of

---

1. After the first industrial revolution in England in the 1780s, "Industry 2.0" refers to widespread electrification and mass production starting in the late 1800s. "Industry 3.0," implemented in developed economies beginning in the 1970s, refers to individual programmable machine tools and robots combined with computerized optimization of overall production and business process. Industry 4.0 "is characterized by the combination of advanced internet and communication technologies, embedded systems and intelligent machines" (Wubbeke et al. 2016, 13).

Made in China 2025 is to upgrade all of China's industries, although it also involves targeting specific sectors such as robotics and 3-D printing. Made in China 2025 continues the strongly nationalist thrust apparent since "indigenous innovation" was first proposed in 2006; it clearly envisions domestic firms replacing foreign firms as suppliers of high-tech equipment and components, and various reference documents associated with the plan contain numerous explicit targets and objectives of this sort.

"Internet Plus" is a broader, but less detailed program that overlaps with Made in China 2025 in industrial sectors. Internet Plus essentially envisages government supporting the application of the Internet to everything: health care, government, transportation and power infrastructure, education, and of course, e-commerce. Both programs are ambitious, and both serve as top-level guidance that triggers concrete implementation measures by ministries and local governments.

15.5.4   Proliferation of Plans and Programs

Made in China 2025 and Internet Plus are motivated by a broader vision than the sector-specific targeted interventions that characterized the SEI program. It is important to stress, therefore, that these programs do not replace the SEIs, which remain in force. Rather, the 2015 programs supplement and reinforce the SEIs. As a result, the proliferation of government programs produces an extremely complex policy landscape. Renewed government activism also gives renewed salience to the five-year plans, which are now tasked with incorporating technoindustrial and environmental objectives and thus take on renewed importance in the economy (Kennedy and Johnson 2016). At least 30–40 central government plans detail how the five year plans and broader strategic plans should be implemented; and literally hundreds of local government plans have an effect as well. Thus, techno-industrial policy has become an important driver of increased government intervention in the economy overall.

Promotion of high-technology industry is arguably the central economic development policy of the Chinese government today. Technology development is the unifying thread that links many aspects of contemporary economic policy, including trade policy and human resource policy. Thus, each of the many strands of policy is taken very seriously by officials and planners at all levels, as well as by entrepreneurs.

15.6   A Multistranded Program of High-Technology Development

The ambitious objectives of China's industrial policies are to be achieved through a full spectrum of policy instruments. Policy-makers deploy qualitatively different instruments that overlap and affect many of the same enterprises simultaneously. For example, Xu, Zhou, and Sun (2013) counted and classified the policies adopted by the central government to support SEIs and showed that the central government promulgated 363 policies to support SEIs during the 30 months between January 2011 and June 2013. The same research group showed that in the wind-power industry, a constantly changing mix of research subsidies, tax breaks for imported components, localization requirements, tax exemptions, and differential power tariffs shaped the incentive environment (Zhou et al. 2013). These policies attempt to align incentives of government and corporate actors in support of the development of knowledge-intensive industry.

15.6.1 Financial Support

A barrage of specific policies, only some of them described here, have the objective and cumulative effect of providing financial support to high-tech industry.

15.6.1.1 Tax Breaks

A whole range of amendments to the tax code have been enacted to make expenditure on R&D virtually costless for the enterprise: a partial tax deduction for R&D expenditures; tax exemption for all income from the sale of new technologies and related consulting services; and tax exemption for imports of equipment used in R&D and not available in China.

15.6.1.2 Subsidized Credit

Varieties of low-cost credit include a domestic fund to support small and medium high-technology enterprises; interest subsidies for specific projects by large enterprises; and support to high-tech exports from the Import-Export Bank.

15.6.1.3 Procurement Preference

Domestic high-tech firms are entitled to a general preference in government procurement. In some cases, government procurement policies are specifically targeted to support domestic IT development, as in the case of ID cards with embedded chips.

15.6.1.4 "High-Technology Enterprise" Status

Enterprises that qualify for "high-technology" status enjoy a lower corporate income-tax rate (15% instead of 30% national tax). High-technology status also opens the door for targeted grants for specific projects, typically funded either by a central ministry or a local government. Local government support may also include lower land and utility prices. High-technology firms early on were allowed to set aside 35% of the net value of increased assets for stock options or other rewards for innovators and entrepreneurs.

15.6.2   Investment Funds

Around the turn of the century, a small but lively venture-capital industry was established in China. It had the peculiarity that most of the funds came directly or indirectly from government agencies, but with a significant role for a few foreign venture capitalists. Domestic private funds gradually became substantial as well. Provisions to allow listing of new high-tech companies on existing stock exchanges were made in the early 2000s, and new listing venues were established (chapter 19). In this way, venture capital had an exit option through public listing.

In 2013, the government carried out a broad, closed-door reassessment of technology policy, presumably reflecting some dissatisfaction with what was viewed as the relatively slow development of SEIs. The most evident policy outcome of this review has been an increased commitment to sectoral investment funds. It was thought that patient and forgiving state-financed equity investors would have more flexibility to attract competing business development proposals, invest at different stages of the corporate life cycle, and in general improve the efficiency of government investment in new technology enterprises. This approach has led to a renewed surge of funding into high-technology industries. Although there is no overall accounting, it is clear that the commitment is extremely large. According to Kennedy and Johnson (2016, 27), an incomplete count as of the end of 2015 turned up fund commitments of 2.18 trillion RMB ($328 billion). A particularly favored sector has been semiconductors, for which national, provincial, and municipal governments have all established funds. Yoshida (2017) reports total commitments to IC funds of 465 billion RMB ($70 billion). To be sure, these are commitments, rather than actual investments; nonetheless, the amount of money flowing into new investment is certain to be large.

15.6.3   Demand-Side Policies

The SEI program included the systematic use of government resources to support demand for emerging industries. These programs had their roots in the government procurement programs developed as part of the "indigenous innovation" program of the MLP. Today, the government is the primary (or sole) customer for some SEIs, such as satellites. For others, such as commercial aircraft, state-owned enterprises serve as lead customers, putting in orders for as-yet-untested aircraft. Policy provides support for broad-based demand as well; for example, purchases of electric vehicles and plug-in hybrids receive generous tax breaks and rebates, and policy-makers raised the feed-in tariffs received by solar and wind electricity generation to support those industries.

15.6.4   Regulatory Environment

The regulatory framework is an essential part of the institutional ecology that supports innovation. As China has moved to a firm-based and predominantly market-based system, regulations have played an ever more important role. At the same time, regulatory institutions have become an increasingly important part of industrial policy.

15.6.4.1   Technical Standards

Chinese policy-makers established an array of technical standards, an essential part of the regulatory state. Often this was done to create a competitive advantage for domestic firms. Efforts included next-generation DVDs, third-generation digital telephony (TD-SCDMA), and encryption (Linden 2004). The TD-SCDMA telecom standard was assigned to China Mobile, the largest carrier, giving them a head start in the 3G market.

15.6.4.2   Protecting Intellectual Property

China entered the reform era with no mechanism for the protection of intellectual property rights. In the 1980s, China created a patent office—the State Intellectual Property Office (SIPO)—and a legal and regulatory framework to protect intellectual property, including dedicated intellectual property tribunals in Beijing and Shanghai. This institutional apparatus conforms with international standards and law and is intensively used (see below).

15.6.4.3   Control of the Internet

As is widely recognized, China exerts much stronger national control of the Internet than any other economically significant country. This control obviously fulfills many different government objectives. One important effect of this control is that it prevents foreign companies such as Google, Facebook, and Microsoft from establishing businesses in China, and protects domestic firms, most notably Alibaba, Baidu, and Tencent (Tengxun). All three of these giant firms are private start-ups with formidable capabilities. They are giants with potential global competitive strength, but they also benefit from nearly complete domestic market protection due to China's Internet regulations.

15.6.4.4   Light Touch Regulation of Emerging Segments

In contrast to the rather strict regulatory control exercised over some parts of the Internet, Chinese policy-makers are willing to absorb some of the risk of innovation by adopting regulatory forbearance in some emerging segments. The best example is the growth of financial services over the Internet, sometimes called "fintech." Given the huge Internet base in China, this is a promising area. Chinese regulators have allowed Internet giants like Alibaba to launch payment services and money-market funds (chapter 19). Peer-to-peer lending platforms have proliferated. These fintech developments have been allowed to proceed with little oversight or prudential regulation. Regulators have clearly been influenced by the developmental potential in these emerging segments.

15.6.5   Asymmetric Use of Institutions to Promote Domestic Enterprises

The developments described in the previous sections were essential to the creation of an institutional framework supportive of innovation. At the same time, virtually as soon as these institutions were created, they began to be used as instruments to protect and privilege domestic enterprises. This was apparent first with technical standards, which were intentionally set up to leverage the advantage of the large Chinese domestic market and give domestic firms a head start in responding to domestic market demand. The Chinese mobile telephone network operated a separate 3G TD-SCDMA system incompatible with both major global standards for several years starting in 2009, until the movement to 4G and now 5G made the 3G standards obsolete. Chinese intellectual property (IP) courts, especially in the early years, made it difficult for foreign firms to make claims and awarded extremely small damages when a claim was finally established against a domestic firm. Chinese IP courts have improved substantially since that time, but local protectionism is still a significant problem. Long and Wang (2015) found that (domestic) plaintiffs were significantly more likely to receive positive judgments in IP courts in their home jurisdiction than they were in external jurisdictions. Article 55 of China's Anti-monopoly Law deals loosely with the connection between intellectual property and antitrust. The requirement that "essential" patents should be licensed on "Fair, Reasonable, and Nondiscriminatory (FRAND) terms" is worldwide but has sometimes been interpreted more strictly in China than elsewhere, to the detriment of foreign firms. In short, the creation of a regulatory framework, while generally proinnovation, has also given those in charge of Chinese industrial policy a new set of tools for intervening in specific sectors and nurturing domestic firms.

15.6.6   Multiple, Overlapping Incentives

The combined evidence from the previous sections makes it clear that policy-makers use the full spectrum of policy instruments. China's overall technoindustrial policy stance is made up of an overlapping and reinforcing combination of supply-side, tax, regulatory, demand-side, and investment policies.

15.7   Outcomes

As discussed in section 15.1, the outcome of the knowledge production function should be examined from two standpoints. From an economic standpoint, we are most interested in whether innovation contributes to the total factor productivity of the economy (in aggregate or in specific sectors). With the current state of our knowledge, it is not yet possible to do this. Technology policies are too complex and too recent to be subject to the detailed studies required to quantify inputs and output. Moreover, policies have both positive and negative effects (section 15.8), which need to be carefully studied. It is too early to tell what impact China's enormous technology effort is having on the Chinese economy. From a technology standpoint, we are interested in the outputs that indicate new knowledge creation, even if this has not yet contributed to the economy's increased productivity. We cannot measure knowledge directly, but two important proxies for new knowledge creation are patents and scholarly articles.

15.7.1   Patents

Patents serve as a useful intermediate indicator of knowledge production. The number of invention patent applications provides striking evidence that China now takes intellectual property seriously. In the United States, the number of patents has doubled since 2000 to almost 600,000. In China, applications skyrocketed to 1.3 million in 2016 (figure 15.5). In the United States, about half of patent applications have been filed by foreign companies or persons since 2008. In China, while about half of patent applications were filed by foreign companies until 2004, domestic applications have accelerated since then and now account for 88% of invention patent applications.[2]

However, Chinese patent applications have been driven upward by government policies to incentivize patents. These are pervasive and generous. Most work units provide cash bonuses for patent applications and pay all associated costs. Enterprise patent applications help firms achieve coveted "high-technology enterprise" status, which lowers their tax rate. Government officials even have total patent applications from their region as one of their success indicators. Inevitably this means that there are incentives to patent items that are unrelated to actual innovation value. To put it plainly, there are many junk patents. Hu, Zhang, and Zhao (2017) found that the

---

2. Only invention patents are considered here, but note that China also issues design and utility patents. These are not reviewed by patent examiners and are not generally comparable with patents in other systems. Applications are generally taken as a better indicator of patenting activity than patents granted because although most applications are ultimately granted, the lag is substantial.

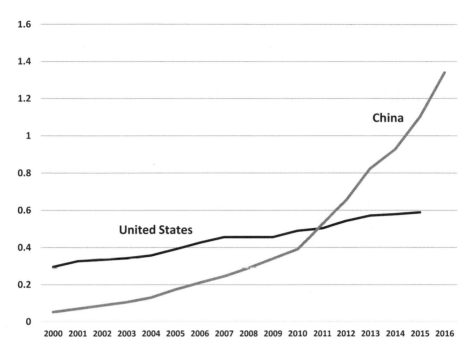

Figure 15.5
Invention patent applications, United States and China (millions).
Sources: State Intellectual Property Office of the PRC, accessed at http://www.sipo.gov.cn/; U.S. Patent and Trademark Office, accessed at https://www.uspto.gov/web/offices/ac/ido/oeip/taf/us_stat.htm.

increase in patents has come primarily from firms that had not patented previously, and that the correlations between patents and both R&D inputs and labor productivity outputs have weakened. For these reasons, it would be foolish to think that China in some sense surpassed the United States in 2011 when it received a larger number of patent applications. More accurately, Chinese patenting demonstrates Goodhart's law: "When a measure becomes a target, it ceases to be a good measure."

Boeing and Mueller (2016) developed an index of patent quality based on how often a patent was cited in subsequent patent applications. They found that the quality of Chinese patents was 44.9% of the average quality of non-Chinese patents in 2001 and declined to 30.4% in 2009. However, this measure may suffer from bias resulting from the dominance of the English language in most of the world scientific community, leading to fewer citations of Chinese-language patents. The value of patents likely varies enormously across sectors. At one extreme, China accounts for 10% of the world's life sciences patents but only 2% of new drugs launched, perhaps indicating low patent value (McKinsey Global Institute 2015, 95). On the other hand, the Fraunhofer Institute studied Chinese patents in the field of "Industry 4.0" (section 15.5.3). They found that China filed the highest number of patents of any nation. They then followed up with a detailed analysis of individual Chinese patents which they found to include "highly innovative inventions … especially energy-efficient wireless sensor networks and network structures" (Fraunhofer Institute 2015). The Chinese patent harvest should be discounted somewhat, but certainly not entirely: knowledge creation is growing rapidly.

15.7.2   Scholarly Articles

Chinese authors accounted for 12.2% of global scientific papers in 2011, up from 0.2% in 1980; since 2007, China has produced the second-largest number of scholarly articles annually, after the United States. Citation counts are a fundamental way to evaluate the influence of scholarly articles (or patent quality). We expect citations to lag the number of articles for China, both because China is a developing country—so the overall quality of scientific production should be lower than in advanced countries—and because the growth of publishing has been very rapid so awareness may lag. In fact, China is number four in national citation counts. Fu, Frietsch, and Tagscherer (2013) developed several useful indicators with data through 2009. They found that the rate at which a Chinese article is cited was below the global average, but moving up steadily. Thus, alongside dramatic quantitative growth, there has also been steady qualitative improvement. In other words, China has certainly not caught up with the advanced economies—China nationally ranks number 78 in the citation frequency count—but the process of catch-up that appears in the quantitative indicators does not disappear when qualitative indicators are used as well.

15.8   Technology Policy Issues

Nearly every aspect of Chinese technology policy is changing rapidly. The fundamental questions about innovation and innovation policy provide a rich agenda going forward. Some of the most important questions include the following:

What is the appropriate level of spending? Although nearly all developed countries have programs to encourage the emergence of new industrial sectors, the scale of these program is much smaller than in China. For example, the German Industry 4.0 program consists primarily of a technology road map, accompanied by about $180 million in funding through 2016 (Wubbeke et al. 2016, 7). The U.S. federal government spends about $50 billion annually on scientific research, with the National Institute of Health the largest recipient. Neither the United States nor Germany spends more than a few billion dollars annually on industrial promotion. China is devoting up to a hundred times as much money to industrial promotion.

What is the rate of return to investments in technological promotion? At present, it is impossible to calculate either the overall investment China is making or the magnitude of the return these investments are getting. As more information becomes available, the apparent rate of return will help answer the previous question.

How distortionary is government intervention? Businessmen generally welcome government subsidies if they are recipients. However, government industrial policy generally provides subsidies and implicit guarantees to some investors and attracts excessive entry. This creates waste and distorts incentives for the healthy development of the industry. The experience of the Chinese solar-panel industry demonstrated exactly these effects. Massive entry led to a rapid reduction in unit production costs (fostering global solar power growth) and the rise of several Chinese firms to global prominence. However, the large majority of firms entering this industry went bankrupt, and billions of dollars of misplaced investment had to be written off. The industry awaits a careful assessment of costs and benefits. Given these distortions, will the innovator with the best idea be successful against competitors with deep government support? Is it worth the innovator's while to even try?

What is the trade-off with international cooperation? The emphasis on domestic investment and protecting and nurturing domestic firms is a fundamental characteristic of Chinese technology policy today. This inevitably implies a deemphasis on the opportunities of technology import and technological cooperation. Developing nations are engaged in complex relations of cooperation and competition with MNCs. On the one hand, MNCs wish to retain control of their IP to appropriate the gains from innovation. On the other hand, MNCs have strong incentives to cut costs within their global production networks, and that implies shifting work to lower-cost domestic firms if they can do it more cheaply. In the old days of the 1990s, it was primarily low-technology stages of the manufacturing process that were "outsourced," so China was temporarily in a low-skill "ghetto." However, today, processes of vertical specialization, or "modularity," have progressed further than in the past, and the same forces that led firms to slice up and relocate the manufacturing value chain are creating opportunities to outsource more highly skilled manufacturing, as well as knowledge-intensive services, such as software, engineering, and R&D. These activities then provide a new pathway to technological upgrading. However, for MNCs to be comfortable with this process, they must trust the Chinese cooperating firms to respect their IP and must have faith in a legal system that protects IP in case of a breakdown in trust. Does the aggressive favoritism given to domestic firms inadvertently hurt China by slowing the transfer of frontier technology within global production networks? More broadly, in the face of dramatic global technological change, it appears that additional efficiency gains can be reaped by a deeper division of labor between dynamic Chinese and global firms, allowing the market to determine the balance of cooperation and competition. Does Chinese innovation policy allow for those gains?

15.9   Conclusion

The pace of technological change in China is impressive and is likely to accelerate. As we have seen, China has now mounted a substantial technology effort that works through diverse channels. Policy-makers have been flexible and adaptive in their approaches. The human resource base is now growing rapidly from a relatively low base, and this growth shows every sign of accelerating. The institutions and incentives that support technology adoption have changed dramatically in just the past few years. At the same time, China is moving away, at the margin, from close cooperation with multinational firms. The resulting prospect is one of rapid rise but also increased friction over a variety of industrial and technological issues.

Whatever the ultimate impact of China's technology and industrial policies, it is important to recognize the many advantages China has in innovation. First, China is an enormous lead market. New inventions have their greatest economic impact when they are successfully tailored to the needs of a mass market. During the nineteenth and early twentieth centuries, the United States gained a formidable first-mover advantage from the size and high income level of its domestic market. Today, China has a similar advantage in market size and is overcoming its past disadvantage of low per capita income. This advantage is most obvious in mobile Internet. Since China has by far the largest number of mobile phones in the world (1.27 billion subscribers at the end of 2015), its companies are best positioned to develop the specific application that ends up being most popular globally.

Second, China has an enormous manufacturing base. A great deal of innovation is cost-reducing innovation that occurs through learning while doing, especially in manufacturing. China's manufacturers will create a continuous stream of productive innovation that will diffuse rapidly in the dense production clusters where China's factories are concentrated. Good government policy can reinforce this but not substitute for it.

Finally, China has an entrepreneurial and risk-taking population. A recent innovation in China that exemplifies all three of these factors is the "internet of bicycles." Several competing firms—Mobike, ofo, Ubike, and others—have created systems through which users locate bikes for hire by using GPS on their mobile phones. Users can immediately reserve the bikes and then scan a QR code on the bike within 15 minutes to unlock it and start charging the payment card. The user then rides the bicycle away and can leave it wherever he or she likes, the battery having been recharged in the meantime by the user pedaling. This is a truly innovative business model that involves no core technologies, no government policy, and no subsidies. Competing firms as of 2016 are scaling up rapidly, knowing that the one that best serves the consumer will win the China market and perhaps expand to the whole world.

Bibliography

Suggestions for Further Reading

The literature on technology and innovation in China is rich and enormous. McKinsey Global Institute (2015) is an original and refreshing take. Wubbeke et al. (2016) puts recent Chinese policies in a broad comparative framework, with excellent graphics.

References

Boeing, Philipp, and Elisabeth Mueller (2016). "Measuring Patent Quality and National Technological Capacity in Cross-Country Comparison." ZEW Discussion Paper no. 16-048 (June). Accessed at http://ftp.zew.de/pub/zew-docs/dp/dp16048.pdf.

Breznitz, D., and M. Murphree (2011). *Run of the Red Queen: Government, Innovation, Globalization, and Economic Growth in China*. New Haven, CT: Yale University Press.

Chen, Ling, and Barry Naughton (2016). "An Institutionalized Policy-Making Mechanism: China's Return to Techno-industrial Policy." *Research Policy* 45:2138–2152.

Cliff, Roger (1998). "China's Potential for Developing Advanced Military Technology." July 8. Santa Monica, CA: Rand Corporation.

Feigenbaum, Evan (1999). "Soldiers, Weapons and Chinese Development Strategy: The Mao Era Military in China's Economic and Institutional Debate." *China Quarterly* 158 (June): 285–313.

Fraunhofer Institute (2015). "Analysis of Industry 4.0 in China: Analysis of Chinese Patenting Activities." March 30. Accessed at https://www.iao.fraunhofer.de/lang-en/about-us/press-and-media/1218-industry-4-0-china-moves-into-the-fast-lane.html.

Fu, Junying, Rainer Frietsch, and Ulrike Tagscherer (2013). "Publication Activity in the Science Citation Index Expanded (SCIE) Database in the Context of Chinese Science and Technology Policy from 1977 to 2012." Fraunhofer ISI Discussion Papers Innovation Systems and Policy Analysis no. 35 (August). ISSN 1612-1430. Karlsruhe.

Grow, Roy F. (1984). "Soviet Economic Penetration of China, 1945–1960: 'Imperialism' as a Level of Analysis Problem." In Steven J. Rosen and James R. Keith, eds, *Testing Theories of Economic Imperialism*, 261–281. Lexington, MA: Lexington Books.

Gu Yuefang (1996). "On the Position of Technology Import in the Process of Industrial Development." In Jiao Xionghua, ed., *Zhongguo Jishu Yinjin de Jingyan yu Tansuo* [An exploration of China's technology import experience], 8–45. Beijing: Zhongguo Biaozhun.

Hu, Albert, Peng Zhang, and Lijing Zhao (2017). "China as Number One? Evidence from China's Most Recent Patenting Surge." *Journal of Development Economics* 124:107–119.

Kennedy, Scott, and Christopher Johnson (2016). *Perfecting China, Inc.: The 13th Five-Year Plan*. Washington, DC: Center for Strategic and International Studies.

Linden, Greg (2004). "China Standard Time: A Study in Strategic Industrial Policy." *Business and Politics* 6 (3): Article 4.

Liu, Xielin (2009). "National Innovation Systems in Developing Countries: The Chinese National Innovation System in Transition." In Bengt-Ake Lundvall, Jan Vang, K. J. Joseph, and Christina

Chaminade, eds., *Handbook of Innovation Systems and Developing Countries*, 119–139. Cheltenham: Edward Elgar.

Long, Cheryl, and Jun Wang (2015). "Judicial Local Protectionism in China: An Empirical Study of IP Cases." *International Review of Law and Economics* 42:48–59.

McKinsey Global Institute (2015). *The China Effect on Global Innovation* (October). Accessed at http://www.mckinsey.com/business-functions/strategy-and-corporate-finance/our-insights/gauging-the-strength-of-chinese-innovation.

Mu, Qing, and Keun Lee (2005). "Knowledge Diffusion, Market Segmentation and Technological Catch-up: The Case of the Telecommunication Industry in China." *Research Policy* 34 (6): 759–783.

Perez, C., and L. Soete (1988). "Catching-up in Technology: Entry Barriers and Windows of Opportunity." In Giovanni Dosi, ed., *Technical Change and Economic Theory*, 458–479. London: Pinter.

SAC (Annual). *Zhongguo Tongji Zhaiyao* [Statistical abstract of China]. Beijing: Zhongguo Tongji.

Segal, Adam (2003). *Digital Dragon: High-Technology Enterprises in China*. Ithaca, NY: Cornell University Press.

SYC (Annual). *Zhongguo Tongji Nianjian* [Statistical yearbook of China]. Beijing: Zhongguo Tongji.

Technology Statistics Office, NBS (National Bureau of Statisdtics) (1990). *Zhongguo Kexue Jishu Sishinian, 1949–1989* [Statistics on science and technology of China, 1949–1989]. Beijing: Zhongguo Tongji.

Wan, Gang (2009). "Develop the Newly Emerging Strategic Industry; Seize the Commanding Heights of a New Round of Development." *Keji Ribao* [Science and technology daily], October 25.

Wang, Huiyao, and Yue Bao (2015). *Reverse Migration in Contemporary China: Returnees, Entrepreneurship and the Chinese Economy*. New York: Palgrave Macmillan.

Wang, Huiyao, David Zweig, and Xiaohua Lin (2011). "Returnee Entrepreneurs: Impact on China's Globalization Process." *Journal of Contemporary China* 20 (70): 413–431.

Wubbeke, Jost, Mirjam Meissner, Max J. Zenglein, Jaqueline Ives, and Björn Conrad (2016). "Made in China 2025: The Making of a High-Tech Superpower and Consequences for Industrial Countries." Berlin. MERICS Papers on China, no. 2. Accessed at https://www.merics.org/en/merics-analysis/papers-on-china/made-in-china-2025/.

Xie, Wei, and Steven White (2004). "Sequential Learning in a Chinese Spin-off: The Case of Lenovo Group Limited." *R&D Management* 34 (4): 407–422.

Xu Guannan, Zhou Yuan, and Sun Lihong (2014). "A Retrospective Analysis of Policies Relating to the Strategic Emerging Industries in the First Half of the 12th Five Year Plan." In China Engineering Technology Development Strategy Research Academy, ed., *Zhongguo Zhanlue Xinxing Chanye Fazhan Baogao* [China strategic emerging industries development report], 128–136. Beijing: Kexue.

Yoshida, Junko (2017). "Much Ado About China's Big IC Surge: Myth and Reality of China's IC Fund." *EE Times*, June 22, 2017. Accessed at http://www.eetimes.com/document.asp?doc_id=1331928.

Zhou, Y., G. Xu, T. Minshall, and J. Su (2013). "A Policy Dimension Required for Technology Roadmapping: Learning from the Emergence of Chinese Wind Turbine Industry." *International Journal of Environment and Sustainable Development* 12 (1): 3–21.

Zweig, D., and H. Wang (2013) 'Can China Bring Back the Best? The Communist Party Organizes China's Search for Talent." *China Quarterly* (215): 590–615. doi: 10.1017/S0305741013000751.

Export goods for sale in the domestic economy, Wangfujing, Beijing 2006.

In the past 40 years, China has transformed from an isolated economy into the world's biggest trading nation. China became the world's largest exporter in 2009 and the world's largest trader (exports plus imports) in 2012, surpassing Germany and the United States, respectively. China has now achieved a degree of openness that is exceptional for a large, continental economy. At its peak in 2006, China's total goods trade (exports plus imports) amounted to 65% of GDP, far higher in that year than the level in the United States (21%), Japan (28%), or India (32%). Since 2006, trade has ebbed as a share of China's rapidly growing GDP and has risen in India and Japan—but there is no doubt that trade will continue to be a crucial dynamic sector driving China's growth and modernization.

Basic economics teaches that countries benefit from trade. Economies with different factor endowments gain when they can trade with each other. Economies tend to export products that intensively use their abundant factors of production and import goods that intensively use their scarce factors of production. China provides abundant evidence of this general principal. China's labor-rich and land-poor economy benefited enormously from the opening to trade after the 1970s that unleashed a flood of labor-intensive exports (clothing, shoes, and toys) while enabling the import of essential food and raw materials. As integration deepened, China was able to import sophisticated machinery that was capital- and technology intensive. China's rapid growth would have been inconceivable without this trade. Exporting enabled the labor-intensive manufacturing sector to expand more rapidly than any other part of the Chinese economy, generating employment and income, while imported supplies of raw materials and embedded technology enabled China to rapidly cut costs and improve efficiency.

International trade facilitated the growth miracle in another way: by giving Chinese businesses a virtually inexhaustible market, it allowed structural transformation to roar forward without impediment. Market saturation was not an obstacle, and Chinese exports spread to every corner of the globe. Finally, besides the huge direct benefit of trade, the desire to access those benefits was a major indirect driver of market-oriented reform in the domestic economy. Trade liberalization was an integral part of China's economic reform process from the beginning. After years of trade growth, a new phase of trade policy reform began when China entered the World Trade Organization (WTO) on December 11, 2001. WTO entry also symbolized China's coming of age as a participant in the global economic community. An enormous systemic transformation was necessary to convert China from one of the world's most economically isolated economies into a global economic player. International opening and domestic economic reform were complementary processes that are often paired in a single term to describe the post-1978 period: "reform and opening" (*gaige kaifang*). This chapter traces both the quantitative growth of trade and the institutional changes that made it possible.

In today's global economy, trade and investment are increasingly closely linked. In China, trade was driven by foreign investment that was itself part of an East Asia–wide economic restructuring (see chapter 17). China adapted a package of liberalization policies to take advantage of the opportunities that it faced. China developed close relations with existing exporters in Hong Kong and Taiwan and crafted a dualistic trade regime under which it could adopt relatively liberal rules on export-processing trade while still protecting domestic markets. These rules enabled China to integrate closely into the cross-border production networks that were developing at this time. Today, all the key characteristics of China's trade are readily comprehensible in terms of these networks: commodity composition, technological sophistication, and international partner composition. The chapter concludes with some observations about China's future trade growth.

16.1   Background

16.1.1   Early Days

In the early days of the People's Republic of China, from 1949 through 1960, China dramatically reoriented its trade away from the Pacific and toward the Soviet Union. Although the traditional Pacific trade was shut down, China remained open to trade and aid, which now came almost entirely from the Soviet bloc. More than two-thirds of China's trade between 1952 and 1960 was with Communist Party–led countries, and 48% was with the Soviet Union alone. Trade was a leading sector in China's economic transformation; total trade grew to about 12% of GDP in 1955. China imported industrial materials such as steel and diesel fuel, as well as machinery, most crucially the complete industrial plants that were the centerpiece of China's First Five-Year Plan (1953–1957; see chapter 4). China exported textiles and processed foods, and the Soviet Union extended credit that supported moderate Chinese deficits. The Great Leap Forward (GLF) (1958–1960) at first encouraged further growth in trade with the socialist countries as China's frenzied investment drive increased its demand for imported machinery.

16.1.2   Economic Isolationism

The economic crisis and famine that followed the collapse of the GLF led to dramatic changes in every aspect of China's economy. China began a long, slow retreat into international economic isolation. The break with the Soviet Union after 1960 meant the virtual end of trading relations with China's biggest trade partner. Imports from the Soviet Union dropped sharply, and by 1970, trade with the Soviet Union accounted for only 1% of total Chinese trade. Trade did not grow at all between 1959 and 1970: exports were exactly the same in 1970 as in 1959 ($2.26 billion). Imports of industrial goods were curtailed sharply in the immediate post-GLF crisis, and scarce foreign exchange was diverted to desperately needed grain imports. The early 1970s were thus the low point of China's relations with the world economy; imports and exports together were only 5% of GDP in 1970 and 1971. At the same time, relations with the West remained distant and on occasion threatening. China was on a war footing through 1971 and intentionally encouraged regional self-sufficiency within China as well as internationally. The foreign-trade system provided insulation from world market forces.

China adopted conscious policies of self-reliance. In fact, China had little to export during this period. In the wake of the GLF, China's households were perilously close to the subsistence margin, and the food and light consumer goods that China had previously exported were now in short supply domestically. Scarce foreign exchange was used to import grain from Canada, Australia, and Argentina, while the remaining foreign exchange available had to be carefully husbanded to enable the import of a few critical industrial materials, including petroleum and steel. The output from China's new heavy industries was not of good-enough quality to find foreign markets. In any case, preoccupied with the Cultural Revolution, China had little information on foreign markets. A quarter of China's exports went to tiny Hong Kong, the largest market. Cut off from its supplies of Soviet technology, China made do with a few small, selective purchases from suppliers of new technology in Japan and Europe.

In the mid-1970s, the economy began to recover from the worst of the Cultural Revolution. Supplies of light consumer manufactures, especially textiles, began to increase and become available for export. Even more important, petroleum output from China's main field at Daqing began to increase rapidly, and China started to export oil. It was obvious that China could reap substantial gains from reengaging with world markets. But how would this be done? As foreign-exchange earnings began to increase, China rapidly stepped up its technology purchases from the West and Japan. Fertilizer plants and steel mills were at the front of the queue of desperately needed technology items. These trading relationships seemed set to continue growing, and ambitious technology-import programs multiplied in 1977–1978. But when oil-field development programs fell through, it was unclear where the foreign currency needed to pay for the imports would come from. China for the first time was forced to confront the inherent problems created by its command-economy trading system. Driven initially by a serious short-run foreign-exchange crisis, China began to systematically open its economy.

16.1.3   China's Emergence as a Trade Power

In 1978, China began a remarkable 30-year process of economic opening. The results are displayed graphically in figures 16.1 and 16.2. As shown in figure 16.1, trade responded quickly to policy reforms at the end of the 1970s and grew at a sustained rapid pace. By 2001–2002, both exports and imports had increased their share of GDP from 5% to 20%, transforming China's economy in the process. Even given this performance, what happened next was remarkable: China's trade growth accelerated after 2002 in the wake of WTO membership and successful reforms. Exports soared to 35% of GDP in 2006–2007, outpacing imports and

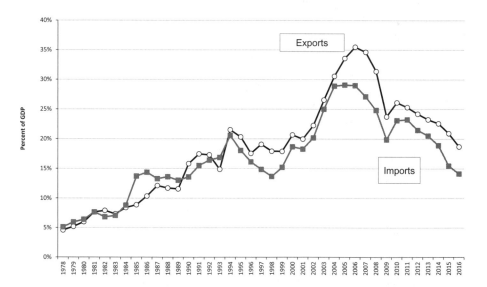

Figure 16.1
Exports and imports (share of GDP).
Sources: *SYC*, updated from General Administration of Customs.

opening up a large merchandise trade surplus for the first time (peaking at 7.4% of GDP in 2007). Figure 16.2 shows that by 2001–2002, China had just caught up with average world levels of trade openness (as measured by the export/GDP ratio). After 2002, it soared ahead, becoming substantially more open than the world average, a remarkable outcome given China's large size and continental character (usually associated with lower trade ratios). Since 2007, China's trade ratios have dropped substantially. They fell quickly during the global financial crisis of 2008–2009, stabilized, and then fell rapidly again after 2014. By 2016, they had returned to approximately where they were in 1998–1999. China's merchandise trade surpluses declined to below 3% of GDP after 2010 but widened again because of the drop in commodities prices after 2014. Figure 16.2 sheds additional light on these changes. China's export ratio has dropped back below the world average (perhaps to a more predictable place for a large continental economy). However, it may be surprising to see that China's share of world exports continued to inch upward until 2015 (shown by the dashed line). The explanation is this: since the global financial crisis of 2008–2009, world trade and China exports both grew slowly (until 2014) and then declined (until 2016). However, in the rest of the world,

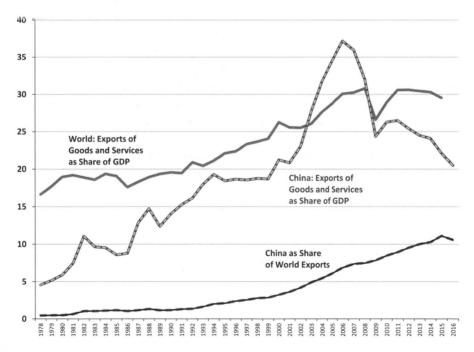

Figure 16.2
China's exports in global context.
Source: World Bank, World Development Indicators (WDI).

GDP growth has also slowed dramatically, so the export/GDP ratio has been stable, while Chinese GDP has continued to grow moderately rapidly, so exports as a share of GDP have declined.

16.2   Reforming the Trade System

16.2.1   The Challenge

The foreign-trade system that Chinese leaders sought to reform in the late 1970s was a typical Soviet-style command-economy trading system that had been adapted to serve China's economic isolation. The domestic economy was rigorously separated from the world economy by what we might term a "double air lock" that controlled flows of both goods and money. The first air lock was the centrally controlled foreign-trade monopoly. Twelve national foreign-trade companies (FTCs) exercised monopolies over both imports and exports. Only authorized goods were allowed to pass through this layer of control. The second air lock was the foreign-exchange system. The value of the Chinese currency (the renminbi, RMB, or yuan) was set arbitrarily, and it was not convertible. Individuals could not exchange renminbi for foreign currency without special authorization, which was very difficult to get. Overlapping, redundant controls covered the flows of both goods and money. The only way to navigate this tangle of administrative controls was to be included in the foreign-trade plan.

The double-air-lock system was designed to insulate the domestic economy from the world economy while allowing a few key commodities to pass through the air locks. The FTCs bought and sold domestic commodities at planned prices and world commodities at world prices. When imports passed through the air lock, they were repriced in accordance with domestic planned prices, and the FTCs regularly cross-subsidized money-losing products with revenues from profitable ones. The socialist price system was thus completely insulated from the influence of world prices. As discussed in chapters 4 and 20, socialist prices were set so as to privilege the state-owned industrial system. Low relative agricultural prices and high industrial prices were used to concentrate profits in state-owned factories, where they could be harvested for the government budget. If world market forces had been allowed to affect domestic prices, they would have gradually eroded the socialist price system and the government's traditional institutions for mobilizing resources. The socialist price system is an extreme version of the price relationships created by the common "import-substitution-industrialization" (ISI) development strategy. In ISI strategies, developing countries erect barriers against industrial imports, thereby protecting their new industries and (they hope) fostering industrialization. In China as well, one of the functions of the traditional foreign-trade system was to protect state-owned industries.

In this system of control, foreign trade served the interests of China's planners, who had simple preferences. The purpose of foreign trade was to import goods that could not be produced by Chinese firms and that would resolve domestic shortages or bottlenecks (food or raw materials) or bring in modern technology (embodied in industrial machinery). Exports were viewed as a sort of necessary evil, required because exporting was the only way to pay for imports. If planners deemed goods "not needed" for the domestic economy, they could be exported, but the cost of producing export goods was largely irrelevant, while the import of nonessential goods was severely restricted.

When Chinese planners stepped up the pace of technology imports in 1978–1979, they quickly overshot their supply of foreign exchange. Foreign-exchange reserves, small to begin with, melted away at alarming speed. Foreign-trade reforms then began in an urgent attempt to increase and diversify sources of foreign exchange. Luckily, China was surrounded by dynamic, export-oriented market economies, including Hong Kong. China turned to these dynamic neighbors as it sought to begin opening up.

16.2.2   Initial Reform Steps

Rather than tackle the enormous task of transforming the whole foreign-trade system, Chinese policy-makers initially took modest but innovative steps to open up new trade channels in the southern provinces of Guangdong and Fujian in 1978–1979. The objective was to make use of the proximity of these provinces to Hong Kong and, to a lesser extent, Taiwan. At this time, Guangdong Province was only a second-tier player in China's foreign trade, accounting for one-seventh of China's export revenues in 1978. Neighboring Hong Kong, however, was already a huge trading power. In fact, tiny Hong Kong exported as much as all of mainland China at this time. China's first step in opening came in 1978 when Hong Kong businesses were allowed to sign export-processing (EP) contracts with Chinese firms in the Pearl River delta. For example, a Hong Kong firm would ship fabric to a Chinese rural firm and have it sewn into shirts. The Chinese firm would be paid a processing fee, while the Hong Kong firm would own the fabric and shirts at all times, so they did not have to pass through the foreign-trade system's air locks at all. In this way, the export-production network already created by Hong Kong could expand into China, but Chinese industrial firms were not exposed to import competition (since it was required that the goods produced be exported).

Shortly thereafter, four special economic zones (SEZs) were set up in Guangdong and Fujian. The SEZs—described more fully in chapter 17—gave foreign businesses a foothold for their EP trade. Like other export-processing zones, the SEZs allowed imports in duty-free as long as they were used in the zone to produce exports. As in other developing countries, policies like the SEZs and export processing allowed

China to selectively promote exports alongside what was still primarily a system of import-substitution industrialization. The zones were enclaves that did not overly threaten the system of domestic protection. Guangdong and Fujian Provinces were also given special powers within the existing foreign-trade system. The provincial divisions of national FTCs were granted autonomy, as well as the right to retain foreign-exchange income they generated. Provincial authorities developed strong incentives to expand trade, and officials in both provinces became well known for their willingness to bend rules to facilitate trade. The special provisions, the incentives, and, above all, the proximity of Hong Kong fundamentally transformed Guangdong Province and made it into an export powerhouse. For the next 15 years, exports from Guangdong and Fujian grew twice as rapidly as those from the rest of China. Those provinces were fundamentally transformed from economic backwaters into crucial nodes in the global trade economy. Moreover, as we will see later, these two key early steps—reliance on Hong Kong as an intermediary and the importance of EP trade—have continued to shape China's trade development in important respects.

16.2.3   Liberalizing the Foreign-Trade System

By the mid-1980s, having created some initial breaches in the traditional system in Guangdong and Fujian, Chinese policy-makers began the task of liberalizing the main national trading system. Despite some occasional missteps (imports surged more than 50% in 1985), between 1984 and 1986, reformists created a provisional modified trade system. There were four key elements: (1) setting a realistic exchange rate, (2) demonopolizing the trading system, (3) liberalizing import prices, and (4) setting up a normal tariff system. Within a few years, they had transformed the rules for trade, largely dismantled the old foreign-trade monopoly, and created a framework for the subsequent growth of trade and investment. The policy stages in this transformation are worth noting:

a. Devaluation. A realistic currency value is a prerequisite for successful trade reform. Before reform, China, like most socialist and ISI economies, maintained an overvalued currency. In 1980, the official rate was 1.5 Chinese yuan to the U.S. dollar; at this rate, it was generally not profitable to export. Trade liberalization could not take place because at this unrealistic exchange rate, no company could make money exporting, while the demand for cheap foreign exchange to import was enormous. Figure 16.3 shows that by 1986, the official exchange rate for the RMB had declined by 57% in real terms against the dollar.[1] Figure 16.3 also shows that on the

---

1. The real exchange rate adjusts for inflation in both economies, using the consumer price index in China and the GDP deflator in the United States. Note that changes in the currency value affect the calculations of openness reported earlier in this chapter. Devaluation makes an economy appear more open because the value of the GDP denominator (measured in domestic currency units) declines

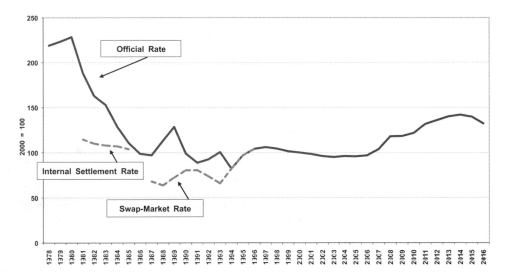

Figure 16.3
Real dollar value of the renmibi (2000 = 100).
Sources: Annual nominal RMB/USD rate, deflated by the Chinese CPI and U.S. implicit GDP deflator;
SYC and Saint Louis Federal Reserve Bank.

way to devaluation, Chinese policy-makers twice introduced dual exchange-rate systems. The first time, between 1981 and 1985, an "internal settlement rate" made it profitable for trade companies within the foreign-trade monopoly to export. The second time, policy-makers created a "swap market"—a lightly regulated secondary market—where exporters outside the foreign-trade system could sell their foreign-exchange earnings. In this market, dollars went for a higher RMB price, thus contributing to a further, market-driven devaluation of the yuan. These dual exchange-rate systems were examples of the dual-track reform strategy applied to foreign trade.

In 1994, another stage of reform further devalued the official rate and unified it with the swap-market rate at 8.6 to the dollar. At the same time, access to foreign exchange was dramatically liberalized, and the currency was made convertible on the current account at that time.[2] This brought the overall and official rates to their lowest level in the reform era; markets for foreign exchange stabilized, and exports

---

relative to the trade numerator (measured in dollars). Also, focusing on the RMB exchange rate with the U.S. dollar does not account for changes in the value of the dollar relative to other world currencies.

2. "Convertible on the current account" means that anyone with a verifiable transaction on the current account (i.e., export, import, service transaction, or profit/interest payments) can purchase foreign exchange by showing proof of that approved transaction.

and imports both jumped (figure 16.1). Subsequently, the exchange rate was essentially pegged to the dollar, remaining at 8.27 through mid-2005. Changes in real rates between 1994 and 2005 were due entirely to differentials in domestic inflation rates (later changes are discussed below).

b. Demonopolization of the foreign-trade regime. The number of companies authorized to engage in foreign trade was allowed to expand dramatically. Industrial ministries were allowed to set up FTCs; the provincial branches of the former national foreign-trade monopolies became independent; and many local governments and SEZs set up trading companies. By 1988, there were 5,000 FTCs, every single one of which was state owned. Direct export and import rights were also granted to some 10,000 manufacturing enterprises. Exports were liberalized much more rapidly than imports. Equally important, there was a steady shift away from the trade plan and in the direction of financial incentives. The old export procurement plan was abandoned in 1988. Foreign-exchange targets and contracting systems similar to those used in industry were applied to FTCs (see chapter 14). Provinces contracted to make fixed annual payments of foreign exchange to the central government and retained all foreign exchange earned above the contract.

c. Liberalizing prices. World prices were gradually allowed to influence domestic prices. On the export side, competing FTCs became much more cost sensitive: exporting predominantly on their own account, FTCs recontracted with domestic enterprises in an effort to lower costs. FTCs sought out cheap producers of labor-intensive goods, which were often township and village enterprises (TVEs). The share of exports produced by TVEs increased rapidly, accounting for one-fifth of procurements by FTCs by the mid-1990s. On the import side, the system steadily adapted to transmit world price signals to the domestic economy. Imports began to be priced according to the agency system, in which domestic prices equal the world price plus a commission paid to the importer, instead of being assigned a domestic planned price equivalent. Stronger incentives pushed trading companies to adapt to opportunities that were increasingly shaped by world prices.

d. A system of tariffs and nontariff barriers. Chinese reformers proceeded cautiously. They were wary of making mistakes and afraid of import surges, trade deficits, and hard-currency debt. Therefore, even as reformers dismantled the planned trade system, they erected high tariff walls and substantial nontariff barriers to maintain a degree of protection of the domestic market. Under the old air-lock system, tariffs had existed but had been irrelevant because the FTCs would carry out the trade plan, and revenues and tax payments were redistributed later as necessary. In the early 1980s, a new tariff system was introduced that set high tariffs for the next two decades. According to the analysis of the World Bank (1994, 56, 67), China's tariffs were similar to those of other highly protected developing countries. The unweighted mean tariff was 43%, and the trade-weighted mean tariff was 32% (the same as that of Brazil at that time). Equally important were nontariff barriers (NTBs). The same World Bank study found that 51% of imports were subject to one or more of four different overlapping nontariff barriers. Indeed, NTBs and tariffs were "used in a complementary fashion to achieve the government's objectives" (67). For example, nonessential consumer goods had high tariffs, while consumer "essentials" were "canalized" to monopoly FTCs administered by the central government. Overall, the most important NTB was simply that import rights were primarily reserved for the state-owned FTCs. Manufacturing enterprises sometimes had limited trading rights but were authorized to import only for their own production needs. Overall Chinese imports were regulated by a combination of tariffs, quotas, and administrative guidance exercised over state-owned trading companies.

After the mid-1980s, China had in place a system of high tariffs, multiple nontariff barriers, and abundant administrative discretion that in many ways was typical of a developing country pursuing an ISI strategy. This was far better than the previous planned system. Steady reforms created an essential minimum of flexibility that allowed access by new exporters and transmitted world prices to the economy. But this partially reformed system was by no means liberal enough in itself to create the dramatic Chinese export success. Instead, the most important such measure was the creation of an entirely separate export-processing trading regime, which allowed exporters to simply bypass the old centralized foreign-trade monopoly.

16.3   A Dualist Trade Regime: The Strange Career of Export-Processing Trade

The early experiments with export-processing contracts that had begun in Guangdong Province as early as 1978 gradually grew into a full-blown export-processing regime. After 1986, recognizing the opportunities for China in the ongoing restructuring of Asian export-production networks, Chinese policy-makers started supporting the "Coastal Development Strategy." All types of firms in the coastal provinces, including TVEs, were allowed to engage in processing and assembly contracts. Foreign investors began to move into China's coastal provinces on a large scale, and they were allowed to adopt a more flexible variant of export-processing contracts in which they took ownership of components and raw materials imported duty-free. By the late 1980s, China had established what were, in essence, two separate trading regimes. EP or export-processing trade grew rapidly and soon surpassed "ordinary trade" (OT) in size, notwithstanding the significant reforms that had been made in the OT system.

These two trading systems exist to the present day. However, their functions and relative roles have changed in surprising ways. Originally introduced as a makeshift way to allow Hong Kong businesses to employ cheap Chinese labor to sew blue jeans, EP trade has morphed into a massive system that is an integral part of virtually all global high-technology production networks, particularly electronics. Precedents for the Chinese EP regime can be found in the trade strategies followed by East Asian forerunner economies, but what is unusual is the sheer scale on which these provisions were introduced in China. In most countries, such concessionary provisions are circumscribed within a designated and strictly policed EP zone. In essence, China created a gigantic EP zone throughout the entire coastal region. Although China's SEZs attracted a lot of attention, it is arguably more important that the boundaries of the EP regime extended far beyond the SEZs, to wherever an export-oriented firm was located.

The exemption from duties on imported inputs provided a significant cost advantage to firms in the EP regime. More important was that under the EP regime, exporters—predominantly foreign-invested enterprises (FIEs)—were allowed to sidestep the entire complex and unwieldy apparatus of import controls, canalization, and regulatory monopolies that restricted development of trade under the OT regime. Given these advantages, EP trade grew much more rapidly than OT trade. Figure 16.4 shows the enormous difference these factors made. The EP regime and FIEs together were the motors of China's export expansion. Figure 16.4 shows that EP trade climbed to 56% of total exports in 1996; it thus accounted for two-thirds of the increase in exports to that date. EP exports maintained this share through 2005 and only then

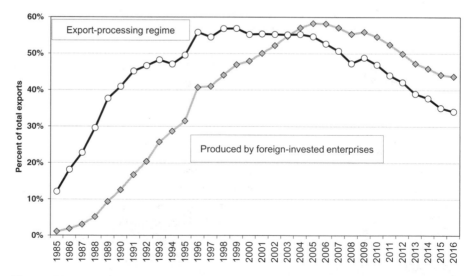

Figure 16.4
Share of exports from export-processing regime and foreign-invested enterprises.
Source: General Administration of Customs.

began a long, steady slide. FIEs, the largest number of which are from Hong Kong and Taiwan, have almost automatic access to the EP system and often received special tax concessions as well (chapter 17). FIEs inexorably increased their share of total exports in every year, starting from only 1% in 1985, reaching 58% in 2005, and maintaining roughly that share through 2010. From a small base, FIEs gradually became important players in China's export growth, and between 1992 and 2005, they accounted for fully 63% of incremental exports. Clearly, the liberalization of the environment for foreign investment played a fundamental role in China's export success. The flip side of FIE export growth was the relatively less impressive performance of domestic firms. Ironically, domestic exporters had to wait for WTO membership to kick in before they could fully realize their export potential.

Processing trade got a new lease on life after the turn of the century, when it became the preferred mode for businesses producing electronics hardware for export. Complex electronics goods like desktop and laptop computers, smartphones, and telecommunications equipment were and are assembled in China's coastal regions. These products require large quantities of imported high-tech components, particularly central processing units and other semiconductors, as well as flat-panel displays (chapter 15). Thus the processing trade system was key to the integration of China's high-tech economy with that of Taiwan, Korea, and Japan and the creation of a pattern of triangular trade (described later).

After 2005, the share of both EP exports and FIE exports began a long, slow, steady decline. Of course, declining share is not the same thing as declining trade, and EP exports expanded through 2014, when they were double, in dollar terms, what they had been in 2005. Moreover, a certain part of the declining share of EP trade has been taken up by trade through bonded zones (special areas that for legal purposes are outside the domestic customs regime). These accounted for 7% of exports in 2014. Thus, although EP trade is no longer the driver of China's export expansion, it still constitutes one of the largest trading systems in the world, and it grew until 2014 (exports in all categories were lower in 2016 than in 2014).

Until recently, Chinese policy-makers thought of EP trade as a second-best type of trade, from which Chinese domestic firms do not benefit adequately. EP firms are often described as being stuck in the low-value-added links of production chains, of which U.S. high-tech giants are often the architects. To a certain extent, the relative decline of EP trade is due to this feeling. It is empirically accurate that, particularly in electronics production networks, Chinese firms are typically concentrated in labor-intensive assembly stages. However, this specialization reflected China's relative factor endowment when it was rapidly integrated into these networks. Only in 2016 did the Chinese government awake to the importance of EP exports and the possibility of expanding and upgrading those links. In any case, the more important reason for the relative decline of EP trade is that in the wake of China's WTO membership, the overall trade environment became far more open. We now turn to those changes.

16.4   WTO Membership and Steps to an Open Economy

From the mid-1990s, building on its achievements in creating a functioning trading regime, China began to move in the direction of a genuinely open economy. Membership in the WTO was a powerful motivating factor. Reforms undertaken before WTO accession in order to strengthen the case and prepare the economy for WTO membership were nearly as important as those undertaken afterward. The 1994 foreign-exchange reforms were part of the coordinated package of fiscal, financial, and trade reforms that were rolled out simultaneously at the end of 1993 and the beginning of 1994 (chapter 5). These unified the foreign-exchange market and greatly liberalized access to foreign exchange. One of the advantages of policy coordination was that the national taxation system was shifted to a much larger reliance on the value-added tax (VAT). The rules of the WTO permit exporters to rebate VAT on exports. Initially, the intention of reformers was to move quickly to full currency convertibility, including on the capital account, and establish a "managed float" for the Chinese currency. In this system, a flexible exchange rate would adjust to changes in supply and demand for foreign exchange, but the central bank would still intervene in the foreign-exchange market on occasion to stabilize the currency.

These plans were never realized, even though WTO membership went forward. In the macroeconomic turbulence that followed the Asian financial crisis of 1997–1998, all Asian currencies, including the RMB, came under intense downward pressure. The "managed float" gradually became a de facto fixed exchange rate vis-à-vis the U.S. and Hong Kong dollars. When Chinese exports started to grow rapidly after 2002, the fixed exchange rate, the lack of capital-account convertibility, and the relatively low value of the renminbi remained in place, setting the stage for the development of large trade surpluses after 2005 (figure 16.1; discussed in section 16.4.3).

16.4.1   The Changing Significance of WTO Membership

When China formally applied to rejoin the General Agreement on Tariffs and Trade (GATT, the forerunner of the WTO) in 1986, it seemed that the process might be quick and relatively painless. After all, China was at that time a pioneer of market reforms and was looked on in the West at least as favorably as Poland and Hungary, already GATT members. But it was not until 15 years later that China finally became the 143rd member of the WTO, on December 11, 2001. During those protracted negotiations, both China and the world trading institutions changed in fundamental ways.

The Uruguay Round negotiations that created the WTO in 1996 signaled a fundamental shift in the terms of global trade negotiations. Earlier agreements had been restricted to a clearly delineated "foreign-trade sector," and negotiations had focused on border taxes and restrictions. After 1996, negotiations increasingly concerned domestic regulation in the negotiating economies. In part, this shift came about because modern developed economies are now primarily service economies, and so international agreements understandably go beyond the former focus on internationally traded goods. Since services almost always involve some physical presence at the point of delivery, agreements about trade in services inevitably involve negotiations about regulation and investment conditions in the receiving, or importing, country. During the Uruguay Round, trade liberalization was achieved by a "grand bargain" between developing and developed countries: Developing countries got the promise of greater access for their agricultural products and light manufactures, especially textiles, and textile import quotas were eliminated in developed-country markets. Developed countries got the promise of improved access for, and protection of, their corporations operating in developing-country economies. This grand bargain cleared the way for the creation of the WTO and the extension of trade negotiations into new areas relating to services, investment, and intellectual property rights. This was exactly the bargain that China was required to make as a condition for WTO membership: granting broader and fairer access to its economy in exchange for greater access for its light manufactured exports to other countries. The terms of this complex bargain involved a vastly more complicated negotiating process than had initially been anticipated.

16.4.2   China's WTO-Driven Trade Reform

On the trade side, the most fundamental issue from the beginning was the requirement that China open up its OT regime. Most important was China's commitment to extend trading rights without restrictions, including giving trading rights to domestic and foreign private companies. Eventually, these new provisions were included in a foreign-trade law effective July 1, 2004. Under this law, the Chinese government no longer restricts trade to a limited number of state- owned FTCs. An exception is made for a few agricultural commodities where state trading is still permitted. In those cases, China committed to a system of tariff-rate quotas (TRQs) for specific products, agreeing to lower tariffs, but only to a certain ceiling to protect against import surges. The accession agreement specifically commits China to distribute a minimum share of the TRQ allocations to nonstate traders. The commitment to a more accessible trade system was the most important component of WTO accession in the foreign-trade arena.

Next most important were commitments to lower tariffs. China began lowering tariffs in preparation for WTO membership immediately after the foreign-exchange reforms of 1994, well before the actual agreements were finalized. The average nominal tariff was reduced in stages from 43% in 1992 to 17% in 1999, the year when the breakthrough in WTO negotiations finally came. In the agreement, China committed to lowering average industrial tariffs to 9.4% by 2005; this rate was achieved in 2004. The agreement lowered average agricultural tariffs to 15%, a rate that was also easily achieved.

16.4.3   The Impact of China's WTO Membership

WTO accession provoked substantial anxiety among Chinese policy-makers and, to a certain extent, the Chinese public. There were worries about whether Chinese industries were competitive with sophisticated foreign firms, and whether Chinese agriculture could withstand an onslaught of imported food. These worries turned out to be unfounded. Chinese industry responded well to the competitive challenge of import liberalization, and even the automobile industry (the focus of many fears) entered a golden age of expansion after WTO membership. Perhaps most striking is that far from being deluged by rapid import growth, China experienced a surge of exports in the wake of WTO membership that changed China and the world. Without FTCs acting as gatekeepers to the world market, Chinese domestic firms seized the opportunity for rapid expansion (see table 16.1).

The productivity surge in the wake of WTO membership was not well anticipated, and policy-makers were slow to respond. As figure 16.1 shows, China's exports surged from 2003 through 2007, while import growth lagged after 2004. A very large trade surplus opened up, averaging 7% of GDP from 2006 through 2008.[3] At this time, China's exchange rate had been fixed against the U.S. dollar since the Asian financial crisis (1997–1998), and it began to appreciate slightly only after July 2005, when the nominal peg was loosened. As figure 16.3 shows, the real value of the RMB was still significantly below its levels in 1997–1998 as late as 2005. (Given an unchanged nominal exchange rate, the real value was lower because inflation had been lower in China than in the United States.) Appreciation of the RMB would have helped moderate the growth of the trade surplus and keep global trade more balanced.[4] In fact, this is what happened after RMB appreciation began in earnest in November 2007. In 2009, China launched its massive stimulus program, and this expansion in domestic demand (which increases imports), combined with RMB appreciation, brought the surplus back down to manageable levels by 2010. In 2011, the Chinese surplus in

---

3. There is no absolute standard for a large surplus or deficit, but a widely accepted rule of thumb is that anything above 4% of GDP is unambiguously "large."

4. Currency appreciation makes a country's exports more expensive (and therefore less competitive) and imports less expensive (and therefore more attractive). Therefore, after a lag, appreciation reduces a trade surplus or increases a trade deficit, all else held constant.

Table 16.1
Chinese exports: Share of total by firm ownership.

	1995	2005	2016
State-owned enterprises	66.7%	22.2%	10.3%
Foreign-invested enterprises	31.5%	58.3%	43.7%
Private domestic firms	0.2%	14.7%	43.6%
Collective and other	1.5%	4.8%	2.4%

Sources: *China Customs Statistics* (1995, 12; 2005, 12); General Administration of Customs.

goods trade had declined to 2% of GDP, before widening again to 4.6% of GDP in 2016.

This period of explosive Chinese trade growth created a significant shock in global trading relationships. Large trade surpluses from large trading countries cause major trade tensions, and there is no global mechanism to induce countries to reduce such large surpluses. During 2006–2008, many countries, including the United States, urged China to let its currency appreciate more rapidly, but China rejected these criticisms as unwarranted interference in domestic policy-making. In the United States, imports from China tripled between 2001 and 2007, creating substantial economic dislocation. The U.S. bilateral trade deficit jumped from $83 billion in 2001 to over $259 billion in 2007 (according to U.S. Customs data). This rapid change overwhelmed the domestic adjustment process in the United States. Autor, Dorn, and Hanson (2013) showed that local labor markets in the United States that were most exposed to competition from Chinese imports lost the most, and that trade-related job losses were not made up by increased employment in nontraded or export-oriented sectors in those localities. In other words, the frictions involved in adjusting to trade were costlier and longer lasting than economists typically expect. As a result, the costs of trade were large and persistent, as well as geographically concentrated. The gains from trade to the United States were also large, but they were spread over all U.S. consumers (in the form of lower prices) or taken as higher profits of U.S. firms importing goods. Since this episode was followed immediately by the global financial crisis, there was no opportunity for economic growth in the United States to reduce the adjustment costs.

16.5   Composition of Trade

Each stage of the liberalization of China's foreign-trade system has been associated with a surge in exports and imports. The result has been an extraordinarily diverse basket of export goods, combined with an import basket dominated by resources, intermediates, and components.

16.5.1   Exports

After 1979, exports at first grew rather indiscriminately. As late as 1985, petroleum was China's largest single export, accounting for 20% of export earnings. Between 1985 and 1995, the systemic changes described in section 16.2.3 drove a dramatic shift to the export of labor-intensive commodities and a correspondingly large decline in natural-resource-based exports. One of the marks of the inefficiency of China's foreign-trade regime before liberalization was that light, labor-intensive manufactures were a small share of China's exports despite China's obvious factor endowments. However, by 1995, all of China's top export commodities were labor-intensive manufactured goods, most strikingly textiles and garment exports, footwear, sporting goods, and miscellaneous manufactures.

The renewed liberalization of the trading regime signaled by WTO accession led to another surge in China's trade. The growth of traditional labor-intensive manufactures, particularly garments, remained robust. Aided by the end of textile import quotas in 2004, production and exports shifted to China. The post-WTO surge was also associated with a dramatic increase in the share of machinery and electronics, from 22% in 1995 to 47% in 2007, after which it leveled off. In other words, having already shifted to encompass labor-intensive manufactures, China's exports now deepened to include manufactures that are much more capital and technology intensive. This has left China exporting an extraordinarily broad range of manufactures, an export composition more typical of a developed country. Openness initially led to an export bundle that strongly reflected China's fundamental factor endowments; then, as development continued, that export bundle broadened smoothly to include goods that embodied increasing capital and technology. The most important exports and imports in 2016 are shown in table 16.2.

Rising wages for semi-skilled and unskilled workers are eroding the cost competitiveness of China's labor-intensive exports. Overall, labor-intensive manufactures made up 27.7% of China's exports in 2016, down from 33.5% in 2003. The decline was concentrated in textiles and garments, which declined to 12.5% of exports in 2016 from 18% in 2003. All other labor-intensive manufactures—shoes, toys, sporting goods—have almost maintained their share, slipping only from 15.5% to 15.2% over the same period. Shifts in competitiveness are manifesting slowly. In part, this is because some labor-intensive production has migrated inland, where wages are lower (section 16.8); in part, it reflects the excellent trade infrastructure and network of suppliers that helps keep overall costs low in China. As table 16.2 shows, electronics products are still important, and have retained their share unchanged. Machinery and industrial materials, such as steel, have increased their share of exports. China's export composition shows a steady shift away from labor-intensive products toward capital-intensive products over the past decade. However, these shifts should be

Table 16.2
Top import and export categories, 2016 (billions of US$).

	Imports	% of total		Exports	% of total
Semiconductors	227.0	14.3	Computers, components,	163.2	7.8
Petroleum and products	144.1	9.1	LCDs		
Autos and auto parts	74.4	4.7	Clothing	157.8	7.5
Agricultural products	69.1	4.4	Telephone handsets	117.1	5.6
except grain			Textiles	105.0	5.0
Computer components, LCDs	59.2	3.7	Agricultural products	72.6	3.5
Iron ore	57.7	3.6	Semiconductors	61.0	2.9
Copper and copper ore	47.1	3.0	Finished steel	54.5	2.6
Grain	41.5	2.6	Furniture	47.8	2.3
Plastic raw materials	41.3	2.6	Shoes	47.2	2.3
Coal	24.5	1.5	Automobile parts	45.6	2.2

Source: General Administration of Customs.

understood in the context of rapid growth: exports in 2016 were five times what they had been in 2003, and even textile and garment exports were 3.3 times greater. From the standpoint of the global market, Chinese competitiveness is still formidable, even in traditional labor-intensive manufactures.

16.5.2   Imports

Imports have continued to be concentrated in resources and capital- and technology-intensive products. The larger volume of these imports has increased China's gains from trade. Many of the most important Chinese imports serve essentially as land substitutes, stretching China's limited land endowment. However, the composition of these imports has shifted significantly in the past decade. In 2003, 23.9% of China's imports were capital-intensive commodities, often produced in heavy, process-technology industries: steel, chemicals, synthetic fibers, and plastic raw materials. These commodities have declined to 17% of China's imports, reflecting the substantial growth of China's heavy industrial base.[5] Instead of importing these processed industrial materials, China now imports an extraordinary quantity of natural resources and mining products: 34.2% of total imports, more than double the 16.1% share in 2003. The most important category comprises oil and gas, accounting for 10.1% of total imports. Metallic ores—primarily iron and copper—make up 6.6% of imports. Finally, food, beverages, and oilseeds make up another 5.8% of imports. These capital- and land-intensive products account for over half of imports. The next

5. SITC categories 5 and 6, excluding 65 textiles.

major category of imports consists of skill-intensive commodities including machinery, transport machinery, and electronics. Electric and electronic equipment—mostly high-tech components for hardware assembled in China—account for 28.5% of imports.

Chinese trade overwhelmingly corresponds to comparative-advantage principles and is likely of enormous benefit to the Chinese domestic economy. China has a substantial impact on world markets for several of these commodity groups: copper, iron ore, fertilizers, and, increasingly, petroleum. These are areas where Chinese demand moves world markets.

16.5.3   Service Trade

China's service trade—exports and imports—has grown gradually over 30 years from 2% of GDP in the mid-1980s to 6.4% of GDP in 2015. China's service trade has three distinctive features. First, the overall size of China's service trade as a share of GDP is only half the world average (13%). Service trade as a share of GDP increases with GDP per capita, so the contrast is not quite so sharp when China is compared with middle-income country average (8.8%), but it is still striking. Second, among 2015 services the biggest service import was "travel and tourism" (56%), much higher than the world average (28%). It follows that nontravel service imports are a much smaller share of GDP than world averages (1.7% versus 4.7%). Third, since 2012 the service trade has consistently been in deficit of over 1% of GDP (1.2% in 2015). The service trade deficit can be set beside the consistent surplus in goods trade, reducing China's overall current account surplus. However, 90% of the service deficit accrues to the travel and tourism sector; all other service sectors combined are close to balance.

How do we explain these patterns? First, the large size of travel imports is at least partially a real phenomenon, reflecting the explosion of Chinese travel abroad and the large number of Chinese studying abroad (educational expenses abroad are included in travel). However, the very large recorded expenditures per traveler suggest that this item disguises some capital flight, as the opportunity of travel is used to purchase assets abroad (chapter 17). Taking account of this special factor, it is clear that service trade in general has fallen behind the robust pace set by growing goods trade. This seems to indicate that service-trade liberalization has lagged the liberalization of the goods trade. For many countries, business services, finance, and insurance are the largest service imports, but for China these are quite small. Since service trade often requires a physical presence, and thus investment, in the importing country, small service trade is plausibly related to slow liberalization of the investment environment for services (chapter 17).

16.6   Technological Sophistication

The rapid increase in China's export of electronics goods, especially laptop computers, is truly impressive. Does this trend mean that China is becoming a technology power? From an uncritical look at the data, particularly the share of China's exports classified as "high technology," the answer would seem to be "Yes." As shown in figure 15.4, China is by far the world's largest exporter of "high-technology" goods and accounts for nearly all the increase in global high-technology exports since the turn of the century. Thus China seems to have not only a strikingly diverse export economy, but also one that is unusually sophisticated.

However, this conclusion is based on misleading data. Virtually all the high-tech electronics goods that China exports are produced under the EP trading regime, and more than 85% are produced by FIEs. Electronics production worldwide is carried out through global production networks, chains that link production, research, and services that are performed in many different countries. China is already an integral link in many of these production networks. But inspection of the products exported and the processes carried out in China reveals that China is overwhelmingly concentrated on the final assembly stage of production. This is a labor-intensive, medium-skilled activity, not a high-tech activity. Classification of China's exports by technological level can thus be extremely misleading because while the final product is technologically sophisticated, the actual value added in China is not (e.g., for a laptop computer). Indeed, from the standpoint of value added in China, the activity is more usefully grouped with other labor-intensive products, such as garments and toys. Upward, Wang, and Zheng (2013) found that electronics goods were the largest single contributor to Chinese manufactured exports but had the lowest share of domestic value added in export value (36%) of any sector.

The distinction between value added in export production and gross value of exported commodities is important and has been the subject of much recent empirical work (Koopman et al. 2010; Koopman, Wang, and Wei 2012). For every economy, value added in export production is less than the gross value of exports, but this difference seems to be especially large in China, probably because of the history of reliance on EP trade. Upward, Wang, and Zheng (2013) found that the share of domestic value added in China's manufactured exports was 53% in 2003 and increased to 61% in 2006. Although they asserted that this is relatively low in an international context, the growth rate is rapid. These adjustments influence our judgments of China's trade sophistication, diversity of exports, and degree of openness, in each case causing us to lower our estimate. However, the rapid pace of increase of domestic value added indicates that China is rapidly climbing the ladder of sophistication. By the time our measures have been comprehensively improved, China may have already changed the patterns the measures are designed to analyze. The rapid increase in domestic value added demonstrates some of the benefits of participation in global production networks. China started off in low-value-added stages of production, but its participation turns out to have been a good way to facilitate technological borrowing, benefiting from learning by doing, and generating spillovers for domestic firms.

16.7   Trade Partners

The pattern of China's trade partners also reflects the history described above (see table 16.3). China runs huge trade deficits with Korea and Taiwan and huge trade surpluses with the United States, the EU, and Hong Kong. In the case of Hong Kong, the surpluses are a secondary phenomenon, matched by Hong Kong's surpluses with the United States and the EU. These flows reflect the patterns of import of components and subassemblies from Taiwan and Korea (and, to a lesser extent, Japan), followed by assembly and reexport, primarily to developed-country markets (including Japan). This triangular pattern is strongly characteristic of China's trade and reflects the close linkages between foreign direct investment and trade (since the exporting

Table 16.3
China's largest trading partners, 2015 (billions of US$).

	Exports	Imports	Total trade	Surplus
United States	502.6	150.5	653.2	352.1
Japan	160.6	143.1	303.7	17.5
Hong Kong	261.1	12.8	273.9	248.3
Republic of Korea	90.2	174.6	264.8	−84.3
Germany	103.3	87.7	191.0	15.7
Taiwan	44.9	143.3	188.2	−98.4
Australia	46.3	73.9	120.2	−27.6
Malaysia	33.2	53.3	86.5	−20.0
United Kingdom	63.0	18.9	81.9	44.1
Thailand	40.9	37.2	78.1	3.7
Brazil	30.7	44.3	75.1	−13.6
India	61.6	13.4	75.0	48.2
Viet Nam	49.4	25.1	74.6	24.3
Singapore	42.1	27.6	69.7	14.6
Netherlands	38.4	8.8	47.2	29.6

Source: *SYC* (2016, table 11-6).

firms in China are often subsidiaries of firms from Taiwan or Korea). The rapid internationalization and geographic redistribution of production networks in the wake of China's adoption of the EP trading system created this triangular trade.

16.8   Accommodating Structural and Regional Change

Growth of trade has accommodated the structural changes described in chapters 6 and 7 of this volume. Long-distance migration from interior provinces to the booming export-manufacturing zones of the coast has been a central part of the Chinese developmental experience and a key driver of structural change. The steady expansion of the export sector permitted the steady expansion of urban employment during the period when labor supply was growing rapidly. Most important, export expansion allowed the high-investment, rapid industrialization growth strategy to roar forward without impediment as people and production moved to export areas.

Foreign trade unsurprisingly benefits the coastal regions of China, and the coastal provinces grew significantly more rapidly than inland provinces on the strength of trade-related demand through 2006 (section 2.6). Different coastal regions, however, responded to the stimulus of trade at different times and in different ways. In the early years, trade provided an enormous stimulus to the southern coastal provinces of Guangdong and Fujian. Table 16.4 shows that the share of China's total exports produced in the Southeast—the coastal provinces of Guangdong, Fujian, and Hainan—rose dramatically from 16% in 1978 to 45% in 1995. These provinces benefited the most from preferential policies during the 1980s and from the growth of foreign investment and EP trade. Guangdong, in particular, was encouraged to take "one step ahead" of the rest of the economy and become an economic showcase—perhaps even to become a "Fifth Tiger," following the "Four Tigers," the newly industrialized

Table 16.4
Regional shares of China's exports.

	1978	1995	2005	2010	2016
Southeast	16%	45%	36%	34%	36%
Lower Yangtze	35%	21%	38%	42%	37%
Northeast / North Coast	40%	22%	18%	17%	15%
Rest of China	9%	11%	7%	8%	13%

Source: *SYC* (2016, table 11-9); *SAC* (2017, 96).
Southeast: Guangdong, Fujian, and Hainan.
Lower Yangtze: Shanghai, Jiangsu, and Zhejiang.
Northeast/North Coast: Shandong, Beijing, Tianjin, Hebei, Liaoning, Jilin, and Heilongjiang.

economies of Korea, Taiwan, Hong Kong, and Singapore. During this initial period, the rise of the Southeast eclipsed the growth of the region that had traditionally been China's richest and most sophisticated economic macroregion, the Lower Yangtze (chapter 2). The Lower Yangtze grew robustly in the 1980s but was not oriented toward foreign trade in the same way as the Southeast.

However, after the mid-1990s, the Lower Yangtze came roaring back. Powered by significant inflows of foreign investment (see chapter 17), the Lower Yangtze saw its share of Chinese exports increase significantly, climbing back above its previous high to 42% in 2010. The share of the Southeast, by contrast, declined to 36% in 2005, before stabilizing. During this period, its exports continued to grow at a pace that would be considered quite healthy in most economies, and it managed a significant technological upgrading in the Shenzhen SEZ (section 15.4.4).

Inland provinces remained second-tier players until 2010, when their share of exports was still only 8%. However, after 2010 several large exporters began to move inland in search of lower wages. Chongqing, Sichuan, and Henan increased exports very rapidly through 2014 as national policy supported their bids for some of the large electronics assemblers. In 2016, inland provinces produced 13% of China's exports. Thus, China's export miracle has in fact been composed of three successive waves: the Southeast, the Yangtze Delta, and the inland provinces taking the lead in export expansion in different periods.

The areas left outside this story have been the closely linked Northeast and northern coastal regions (section 2.3), whose relative share has declined steadily. These northern regions were a major force in China's trade in the 1980s, with their diversified heavy industrial base and petroleum. However, their share had slipped to 15% by 2016, and the three provinces of the Northeast now produce only 2.6% of China's exports. The region is in danger of becoming economically marginalized. By contrast, both the Lower Yangtze and southeastern China have maintained their positions in China's export economy. Guangdong Province is still the single largest exporting province, and has the highest export/GDP ratio, at 55% in 2016. This is well below its peak in the mid-1990s, when the value of exports (a gross value) was more than 100% of GDP (a net concept). Guangdong is not as export-dependent as Malaysia or Thailand (67% and 69% respectively), but is similar to export powers such as Korea or Poland (42% and 52%). The Lower Yangtze has an export/GDP ratio of 34%, about the same as Mexico (38%). Inland China, with exports just under 6% of GDP, is considerably less export-oriented than Brazil, at 12.5%. There are dramatic differences in the degree of openness and of trade dependence among China's regions.

16.9   Conclusion

China has achieved trade success through a combination of domestic economic reform and restructuring and an astute accommodation of the opportunities created by East Asian economic restructuring and foreign investment. Its achievement is especially impressive given how far China has come: from one of the most closed economies in the world, China has developed into the most open large economy in the world, and it has done so with a minimum of disruption and trade-related economic distress. China is like an economic union of a very open coastal economy and a less integrated inland economy, for example, a union of Malaysia and Brazil. Moreover, the very high trade/GDP ratios of economies like Malaysia or Thailand are achieved precisely because those countries are integral parts of cross-border global production networks, especially prominent in electronics. Those networks involve high-value items crossing borders as trade in order that relatively simple processing activities can be performed in different locations. This means that the value added in the export sector is small relative to the value of the trade flows. Of course, this is exactly the kind of activity that the Chinese dualistic trade regime was designed to encourage in the first place. But this outcome reminds us that the trade/GDP ratio is an index of openness, not a measure of the size of the traded-goods sector. Actual Chinese value added in the export sector is a smaller share of total national value added than might have been guessed just by taking clues from the trade/GDP ratio.

China's trade growth has enormous momentum. Since about 2005, wages of unskilled workers have climbed rapidly, and the cost competitiveness of labor-intensive manufactures has eroded. Moreover, the slowing global economy means that demand from developed countries can no longer be expected to grow as robustly as in the past. Therefore, foreign trade is unlikely to be as conspicuous a leading sector in the future as it was in the first decade of the twenty-first century. Whereas between 2000 and 2007, net exports (exports minus imports) were growing steadily, adding to aggregate demand, net exports declined (with the shrinking trade surplus) from 2008 through 2014. This means that trade has been making a net negative contribution to aggregate demand. These important structural changes will have enormous implications for China's trade growth in the future.

However, China continues to have strong trade competitiveness. Trade-related infrastructure in China is among the very best in the world (chapter 2). WTO-related liberalization lowered transaction costs, as well as import costs, as access to trading opportunities multiplied. In the years since WTO accession, a more open and integrated trade regime has propelled China to the front ranks of world traders. Because China's factor endowments vary significantly from those of the developed countries, China has a lot to gain from globalization. Its labor-rich and land-scarce economy will continue to benefit greatly from exchange based on comparative advantage, while its dynamic and relatively well-educated labor force can quickly absorb technology and skills by observing and imitating global best practice. China has more to gain from globalization than any other economy in the world except perhaps the United States.

Bibliography

References

Autor, David H., David Dorn, and Gordon Hanson (2013). "The China Syndrome: Local Labor Market Effects of Import Competition in the United States." *American Economic Review* 103 (6): 2121–2168.

General Administration of Customs. "China Customs Statistics Network." www.chinacustomstat.com /aspx/1/index.aspx.

Koopman, Robert, William Powers, Zhi Wang, and Shang-Jin Wei (2010). "Give Credit Where Credit Is Due: Tracing Value Added in Global Production Chains." Working Paper no. 16426, National Bureau of Economic Research, Cambridge, MA.

Koopman, Robert, Zhi Wang, and Shang-Jin Wei (2012). Estimating Domestic Content in Exports When Processing Trade Is Pervasive." *Journal of Development Economics* 99:178–189.

SAC (Annual). *Zhongguo Tongji Zhaiyao* [Statistical abstract of China]. Beijing: Zhongguo Tongji.

SYC (Annual). *Zhongguo Tongji Nianjian* [Statistical yearbook of China]. Beijing: Zhongguo Tongji.

Upward, Richard, Zheng Wang, and Jinghai Zheng (2013). "Weighing China's Export Basket: The Domestic Content and Technology Intensity of Chinese Exports." *Journal of Comparative Economics* 41:527–543.

World Bank (1994). *China: Foreign Trade Reform*. Washington, DC: World Bank.

The "openness" of an economy is measured not only with respect to exports and imports, but also with respect to inflows and outflows of capital. China has become more open to capital flows since 1978, but the process has been more difficult and less complete than the opening to trade has been. During the first two decades after 1978, China opened widely to incoming foreign direct investment (FDI), while other types of capital flows were still generally restricted. Since the mid-1990s, China has consistently been one of the world's most important destinations for FDI, and FDI has played an essential role in China's industrialization and in the overall process of reform.

In the twenty-first century, the relationship between FDI and the rest of the economy has begun to shift in fundamental ways. FDI has continued to grow, but much more slowly than overall GDP, and as a result, the relative weight of incoming FDI in the economy has been declining for years. Even as the relative weight of incoming FDI has decreased, new forms of inward and outward investment have grown in importance. When FDI poured into China, the overall capital account in China was closed: most kinds of financial investment in both directions were restricted. Today, some of those restrictions are being lifted as China moves toward an open capital account. At the same time, China's high saving rate has combined with slowing domestic growth to drive China's emergence as one of the world's largest sources of outbound investment. Chinese savings have flowed out of China in three primary forms, in successive waves. First, Chinese accumulation of official foreign-exchange reserves became very large from 2003 through 2011; second, Chinese outbound FDI increased very quickly after 2007; and third, diverse financial flows, both official and private, began to come out of China after 2011. As of 2016, China was a major source of saving and investment on a global scale. The first half of this chapter describes and analyzes FDI in China; beginning with section 17.7, the perspective is broadened to consider all important incoming and outgoing capital flows.

17.1   FDI in the Chinese Economy

Foreign direct investment is just one item on the capital account, along with portfolio investment (stocks and bonds) and other investment (including bank lending). However, until well into the twenty-first century, FDI was the only quantitatively significant form of capital inflow to China. FDI began to pour into China after 1992, and China became by far the largest developing-country host of FDI, accounting for about one-third of total developing-country FDI. The global manufacturing networks created by FDI in China reshaped China and the world and continue to play a critical role in the world economy.

17.1.1   Overall Trends

Foreign direct investment had been important in China's early industrialization: the famous Bund on Shanghai's riverfront preserves a vivid physical reminder of the prominent role foreign companies had in 1930s Shanghai. However, after 1949, China closed to FDI, with the minor exception of a few joint ventures operated with other socialist countries that were wrapped up in the late 1950s. When China decided to accept foreign investment in 1978, it broke sharply with socialist orthodoxy by establishing special economic zones (SEZs) in 1979 and 1980. Following this breakthrough, though, policy and institutional changes were cautious, incremental, and geographically localized through the 1980s. Incoming FDI grew during the 1980s and wrought important changes in the regional economies of Guangdong and Fujian, but nationwide, the impact of FDI was moderate through the 1980s. As figure 17.1 shows, beginning in 1992–1993, the stream of incoming FDI turned into a flood. Investors from Hong Kong moved in first, but investors from other countries followed close behind. Huge FDI inflows then fundamentally transformed the Chinese economy.

Chinese policy changes lay behind the upsurge of investment in 1992–1993. Policy dramatically expanded the types of FDI that were acceptable. Until that time, China had largely confined incoming FDI to export manufacturing (as well as geographically to the southeast coast); access to the Chinese market had been dribbled out to only a few selected foreign firms. From 1992, China began selectively opening its domestic marketplace to foreign businesses and relaxing geographic restrictions. Manufacturers were increasingly granted rights to sell their output on the Chinese market and new sectors such as real estate were opened to foreign participation. For the first time, the huge potential size and rapid growth of the Chinese market played a direct role in attracting foreign investment. In addition, the 1992–1993 policy changes were especially consequential because for over a decade, China had been gradually building credibility with foreign investors, gaining experience

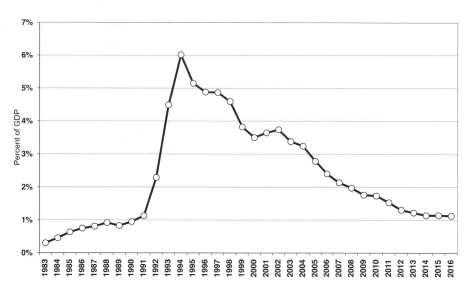

Figure 17.1
Foreign direct investment (share of GDP).
Source: *SYC* (2016, table 11-13; and earlier volumes).

while liberalizing and building institutional infrastructure. When Deng Xiaoping made his famous "Southern Tour" in the spring of 1992, he dissolved the anxiety about China's overall policy direction that had lingered since the Tiananmen incident, and foreign investors were quick to respond because the institutional foundations and FDI-friendly policies had already been put in place.

Figure 17.1 shows the dramatic rise and sustained fall of foreign direct investment as a share of Chinese GDP. During the 1980s, although FDI never exceeded 1% of GDP, inflows crept steadily upward and then surged to 6% of GDP in 1994. Since that time, FDI has grown more slowly than nominal GDP, stepping down to 3% to 4% of GDP between 1999 and 2004 and then trending steadily down to just over 1% in 2014–2016. These ratios can be situated in the context of two other Asian models of policy toward FDI. In the "Northeast Asian" pattern, characteristic of the Asian forerunner economies of Japan, Korea, and Taiwan in the 1950s through the 1980s, incoming FDI was always restricted and was considerably less than 1% of GDP. These countries allowed selective entry of FDI as a part of their national industrial policies. After the late 1990s, Korea, Japan, and Taiwan all relaxed controls over FDI, but inflows have never amounted to as much as 2% of GDP in these countries. By contrast, in the "Southeast Asian" model, the export-driven economies of Malaysia, Thailand, the Philippines, and Indonesia have generally welcomed FDI and inflows around 4% to 6% of GDP have been common. Generally speaking, then, China went from a closed economy to a "Southeast Asian" pattern of openness to FDI, particularly in export-oriented manufacturing. Today, it seems to be returning to a "Northeast Asian" pattern in which reliance on incoming FDI is curtailed and shaped by industrial policy.

Regional differences in Chinese FDI are large. During the decade of peak importance of FDI in China, from 1993 through 2002, many regions of China were substantially more open to FDI than a "typical" Southeast Asian nation. For those ten years, annual inflows of FDI averaged 12.7% of GDP in the three southeast coastal provinces of Guangdong, Fujian, and Hainan; 8.3% of GDP in Beijing and Tianjin; and 7.6% of GDP in Shanghai and Jiangsu. Thus, the open areas of China accepted proportionately about twice as much FDI as even the highly open economies of Southeast Asia. These regional economies were fundamentally transformed by incoming FDI. The remainder of China was much less affected: the 18 inland provinces with hosted annual incoming flows of FDI equal to 1.4% of GDP on average during that decade.

In absolute terms, incoming FDI continued to increase through 2011, before leveling off (figure 17.3). As China's GDP has grown rapidly—and the Chinese currency appreciated between 2005 and 2014 (figure 16.3)—the ratio of incoming FDI to GDP has declined steadily and seemingly converged toward 1% around 2016. FDI no longer has the transformative impact it had in the 1990s and China is, to some degree, less open to FDI than it was 20 years ago. This certainly reflects a less welcoming policy toward foreign investment from China.

However, foreign investment still has enormous importance in China. In many sectors, foreign firms are now well established and able to fund their expansion through retained profits. In theory, re-invested profits of foreign firms should be counted in incoming FDI, but they are almost certainly undercounted in Chinese statistics. The policies that once kept FDI bottled up in export-oriented sectors and regional enclaves are now long gone, and foreign-invested enterprises (FIEs) are deeply embedded in many sectors of the Chinese economy. Enright (2017, 37) calculates that domestic sales of FIEs surpassed export revenues in 2005, and that by 2013 domestic sales were 2.7 times that of exports. As we discuss in section 17.5, the foreign enterprise impact is especially notable in manufacturing.

17.2   "Zones": Gradual Liberalization of the Investment Regime

China used the establishment of special zones to pioneer the liberalization process. Today, zones still exist and carry out important functions, but their role in the national economy has changed dramatically.

17.2.1   The Function and Significance of Special Economic Zones (SEZs)

One of the peculiarities of China's FDI landscape is the proliferation of special investment zones of various kinds. The establishment of the first Special economic zones
(SEZs) in China in 1979 was a strikingly visible signal of commitment to economic
opening, and China has subsequently marked every major wave of liberalization with
the establishment of a new batch of zones. The most recent batch, led by the Shanghai Pilot Free Trade Zone, was launched in 2013 to test implementation of a new, more
liberal regime with respect to services and financial transactions. Over time, special
zones have become "less special" as concessionary policies for foreign investors
have been scaled back across the board. Even so, much foreign investment is still
located in zones of various kinds, and the rules of business are still subtly different
inside the zones. Why does Chinese policy have this proclivity for special zones? The
SEZs exemplified the pattern of Chinese policy-making during the first era of reform
(as described in chapter 5): dual-track, incremental reforms that started by creating a
new system alongside, or in the interstices of, the existing one. Moreover, they are
consistent with the dualistic system that was such a prominent feature of the trading
regime (chapter 16). Zones permitted rapid incremental progress within the confines
of an initially rigid system.

Deng Xiaoping's endorsement of the SEZs 1979 and 1980 meant that they became
a symbol of the government's commitment to external liberalization. Zones permitting foreign businesses free operation in China were inevitably sensitive because of
China's history of foreign concessions. Conservatives opposed to economic reforms
could easily portray zones as a derogation of China's sovereignty. Precisely for this
reason, the establishment of the SEZs served as a powerful commitment device. By
demonstrating to foreign businesses that China would maintain an open environment
in a specific, easily monitored, location, the SEZs enhanced the credibility of the
reform process. At the same time, zones played a powerful symbolic role whenever
the reform policies were contested: on two subsequent occasions (1984 and 1992),
Deng Xiaoping traveled to the Shenzhen SEZ and endorsed its operation as a pre-
lude to a further wave of liberalization.

17.2.2   The Role and Proliferation of SEZs

The initial SEZs were similar to the export-processing zones (EPZs) that had spread
in Asia since the 1970s: they were regions in which foreign investment was encouraged by lower tax rates, fewer and simplified administrative and customs procedures,
and, most crucially, duty-free import of components and supplies (see box 17.1). Thus
the SEZs were part of the early development of the export-processing regime
described in chapter 16. But the SEZs also went beyond the other Asian EPZs (see
box 17.2). Because they also served as test beds for domestic economic reforms, they

Box 17.1
How Chinese SEZs are similar to Asian EPZs.

China's special economic zones are a type of export-processing zone. The first export-processing zone in Asia was established at Kaohsiung in Taiwan in 1965. By the 1980s, there were 35 EPZs in Asia, and most countries had them. A strikingly successful example has been the Penang Free Trade Zone in Malaysia, which initiated the development of Malaysia's substantial electronics industry. All Asian EPZs offer an essentially similar set of incentives for investors. First, components and raw materials can be imported duty-free and without administrative formalities; and exports leave the zone without export or sales taxes. Thus the zones are outside the country in which they are located insofar as normal customs procedures are concerned. Second, tax holidays on company incomes are typically granted for a period of 3 to 10 years. Third, the administrative procedures are streamlined, often through a "one-stop-shop" coordination of permits and usually through exemption from restrictions on foreign ownership and employment of foreign nationals that might apply in the rest of the economy. Fourth, the zone often operates as a commercial entity, building infrastructure and supplying utilities—often at a subsidized rate—to the foreign firms.

Asian EPZs offered a way to move toward export promotion without fundamentally overturning the structure of protection in place for domestic manufacturers. EPZs produced benefits in employment created and foreign exchange earned, but at the cost of giving up significant tax revenues and forgoing potential linkages to the remainder of the domestic economy. Many EPZs started slowly and ended up costing more than initially envisaged, but the policies have typically been seen as ultimately successful in most of the countries that have tried them. EPZs initially attract "footloose" investors in such sectors as garments and electronics assembly because of low wages and easy conditions for moving goods in and out. To varying degrees, some zones have been able to move beyond a few initial industries and contribute to a broader-based process of industrialization. Chinese SEZs share all these fundamental characteristics with other Asian EPZs.

inevitably had a broader role to play in China's economic evolution. For example, wholly owned foreign subsidiaries were permitted in the SEZs long before they were allowed elsewhere. Moreover, since each of the four initial SEZs was intended to appeal to an economically significant group of overseas Chinese (chapter 2), they connected with important groups who were potential investors. For all these symbolic and systemic reasons, the SEZs had great importance for China's economic reform.

A dramatic proliferation of zones began in the 1980s. Hainan Island was designated an SEZ, and the existing SEZs at Zhuhai, Shantou, and Xiamen were expanded enormously. Broad expanses of territory were subsequently declared open to foreign investment, including substantial rural areas. At the beginning of the 1990s, the second period of accelerated reforms was announced by the creation of another special economic zone. The Pudong (East Shanghai) Special Zone served as an advertisement and a commitment device by creating an SEZ in the heart of China's most developed region for the first time. Slightly larger than Shenzhen, Pudong possessed a population of 1.1 million even before development began. By the turn of the century, there were hundreds of zones, including 6 SEZs (the 4 original ones, Hainan, and Pudong), 54 national-level economic and technological

Box 17.2
How Chinese SEZs differ from Asian EPZs.

Chinese SEZs were bound to be more "special" than other Asian EPZs. Other Asian EPZs were established in economies that were basically market economies, albeit sheltered from world markets and competition by import-substitution-industrialization (ISI) policies. Chinese SEZs were created in a planned, bureaucratic economic system, so the difference between the rules of the game in the SEZs and those in the domestic economy was bound to be large.

• The SEZs often served as laboratories for experiments with economic reforms. For example, the Shenzhen SEZ was an early pioneer of both flexible wage systems (no limits on incentive payments) and tender bidding for construction projects. Experiments with development of land markets through leasehold and with equity markets have also been significant.

• The SEZs were governmental bodies with unusually high levels of autonomy compared with EPZs. During the early years, SEZs were allowed to retain much of the tax, customs, and foreign exchange revenues generated within them.

• The SEZs had multiple functions. They were seen as windows on the world, absorbing advanced experience in technology, administration, and business. Shenzhen in particular has been developed as a comprehensive site, including tourism, housing, and other services for Hong Kong people.

• Chinese domestic enterprises have also had a substantial incentive to invest in the SEZs. By setting up their own subsidiaries—even if they are not joint ventures with foreign businesses—Chinese domestic enterprises enjoy greater administrative flexibility, lower tax rates (15% income tax rather than 30%), and less complicated access to the outside world.

Because of their multiple roles and greater importance to the domestic economy, it is not surprising that China's SEZs are much bigger than other Asian EPZs, as the following table shows:

Size of China's S and Asian EPZs (square kilometers).

	Initial 1980 size	Size in 1990
Shenzhen	327.5	327.5
Zhuhai	6.8	121.0
Shantou	1.6	52.6
Xiamen	2.5	131.1
Kaohsiung, Taiwan		0.7
Penang, Malaysia		1.2
Batam Island, Indonesia		36.6
Bataan, Philippines		3.4

development zones, 53 nationally recognized high-tech industrial zones, and 15 bonded zones (in which commodities can be legally parked outside the country's customs borders).

These zones had the authority to provide tax concessions to foreign investors. It was common for zones to give tax holidays (three years with no income tax) and then reduced income tax rates. Most foreign firms were being charged a statutory rate of 15% on profits, at a time when the rate for domestic firms was 30%. Moreover, zones typically organized their own infrastructure and construction companies to provide up-to-date services for foreign investors. Given the competitive relationship among local governments (section 5.4), zones were convenient instruments to attract foreign investment. Local governments would even go so far as to provide cheap land and low utility rates to desirable FIEs, thereby contributing to local output and employment.

After 2013, several new Free Trade Zones were launched in conjunction with the rejuvenation of economic reform pursued under Xi Jinping and Li Keqiang. The most important was the Shanghai Pilot Free Trade Zone. The Shanghai FTZ was designed to test several innovations. Foreign businesses were allowed to operate wholly owned subsidiaries in service sectors generally closed to foreigners elsewhere in China, including hospitals, logistics, and insurance. Financial regulations were considerably less rigid, and firms were encouraged to establish unified financial centers for their China operations that could be legally offshore in most respects. The Shanghai FTZ also pioneered the use of a "negative-list" system, in which foreign firms were allowed to operate in any sector except those explicitly restricted by the negative list. Some of the innovations of the Shanghai FTZ were also allowed in FTZs set up in Tianjin and Guangdong (Qianhai Financial District and other associated zones). Early progress in these zones was slow, disappointing initially high expectations of rapid progress. However, it is too early to assess the ultimate impact of these new FTZs.

17.2.3   Normalization of the Rules in SEZs

Competition among zones and regions for FDI was accepted as normal in the early stages of China's opening, but as China's domestic enterprises strengthened, the government became less interested in providing preferential treatment to foreign firms. Although the tax reform of 1994 unified tax rates for domestic firms, it wasn't until 2008 that a unified enterprise income tax law applied to FIEs as well. A uniform national profit tax rate of 25% for domestic and foreign firms was instituted and gradually phased in by 2012. Around the same time, FIEs were brought into the system of local infrastructure taxes, social security and other payroll taxes, and educational surcharges. As the potential for special treatment has narrowed, special zones have inevitably become less special. However, special zones still exist and have substantial impact on the business environment for individual firms. Local governments still use the zones to attract foreign investment. In 2017, the inland province of Henan is spending billions to build a special bonded zone to attract the assembly of iPhones, carried out through a large investment by the Taiwan-based electronics assembler Foxconn. The most important functions of special zones are still intact.

17.3   The Impact of FDI

FDI has a multifaceted impact on the host economy. While FDI is a source of saving and investment, it differs from other capital flows in that it involves control over ongoing operations by the investor. FDI brings a bundle of skills and knowledge, such as management experience, marketing channels, production technology, and supply-chain management. Moreover, FDI is typically thought of as "patient capital" that remains in the host country over the long term, relatively unaffected by short-term fluctuations in economic conditions.

17.3.1   Contribution to Aggregate Saving and Investment

FDI is a form of fixed capital formation financed by foreign companies. It contributes to saving and investment and thereby facilitates structural change. This aspect of FDI is important for many developing countries but much less significant for China because of China's high domestic saving and investment rate. Chapter 7 discussed China's extremely high domestic investment rate. During the 1993–2002 decade of peak relative importance of FDI, it accounted for over 10% of total investment annually for of ten successive years. The decadal average of 13% of investment is close to—but slightly below—developing-country averages. According to UN figures, all developing countries excluding China experienced incoming FDI equal to about 15% of gross fixed capital formation in 1999–2001. Since that time, overall investment in China has climbed while FDI has waned, so FDI has accounted for less than 3% of total fixed investment since 2012. FDI in China is not an important contributor to aggregate saving and investment today.

17.3.2   Contribution to Foreign Trade

The largest and most unambiguous contribution of FDI to the Chinese economy came through its contribution to trade. The earliest foreign investors were exporters of light manufactures from Hong Kong and Taiwan. They sought in the China mainland cheap labor and facilities, and they brought extensive experience with developed country markets and managing supply and logistics. Chapter 16 described the central role that FIEs played in China's export expansion in the 1990s. Between 1992 and 2005, almost two-thirds of the increment to China's exports came from FIEs. In the early 2000s, a second wave of export restructuring brought to China the assembly of electronics hardware for export. This wave of FDI brought sophisticated production technology and familiarity with high-tech production networks to China. The quadrupling of exports between 2002 and 2007 would have been inconceivable without this investment.

17.3.3   Technology Transfer

As described in chapter 15, FIEs were the largest source of new technology in Chinese industry through the turn of the century, after which China's domestic R&D effort accelerated and surpassed the contribution from foreign investment. FIEs contribute to improving productivity in the economy even if they retain the economic benefits of their proprietary technologies. In addition, FIEs have a clear demonstration effect. Domestic firms can quickly understand and copy the business model of most FIEs. The circulation of workers and managerial personnel among firms—which takes place at a high rate in China—spreads hard and soft technologies from FIEs to domestic firms. In the first wave of FDI into China, this emulation was especially important. China had been cut off from all types of knowledge of global business for decades; the early-mover Hong Kong and Taiwan firms had rich experience of developed-country markets and modern business practices. Those early investors brought with them simple production technologies for garments, toys, and shoes that were relatively easy to imitate. As FIEs brought more sophisticated technologies, the learning of new technologies continued to take place, but proceeded through more complex mechanisms.

17.3.4   Competition and Emulation

Foreign firms provide competition for domestic firms. This competition pushes down product prices and cuts into profit margins, forcing firms to respond. Not all local firms can respond effectively, and some are forced into bankruptcy. However, surviving firms display increased productivity improvement as they respond to competition. Brandt et al. (2017) showed that productivity improvement in Chinese industry during the 1995–2007 period was greatest in sectors where WTO-related tariff reductions were greatest. Competition from FIEs is similar, with the additional circumstance that domestic competitors are often in close proximity to FIEs, and can benefit from direct observation and from hiring workers with experience in the FIE.

17.3.5   Spillovers and Upgrading

One of the most important spillover mechanisms is supplier relations. Medium- and high-technology industries typically have complex networks that link suppliers to final assembly firms. When these manufacturers of final goods first moved to China, they imported most of their supplies. Automobiles, for example, at first assembled imported "kits," and computer manufacturers assembled imported components. Initial spillovers of skills and technology were limited. However, FIEs in competitive industries face complex and somewhat contradictory incentives.

On one hand, FIEs have an incentive to protect their core technologies, intellectual property, and business models. The spillover of knowledge to competitors weakens a firm. Foreign companies often elect to keep their most sensitive research and development and intellectual property in the home country (where, to be fair, high-quality research can often be carried out more efficiently). Electronics firms especially often manage production chains in which a few core components embody the most valuable intellectual property, and these technologies can be relatively easily screened from the adjacent processing and assembly steps. For example, this is obviously the case with respect to central-processing units for desktop and laptop computers. China's export-processing (EP) trade regime makes it easy for firms to import a small number of high-value components. These business adaptations protect the investing firm but also limit the positive spillovers from FDI to domestic Chinese firms.

On the other hand, in competitive industries such as these, no manufacturer can maintain such a high-cost business model for long. Producers will also work to qualify and upgrade domestic suppliers in order to lower their costs. The spillover of knowledge to suppliers improves the FIE's competitive advantage, while fostering development in the economy. Auto manufacturers, for example, quickly saw the need both to persuade their partner firms producing parts and subassemblies to invest in China and to help domestic firms develop into low-cost suppliers. This provided a potent impetus to create a network of supplier firms, both domestic and foreign owned, to supply the auto industry. Domestic Chinese auto parts companies, including Wanxiang, emerged from this market environment. Final-product firms in competitive industries have a strong incentive to help local, low-cost suppliers qualify in terms of quality and reliability.

17.4   Sources of Investment in China

17.4.1   Main Source Regions

China is distinctive as a host country for incoming FDI in that most of the investment comes from its near neighbors and a limited share from developed countries. This is an important real feature of Chinese FDI, but it is also overstated by the way China collects FDI data. According to official Chinese data, Hong Kong is indisputably the biggest investor in China, accounting for 52% of the cumulative total from 1985 to 2016 ($934 billion out of $1.8 trillion). Equally striking is that the developed-country triad of the United States, the EU, and Japan has accounted for only 17% of incoming FDI, about $300 billion. Also noteworthy is the prominent role played by Taiwan, Korea, and, especially recently, Singapore.

Chinese FDI data report the place of legal registration of the company carrying out the investment, not that company's ultimate home. The British Virgin Islands (B.V.I.), the Cayman Islands, and Samoa—well-known "free ports" and tax havens—have been big investors in China. Indeed, B.V.I. was the second-largest investor in China from 1985 through 2016. The rank of source countries in cumulative investment, according to Chinese data, has been Hong Kong, B.V.I., Japan, Singapore, United States, Taiwan, and Korea. However, this listing is unrealistic, and in particular understates the importance of Taiwan, which is known to have channeled a large proportion of its outgoing investment through these tax havens. Given the impossibility of untangling the data, figure 17.2 shows investment from four source regions. In this figure, Taiwan, Korea, and Singapore are aggregated with tax-haven jurisdictions to show roughly the importance of these near neighbors (of course, other source countries besides Taiwan may also channel investment through tax havens). Korean investment is also quite large: according to official Chinese data, it has surpassed that of Japan and the United States in some years. The Korean company Samsung is the largest single corporate investor in China.

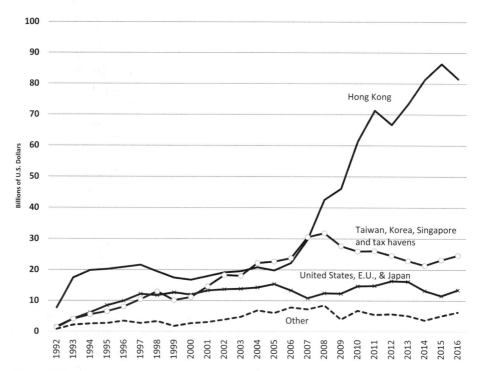

Figure 17.2
Main FDI source regions.
Source: *SYC* (2016, table 11-14; and earlier volumes).

U.S. investment in China is substantially greater than the amounts shown in Chinese data. According to Chinese records, the United States invested $77 billion in China between 1990 and 2015. However, Hanemann, Rosen, and Gao (2016) independently compiled a record of FDI in China by companies with U.S. headquarters, using commercial databases, press reports, and individual company disclosures, and counted total U.S. FDI in China was $228 billion in the same period, three times the Chinese figure.[1] Taiwan, the United States, the United Kingdom, and Hong Kong all have a relatively high propensity to route investment through free ports as well as through Hong Kong and Singapore subsidiaries. The figures strongly suggest that the United States accounts for about 10% of incoming Chinese FDI rather than the 4.6% shown in Chinese data. A plausible reconstruction of the actual ranking of ultimate sources of Chinese FDI would be Hong Kong, United States, Taiwan, Japan, Korea, and Singapore.

The largest sector for U.S. investment was information and communications technology (ICT), including hardware, software, and information technology services; the next three sectors were chemicals and materials, energy, and automotive and transport equipment. American corporations prefer to invest in Shanghai, which hosts $53 billion in U.S. FDI, followed by Beijing at $36 billion. This shows that U.S. investors are less deeply involved in the export-oriented investment networks that dominate Guangdong and Fujian and more oriented toward the Chinese domestic market.

As China's industrial policies have become more interventionist since 2005 (chapter 15), developed-country investors have been disproportionately affected, and their share of incoming investment has declined. U.S. investment has drifted downward since 2012, while Japanese investment has also been affected by the souring of relations between China and Japan. Investment from the European Union has held up comparatively well. However, we can judge that FDI in China today does not fully exploit the potential for developed-country inflows, and especially large potential complementarities between Japan and China remain unexploited. This is in contrast to the 1990s, when FDI played a predominant role in sparking a new wave of industrialization and technological upgrading.

17.4.2   The Special Role of Hong Kong

Hong Kong is not just the largest investor in China; its role is special in almost every respect (for example, with respect to outgoing investment; see section 17.6). On July 1, 1997, the former British colony of Hong Kong became a special administrative region

---

1. The figures are not fully comparable, since Hanemann, Rosen, and Gao included some types of financial transactions that are excluded from the Chinese data.

(SAR) of China. Thus China's largest foreign investor is not really foreign. However, there are abundant reasons to treat Hong Kong as "foreign" beyond habitual practice. Hong Kong has a dramatically different economic and administrative system from that of China; it has a much higher level of economic development than the rest of the mainland; the SAR government has decision-making authority over virtually all important economic decisions, including trade regulations; and, in recognition of this, Hong Kong has long been an independent member of some international organizations, including the World Trade Organization. Given these factors, the classification of Hong Kong as a foreign investor in China is a welcome triumph of common sense.

From the 1950s through the 1970s, Hong Kong grew from a trade entrepôt to a manufacturing, finance, and trade center of formidable efficiency. As Hong Kong continued to grow in the 1980s, it was natural that manufacturing firms would seek additional space outside the crowded center city. But because Hong Kong is so small, urban growth inevitably meant relocation of firms a few miles away to China. When a Hong Kong factory moves to the suburbs, it creates "foreign" investment. Hong Kong's proximity to China also means that its investors tend to have better information about policy changes inside China than do investors in other countries. Hong Kong businesses move quickly to take advantage of new opportunities in China when policy shifts. Hong Kong is also the home of many subsidiaries of corporations based elsewhere. In 2015, there were 1,400 foreign-company regional headquarters in Hong Kong (including 307 from the United States, 238 from Japan, and 137 from China). Investment originating elsewhere but channeled through Hong Kong shows up in Chinese data as Hong Kong investment. Parent companies located in China sometimes channel investment from their subsidiaries back into China or even create subsidiaries for this purpose, so-called "round-tripping." Chinese firms may be motivated by the desire to gain access to concessionary tax and other advantages enjoyed by foreign-invested firms, and also by the autonomy and anonymity that come from channeling funds through Hong Kong subsidiaries. But here we must be careful. The Hong Kong economy has long been the headquarters of several large firms that are owned by Beijing. Firms such as China Resources and China Merchants (owned by the Chinese Ministry of Commerce and the Ministry of Transportation, respectively) have been active in Hong Kong for more than 50 years. These firms are big investors in China, but their activities cannot be reduced to simple round-tripping.

Since 1997, when it became a Special Administrative Region of China, Hong Kong's restructuring has been especially thorough because it has shed many industrial functions altogether and has moved into greater specialization in services, particularly business services—finance, accounting, and marketing—as well as transport and telecommunications. In 2003, China and Hong Kong signed the Closer Economic Partnership Agreement (CEPA), which gave Hong Kong firms special rights and privileges on the mainland. Additional supplementary provisions have augmented the original agreement nearly every year since. In theory, CEPA gives Hong Kong firms extraordinary first-mover advantages in China service sectors in which Hong Kong already has experience and an obvious comparative advantage. Yet so far, the impact of these provisions has been limited with respect to Hong Kong firms taking a prominent role on the mainland. It is unclear whether this reflects informal understandings, regulatory discrimination, or a preference among Hong Kong firms for working out of their existing headquarters. However, closer economic relations have brought much more mainland activity to Hong Kong and have contributed to the steady growth of Hong Kong's service economy.

17.4.3   The China Circle

The close economic association among the economies of the People's Republic of China, Hong Kong, and Taiwan warrants calling them the "China Circle." The basis for the emergence of the China Circle was the success of Taiwan and Hong Kong in developing labor-intensive manufactured exports during the 1960s and 1970s, particularly to the U.S. market. Both economies produced an enormous range of light, labor-intensive manufactures, beginning with plastic flowers in Hong Kong and extending through a vast range of sporting and travel goods to the huge garment and footwear sectors. This success had an important demonstration effect on China from the beginning of the reform era because Chinese policy-makers observed it and sought to emulate and repeat it through economic reform. The export success of Taiwan and Hong Kong began to have a much more direct effect on the mainland in the mid-1980s, when it began to drive a restructuring of East Asian production networks. Exporters found that increasing wages and costs, magnified by currency realignments, were creating "push" to move production to lower-wage locations.

The opening of China to foreign investment at this time created a dramatic opportunity to transfer labor-intensive export production to the People's Republic. This development, described in chapter 16, was part of a worldwide trend toward increasing intraindustry trade. In China, it required massive investment from Hong Kong and Taiwan to be realized. The trend toward the geographic dispersion of production chains leads to an increasing share of international trade that is made up of intermediate and capital goods and to increasing FDI to build the required networks. This process was particularly powerful in the China Circle because transaction costs for Taiwan and Hong Kong firms to operate in the PRC were low. Proximity, aided by common language and customs, made doing business on the mainland easy and cheap once the mainland's economic system opened up. Production chains were quickly created that crossed political boundaries and allowed Hong Kong and Taiwan to specialize in high-value services and technology-intensive production, while much of the ordinary manufacturing moved to the PRC.

This restructuring moved remarkably quickly in traditional labor-intensive manufacturing, such as garments and footwear, and was basically completed by the early 1990s. For example, Taiwan firms moved their footwear production to the mainland, and, in the United States, imported shoes from China "displaced" imported shoes from Taiwan. In the personal computer industry, production of keyboards and power-supply units (the most labor-intensive products) were the first to move to the mainland because the cost advantages were most marked. They were followed by production of monitors and motherboards and, after 2002, assembly of the desktop and laptop computers themselves.

The foreign-invested firms that account for 85% of China's high-technology exports are often Taiwan firms even when the products have U.S. brands. Taiwan firms such as Foxconn and Quanta assemble high-tech equipment in their factories in China and have stable contracting relationships with U.S. firms such as Apple, Dell, and Hewlett-Packard. Several large Taiwan-based exporters from the mainland are engaged in assembling valuable components into high-value final products. Foxconn is the largest and best known. Smartphones and desktop and laptop computers make up a big share of the total; contract manufacturing of a range of final consumer products accounts for most of the rest.

As manufacturing production moved to the Chinese mainland, the southern coastal provinces industrialized rapidly, while Hong Kong deindustrialized. The Hong Kong industrial labor force peaked at just below 1 million and has since lost 90% of those manufacturing jobs. Taiwan held on to a sophisticated manufacturing sector, but employs fewer workers than before. Taiwan's remaining manufacturing is now closely integrated with facilities on the mainland. This explains Taiwan's prominent role in China's incoming FDI.

Hong Kong and Taiwan have both experienced substantial success in upgrading to higher-skilled activities while simultaneously experiencing steadily rising incomes and relatively low unemployment. The pathway for this skill upgrading was quite different in Hong Kong and Taiwan. Hong Kong moved into services and out of industry; Taiwan upgraded and reorganized its industry, but has been only partially successful as a business operations and financial center. Taiwan and Hong Kong both experienced dramatic success moving into the ranks of the high-income economies but are today struggling with slower growth and the onset of aging societies.

17.5   The Sectoral Composition of FDI and WTO

Manufacturing has been a much larger part of FDI inflows into China than it is for FDI inflows in the rest of the world. Manufacturing accounted for more than half of Chinese FDI inflows consistently until 2010, and 70% in 2003–2005. Only after 2012 did the share of manufacturing drop sharply from 44% in that year to 31% in 2015. In comparative terms, this is unusual: Manufacturing accounted for only 38% of the stock of FDI in developing countries at the end of 2002, while services accounted for 55%. Real estate is the second most important sector for foreign investment, accounting for over 20% of incoming investment since 2008.

These numbers imply that services are a comparatively small share of investment in China, particularly when real estate is excluded. Typically, less than 30% of China's incoming FDI has been in services, although this ticked up in 2015 to 41%. This is a substantial contrast with the rest of the world, where wholesale and retail trade, transport and telecommunications, and finance are all large parts of investment. To a large extent, this can be explained by the restrictions that China has maintained on foreign entry into the most important service sectors. China's accession to the WTO involved commitments to dramatically lower those barriers, and it was widely anticipated that the impact of WTO membership would be most dramatic in opening service sectors. However, there has been a long delay before this impact has become evident in the investment numbers. Although WTO accession had a major impact on the way in which trade was conducted, the impact on foreign investment was apparently much more limited, at least in regard to the sectoral composition of investment.

17.6   Outbound FDI

China was an attractor of FDI for more than a decade before it began to permit, and then promote, outward FDI (OFDI). At first, OFDI targeted natural resources and was dominated by the state-owned enterprises (SOEs), especially large central SOEs. Gradually the gates opened further, and the trickle of OFDI became a flood. After the onset of the global financial crisis, Chinese policy-makers began to see that a range of attractive assets were available globally, not limited to natural resources. As figure 17.3 shows, China's OFDI has increased extraordinarily rapidly for the past decade, and OFDI surpassed inward FDI by a considerable margin in 2016.

As outflows have increased, private firms have begun to play a bigger role, and investment has expanded beyond resources into many other manufacturing sectors. The motives of Chinese OFDI have diversified, as Chinese firms have sought to

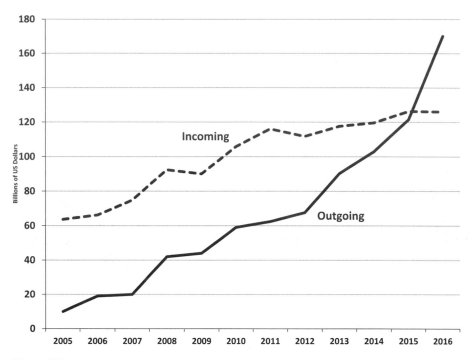

Figure 17.3
China FDI: Incoming and outgoing.
Sources: Incoming: *SYC* (2016, table 11-13); Outgoing: Ministry of Commerce, http://www.mofcom
.gov.cn.

acquire expertise abroad (through acquisitions), as well as gain access to resources and markets. As is the case with incoming FDI, Chinese official data on OFDI reveal the special role of Hong Kong. More than half of Chinese OFDI goes initially to Hong Kong, testifying to its continuing importance as a channel for outgoing as well as incoming investment. Unfortunately, these data tell us little about the actual distribution of Chinese OFDI, either geographically or in sectoral composition. As a result, several projects have sprung up to track Chinese OFDI on the basis of press reports and regulatory filings. These have located investment projects that aggregate to a total similar to Chinese official totals, and yield a very different picture of the destination of Chinese OFDI. The AEI (2016) database of cumulative Chinese OFDI from 2005 through mid-2016 found that the United States was the top destination with almost $130 billion; Australia was second ($81 billion), followed by Canada ($45 billion) and Brazil ($39 billion). Moreover, the U.S. share increased strongly in 2015 and 2016. The U.S. data collected by Hanemann, Rosen, and Gao (2016) show a similar pattern. Flows of incoming Chinese investment in the United States caught up with U.S. flows of investment into China in 2013, ran at about $15 billion per year from 2013 to 2015, and then soared to an astonishing $46 billion in 2016 (Hanemann and Gao 2016). Although China's stock of completed FDI in the United States is still only about a third of the U.S. stock of FDI in China, it has been growing much faster.

China is a newcomer to overseas investment, which is complex and costly, and China's investments have suffered a number of setbacks. China's early OFDI strategy revolved around seeking resources abroad and was led by state-owned firms. After the collapse in global energy and resources prices in 2014, many of these investments are set to lose substantial amounts of money. Several large-scale resource projects in Australia have failed rather spectacularly, and a large investment in Canadian oil sands will never pay off with oil prices at their current levels. Since 2014, OFDI in resources has declined, and investments in finance and technology have grown rapidly. Even so, as of mid-2016, 38% of China's cumulative OFDI was in energy and power, mostly petroleum, and 16% in metals, mainly ore extraction. Real estate (10%), transport (8%), and finance (8%) followed. Moreover, a comparatively high share of China's OFDI projects are "troubled," that is, unable to complete the transaction (AEI 2016).

The vast majority—over 80%—of Chinese investment projects have been mergers and acquisitions (M&A), with a relative handful of greenfield investments. While the majority of FDI in all developed countries consists of M&A, greenfield investments are especially welcome by host countries. Greenfield investments obviously create new jobs, since new facilities are built and operated by the foreign investor. Moreover, an important motive for M&A is to acquire skills and technologies possessed by the firm being bought. China has embarked on an expensive effort of government-led technology development, and overseas acquisitions are a part of that effort. This combination of attributes means that Chinese OFDI has become controversial in host countries such as the United States. Indeed, there are legitimate discussions about the net costs and benefits of FDI in both directions.

As OFDI has shifted out of resources, it has also shifted to a more diverse ownership base. Since 2013, nonstate firms have accounted for three-quarters of Chinese investment in the United States (Hanemann and Gao 2016). The diversification of ownership of OFDI is a highly positive development. However, this achievement has been somewhat undermined by its dependence on a handful of deep-pocketed, politically connected private firms. This issue burst into the open during the first half of 2017, when four firms were subjected to special bank audits and instructed to reduce leverage. These four firms—Anbang Insurance, Dalian Wanda Group, Fosun Group, and Hainan Airlines—accounted for $55 billion, or 18% of total Chinese overseas acquisitions in 2015–2016 (Wei and Deng 2017). Each arguably had privileged access to bank credit because of real or perceived connections to influential politicians. The result of the financial regulatory crackdown was that OFDI dropped 48% in the first half of 2017 to $39.2 billion, according to official Chinese figures. If these policies are maintained as expected, 2017 OFDI will reverse the pattern of rapid growth shown in figure 17.3 and drop substantially below China's incoming FDI.

17.7   The Balance of Payments and the Capital Account

The balance of payments covers all sources and uses of foreign exchange. It is divided into the current account and the capital account. The current account is dominated by trade in goods and services (chapter 16). The capital account, which involves transfer of ownership claims, is covered in this chapter. FDI is an important part of the capital account, but it is only one component among many. Countries that have open capital accounts allow relatively free buying and selling of securities (stocks and bonds) and bank lending by domestic residents and foreigners. As a result, financial flows through these channels can be large. China does not have an open capital account, although it moved in that direction in 2013–2015. That means that capital-account transactions other than FDI through these formal channels have been relatively small. Private portfolio flows, for example, have been tiny. However, this should not lead to the conclusion that non-FDI capital flows have been zero. Transactions that look suspiciously like financial transactions show up in other components of the balance of payments. For example, "errors and omissions" is a large item that has sometimes been positive and sometimes negative; short-term trade credits have also been large in some periods. Figure 17.4 shows one way to simplify China's balance of payments. It classifies all of China's foreign exchange transactions into four categories, shown by four lines. The four categories are: (a) the balance of trade in goods and services, (b) net FDI, (c) accumulation of official foreign exchange reserves, and (d) "all others." By definition, the four sums shown sum to zero in each year.

Two large components of the balance of payments shown in figure 17.4 have consistently been positive. The balance of trade in goods and services has generally been about +2% to 3% of GDP, although it surged higher between 2005 and 2009, when it averaged 6.8% over five years (as discussed in chapter 16). Net FDI has been positive, before drifting down gradually and then turning negative in 2016 (note that balance of payments data on FDI differ from the Ministry of Commerce data used in previous sections). The circle-line shows changes in official foreign exchange reserves. An increase in official reserves shows up as a negative number, that is, it corresponds to a capital outflow. When the central bank accumulates reserves, it invests the money in low-risk securities, such as U.S. Treasury bonds. Thus the increase of official reserves is a special kind of capital outflow, since a domestic actor is purchasing foreign securities. Finally, figure 17.4 shows a constructed "all others" category. The first component of "all others" is the net balance of all items from the capital account, *except* for FDI. To this are added three items that do not appear on the capital

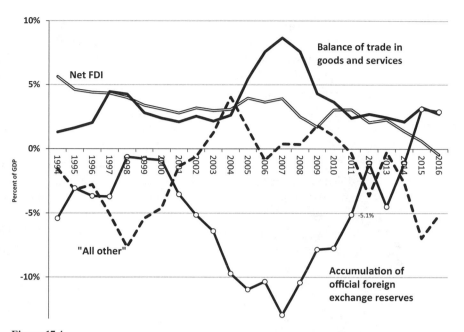

Figure 17.4
Simplified balance of payments.
Source: Consolidated and simplified by author from State Administration of Foreign Exchange, http://www.safe.gov.cn/wps/portal/english/Data/Payments.

account, but which in the Chinese case appear to serve as conduits for informal flows of financial capital. The first two are net factor income and remittances, which appear on the current account (as payments for factor services). The final component is net errors and omissions. Normally these very different items belong in different categories of the balance of payments. However, inspection of the balance of payments reveals that there is considerable fluctuation in the size and direction of these items, and that they tend to move together. This suggests that individuals and businesses, in the absence of capital-account convertibility, use many different channels to move money into and out of China. This omnibus "all others" category can be taken as the net value of all the flows of liquid capital in and out of China. While the trade balance and FDI accounts are consistently positive; and official reserve accumulation was negative until 2014, this "all other" category swings broadly from negative to positive and back. Because the items in the "all others" category are highly variable, they are sometimes referred to as "hot money," or speculative capital.

Figure 17.4 shows that despite China's nominally closed capital account, financial flows are actually extremely large and highly volatile. In general, three periods emerge from looking at the "all other" capital balance. From 1994 through 2002, capital was generally leaving China. From 2003 through 2010, capital flowed into China on a large scale, attracted by China's booming economy and further encouraged by expectations of RMB appreciation. During this 2003–2010 period, China had a large trade surplus and a large private capital inflow. To balance the accounts and restrain or prevent currency appreciation, the Chinese central bank bought up massive amounts of foreign exchange. For the years 2004 through 2010, China's foreign-exchange accumulation averaged 10% of GDP annually.

During the third period, from 2012 through 2016, a dramatically different picture emerged. The trade surplus returned to a historically more normal 2% to 3% of GDP. More important, "all other" capital flows turned negative and grew large. On balance, speculative capital flowed out of China, and this flow became quite large in 2014–2016. As a result, official reserves reached a peak in June 2014 and then began to decline, dipping to just over US$3 trillion at the end of 2016 (figure 17.5). Normalized by China's GDP, outflows during the first and third periods were similar, but in absolute terms the sums were much bigger in 2015 and 2016. In 1998, the year of the largest proportionate outflow, the total amount was only US$79 billion, whereas in 2015 and 2016 outflows estimated by this broad measure were enormous, $769 billion and $647 billion respectively.

China has maintained restrictions on capital-account convertibility. That is, while an exporter or importer can freely convert RMB to foreign exchange with presentation of trade documents, individuals and businesses cannot simply buy or sell large amounts of domestic or foreign currency. In theory, therefore, we should expect other kinds of capital flows reflected in the balance of payments to be quite small. However, this expectation is false. Despite the nominal lack of convertibility on the capital account, liquid capital flows to and from China are in fact quite large.

17.8   Accommodating Capital Outflows

Building on the analysis in the previous section, we can further generalize the picture of the balance of payments. For all countries, the balance of payments accounting identity tells us that the current account surplus equals net capital outflows. Countries that import more than they export must borrow to finance their consumption, and countries that export more than they import must extend credit to allow the rest of the world to buy their output. Furthermore, capital outflows equal the surplus of domestic saving over domestic investment. Since China's current account has been in surplus for the past 20 years, China must have been experiencing capital outflows of the same magnitude. This should not be surprising. We have already seen that China has an extraordinarily high domestic saving rate (chapter 7). Moreover, as

China moves out of the miracle-growth era, domestic investment opportunities become more difficult to locate and total investment as a share of GDP has declined by almost four percentage points since 2011. In this view, China has a persistent saving "surplus," and these savings become capital outflows through different channels, depending on economic conditions and government policy. Indeed, China has adopted three successive and very different policy regimes to channel these outflows.

17.8.1 Official Reserves Accumulation

During the first decade of the century, China ran a current-account surplus and experienced a net inflow of private capital, including FDI and the "all other" aggregate shown in figure 17.4. This implies that China must have been accumulating official foreign-exchange reserves to offset these twin surpluses. That is indeed the case. As figure 17.5 shows, between 2004 and June 2014, China increased its reserves from under $500 billion to $3.99 trillion. Thus all of the net (public and private) outflow was realized in the form of additions to official foreign-exchange reserves.

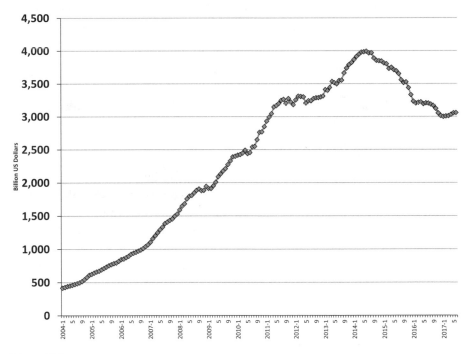

Figure 17.5
China: Official foreign-exchange reserves.
Source: State Administration of Foreign Exchange.

It is doubtless better to have $4 trillion in reserve than not to have $4 trillion. However, accumulating such a large sum of official reserves creates three important problems.

1. Accumulating reserves is equivalent to keeping your currency from appreciating (since the central bank is printing as much additional domestic currency as required to purchase for foreign exchange at a given price, thus keeping the value of the domestic currency from rising). Preventing appreciation facilitated the increase in the trade surplus to 8% of GDP in 2007, which was associated with misallocation of resources and friction with trading partners.

2. Rapid reserve accumulation makes it difficult to run a coherent domestic monetary policy. Excess emission of domestic currency contributes to inflationary pressures and requires the central bank to sterilize the monetary impact (see chapter 18).

3. This vast sum of money is invested in a limited range of low-risk, low return securities, especially U.S. Treasury bonds. Official reserves, in order to be useful reserves, need to be in a safe and highly liquid investment. Unfortunately, there are not many such investments in the world, and U.S. bonds dominate the available supply. This means that the return on reserves is low, and, more important, the investment is not very diversified.

For these reasons, Chinese policy-makers gradually achieved agreement that $4 trillion in reserves was more than China needed. They began searching for a more liberal regime that would permit multiple forms of capital outflow and generate higher and more stable returns.

17.8.2 "Go Out": Outgoing Direct Investment

China began to promote OFDI around 2005, but the liberalization of access to OFDI opportunities came later, especially after 2011. In a sense, the "Going Out" policy discussed earlier represents an effort to seek other forms of capital outflow that would generate higher returns, a more diversified investment structure, and other strategic and economic benefits. The "Go Out" policy has lowered barriers to companies seeking to invest abroad, and support is often available for OFDI from banks and other financial institutions. This intentional policy involved less government control over the outflows and a steady diversification of ownership types, as well as destination countries and sectors.

17.8.3 Sovereign Wealth Funds

In addition, China seeks government-sponsored channels for investment abroad. China has now established two large sovereign wealth funds (SWFs), which invest for the long-term interest of the government and the nation. Not all the investment of these SWFs is foreign, and we do not have good data on the composition of their assets. However, these are big SWFs, and foreign assets are a significant part of their investments. The China Investment Corporation had $747 billion in assets in mid-2015, while the SAFE Investment Company had $568 billion. This ranks them third and sixth, respectively, among global sovereign wealth funds (SWFI 2016). These SWFs are authorized to hold considerably less liquid—and potentially much higher yielding—securities than the foreign-exchange reserve fund.

17.8.4   New Multilateral Financial Institutions

In a further step, China in 2015 sponsored the creation of a number of new mutilateral financial institutions in which China has a preponderant voice. The Asia Infrastructure Investment Bank (AIIB) is a new regional investment bank, similar in character to the World Bank and the Asian Development Bank. However, China contributed 30% of the capital (and votes 26.1% of the shares). Since, as in other multilateral financial institutions, a supermajority is required for important decisions, China has a veto, and it also secured the appointment of a Chinese national as the first head. The AIIB could eventually help channel a significant amount of Chinese saving to investment projects around the Asian periphery. A somewhat similar institution, the BRICS Bank (recently renamed the New Bank) is expected to play a similar role for the BRICS (Brazil, Russia, India, China, and South Africa). For China, these institutions are means to facilitate the flow of Chinese domestic saving abroad, and it is hoped that they will encourage the selection of higher-quality projects through the application of sophisticated financing and appraisal and evaluation techniques. These new financial institutions—so far, quite small—are envisioned to play a role alongside state-owned banks in financing infrastructure projects in China's neighboring countries. The program called the "Belt and Road Initiative" seeks to provide official Chinese funding and guide private capital flows to China's neighbors.

17.8.5   Re-Regulating Capital Outflows

A third phase of regulating large capital outflows began in late 2016. As shown in figure 17.4, outflows of speculative capital became extremely large in 2015–2016. The outflow of "all other" speculative capital totaled an astonishing $1.4 trillion over two years, more than 10% of annual GDP. To maintain currency stability in the face of these massive outflows, the Chinese central bank had no choice but to draw down official foreign exchange reserves at a rapid pace. Between June 2014 and January 2017, China's official reserves declined exactly $1 trillion, and fell to the $3 trillion that seemed to define policy-makers' comfort level. Administrative regulations that limited capital outflows, which had been significantly dismantled during the previous few years, were hastily re-imposed. The result was a quick end to foreign exchange losses in 2017, shown in figure 17.5. This brought a sudden close to one chapter in China's ongoing story of capital account liberalization.

The 2014–2016 episode of liberalization and large capital outflows ran into many of the problems that have bedeviled attempts at capital account liberalization in many developing countries. Thorough financial reforms (discussed in chapter 19) will open an economy up to capital flows in both directions, but they can only work if they have made domestic financial markets attractive to foreign investors as well. China under all conceivable scenarios will be exporting capital (since its saving rate is so high). Regulation cannot prevent these outflows nor is it likely to be able to confine them to government-controlled channels. Only if robust capital inflows emerge to offset a portion of the overall capital outflows will China be able to move forward with further liberalization. That in turn will require more thorough reform of China's stock and bond markets than has been yet achieved.

17.9   Conclusion

Capital flows, in and out, have had a major impact on China's economy notwithstanding the lack of formal capital account convertibility. The preceding pages have made clear that FDI has had a major impact, transferring manufacturing capability, jobs, and export markets to China. The close integration of China and other East Asian economies—especially the China Circle economies of Taiwan and Hong Kong—created extremely competitive, flexible, and low-cost manufacturing networks. China today is becoming a large-scale capital-exporting country. The scale of China's export of savings is likely to have a profound impact on the global economy. If it is managed well and takes place through stable and transparent mechanisms, it will be of enormous benefit to a global economy where saving and investment rates today are far too low. In addition, if a successful program of capital-account opening is carried through, large two-way flows will emerge as foreign investors also seek to diversify into China's securities markets (stocks and bonds). If savings come out of China through erratic or underground channels, the destabilizing impact on the world economy could be substantial.

China today is poised between a nationalist impulse that has gradually and subtly but unmistakably limited the access of foreign investors to many areas of the domestic economy and a reformist impulse that recognizes that the largest breakthroughs in China's move to a market economy have been accompanied by greater openness to foreign businesses as well. The predominance of FDI among China's external capital sources is exceptional; it implies that China's openness as measured by exposure to FDI is greater than its openness in other dimensions. Further major choices confront China's policy-makers: Will openness again be a part of China's new reform initiative? Will the Shanghai Free Trade Zone play a role in the current wave of reforms that resembles that played by Shenzhen and the other SEZs in the 1980s or Pudong in the 1990s? Will China's service sectors become more open to investment as China seeks to upgrade to a more sophisticated and prosperous economy? Will China's tentative moves toward an open capital account bear fruit? The future direction of the global economy depends on the answers to these questions.

Bibliography

Suggestions for Further Reading

Enright (2017) is a comprehensive update and written in a lively style. Hanemann, Rosen, and Gao (2016) is both an up-to-date accounting of Chinese investment in the United States and a cogent discussion of investment issues. The annual *World Investment Report* from UNCTAD has global data and good discussions of current issues.

References

AEI (American Enterprise Institute) (2016). "China Global Investment Tracker." Accessed at https://www.aei.org/publication/chinas-outward-investment-explodes-and-peaks/.

Brandt, Loren, Johannes Van Biesebroeck, Luhang Wang, and Yifan Zhang (2017). "WTO Accession and Performance of Chinese Manufacturing Firms." *American Economic Review* (forthcoming). Accessed at https://www.aeaweb.org/articles?id=10.1257/aer.20121266.

Enright, Michael J. (2017). *Developing China: The Remarkable Impact of Foreign Direct Investment*. New York: Routledge.

Hanemann, Thilo, and Cassie Gao (2016). "Record Deal Making in 2016 Pushes Cumulative Chinese FDI in the US Above $100 billion." December 30. Accessed at http://rhg.com/notes/record-deal-making-in-2016-pushes-cumulative-chinese-fdi-in-the-us-above-100-billion.

Hanemann, Thilo, Daniel H. Rosen, and Cassie Gao (2016). *Two-Way Street: 25 Years of US-China Direct Investment*. New York: National Committee on U.S.-China Relations and Rhodium Group. Accessed at http://rhg.com/reports/two-way-street-25-years-of-us-china-direct-investment.

SWFI (2016). "SWFI League Table of Largest Public Funds." Sovereign Wealth Fund Institute. Accessed at http://www.swfinstitute.org/fund-rankings/.

SYC (Annual). *Zhongguo Tongji Nianjian* [Statistical yearbook of China]. Beijing: Zhongguo Tongji.

UNCTAD (United Nations Conference on Trade and Development) (Annual). *World Investment Report*. New York: United Nations. Accessed at http://unctad.org/en/Pages/DIAE/World%20Investment%20Report/World_Investment_Report.aspx.

Wei, Lingling, and Chao Deng (2017). "Xi's Sign-Off Deals Blow to China Inc.'s Global Spending Spree." *Wall Street Journal*, July 23. Accessed at https://www.wsj.com/articles/chinas-latest-clampdown-on-overseas-investing-has-president-xis-approval-1500802203.

VI MACROECONOMICS AND FINANCE

Headquarters of the People's Bank of China, Beijing 2006.

18 Macroeconomic Policy: Instruments and Outcomes

Capable macroeconomic policy is an essential part of successful development. Macroeconomic policy failures derail growth, but successful macro policy is often invisible as problems recede into the background. This chapter covers the demand side of the economy, as well as short-run fluctuations, money and prices, and the tools of fiscal and monetary policy. While most of this volume covers the long-term changes in the supply of capital, labor, technology, and institutions that make up China's growth, this chapter examines short-term changes in demand and money and their interaction with long-run growth. The main topic of the volume is the "real" economy; this chapter discusses "nominal" and financial variables. This chapter is complementary to the description of the real economy that makes up most of this book, and it sets the stage for the discussion of financial and fiscal institutions in chapters 19 and 20.

Macroeconomics does not command the same high degree of consensus that some other areas of economics can claim. Macroeconomists make use of many different theories and methodologies in order to illuminate different parts of the macroeconomy. This chapter takes a selective and practical approach, focusing on a few aspects of macroeconomics that throw light on the most distinctive aspects of China's experience. It begins by reviewing a few core ideas of macroeconomic analysis and relating them to overall Chinese experience. It then tells the tumultuous story of China's macroeconomy in the twenty-first century, concluding with a simple characterization of China's macroeconomic policy. In this century, China has used the policy instruments of Keynesian economics in a coordinated way to drive growth at the fastest feasible rate. This "super-Keynesian" approach is in tension with the economy's lower growth potential after the miracle-growth era.

18.1 The Objectives of Macroeconomic Policy

Good macroeconomic policy is that which provides full employment of resources and stable prices, that is, growth with low inflation. Shocks to the economy are inevitable and can be negative or positive, domestic or foreign. Macroeconomic policy must be resilient in the face of these shocks. Since these goals are commonsense and widely shared, it is easy to recognize good macro policy when it is successful. However, when things go wrong, it is difficult to get macro policy back on track. Policy-makers have a limited number of tools: monetary policy, fiscal policy, and sometimes exchange-rate policy. There are trade-offs among different objectives and among different tools with different time lags. In principle, both monetary and fiscal policy can help achieve the goals of macroeconomic policy. In practice, for reasons discussed below, most of the attention of macroeconomists since the 1980s has been paid to monetary policy and the role of central banks.

Most of the world's central banks are assigned one or two fundamental objectives: price stability (always) and full employment of resources (sometimes). Stabilization is achieved as an offshoot of the measures taken to reach the inflation and employment targets. Price stability typically means a low rate of inflation. High inflation is costly, particularly because it tends to accelerate. China (like Germany) has a historic memory of hyperinflation, and policy-makers and the public are strongly averse to high inflation. However, zero inflation or deflation (declining prices) is also undesirable. Deflation is harmful because it causes consumers to delay purchases and might cause a downward spiral of lower sales and depressed output. A little inflation makes it easier for businesses to smoothly carry out the continuous adaptations of individual prices necessary in a market economy. Thus an inflation rate around 1% to 2% is usually considered just right, not too hot and not too cold.

Full employment of resources means that actual output is at or near maximum potential output. However, it is not easy to measure potential output, especially in an economy undergoing rapid structural and institutional change, like that of China. In practice, most countries evaluate full utilization of resources by monitoring either the unemployment rate or the growth of total output (GDP) compared with some judgment of the economy's potential growth rate. The most desirable labor unemployment rate will never be zero, since some "frictional unemployment" is necessary if people are changing jobs or searching for better jobs. In the United States, the Federal Reserve Board usually considers unemployment of around 5% to be consistent with full employment.[1] In China, labor markets are more fragmented and unemployment statistics are unreliable, so there is no single unemployment rate that policy-makers can consistently use. However, policy-makers can and do monitor other indicators of labor-market conditions. For example, since 2009 they have paid close attention to changes in the flow of rural-to-urban migrants as an index of the adequacy of urban employment opportunities.

---

1. See http://www.federalreserve.gov/faqs/money_12848.htm. Note that the U.S. Fed does not use a single unemployment number, explicitly stating that labor markets are multidimensional and cannot be captured in a single statistic.

Different countries have very different potential growth rates. According to a set of estimates by an International Monetary Fund (IMF) team, potential growth in advanced countries has varied from 1.3% to 2.4% over the past 20 years (with the United States somewhat higher than Germany or Japan). Today, large developing countries (including China) have a potential growth rate between 5% and 7.4% (IMF 2015). Clearly, China's economy was capable of more than 10% annual growth for decades, but this was achieved in the special context of the miracle-growth era (rapid employment growth, high investment, and rapid institutional change and productivity growth; see chapter 7). All economists agree that China's potential growth has declined since about 2010, but there is no widespread agreement on the current potential growth rate: estimates range as high as 8% and as low as 4%. Thus macroeconomic policy-makers have an extremely difficult task trying to determine the "right" growth rate to target. The growth target set in the 13th Five-Year Plan (2016–2020) implies a 6.5% annual growth rate.

Macroeconomic policy cannot push real growth above the potential growth rate. If policy—say, on the growth of the money supply—is set above the potential growth rate, the result will be excess money and credit, too much inflation, and potentially financial distress. If policy is targeted below the potential growth rate, it may lead to excessively high interest rates, discourage desirable investment projects, and potentially cause a recession. Therefore, it is important to get the potential growth rate right. Attempts to push the growth rate above potential might succeed for a year or two but will ultimately fail. Moreover, such attempts can have a high cost because of the difficulty in getting policy back on track once it is derailed.[2]

Macroeconomic policy is sometimes called "stabilization policy." This term emphasizes that even when policy-makers have achieved price stability and sustainable growth, their policies will constantly be disrupted by various shocks. For example, the global financial crisis (GFC), emanating from the United States in 2008–2009, created an enormous external shock to which macroeconomic policy-makers all over the world were forced to react. Policy-makers everywhere adopted much more expansionary policies (both monetary and fiscal). China's reaction was especially vigorous; it increased the fiscal deficit and pumped a massive amount of bank credit into the economy. Policy-makers should generally respond to a negative demand shock in this way with a shift toward expansionary policies. There are also positive demand shocks, and policy-makers should generally respond to them with a shift toward contractionary policies to keep the economy from overheating. Shocks can also occur on the supply side: negative when supply is interrupted

---

2. Indirectly, and over the long term, macroeconomic policy can nudge the real growth rate up or down. If macro policy is stable and successful, it will gradually bring more production factors into the economy, including marginal workers attracted into the labor force by higher wages, and additional fixed capital created because investment projects have consistently paid off.

and positive when productivity improves because of institutional changes or new technologies. Long-term growth will be faster when macroeconomic policymakers neutralize shocks and prevent them from interrupting the development process.

18.2   A Snapshot of China's Macroeconomic Record, 1978–2016

Does China's macroeconomic record display full employment and stable prices? Generally, the answer to this question is "Yes" when we take into account the special circumstances of a developing and transitional economy. Effectively managing macroeconomic policy during the transition to a market economy is demanding and difficult. Fiscal and monetary policy are both subject to extraordinary challenges, while policy-makers initially lack proper tools for modern monetary and macroeconomic management. Macroeconomic instability in the transitional economies of Eastern Europe and the former Soviet Union contributed to high inflation and then large recessions. By contrast, China was generally able to navigate around the largest macroeconomic pitfalls. To be sure, the first 20 years of economic transition were marked by three serious inflationary cycles through the mid-1990s. However, bursts of high inflation were controlled reasonably quickly; household financial savings generally maintained their value; and, most important, expectations about the future were not plagued with the extreme uncertainty that can follow from serious macroeconomic disruption.

In regard to price stability, figure 18.1 clearly shows that after turbulence in the 1980s and 1990s, China made the transition to a new inflation regime after 1997. Inflation was much lower and less variable than in the previous period. The average inflation rate dropped from 10.1% (1983 through 1996) to 2.0% (1997 through 2016), while the standard deviation of the monthly inflation rate dropped from 7.8 percentage points to 2.4 percentage points. This was a major achievement that corresponded to the establishment of a true central bank—the People's Bank of China (PBC)—and the achievement of monetary discipline. As we will see, the PBC gradually developed a range of instruments to manage monetary policy. China's post-1978 macroeconomic policy regime has been generally successful in achieving an environment of moderately low inflation.

The record with respect to full employment is more complex. Obviously, China's high growth rate shows that macroeconomic policy has been successful in accommodating and supporting growth. Moreover, China has not experienced a major recession since 1990, and even the 2008 global financial crisis produced only a short-term downturn in the Chinese economy. From this standpoint, then, China's long-term macroeconomic record has been excellent. Rapid growth and full employment of resources have been achieved with moderate inflation, especially since 1997. This statement should be qualified somewhat. At the beginning of transition in 1978,

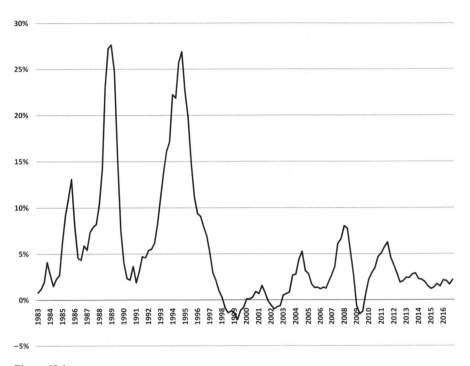

Figure 18.1
Consumer inflation, 1983–2016.
Source: Monthly data from National Bureau of Statistics, consolidated into quarterly, http://www.stats
.gov.cn/tjsj/zxfb/201701/t20170110_1451700.html. There are no usable inflation data before 1983.

resources—especially labor—were pervasively under-utilized. Many workers were
bottled up in the countryside with inadequate land or tools. In the cities, disguised
unemployment—people with jobs but nothing to do—was a serious problem, especially in 1978–1982. In a later episode, open unemployment surged in 1998–2002
(chapters 5 and 9). However, open unemployment declined quickly after 2002, and
even in the midst of the global financial crisis, demand for workers remained robust.
Thus "full employment" in China should be seen as a dynamic achievement, coming in the context of a steady improvement in the economic system's capacity to use
human resources, rather than successful minimization of a static "unemployment
rate." The former is the more important long-run achievement, even though the lat-
ter might make life simpler for macroeconomic policy-makers in the short run. Today,
labor-force growth has dropped rapidly, while overall demand for labor is still high,
and there are not as many reserves of underutilized labor as before. This creates a
new dynamic in labor markets: unemployment may become less of a problem, but
macroeconomic policy-makers may eventually face a more challenging trade-off
between unemployment and inflation.

18.3   The Demand Side and Macroeconomic Policy Instruments

18.3.1   Final Demand Components—Expenditure-Side GDP

The demand side of the economy can be analyzed in terms of its principal components. As box 7.1 showed, there are three different but mutually consistent approaches to accounting for GDP. The "expenditure approach" corresponds to demand-side analysis of the economy. The most common expression of the expenditure approach is that overall, or aggregate, demand consists of four final demand components: consumption (C), investment (I), government expenditure (G), and net exports ($X - M$). This is succinctly expressed as a formula:

$$Y = C + I + G + (X - M).$$

Each of the final demand components has different characteristics, and each is influenced by a different macroeconomic instrument, if it can be influenced at all. The first component, consumption, is relatively stable and is the least subject to influence by macroeconomic policy instruments. Consumption is funded from household income and responds in predictable ways to the level and growth of income. Investment is far more volatile. It responds to expectations about the future and can be influenced by the level of interest rates and borrowing costs. One of the main channels through which monetary policy works is by influencing investment demand. Government adds to demand through spending and subtracts from demand through taxation. The net fiscal balance, taxation minus spending, is the most direct index of fiscal policy. Finally, net exports are influenced by exchange-rate policy: a lower value for the domestic currency encourages exports and discourages imports, thus increasing net exports; this increase is expansionary. Three macroeconomic policy instruments—monetary, fiscal, and exchange-rate policy—thus correspond to three of the four components of aggregate demand.

18.3.2   Demand-Side Sources of Growth in China

The expenditure-side GDP accounts can be used to produce an analysis of the demand-side sources of growth in the economy. Chinese statisticians do not report a separate "government" account but rather break consumption down into household consumption and government consumption (however, there is no parallel breakdown for investment). This leaves us only three components of final demand to work with. By tracking the increase in each of these components, we can derive the three demand-side components of growth. This is done in figure 18.2. (The contribution of a component equals its share in aggregate demand in the initial year times its growth rate; for example, if consumption is 60% of GDP and grows at 10%, its

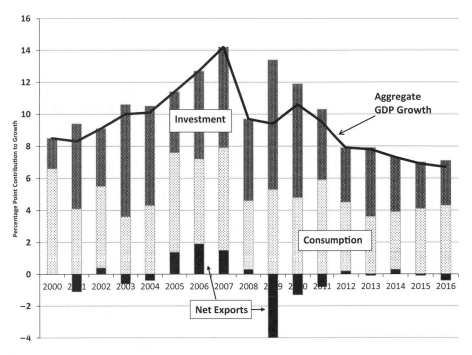

Figure 18.2
Demand-side components of growth.
Source: *SAC* (2017, 37).

contribution to growth is $0.1 \times 0.6 = 0.06$ or 6 percentage points.) We find that consumption has made a generally stable contribution to growth of 4 to 5 percentage points of GDP, occasionally rising as high as 6 percentage points. By contrast, net exports added very substantially to growth in 2005 to 2007 and then swung strongly negative in 2009–2010 as China worked up a very large trade surplus and then drew it down during the GFC. Investment made an extremely large contribution to growth in every year. During 2005 to 2007, when growth peaked at 14%, all three demand components were making a large contribution, and investment's contribution increased from under 4 to over 6 percentage points. In 2009, investment's contribution soared to almost 8 percentage points, almost fully offsetting the reduction in growth of 4 percentage points caused by the shrinkage in net exports. Since 2011, the contribution of net exports has fluctuated around zero, while the contribution of investment has declined. Consumption growth has remained robust, but it has not accelerated enough to offset the declining contribution of investment, which fell just below 3 percentage points in 2015. The evolution of demand-side components of growth provides a quick snapshot of growth drivers; the specific episodes are discussed further in section 18.6.

18.3.3   The Usefulness of Macroeconomic Policy Instruments

In principle, China's macroeconomic policy-makers can steer the economy through three instruments: monetary policy, fiscal policy, and exchange-rate policy. We can summarize their effects as follows: Policy provides more stimulus (is more expansionary) when (1) monetary policy lowers interest rates or increases the growth of money and credit, (2) fiscal policy yields a larger budget deficit, and (3) the domestic currency depreciates (or is set at a lower value). Conversely, policy is more contractionary when interest rates rise and money and credit growth slow; when the budget deficit is reduced; and when the currency appreciates. In practice, monetary policy is by far the most effective of the three, and there are significant limits on the use of fiscal or exchange-rate policy. This is parallel to the situation in developed economies, but for different reasons.

Fiscal policy ought to have great advantages as a macroeconomic policy instrument. The principles behind fiscal policy are simple, and the government might be presumed to have its hand directly on the levers of expenditure and taxation. In practice, very few developed economies can use fiscal policy effectively. Checks and balances imposed by the political process make it difficult to quickly raise or lower either expenditures or taxation, so there are long lags before fiscal policy becomes effective, and it is often too late. Moreover, high government debt levels have made many countries reluctant to run additional fiscal deficits, even when interest rates are low. Neither of these factors is significant in China. Instead, a major problem with fiscal policy in China is that the boundaries of fiscal accounts are vague. First, the government collects large tax-like levies in funds that have growing balances, creating a kind of shadow budget surplus. For example, social security funds are large and growing and are not included in budgetary accounts. There is also a budget-adjustment fund used to transfer surpluses from good years to bad years, a good practice, but not necessarily accounted for properly in calculating the overall fiscal stance. Second, the government carries out many fiscal-like expenditures through the state-owned banks, particularly the China Development Bank. These expenditures show up on the banking system's balance sheet even though they are the direct result of government spending decisions. Because of these factors, fiscal policy can only rarely be used as a separate macroeconomic policy tool, and instead, policy-makers have simply tried to adjust fiscal balances in a way that is consistent with their macroeconomic objectives at the time (section 18.6.1 and figure 18.3).

Exchange-rate policy is even more encumbered. Through most of China's recent history, policy-makers have set the exchange rate and defended it with interventions in the foreign-exchange market, thereby accumulating or drawing down official foreign-exchange reserves (chapter 17). From the standpoint of macroeconomic policy, though, this has been possible only because through most of this period, the Chinese capital account was predominantly closed. As the capital account has been progressively opened, the ability of macroeconomic policy-makers to maintain both the policy setting they want and a fixed exchange rate has steadily declined.[3] Moreover, national leaders have set the exchange rate with an eye toward the competitiveness of exporters (a developmental and not a macroeconomic policy objective). Thus, even when the exchange rate was an instrument that could be manipulated, it could never be used effectively as a constructive component of macroeconomic policy.

As a result of these factors, most of the burden of day-to-day macroeconomic and stabilization policy has been placed on the central bank. Again, this is similar to the situation in developed market economies. Control of the money supply is thus perhaps the most fundamental instrument of macroeconomic policy. Monetary policy is discussed next and receives the bulk of the attention in the following sections. Later, in sections 18.5 and 18.6, the discussion of macroeconomic policy in practice is broadened to include all three macroeconomic instruments.

18.4   Money and Monetary Policy

18.4.1   Fundamentals of Monetary Economics

It is the job of the central bank to supply the appropriate quantity of money to fulfill the demands of the economy. The money supply must provide acceptability and stability. By acceptability, we mean that money must be broadly accepted as payment for goods and services but also, in a modern economy, provide liquidity in financial transactions. That is, there must be a form of money available that is useful in making and repaying loans and buying and selling assets. The central bank's job is to ensure the ample provision of these liquidity services. Stability refers to the need for money to maintain its value over time. Since governments gain real power and resources from the issuance of money, they are often tempted to create too much of it. Excessive money creation leads to excess inflation, which destabilizes expectations about the future. The appropriate money supply is that which provides a stable monetary value that is widely acceptable for a variety of complex intertemporal transactions.

---

3. This is the "impossible trinity," the finding of economists that no economy can simultaneously have all three of a fixed exchange rate, an open capital account, and monetary policy autonomy. Most developed economies have open capital accounts and monetary policy autonomy and allow their exchange rates to be determined by market forces.

It is hard to determine the appropriate quantity of money for any economy. However, it is much easier to understand the increase in money supply needed to accommodate a growing economy. One way to begin the discussion is to look at the monetary identity that describes the quantitative relation among money, prices, and real economic activity. The supply of money multiplied by the number of times it is used in a year equals the nominal value of all transactions undertaken that year:

$$MV = PT;$$

that is, money (M) times the velocity of its circulation (V) equals the overall price level (P) times the volume of transactions (T). The volume of final demand transactions is the same as GDP.

Although this is just an identity, we can wring some meaning out of it. First, rearrange terms so that the price level equals the money supply times the velocity, divided by real output:

$$P = MV/T.$$

We are interested in growth rates, so first convert to logs:

$$\ln P = \ln M + \ln V - \ln T.$$

Using the shortcut introduced in chapter 7, note 7,[4] we can convert logs into percentage growth rates:

$$G_P = G_M + G_V - G_T.$$

This tells us that the rate of inflation (G_P) equals the growth of the money supply minus the growth of the real economy (G_T) plus changes in velocity (G_V). If velocity is constant, G_V equals zero. Strict adherents of the quantity theory of money argue that both V and T are stable and predictable, so the relationship between M and P is one of stable causality. In this simplified world, if the potential growth rate is 6%, M growth can be set at 8% to generate an optimal 2% inflation rate. This generates a simplified—indeed, oversimplified—monetary growth rule.

In the real world, the relationship is much more complicated. The GDP growth rate is not known with certainty, and unanticipated shocks affect every part of the relationship. However, the equation tells us that the appropriate growth of the money supply over the long run will be that which accommodates real growth, shocks to the velocity of circulation, and the desired (low) rate of inflation. For further discussion, it makes sense first to divide reality into normal "good" times and disruptive "bad" times.

---

4. If X is a number near 1, then the approximation $\ln(X) \approx X - 1$ is roughly correct.

18.4.2   Monetary Policy in Good Times

"Good times" can be defined as a stable period in which the velocity of circulation changes in moderate and predictable ways. Policy-makers will have a straightforward path toward achieving their preferred targets for inflation and real growth. Even so, there will be shocks to supply and demand and perhaps to the financial system (to velocity). If policy-makers act to increase the growth of money, they can expect that in the short run, policy will increase both inflation and the real growth rate:

$$G_P + G_T = G_M + G_V.$$

In other words, policy-makers can increase nominal GDP growth ($G_P + G_T$), but they do not know with certainty what the composition of this nominal GDP growth will be (the distribution between G_P and G_T). To what extent will it raise real growth (by raising demand and bringing in underemployed resources)? To what extent will it simply increase inflation? They know only that over the medium run, they cannot raise real growth above the potential growth rate, and any monetary growth above that will just create more inflation. Of course, policy-makers wish that they could separately target inflation and real growth, but in practice they do not have this capability. They must choose a money-supply policy that gets them closer to both their inflation and real growth targets. There is always some trade-off between these two different objectives. If the inflation rate is too high, policy-makers must reduce the growth of the money supply; if real growth is too low, policy-makers must increase the growth of the money supply.

This general principle is sometimes reflected in decision rules prescribed for central bankers. The idea behind the decision rule is that the behavior of central bankers should be transparent and predictable. The most prominent such rule is the Taylor rule, which instructs central bankers to adjust their interest-rate targets in a rule-bound way to deviations from their explicit output and inflation targets. When the inflation rate provides an adverse shock and is higher than its target, the central bank should raise the nominal interest rate as much as the inflation shock and more. Increasing the nominal interest rate by the inflation increase merely holds the real interest rate constant (since the real rate equals the nominal inflation rate minus inflation), while increasing it above the inflation increase raises the real interest rate and moves monetary policy in a contractionary direction. A similar rule applies to GDP growth below the targeted growth rate (or unemployment above the target), which calls for lower interest rates. Whether or not a central bank explicitly follows a Taylor rule, it is a good description of the trade-off central banks are constantly making in practice. Their efforts are constantly being disrupted by shocks to the economy, but if they are successful, they systematically buffer those shocks and enable a growth rate as close as possible to the potential growth rate.

18.4.3   Monetary Policy in Bad Times

In "bad times," there are sudden large, unpredictable changes in the demand for money and in its velocity of circulation. When a large negative shock hits an economy, it can cause a wave of payment failures or even bankruptcies. Other firms respond to these payment difficulties by increasing their demand for money, that is, by unwinding existing investments ("cashing out"). They do so for two reasons: they are afraid that other firms may not be able to pay them (so they need more cash), and other firms may be uncertain about their ability to pay in turn (so they need to show more cash as collateral). This causes a sudden spike in demand for money and an equally sudden drop in risk appetite. The price of risky assets can drop quickly.

Central bankers must be prepared to step into this crisis situation and provide abundant temporary liquidity. In the monetary identity, the velocity of circulation drops, so G_V suddenly becomes a large negative number, and G_M must increase rapidly to keep real growth and the inflation rate in positive territory. Liquidity crises like these seem to be inherent parts of a market system, and monetary authorities must retain the flexibility to respond to them quickly. Good monetary policy emerges when central bankers react appropriately in both good and bad times.

18.4.4   Base Money and the Money Multiplier

The previous section describes the money supply as if it were something the central bank could set directly and unilaterally. In fact, China, like most market economies, operates a "fractional reserve" banking system, which means that the money supply is created through an interaction between the central bank (the government) and the commercial banking system (businesses). The central bank has the dominant hand in the process because it controls the creation of so-called "base money" and also sets the parameters of the banking system that determine the final money supply through the "money multiplier." The commercial banks play their role in the system simply by maximizing profit under the conditions set by the central bank.

Central-bank decisions create "base money" or "high-powered money." Base money consists of the sum of currency in circulation (cash) and commercial bank deposits with the central bank. To oversimplify a little, the bank creates this money by either (1) lending to the government or commercial banks, or (2) buying foreign exchange.[5] This is the beginning of the process that determines the total money supply. Commercial banks then turn base money into broad money by relending base money (created by the central bank) and thus multiplying the amount of money in circulation. How much commercial banks can lend is determined by the regulations that govern the commercial bank sector. In any fractional reserve system, commercial banks are required to maintain deposits at the central bank equal to a fixed proportion of their total deposits. Since commercial banks want to loan out as much as they can in order to make more profits, they will expand lending until they are as close to the required reserve ratio as is prudent. In turn, the loans one commercial bank makes create new deposits at the borrower's bank. The initial borrower's bank then lends out as much of this new deposit as possible. When the funds circulate through the entire commercial bank system, the result is a "money multiplier" that predictably links broad money to base money. For example, a commonly used definition of broad money is M2, which consists of (1) currency in circulation, (2) bank deposits that can be used directly to make payments (checking accounts), plus (3) other commercial bank deposits that can be quickly converted to cash or other checkable accounts.

The money multiplier directly determines the size of bank deposits. The fractional reserve rule can be described as follows:

R / bank deposits $\geq rr$,

Where R is commercial bank deposits with the central bank, the main component of base money (or high-powered money), and rr is the required reserve ratio. After all banks have increased their lending to the maximum permitted, we get the following, rearranging terms:

bank deposits $\leq R$ / rr.

Since the central bank sets both R (base money) and rr (the reserve requirement), it has established the upper limit on the bank-deposits component of broad money.[6] The money multiplier is $1/rr$. For example, if the rr is 0.05, total commercial bank deposits will be 20 times official reserves, and the money multiplier is 20. If the rr is 0.2, the money multiplier will be 5, and commercial bank deposits will be 5 times official reserves.

---

5. Put another way, base money is a liability on the central bank's balance sheet. Central-bank assets consist of holdings of gold and foreign exchange, central-bank lending to commercial banks, and central-bank lending to the government. As in any accounting framework, total assets are equal to total liabilities, and the central bank creates new money (liabilities) whenever it purchases new assets.

6. Currency in circulation is part of base money, but in this simplification it is taken to be separately determined by transaction needs and so does not influence the money multiplier.

Central banks have three basic policy instruments to control the money supply:

1. Directly supplying base money. The central bank buys government bonds or foreign exchange, increasing deposits, reserves, and the money supply.

2. Raising or lowering official interest rates, thus indirectly changing the supply of base money. The central bank provides credit to commercial banks, so lowering the interest rate will increase borrowing by commercial banks from the central bank. The increase in commercial bank deposits at the central bank increases the supply of base money.

3. Changing the money multiplier. The central bank can change reserve requirements. The reserve ratio is like the fulcrum of a lever; adjusting the fulcrum produces big changes in the final money supply.

The choice among these instruments will depend on specific conditions. In a country with a developed financial system and stable macroeconomic conditions, adjustments in the interest rates and modest purchases or sales of treasury bonds will typically be sufficient. When conditions change more rapidly, large purchases of treasury bonds or changes in the reserve requirement may be needed to achieve larger effects. In a developing country like China, more crude but effective measures may be necessary.

18.5   Special Features of China's Monetary System

The preceding principles of money formation apply to all modern economies. Three distinctive features of China's system are highlighted here.

First, in China, quantity instruments are more important than interest-rate instruments. For many decades, interest rates in China were tightly controlled and played almost no role. Chinese financial markets had few clear interest-rate benchmarks until about 2015. Conversely, the Chinese central bank, the People's Bank of China (PBC), uses quantitative monetary policy instruments regularly and much more aggressively than developed market economies do. In addition, changes in base money, driven by changes in foreign-exchange reserves, have been large. Partly as a result, the PBC has regularly adjusted the required reserve ratio. For this reason, the equation that determines the money multiplier is directly relevant to China, one of the few economies in the world where economists watch the reserve ratio and speculate about changes in it on a weekly or monthly basis. In important macroeconomic policy episodes, quantitative actions have played a big role. Today, most administrative interest-rate setting has been phased out, and controls over bank-deposit rates were finally removed in 2015 (chapter 19). Nonetheless, informal interventions ("window guidance") over interest rates remain, and quantitative measures are important.

Second, since the beginning of the reform process in 1978, China has undergone a consistent process of monetization. That is, the velocity of circulation of money has declined consistently over the long term. Alternatively stated, the money supply has consistently grown faster than nominal GDP, even though inflation has generally remained low. Early on, this was easy to understand, since China was coming out of an almost cashless socialist economy, especially in the countryside. Few households had significant holdings of money, and small businesses that used cash were basically nonexistent. However, even after the economy would seem to have become fully monetized, around 2005, broad measures of money have continued to grow faster than GDP. This may make life easier for monetary policy-makers, since they have more slack to increase monetary growth, but it complicates their work as professionals, since it is hard to know the appropriate benchmarks for the speed of money supply growth. Recall the monetary identity: policy-makers should keep the money supply growing fast enough to accommodate real GDP growth and the reduction in velocity (but not much faster than that, in order to keep inflation low). This has added a layer of uncertainty about appropriate money-supply growth.

Third, the Chinese central bank, the PBC, is not autonomous. Most other market economies have independent central banks because it has been found that monetary policy is more successful and consistent when central bankers are insulated from political concerns. Strong norms protect central bankers from political interference, even by the national chief executive. This is not true in China: monetary policy decisions are made by the premier and are ratified by the Standing Committee of the Communist Party Politburo. This has two separate effects: specific monetary policy decisions must be cleared with the premier; and the PBC does not have the authority to announce a set of long-run targets or decision rules (like the Taylor rule). These features impede effective monetary policy. In practice, the PBC is extremely influential and often will have the premier's ear. The PBC has great expertise in macroeconomic issues and has been led by effective and persuasive technocrats (PBC head Zhou Xiaochuan served from December 2002 through 2017). Still, at the end of the day, the PBC must carry out the macroeconomic policy directives set by the central government and the Communist Party.

18.6   Chinese Monetary Policy in Practice: Three Episodes

We saw earlier that China's long-term macroeconomic performance since 1997 has been positive. In this section, we examine three episodes that illustrate the most important aspects of policy-makers' choices: (1) the control of inflation in 1996–1998, (2) the positive shock of entry into the World Trade Organization in 2003–2004, and (3) the shock of the global financial crisis in 2008–2009. Macroeconomic policy management includes providing long-term stability, but also adjusting to both positive and negative shocks.

18.6.1   Controlling Inflation and Adapting to Real Shocks, 1996–1998

As shown in figure 18.1, 1997 was a turning point in China's inflation performance. The high and volatile inflation before 1997 was typical of countries transitioning out of socialism. Decades of growth under controlled prices led to a buildup of frustrated purchasing power for many commodities, so the relaxation of price controls almost inevitably led to inflation. Moreover, the decentralization of economic power that was part of the reform process inevitably increased aggregate demand. When enterprises and local governments have soft budget constraints, they have strong demand for investment ("investment hunger") and also wish to increase wages and bonuses for managers and workers. When they are given more authority, they overspend. Thus reform-driven decentralization produces some of the same macroeconomic cycles we observed in the socialist period (chapter 4). The common feature is decentralization in the presence of soft budget constraints. There were some special features of the Chinese cycle that took place from 1992 to 1997: Deng Xiaoping's "Southern Tour" in early 1992 set off a scramble for deals and projects among local governments and state-owned enterprises (SOEs) that understood that the old system of planned controls was collapsing. In this environment of extreme soft budget constraints, inflation soared again.

In response to this challenge, Zhu Rongji developed a policy regime in the late 1990s that was a combination of orthodox macroeconomic policy and deep systemic reform. The PBC was made into a true central bank, an essential step that strengthened and rationalized the bank's control over aggregate lending and over the money supply. While central policy-makers had always been able to end cycles by imposing draconian controls on finance, now, for the first time, they had instruments they could use to guide the economy to a soft landing. At the same time, the fact that SOEs were losing money and the central government was experiencing a serious revenue crisis created a political environment supportive of a strict macroeconomic policy regime.

In these conditions, Premier Zhu Rongji began to steadily restrict the growth of credit and money. Doing so meant imposing hard budget constraints on commercial banks, which in turn imposed hard budget constraints on the industrial SOEs that were their primary clients. In other words, commercial banks began to insist on repayment. At the same time, tighter monetary policy inevitably lowered both inflation and the real growth rate (section 18.4.2), creating economic forces that pressured SOEs and pushed many state firms into bankruptcy. With this combination of political will and effective instruments, Zhu was able to manage the disinflation process toward a soft landing while also forcing a necessary but painful restructuring on the state sector.

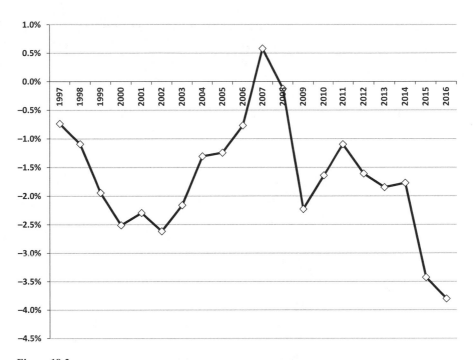

Figure 18.3
Fiscal surplus or deficit (percent of GDP).
Sources: Definition of fiscal surplus and deficit follows Ministry of Finance, which makes extensive use of reserve deposits. *SAC* (2017, 69); and Ministry of Finance, mof.gov.cn.

Just as this policy was gaining traction in the second half of 1997, the Asian financial crisis erupted in Thailand. Over the next two years, economic activity in much of East Asia plummeted. Although China was spared the worst, China's exports stopped growing, and there was additional downward pressure on the economy. In fact, the inflation rate fell into negative territory during 1998–2000, so that contractionary policy overshot to a certain extent (figure 18.1). Zhu's response was to maintain the tough monetary stance but increase fiscal spending, primarily on infrastructure investment (figure 18.3). The deficit increased from below 1% of GDP in 1997 to 2.5% in 2000, marking the first intentional use of the fiscal deficit as a macroeconomic policy instrument in China. This policy mix worked reasonably well, and the economy was clearly recovering by 2000. Although the downsizing of the state sector was painful, it laid the groundwork for the quick and healthy recovery that followed.

18.6.2   WTO Entry: A Positive Shock

China's entry into the World Trade Organization and the gradual phasing in of WTO-related provisions between 2001 and 2004 led to the creation of a new trading regime for China (chapter 16). In particular, new rules greatly improved the access of Chinese firms, especially private firms, to world markets. Part of this improved access came from the concessions made by other WTO members to open their markets to Chinese goods, but much more important was that China liberalized its trading system to allow access to virtually all domestic firms. The combination of a more open trading system, increased competition, and the dramatic industrial restructuring of the Zhu Rongji era caused a surge of productivity (Brandt et al. 2017). Supply-side shocks are especially challenging for macroeconomic policy-makers because they send opposite signals on growth versus inflation.[7] In this case, growth accelerated because of both the positive demand shock of increased net exports and the supply-side shock of improved productivity. With countervailing effects, inflation, after a brief spike in 2004, quickly moderated. It was difficult for the PBC to know which instruments to deploy.

Under these circumstances, the increased competitiveness of China's exports led to a steadily increasing export surplus, which gradually became the most important macroeconomic fact. Policy-makers could have responded by adjusting the exchange rate to increase the value of the Chinese currency. However, Premier Wen Jiabao insisted that China's exchange rate should remain stable, overruling the PBC, which was known to favor appreciation. This decision inevitably implied that China would accumulate official foreign-exchange reserves (since the demand for RMB to buy exports surpassed the demand for dollars to buy imports and the capital account was restricted). By the end of 2004, the PBC was purchasing $20 billion of foreign exchange every month. Inevitably, this meant a rapid increase in the domestic money supply. As the PBC bought foreign exchange, it paid out RMB, increasing the high-powered (base) money supply. In order to prevent the overall money supply from growing too rapidly, the PBC raised the required reserve ratio in steps from 6% to 17.5% between 2002 and June 2008. In other words, the money multiplier decreased from about 13 to under 6 (that is, from $1/.06$ to $1/.175$). Quantitative instruments played the dominant role in Chinese monetary policy during this period. The PBC first tried to reduce the growth of base money by "sterilizing" the increase in foreign-exchange reserves (selling bank bonds to sop up deposits). This was not enough, so the PBC raised the required reserve ratio. Quantitative measures can be a crude but effective means of monetary control.

In mid-2005, the link to the U.S. dollar was broken, and the RMB began a gradual appreciation. However, the pace of appreciation was initially slow. The trade surplus continued to widen through 2007, and economic growth and inflation were both accelerating. Moreover, monthly PBC purchases of foreign exchange reached $40 billion. Macroeconomic policy-makers tightened fiscal policy (figure 18.3), but

---

7. This is most intuitive with an adverse supply-side shock, such as an increase in oil prices: the shock increases inflation, which tells policy-makers to tighten the money supply, but it slows growth, which tells policy-makers to expand the money supply.

they were clearly falling behind the curve. Inflation accelerated above the 5% warning line. Finally, in the last quarter of 2007, policy-makers shifted to full inflation-fighting mode. The RMB was allowed to appreciate rapidly for the first time, and monetary policy tightened. By this time, China was using all three main policy instruments in coordinated fashion: fiscal, monetary, and exchange-rate policies were all tightening. The repercussions were quick in both the stock market and the housing markets, where bubbles burst and asset prices fell. The PBC was preparing additional contractionary steps in mid-2008 when the economic landscape was suddenly overturned by the eruption of the global financial crisis thousands of miles away in New York City.

18.6.3   The Global Financial Crisis, 2008–2009

China's response to the global financial crisis (GFC) of 2008–2009 was remarkably quick and decisive. The collapse of Lehman Brothers on September 15, 2008, marked the beginning of full-fledged crisis. Within two months, China had completely reversed its macroeconomic policy orientation dating from the preceding inflationary period and had announced a 4 trillion RMB ($580 billion) fiscal stimulus program. Even more impressive, within another six weeks, money was actually flowing to construction projects around the country. During 2009, China's prompt and aggressive policy-making began to have an unmistakable effect on China's economy and the world.

18.6.3.1   The Initial Stimulus Response

China's announcement of a 4 trillion RMB fiscal stimulus program caught the world's attention and ever since has served as a shorthand for the Chinese response (table 18.1). In some respects, this is unfortunate since the fiscal program was less than it initially appeared. It included 1 trillion RMB in funds that had already been authorized for reconstruction after the May 2008 Sichuan earthquake. Outlays were scheduled over three years and amounted to under 2% of GDP per year. Indeed, the fiscal deficit never expanded much beyond 2% of GDP (figure 18.3), and the fiscal stimulus program was dwarfed by the flood of credit that the government's proactive policy stance unleashed. Still, the clear formulation contributed to confidence, and the emphasis on infrastructure construction promised a response that was both appropriate to the macroeconomic environment and positive for long-run development.

The main characteristic of the stimulus was the unity of fiscal and monetary policy. China ramped up extremely rapid responses in both the fiscal and monetary dimensions; however, in aggregate terms, the monetary response was far larger than the fiscal response. The excess (above-normal) lending in just the first half of 2009 was equal to 14% of GDP. This far overshadowed the fiscal program and constituted proportionally one of the largest stimulus packages in the world. The U.S.

Table 18.1
Stimulus package investment plan (November 2008).

	Billions of RMB	Composition
Earthquake reconstruction (previously committed)	1,000	25%
Transport and power infrastructure (railroads, roads, airports, electricity grid)	1,800	45%
Rural village infrastructure	370	9%
Environmental investment; natural areas	350	9%
Affordable housing	280	7%
Technological innovation and structural adjustment	160	4%
Health and education	40	1%

Source: Naughton (2009).

fiscal stimulus package passed in 2009 was about 9% of GDP and stretched over several years. The Chinese stimulus was bigger and concentrated in 2009.

18.6.3.2   Rapid Uptake

The response to the November 2008 stimulus decision was remarkably rapid. By January 2009, there were clear signs of increased investment activity. Why was this response so rapid? In part, it was because China employed much more than the standard tools of macroeconomic policy. Behind the scenes, Communist Party channels were used to encourage or even mandate an urgent response. Provincial governments and ministries were brought to meetings and told to "make every second count." Meetings at the county level followed within a week. Furthermore, the fact that the banking system was predominantly state owned now came to the fore. State-owned commercial banks were instructed to carry out a relaxed credit policy to support increased investment. Budget constraints on the banks were quickly relaxed. The China Development Bank rolled out a program of long-term loans in which interest rates were subsidized in some cases. In other words, an extensive repoliticization of the financial system and investment decision-making was an important part of China's stimulus response.

18.6.3.3   Local-Government Response

Why were local actors eager to borrow and initiate new investment projects in the most uncertain period of a major economic crisis? We would not expect private actors to behave in this manner. Private investment demand ordinarily would drop in the face of reduced external demand and increased uncertainty. However, the main borrowers were not ordinary business units but local governments with very different objectives and incentives. The distinctive political economy of China's local governments was described in section 5.6, where it was stressed that local governments were strongly entrepreneurial actors whose leaders were evaluated and promoted on the basis of the success of local economic development. This fundamental feature affected the uptake of macroeconomic policy. A typical local government has a queue of projects waiting to be approved. When a negative shock hit the system, local governments could pull a project "off the shelf," more or less ready-made, so the response to the increased availability of credit was rapid.

In the crisis mentality of 2009, local governments were allowed to develop government-sponsored corporations to carry out investment projects. These corporations—often called "local-government funding vehicles"—have always existed in China, but the central government has generally kept them on a short leash, worried that they could be used to circumvent the oversight of local spending. During the crisis, caution was abandoned, and local governments were encouraged to set up investment companies that could move quickly to implement stimulus measures. With abundant credit resources and receptive local governments, these local-government funding vehicles expanded rapidly during 2009, adding an estimated 10 percentage points of GDP debt to their balance sheets in a single year.

18.6.3.4   Legacies of the Chinese Stimulus Program

The 2009 stimulus program thus has an extremely complex economic legacy. On one hand, the program buffered China from the impact of the GFC and kept growth strong. GDP growth, after briefly dropping close to zero at the end of 2008, rebounded to 9.2% for all of 2009. Following on the explosive growth of the 2003–2007 period, this achievement cemented China's emergence as the second-largest economy in the world. Moreover, Chinese policy contributed to global economic recovery. Chinese demand for imports began to recover in the second quarter of 2009, signaling to world markets the possible end of the downward spiral of the previous six months. The big negative contribution that net exports made to China's growth in 2009–2010 (figure 18.2) was a positive contribution to the rest of the world, rebalancing the global economy and contributing to the recovery of global demand. China "gave back" the increase in net exports that had fed its growth in 2005–2007 in a way that was timely and significant.

However, the stimulus also had substantial long-term costs. The most important was the repoliticization of the economy referred to earlier. Relaxing oversight of local governments and encouraging them to borrow inevitably led to the reinstatement of local-government soft budget constraints. Local governments clearly realized that they did not have to bear any risk from their investment decisions. This meant that their investment demand was "insatiable," and the system created what Kornai (1980) called "investment hunger." This partially reversed one of the signature achievements of the Zhu Rongji era, the creation of hard budget constraints for SOEs, banks, and local governments.

These considerations might not have been important if stimulus measures had been quickly reversed once recovery was in process. Already in mid-2009, it was clear that the stimulus, while successful, had been larger than expected and was not under control. Credit growth was gradually reined in, but there was no effort to withdraw liquidity or shut down projects still in the early stages of construction. On the contrary, policy-makers seemed to embrace the increased impact of government intervention. They were justifiably proud of the economy's overall performance, which seemed to validate a new stage of government activism. Moreover, the GFC had damaged the reputation of the American model of laissez-faire and of those Chinese economists who supported it. Perhaps as a result, no major steps were taken to reverse the politicization and soft-budget-constraint environment. The institutional characteristics of the Chinese system made it easy to open the credit spigot quickly, but it has not been easy to close the spigot quickly once it was opened.

As a result, China emerged from the stimulus program with a large financial overhang. Debt of local-government financing vehicles continued to grow even after the immediate crisis had passed. According to a very conservative accounting from the National Audit Office, debt owed by local governments and their local-government funding vehicles increased steadily and reached 18.5% of GDP in mid-2013. China came into the GFC with very low government debt, but after the rapid run-up in the GFC, China is now at a medium debt level. Moreover, inflation pushed up briefly in 2011 because of lax monetary conditions. Despite its overall success, then, the stimulus program bequeathed a significant negative legacy as well.

18.7   Macroeconomic Policy After the High-Growth Era

As described throughout this book, China for the past several years has been undergoing a transition from a high-growth phase to a more moderate growth path. This means that the growth of potential output from year to year is quite different from what it was in the past. Potential output used to grow 10% or more in a single year, whereas in 2016–2017, potential output is probably growing in the range of 6% to 7%. This shift of growth trajectory counts as a shock, but it is a particular type of shock. The changes in potential output growth happen quite gradually. The slowdown in labor-force growth, for example, has extended over decades. In some respects, therefore, it ought to be possible to adjust macroeconomic policy to the new normal. However, dealing with a growth slowdown is much more difficult than it might initially appear.

There are at least three reasons why the growth slowdown presents unusual challenges. First, it is hard for policy-makers to quantify and accept the fact that growth potential has suddenly diminished. They see what is on the surface, that new industrial capabilities have been created and living standards have improved, and wait too long before adapting to changing economic conditions. Second, growth slowdown creates additional problems because of the relationship between investment and the rest of the economy through various "accelerator" effects. As long as final demand is growing rapidly, investment demand is correspondingly robust. In turn, that investment demand reinforces demand upstream for industries that supply investment projects. When final demand growth slows, it whipsaws upstream demand. For example, as demand for steel flattens, demand for investment in new steel mills drops suddenly (potentially to zero). The profitability of a whole class of investment projects declines. These effects have the potential to transform a gradual slowdown into a sharp contraction. Third, partly as a result of the previous points, there will often be a buildup of financial problems. The composition of investment demand changes rapidly, and overall private investment demand declines. Policy-makers support new public investments (in order to sustain rapid growth as long as possible), while private investors discover some of their existing projects were based on now disappointed expectations. This can lead to a buildup of unprofitable investment projects and nonperforming loans, creating new challenges for monetary policy authorities, who are responsible for the overall health of the banking system.

These problems presented challenges to policy-makers in previous cases of growth slowdown, for example, in Japan in the early 1990s (the second phase of Japan's slowdown, to be sure) and Korea in the late 1990s, and are now popping up in China in 2016–2017. So far, the general response of China's policy-makers has been to try to keep the growth rate high. This is evident in figure 18.4, which shows the growth rate of credit and nominal GDP. Credit surged above 30% growth during the GFC. It has since come down, but only to about 15% annual growth, where it has consistently remained since early 2011.[8] At first, in 2010–2011, this rapid growth of credit seemed to be causing inflation, and for a while, the PBC brought the growth of credit down below the growth of nominal GDP. Since then, however, the growth of nominal GDP has fallen substantially because of both the real growth slowdown and the global decline in commodity prices that has pushed down Chinese industrial prices (and pushed the GDP deflator virtually to zero in 2015). The result is that credit and money are growing much more rapidly than nominal GDP, but so far this has not caused inflation. This is a worldwide phenomenon, due to falling prices of commodity markets and general excess capacity. At the same time, as figure 18.3 showed, fiscal policy has become quite expansionary, with a deficit even bigger than that during the GFC.

8. Other components of total credit have grown much more rapidly. See the discussion in chapter 19.

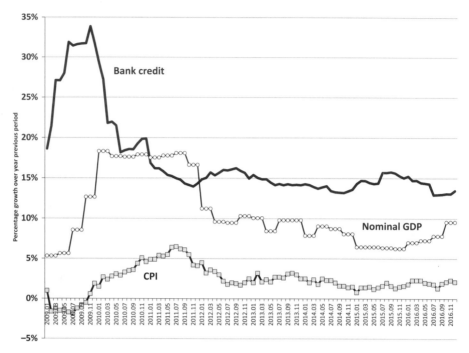

Figure 18.4
Growth of credit and nominal GDP (2009–2016).
Sources: Monthly growth of bank credit, People's Bank of China, pbc.gov.cn; quarterly GDP data and monthly price data, National Bureau of Statistics, http://www.stats.gov.cn/tjsj/zxfb/201601/t20160120 _1306759.html.

In short, since 2012, Chinese macroeconomic policy has been consistently expansionary, trying to prevent the slowdown of the economy. All three of the main macroeconomic policy instruments were at an expansionary setting through the end of 2016. Bank credit has grown rapidly and, as chapter 19 shows, other forms of credit have grown much more rapidly. Fiscal deficits expanded in 2015 and 2016. Currency depreciation was allowed until the policy became unsustainable in late 2016. Thus macroeconomic policy-makers are leaning hard against the tendency of the economy to slow down after the end of miracle growth. This suits the political orientation of leaders but contributes to softer budget constraints and worrisome growth of debt. From a global standpoint, expansionary Chinese policy has probably been beneficial, helping stabilize expectations and prop up demand in the face of protracted and mostly unanticipated sluggish growth. However, these conditions suggest that China is vulnerable to a change in macroeconomic conditions. If global price trends significantly reverse, Chinese macroeconomic policy-makers will face a harsh trade-off between higher inflation and slower growth.

18.8   Conclusion

China has overall been successful in adapting macroeconomic policy instruments to an increasingly marketized environment. Rapid growth and generally stable prices are the benefits that come from effective macroeconomic policy. Overall, the transition from the command economy was made with only moderate episodes of inflation and avoided a destabilizing sense of unfairness. To some extent, macroeconomic policy-makers benefited from favorable conditions in the Chinese economy due to the success of economic reform. The demand for money increased throughout the reform era (the velocity slowed down), allowing the system to absorb a fairly rapid overall monetary growth rate. The upward shift in monetary demand was presumably due to the high Chinese household saving rate and the rise of unincorporated businesses and the informal economy. The steady improvement in utilization of resources, above all, labor resources, also created favorable conditions for macroeconomic policy. In other words, the successes of macroeconomic policy in China should not be taken in isolation but rather should be understood as an integral part of a generally successful program of reform and market transition.

The reliance of the PBC on primarily quantitative instruments has been a distinctive feature of Chinese monetary policy and also a source of frustration for the PBC. Financial reforms—covered in chapter 19—envisage a transition toward a system of market-determined interest rates. There has been significant progress in this direction, particularly since 2015. Interest-rate benchmarks for the interbank lending market and for "repos" (short-term lending of Treasury bills) have developed and are publicly available. The PBC has developed experience in injecting and withdrawing liquidity from financial markets through lending facilities, repos, and reverse repos. Still, required reserve ratios for commercial banks are still very high, at 17%. In January 2017, the PBC reduced that reserve requirement to 16% for 28 days to provide liquidity for the New Year, showing that short-term manipulation of reserve requirements is still part of the PBC toolbox. The PBC clearly welcomes the change to a diversity of instruments. The diversification enables the PBC to move away from quantitative instruments and adopt more indirect (and less distortionary) interest-rate policies instead. Indeed, the PBC's heavy reliance on quantitative tools was in part forced on it by the need to manage dramatic changes in foreign-exchange reserves (which create base money), changes that the PBC would have preferred not to have to deal with. Today, the PBC faces a more challenging environment, but also deploys a much broader and more effective range of instruments.

Finally, if we characterize the overall macroeconomic policy stance in China since the turn of the century, we might say that it has been "super-Keynesian." After the experience with Zhu Rongji's orthodox contraction and reform policies, macroeconomic policy has been characterized by a prompt and mutually consistent use of Keynesian instruments for macroeconomic management. Monetary, fiscal, and exchange-rate policy have been used together to achieve desired outcomes. Moreover, policy has consistently stimulated increases in aggregate-demand components in order to keep growth high. For example, in the face of the positive WTO shock, policy-makers resisted allowing the currency to appreciate, ensuring that net exports (a large trade surplus) would make a big contribution to rapid growth. When the GFC caused a rapid change in economic conditions, an extremely forceful increase in investment—driven by both fiscal and monetary expansion—more than compensated for the reduction in net exports. This episode in particular could be called super-Keynesian because the speed and effectiveness of the expansionary impulse were in line with Keynesian prescriptions. Finally, since 2011, money and credit policy has given priority to keeping the growth rate as high as possible in the face of structural changes tending toward lower growth. So far, these super-Keynesian policies have kept Chinese growth rates among the highest in the world. These policies have both benefits and costs. The benefits are evident in today's high growth rates, while the costs mainly take the form of latent vulnerabilities in the financial system. These are discussed in chapter 19.

Bibliography

Suggestions for Further Reading

The literature on macroeconomics in China is not very accessible. Ma (2015) is a good example of a macroeconomist arguing a strong policy position with clear analysis and data. King (2016) on monetary policy in general is highly readable and is the source of the distinction between monetary policy in good times and in bad times.

References

Brandt, Loren, Johannes Van Biesebroeck, Luhang Wang, and Yifan Zhang (2017). "WTO Accession and Performance of Chinese Manufacturing Firms." *American Economic Review* (forthcoming). Accessed at https://www.aeaweb.org/articles?id=10.1257/aer.20121266.

IMF (International Monetary Fund) (2015). *World Economic Outlook*, April, 73–75, 83.

King, Mervyn (2016). *The End of Alchemy: Money, Banking and the Future of the Global Economy*. Boston: Little, Brown.

Kornai, J. (1980). *Economics of Shortage*. Amsterdam: North-Holland.

Ma Guonan (2015). "A Compelling Case for Chinese Monetary Easing." Bruegel Policy Contribution, issue 2015/06 (April).

Naughton, Barry (2009). "Understanding the Chinese Stimulus Package." *China Leadership Monitor*, no. 28 (Spring). Accessed at http://www.hoover.org/publications/clm/issues.

SAC (Annual). *Zhongguo Tongji Zhaiyao* [Statistical abstract of China]. Beijing: Zhongguo Tongji.

The Financial System

The Chinese financial system is currently undergoing momentous change. Long dominated by state-owned banks, the financial system today is evolving rapidly into a more diverse system with multiple actors and substantial market dependence. This is not an orderly process. It is driven by powerful and sometimes contradictory forces, including financial innovation, new Internet technologies, rent-seeking individuals, market-oriented reforms, and pressure from top policy-makers to provide liquidity to support growth. This process creates new opportunities and also new risks.

An efficient financial system fosters growth and prosperity, while flaws in financial systems are the most important causes of economic crisis and the recessions caused by financial crises. Earlier chapters have emphasized the role of high saving and investment in China's growth, but saving and investment can play their role effectively only with a well-functioning financial system.

The first two sections of this chapter set the scene, introducing some basic finance concepts, and discussing China's high-saving economy and some reasons for high saving. Sections 19.3 through 19.6 review the four major components of China's financial system: banks, stock markets, bond markets, and shadow banks. Section 19.7 describes the liberalization and diversification process that has gathered steam since 2013. Liberalization has allowed an increasing volume of saving to escape from the regulated and repressed formal financial system into lightly regulated "shadow-banking" sectors. This process has not been smooth, and section 19.8 describes some of the risks posed by growing debt and leverage in the Chinese system.

19.1 Building Block Concepts

The financial system channels savings into investment by matching savers with investors. In the process, the financial system steadily creates new financial assets (such as bank deposits, stocks, and bonds) as the economy develops. The pool of savings—created by the act of saving—grows more rapidly than GDP, and so the ratio of financial assets to GDP increases. This process is called "financial deepening." As financial deepening proceeds, a more diverse set of financial assets develops. Savers want assets with different risk characteristics. Some savers are willing to bear high levels of risk in search of high returns, while others purchase insurance to reduce their risk. Borrowers are willing to offer different interest rates to get funds under different conditions. The diversification of financial assets is called "financial broadening." The processes of financial deepening and broadening are ongoing, since financial innovation continuously creates new asset types that combine risk and return in new ways.

There are two main types of financial institutions that transfer funds from savers to investors: banks and capital markets. Banks provide indirect finance. A bank sets itself up as an intermediary, taking deposits from savers and providing loans to investors. The bank converts the maturity of funds (using short-term money to make long-term loans), and specializes in evaluation of the risk and return of potential borrowers. Capital markets, for stocks and bonds, provide direct finance. Borrowers obtain funds directly by selling bonds (fixed-income securities) or stocks (ownership claims). Financial broadening usually encompasses an increase in the relative importance of direct finance, that is, of capital markets. However, all modern financial systems combine direct and indirect finance. Companies access funds both from capital markets and from banks.

19.1.1   China: Financial Deepening Under Bank Dominance

Until around 2009, the financial system in China could be summarized in two words: "deep" and "narrow." As China reformed, households and unincorporated businesses increased their savings and put them in banks. The banking system became the dominant financial channel and intermediated household surpluses to businesses to be invested. One index of the depth of a financial system is the ratio of "broad" money, M2, consisting of currency in circulation plus demand and savings deposits, to GDP. As figure 19.1 shows, this ratio increased very rapidly from 32% of GDP in 1978 to 162% in 2003, paused for several years, and then resumed its increase to 211% in 2016. This ratio is higher than in other high-saving East Asian economies and much higher than in most other economies. By the end of 2016, the Chinese banking system was the largest in the world, having surpassed that of the entire Eurozone (Wildau 2017).

However, for most of the post-1978 period, financial deepening was not accompanied by financial broadening or diversification. Bank deposits and lending were the dominant form of intermediation, accounting for 80% of the funds provided to the corporate sector. Corporate bonds were practically nonexistent until after 2010. A stock market was created in the 1990s, and fluctuated enormously in importance over

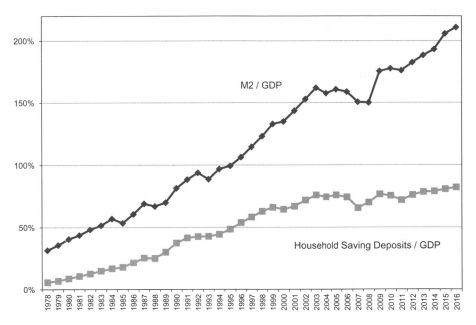

Figure 19.1
Financial deepening: M2 and household saving.
Source: People's Bank of China, accessed at http://www.pbc.gov.cn/diaochatongjisi/116219/116319/3013637/3013641/index.html.

the succeeding 25 years, but overall has been much less important for raising funds than the banking system. China's financial system has thus been "narrow." This system only gradually began to change after 2009, as described in section 19.6. Even today, the financial system is bank-dominated, and since nearly all the important banks are state owned, China's financial system is also state dominated.

19.1.2   Financial Repression

A sub-set of narrow, bank-dominated financial systems consists of those characterized by "financial repression." In a financially repressed system, savers receive very low returns and have little choice. The real interest rate on bank deposits, after accounting for inflation, is usually negative. Banks and their clients benefit from access to these cheap funds, and the government steers credit toward favored borrowers. To make a system of financial repression work, households are generally restricted in their ability to purchase financial assets other than bank deposits. Some degree of financial repression characterizes many developing countries.

Generally speaking, China's financial system has been one of financial repression. Over the long term, it has served to channel low cost funds from households to businesses, and especially to state-owned enterprises (SOEs). But here we must be careful. First, there are degrees of financial repression, from mild to very severe. Second, although financial repression works to the advantage of the government and disadvantage of savers, it is often something governments stumble into unintentionally. In particular, macroeconomic policy mistakes often lead to financial repression when governments try to protect their interests and objectives in an inflationary environment. Third, different styles of financial repression can exist at different times. Sometimes the banks themselves are the biggest beneficiaries of financial repression, but sometimes the benefits flow to their clients, especially SOEs. These cautions lead us to expect that financial repression is not a permanent characteristic of the Chinese system, but rather a recurrent feature of fluctuating intensity. These issues are discussed later in this section and in section 19.6.

We normally expect that a financially repressed system would be shallow: facing low returns and little choice, households should save less. However, we have already seen that China's financial system is unusually deep, and section 19.2 will describe China's very high saving rate. In one important respect, China has been successful in protecting the interests of savers. The relatively stable macroeconomic environment (chapter 18) means that most savers have been able to at least maintain the value of their bank balances. During periods of high inflation through 1997, household term-saving deposits have been paid supplemental interest to match the increase in the consumer price index, protecting the value of deposits. This is in contrast with the experience of most transitional economies, where the sudden release of prices in the face of pent-up inflationary pressures led to a surge of inflation that wiped out the value of savings deposits. China's more cautious approach to transition averted this kind of financial demolition. Thus, the development of China's deep financial system contrasts with what happened, for example, in Russia, where broad money (M2) declined from 80% to only 20% of GDP between 1990 and 1993. In those economies, financial systems shrank even more rapidly than the overall economy declined, and they had to be rebuilt from the ground up.

Indeed, through 1997 China was protecting the interests of savers while continuing to provide low-cost funds to SOEs (which did not pay supplemental interest on their loans when inflation surged). This was only possible because the banking system itself was bearing the costs of subsidizing SOEs. By the end of the 1990s, bank resources had been depleted, were technically bankrupt, and had to be rescued by a massive write-off of bad loans and recapitalization. That bank bail-out is discussed in section 19.3.4. Subsequently, a new version of financial repression was instituted that, intentionally or unintentionally, protected the interests of the banks and allowed them to maintain profitability and rebuild their capital. This style of financial repression was maintained until about 2013, and after that the privileged position of banks gradually began to erode (sections 19.6 and 19.7).

19.1.3   Costs and Benefits of Financial Repression

Some economists argue that financial repression has benefits. Financial repression serves as a mechanism to pump resources into investment in ways subject to government influence. During the high-growth era, the government may have had a good idea of the kind of infrastructure investment necessary to drive growth, and financial repression may have helped concentrate investment in essential projects. Japan and Korea both had financially repressed financial systems during their high-growth eras. It is even possible to interpret the command economy as a very extreme form of financial repression. However, financial repression has substantial costs, of which three are most important:

1. Investment is misallocated. Since lending rates are low, low-productivity projects sponsored by the government appear profitable. Bank credit must be rationed, and the criteria for the rationing are rarely clear. Higher-productivity projects sponsored by small-scale and private actors cannot get funding, even though they are willing to pay higher interest rates.

2. Income is transferred away from households, and consumption is depressed. Chinese households savings deposits are about 1.25 times household disposable income; if interest rates on those deposits were 2 percentage points higher, household income would increase by 2.5%, and most of this would be shifted from investment to consumption. Reducing financial repression would contribute to rebalancing the economy by increasing consumption demand.

3. Volatility in asset markets increases. Households have few options to diversify and get a decent return on their saving. Frustrated households seek other outlets for their saving, especially housing. Whenever it appears that alternate channels for investment are opening up—for example, when the stock market seems to be opening up—households quickly shift into that arena, causing short-term bubbles that draw in even more funds. Financial repression makes problems of high housing prices worse.

It seems that the costs of financial repression are lower during the high-growth period, but increase after high growth is over.

19.2   Saving

China is an extremely high-saving economy, and this characteristic is fundamental to many aspects of the economy. For example, it explains how China is able to maintain such a high investment effort without relying on foreign saving and it is also essential to understanding the financial system.

19.2.1   The Flow-of-Funds Table

The distribution of income among the household, business, and government sectors is called the "primary income distribution" and is shown here in a simplified "flow-of-funds" table (table 19.1). The flow of funds is a way of looking at gross domestic product through the income approach (we looked at the production approach in chapter 7 and the expenditure approach in chapter 18). This divides the national economy into households, businesses (financial and nonfinancial), and government, and looks at the income of each of these big sectors.

Business produces the bulk of GDP. It transfers income to households through wages and profit distribution and to government through taxes. The household sector (column 1) includes unincorporated household businesses. Households defined in this broad way—which include farms and small shops and service businesses—produce a very substantial amount of total value added (15.7 trillion RMB, or 24% of the national total). In addition, households receive wages and other payments from business and government. This broadly defined household sector has a very high saving rate, 38% of net income. The household sector invests quite a lot in its own assets, including housing and household businesses, but even after this investment, households have a net surplus of 7.2 trillion RMB, which is available to be loaned to, or invested in, the business sector. The primary job of the financial sector is to facilitate this investment.

After business pays out wages and taxes, it is left with a net disposable income—or retained, after-tax profit—of 13.2 trillion RMB. By definition, businesses cannot "consume" (only individuals can consume, so businesses distribute money to individuals, such as owners), so all the 13.2 trillion RMB is saving. This is not enough to fund its desired investments, so businesses borrow 5.6 trillion RMB (9% of GDP) from the household sector. The financial system helps businesses to access this

Table 19.1
Simplified flow of funds.

	Household (trillions of RMB)	Business (trillions of RMB)	Government	Total domestic
Value added	15.7	43.9	4.8	64.4
Total disposable income	39.1	13.2	12.2	64.5
Savings	14.9	13.2	3.6	31.7
(Saving rate)	38%	100%	29%	49%
Gross capital formation	7.7	19.3	3.4	30.3
Net financing + acquisitions	7.2	−5.6	−0.2	1.4

Source: *SYC* (2016, table 3-21).

financing flexibility and at low cost. Finally, government is also a large saver and even has a small saving surplus. Although China runs a general budget deficit, this is more than offset by the surplus accumulating in various government funds, such as the social security fund balances deposited in the bank.

The flow-of-funds table shows that China saves a lot: 49% of national income in 2014. The high saving rate can be mechanically explained by three factors. First, the household saving rate is high, and households account for almost half of total saving. Second, business income is a relatively high share of national income, and all of business income is saved and re-invested. Corporate net income was 21% of GDP in 2014 in China, compared to about 10% of GDP in 2013–2015 in the United States, during a period of historically high profits; the long-term average is close to 6% (Yardeni and Johnson 2015). Third, the fact that government is a net saver also obviously contributes to high national saving.

19.1.2   High Household Saving Rate

Economists have advanced several explanations for China's high household saving rate, without coming to a general consensus. Five important explanations have been advanced:

1. The large number of unincorporated businesses pushes up household saving. In all economies, unincorporated businesses have high saving rates. Small businesses often have difficulty accessing credit (in China and elsewhere) and must grow their businesses through retained earnings.

2. Rapid household income growth causes households to save more. Chapter 10 showed that urban household income growth has been around 7.5% per year for 30 years. Whenever household income growth is rapid, saving rates rise. Why does this occur? Economists agree that households work with a set of expectations about their lifetime or "permanent" incomes. When incomes rise rapidly, households update their expected lifetime income more slowly than their short-term income is changing. They expect to spread consumption over their lifetimes by saving in high-income periods, and they may also raise their target household wealth. People cautiously adapt to improving income. The natural effect of habit in human behavior strongly reinforces this factor. Consumption habits change slowly, particularly those habits of prudence and frugality formed when incomes low.

3. Life-cycle saving interacts with the demographic dividend to create decades of high saving. The concept of life-cycle saving was introduced in chapter 8, arguing that households will smooth out consumption over the lifetime of family members. Since income peaks between 30 and 55, we expect households to save more when the share of the population at peak income-earning years is high, as it has been in China since the 1990s. Later, households will dis-save when there are large numbers

of elderly. However, microeconomic studies of Chinese saving (i.e., those using individual household data) have not been able to demonstrate this relationship. Saving remains high even when the head of the household is elderly (Chamon and Prasad 2010; Modigliani and Cao 2004). Because the evidence for life-cycle saving is weak, economists have sought other explanations.

4. Chinese households may experience an unusually high demand for precautionary saving. This argument is based on the rapid decline in government social security during the 1980s and 1990s combined with the shift to single-child households. In this view, Chinese parents traditionally relied on their children (specifically their sons) for social security in old age. The rapid reduction in fertility rates has meant that fewer parents can depend on their children for support when they are elderly or sick. Most rural households have no government support to look forward to, and the proportion of urban dwellers covered by generous state-enterprise pensions has declined slowly.

5. Chinese households may save more because of distinctive rules governing new household formation. As young couples contemplate marriage, they face a widely accepted norm that the husband's family should provide a home (apartment or house) for the new married couple. This expectation, it is argued, raises saving among all members of the extended family, who chip in to provide the young couple with the real estate asset. Age at first marriage is increasing (according to the 2010 census, almost 27 for men and 25 for women), and housing is expensive, especially in big cities, so external conditions mean that this explanation is plausible. According to one large-scale survey, 52% of unmarried women believe that home ownership is a prerequisite for marriage ("Love and Marriage" 2012). Wei and Zhang (2009) argued that males in an increasingly competitive marriage market must accumulate substantial financial resources by the time they are (for example) 30. This saving dynamic is very different from the traditional life-cycle saving model and also from household saving patterns in the United States.

Both the precautionary-saving motive and the household-formation motive display the strong influence of China's one-child policy. Rapid change in household characteristics, triggered by government actions, has induced large changes in household saving behavior. Choukhmane, Coeurdacier, and Jin (2013) argued that a key may be found in analyzing the response of different generations to the one-child policy. Older generations have increased their precautionary saving, while younger generations save for household formation; the result has been higher saving across the board that does not correspond to the ordinary predictions of the life-cycle saving model.

The explanation of China's extremely high household saving rate is essential if we are to resolve a paradox of China's financial system. Returns to financial saving have been low for the past decade, due to financial repression, but Chinese households have continued to save at high rates. This apparent contradiction can be resolved only if we find that Chinese households have an unusually high propensity to save. The five factors enumerated here may help explain that high saving propensity. In the future, the fundamental dynamic of the life-cycle process may re-assert itself, and household saving rates in China would gradually decline from today's highs.

19.3   The Chinese Banking System

China's banking system has evolved continuously over the past 40 years. In the command economy, there was a banking system, but there were no stock and bond markets at all. Restructuring this banking system was one of the most urgent tasks of the early reform era. By the early twenty-first century, a strengthened banking system had emerged as the dominant part of the financial system.

19.3.1   The Command-Economy Banking System

China had a fully developed set of financial institutions under the command economy. Although the banking institutions looked like those in a market economy, they performed completely different functions. Intermediation from households to businesses was insignificant. First, household income was controlled so strictly that households rarely had any surplus income to save: financial saving through the 1960s and 1970s averaged under 3% of household income, compared with over 30% today. Second, there were few household businesses and many command-economy institutions replaced money-based transactions. The rural collectives—then the largest part of the economy—transacted directly with government commerce and distributed money to households only once, at the end of the year.

Overall, the command economy financial system was remarkably shallow. The government-run banks provided trade credit and payment services to facilitate the exchange of goods, but no long-term lending for investment projects. The financial system was purely "passive," meaning that important economic decisions were never based on financial considerations. Decisions about which investments to undertake were made by planners and were financed from the government budget; banks merely accommodated the physical flows that the planners arranged. In the days of the planned economy, these banks were subdivisions of a single government bank, sometimes dubbed the "monobank" because it was a single organization with a monopoly on financial business. With the sole exception of the tiny Rural Credit Cooperatives (RCCs), the monobank held all the assets in the financial system. The monobank kept the books on transactions among divisions of the state-run economy, and a large retail banking network mainly served to siphon off meager household savings for the benefit of the state-run economy. Although the system was inefficient, it had an enormous network that reached into every town in China and provided a nationwide system of payments transactions.

19.3.2   Creation of an Institutional Framework for the Banking System

During the 1980s and 1990s, China had to remake its banking system to serve the needs of a market economy. The first step was to break up the monobank and transform it into a set of diverse institutions with different goals and functions. During the 1980s, the People's Bank of China (PBC) was separated from the rest of the monobank and began a long process of conversion into a true central bank. Four state-run commercial banks—the "Big Four"—were carved out of the monobank and given independent identities and designated sectors. In 1994–1995, new laws were passed that provided a legal framework for the commercial banks and the PBC. Three "policy banks" were set up to take over the government-directed lending of the Big Four, freeing them to become truly commercial banks. The China Bank Regulatory Commission (CBRC) was established in 2003, completing the institutional setup. Entry of carefully vetted local and joint-stock banks was authorized, and a few foreign bank subsidiaries were allowed as well. Thus, shortly after the turn of the century, China had developed a full complement of banking institutions, including a central bank (the PBC), a regulatory body (the CBRC), and a diverse set of commercial banking and nonbanking institutions.

19.3.3   The Makeup of the Banking System

The long-term story of the evolution of the banking system is the decline of the share of the previously monopolistic Big Four to only 39% of total banking system assets in 2015 (table 19.2). However, the full story is more complex. The financial sector has not simply "grown out of the plan" by opening up to entrants. On the contrary, new entrants have been carefully vetted, and nearly all of them have close ties to the government, either central or local. None of the important banks are truly private; only in 2014 were a few tiny private banks granted legal recognition. At the same time, the Big Four have restructured ("equitized") and grown and are now among the largest and most profitable banks in the world.

19.3.3.1   Equitized Large State Banks

The equitized large state banks are the original Big Four state-run commercial banks and the Bank of Communications. These are huge organizations, with hundreds of thousands of employees and branches nationwide, and are the dominant deposit-taking institutions. Each has a distinct personality rooted in its history. The Industrial and Commercial Bank of China (ICBC) took over the urban bank branches of the

Table 19.2
Banking-sector assets (by type of bank).

	Number	Employees	2003	2007	2010	2013	2015
Policy banks	3	62,947	7.7%	8.1%	8.0%	8.3%	9.7%
Equitized large state banks	5	1,730,291	58.0%	53.7%	49.2%	43.3%	39.2%
Joint-stock commercial banks	12	402,432	10.7%	13.7%	15.6%	17.8%	18.6%
City commercial banks	133	370,124	5.8%	6.5%	8.2%	10.0%	11.4%
Rural banks and RCCs	2,303	859,248	9.7%	10.5%	11.2%	12.1%	12.4%
Nonbank financial institutions			3.3%	1.8%	2.2%	2.6%	3.3%
Foreign banks	40	46,730	1.5%	2.4%	1.8%	1.7%	1.3%
Postal Savings Bank			3.2%	3.3%	3.7%	4.1%	4.2%

Source: CBRC (2015, 192, 202).

old monobank—it is today the largest bank in the world by assets (and third largest in market capitalization). The Construction Bank (CCB) evolved out of the parts of the monobank that focused on project financing, while the Bank of China (BOC) evolved from the foreign-trade and foreign-exchange departments of the monobank. Today, the CCB and BOC possess higher levels of expertise and fewer branches, and they have restructured most rapidly. The Agricultural Bank of China (ABC) faces the most challenging economic environment because it operates in the lower-income rural sector and retains a large staff. All of the Big Four are listed on stock markets, but the government maintains a controlling stake. Although the Big Four have steadily declined as a share of the total, their conversion to profitable commercial banks, discussed in section 19.3.4 must be judged a success.

19.3.3.2 Policy Banks

While the Big Four have shrunk in relative terms, the three policy banks have steadily gained share. The China Development Bank (CDB), the Agricultural Development Bank, and the China Export-Import Bank make up the part of China's banking system under the most direct government control. All three of the policy banks are 100% owned by the Chinese government through various intermediaries. Originally set up in 1995 to shield the Big Four from political influence by relieving them of their policy lending responsibilities, the policy banks have played a large and increasingly important role since 2003, powered by the revival of government industrial policy. The China Development Bank (CDB) is by far the largest and most important of the three, with 12.6 trillion RMB in assets in 2015. All three development banks play important roles; for reasons of space, only the CDB is discussed here.

The CDB's core mission is to provide long-term financing for large infrastructure projects and priority heavy industries (Sanderson and Forsythe 2012). Many projects are assigned directly to the bank by the central government, often by the State Council. The CDB has funded the massive Three Gorges Dam, the strategic emerging industries (chapter 15), and affordable-housing initiatives. The CDB also makes large international loans (Downs 2011), and is a major funder of the Belt and Road Initiative designed to expand China's infrastructure connections abroad. In 2014, the CDB had US$267 billion of foreign-currency-denominated loans, more than the total loan portfolio of the World Bank

CDB funds do not come from deposits but from CDB bonds that are bought predominantly by the commercial banks. Since commercial banks are required to buy CDB bonds, these bonds amount to an implicit tax on the banking system. Despite its close ties to the government, the CDB has tried hard to build a high-quality professional organization; it is well run and enforces financial discipline on its borrowers. It is also sometimes very inventive. The CDB created the local-government financing vehicles (LGFVs) described in chapter 20. In 1998, the CDB helped a city government capitalize a new company with land rights and ongoing investments. This investment company then expanded borrowing by promising lenders return from future land sales, backstopped by local-government guarantees. The arrangement spread, and when the global financial crisis arrived in late 2008, this framework was used for the massive stimulus program.

19.3.3.3   Joint-Stock Commercial Banks

Twelve joint-stock commercial banks (JSCBs) were set up after 1986 (the Bank of Communications graduated from JSCB status to become the fifth equitized state bank). Each JSCB is a new entrant with a nationwide network and is relatively unburdened by baggage from the planned-economy era. The JSCBs have younger, more highly trained staffs and fewer bad loans on their books. They have steadily gained market share, reaching 18.6% of total banking-system assets in 2015. The JSCBs are generally listed on the stock exchange, so the public holds a minority of shares, while the government maintains a strong influence usually through indirect holdings by SOEs or government agencies. The JSCBs have pioneered new business approaches. The equitized large banks are more or less forced to be generalists, serving all types of customers, but the JSCBs have been free to carve out specialized business models. For example, JSCBs have taken the lead in developing credit-card programs, helped by alliances with foreign banks.

19.3.3.4   City Commercial Banks

The 133 city commercial banks grew out of urban credit cooperatives set up in the 1980s to provide services to small-scale urban firms. Most city commercial banks operate in a single region and are often controlled by the local government. With local-government sponsorship, city banks have grown rapidly to 11.4% of total assets in 2015, even though they often have weaker management and lower asset quality than JSCBs.

19.3.3.5   Rural Commercial Banks and Rural Credit Cooperatives

The rural credit cooperatives (RCCs) were the only financial institutions in the command-economy period that were not part of the monobank. They provided trade finance to the countryside and allowed farmers to purchase modern agricultural inputs. The RCCs thrived during the early phase of rural reform, channeling local savings into highly profitable TVEs. After a flourishing 1980s, the RCC network began to be plagued with bad debt and managerial problems in the 1990s. RCCs were often called on to make policy loans to support low-income agriculture, and their far-flung network of small-scale credit organizations was inherently expensive. After 2003, policy-makers pumped money into the RCCs and encouraged them to merge into cooperative banks or commercial banks. This program succeeded in moving RCCs out of the crisis zone, although sometimes at the cost of their capture by local governments or private businessmen. By 2015, these entities had increased their share of banking-sector assets to 12.4% (table 19.2).

19.3.3.6   Other Banking Sector Institutions

The five bank types described above have consistently accounted for 91–92% of bank assets from 2003 through 2015. Other financial institutions include the Postal Savings Bank, which was set up in emulation of Japan's (troubled) postal banking system. Nonbank financial institutions include leasing and automobile credit companies, trust companies, and credit-guarantee companies, all of which play an important role in niche areas of the financial system.

What about private banking? The failure of foreign banks to make a serious dent in the Chinese market is obvious in table 19.2: foreign-funded banks peaked at 2.4% of banking assets in 2007 and slipped to only 1.3% in 2015. This poor performance is directly attributable to the regulatory apparatus the Chinese government set up to hobble foreign banks: very high capital requirements and limitations on fund-raising ability in RMB (especially important given weak branch networks). In 2014, Chinese regulators approved five private banks. Two were set up as "Internet only" banks, including one controlled by Alibaba's Ant Financial Corporation. Three of these private banks are in new pilot trade zones. Of course, private banking activity is rife in the Chinese economy, but it does not usually have a firm legal basis. There is a vast informal lending sector in China (Tsai 2004). Private "underground banks" play an important role in providing quick, short-term, and expensive credit to businesses and households in need. The private element in the organized banking system is remarkably small.

19.3.3.7   Banking-Sector Makeup: Conclusion

The banking sector has gone through a remarkable process of diversification, and there are now banks that can meet almost any kind of need. The system is vastly more professional than it was 20 years ago and has generated large profits for over a decade. At the same time, the financial system is still almost as completely controlled by the government as it was a decade ago, and private and foreign ownership correspondingly limited. The banks subject to central government control—the policy banks, the equitized large state banks, and the Postal Saving Bank—together still accounted for 53% of banking-sector assets in 2015. Moreover, another 42% of assets were owned by the city commercial banks, with their close ties to local governments, or the JSCBs and the rural banks that have substantial government stakes and maintain close links to local governments. China has diversified its banking system while maintaining pervasive government influence. Indeed, two categories that have grown especially rapidly—policy banks and city commercial banks—display *increased* government influence. The policy banks explicitly carry out central government mandates, while the city commercial banks possess a degree of local monopoly power due to local government favoritism. Perhaps because of persistent government control, private and small-scale businesses continue to report difficulty in accessing banking services, notwithstanding nominally favorable policies.

19.3.4   The Bailout and Restructuring of the Banking System

During the period of "reform without losers" (1978–1993), the banking system played the key role in protecting inefficient firms from the consequences of increased competition. Soft budget constraints implied continuous bank lending to unviable clients, keeping many "zombie firms" alive. A large buildup of nonperforming loans (NPLs) inevitably occurred, and by the mid-1990s, the banking system was in desperate shape (Lardy 1998, 92–127). Finally, the Asian financial crisis in 1997–1998, which imposed huge costs on previously well-performing economies, such as Korea and Thailand, brought home the risks of using the banking system to prop up SOEs and policy-makers determined to inject sufficient resources into that system to avert crisis.

19.3.4.1   Bailout and Restructuring

In a remarkable sustained effort, between 1998 and 2006, China pumped money into its banking system, restructured it, and returned it to basic financial health. Essentially, a four-step process was followed:

1. Harden the banks' budget constraints. In an intensely political process, the government signaled strongly that it was willing to bear the costs of a major shrinkage

of the state sector. As described in chapters 5 and 18, control over the banking system was centralized. Lending officers were made personally responsible for their portfolios and harshly penalized for creating new bad loans. The primary objective was to plug the flow of resources to loss-making SOEs, but the only way to achieve that was to create a tough new incentive environment to stem the flow of resources into and out of the banks.

2. Massive NPL bailout. The government injected billions of RMB into the banking system to relieve it of the burden of legacy NPLs. In 1998, the government issued 270 billion RMB in special bonds and injected the capital into the commercial banks. When that was not enough, four state-run asset-management companies (AMCs) were established, one for each of the Big Four commercial banks. The AMCs purchased nonperforming loans at face value from the Big Four commercial banks for a total of 1.4 trillion RMB. The banks were relieved of about half their overall NPL burden at a cost of about 15% of 2001 GDP.

3. Bank restructuring. Banks had to begin an internal restructuring process on their own. They had to use their own financial resources (profits and loss provisioning) to write off recently generated NPLs and significantly improve internal management, auditing, and controls. Finally, they had to slim down and become more efficient. The Construction Bank was the leader; it sold or wrote off billions in bad loans, laid off a quarter of its staff, closed one-third of its branches, and invested heavily in information technology and a more tightly managed organizational structure. Then, and only then, were it and the BOC judged to have done enough to qualify for recapitalization.

4. Recapitalization and stock-market listing. At the end of 2004, the CCB and the BOC received US$45 billion for recapitalization from China's foreign-exchange reserves (that is, essentially from the central bank). A new entity called the Huijin Corporation was established as a bank holding company (parallel to SASAC for industrial firms). The cash infusion was used as equity capital, and the CCB and the BOC were restructured into joint-stock corporations, initially wholly owned by the Huijin Corporation. Next, strategic stakes in the CCB were sold to international investors, specifically the Bank of America (8.7%) and the Singapore sovereign wealth fund Temasek (6%). Finally, in October 2005, the CCB was listed on the Hong Kong Stock Exchange, where it sold 12% of its shares in an initial public offering. The successful offering valued the CCB at an enormous US$67 billion. The CCB remained more than 70% owned by the central government, but it received a major infusion of money and skills, and its performance since has been tracked by its share price. The other state-owned banks followed suit: the BOC and the ICBC in 2006, and the Agriculture Bank in 2010.

19.3.4.2   Assessment

Overall, the restructuring of China's banking system was an enormous achievement. Table 19.3 (page 509) shows that the operation removed a large part of the enormous NPL burden from the Big Four banks. A liquidity crisis was averted and the ground prepared for more fundamental banking reform. Each of the Big Four also absorbed substantial managerial expertise from their foreign banks stakeholders, most of whom substantially reduced their holdings in the wake of the 2009 global financial crisis.

The process was extremely expensive: in total, about 3.5 trillion RMB in NPLs was written off, almost exactly one-third of GDP. Some accounting tricks helped get rid of the NPLs. The AMCs originally funded the purchase of NPLs by issuing bonds guaranteed by the central government and sold to the commercial banks. The AMCs could only recover a portion of the NPLs' face value (24% as of early 2006), after which the AMCs themselves had to be bailed out by a combination of tax breaks, debt forgiveness, and the repurchase of ownership stakes by the banks. Nevertheless, NPLs were safely warehoused and separated from ordinary bank business.

A certain amount of accounting sleight of hand occurs in any bailout procedure. The key feature is that a bailout must solve two contradictory problems: the "stock" problem and the "flow" problem. The existing stock of bad loans already on the bank's balance sheets primarily reflects the legacy of past bad decisions. They should be written off as quickly as possible. The flow problem refers to the need to prevent new loans from repeating past mistakes and becoming new NPLs: the banking system must adopt rigorous and commercially sound practices going forward. The first action is a bailout, while the success of the second depends on convincing the banks that there will be no more bailouts, that is, enforcing a credible "never-again" policy. This results in a time consistency problem: if you are willing to bail out the banks now, how can you credibly commit to not doing so in the future? What will prevent the banks from replicating past behavior (the soft budget constraint) and creating new bad loans?

In practice, radical economic reforms helped answer the credible-commitment problem. Only NPLs created before 1996, before serious SOE reforms, were eligible for purchase by AMCs. A kind of firewall was set up between the "old bad" lending decisions and the "new better" lending after market reforms. This "never-again" approach was at least partly credible. Moreover, the banks emerged from restructuring very different creatures, with better accounting, incentives, and transparency. It was possible to believe that the bailout was a one-time event, incurred in the course of economic reform. Finally, as growth accelerated, the warehoused old NPLs became an easily managed burden on a much bigger economy.

19.4   Capital Markets: Equity

Equity markets are an important and highly visible part of a modern financial system. In a market-based system, equity markets perform three essential functions: they (1) provide an important channel for corporate finance; (2) serve as a market for corporate control, giving outsiders the ability to buy an undervalued company and replace its management; and (3) provide a sensitive evaluation of managerial performance that can be linked to managers' compensation.

19.4.1   Overview of the Chinese Stock Market

China's experience with stock markets has been uneven. China's stock markets were initiated with the help of local-government policy entrepreneurship when the municipalities of Shanghai and Shenzhen in the late 1980s invested resources in building stock-market institutions, hoping to get central-government approval later. In 1991, the central government gave its blessing when the development of the Shanghai Stock Exchange was folded into the accelerated development of Shanghai's Pudong Special Zone. In the late 1990s, Chinese stock markets were given the go-ahead for rapid expansion and are today among the largest exchanges in the world by market capitalization and turnover. China established a technically efficient system of market operation, such that tens of millions of individuals trade stocks securely, with central custodial accounts and few glitches or crashes. Disclosure of information is far better for listed firms than for nonlisted firms.

After 2012, markets for small-scale and start-up firms were opened, filling a huge hole in the stock-market system. Overall, China has created a multilevel equity market for small companies, which can be envisioned as a pyramid. At the apex are the main boards in Shanghai and Shenzhen. The main boards list 2,797 companies (end of June 2015). The next tier is the small- and medium-enterprise market, which lists tens of thousands of companies. Below this, the ChiNext Market was set up in October 2009 at the Shenzhen Stock Exchange to list companies in high-growth sectors like electronics and pharmaceuticals. Finally, an over-the-counter (OTC) market that is similar to the OTC Bulletin Board in the United States was established in 2015 to enable share transfers of companies that do not meet the listing requirements of other boards. Overall, then, China has developed large and diverse equity markets from the ground up.

Nevertheless, certain important problems have never been solved. The majority of large-capitalization firms on the Shanghai exchange are still state controlled. As part of the conversion of traditional SOEs to joint-stock and limited-liability corporations (chapter 14), stock markets provided an opportunity for "partial privatization," in which an SOE was listed on the exchange and a minority stake was sold to the public. This introduced new shareholders into the firm, provided a channel for better information disclosure, and was the first step in a process that could potentially lead to further privatization. Certainly, stock-market listing created a new source of funding for SOEs, which received the revenues from the initial public offerings (IPOs). Parent companies maintained control through their majority stakes while making money from the sale of a minority share. This seemed like a pure win-win proposition.

It was on this basis that China's stock markets grew rapidly. However, the combination of government control and sale of minority stakes turned out to be the "original sin" that has hobbled the healthy development of the stock market ever since. State-owned parents have only rarely released their control of listed firms, and the Chinese stock exchange has never become a market for corporate control. Partly as a result, the market has remained extremely dependent on government policy decisions. Huge fluctuations have occurred as expectations of policy change fluctuated between optimism and pessimism. Movements of individual stocks are highly correlated, as all partake of the boom and bust cycles (rather than being determined by individual company fundamentals). Figure 19.2 shows the growth of the Chinese stock market (Shanghai and Shenzhen combined), scaled to GDP, and displays the pattern of boom and bust that has bedeviled the Chinese market. Stocks soared in 1993, 2000, 2007, and 2015, only to collapse each time. While emerging-market stock markets generally display high volatility, the Chinese pattern is extreme even within the emerging-market context.

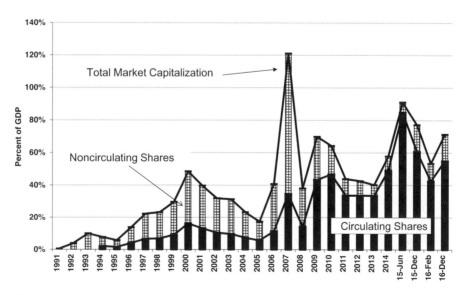

Figure 19.2
Stock-market capitalization as share of GDP.
Source: China Securities Regulatory Commission, http://www.csrc.gov.cn/pub/newsite/sjtj/.

19.4.2   Limitations on Control and Circulation

In almost all cases, when SOEs were listed, the government and the corporate parent of the enterprise retained a majority of the equity in the firm. Worried about insider privatization, the government declared that these shares would simply not be allowed to circulate. Through 2007, the majority of shares were in a legal category of "noncirculating" shares (figure 19.2). In 2007, a program was adopted that allowed companies to convert their noncirculating shares to circulating status if the external shareholders agreed (optimism about this program was one of the drivers of the 2007 stock-market boom). The program succeeded: most shares were converted, and noncirculating shares were less than 10% of the total by mid-2015. However, although the number of shares legally classified as noncirculating declined, most of these shares did not in fact circulate since most government and SOE shareholders held on to their shares to retain control. Nor was this the end of the story. The stock market enjoyed a spectacular run-up in the first half of 2015, peaking on June 12. Market correction after June 12 turned into panic, and the main indexes dropped 40% in days. The government then intervened to stop market rout. SOEs were instructed to hold on to their current shares, and other state-owned entities began to buy up shares on the market to support the price.

As a direct result, the proportion of noncirculating shares increased after June 2015. An opportunity to put the stock market on a fully market basis was lost, and the problem of an overhang of government-owned shares was worsened. It is striking that the Chinese government took these actions even though the market decline was not as large as that experienced in 2007–2008, during which the government did not intervene.

Privatization through several successive tranches of stock sales had been successfully adopted in several Western European countries, but this has generally not happened in China. Given that majority control has remained firmly in government hands, private shareholders have no possibility of gaining control over most companies. Management need not fear a hostile takeover, and the stock market's role in improving corporate governance is limited. The Chinese stock exchanges have not served as a market for corporate control.

19.4.3   Rationing Access to a Policy-Driven Market

Listing on a stock market is lucrative, so the demand for permission to list is large. Since the creation of China's stock market, regulators have formally or informally rationed the right to list. It is not enough that a firm meet the requirements for listing; it must also compete for the favor of regulators in gaining permission. This necessity produces a further distortion of the market's ability to value companies accurately. New IPOs were suspended after the 2011 market decline, not resumed until 2014, and then suspended again after the June 2015 crash. In principle, regulator permission is no longer required, but there is a big backlog of firms waiting to list.

Because the supply of desirable shares is limited, prices have tended to be very high. At each of the market's peaks (in 2000, 2007, and 2015), Chinese shares became extremely expensive, with a price/earnings ratio above 40. (In comparison, the U.S. S&P 500 price/earnings ratio has historically been between 15 and 25.) Of course, rapidly growing companies should have higher price/earnings ratios to account for higher expected future earnings, but Chinese A-share valuations have been very rich even after this is taken into account.

In this environment, the Chinese stock market inevitably is driven primarily by changes in government policy. Studies have shown that market fluctuations are better explained as reactions to government policy changes, particularly those that affect liquidity in the markets, than as reactions to changes in underlying fundamentals of individual companies. Since access to the market is rationed by the regulator, the market often seems to be allergic to policy changes that will increase the supply of state shares (since increased supply will drive down share prices) while welcoming measures that will increase liquidity (driving up prices). Investors are forced to gamble that the Chinese government will adopt policies to further development of the stock market; conversely, investors have been deterred since the 2015 market rescue by concerns that the government will dump shares when the market starts to rise.

19.4.4   Market Participants

Some of the characteristics of the Chinese market—volatility, high turnover, and policy-driven moves—are plausibly related to the composition of market actors. Institutional investors, such as mutual funds, pension funds, and insurance companies, contribute to the healthy development of the market because they serve as "patient" owners with a long-term interest in improving corporate governance and performance. However, the share of institutional investors in the Chinese market is low. According to China Securities Regulatory Commission (CSRC) statistics, at the end of 2014, only 14% of total shares were held by "professional institutions," which includes institutional investors: mutual funds (5.9%); insurance companies (3.9%); qualified foreign investment institutions (QFIIs) (1.7%); trusts and enterprise funds (1.5%); and the Social Security Fund (1.2%) (CSRC 2014, 21–22).

It is sometimes said that individual investors dominate the Chinese market, but in fact they hold 25% of total shares, while 61% of shares are held by "general institutions," which contain two large categories: (1) parent companies of listed firms, and (2) "private investment funds" and investments managed by securities firms. Securities firms have substantial assets under their control, about 15% to 20% of total A-share market capitalization according to different estimates. These behave more like hedge funds than mutual funds.

19.4.5   New Liberalization Policies

A major push to expand and liberalize China's stock markets developed in the wake of the November 2013 Third Plenum. Three main points from this effort (State Council 2014) are worth noting.

First, the smaller exchanges were expanded and liberalized, with relaxed capital and profitability requirements for listing but stricter rules on information disclosure. Second, any company that meets objective standards of capital, profitability, and information disclosure should in principle be allowed to list on the main boards; rationing of listing slots would come to an end. Third, China's stock markets are to be internationalized, that is, opened to foreign investors.

This entire program was essentially frozen in the wake of the summer 2015 market meltdown. Nevertheless, several important institutional steps were taken that have the potential to revitalize the Chinese stock market if and when they are resumed. In November 2014, the Shanghai–Hong Kong Stock Connect began to operate, a program that allows investors in China and Hong Kong to purchase shares directly in the other jurisdiction through their home brokers. Hong Kong investors are not required to have Hong Kong residence, so this effectively opens up China's stock market to anyone willing to work through a Hong Kong intermediary. If listings resume, government shareholding begins to be reduced, and the market stabilizes or increases in value, the market could spring back to life. In particular, China's stock markets have been brought to the threshold of internationalization, but actual international ownership of shares is still less than 2%, whereas full internationalization would probably imply that around 20% to 45% of China's shares would be owned internationally.

19.4.6   Comparative Evaluation of China's Stock Market

Since the end of 2013, the Chinese stock market (Shanghai and Shenzhen) has fluctuated in value from 40% to 100% of GDP, a range similar to the levels in India (69%), Indonesia (43%), Japan (62%), and Korea (97%). However, given the extraordinary depth of China's financial system and the presence of an M2 money supply that is more than twice GDP, it is clear that the stock market is underperforming. Even this comparison is slightly misleading because it treats the large volume of effectively noncirculating shares as having the same value as circulating shares. Despite its overall large volume and global impact, the Chinese stock market is still a laggard in the Chinese developmental context.

19.5   Capital Markets: Bonds

In developed market economies, bond markets are often bigger than stock markets, and bond-market capitalization is typically larger than GDP. In the United States,

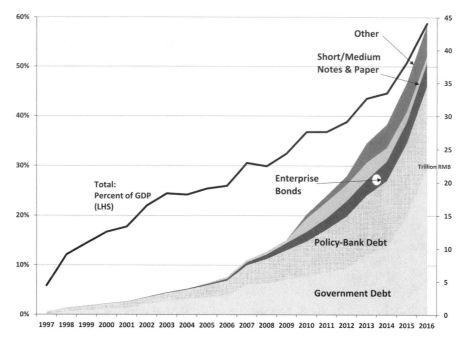

Figure 19.3
Value of bonds outstanding (right-hand axis) and share of GDP.
Source: China Central Depository and Clearing Company, www.chinabond.cn.com.

the bond market is worth about $40 trillion, or 2.2 times U.S. GDP. In China, there were virtually no bonds outstanding through the end of the 1990s, but the market has grown steadily since then. As figure 19.3 shows, growth accelerated after 2006, and by the end of 2016 the total market was 43.7 trillion RMB, or 60% of GDP. In terms of volume, this puts the Chinese market in the global big leagues, but scaled to China's GDP, it is still of moderate size. In addition, China has set up a centralized registry, standards for disclosure documents that are freely available on the Web, and several domestic bond-rating agencies. Although China's bond-market development has lagged behind the banking system and the stock market, it has the potential to develop quickly in coming years.

19.5.1 Bond Issuers

A fundamental feature of China's bond market is that almost all the sellers of bonds are government actors. As of the end of 2016, 51% of the bond market was government debt, and another 28% was from the state-owned policy banks. (The China Development Bank alone accounts for 71 trillion RMB in outstanding bonds, 16% of the total market.) If agencies with official government backing are included, a total of 82% of bond-market capitalization is government debt by a broad definition. Thus the bond market serves primarily as a channel of funds to a few government borrowers.

Conversely, amounts of corporate or enterprise bonds are modest, just under 5% of GDP. By contrast, in the United States, corporate bonds are over 50% of GDP, and various kinds of mortgage and asset-backed securities are even larger. Moreover, in China, issuance of corporate bonds must be approved on a case-by-case basis by national regulatory bodies, in particular, the National Development and Reform Commission, the former planning agency. This has meant that state-owned enterprises have accounted for almost the entire volume of corporate debt. Conditions for issuance of corporate bonds are being liberalized, but their share in the overall bond market actually declined a few percentage points from 2014 to 2016.

Local-government debt, or municipal bonds, grew rapidly after 2015. Local governments and their funding vehicles (LGFVs) that had borrowed from banks during the global financial crisis (GFC) had been struggling to make interest payments ever since. In 2015 and 2016, local governments converted a whopping 8 trillion RMB in debt into bonds, pushing their outstanding debt up to parity with the central government (section 20.6).

19.5.2 Bond Markets and Bondholders

Government and policy-bank debt is allocated to commercial banks, who are required to accept it. As a result, commercial banks hold about 80% of policy-bank debt and 70% of government debt. Commercial banks typically hold this debt to maturity. This debt plays a significant role in the financial system. The debt is considered a safe asset in the evaluation of bank capital adequacy. A large and reasonably liquid interbank market has grown up, in which the dominant form of transaction is a "repo" (reverse purchase agreement), in which banks "borrow" a security from another bank in return for cash and a promise to return it (that is, the long-term bond serves as collateral for banks borrowing short-term money). This has allowed a fairly efficient interbank market to develop and permits banks to develop different business strategies predicated on their access to this market. This interbank market is enormous and increasingly plays a role in the overall financial system since it sets some key interest rates on a continuous, market-determined basis. Access to this market was extended during 2016 to various foreign investors, who may in the future increase their current tiny holdings of less than 2% of the market.

However, the interbank market does nothing to diversify funding sources for nonfinancial corporations. The market for corporate bonds is small (4.8% of GDP at the end of 2016), and generally restricted to SOEs. However, it operates in a completely different way from the interbank market. A large majority of corporate bonds trade on the Shanghai and Shenzhen exchanges; bonds turnover much more frequently, and interest rates on individual bonds can diverge substantially. About half the outstanding value is held by investment funds, and another quarter is registered with the exchanges themselves. This market can begin to provide corporations with funding options if it is allowed to expand.

19.6   Shadow Banking

Shadow banks are institutions that do the same thing as banks but without being subject to the same regulatory oversight as banks. That is, shadow banks perform financial intermediation, converting short-term funds into long-term loans, and taking on various kinds of risk. Shadow banking is diverse and hard to pin down. Even banks can engage in shadow banking, but when they do so the activity is off their balance sheets, which means they are not subject to the same capital requirements and other restrictions. In fact, even China's large state-owned banks have been enthusiastic participants in shadow-banking activities. To understand this phenomenon, we need to return to the discussion of financial repression begun in section 19.1.2

19.6.1   The Post-2003 Wave of Financial Repression in China

The post-2003 version of financial repression has its roots in the Chinese effort to restructure and recapitalize the banking system after the late 1990s. Before that bailout, the banking system had been used for decades to support the SOE sector, so lending rates were kept low. This meant that Chinese banks had very small spreads between interest rates on loans and those on deposit rates; taking deposits and making loans were not particularly profitable, and SOEs got most of the benefit of financial repression. In June 1999, as policy-makers got serious about bailing out the banks, spreads between one-year lending and deposit rates were pushed up to 3.6 percentage points and were kept above 3 percentage points until June 2012. Banks could pay 2% for term deposits and loan them at 5%, which was quite a profitable business. Policy-makers wanted to strengthen the banking system, so they were content to let the banks benefit from financial repression.

Figure 19.4 shows this phenomenon from the perspective of average households. Nominal deposit rates in China were generally low and were rarely changed (staying in the 2%–4% range after 1999). As a result, changes in the real interest rate (the nominal interest rate minus the change in the consumer price index) were driven by changes in the inflation rate. A bout of deflation in 2003 caused real interest rates to spike, but afterward real interest rates fluctuated around zero (and turned significantly negative when inflation accelerated). Overall, between the end of 2003 and the end of 2013, the average real interest rate was −0.34%, so a deposit of 100 RMB in 2003, after adding interest payments, had only 96.65 RMB of purchasing power 10 years

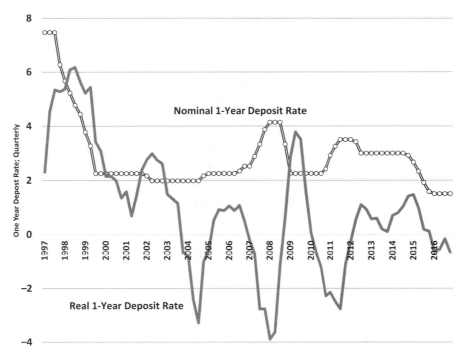

Figure 19.4
Nominal and real deposit rates (1997–2015).
Sources: *SAC* (2016, 166; and earlier volumes); People's Bank of China, pbc.gov.cn.

later. Financial repression was transferring wealth from households to the banking system. A fairly modest adjustment of nominal interest rates would have been sufficient to keep real rates in positive territory, but by their actions, state policy-makers revealed that they preferred financial repression rather than forcing banks and state firms to pay more for funds.

Banks were happy to reap profits from wide interest-rate spreads, but they faced a problem. Households were much less motivated to deposit savings in the bank; figure 19.1 shows that between 2003 and 2012 household saving deposits growth slowed down. Banks were prevented from competing for deposits because interest rates were capped by regulators and were the same for everybody. Moreover, lending was limited to 75% of deposits. Ambitious and competitive banks and other financial institutions saw an opportunity to match savers and borrowers at higher interest rates and make higher profits. Shadow banking was ready to emerge as a way to attract funds at higher interest rates.

19.6.2   The Emergence of Shadow Banking

Figure 19.5 shows flows of credit through multiple channels in China, including bank loans, various forms of shadow banking, and capital markets. "Total social credit" is the term the PBC uses to cover all flows from financial to nonfinancial sectors. Through 2009, bank credit was the dominant form of financing, as discussed in section 19.1.2. However, after the surge of lending for the 2009 GFC stimulus program was over, financial flows began to diversify. Banks and other financial institutions were already looking for ways to attract more funds. When macroeconomic policymakers reduced bank lending between 2009 and 2011, but the demand for funds remained high, new financing instruments began to proliferate. In 2010–2012, shadow banking surged, providing credit to borrowers outside the normal regulated (and repressed) financial system (Collier 2017). The simplest interpretation is that these funds were escaping from the repressed financial system.

Nonbank financial institutions, particularly trusts, had already pioneered the creation of shadow-bank assets. Banks, competing for funds with deposit rates capped,

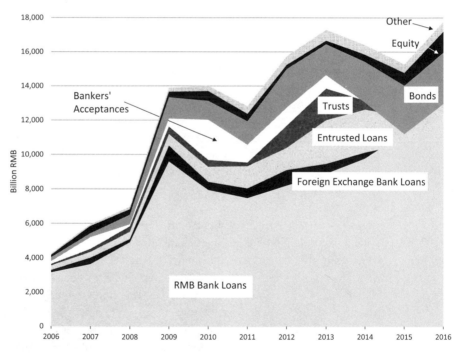

Figure 19.5
Total social financing.
Source: People's Bank of China, http://www.pbc.gov.cn/diaochatongjisi/116219/116319/3013637/3013639/index.html, and earlier years.

began offering "wealth-management products" (WMPs) with higher interest rates. These WMPs were off-balance-sheet packaged products that bundled other kinds of financial assets, sometimes risky and often non-transparent. At the beginning, the five big equitized state banks created more than half of these WMPs, although the JSCBs subsequently moved aggressively to catch up. By moving these deposits off their balance sheets and into special-purpose vehicles set up for this purpose, the banks were able to avoid reserve requirements and quantitative loan limits.

WMPs were a way of attracting new funds (adding to banks' off-balance-sheet liabilities), and using them for profitable new investments (adding to banks' off-balance-sheet assets). How did the funds get used? In the aggregate, at the end of 2013, 39% of WMP funds were invested in bonds and money-market instruments; 27% were in nonstandardized debt, such as entrusted loans and trusts (compare figure 19.5). Another 26% of funds were put in bank deposits (presumably bundled into long-term higher interest accounts) and 6% were in equity-like variable-return instruments (CCDCC 2014, 10, 18). In other words, retail consumers were offered the opportunity to participate in all of the nonbank-loan forms of financing shown in figure 19.5 through WMPs.

Consumers widely believe that WMPs purchased from banks are covered by government deposit insurance, although they are not. Consumers are therefore purchasing riskier, higher-returning saving products without fully understanding the risk they are taking on. Regulators could have squelched this emerging sector, but are also aware that WMPs often provide funds to private and small-scale businesses at higher interest rates. In that sense, WMPs and shadow banking contribute to the diversification and restructuring of the economy that policy-makers would like to see.

Regulators have followed a similar approach of benign tolerance toward Internet-based shadow banks. Internet merchants like Alibaba have built sophisticated online payment systems over the past several years. In mid-2013, Alibaba launched the popular Yu'ebao saving product, essentially an online money-market fund. Seeking to aggressively leverage its advantage in online payments into a banking business, Alibaba offered extremely generous interest rates on Yu'ebao deposits for the first few years. Regulators allowed these experiments to go forward without restriction until 2016. Explosive growth followed: by the first quarter of 2017, Yu'ebao had become the world's large money-market fund. Other innovations, such as peer-to-peer lending, in which Internet intermediaries directly link individual lenders and borrowers, proliferated as well. These innovations create new risks, which are discussed in section 19.8.

19.7   Liberalization and the Marketization of Interest Rates

The huge changes described in the previous four sections are clearly not the result of simple policy choices, but rather are the complex result of multiple forces. Nevertheless, financial policy does have an important effect. In general, policy-makers have attempted to move toward a system of market-set interest rates and fair treatment of different financial organization.

19.7.1   Interest Rate Liberalization

Marketization of bank interest rates is a crucial step in shrinking the big differentials between banks and shadow banks and moving toward a level playing field in the financial system. Controls on lending rates have been gradually relaxed and in October 2015, a nationwide system of deposit insurance was adopted and the ceiling on deposit interest rates was eliminated. Since this major milestone, spreads between lending and deposit rates have declined significantly for all the big banks. However, the big banks have dragged their feet on raising deposit interest rates, and there is some evidence that regulators give "window guidance" to the banks not to raise deposit rates too abruptly, in order to restrain competition.

In a modern diversified financial system, bank deposit and lending rates are components of a system of interest rates. They are important, but they are not the only, or even the most important, interest rates. There is typically a benchmark, short-term interest rate—over which the central bank exerts predominant influence—and beyond this, a complex system of interest rates that are constantly adjusting in response to market forces. This system of interest rates links banks and bond markets very closely. Relations between short-term and long-term rates constantly adjust (the "term structure" of interest rates in the bond market), as does the relationship between rates charged to risky companies and to safe companies (the "spread"). Under these conditions financial intermediation works well and interest rates can be used by the central bank to steer the macroeconomy. As described in chapter 18, China is moving in the direction of reliance on interest rates for macroeconomic policy. Today, the closest thing to a benchmark interest rate China has is that which prevails on the interbank funds market. The PBC intervenes directly in this market to smooth fluctuations and manage liquidity. It is striking that the PBC's effort to reduce credit between 2009 and 2011 was largely frustrated by the emergence of shadow banking (figure 19.5). Quantitative controls just weren't working any more, and the envisioned transition to interest-rate–based policy became even more urgent. The PBC was forced to accelerate its steps to create a more integrated system.

Some of the tolerance that Chinese regulators displayed toward financial innovation was scaled back after 2013. As figure 19.5 shows, the net value of trusts outstanding stopped growing after 2013, and the growth of entrusted lending slowed sharply. Internet-based peer-to-peer lending platforms had been rife with fraud and bankruptcy, and regulators finally started to crack down in 2016. A broad crackdown began in 2016 as well on so-called "universal life insurance" policies, thinly disguised fund-raising vehicles that allowed insurance companies to raise and invest enormous sums of money quickly. Even the internet-based money-market funds such as Yu'ebao began to face new disclosure and regulatory requirements. So far, these new regulatory measures do not attempt to close off financing channels outside formal bank deposits and loans, but seek to drag them into the daylight and expose them to more regulatory scrutiny. If these measures can be combined with further liberalization of the stock and bond markets, it would represent a major step forward toward a market-based financial system.

19.7.2   Market-Driven Disintermediation

It is clear that unprecedented market forces are disrupting the traditional role of banks. The elimination of administrative controls on interest rates creates new competition within the banking system, while traditional boundaries between different types of financial businesses were already eroding, increasing competition (Zhang and Liu, 2015). Traditional trust companies had been used to managing money and making investments for other companies and rich individuals. Securities companies had combined fund management with traditional brokerage business. After 2012, though, banks (especially urban commercial banks) and insurance companies were allowed to set up fund management companies. Increased competition among brokerages has driven brokerage commissions down to a tiny fraction of what they had been. As competition has deepened, the enforced shift to interest-rate and liquidity management by the PBC forced banks and others to become much more nimble and interest-rate responsive. Beginning in 2013, occasional liquidity shocks have created sharp interest-rate spikes on the interbank market. The sudden emergence of online banking, following the creation of Yu'ebao in June 2013, further disrupted financial markets. The result has been pressure on the traditional business of banks. It seems unlikely that financial repression can serve such a competitive onslaught.

19.8   Conclusion

It should be clear that financial-market reforms are creating powerful forces that are eroding financial repression and displacing the banking system from its heretofore overwhelming dominance of the financial system. These changes are also creating new sources of risk.

19.8.1   Increasing Financial Risk

The dramatic changes occurring in the Chinese financial system have increased the short-term financial risks in the Chinese economy. It is widely recognized in the comparative literature that risks are highest during the process of liberalization and systemic change: investors move large amounts of capital to reposition themselves, regulators are inexperienced, and mistakes are made. This general principle is relevant to China today, and there are three additional reasons for heightened concern.

19.8.1.1   Aggregate Debt Has Increased Very Fast

China's overall debt level has increased quickly. There are many different ways to calculate aggregate debt levels, but according to the broadest definition by the IMF (2017, 19–20), China's aggregate nonfinancial debt has increased from 179% of GDP in 2012 to 236% of GDP at the end of 2016. This is a remarkably rapid increase in debt, amounting to 14 percentage points of GDP per year. Moreover, the increase in debt is across the board: nonfinancial corporations, households, and government have all experienced rapid increases in overall debt levels. To a certain extent, debt is simply the obverse side of financial deepening and high saving rates. Therefore, we expect the debt to GDP level to increase as development proceeds. However, very rapid increases in aggregate debt of this sort are strongly associated with increased risk of financial crisis. There have been previous cases of countries increasing aggregate debt at rates similar to that of China in this period, and they have almost all been followed by financial crisis.

19.8.1.2   Hidden Leverage and Inappropriate Guarantees Make the System Vulnerable

The rapid increase in new types of borrowing and lending creates heightened risk because it is simply impossible to know where leverage is concentrated in the system. Leverage allows investors to increase their returns by borrowing a portion of the purchase price of an asset, but it also magnifies risk, especially when short-term funds are borrowed to finance long-term investments. Short-run fluctuations in the availability of funds, or in the value of the underlying asset, may suddenly make investors insolvent or illiquid. Moreover, debt among financial institutions—not included in the aggregate debt data in section 19.8.1.1—has also increased rapidly and clearly leads to high leverage rates among shadow-banking institutions.

Investors are particularly likely to take these risks if they believe they will get "bailed out" by government. In fact, Chinese government behavior frequently seems to indemnify investors against some risks. For example, regulations are quite clear that WMPs and other new products cannot offer guarantees and must explain risks to customers, but in practice, politicians and regulators often try to find solutions to avoid messy defaults. There are many cases of banks bailing out "their"

WMPs in order to protect their reputation and last-minute rescues organized by local governments and their agents. Politicians have a strong preference for stability, and do not wish to provoke protests by angry investors. These actions provide implicit guarantees that lead investors to take riskier gambles.

19.8.1.3 Previous Bad Investments Remain Unresolved

There is anecdotal evidence that many bad investments associated with the financial crisis and the subsequent growth slowdown remain unresolved. It is not surprising that investments made for stimulus purposes in 2009 will often fail to pay back their initial capital. Moreover, we should expect that the dramatic change in economic conditions accompanying the end of the high-growth era would lead to many investment mistakes. So far, Chinese policy-makers have not restructured these debts and removed them from the books. Instead, they are constantly rolled over ("evergreened"), incomplete projects continue to suck in new money, and aggregate debt increases rapidly. Indirect verification of these problems is provided by the increase in nonperforming loans after 2012 shown in table 19.3.

Within the banking system, budget constraints, only recently hardened by the Zhu Rongji regime and its bank restructuring, became softer during the GFC. During early 2009, banks were ordered to lend without restraint to local-government investment projects for stimulus purposes. The implicit "never-again" clause for bailouts was violated, and banks were again asked to follow government orders and lend to clients (especially local governments) without regard to solvency or repayment.

Table 19.3
Nonperforming loans in China's banking system.

	Large state-owned banks*			All commercial banks		
	Billions of yuan	% of loans	% of GDP	Billions of yuan	% of loans	% of GDP
2002	2,088.0	26.2	17.3			
2007	1,115.0	8.1	4.2	1,270.2	6.1	4.7
2008	420.8	2.8	1.3	563.5	2.4	1.8
2012	309.5	1.0	0.6	492.9	1.0	0.9
2015	700.2	1.7	1.0	1,274.4	1.7	1.9
2016				1,512.3	1.7	2.0

Sources: China Bank Regulatory Commission website, CBRC.gov.cn; and CBRC *Annual Report* (various years).
*Includes Bank of Communication after 2010.

19.8.1.4   Assessment

The increase of financial risk is real, but does not make financial crisis inevitable. It should be recognized that the core banking system is well capitalized, and has made substantial provisions against bad loans. Moreover, government guarantees for individual depositors are explicit and reliable. Despite increased competitive pressure, the state-run banks remain reasonably healthy. Moreover, government policy-makers are well aware of the elevated risks, so it is unlikely that they would be taken by surprise by any particular incident. Finally, because virtually all the debt is held domestically, policy-makers have more policy instruments at their disposal to deal with crises than would be the case if foreign debt was involved. Policy-makers still have some time to reduce risk by improving regulatory oversight and moving to liquidate bad debts in an orderly fashion.

19.8.2 The Emerging Financial System

The Chinese system is evolving in new and difficult-to-predict directions. The traditional way to describe financial systems is to divide them into two main types based on the relative importance of banks and capital markets. "Bank-dominated" financial systems rely on banks to provide most financing to corporations and to monitor corporate performance. Financial systems that rely predominantly on capital markets, often labeled "Anglo-American," raise capital primarily from capital markets and rely on investors to "vote with their feet," buying and selling a company's securities because of their confidence (or lack of it) in the company's management.

The Chinese system has been bank dominated, but it does not fit that traditional category. Chinese banks have been weak overseers of the corporate sector—they have never been allowed to directly own equity, except under some special circumstances when bad debts are being restructured. Moreover, since Chinese banks are predominantly state owned, they have internal governance issues. The issues were aggravated by the instruction to loan indiscriminately during the 2009 stimulus response to the global financial crisis. But if China's banks are weak, China's capital markets have not yet grown into a comprehensive alternative. Developing much later, and still hobbled by government restrictions and limitations, stock and bond markets have grown but without achieving the maturity and stability required for them to play their full role in the financial system. This huge but immature system is now being buffeted by a set of changes arising from the Internet, as many types of financial transactions migrate online. We should expect to see continued rapid change in China's financial system, even as policy-makers search for greater stability.

Bibliography

Suggestions for Further Reading

Armstrong-Taylor (2016) is a lucid and up-to-date account of China's financial system that makes even the most difficult issues approachable. Walter and Howie (2012) add some terrific anecdotes and pointed criticism. For the comparative context of financial systems and economic development, see Levine (1997) and Allen, Chui, and Maddaloni (2004).

References

Allen, Franklin, Michael Chui, and Angela Maddaloni (2004). "Financial Systems in Europe, the USA, and Asia." *Oxford Review of Economic Policy* 20 (4): 490–508.

Armstrong-Taylor, Paul (2016). *Debt and Distortion: Risks and Reforms in the Chinese Financial System.* London: Palgrave Macmillan.

CBRC (China Bank Regulatory Commission). *Annual Report.* Beijing: China Bank Regulatory Commission.

CCDCC (China Central Depository and Clearing Company). (Annual). *Zhongguo yinghangye licai shichang niandu baogao* [China banking wealth management market annual report]. Beijing: China Central Depository and Clearing Company.

Chamon, Marcos, and Eswar Prasad (2010). "Why Are Saving Rates of Urban Households in China Rising?" *American Economic Journal: Macroeconomics* 2 (1): 93–130.

Choukhmane, Taha, Nicolas Coeurdacier, and Keyu Jin (2013). "The One-Child Policy and Household Savings in China." Accessed at http://econ.sciences-po.fr/sites/default/files/file/draft_ocp_130213.pdf.

Collier, Andrew (2017). *Shadow Banking and the Rise of Capitalism in China.* Singapore: Palgrave Macmillan.

CSRC (China Securities Regulatory Commission). *Annual Report.* Beijing: China Securities Regulatory Commission.

Downs, Erica (2011). *Inside China, Inc.: China Development Bank's Cross-Border Energy Deals.* Washington, DC: Brookings Institution.

IMF (International Monetary Fund) (2017). People's Republic of China, 2017 Article IV Consultation. Washington, DC: International Monetary Fund. Accessed at https://www.imf.org/~/media/Files/Publications/CR/2017/cr17247.ashx.

Kodres, Laura E. (2013). "What Is Shadow Banking?" *Finance & Development* 50 (2). Accessed at http://www.imf.org/external/pubs/ft/fandd/2013/06/basics.htm.

Lardy, Nicholas R. (1998). *China's Unfinished Economic Revolution.* Washington, DC: Brookings Institution.

Levine, Ross (1997). "Financial Development and Economic Growth: Views and Agenda." *Journal of Economic Literature* 35 (2): 688–726.

"Love and Marriage in Modern China: Survey Reveals Latest Trends" (2012). December 30. Accessed at http://www.echinacities.com/news/Love-and-Marriage-in-Modern-China-Survey-Reveals-Latest-Trends.

Modigliani, Franco, and Shi Larry Cao (2004). "The Chinese Saving Puzzle and the Life-Cycle Hypothesis." *Journal of Economic Literature* 42:145–170.

PBC (People's Bank of China). (Quarterly). *Monetary Policy Report.* Beijing: People's Bank of China.

SAC (Annual). *Zhongguo Tongji Zhaiyao* [Statistical abstract of China]. Beijing: Zhongguo Tongji.

Sanderson, Henry, and Michael Forsythe (2012). *China's Superbank: Debt, Oil and Influence—How China Development Bank Is Rewriting the Rules of Finance.* New York: John Wiley and Sons.

State Council (2014). "Views on Accelerating the Healthy Development of the Capital Market." *Guofa*, May 8, 17.

SYC (Annual). *Zhongguo Tongji Nianjian* [Statistical yearbook of China]. Beijing: Zhongguo Tongji.

Tsai, Kellee S. (2004). *Back-Alley Banking: Private Entrepreneurs in China*. Ithaca, NY: Cornell University Press.

Walter, Carl, and Fraser Howie (2012). *Red Capitalism: The Fragile Financial Foundation of China's Extraordinary Rise*. Rev. ed. Hoboken, NJ: Wiley.

Wei Shang-Jin, and Xiaobo Zhang (2009). "The Competitive Saving Motive: Evidence from Rising Sex Ratios and Savings Rates in China." NBER Working Paper no. 15093 (June).

Wildau, Gabriel (2017). "China Overtakes Eurozone as World's Biggest Bank System." *Financial Times* [London]. March 5. Accessed at https://www.ft.com/content/14f929de-ffc5-11e6-96f8-3700c5664d30.

Yardeni, Edward, and Debbie Johnson (2015). "Corporate Profits in GDP." Yardeni Research, August 28. Accessed at www.yardeni.com/pub/ppphb.pdf.

Zhang, Lizhou, and Liu Lanxiang (2015). *Zhongguoshi Touhang (Chinese-Style Investment Banking)*. Beijing: China CITIC Press.

20 The Fiscal System

The fiscal budget is the most direct instrument a government has for influencing a market economy and achieving its social and economic goals. In developed market economies, there are generally no "plans," just budgets. Budgets are the focus of intense politicking and lobbying, and there are multiple access points in the executive and legislative branches through which different social groups and interests seek to influence budgetary outcomes. In the command economy, by contrast, the budget was almost irrelevant; the most important decisions were made in the plan, and the budget simply accommodated those decisions by assigning financial flows that were consistent with the plan. As China transitioned out of the command economy, it improvised a fiscal system in response to immediate needs but deferred many problems to the future.

When the reform process in China began in 1978, the government controlled one-third of GDP in the form of budgetary revenues, a substantial share. Economic reform led to the gradual erosion and ultimately the virtual collapse of the command-economy budgetary arrangements. By the early 1990s, China was in deep fiscal crisis. Beginning with the fiscal reform of 1994, the budgetary system was reconstructed on a completely new basis, compatible with a market system. Overall, this reconstruction was an enormous success: Chinese consolidated budget revenues (combining central and subnational governments) increased steadily after 1995 and doubled as a share of GDP by 2012 (figure 20.1); they then leveled off at around 22% of GDP, and declined slightly in 2016. When the doubling of the budget's take of GDP is combined with rapid GDP growth, the U.S. dollar value of Chinese budgetary revenues (converted at exchange rates and taking into account RMB appreciation) increased from $113 billion in 1995 to $2.4 trillion in 2016. For comparison, U.S. federal government on-budget revenues, excluding Social Security, were $1.97 trillion for 2012. Less than two decades after the country faced a potential crisis of state capacity, the Chinese system was awash in cash.

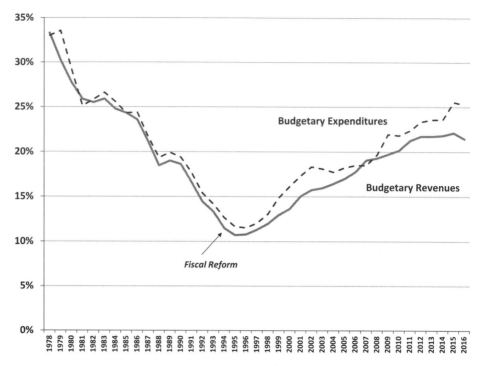

Figure 20.1
Budget share of GDP.
Source: *SAC* (2017, 69).

Despite this achievement, the Chinese fiscal system still faces tremendous challenges and has deep built-in defects. The fiscal reform of 1994 solved the most pressing issues facing China, but more than 20 years later, the same fiscal system has been adapted and repurposed but not fundamentally restructured, and it is now looking somewhat dilapidated and structurally unsound. The most immediate problems concern the division of resources and responsibilities between the central government and local governments. As discussed later, China's fiscal system has a peculiar and paradoxical characteristic: formally highly centralized, it is highly decentralized in regard to actual expenditures. Local governments never had an adequate revenue base after the 1994 fiscal reform, and the problem has become progressively more serious. A major new round of fiscal reforms was advanced in 2014 but this initiative quickly bogged down, and it is uncertain whether it will move forward.

The first three sections of this chapter examine three basic questions of public finance as they apply to China: How should the government be funded? What expenditures are most important? How should revenue and expenditure responsibilities be divided among central and local governments? Sections 20.4 through 20.6 then discuss three major challenges: the dependence of local governments on fiscal transfers, the unhealthy dependence of urban governments on land sales and development, and the management and consolidation of local government debt. The chapter concludes by placing these issues in the context of China's next round of fiscal reforms. Are China's taxes too high? How can a new, more sustainable budgetary system be developed?

20.1   Revenue and Taxation

20.1.1   How Should the Government Be Funded?

How does a government raise sufficient revenue to provide the goods and services its people demand? This is a formidable problem, particularly early in the development process. Governments in underdeveloped economies that are rural and overwhelmingly small scale have little capacity to collect revenues (Besley and Persson 2013). They typically rely on taxes collected on foreign trade or a few monopoly goods (such as salt in traditional China) or on printing money (seigniorage). The Chinese system under the command economy should be seen from this perspective: almost all budgetary revenues were raised from tens of thousands of state enterprises with monopoly powers rather than hundreds of millions of households. State-owned enterprises (SOEs) were profitable because they had de facto monopolies in given markets, government control of the price system was used to concentrate revenues in those firms, the government then harvested revenues from them, and entry and competition were prohibited. The details of tax rates and the nonexistence of a professional tax administration were irrelevant. This system eroded and then essentially collapsed between 1978 and 1994. New firms entered the most lucrative markets, competition spread rapidly through the economy, and without state monopoly profits, there was no money to run the government.

China in the 1990s had to build a modern fiscal system more or less from scratch. The first question, therefore, is, how do we achieve an effective and fair tax system that is compatible with a market economy? The economics of public finance provides some answers to this question: The tax base should be broad; tax rates should be as even as possible; and the system should be feasible given the country's level of development. A broad tax base is important because it (1) permits tax rates to be as low as possible for a given level of need; and (2) spreads the tax over as many taxpayers as possible, so it is fairer. These two traits—that taxes be low and fair—are desirable in themselves but also contribute to the economic efficiency of a tax system. Any system for funding government activity imposes direct and indirect costs on the economy. The direct cost of taxation is simply that we have to pay the taxes; we do not get any government services for free. To this we add the indirect cost—the excess burden—that comes from the fact that taxation drives a wedge between a good's cost and its price and therefore disproportionately discourages the consumption of the taxed good. Occasionally, this is a desirable outcome: high cigarette taxes discourage smoking. More often, it is an unintended cost that comes from taxing something that is relatively visible and hard to move or conceal; thus most societies tax work because employment relations are usually well documented, and almost everybody has to work.[1]

As countries develop, they collect more in taxes. According to Baunsgaard and Keen (2010), low-income countries collect an average of 14.5% of GDP in taxes; middle-income countries collect 18.7%, and high-income countries collect 32.5%. Thirty high-income OECD countries in 2012 collected 22.4% of GDP in ordinary taxes and 10 percent of GDP in social security contributions, for a total of 32.4% (OECD 2014, excluding four countries that consolidate social security accounts). The key innovations that allowed developed countries to collect so much were the two important taxes introduced during the early twentieth century: the personal income tax (with tax withholding) and the value-added tax (in every developed country except the United States). These two taxes effectively broaden the tax base, but they are quite difficult to implement before a certain stage of development: not until most workers have regular jobs and payments are made through the banking system does it begin to be cost effective to collect these taxes. Capacity to collect fiscal revenues grows along with economic development.

20.1.2   The Tax Reform of 1994

The Chinese government in 1994 enacted a sweeping reform of the fiscal system that standardized the taxation system, creating a nearly uniform value-added tax and a profit tax that applied equally to all ownership forms. The fiscal reform had three crucial elements: new taxes, a tax-assignment and sharing system, and a new central-government taxation agency. The most important new tax was the value-added tax (VAT) levied on most manufactured goods at a uniform rate of 17%. Very small private enterprises without regular bookkeeping systems were to pay a tax of 6% of gross sales in lieu of VAT. A 33% profit tax was introduced, with uniform rates for state, collective, and private enterprises. Only foreign-invested firms were left with their original, concessionary tax deals, and they were integrated into the system when a uniform 25% corporate income tax was phased in for everybody between 2008 and 2012. The system of personal income taxes was unified and made slightly more

---

1. It is peculiar that almost all governments tax work (a good) but are generally resistant to taxing, for example, carbon emissions (a bad).

rigorous. A "consumption tax" (actually a luxury or excise tax) was introduced for cigarettes, alcohol, and a few other luxuries. Several minor local taxes were introduced (or, more accurately, regularized). In return, the previous system of industrial and commercial taxes was abolished, and the SOE profit contract system was eliminated.

The merging of the product tax and much of the business tax into the VAT and the adoption of only two rates for the VAT significantly reduced the variation in tax burdens due to differential tax rates. Since the VAT was now collected by a central-government agency, local governments could no longer give VAT tax relief to favored enterprises. These changes have made the tax system more transparent, and less costly to administer.

Most crucial, perhaps, is that the fiscal reform worked. That is, as the opening section of this chapter showed, the tax reform provided the foundation for a sustained growth in budgetary revenues. China jumped from being below the low-income average to being above the middle-income average, according to Baunsgaard and Keen's (2010) averages, and by some standards even exceeds the OECD level (see section 20.7). At the same time, as detailed below, it improved the fiscal standing of the central government. The fiscal reform of 1994 solved the fiscal crisis that China had faced at the beginning of the decade.

20.1.3   Revenues Today

In the more than two decades since the 1994 fiscal reform, China's revenue base has changed relatively little. As Table 20.1 shows, China relies on a broad array of taxes. Although the VAT is the largest single source of revenue, it is by no means predominant. A very large share of tax revenue is derived from levies on transactions. Even the several taxes listed as "land and resource" taxes are levied only when land or resources are sold. Thus China relies primarily on "indirect" taxes that are collected from one party of a transaction, not necessarily the person ultimately paying the tax.

"Direct taxes"—those levied directly on the person ultimately paying—are a correspondingly small part of Chinese revenues. Most striking, the personal income tax accounts for only 5% of budgetary revenues, in contrast to the 40% the income tax contributes in most developed countries. The income tax is small because (1) it is levied on income after a monthly deduction set in 2011 at 3,500 RMB, which was just over the average urban wage in that year, so less than half of wage earners are affected; and (2) little effort is made to collect income tax on nonwage income. These features mean that the income tax plays almost no role in equalizing income (chapter 10). Property taxes paid annually do not exist, except in two pilot cities (and even those have numerous exemptions). Thus, China has a high overall tax rate without fully using two of the biggest income-raising taxes, income tax and property tax;

Table 20.1
2014 fiscal revenues by type.

	Percent of total revenues
Tax revenues	**85**
VAT	22
Other business and service taxes	21
Product and trade taxes	4
Land and resource taxes	10
Stamp and contract duties	4
Profit tax	18
Personal income tax	5
Nontax revenues	**15**

Source: Ministry of Finance website, http://yss.mof.gov.cn/2014czys/201507/t20150709_1269855.html.

only the VAT is a broad-based tax. As discussed later, China does levy high payroll taxes, but these go directly into the social security fund, and are not counted in government tax revenues.

20.2   Expenditures

20.2.1   What Goods and Services Should the Fiscal System Provide?

In a market economy, we can rely on private individuals and companies to produce ordinary goods. Governments should provide outlays in three situations in which the market does not work efficiently or different outcomes are desired: public goods; goods with positive externalities; and socially favored redistribution. Public goods are goods and services that are "nonexcludable" and "nonrival." Because public goods are nonexcludable, citizens cannot be charged user fees and excluded from enjoying them if they do not pay. The clearest example is national defense. Because public goods are nonrival, one additional person enjoying the good does not detract from other people's enjoyment, so there is no real social cost to providing an extra unit (and the price should be zero). Personal security is a good example: my increased sense of personal security does not detract from yours (and may add to it). Therefore, the government should provide collective and individual security to its citizens without charging them directly for the service.

Second, governments may provide goods when there are clear positive externalities. For example, research and development provides benefits to society through the diffusion of new technologies, from which the researcher cannot appropriate all the benefits. Without government support, research would be underprovided, and government subsidies or funding are appropriate.

Third, governments can redistribute income. Redistribution occurs not just from rich to poor but also from healthy to sick and from working people to the young and to retirees. Indeed, in virtually all societies, the largest component of redistribution is from the currently working to the currently retired.

Different political systems make different decisions about which goods and services are provided and particularly on the degree of redistribution that they prefer. Take government funding of education, for example. Education is not a public good, since most of the benefits go to the individual receiving the education, and it is excludable and at least partially rival. However, all governments fund education for two basic reasons. First, they want to redistribute resources to the young, who consume most education before starting their working lives; and second, education has positive externalities by enabling more sophisticated cooperation. A highly skilled worker is even more productive when she has a cohort of skilled coworkers and a set of educated customers, and it becomes easier for society to adopt more productive technologies. Some societies emphasize equality of initial access (which ends up providing subsidies to families who can afford to pay full prices), while some societies emphasize cost recovery from those receiving education (which ends up burdening graduates with repayment responsibilities).

20.2.2   Restructuring Budget Expenditures

From this perspective, it is immediately apparent that Chinese budgetary outlays in the command-economy period were profoundly irrational. In the prereform era, the Chinese government spent an enormous amount of time and resources doing things that the free market could do with minimal intervention. The largest component of outlays was investment, but most investment went to ordinary industrial facilities, like steel mills and machinery plants, rather than public goods like infrastructure. During the reform, the Chinese government stopped trying to do everything and focused government resources on the things that only government can do well.

As figure 20.2 shows, from 1978 through the low point in 1995–1996, the government cut back on investment, subsidies, and military expenditures. Investment in private goods was turned over to the business sector. Subsidies were an especially regressive form of expenditure since they went predominantly to relatively high-income urban workers, protecting them from the impact of increased food prices. Military outlays were heavy for an economy the size of China's in 1978.[2] These were all cut back, while core government outlays for administration and social services were successfully protected ("current civilian" in figure 20.2). Then after 1995,

---

2. Most analysts believe that officially classified military expenditures in China understate the full investment of resources in the defense sector, and that substantial outlays are classified as administration, science and technology, and investment.

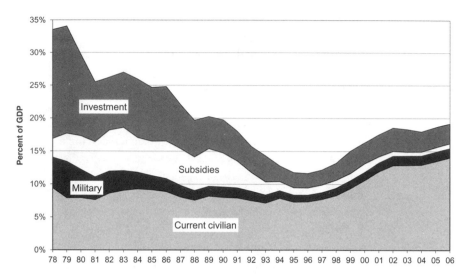

Figure 20.2
Types of budgetary outlays.
Source: *SYC* (2005, 280–281; and earlier volumes).

outlays for administration, education, and pensions and social security all increased rapidly, while outlays for investment, subsidies, and the military have all been held constant as a share of GDP. Thus, after 1994 budgetary expenditures also began to fund activities in ways that converge to the government's roles in other market economies.

20.2.3   Is China Becoming a Welfare State?

Through 2006, though, even after the fundamental realignment of budgetary expenditures, the Chinese government was spending relatively little on social services.[3] The legacy of budgetary shortage combined with the relatively young population kept social outlays low. Table 20.2 shows that budgetary expenditure for three important social welfare outlays was quite small as a share of GDP in 2006, but subsequently grew rapidly. Expenditure on education in 2006 was 2.5% of GDP, which was still quite low in comparative terms. Chinese policy-makers repeatedly targeted 4% of GDP for education, seeing this as the international norm, and outlays in fact jumped to 3.9% of GDP in 2012 before leveling off. Health expenditure, at 0.6% of GDP, was even further below global norms in 2006, and began a sustained rise to 1.8% in 2016. Finally, government expenditures on low-income housing—which did not exist

3. The classification of budgetary expenditures changed after 2006, so it is impossible to directly compare pre- and post-2006 outcomes.

Table 20.2
Budgetary expenditures on social services.

	2006	2012	2016
	Billion RMB (percent of GDP)		
Education	546.4 (2.5%)	2,124.2 (3.9%)	2,805.6 (3.8%)
Health	142.1 (0.6%)	724.5 (1.3%)	1,315.4 (1.8%)
Public housing	n.a.	448.0 (0.8%)	677.6 (0.9%)

Source: Ministry of Finance website, http://yss.mof.gov.cn/2016js/201707/t20170713_2648981.html.

as a budgetary category in 2006 and is presumed close to zero—reached 0.9% of GDP in 2016. Total spending in these three social welfare categories doubled from 3.1% of GDP in 2006 to 6.4% in 2016.

A similar large increase is evident with respect to pension outlays, which are not fully integrated into the budget. Pensions for SOE retirees and other fully vested urban enterprise workers are paid from the Social Security fund. Outlays from this fund increased from 2.2% of GDP in 2006 to 4.6% of GDP in 2016. In addition, the government budget pays the pension of retired civil servants and public services undertakings. These outlays increased to 0.7% of GDP in 2016 from an estimated 0.25% a decade earlier. The increase in basic pension outlays has been driven by the beginning of population aging, but more important currently has been the policy decision made at the end of the 1990s to allow nearly universal early retirement among the urban population (chapters 8 and 9). The number of retirees enjoying a full pension doubled in the decade after 2005 and reached 101 million in 2016. Moreover, pensions have been increased annually for more than a decade, so benefits are relatively generous. We can use these numbers to get a general sense of the Chinese government's shift in the direction of a welfare state. Total government pension outlays increased from 2.45% to 5.3% of GDP between 2006 and 2016. If pension outlays are added to the budgetary social service outlays shown in table 20.2, the total goes from 5.6% of GDP in 2006 to 11.7% of GDP in 2016. This is quite a substantial increase, particularly when we recognize that population aging has scarcely begun.

In nearly all these areas, a similar pattern of incremental policy-making adapted to China's urban-rural divide is in evidence. As chapter 6 showed, urban residents (with urban *hukou* and employment) have long had a generous system of social welfare entitlements. The innovation in the past decade has been the creation of separate, initially less generous systems of social spending for the rural and rural-urban migrant populations. These programs started small. For example, the expansion of rural education started with textbook subsidies in 2001 and was abruptly expanded to provide free primary and middle schools in 2006. The rural New Cooperative Medical System (NCMS) started in 2003 with an annual fiscal subsidy of 20 RMB per participant, which grew steadily for more than a decade to 420 RMB per participant in 2016, and the program reached more than 800 million participants (Wong 2016). This figure is greater than the number of rural residents, showing that large numbers of rural-to-urban migrants have enrolled as well.

There are now three separate programs of government health insurance. To the long-standing system for urban employees was added not only the rural NCMS (2003) but also an insurance program based on urban residence (2007) that primarily serves the elderly, children, and students not covered by the employee-based system. The employee-based system is administered by the Ministry of Human Resources and funded through payroll deductions, so it is much richer than the other two, which are funded from government expenditures. The NCMS is administered by the Ministry of Health, and funds are pooled at the county level, while the funds for the urban systems are pooled at the city level. There are literally hundreds of different "risk pools" (counties or cities in which funds are combined) with different funding availability and ability to bear shocks (Meng et al. 2015). China has set a goal of consolidating systems by 2020, but although that is possible, it poses enormous administrative and financial challenges. Bringing the rural system up to the level of the employee-based system through consolidation would be extremely costly.

An analogous situation exists with respect to retirement programs. A separate new program for urban and rural workers not part of the existing worker-staff retirement program was inaugurated in 2014. In principle, the program covered 508 million participants in 2016. Like the NCMS, the program is based on individual contributions plus government subsidies. Although the initial level of contributions and subsidies is quite low, if the program follows the same trajectory as the medical insurance programs, the ramp-up could be quite steep. Again, the declared objective is to reach some kind of universal consolidated system by 2020. For a pension program, the challenges to raising everyone to the level of the first tier urban pension system are even greater than for medical insurance. China's life expectancy has been increasing rapidly and is now over 75, and the proportion of elderly is increasing rapidly. In the existing worker-staff pension program, almost everyone can retire at 60, and many retire earlier. Benefits are generous and have been adjusted upward for inflation annually for the past 15 years. Consolidation of pension programs at this level of coverage would probably be too big a financial burden. Yet the existing pension program needs to incorporate more currently employed workers. The number of retirees is rapidly growing, and there are only three currently employed workers under the old system for each retiree. In the long run, the system must add migrant and informal workers if it is to be financially viable.

China's social expenditures are still too low to qualify China as a full-fledged welfare state, but there has been dramatic movement in that direction. Current outlays have increased significantly and there has been a dramatic expansion in eligibility and, potentially, entitlement. Generous eligibility combined with a rapidly aging population may indicate that China is on track to become a welfare state within a decade or two. These emerging systems of social welfare have begun to rebuild the system of social insurance that collapsed when the rural collectives fell apart in a way that is potentially appropriate to China's middle-income and predominantly urban society. The system is beginning to transfer resources from young to old and from healthy to sick. However, it still does very little to distribute resources from rich to poor. The top tier of the system provides generous benefits to urban workers, who now often retire in their mid-50s. To be sure, 59 million migrant workers participated in the urban-employee pension scheme as of 2016, but the large majority are still outside it. Overall, then, these are still very much dual-track systems, and the actual outlay of government resources has just begun to trickle over to rural people.

20.3   Central and Local Budgets

20.3.1   How Should Revenue and Expenditure Responsibilities Be Divided Among Governments?

Every large country faces difficult choices between centralization and decentralization of government functions. In the assignment of fiscal responsibilities, there is a fundamental trade-off between centralized and local responsibility. One basic principle is that management should be "as local as possible," so the government can respond easily to citizens' preferences and values. Exactly what public goods should be delivered and in what amounts? Is the marginal value of tax equal to the marginal value of benefits? (That is, are we "overtaxed" or "underprovided with public goods"?) With full local responsibility, local governments should be responsible both for the provision of public goods, like education and personal security, and for taxation so citizens can see the link between their tax payments and the services they receive. This is especially important if different regions have different preferences for the level and quality of public services they demand.

To be effective, though, decentralization requires good-quality local governance. That in turn requires that local governments have adequate, trained personnel and the capacity to collect revenues and deliver services efficiently. Even with that capacity, effective decentralization requires (1) transparency and accountability to the local population, (2) autonomy of local-government operation, (3) clarity and transparency of central-government mandates and entitlements given to local governments, and (4) central-government capacity to monitor and audit (Bahl 1999). Each of these areas presents substantial challenges for China.

Certain public goods by their very nature entail central-government provision. The most obvious example is national defense. In addition, the legal and regulatory framework that governs the country is a fundamental public good that should be applied under uniform principles nationwide. Some public services, such as social security, may rely on a minimum standard of provision that should be the same everywhere. Finally, only the central government can redistribute resources across regions. For all these reasons, central-government provision of services will be preferred to local control in certain policy areas.

Finally, each level of government should have control of sufficient revenue to cover the expenditures for which it is responsible. The central government can achieve some of these competing objectives by maintaining a system of intergovernmental transfers. These transfers should be predictable, transparent, and rule driven. Otherwise, conflicts between levels of government are inevitable, politicking and lobbying will be incessant, and unsustainable fiscal arrangements with unclear responsibility are likely to emerge. In the federalist system of the United States, arrangements have evolved over more than two centuries. The national and local governments each have their own independent powers, (incompletely) specified in the Constitution, and each level is accountable directly and separately to the electorate. Even so, there are many highly contested areas of intergovernmental responsibility. In areas such as education and health insurance, there are ongoing debates both about federal expenditures and about unfunded mandates. China faces parallel issues, but under a very different governmental system. How can China achieve an assignment of revenues and expenditure responsibilities that is efficient and compatible with the goods and services it wants to deliver?

20.3.2   Center and Local: The Paradox of China's Fiscal System

The Chinese fiscal system—indeed, the entire governmental system—is integrated and hierarchical. The government is organized into five levels: nation, province, prefecture, county, and township. These are relations of hierarchy and subordination: superior levels of government generally have the right and ability to issue instructions to subordinate levels. Local governments have no autonomous rights to levy taxes and, until recently, were forbidden to borrow (although they did so anyway). The central government sets all tax types and tax rates. Moreover, the central government provides the local levels with a detailed set of budgetary guidelines and instructions and prepares an integrated set of budget accounts that consolidate central and local revenues and expenditures. By all these indicators, China's fiscal system is highly centralized. Moreover, the centralization of the fiscal system is reinforced by the centralization of the political system. Heads of provinces are appointed by the central government, or, more precisely, by the central Communist Party. Performance indicators are set by the central Communist Party Organization Department, and career paths are clearly in the hands of superiors. The rules and parameters of the fiscal system are set in a highly centralized fashion.

It is surprising, then, to discover that in regard to expenditure, the Chinese fiscal system is one of the most decentralized in the world. In 2016, the central government carried out less than 15% of total expenditures. The remaining 85% of expenditure was carried out by the four subnational levels of government: province, prefecture, county, and township. As figure 20.3 shows, local government expenditures have grown steadily as a share of GDP since the 1994 fiscal reform; central expenditures, however, plateaued in 2000–2003, and have since declined as a share of GDP. Expenditure is more decentralized in China than, for example, in India or the United States, in both of which the central government accounted for more than half of total expenditures (Goyal, Khundrakpam, and Ray 2004; OECD 2014). Along with the decentralization of expenditure goes responsibility for policy mandates: China depends on local governments to execute many national policies. Thus local governments in China dispose of a lot of resources but have even more responsibilities.

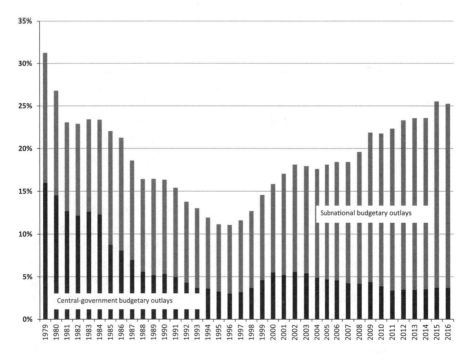

Figure 20.3
Central and local budgetary expenditure (share of GDP).
Source: *SAC* (2017, 70).

Local governments are not accountable to local electorates because they are appointed from above. Although efforts have been made to increase transparency of local budgets, these still fall far short of democratic accountability. Accountability is upward, not downward. Inevitably, this means substantial "agency loss." Thus, local governments in practice have substantial leeway to interpret policy mandates and determine priorities. The paradox of China's fiscal system is that it is formally highly centralized but at the same time highly decentralized in practice.

Two factors have made the tension between centralization and decentralization in the Chinese budgetary system particularly acute today. First, the 1994 fiscal reform never did provide local governments with an adequate tax base. Policy-makers were focused on resolving the center's fiscal difficulties, so they awarded rights over most tax types to the central government and created the centrally controlled State Administration of Taxation (SAT) with the power to collect the most important taxes, including the VAT. This resolved the center's budgetary problems at the cost of weakening local governments' tax-collection capability. The subsequent reduction in rural fees and irregular levies (section 20.4.1) made this problem even more critical. Second, the shift in the composition of expenditures toward greater social welfare (section 20.2.3) has increased the expenditure responsibility of local governments. Traditionally, local governments in China had responsibility for all local-government services, including health, education, police, and courts. As these expenditures have grown, local-government expenditure responsibility has naturally increased. It is particularly surprising that local governments have responsibility for administering retirement and social security programs, which are a central-government responsibility virtually everywhere else in the world. There has been no fundamental rethinking of expenditure assignment since 1994, and so the tension between the center and local governments on the revenue and expenditure sides has steadily increased.

20.3.3   Central-Local Fiscal Relations

The 1994 fiscal reform solved the disparity between central and local resources and responsibilities by creating an ad hoc system of transfers from the central government to local governments. The center government collects the lion's share of revenue and local governments are dependent on the center for budgetary transfers. As shown in figure 20.4, China has had three different systems linking central and local budgets since the beginning of the reform era. At first, the central government was dependent on revenues transferred from local governments, a peculiar legacy of the Maoist decentralization of the Cultural Revolution period. During an intermediate period, 1985–1993, the central government spent about the same share of outlays as the share of revenues it took in, as transfers in both directions between the center and localities balanced out almost exactly. In the post-1994 system the

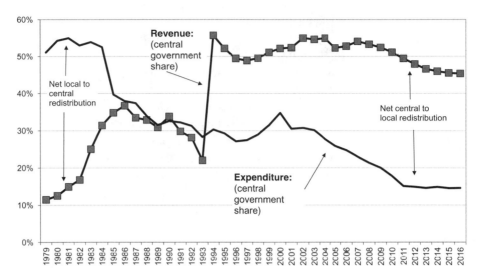

Figure 20.4
Central-government share of budgetary revenue and expenditure.
Source: *SAC* (2017, 70).

central government collects about half of all revenues, and then transfers most of these revenues to local governments. In 2016, central to local transfers amounted to 9.8% of GDP. This arrangement both enhances the central government's overall financial position and gives it a strong bargaining position vis-à-vis local governments.

This system was created through "tax assignment." Central-government taxes included the consumption (luxury) tax, customs duties, and most direct and indirect taxes on central-government-controlled sectors (railroads, financial institutions, and some large centrally controlled enterprises). Provincial taxes included direct taxes on local enterprises, as well as a number of relatively modest taxes, including real estate and property taxes, and pollution and resource fees. The key provision was the designation of most VAT revenues as "shared income," with 75% going to the central government and 25% to the local government. Under this system, the new central SAT first collects the bulk of revenues—including all VAT revenues—and then shares them with the provinces.

A system of intergovernmental transfers gradually evolved to rectify the "vertical imbalance," that is, the disequilibrium between the activities assigned to each level of government and the resources available to that level of government. Right after 1994, the central government was focused on rebating enough of the VAT revenues to keep each province's total revenues from declining after the reform. Over the subsequent two decades, a much larger system of transfers was gradually improvised to cover expanding policy mandates. These included "earmarked transfers" for specific projects, often those involved in regional development policy, as well as "general transfers" designed to equalize budgetary resources among regions. Remarkably, there has never been a systematic overhaul of the system of transfers, and there is no set of rules or principles that governs the transfer process. There is a common misunderstanding that these transfers show that local-government revenues are inadequate. In fact, there is nothing wrong with local governments being dependent on transfers from higher levels of government. Germany, for example, runs just such a system. But it is critical that a system of this kind be clear, transparent, and predictable. The current Chinese system is none of these, although Chinese policy-makers are now trying to move in that direction.

20.4   Rural Government Budgets

In China, rural areas have always had a thinner revenue base than urban areas. Rural regions were poorer to begin with, and rural command of resources was further reduced by policies of urban bias that kept the price of rural goods low and concentrated revenues in urban industries (chapter 6). For most of the command-economy period, rural public goods were provided by agricultural collectives that were not part of the formal governmental or fiscal system (chapter 11). After the rural collectives dissolved in the 1980s, local governments tried to shore up the rural fiscal system with a variety of extrabudgetary funds and irregular fees.

20.4.1   Fees and Extrabudgetary Funds and Their Abolition

Local governments during the 1980s and 1990s imposed numerous fees and levies on farmers. Some of these were user fees; others were tied to the provision of an important local public good or service. However, since these fees were irregular and imposed at local discretion, there was little to prevent a corrupt local official from arbitrarily imposing a new fee to fund his own administrative expenses. By the late 1990s, collection of taxes, fees, and charges in rural areas had become the major source of rural discontent. Some fees were reasonable, for schools and hospitals, but others were murky or unpopular, such as those for coercive family-planning operations. In the early twenty-first century, the central government decreed that all fees were illegal except those on a short approved list. Fees for education, family planning, road building, and welfare were all abolished. The central government began to provide transfers to compensate local governments for the fees they were relinquishing. At first, these transfers were provided only to poor provinces as part of regional development policies. For example, the Western Development Program after 2001 included subsidies for administrative personnel and education in poor western counties. This type of ad hoc redistribution gradually expanded to cover more regions (such as central provinces) and an increasing list of social objectives.

The central government promulgated a set of objectives for rural policy and increasingly demonstrated willingness to fund the needed programs. The pioneering effort was to make six years of education available nationwide without tuition charges. Along with education, the government began to contemplate a series of policies grouped together as the "New Socialist Countryside" (chapter 11). These included, for the first time, extension to the countryside of a nearly uniform but barebones system of social welfare services. A uniform system of minimum welfare payments was extended nationwide; the NCMS health insurance package was adopted; and some very basic retirement programs were established. Each of these required some contribution from the central government in all but the richest provinces.

Between 2004 and 2006, agricultural taxes were abolished nationwide. This was a momentous policy change. The agricultural tax had been in place for millennia. For the first time, the Chinese government could finance its activities without putting the cost on farmers, the poorest class of society. For local governments, the abolition of the agricultural tax had the same type of impact as the abolition of irregular fees. Villages had less of their own resources, and were more dependent on the central government, which was now increasingly steering money toward specific targets.

20.4.2   New Structure of Power at the Rural Grass Roots

Central-government transfers must go through five levels of government, described in section 20.3.2. Of these five, explicit national policy governs only the fiscal relations between the center and the provinces. Below the province level, budgetary transfers and relations of responsibility over expenditure have been constantly adjusted through an informal bargaining process. County-level governments have emerged from this process comparatively much richer, because they became the conduit through which central-government money flowed. The county share of total consolidated budget expenditures increased from 26% in 2000 to 46% in 2013, while revenues declined, and the gap was financed from above. Counties, in the aggregate, spend three times as much as the central government in China.

County governments increasingly loom large in the life of rural residents. County governments are in charge of distributing revenues downward to townships and villages, increasing the voice of county-level officials, and they determine the concrete policies of the New Socialist Countryside. Townships and villages saw their tax bases shrink, and they were more subject to the influence of superior county-level governments. Village democracy became less salient in the lives of villagers because the oversight over village budgets that their elected councils exercised was less important. At the village level, an increasingly centralized budgetary system has meant more resources but less local control.

20.5   Urban Government Budgets

The budgetary position of urban governments was quite different from that of rural governments. Cities can be at any subnational level of the Chinese governmental hierarchy: there are 4 province-level cities (Beijing, Shanghai, Tianjin, and Chongqing), 30-some "vice-provincial" and prefecture-level cities (e.g., Wuhan, Fuzhou, and Qingdao), hundreds of county-level cities, and thousands of township-level towns. The general rule is that the higher in the hierarchy, the greater the budgetary resources and the higher the managerial autonomy. In the command-economy system, cities had resources because they had control over profitable local state-owned firms, and those resources were adequate in an era when city governments refrained from large-scale redevelopment and frugally maintained the traditional urban cityscape.

20.5.1   Municipal Governments and the Challenge of Urbanization

Municipal governments had to surrender a portion of their existing revenues in the 1994 fiscal reform. Moreover, the local SOEs that remained under their control were predominantly medium-sized enterprises that were exposed to the brunt of competition and were not profitable. In exchange for their loss of control over revenues, municipal governments in the 1990s were given substantial autonomy. They had to carry out the restructuring and downsizing of SOEs in the late 1990s and, in some cases, grapple with major unemployment problems. They had to develop urban development plans.

The Chinese fiscal system was never explicitly adapted to provide the resources needed for urbanization (Wong 2013). Migrants began to pour into the cities after the turn of the century, and a housing boom steadily gathered steam. While the central government focused on providing resources in the countryside to permit the expansion of social programs, city governments were left on their own to develop the resources for urbanization. They found a solution in land development.

20.5.2   Land-Driven Local Government

City governments discovered that their control of urban land could generate the resources they needed for urbanization. Chapter 6 described the nature of urban-government control of land. As the representative of the "state" that formally owns all urban land, city governments were in an advantageous position to begin with. However, the crucial lever of control and source of resources was the city government's monopoly control of the conversion of rural land to urban land eligible for development. Rural people are strictly forbidden to develop agricultural land for

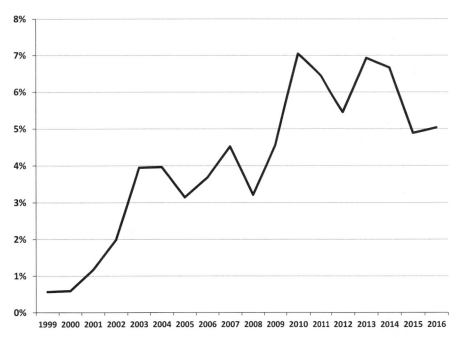

Figure 20.5
Local-government land revenues (share of GDP).
Sources: Through 2010, Huang (2012); from 2011, Ministry of Finance website, http://zhs.mof.gov.cn
/zhengwuxinxi/zonghexinxi/201604/t20160401_1934261.html.

urban uses.[4] They must instead sell their land, and the only entity authorized to purchase that land is the city government. In practice, then, city governments purchase developable land from farmers (exploiting their monopsonistic position to buy low), install infrastructure, and sell the land-use rights to developers (exploiting their monopolistic position to sell high).

This key structural position has meant that local governments have been able to consistently raise substantial sums of money from the sale of land. Figure 20.5 shows that local governments generated between 5% and 7% of national GDP annually in land revenues after 2010 (revenues grew rapidly, but data coverage in earlier years may also have been incomplete). For many cities, these land revenues, which are not incorporated into their formal budgets, are as big as or bigger than all other forms of locally generated revenue put together. City governments in China have become land

---

4. Since 2015, villages have been allowed to develop land that had already been set aside for township and village enterprises or housing. At the same time, restriction on land zoned agricultural have been tightened.

developers; their resources and achievements are inseparable from their success in developing land.

This system has many shortcomings. Most clearly, it continuously involves local-government officials in direct, microeconomic interventions in the economy. Local governments have strong interests. Since local governments also have strong regulatory and policy responsibilities, the potential for conflict of interest is great. Moreover, the dependence on land inevitably makes it more difficult for the city government to develop a clear arm's-length relationship with the market. Local-government entrepreneurship has been a crucial characteristic of China's economic reform from the very beginning. With land dependence, however, this entrepreneurship can take on an extremely unhealthy form.

Local-government officials respond to the incentives they face. Land revenues loom large in the total resources available to them, and successful land development is one obvious area in which an energetic local official can raise funds. What objectives do local officials seek to achieve? Crucially, local officials work in the context of a hierarchical, centrally managed bureaucratic system. As described in section 5.6, that system provides strong and explicit incentives for long-term career success. Local officials are strongly incentivized to grow local GDP and increase local budgetary revenues. By contrast, local officials have no direct accountability to local residents, other than making sure that they are reasonably content and not given grounds to disturb social order. Thus local officials have strong incentives to build and develop and only very weak incentives to provide high-quality services to urban residents. Moreover, as discussed in chapter 6, city officials gain nothing from incorporating migrants into the city economy. Thus they overemphasize the urbanization of land and obstruct the urbanization of people. An obsessive focus on land development by local officials is thus an entirely rational response to the incentive system that they face. This distorts the urbanization process by encouraging physical overexpansion and human underexpansion of the city fabric.

The land-based municipal finance system has provided adequate resources for urban development, but it has many disadvantages. It fosters government intervention in and distortion of the local economy. For this reason, it also encourages corruption and insider dealing. Finally, it creates an undesirable pro-cyclical pattern in municipal finances: when times are good, city coffers are full and city expenditures grow rapidly, but when times are bad, city revenues drop disproportionately, and it is difficult for cities to help the local economy. Indeed, when the 2008–2009 global financial crisis hit, the return to urban land-development activities would normally have declined sharply, leading local government to pull back on investment. In order to prevent this pro-cyclical response—which would have worsened the downturn—central policy-makers encouraged local governments to take on new debt, in the process creating a serious problem of local-government debt.

20.6 Local-Government Debt

Until 2014, local governments in China have had no legal power to borrow money and go into debt. Despite the clear legal prohibition, local governments have always borrowed money. The most common way for a local government to circumvent the prohibition on borrowing has been to set up a local investment company or development fund and then encourage the company to borrow, backed by an explicit government guarantee. Indeed, it is hard to imagine local governments playing the kind of entrepreneurial and developmental roles that they routinely play in China unless they set up some kind of corporate entities to raise funds and carry out development activities. (State-owned enterprises are certainly legal in China, so the legitimacy of such vehicles is not in question, but there is no legal basis for local governments guaranteeing debt.) Such operations have a long history in China, but during most periods the central government has vigilantly monitored and limited such activities.

During the 2008–2009 global financial crisis (GFC), the attitude of the central government shifted from cautiously restraining local-government investment vehicles to actively promoting them. As described in chapters 18 and 19, new local-government funding vehicles (LGFVs) proliferated as instruments for local governments to accelerate investment as quickly as possible. State-owned banks were urged to lend generously and to keep the money flowing. These steps led to a rapid explosion of the debt of LGFVs, which doubled from year-end 2007 to 2009, from 4.5 trillion RMB to 9 trillion RMB, with over 80% of the funds coming from the banking system (Fan and Lv 2012). Almost overnight, a serious local-government debt problem was created. The National Audit Office (NAO) conducted a thorough study of local-government debt as of June 30, 2013, and discovered a total of 10.89 trillion RMB for which local governments had direct repayment obligations and a further 2.7 trillion RMB in debt that the government had guaranteed, plus 4.3 trillion RMB of potential or contingent liability (NAO 2013). The NAO estimates are conservative, covering documented and verifiable debts, and lead to a calculation of direct local-government debt equal to 18.5% of 2013 GDP and all three categories together at 30% of GDP.

More alarming than the total volume of this debt is the fact that it existed in a kind of legal never-never land. Local governments cannot legally borrow or guarantee debt, but the NAO published detailed figures on the borrowing and guarantees of local government. Responsibility for the debt is diffuse (the central government encouraged it at the time); procedures for managing debt are weak to nonexistent; and procedures for sorting out debt and declaring default are unknown. The underlying income-earning potential of the assets held is dubious. A very small proportion of LGFVs own projects that generate a steady revenue stream, for example, toll highways or water-treatment plants. About half hope to repay debt through land sales: LGFVs are the instruments through which local-government land dependence is realized. If the value of land drops, these debts will be extremely difficult or impossible to repay. Acknowledged local-government debt exceeds the volume of central-government treasury bonds circulating in China, and there are additional debts beyond these liabilities

A comprehensive effort to manage local government debt was launched in 2014. A revised Budget Law gave local governments the formal right to borrow in their own name under strict central-government oversight. This allowed local governments to issue "municipal bonds" within an allocated quota. The next step was to convert existing debt into new municipal bonds as well. The ultimate objective was to create a municipal-bond market in China. In this market, investors would be able to assess the risk and return of individual local-government borrowers and the municipal-bond market would ultimately serve as an alternative to land-driven local budgets.

The ambitious effort to restructure existing local-government debt quickly ran into obstacles. When the Jiangsu fiscal authorities tried to sell municipal bonds, they discovered that potential bond buyers disagreed about the risk—and therefore the interest rate—at which local debt should be sold. Local officials did not want to pay higher interest rates, and central policy-makers were impatient to carry through the restructuring as soon as possible. The result was that policy-makers simply directed the state-owned banks to repurchase the loans on their books that they had extended to local governments, but in the form of bonds. During 2015 and 2016, a total of 8 trillion RMB of local-government debt—more than 10% of GDP—was converted into local bonds, placed on the bank balance sheets, and made the explicit responsibility of provincial governments.

The restructuring program lowered the interest-payment burden on local governments, moved them closer to solvency, and slapped an implicit central-government guarantee on the debt, removing a potential source of financial risk. However, only a tiny proportion of the debt was sold on to an exchange-based market, where investors would have been able to discover the risks and returns (or "spreads" above national government bonds) associated with the borrowing of specific local governments. The effort to quickly provide an alternative to land-driven finance was stymied. LGFVs have continued to borrow from banks, although it has technically been forbidden. Many of the problems associated with the old system are still evident and may grow worse if the government cannot control future borrowing. On the positive side, new debt instruments have been created, and future borrowing within the authorized quotas will provide new supply to the market. It may eventually grow into a new and more reliable source of funding for local governments.

20.7   Fiscal Reform and Overall Economic Reform

Beneath the surface of the fiscal system put in place in 1994, it looks increasingly cobbled together with numerous ad hoc adaptations made to a system rushed into place in response to crisis. Remarkably, more than 20 years later, despite massive growth, rapid urbanization, and dramatic shifts in the composition of budgetary expenditures, the same basic system is still in place. In the summer of 2014, then finance minister Lou Jiwei laid out a comprehensive program of fiscal reform that was accepted by top policy-makers and that would address some of the main issues in the current system.

Lou envisioned a three-stage reform. The first stage, in 2014–2015, was to establish new transparency and better standardized budgetary management procedures; oversight by the National People's Congress and local people's congresses; and new procedures that would allow supervised local-government borrowing, clarify rules for intergovernmental transfers, and introduce greater transparency. Most of these budgetary management provisions were included in the new Budget Law adopted in 2014. However, the second and third stages of fiscal reform immediately ran into obstacles. The second stage envisioned new taxes. Many of the existing transaction taxes would be canceled, and a greater reliance on direct taxes—the income tax and the property tax—would replace them. The third stage of reform would create a new central and local revenue- and expenditure-sharing system based on the new taxes adopted. Under the new system, local governments would gain control of some new revenue streams, and the central government would take over certain expenditure responsibilities from local governments, perhaps including social security and education.

The changes proposed by the minister of finance, if carried through, would amount to a fundamental restructuring of the Chinese fiscal system. The details of the new taxes and expenditure responsibilities were never released, probably because they were the subject of intense debate and political maneuvering. As of the end of 2016, progress on the second and third stages was seriously behind schedule, and the ultimate fate of the program is unknown. Nevertheless, the reform proposal raises the most fundamental issues that must be addressed in any fiscal program. Two fundamental issues are related to the discussion of public finance with which this chapter began: How big should the Chinese government be? And how should revenue and expenditure responsibilities be divided among central and local governments?

20.7.1   New Taxes: How Large Should China's Budget Be?

How big is China's government today? Section 20.1 described the strong recovery of China's formal budgetary revenues and showed they are now relatively large compared to other middle-income countries. However, the subsequent discussion has

Table 20.3
2014 fiscal and quasi-fiscal revenues.

	Billions of RMB	Percent of GDP
Total budgetary revenues	13,690	21.8
Local-government land revenues	4,294	6.7
Social insurance premiums	3,982	5.4
SOE profits (after tax)	3,087	4.8
Total	25,054	38.7

Source: Naughton (2017, online appendix).
Notes: Fiscal subsidy to social security fund deducted to avoid double counting.

referred to other forms of revenue that are not included in formal tax revenues, in particular urban land revenues and social insurance revenues. These fit into a "gray zone" where officials control funds and off-budget resources. It is reasonable to group these funds with formal budgetary revenues, and compare this total to other countries. Table 20.3 shows the main categories, including the after-tax profits of SOEs (both financial and nonfinancial enterprises). In addition to 21.8% of GDP in formal taxes and non-tax budgetary revenue, local governments raised the equivalent of 6.7% of GDP in land revenues, and social insurance contributions amounted to 5.4% of GDP. After-tax profits of SOEs, potentially influenced by government officials, amounted to another 4.8% of GDP, for a total of 38.7% of GDP. (Alternately, if SOE revenues are excluded, the total is 33.9% of GDP.)

These figures are close to the OECD (rich country) averages reported in Baunsgaard and Keen (2010). Not considering social insurance contributions, government revenues in China, according to this expanded definition, amounted to 33.3% of GDP, which is well above the OECD average of 22.4% of GDP. Social insurance contributions in China are 5.4% of GDP, compared to the OECD average of 10%. Aggregating social insurance contributions with broadly defined government revenues, the 2014 Chinese figure of 38.7%—or 33.9% without SOEs—is above the 32.4% average total of OECD countries. China is a middle-income country that is taxed at the level of a rich country.

This broad accounting gives us a new perspective on the problems of fiscal reform. New direct taxes, such as an expanded income tax and a property tax, would be more efficient and potentially fairer than existing taxes. However, it is not easy to impose a new set of burdensome taxes on people, especially when their overall tax burden is already relatively high. This is exactly the case in China.

The broad perspective also helps understand China's situation with regard to social insurance. China's pension program is already large. The Chinese budget puts money directly into the social insurance fund, and also pays pensions directly to retired civil servants. Together, these contributions amount to another 1.4% of GDP, so along with individual contributions, the total revenue raised for social insurance totals 6.8% of GDP. This is not too far behind the OECD average, which is remarkable, considering that China is at a much lower level of income, is at the very beginning of the population aging process, and only covers urban residents who are only half the population. China's social security system has other unusual features. It is funded through a payroll tax with fairly high rates, but low coverage. Individuals and employers both have fairly strong incentives to evade the program, and the number of covered employees is only three times the number of retirees. In addition, social security funds and the responsibility to pay pensions to local residents are controlled by local governments. In almost every other country, social security is a national program with at least one tier of uniform treatment.

Section 20.5 described some of the shortcomings of the system of land-dependent urban finance. Ideally, future fiscal reforms would wean local governments from their dependence on revenues from the sale of land. Local property taxes encourage city governments to provide better public services and welcome newcomers because both tend to push up property values. In contrast, land-development revenues can be raised only one time for each plot of land, encouraging the most lucrative short-run projects and attracting only the wealthiest newcomers. Moreover, property taxes are the local-government revenues that are most directly linked to the provision of local public goods. Clearly, tax reform cannot simply pile new taxes on top of the existing ones; it must imply the reduction of many indirect taxes and the elimination of land revenues as a type of local-government revenue. A successful tax reform would be one that relied on increased direct taxes—the income tax and the property tax—while lowering other taxes and not increasing the overall tax burden. This is completely feasible but presents daunting technical problems of sequencing, the timing of tax phase-ins and phase-outs, and the division of revenues between the center and local governments.

20.7.2 Creating a New System of Intergovernmental Transfers

As the difficult process of determining new taxes and tax rates is accomplished, policy-makers must also determine a new division of responsibility between central and local governments. The two most obvious candidates for a recentralization of responsibility are social security and education. Most countries have centralized social security administrations, and some countries—but not the United States—have centralized educational systems. It would not be surprising if China opted for a centralized solution in these two areas.

Even with some expenditure responsibilities recentralized, there will be a need for an ongoing program of intergovernmental transfers. The current system needs to be overhauled. The 2014 fiscal reform program produced much more information about the various programs of intergovernmental transfers and developed a relatively transparent system for disclosing the most important transfers. This was an important step forward in what will be a long-term process of putting the transfer system on a regular and rule-driven basis. The system of "general transfers," has gradually been expanding, and accounted for 56.8% of total transfers in 2015 (MOF 2016, 61). General transfers tend to be partially rule-driven transfers for broad public policy purposes, such as education, health, and administration. However, even within categories like "general transfers," there are many different items and formulas, including ad hoc differences between inland and coastal provinces. As new funding programs were set up, relatively wealthy coastal provinces were often asked to pay for expenditures themselves, whereas poorer inland and western provinces were provided transfers from the center. "Earmarked transfers" are even more tailored to specific projects and objectives, and while they have been reduced, they were still 43.2% of total transfers in 2015.

The current system has a number of disadvantages, two of which are most significant. First, since the transfer system is not guided by a coherent developmental framework, it does not systematically transfer income to lower-income regions on balance. Poor regions get special treatment to help them pay for social outlays, but these can be swamped by the impact of earmarked transfers that end up going disproportionately to richer areas. Second, because transfers are not rule driven, they have perverse incentive effects. Local-government officials have strong incentives to be seen as "needy" by upper levels of government. The ongoing budgetary reform envisions a clear, rule-driven system of transfers to make sure that each locality can afford to pay for education, health, and other essential social services. It will also have to replace land revenues and adjust for a radically different structure of taxation.

20.8   Conclusion

Overall, China's fiscal system has performed a remarkable job. It was created from nothing in the wake of economic reform, provided adequate revenues to build China into a middle-income economy, and allowed China to bridge the gap between a command economy and a market system. In the process, the system was also adapted to provide a modicum of regional burden sharing. Today, the budgetary system is too large, too inefficient, and too opaque to serve the upper-middle-income society that China has now become. Recognition of these facts has already triggered a major new round of fiscal reforms, but they will require much time and effort to restructure the fiscal system and redefine the relationship between the government and the economy. A thorough fiscal reform has the potential to unlock new sources of productivity growth in the economy.

Bibliography

Suggestions for Further Reading

Wong (2013, 2016) goes deeper into the problems of the Chinese fiscal system, while Besley and Persson (2013) put it into an illuminating international context. Su and Tao (2017) is a hard-hitting critique of the urban land and fiscal systems.

References

Bahl, Roy (1999). *Fiscal Policy in China: Taxation and Intergovernmental Fiscal Relations*. San Francisco: The 1990 Institute.

Baunsgaard, Thomas, and Michael Keen. (2010). "Tax Revenue and (or?) Trade Liberalization." *Journal of Public Economics* 94 (9–10): 563–577.

Besley, Timothy, and Torsten Persson (2013). "Taxation and Development." In *Handbook of Public Economics*, vol. 5, 51–110. Amsterdam: Elsevier.

Fan, Gang, and Yan Lv (2012). "Fiscal Prudence and Growth Sustainability; An Analysis of China's Public Debts." *Asian Economic Policy Review* 7:202–220.

Goyal, Rajan, J. K. Khundrakpam, and Partha Ray (2004). "Is India's Public Finance Unsustainable? Or, Are the Claims Exaggerated?" *Journal of Policy Modeling* 26 (3): 401–420.

Huang, Xiaohu (2012). "The Time Is Ripe to Reform the System of Government Land Management" [in Chinese]. *Gaige* [Reform], 6, 137–147.

Meng, Qingyue, Hui Fang, Xiaoyun Liu, Beibei Yuan, and Jin Xu (2015). "Consolidating the Social Health Insurance Schemes in China: Towards an Equitable and Efficient Health System." *Lancet* 386 (October 10): 1484–1492.

MOF (Ministry of Finance) (Annual). *Zhongguo Caizheng Nianjian* (Finance yearbook of China). Beijing: Zhongguo Caizheng Zazhishe.

MOHRSS (Ministry of Human Resources and Social Security) (Annual). *Renli ziyuan he shehui baozhang shiye fazhan tongji gongbao* [Statistical report on the development of human resources and social insurance]. Accessed at www.mohrss.gov.cn.

NAO (National Audit Office) (2013). "Audit Result for National-Government Debt." December 30. Accessed at http://www.audit.gov.cn/n4/n19/c45343/content.html.

Naughton, Barry (2017). "Is China Socialist?" *Journal of Economic Perspectives* 31 (1): 1–23.

OECD (Organisation for Economic Co-operation and Development) (2014). *Revenue Statistics 2014*. Accessed at http://www.oecd-ilibrary.org/taxation/revenue-statistics-2014_rev_stats-2014-en-fr.

SAC (Annual). *Zhongguo Tongji Zhaiyao* (Statistical abstract of China). Beijing: Zhongguo Tongji.

Su, Fubing, and Ran Tao (2017). "The China Model Withering? Institutional Roots of China's Local Developmentalism." *Urban Studies* 54 (1): 230–250.

SYC (Annual). *Zhongguo Tongji Nianjian* [Statistical yearbook of China]. Beijing: Zhongguo Tongji.

Wong, Christine (2013). "Paying for Urbanization in China: Challenges of Municipal Finance in the Twenty-First Century." In Roy Bahl, Johannes Linn, and Deborah Wetzel, eds., *Financing Metropolitan Governments in Developing Countries*, 273–308. Cambridge, MA: Lincoln Institute of Land Policy.

Wong, Christine (2016). "Budget Reform in China: Progress and Prospects in the Xi Jinping Era." *OECD Journal on Budgeting* 15 (3): 27–36. doi:10.1787/budget-15-5jm0zbtm3pzn.

Shanghai 2005, from the Jinmao Tower in Pudong. Compare front cover image, which looks down on this vantage point.

Economic activity—indeed, all human activity—takes place within an enabling natural environment. "Natural capital" provides a stream of services without which no economic activity could take place. Often, these services are unpriced, so they seem to be free and are taken for granted: air to breathe, water to drink, and complex networks of diverse plants, animals, and microorganisms that provide food to eat. Almost always, countries undergoing industrialization deplete and damage their natural capital, and China has not been an exception. The quality of China's air, water, and living resources has been severely degraded over the past century. Now China is struggling to repair the damage and move on to a sustainable development path.

China's natural endowment is extraordinarily rich, as its large traditional population attests. Environmental degradation began in historical times, though. A hundred years ago, most of China's forests had already been stripped away, and China had almost no pristine wilderness areas. Maoist economic policy in turn was heedless of the value of the environment. Yet for all that, the most damaging environmental destruction has come during the acceleration of growth in the post-1978 reform era. Massive industrialization in China after 1978 has created challenges far greater than those of the Maoist era. China has transformed from an energy midget into an energy giant. Meanwhile, traditional agricultural practices of recycling organic waste products into the soil have been displaced by a modern, chemical-intensive, and highly polluting agriculture. There is no question that China today faces a severe environmental crisis. How serious are China's environmental problems today? Has China's economic growth been purchased at an unacceptably high environmental price? Do environmental problems threaten to undermine the progress being made toward a higher quality of life for the majority of Chinese citizens?

Economists frequently view environmental issues through the lens of the "environmental Kuznets curve." According to this conception, pollution and other environmental problems worsen during the early stages of modern economic growth and then begin to diminish as a country reaches middle-income status. Pollution graphed against GDP per capita looks like an inverted U. There are both preference and technology-related arguments for this pattern (Stern 2004). In regard to preferences, poor people understandably place priority on economic growth to increase income and consumption. At first, people need more private goods, and a growing industrial sector responds, producing pollution that at first elicits little protest. As household incomes grow into middle-income ranges, people begin to demand a better personal environment. Public environmental quality is a "luxury good," demand for which increases more than proportionally as incomes grow (income elasticity is greater than one). Citizens begin to demand that governments provide the public goods of clean air and water more effectively. In China today, broad-based popular demand for a better environment is clearly evident. More than 70% of Chinese responding to a 2016 Pew poll said that both air and water pollution were big problems, and 65% agreed that "We should reduce air pollution even if it means slower economic growth" (Pew Research Center 2016). In regard to technology, early stages of industrialization often involve the spread of relatively crude production techniques that are easily mastered but dirty and that fail to use many by-products. Subsequently, as technological capabilities grow, access to cleaner and more efficient production techniques spreads. Government regulatory capacity improves, so new administrative tools are available to restrain polluters. These factors all apply to China.

In fact, there is not one single Kuznets turning point but rather numerous turning points that must be navigated. China's environment is a massive topic that would require volumes to cover adequately. This chapter sketches a few of the most important interactions between the economy and the environment. We begin with the energy baseline, and China's biggest problem: coal. China is currently undergoing an energy transition, and we ask whether this is the beginning of dramatic reductions in coal consumption and carbon emissions. Section 21.2 provides an overview of China's energy and environmental policy over the past two decades, and also explains why the period after 2015 presents a dramatic opportunity that may see the beginning of significant improvement in China's environment. Section 21.3 addresses pollution, and proceeds to the most important issue areas: air, water, and soil. The final section considers global warming and sustainability.

21.1   The Energy Baseline and the Coal Problem

21.1.1   Energy Composition

Sustainability begins with energy. China is an energy giant, the biggest producer and consumer of energy of all kinds (table 21.1). It has long been the world's largest producer and consumer of coal; it is now the world's largest producer of hydropower

Table 21.1
Energy consumption, 2016.

	Total consumption	Percent of total energy consumption					
	Million TOE	Oil	Natural gas	Coal	Nuclear energy	Hydroelectric	Renewables
China	3,053	19.0	6.2	61.8	1.6	8.6	2.8
Brazil	298	46.6	11.1	5.5	1.2	29.2	6.4
India	724	29.4	6.2	56.9	1.2	4.0	2.3
Japan	445	41.4	22.5	26.9	0.9	4.1	4.2
EU	1,642	37.3	23.5	14.5	11.6	4.8	8.3
U.S.	2,273	38.0	31.5	15.8	8.4	2.6	3.7
World	13,276	33.3	24.1	28.1	4.5	6.9	3.2

Source: BP (2017), "Primary Energy: Consumption by Fuel." BP figures vary slightly from Chinese official data because conversion into comparable standardized units is done differently. Chinese coal-production figures were revised upward by 8% in 2014 after the discovery of previously uncounted output in the 2013 Economic Census. These revisions are incorporated into all data in this chapter.

and, since 2016, of solar and wind power. Not surprisingly, it is the world's largest contributor to global warming by a substantial margin. China is also the world's largest oil importer. Clearly, prosperity and environmental quality can go together only if energy is used efficiently and if the externalities of different kinds of energy use are incorporated into production and investment decisions.

China's energy production and consumption are dominated by coal. All fossil fuels are exhaustible, and all contribute both to local air pollution and to global warming. Coal is particularly problematic because it is intrinsically much dirtier than oil and gas. China is far and away the largest coal user in the world. China pulled almost 4 billion tons out of the ground at the peak in 2013, and accounted for 48% of world production. Moreover, China is more dependent on coal than any other economy in the world except South Africa. Table 21.1 shows that coal accounted for 61.8% of China's energy consumption in 2016. China has been steadily reducing its dependence on coal for a decade, but the process of reducing dependence on coal is inevitably costly and drawn-out. China has reduced coal dependence while India, thus far, has not; while India extracts only one-fifth as much coal as China, Indian coal dependence is now not far behind that of China.

21.1.2   Evolution of the Energy Economy

Figure 21.1 shows the big picture. As the solid line shows, China's energy consumption was 4.36 billion tons (gigatons) of standardized coal equivalent (SCE) in 2016, almost eight times what it had been in 1978. The stacked bars in figure 21.1 show domestic production (above the horizontal axis) and net imports (below the axis). The

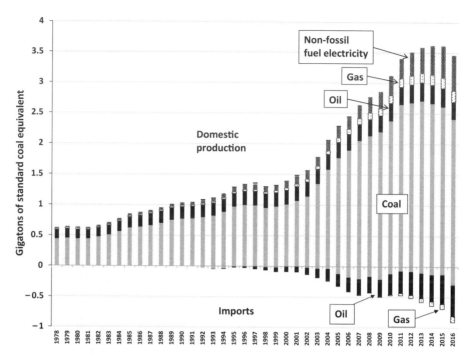

Figure 21.1
Energy consumption: Domestic production and imports.
Sources: *SYC* (2016, tables 9-1, 9-2), updated from *SAC* (2017, 75–76). One ton of standardized coal equivalent (SCE) equates to about 0.7 tons of standardized oil equivalent, or 4.79 barrels of oil.

distance between the top and bottom of the stacked bars equals total consumption after 1992 when imports began. Four significant points emerge from figure 21.1:

Coal dependence. China has traditionally been dependent on coal for more than two-thirds of energy consumption. Back in 1985, coal fulfilled 80% of China's domestic energy needs, while oil was exported. Since then, dependence on coal has declined while the absolute quantity of coal extracted soared. Between 1994 and 2011, raw coal production *tripled*, and approached 4 billion tons a year. Only then did output growth slow and then slip into reverse. Over the past nine years, China has reduced its dependence on coal by ten percentage points, a remarkable achievement. From the recent peak of 72.5% in 2007, dependence declined to 61.8% in 2016.

Turning point in 2013. Energy production and use grew very rapidly after the turn of the century, and total energy consumption grew 9% annually for a decade. Coal production grew in step, and this rapid growth set alarm bells ringing among Chinese policymakers, as well as worldwide because of the impact on carbon emissions.

From 2013, growth of both consumption and production slowed dramatically. Consumption growth dropped to 1.5% annually between 2013 and 2016, while coal consumption declined 3.8% over those three years. The year 2013 is a particularly sharp inflection point for domestic production: domestic coal production was down 11% over the next three years, leading an overall decline in fossil-fuel production. Two-thirds of the widening difference between energy consumption and domestic fossil fuel production between 2013 and 2016 was met by increased energy imports and one-third by increased primary (non-fossil fuel) electricity.

Energy importer. China was an oil exporter in the 1970s and 1980s, but became a net importer for the first time in 1993. Today, it imports substantial quantities of oil, gas, and coal, accounting for 20% of total energy consumption. The most important import is oil. China's oil production grew slowly but steadily for 40 years, and then dipped in 2016 to 4 million barrels a day. The small decline in 2016 dropped China's rank from fifth to eighth largest producer in the world. Since 2013, China has been the world's largest importer, displacing the United States where domestic production has surged. In 2016, China imported 8.2 million barrels of crude and refinery product per day, more than two-thirds of domestic oil consumption. China now imports natural gas through liquefied natural gas tankers as well as transcontinental gas pipelines from Turkestan, Myanmar, and soon, Russia. In response to this increased energy dependency, China has built up a strategic petroleum reserve of 234 million barrels of oil in early 2016.

Rapid growth of renewables. Primary electricity generation—not derived from burning fossil fuels—already accounted for 10% of China's energy use in 2013. By far the biggest part of this was hydropower, but heavy investment in wind and solar power was also essential to boost the share to 13.4% in 2016. For a closer look at renewables, we now consider their share in electric power generation. In 2016, 65% of electricity was still generated by burning coal, and thermal power generation of all types accounted for 71.6%. The non-fossil fuel generation sources accounted were hydropower 19.7%, wind 4.0%, nuclear, 3.6%, and solar 1.1% (CEC 2017). Wind, nuclear, and solar together were 8.7% of electricity, up from under 3% in 2010.

These four dramatic changes provide the basis to understand China's contemporary energy economy.

21.1.3   Efficiency

In 1978, at the beginning of the reform era, the Chinese economy used energy with appallingly low efficiency. Figure 21.2 shows that at the end of the 1970s, China used the equivalent of more than 600 grams of oil to produce $1 of GDP (in 2011 PPP-adjusted dollars). This was three times as much as the average of OECD (rich) countries, which had just brought their consumption down below 200 grams in the wake of the second oil shock. To get an idea of how inefficient this is, consider this comparison: if oil is $60 a barrel (136.4 kilograms), then 600 grams of oil costs $0.26.

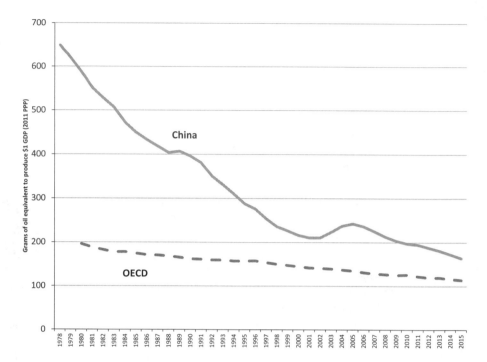

Figure 21.2
Energy use per unit of real GDP (oil equivalent per 2011 PPP-adjusted dollar).
Sources: Energy use is from BP (2016). GDP is annual 2011 PPP GDP from World Development Indicators, last update, August 10, 2016.

China in 1978 had to burn more than 25 cents worth of oil equivalent to produce a dollar's worth of GDP.

As remarkable as that figure is, it is in some ways easy to understand. China had been isolated from world technologies since the break with the Soviet Union in 1960, so its industrial technologies were more than 30 years out of date. Small-scale, inefficient, and polluting facilities were used for energy and industry. Under the command economy, planners directed energy into wasteful and inefficient projects; energy prices were controlled at low levels; and incentives to conserve energy were weak to nonexistent. Chinese planners also mistakenly believed that they had abundant oil, since domestic production had grown very rapidly for 20 years after the discovery of the Daqing oil field in 1959. China's industry in 1978 was overwhelmingly focused on energy-intensive industrial products, such as steel, and energy waste was enormous.

China cut energy use per unit of GDP by two-thirds between 1978 and the end of the twentieth century. This remarkable achievement reflected the confluence of three powerful factors: (1) a fundamental transformation in the system (so that producers had incentives to reduce costs and push up profits); (2) the steady inflow of new technologies from abroad; and (3) a reorientation of output toward consumers and consumer demand, which produced a "lighter" composition of industrial output. As the economy underwent reform, incentives to conserve energy greatly improved. Prices were raised to reflect resource costs, and profit-oriented producers now have incentives to reduce energy consumption and seek new technological solutions.

After the turn of the century, progress in improving efficiency slowed dramatically because of China's industrial surge. New technologies continued to increase energy efficiency, especially in the electricity sector. However, the structure of output, after trending "lighter" for 20 years, now began to swing to a "heavier" orientation. Investment increased, and the housing boom and sustained infrastructure investment pushed up the demand for steel, cement, copper, and chemicals, all voracious consumers of energy. Up through the present, industry has dominated China's demand for energy, particularly electricity. About 70% of energy and electricity are consumed by industry. Thus, the acceleration of heavy industrial growth inevitably increased China's energy use.

Total energy use per unit of output resumed its decline in 2006 and by 2015 required one-quarter as much energy per unit of GDP as in 1978. China's achievement in improving energy efficiency over 40 years has been remarkable. But other countries have not been standing still, and China is still considerably above the OECD average in its use of energy. According to 2014 data, which are available for many countries, China ranked 106th out of 129 economies in the amount of energy needed to produce a dollar's worth of GDP.[1] Only a few large economies, like those of Russia (113) and South Africa (119), were worse. This is primarily because of China's huge manufacturing sector. China today requires 175 grams of oil equivalent to produce a dollar of GDP; developed countries are generally more efficient, and even the profligate United States can produce a dollar of output with 136 grams of oil equivalent. Best practice is defined by the level achieved by the EU (88 grams) and Japan (93 grams).

Market forces have driven much of the improvement in energy efficiency, but government policy has enhanced energy efficiency. The main strands of policy have included closing down small-scale, inefficient producers and concentrating production in larger, more efficient producers, and investing in new technologies that improve productivity. In addition, after 2005, China's five-year plans have included energy saving targets (per unit of GDP), which have generally been binding on local governments. To examine these measures, we need to take a broader look at energy and environmental policy.

1. These comparisons use the World Bank World Development Indicators (WDI), which include many countries. The data in figure 21.2 use Chinese official data, combined with spliced series on PPP-adjusted GDP for consistent intertemporal comparison.

21.2   Energy and Environmental Policy

More efficient energy is generally cleaner energy. The effort to minimize inputs consumed per unit of output usually has as a side effect of lower emissions of waste per unit of output. For China, during most of the past 40 years, the pursuit of market efficiency (profit) has been the main driver of improvements in energy efficiency. That is, the pursuit of environmental objectives in themselves was not the primary driver of policy. However, environmental objectives have slowly become more and more important determinants of policy. Beginning in 2005, with the Eleventh Five-Year Plan, Chinese policy-makers began to signal willingness to pay substantial costs to improve energy efficiency and to reduce pollution. Since that time, Chinese policy-makers have gradually tackled a series of the most critical environmental problems, and these initiatives have begun to bear fruit. As seen in section 21.1, a significant shift in the make-up of the energy industry has been discernable since 2013. Change is gradual, and every society finds it difficult to make coherent energy policy. Energy is essential to the basic functioning of the economy, so interruption of energy supply is simply not an option. Energy relies on extremely expensive and long-lasting infrastructure, so significant changes require a long lead time. Energy is entangled with national security, so decisions are not always made on a least-cost economic basis. Finally, energy creates powerful interest groups that may overwhelm the public interest. These general truths apply to China as well.

21.2.1   Initial Neglect of the Environment During the High-Growth Era

For most of the post-1978 period, the objective of energy policy was to access abundant and diversified energy. Energy was a source of worry. China is an energy giant, but past problems relating to energy development have several times threatened to hold back China's economic development. It is meaningful to remember that China's reform era began with an energy crisis, when the oil China was planning to export to pay for expanded technology imports failed to materialize. Planners worried about energy or electricity shortages to various degrees in 1989–1990, 1995–1996, and 2004–2005.

Before the turn of the century, many policy decisions were made that more or less explicitly traded environmental quality for growth even when the trade-off was relatively costly. China relied on coal, in particular on small-scale coal mines, to maintain industrial growth. In that sense, China continued to "walk on two legs," as the slogan from the Great Leap Forward put it. While the national government was developing large coal mines, local governments and, increasingly, individuals were authorized to develop small-scale coal mines, so the 1980s boom in township and village enterprises included coal. Exploitation of coal deposits by local village collectives and even individuals was allowed, despite the fact that resources were theoretically owned by the state. Since China's coal resources are highly dispersed, small-scale mining boomed in the 1980s and 1990s. As of 1995, coal mines were operating in 1,264 of China's 2,200 counties, and mines run by individuals or village collectives, almost all small scale accounted for 46% of total coal output. China simply followed the same policies with respect to coal that it followed in reform policy more generally, unleashing grass-roots initiative and fostering rapid catch-up growth of the small-scale sector (chapter 14). However, the consequences were dire in the coal sector. With the growth of small-scale mining, China's coal-mining sector underwent technological regression. Miners worked under very poor conditions, and safety measures were practically non-existent. Extraction rates were low and the quality of output poor, and destruction of local land and pollution were serious. The safety record was abysmal: from the 1980s through the mid-2000s coal mining deaths averaged 6,000 per year (IEA 2009, 39–47).

In 1998, Premier Zhu Rongji launched a major effort to close down small mines, especially those out of compliance with rudimentary safety regulations. Local governments responded by reporting that their mines had closed while actually shielding their local producers. The statistical system for coal reporting collapsed, and China initially reported a large drop in coal production between 1999 and 2002. Those data have since been revised upward on three occasions, as successive statistical surveys have each found more small-scale mines in operation (figure 21.1 shows data after the third revision). By 2003, Chinese policy-makers knew that they were producing much more coal than they had believed, and that coal production and consumption were increasing very quickly. This shock contributed to a major change in the approach to environmental policy.

21.2.2   The Birth of Environmental Policy

Chinese policy-makers began to develop a serious environmental agenda in 2005. Of course, awareness of the importance of the environment dated much further back, and an independent Environmental Protection Bureau had been established in 1988. This agency was raised in rank in 1998, even as many industrial ministries were being downgraded, but its chief still did not receive full ministerial status.

It was not until 2005 that Chinese policy-makers began to accept the need to pay significant costs to improve energy conservation and the environment. The data showed energy consumption rising more rapidly than GDP from 2001 to 2005, partly due to the rediscovery of previously hidden small coal mines, but also because some previously closed mines were reopening. There was no denying the seriousness of the situation. China's industrial growth was accelerating, the price of coal soared, and producers were scrambling to expand. The surge in production that would take China from extracting 1.5 billion tons of raw coal in 2002 to over 3 billion tons in 2009 was already underway. Ironically, by 2006, small private and village collective mines accounted for 38% of total output, almost as high proportionally and far higher in absolute terms than before the crackdown (IEA 2009, 44). Policy-makers scrambled to respond.

Drafted during 2005, the Eleventh Five-Year Plan (2006–2010) spoke eloquently about a new development strategy with a "smaller environmental footprint" and moving to a "knowledge-intensive growth path." The Chinese Academy of Sciences published an optimistic report suggesting it would be possible to sidestep the worst of the Kuznets curve and get on a clean development path. The five-year plan put muscle behind its vision with a binding target of a 20% reduction in energy use per unit of GDP. This target was dis-aggregated and given to local governments as an obligatory target. A national climate-change program was adopted in 2007, and a revised Energy Conservation Law in that year specified that conservation of natural resources was a fundamental national policy.

This enhanced policy effort was consistent with other efforts of the Hu Jintao-Wen Jiabao administration (section 5.7). Environmental issues were achieving greater prominence in the public mind along with public health issues highlighted by the SARS crisis and food safety scandals. An important symbolic event occurred in 2004, when Premier Wen Jiabao suspended work on a series of dams projected for the Nujiang (Nu River or Salween) in Yunnan. This river flows through an area of great natural beauty and enormous biodiversity, a rugged area where the upper reaches of three great rivers (the Yangtze, the Mekong, and the Salween) flow in parallel less than 100 kilometers apart. The suspension was a symbolic victory for the nascent environmental movement. Meanwhile, a major spill in the Songjiang River in north-eastern China received significant publicity and shocked the public.

Despite the greater salience of environmental issues, actual progress was extremely uneven. As China's industrial growth accelerated in 2006 and 2007, energy demand and industrial emissions continued to grow rapidly. Aspirations to move to a lighter production structure were set aside. Air pollution continued to worsen in Beijing and throughout north China, at least through 2011. The Ministry of Environmental Protection was raised in rank to full ministerial status in 2007, and given cabinet (State Council) membership, but its performance was widely viewed as disappointing at first. An indicator of continuing ambivalence came when the dams on the Nujiang reappeared in development plans in 2013, only to be suspended again in 2016 (the final decision has still not been made).

21.2.3   A Simplified Political Economy

The fate of environmental policy during most of this period must be understood in the context of the goals of policy-makers and the distribution of power through the political system. During the period of high-speed growth, there was an overwhelming consensus in favor of rapid growth and the high levels of investment needed to sustain it. As described in section 5.6, the administrative system gave local actors strong incentives to pursue growth, and the broader growth coalition was extremely powerful. Even when policy-makers asked local actors to pursue environmental objectives, the system gave those actors every incentive to ignore their requests and continue their headlong pursuit of growth. Central-government policy-makers were themselves conflicted and sometimes did not send unambiguous instructions to local actors.

In the context of the political forces arrayed behind the pro-growth consensus, the Ministry of Environmental Protection (MEP) has been decidedly underpowered. Even as it gathered experience and moved up in the hierarchy, MEP remained weak. With a staff of only 300, the fines it collected were small and sometimes ignored. Fees were frequently rebated to the polluting firm in order to fund investment in pollution abatement, and oversight of actual spending was weak. In 2014, the level of fees was doubled, and a nationwide total of 12.7 billion RMB was collected in 2015 (Shan 2016). While this is not an insignificant amount, it will not have much effect on a 69 trillion RMB economy. National government bureaucracies in charge of energy policy have plenty of power but conflicting agendas. The National Development and Reform Commission (NDRC) is in charge of both the energy and climate-change portfolios, but is also in charge of China's industrial planning and development. A National Energy Commission, was created, but it was subordinate to the NDRC for staffing and dependent on personalities for impact. The NDRC also oversees China's national oil companies, which themselves control enormous financial and material resources, and whose chief executives hold ministerial rank and have networks of powerful friends in the top leadership. Resistance to change was thus profound.

A popular environmental movement has gradually grown up in China and has won some important victories. These include protecting key wilderness sites, and protecting charismatic endangered species such as the giant panda. Local movements have been prominent in blocking the construction of new polluting factories, especially chemical factories, near residential districts. However, the efficacy of the Chinese environmental movement has been hobbled by difficulties in accessing information and by the uncertain legal status of independent citizens' groups. Although the Chinese government acknowledges the need for citizen input, it insists that nongovernmental organizations be registered and affiliated with an official government agency. These limitations have reduced the impact of citizens' movements and have slowed China's transition to a more sustainable development path.

21.2.4   Incremental Progress

With deeply entrenched opponents, limited ability to impose regulations on local governments, and deprived of effective citizen support, China's environmental policymakers have had to choose their battles carefully. After 2005, though, we can identify three important areas in which policy made important contributions to environment improvement. First, environmentalists supported investments in more efficient facilities that contribute to growth while reducing pollution. There has been a remarkable technological transformation of China's electricity sector: today 44% of capacity uses supercritical technology, meaning very high temperature (over 705° Fahrenheit), high-pressure generators that are significantly more efficient and less polluting. This is significantly more advanced than the U.S. fleet, which consists predominantly of older subcritical plants. For example, China has 90 ultra-supercritical units currently in operation, while the United States has precisely one (Hart, Bassett, and Johnson 2017). To be sure, China's modernization at this pace is possible only because large additions of new capacity have been made in recent years, which is not the case in the United States.

Second, China tackled concentrated sources of pollution first. SO_2 is a particularly noxious pollutant causing acid rain and service as a precursor to smog. SO_2 comes mainly from point sources at power plants and factories. Emissions of SO_2 peaked in 2006, and then began a slow, steady decline (*Environmental Statistics* 2016, 43). Investment in industrial and municipal wastewater treatment increased significantly. Point source pollutants were also ripe for the introduction of innovative policy mechanisms, such as pollution fees and cap and trade programs.

Third, environmental regulators have begun to provide more information about environmental issues. The turnaround is especially clear with respect to PM2.5, airborne fine particles less than 2.5 microns in diameter. This suspended particulate is especially hazardous to health, since it penetrates deep into the lung. Despite this, China's MEP did not provide data on PM2.5, perhaps reflecting a historical focus on PM10, the larger sooty particles that were an earlier problem. Filling a data void, the U.S. embassy in Beijing in 2008 installed a roof-top monitor that tweeted hourly PM2.5 levels. After a lag, the MEP "flipped the script by going public with the nation's pollution data and using citizen anger as a lever to force polluters to comply with the nation's environmental regulations" (Hart, Bassett, and Johnson 2017). Today, real-time air-quality data are available for Beijing (and most Chinese cities) at aqicn. org/city/Beijing and in many convenient apps. Public information about pollution increased as public concern mounted due to deteriorating air quality. In the winters of 2013 and 2014, the city of Beijing experienced a series of disastrously bad air-pollution days, when Beijing's air was as bad as that of London during the "killer fog" of the 1950s. Since good information was available on PM2.5 and the government had already promised to reduce pollution, the impact on popular opinion in the national capital was substantial.

In this fashion, environmental policy-makers have made cumulative, incremental changes. This progress was real, but should also not be overstated. Beginning to control sources of pollution is essential, but there is a long road from emissions to ultimate improvement in the environment. To bring fundamental change in China's environmental policy, it took the end of the miracle-growth period and the arrival of a new normal.

21.2.5   A Turning Point: The End of High-Speed Growth

Throughout this text, we have shown that the end of miracle growth was a fundamental turning point for many aspects of the Chinese economy. This is also true for environmental policy and environmental outcomes. The end of the miracle-growth era (after 2010) and the beginning of the new normal of moderate growth fundamentally altered conditions. Figure 21.1 showed that fossil-fuel production peaked in 2013 and has declined since, at least for three years through 2016. This was not the direct result of a specific policy decision, but rather the result of economic changes that strongly reinforced the cumulative impact of incremental environmental policy changes in the preceding years.

The period of high-speed growth came to an abrupt end after about 2010. Although all the environmental ramifications of this shift are not yet clear, it is obvious that the impact will be profound. Structural changes in the economy are now changing the relationship between the economy and the environment. Three closely related structural changes all interact to reduce the adverse environmental impact of economic activity.

1. Slower economic growth: The simple fact of slower GDP growth means that fewer emissions and pollutants are being released.

2. Lower investment: As growth slows, China will gradually invest a smaller share of its GDP in new fixed capital. Indeed, the ratio of investment to GDP peaked in 2011 and has been gradually drifting down ever since. This reduces the demand for energy-intensive industrial goods such as steel and cement.

3. Shift to services: As industrial output reaches peak levels, the growth impetus shifts to services. As chapter 7 described, economies shift toward a postindustrial service economy after about $15,000 per capita GDP (PPP adjusted). China is just beginning this transition. Most services are far less energy intensive and polluting than industry (although transport is an important energy-intensive service).

These three closely related structural factors open up a completely new set of opportunities for China's environmental policy.

The end of the high-speed growth era also induced among policy-makers a search for new drivers of growth. As we saw in chapter 15, since 2006, China has devoted increasing resources to technology and industrial policies, including those focused on "strategic emerging industries" (SEIs). Several of the SEIs are related to cleaner energy, such as solar and wind power, advanced nuclear power, and electric vehicles. Environmental engineering is also an SEI. In emerging industries, there are no entrenched incumbents in developed countries, and Chinese planners believe that China can therefore develop a competitive advantage through aggressive early action. As a result, the government has poured money into new energy sectors with scant attention to short- or medium-term paybacks in the hope that these will be the growth sectors of the future. Governments in the West pursued similar policies during the global financial crisis (2008–2009), but their commitment was steadily scaled back between 2012 and 2016, while China continued and even strengthened these policies.

These policies have led China to pour an enormous amount of money into green technologies. This commitment of resources is certain to have an impact. Photovoltaic electricity capacity jumped especially quickly in 2016 (China Electricity Council 2017). So far, utilization has been low, as delays in connecting this capacity to the electric grid and managing integration have held back generation. However, in the past few years, generation of wind and solar electricity has grown more rapidly in China than in any other nation. The beginning of a shift in China's energy output mix is clearly evident in figure 21.1.

National security considerations also reinforce China's tilt away from fossil fuels. China now depends on imports for about 20% of its energy and two-thirds of its oil consumption. If "new energy" can reduce China's energy dependence, that will give greater peace of mind to policy-makers worried about security. Thus Chinese energy policy reflects many different motivations in addition to those of environmental quality.

These considerations are all essential to understanding China's current environmental situation and its sustainable future. Structural economic changes are driving big changes in relative prices, and changing the calculus for many actors, including businessmen and policy-makers. Just as policy-makers had increased their commitment to environmental goals, they became convinced that environmentally friendly industries could contribute to economic growth and that a stronger push was necessary on energy and environmental issues. The result has been a sea change in the seriousness with which policy-makers treat environmental issues.

21.2.6　Government Policy After the Turning Point

Will the energy transition that China started after 2013 be sustained? We can gain insight by looking at government policy since about 2015. In response to both structural economic changes and to environmental imperatives, policy-makers have favored increased direct central-government pressure on local actors. These actions are consistent with the supply-side structural reform policies introduced in 2016 and mentioned in section 5.8. We can see this new activism in regard to coal, electricity, and environmental goals more broadly.

Central-government planners are very aware that the inability to control small-scale coal mines led to the frustration of government, environment, and safety goals in the past. Since 2013, they have sought to use the slowdown in the economy and the sharp decline in coal prices to ratchet up pressure on small coal. Their objective is to shut down all mines with capacity under 300,000 tons by 2020. This is a major undertaking. According to Duan (2016), mines below this cutoff accounted for 45% of total production in 2005, but the share had already decreased to 22% in 2010 and 10% in 2015. According to the Coalmine Safety Bureau (2016), accidental coalmine deaths dropped from 2.433 in 2010 to 598 in 2015, about a tenth of the rate at the turn of the century. Since the vast majority of accidental deaths are in small mines, this suggests dramatic shrinkage of the small coal sector. Separately, a flurry of safety inspections and financial assistance measures designed to facilitate mine closure rolled out in 2016 (Duan 2016). These facts indicate the central government is intent on keeping the pressure on.

The situation is even more complicated in the electricity sector. Surprisingly, the slowdown in electricity demand was not accompanied by a slowdown in electricity investment. (This reflects the general policy of trying to sustain growth by keeping government investment high, described in chapters 7 and 18). Thus, even as China built the modern efficient plants described in section 21.2.5, small-scale capacity has continued to expand. As a result, capacity utilization has plummeted to extraordinarily low levels. According to official CEC data, on average, Chinese power plants were generating 41% of the time in the first half of 2017, down from a high point of 62% in 2004 (CEC 2017). This reflects wasted investment, and helps explain the deterioration in capital productivity described in chapter 7. However, it also creates an opportunity for the government analogous to that which exists in coal. Under economic pressure already, these small power plants now face a big squeeze from the central government, which wants to close all plants below a certain efficiency cutoff by 2020. However, the same difficult over-capacity problem caused electricity planners to cut down on their uptake of power from solar and wind producers in 2017.

A new environmental protection tax is phasing in at the beginning of 2018 to replace the old system of pollution discharge fees. The new tax is tougher, mandating collection of tax per unit of emission for air, water, solid wastes, and excess noise. Although it does not tax carbon emissions, by creating a formal tax, instead of a fee administered by MEP, it should apply nearly universally and with fewer exemptions (Shan 2016). Finally, during 2016–2017, the Chinese Communist Party sent environmental inspection teams into all provinces. Each team stayed in a province for a month, checking up on environmental enforcement, making sure that top provincial leaders were committed to environmental objectives, and accepting letters and calls from citizens. Taken together, these measures clearly demonstrate the intention of the government to keep the pressure on in enforcing environmental and efficiency goals. Seeing this strong commitment, optimists believe that China has already reached "peak coal" (Ye et al. 2016). It seems clear that China has made the first step in an energy transition, de-linking future economic growth from consumption of fossil fuel. For the energy transition to continue, China will require a fundamental shift in the underlying political economy—the relations between central and local governments—that has frustrated environmental goals in the past. In turn, such a political shift is most likely to occur if the transition to a service-based economy proceeds smoothly and quickly.

21.3   Pollution

Pollution represents the other side of the coin—or perhaps the other end of the pipe—from the energy economy. Economic activity, especially energy use, tends to lead to an increase in emissions, that is, in pollutants dumped into the natural realm. Pollution causes the largest current costs, and these are relatively visible. It is relatively straightforward to count up the costs of pollution in money and excess deaths (World Bank/IHME 2016). Moreover, the economics of pollution are relatively straightforward. Pollution is a negative externality imposed on society. If it is feasible, the proper response is to levy a tax or penalty on the polluter. If this is done, the costs of the activity are internalized and borne by the polluter. At the same time, pollution is the aspect of the environment most susceptible to a degree of optimism based on economic development and changing population preferences. Some types of air pollution will dissipate within days of curtailing the causal emissions: Beijing repeatedly engineers "APEC blue-sky days" when it wants an unpolluted environment for important international meetings. Of course, most pollution problems cannot be so speedily resolved.

China's biggest pollution problems are air, water, and soil. Not coincidentally, in recent years Beijing has issued action plans for each of these, beginning with air (2013), then water (2015), and soil (2016). These plans are ambitious and important. They tend to be heavy on targets and light on instruments and funding, but they do lay out the central government's roadmap and preferred destinations.

21.3.1   Air Pollution

In China's cities today, particularly the larger ones, trends in air quality are shaped by offsetting forces. Industrial emission controls and the shift in household fuel use away from coal have improved air quality. In Beijing, the movement of industry out of the city has also contributed. Pollutants produced by large factories (industrial point sources) have declined, resulting in big reductions in large particulate matter, PM10 and sulfur dioxide. However, the growth of automobile transport, poor vehicle emissions controls, and cross-boundary pollution are causing deterioration in air quality. The resulting outcomes have differed across cities and specific pollutants.

A major source of improvement in air quality has been the reduction in the dispersed use of coal by households and work units. Eighty percent of the urban population now has access to gas for cooking. In rural areas, however, indoor air pollution is still a severe problem. About half of the rural population has unimproved stoves that burn raw coal or wood and produce particulates, sulfur and nitrogen oxides, carbon monoxide, and other pollutants. Indoor air pollutants contribute to high rates of respiratory disease, the leading cause of death in rural areas and the third-leading cause in cities.

Positive trends have been partially offset by other factors. The total number of vehicles in China soared from 5.5 million in 1990 to 192 million in 2016. Auto emission standards and fuel standards have been steadily raised since 2001, but will not finally catch up with U.S. and European standards until 2020. Heavy-duty trucks are suspected of evading the pollution equipment mandated by law. Motor vehicles emit particulates, carbon monoxide, nitrogen oxides (NO_x), and volatile organic compounds. NO_x reacts with other chemicals in the presence of sunlight to form ozone, photochemical smog, and greenhouse gases. Remote sensing reveals that the world's largest global concentration of nitrogen oxides is in the North China Plain. NO_x concentrations declined in most global cities between 2005 and 2014, including Beijing, Shanghai, and Hong Kong. However, in the North China Plain around Beijing, NO_x has continued to increase and this is now the biggest and strongest concentration of NO_x worldwide (NASA 2015; Krotkoff et al. 2016, figure 8).

Most attention today is focused on small particulate matter (PM2.5), which is more hazardous because it infiltrates deeper into the lungs. PM2.5 can be produced by human activity, but in the atmosphere interactions among NO_x, sulfur, and volatile organic compounds (VOCs) also create secondary PM2.5, one of the main components of smog. Smog is highly visible, and awareness is high. Widespread public awareness has triggered a major campaign to reduce PM2.5 in key target zones. In the greater Beijing-Tianjin-Hebei region, 2017 levels should be 25% below 2012 levels; in the Yangtze delta, 20%; and in the Pearl River delta, 15%. National ambient PM2.5 levels plateaued after 2010–2011. There were hopes for a sustained reduction, but the evidence so far is mixed at best. Satellite sensing does not reveal a clear trend, and according to Chinese government ground sensors, the first half of 2017 was significantly worse than 2016.

21.3.2 Costs of Air Pollution

Air pollution damages the health of people exposed to it, lowers the productivity of workers, and degrades natural resources. A number of studies have attempted to quantify the costs of pollution to the Chinese economy. The Global Burden of Disease project relies on satellite measurement to measure main pollutants (PM2.5 and ozone) in a global grid, and uses this to compute annual population-weighted pollutants for countries and regions. When combined with exposure-response relations for human mortality and illness, it produces estimates of the health costs of pollution that are comparable across different regions and countries. Building on this, World Bank/IHME (2016) estimated that all kinds of air pollution in China caused 1.6 million premature deaths in 2013. The majority were due to atmospheric PM2.5, although indoor air pollution was also a large contributor. By this uniform global methodology, China with 19% of the world's population, experienced 30% of world premature deaths attributable to air pollution. A follow-up study (HEI 2016) found that coal burning was the largest cause of China's elevated PM2.5 levels. A study using a novel (and completely different) methodology found roughly comparable results. Chinese government policy provides coal for winter heating north of the Huai River, so there is a discontinuous jump in suspended particulates (including PM2.5) north of the river. The authors used this discontinuity to estimate that this coal-related pollution reduced life expectancy in north China by 5.5 years (Chen et al. 2013). Air pollution imposes severe, immediate costs on the Chinese people.

21.3.3 Water Pollution

Since 1980, the quality of China's surface water and groundwater has deteriorated significantly under the pressure of rapid industrial development, brisk population and urban growth, and increased use of chemical fertilizers and pesticides. As a result, water pollution is now a serious problem for urban and rural drinking water. There are three main categories of water-pollution sources:

1. Industrial waste: Pulp and paper, metallurgical, and chemical factories are the worst polluters. There has been major progress in cleaning up large-scale factories, and today 90% of industrial wastewater from regulated (large-scale) industries receives some kind of treatment. However, smaller factories, including township and village enterprises, often have no treatment facilities at all.

2. Municipal waste: In the 1990s, almost no municipal sewage was properly treated. A major push has been undertaken to improve sewage treatment, and by 2010 China had constructed sufficient capacity to give all municipal waste at least primary treatment.

3. Agriculture: Intensively used nitrogen fertilizers and pesticides are a serious source of water pollution (section 12.6). Poor-quality fertilizers, excessive use of nitrogen fertilizers (relative to phosphorus and potassium), and especially widespread use of cheap ammonium bicarbonate fertilizer, which is readily soluble and easily washed out to streams, lakes, and aquifers, add to the impact. This type of non-point-source pollution is extremely difficult to address. Pesticides, used very intensively, have been implicated in species loss (birds) and has polluted some important water bodies. Animal waste from increasing numbers of intensive pig-raising farms is another major source of biological oxygen-demand and coliform pollution. The ecological balance of Hangzhou Bay is seriously threatened, primarily by agriculture-related runoff.

As a result of these pollutants, water quality is poor, especially in the water-short northern regions. Table 21.2 summarizes the available data. Water quality below class V means that the water is literally toxic, unsuitable even for irrigation, and cannot be safely purified for human uses. Ten years ago, in the Liao, Hai, and Huai systems, half the water was in this category, as well as a third of the Yellow River (see figure 21.3, which shows these river systems). These rivers have all three of the biggest pollution problems. Waters turn eutrophic from biological and chemical oxygen demand; depleted of oxygen, they can support only bacteria and flagellates, but no higher life forms. Persistent heavy metals, such as chromium, mercury, and lead, build up in the water and riverbeds. Chlorinated hydrocarbons (such as PCBs and DDT—banned but still used) build up and are also highly persistent. There has been progress since 2003, particularly in migration out of "below V" into classes IV and III.

Table 21.2
Water-quality class of main river systems, 2015.

	River length (kilometers)	Class I	Class II	Class III	Class IV	Class V	Below V
National, 2003	201,216	5.7	30.7	26.2	10.9	5.8	20.7
National, 2015		2.7	38.1	31.3	14.3	4.7	8.9
Liao, 2003	4,529	1.6	8.8	17.6	8.6	13.5	49.9
Liao, 2015	5,454	1.8	30.9	7.3	40.0	5.5	14.5
Hai, 2003	10,719	3.1	17.3	18.2	6.1	2.8	52.5
Hai, 2015	14,953	4.7	15.6	21.9	6.2	12.5	39.1
Yellow, 2003	13,721	7.6	14.1	11.8	17.7	16.8	32.0
Yellow, 2015	20,545	1.6	30.6	29.0	21.0	4.8	12.9
Huai, 2003	11,621	2.1	8.8	16.8	15.4	8.0	48.9
Huai, 2015	25,904	0.0	6.4	47.9	22.3	13.8	9.6

Source: MEP (2016).

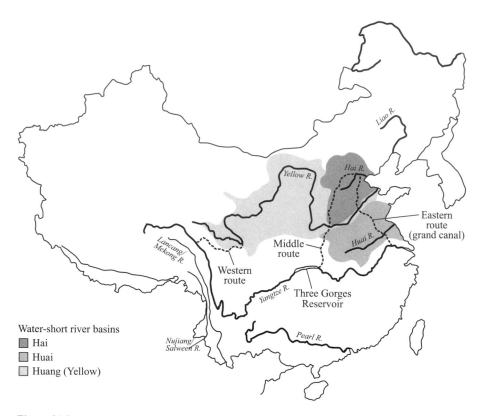

Figure 21.3
Map of south–north water transfer routes.
Source: Liu (1998, 902).

Class IV water can be used for industrial and some recreational purposes but is not fit for direct human contact. Class III is the standard for direct human contact and also for intake into purification for drinking water. Class I is pristine. In northern China, the water in only about half of the river length meets the standard for human contact. Moreover, this is the entire river system; quality is much worse in the downstream, urban areas where most people live. Indeed, some of the measured improvement in quality is due to the addition of sensors in the cleaner upstream segments.

Only 70% of China's river water is of good-enough quality that it can be used to begin the water-purification process that will make it fit for consumption; 30% is unfit for human contact, and of this, almost 10% is toxic. The share of pure water (Class I) has declined by more than half since 2003. These are national figures, and pollution is much worse in northern and northeastern China. The experience in the Huai River basin was especially sobering. Economy (2004) described how a massive toxic spill in 1994 shook up central-government leaders and induced them to launch a huge, coordinated program to clean up the river by 2000. Some 60 billion RMB ($7.2 billion) later, the program had failed utterly to meet its ambitious goals. Twenty years later, the Huai is still one of the most polluted rivers in China, unfit for human contact along 46% of its length (table 21.2).

21.3.4   Water Availability

China currently suffers from a moderate to high level of water stress, including most of northern and northwestern China. Annual renewable freshwater resource per capita in China is 2,093 m^2, less than a quarter of the world average of 8,349 m^2. Moreover, there is much less water per capita in the north, and five northern provinces with 250 million people, including Beijing, rely on underground water for 50% or more of their needs (Wang et al. 2016, 3). Irrigation is by far the biggest human use of water in China, accounting for almost two-thirds of total water use, although the proportion is slowly declining. China has been forced to rely on many unsustainable practices to maintain current supplies of water to its cities and agriculture. Runoff of the northern rivers Huang, Huai, Liao, and especially Hai have declined significantly in the past twenty years. The heavy demands on these rivers intensify the impact of the pollution that afflicts them. A related serious problem is the overexploitation of groundwater. Using underground water supplies (aquifers and groundwater) in such a way that they are gradually depleted is sometimes known as "mining water." This is a very serious problem in northern China. Large amounts of water have been withdrawn from underground sources since the 1970s for tube-well irrigation in the North China Plain (section 12.6). It has become more difficult and costly to extract water from these underground sources. Private entrepreneurs now dig deep wells and sell the water, increasing supply but exacerbating the long-run threat to the sustainability of the water supply.

Cities have been extracting increasing amounts of water. Beijing was originally built in a naturally favored location where five different rivers flowed down from neighboring hills, and 10 billion cubic meters of reservoir capacity was built north and west of the city in the 1950s and 1960s. Today all five of the rivers run dry in dry years, and only one-third of the reservoir capacity is used. The water table in Beijing has fallen more than 50 meters. Coastal cities including Tianjin and Shanghai have experienced major subsidence problems. Depleted aquifers allow saltwater to intrude into water sources near the coast, requiring the abandonment of thousands of wells. These are very serious problems, and solving them will be expensive. Efficiency improvements are possible at nearly every point in the chain of collecting, storing, and delivering water. Currently, charges to farmers for irrigation water cover a fraction of the cost of supplying the water (Lohmar et al. 2003), and incentives to conserve are weak.

One major initiative of the Chinese government is to pump southern water northward to alleviate stress in the North China basin. There are three feasible routes (figure 21.3). The western route is the most expensive but might someday provide the best water quality. The eastern route is the cheapest and was built first but provides the lowest water quality. The middle route was completed and began delivering water to Beijing in 2015. Built at a cost estimated at 500 billion RMB, it takes water from the Han River reservoir at Danjiangkou and delivers it through a 1,000-kilometer concrete culvert to Beijing, only 100 meters lower elevation. Such grand infrastructure projects are expensive and, in the long run, less important than the hundreds of thousands of small-scale improvements in the efficiency with which water is used as delivery systems are upgraded, and as consumers are given stronger incentives to conserve water.

21.3.5   Land and Soil

Soil pollution is significant in China's agricultural regions. Nearby mines and the indiscriminate application of low-grade fertilizers and excessive pesticides have led to a buildup of toxic heavy metals in the soil. In 2013, China used 23% of the world's fertilizers and 44% of the world's pesticides, according to data from the FAO and China's Ministry of Agriculture (MOA). For every hectare of arable land, China uses three times the amount of fertilizer and six times the amount of pesticide as the United States uses. According to MOA surveys, over one-third of the pesticides and fertilizers are wasted in use, due to lack of knowledge or low-quality tools, and the excess application contaminates land and water. An official, multi-year soil-pollution survey was carried out between 2005 and 2013, and it was reported that 19.4% of China's arable land (and 16% of total land tested) was polluted. Cadmium, nickel, and arsenic were among the most common pollutants, and contamination by cadmium—a persistent, toxic heavy metal—was found in 9% of rice samples tested (Zhang and Zhou 2016). The provinces of Hubei, Hunan, Jiangxi, and Sichuan were in a particularly bad shape, with 68% of rice fields across those areas suffering from heavy metal contamination. The government acknowledges the problem and produced an action plan in 2016 but so far has not arranged funding for any actual remediation.

Broader problems of land degradation are often related to appropriate water supply. Too much water at the wrong time causes erosion; too little causes desertification. Erosion is concentrated in western regions of China, where overall water supply is deficient, ground cover is sparse, and seasonal rainfall causes huge soil losses due to erosion. Serious flooding on the Yangtze in 1998 was directly linked to the degradation of the upstream environment due to deforestation and erosion. Desertification is an enormous problem. China, as stressed in chapter 2, is an arid country. West of the Aihui–Tengchong line, much of the land is desert. Ominously, the desert has been moving east, primarily because of the impact of human activity. The overexploitation of grass and forest lands has greatly reduced the regenerative capacity of the land's plant cover. As biological buffer zones have weakened, deserts have spread significantly. Perhaps as a result, sand and dust storms spiked for a period in the early twenty-first century. In March 2002, two huge dust storms blew across northern China, reducing visibility for days and pushing airborne particulate matter over the top of all measurement scales in Beijing. For unknown reasons, these sandstorms subsided after a few years.

The single most important factor aggravating desertification has been overgrazing in the grasslands of Inner Mongolia and other pastoral regions of northern China. The dissolution of the collectives in these areas led to the distribution of herds of grazing animals to individual households and an explosion in the size of herds. The "tragedy of the commons" was exacerbated as each individual household sought to maximize its individual income from animal husbandry. "Shelter belts" of planted trees seek to halt the encroaching desert, but the desert has expanded despite the successful rehabilitation of 5,700 square kilometers through reforestation, grass seeding, and expanded irrigation. Most of the rehabilitation took place in central China, in areas not far from major watercourses. Most of the spread of the desert took place in northern China, especially in the vast border areas populated by herders.

Away from the frontiers of expanding deserts, the efficacy of Chinese sustainability policy has been substantially better. For many years, tree planting has been emphasized as a government policy, as a civic responsibility, and, on several occasions, as a campaign of mass mobilization. Over the long term, this consistent emphasis has had a significant payoff, and China's overall forest cover has grown substantially. The first national inventory, in 1962, found that only 8.9% of China was forested; by 2015, total forest cover had increased to 27% of China (*SYC* 2016, table 8-1). The newly planted forest cover is typically of lower quality and tends to be composed of a relatively small number of fast-growing species, scattered through densely settled parts of China. At the same time, considerable acreage of old-growth forest, with diverse species and big trees, has been lost. By 2013, 14.8% of China's land was protected in some fashion in parks or animal and nature reserves (one of the benefits of mass tourism).

21.4   Conclusion: The Environment, Sustainability, and Global Warming

It is evident that China has an air pollution problem. China suffers disproportionately from the local impact of air pollution, with its 19% of world population incurring 30% of the world health costs. At the same time, China contributed an estimated 27% of global carbon emissions in 2016 (BP 2017), making it by far the largest contributor to greenhouse gases and global warming. While air pollution is no longer worsening, it has just begun to get better, and the health costs may even mount in the future as the population ages and becomes more sensitive to airborne pollutants.

China for years argued that developing countries should not be subject to limits on greenhouse-gas emissions. However, China's position has gradually changed since the mid-2000s, and as part of the Paris accords in 2015, China agreed to reach zero carbon-emissions growth by 2030. If current trends continue, China will reach "peak carbon" well before 2030.

Global warming threatens China directly. Average temperatures have already increased by more than 1° C since the 1960s. Rising sea levels caused by global warming endanger approximately 154 million people in China, more than 10% of the population, plus affiliated infrastructure, located in low-elevation coastal zones. The PRC has one of the highest global exposures to sea-level rise because of its low northern coastline. Fourteen coastal port cities vital for economic commerce and trade will be threatened, including both Shanghai and Tianjin, which are more vulnerable because of local subsidence linked to excessive pumping of groundwater. Local authorities have built extensive seawalls in many places along the coast. However, vulnerability to severe storms and storm surges is still substantial.

The interaction between global warming and water availability is the area of greatest long-run uncertainty. Water availability is already a concern in north China, and it may get worse in the short run. According to some models, rainfall in the North and especially the Northeast will decline, and rain in the South will increase, which would exacerbate the existing water imbalances and the impact of severe coastal events. The glaciers of the Tibetan plateau are the ultimate source of China's rivers and the great rivers of South and Southeast Asia as well. The speed at which these glaciers are shrinking appears to be accelerating, and shrunken glaciers will ultimately cause reduction in the flow of these rivers. Higher temperatures will increase surface evaporation and reduce runoff. The powerful forces may come together in a way that threatens China's water availability.

Environmental degradation has imposed serious costs on the Chinese economy and has reduced the well-being of the Chinese population. Moreover, there is increasing public concern about environmental issues, and that concern has increasingly been publicly articulated. The Chinese government has made important new commitments to environmental improvement. China's growth trajectory is quite different today from what it was a decade or two ago. There are profound economic reasons to move away from the heavy-industry-intensive growth path of the past decade and find a lighter and more sustainable growth path. Moreover, China's embrace of high-technology industry has included a major role for new energy and environmental sectors. The impact of these factors is already evident in the beginning of China's energy transition. To further this transformation China will have to use smart policy-making and bring market forces to bear through efficient tax and regulatory policy.

The challenges of water availability, soil pollution, resilience of the natural environment, and atmospheric degradation and climate change are among the most serious that China confronts. Few natural landscapes remain in the PRC because culturally the emphasis is on managed and reshaped landscapes and the control of ecological processes. In the past, development has focused on maintaining economic growth, often at the expense of the environment. However, the PRC recognizes that increasing levels of environmental degradation are undermining resilience and the capacity to adapt to climate change. In each case, it is easy to see that current practices are unsustainable, but hard to determine how quickly they can be changed. China has entered the turning point of its environmental Kuznets curve, but has not yet passed through that turning point and decisively launched the phase of steady improving environmental quality. There is still an opportunity for improved environmental policy-making to make a significant difference before further environmental catastrophes develop.

Bibliography

Suggestions for Further Reading

Reasonably up-to-date coverage of China is available at Renewable Energy World (http://www.renewableenergyworld.com/index.html) and at the Renewable Energy Policy Network for the 21st Century (www.ren21.net/). Good contemporary overviews include Hove and Enoe (2015) and Ye et al. (2016). HEI (2017) is a lucid and current introduction to the air-pollution aspect of the Global Burden of Disease project, with plenty of attention paid to China. The project's interactive data is current and easily accessible at https://www.stateofglobalair.org/data.

References

BP (British Petroleum) (2017). *BP Statistical Review of World Energy, June 2016.* Accessed at http://www.bp.com/statisticalreview.

CEC (China Electricity Council) (2017). "Comprehensive Flash Report on China's Electricity Industry 2016." January 20. Accessed at http://www.cec.org.cn/guihuayutongji/tongjxinxi/niandushuju/2017-01-20/164007.html.

Chen, Yuyu, Avraham Ebenstein, Michael Greenstonec, and Hongbin Li (2013). "Evidence on the Impact of Sustained Exposure to Air Pollution on Life Expectancy from China's Huai River Policy." *PNAS* 110 (32): 12936–12941.

Coalmine Safety Bureau (2016). *Meikuang anquan shengchan 135 guihua: Zhengqiu yijiangao* [Coalmine safe production thirteenth five-year plan: preliminary draft]. April. Accessed at http://www.chinasafety.gov.cn/newpage/Contents/Channel_5826/2016/0422/268741/files_founder_457118490/1788319668.doc.

Duan, Hongxia (2016). "Windows of Opportunity: Coal Phase-Out in China." International Institute for Sustainable Development. Accessed at https://static1.squarespace.com/static/56fbe6a97da24f416c2f651f/t/57e4325bd1758e426f3cd45f/1474572893183/FFS-Conf-2016-Duan-China-coal-phaseout.pdf.

Economy, E. (2004). *The River Runs Black: The Environmental Challenge to China's Future*. Ithaca, NY: Cornell University Press.

Environmental Statistics (Annual). National Bureau of Statistics and Ministry of Environmental Protection, Compilers. *Zhongguo Huanjing Tongji Nianjian* [China statistical yearbook on environment]. Beijing: Zhongguo Tongji.

Hart, Melanie, Luke Bassett, and Blaine Johnson (2017). "Everything You Think You Know About Coal in China Is Wrong." Center for American Progress, May 15, 2017. Accessd at https://www.americanprogress.org/issues/green/reports/2017/05/15/432141/everything-think-know-coal-china-wrong/.

HEI (Health Effects Institute) (2016). *Burden of Disease Attributable to Coal-Burning and Other Major Sources of Air Pollution in China*. Special Report #20. Boston: Health Effects Institute. Accessed at https://www.healtheffects.org/publication/burden-disease-attributable-coal-burning-and-other-air-pollution-sources-china.

HEI (2017). *State of Global Air 2017*. Special Report. Boston: Health Effects Institute. Accessed at https://www.stateofglobalair.org/report.

Hove, Anders, and Merisha Enoe (2015). "Stronger Markets, Cleaner Air: Integrating Policy and China's Economic and Environmental Prosperity." Paulson Institute, June. Accessed at http://www.paulsoninstitute.org/economics-environment/climate-sustainable-urbanization/research/.

IEA (International Energy Agency) (2009). *Cleaner Coal in China*. Paris: International Energy Agency. Accessed at https://www.iea.org/publications/freepublications/publication/cleaner-coal-in-china.html.

Krotkov, Nickolay, et al. (2016). "Aura OMI Observations of Regional SO_2 and NO_2 Pollution Changes from 2005 to 2015." *Atmospheric Chemistry and Physics* 16:4605–4629. Accessed at www.atmos-chem-phys.net/16/4605/2016/.

Liu Changming (1998). "Environmental Issues and the South-North Water Transfer Scheme." *China Quarterly*, no. 156 (December): 899–910.

Lohmar, Bryan, and Jinxia Wang (2002). "Will Water Scarcity Affect Agricultural Production in China?" In U.S. Department of Agriculture, Economic Research Service, *China's Food and Agriculture: Issues for the 21st Century*, 41–43. Washington, DC: USDA.

Lohmar, Bryan, Jinxia Wang, Scott Rozelle, Jikun Huang, and David Dawe (2003). *China's Agricultural Water Policy Reforms: Increasing Investment, Resolving Conflicts, and Revising Incentives*. U.S. Department of Agriculture, AIB-782, March. Accessed at http://www.ers.usda.gov/publications/aib782/.

MEP (Ministry of Environmental Protection) (2016). *Zhongguo Huanjing Zhuangkuang Gongbao* [Report on China's environmental conditions]. Beijing. May 20. Accessed at http://www.mep.gov.cn/hjzl/.

NASA (National Aeronautics and Space Administration) (2015). "New NASA Satellite Maps Show Human Fingerprint on Global Air Quality." Release 15-233 (December 14). Accessed at https://www.nasa.gov/press-release/new-nasa-satellite-maps-show-human-fingerprint-on-global-air-quality.

Pew Research Center (2016). "Chinese Public Sees More Powerful Role in World." Accessed at http://www.pewglobal.org/2016/10/05/chinese-public-sees-more-powerful-role-in-world-names-u-s-as-top-threat/.

Rohde, Robert A., and Richard A. Muller (2015). "Air Pollution in China: Mapping of Concentrations and Sources." *PLoS ONE* 10 (8): e0135749. Accessed at https://doi.org/10.1371/journal.pone.0135749.

SAC (Annual). *Zhongguo Tongji Zhaiyao* [Statistical abstract of China]. Beijing: Zhongguo Tongji.

Shan, Yuxiao (2016). "The Environmental Protection Tax Will Be the 18th Tax Types on January 1, 2018." *Caixin*. December 25. Accessed at http://china.caixin.com/2016-12-25/101030488.html.

State Council (2014). *Nengyuan Fazhan Zhanlue: Xingdong Jihua 2014–2020* [Energy development strategy action plan, 2014–2020]. State Council Office, November 19. Accessed at http://www.gov.cn/zhengce/content/2014-11/19/content_9222.htm.

Stern, David I. (2004). "The Rise and Fall of the Environmental Kuznets Curve." *World Development* 32 (8): 1419–1439.

SYC (Annual). *Zhongguo Tongji Nianjian* [Statistical yearbook of China]. Beijing: Zhongguo Tongji.

Wang, Jinxia, Qiuqiong Huang, Jikun Huang, and Scott Rozelle (2016). *Managing Water on China's Farms: Institutions, Policies and the Transformation of Irrigation under Scarcity.* Cambridge, MA: Academic Press.

World Bank/IHME (2016). *The Cost of Air Pollution: Strengthening the Economic Case for Action.* Washington, DC: The World Bank. Accessed at https://openknowledge.worldbank.org/handle/10986/25013.

Ye Qi, Nicholas Stern, Tong Wu, Jiaqi Lu, and Fergus Green (2016). "China's Post-Coal Growth." *Nature Geoscience* 9 (August). doi:10.1038/ngeo2777.

Zhang, Yan, and Chen Zhou (2016). "China's Tainted Soil Initiative Lacks Pay Plan." *Caixin English.* June 8. Accessed at http://english.caixin.com/2016-06-08/100952896.html.

Index

Note: Boxes, figures, and tables are indicated by "b," "f," and "t" respectively, following page numbers.